NUGGET COOMBS

A REFORMING LIFE

Born in 1906 and trained as an economist, H. C. Coombs was Governor of the Reserve Bank of Australia from 1949 to 1968. However, the breadth of his activities and his commitment to public affairs over seven decades makes his life story a cameo of Australians' many-sided quest for a better life. Coombs spent his childhood and youth in Western Australia. As Director-General of Post War Reconstruction he advised the Labor governments of the 1940s. In the Menzies years, he added performing arts and tertiary education to his duties in banking. Upon retirement in 1968 he continued to shape arts policy and took up a new reform interest as chairman of the Council for Aboriginal Affairs. Particularly interested in Coombs as an economist, Tim Rowse shows that Coombs understood 'economic rationality' as the socially integrative mission of private and public sector elites. When his Keynesian confidence faltered in the early 1970s, Coombs reformulated his ideas of economy and governance to meet the challenges of environmental degradation and indigenous renaissance. Ceaselessly testing the adaptability of twentieth-century liberalism, and straddling the gap between public servant and public intellectual, Coombs made his career a 'reforming life'.

Tim Rowse was born in 1951 and educated at Sydney and Flinders Universities. Best known for his work in Aboriginal history and policy, Rowse has published eight books since 1978. He has taught at Macquarie University, researched and lived in Central Australia for almost ten years, before arriving in Canberra in 1997. He is currently a Research Fellow in the History Program at the Australian National University.

To
Jan Mackay, Anna Mackay,
Kathleen Rowse and Ian Rowse

NUGGET COOMBS
A REFORMING LIFE

Tim Rowse

CAMBRIDGE UNIVERSITY PRESS
Cambridge, New York, Melbourne, Madrid, Cape Town, Singapore,
São Paulo, Delhi, Dubai, Tokyo, Mexico City

Cambridge University Press
The Edinburgh Building, Cambridge CB2 8RU, UK

Published in the United States of America by Cambridge University Press, New York

www.cambridge.org
Information on this title: www.cambridge.org/9780521677837

First published 2002

A catalogue record for this publication is available from the British Library

ISBN 978-0-521-81783-7 Hardback
ISBN 978-0-521-67783-7 Paperback

Contents

Acknowledgements

I WROTE THIS BOOK and its predecessor with the help of a number of institutions. For five years the Australian Research Council made a grant to the University of Sydney for my salary and expenses. My host there was the Department of Government and Public Administration. During and after my time in that Department I was a Visiting Fellow and then a Fellow of the Centre for Aboriginal Economic Policy Research at the Australian National University. Finally, I finished my writing while in the History Program, Research School of Social Sciences, ANU. I'm grateful to Martin Painter, Graeme Gill, Jon Altman and Barry Higman for their warm support, as the heads/directors of those three 'homes', for my Coombs research. Almost as much a 'home', since I spent so much time there, was the Reserve Bank itself. Allan Seymour, Virginia MacDonald and Cheryl Lindwall make it a pleasure to visit the Bank's archives. I also thank Graeme Powell and staff at the Manuscript Room, National Library of Australia, and the staff of the National Archives, Canberra. Film Australia allowed me to use interview transcripts from their Australian Biography series, produced under Film Australia's National Interest Program, with interviewees Robin Hughes and Frank Heimans.

Dr Coombs supported my research, letting me use his papers, and talking to me at length on several occasions. I had met him before I made my approach – both in an academic setting and over dinner in the Darwin home of our friend Cath Elderton. I was told that he cherished his privacy, so I made it clear when initiating the idea of a biography that what interested me was his public life. I had been well advised. Coombs' reply to my suggestion that I write his biography expressed reservations.

In the past I have discouraged exercises in that mode whether in written or in oral form – recorded interviews etc, when they have been designed to involve me in the work. I believe anyone working in a job which has 'public' responsibilities (whether paid or unpaid) has an obligation to be accountable and therefore to explain the basis on which those responsibilities have been performed. I think that on the whole I have left a reasonable account of my various stewardships and have been ready to supplement that account where necessary and practicable. I dislike being asked to defend or justify or to answer questions in which 'judgment' is involved. Partly because that is the function of others and partly because I am conscious that it is very difficult for a person to be wholly honest in that task. Also such exercises inevitably, whether deliberately or by accident, intrude on 'personal space' – attitudes, beliefs, relationships which I have always tried to protect as private. Few people are capable of articulating the content of their own personal space and I doubt whether I am one of them. I have therefore preferred to 'look outward'.

In a postscript he apologised for sounding 'pompous'.

Coombs' deposited papers do not include items that reveal what he considered to be his private life. Two of his children (Janet and Jim) thought it appropriate that I know a little of Coombs' family relationships, but my consent to Coombs' public/private boundary restrained me from exploring that theme very far. The resulting book is more impersonal than most readers of biographies would wish.

Making a virtue of impersonality, I have cast my study of Coombs' life as an exploration of some themes in Australia's twentieth-century history. In particular I have been stimulated by Paul Kelly's framing of twentieth-century Australian history as the persistence and then dissolution of what he calls 'the Australian Settlement'. The reader will see in my Conclusion that Coombs' political and intellectual itinerary, as I present it, cannot be fitted to Kelly's narrative without our becoming aware how Kelly's influential tale limits our appreciation of the options that have faced and continue to face Australians.

Approaching Coombs' life in this way has determined what I have covered and not covered. There is more of Coombs' public life than I have told here. For example, his restructuring of the external debts of India in a World Bank consultancy in 1972 would make a meaty study for another scholar. And there is more still … a subject difficult to exhaust.

Many people have helped me: Eric Alcock, Kim Armitage, Christine Bapty, Geoffrey Bolton, Nick Brown, John Burton, Ann Capling, Lindsay Cleland, Cecily Close, Janet Coombs, Jim Coombs, Melanie Coombs, Sharon Connolly, Selwyn Cornish, Pam Crichton, Michael Crozier, Dick Denton, Margaret Denton, Robin Derricourt, Barrie Dexter, Frank Fenner, Graeme Gill, Elizabeth Green, Phyllis Hatt, Dorothea Heron, Barry Hill, Brian Honner, Ralph Honner, Ian Hunter, Ken Inglis, Evan Jones, Marilyn Lake, Cheryl Lindwall, Virginia MacDonald, Stuart Macintyre, Janet Mackenzie, Phillipa McGuinness, Leslie Melville, Shannon Murphy-Townsend, Ettie Oakman, Rod O'Donnell, Cecily Osborne, John Pepper, M. John Phillips, Graeme Powell, Geoff Raby, Marian Sawer, Bob Scott, Tom Stannage, Allan Seymour, Arthur Tange, Bob and Myrna Tonkinson, Sean Turnell, Paul Watt and Nancy Williams. I thank them all, and I hope they enjoy the book.

Abbreviations

ABC	Australian Broadcasting Commission (later Corporation)
ACF	Australian Conservation Foundation
ACFTA	Australian Council for the Arts
ACTU	Australian Council of Trade Unions
AIAS	Australian Institute of Aboriginal Studies
ALP	Australian Labor Party
Angau	Australian New Guinea Administrative Unit
ANU	Australian National University
ANZAAS	Australian and New Zealand Association for the Advancement of Science
ASOPA	Australian School of Pacific Administration
CAA	Council for Aboriginal Affairs
CBOA	Commonwealth Bank Officers Association
CDEP	Community Development Employment Projects
CSIR	Council for Scientific and Industrial Research
CSIRO	Commonwealth Scientific and Industrial Research Organisation
CUC	Canberra University College
DLP	Democratic Labor Party
ECOSOC	Economic and Social Council (of the United Nations)
FAO	Food and Agriculture Organisation
F&E Committee	Finance and Economic Advisory Committee
GATT	General Agreement on Tariffs and Trade
IMF	International Monetary Fund
ITO	International Trade Organisation
LGS	liquid assets and government securities
LSE	London School of Economics
NSRB	National Security Resources Board
NUWM	National Unemployed Workers Movement
SAC	Society for Aboriginal Civilisation
UAP	United Australia Party
UNCTAD	United Nations Conference on Trade and Development
VSO	Victorian Symphony Orchestra

Auream Particulam

'What a delightful, comforting, friendly and solid-gold-throughout nickname!'[1]

Why was Coombs known as 'Nugget'?

The name had two connotations, one publicly celebrated, the other privately cherished. 'Nugget' was sufficiently established to be the subject of a friendly thrust in the Perth Modern School paper *The Sphinx*, from 'L.R.' (probably Leslie Rees), at the end of the first term of Coombs' fourth high school year, 1922.

> What connection could have been seen between the lad concerned and a large piece of gold? ... Perhaps the originator was thinking of Boot Polish, or may hap he had in mind the kind of nuggets which are covered in the gold paper off the threepenny chocolates.[2]

It was not the last time that 'Nugget' would have its metallic sense. Alan Renouf recalls the 'affection and respect' of fellow diplomats in 1948.

> I well remember being asked by Clair Wilcox, the leader of the American delegation, why Coombs was called Nugget. I replied that he was so called because he was small and stocky. Wilcox added, 'He is also pure gold.'[3]

In 1964 A. D. Hope made punning tribute to Coombs' work as Chair of the Australian Elizabethan Theatre Trust.

> Without what Generosity affords
> Our show tonight had never reached the boards,
> Eureka's golden hopes would soon decline
> Had she not found a Nugget in her mine.[4]

In 1968, the economist Heinz Arndt and the classicist A. D. Trendall melted Coombs down into eighteen lines of Latin verse, beginning '*Auream particulam/ In forma non gigantem/ Sed in mente maximum*'.[5]

For Coombs, 'Nugget has nothing to do with gold.' As he explained to Roberta Sykes in 1983,

> In the country in W.A. when I was growing up any person, horse, bullock, dog or other creature that was short in the legs and stockily built was called 'Nugget' and every team of horses or bullocks had one. They were believed to be tough and hard working.[6]

To Frank Heimans in 1991 he explained: 'Nuggets are reported to be energetic, vigorous ... you know, not necessarily terribly clever I think.' The name was more generic than individual. 'I didn't have to … tell people that I was called Nugget, soon as they had one look at me – he's a Nugget.[7]

He had never liked his given name Herbert, and 'Bertie' even less, because it signified a comically stupid Englishman. As he put it to that zealous Anglophobe Xavier Herbert in 1974, Herbert 'carries fatuous "Pommy" overtones …'[8] Among the motives we may imagine for Coombs refusing a knighthood was his dread of being known as Sir Herbert. He told Sir Walter Murdoch that a knighthood would be, for him, 'out of character'.[9]

That Coombs emphasised his physical stature in his own explanation of his name is partly what made that sense personal, especially when the alternative, auriferous sense was available for others' public praise. At five feet three inches, Coombs was noticeably shorter than the average Australian adult male. The word 'stature' demonstrates that the body may signify moral qualities. Coombs' shortness could be noted as if it were a defect of character. Less than ten months after he joined Leslie Melville in the Economics Section of the Commonwealth Bank, a superior said of Coombs that his 'defects of stature' were 'offset by a frankness and sincerity of manner and directness of speech.'[10]

Puberty being a ruthless differentiator, small men know their physical destiny from an early age. It must have enhanced Coombs' 'stature' among his peers that he was nimble, fast, dexterous and had a good eye for a rising ball. School sport allowed him to prove the manly worth of his small body. As a result, 'I was almost unconscious of being small.'[11] He played a football code in which height is an asset, but that values as well the nippy little man, the rover. Coombs once drew on his football experience to expound a cherished principle of institutional design. Small task-oriented groups within large organisations are 'the rovers of our social life who can gather up the ball that falls between the clumsy towering ruckmen'.[12]

Coombs' nickname was a personal metaphor, laying the basis of an identity that synthesised physical endowment with moral outlook. To accept and celebrate his shortness secured a viable ego-ideal – the adroit and flexible man, abilities unmapped by others' expectations, power without ostentation. He once remarked of Gough Whitlam: 'big men are not used to being wrong – they find it hard to live with'.[13]

Nugget Coombs: A Reforming Life is preceded by my 2000 study of Coombs' work with Indigenous Australians. I need to say something about the relationship between the two books. *Obliged to Be Difficult* (henceforth *Obliged*) says little about Coombs' life until 1967. *Nugget* is about Coombs from birth to death, but its coverage of post-1967 events overlaps in no way with *Obliged*. Although I have dealt with Indigenous affairs in *Nugget*, I have done so under different thematic headings and by narrating different incidents to those in *Obliged*. I invite readers interested in Coombs' intervention into Indigenous policy to read both books, or at least *Obliged* and pages 284–5, 300–2, 324–9 and 340–52 of this one.

In both books I have presented Coombs' public life as a series of attempts to answer the question: how can liberal government draw heavily on the expertise of policy intellectuals while continuing to honour popular sovereignty?

In *Obliged* the 'popular sovereignty' that he sought to promote was that of the dispossessed Indigenous Australians who had not been party to the federal compact of 1901, and who were only just beginning to emerge, in the 1960s, from beneath an intrusive apparatus of 'protection' and citizenship training. The characteristic dilemma of the 'self-determination' liberalism of which Coombs was an exemplary exponent was to promote instruments of Indigenous choice without pre-empting, by the design of those instruments, the field of Indigenous choices. The dilemma became evident in a number of ways that I highlighted in *Obliged*: in tensions between local and national Indigenous agencies, in Coombs' differences of opinion with Charles Perkins, in Coombs' ambivalence towards large Indigenous agencies such as the Northern Territory Land Councils, in his expectation that Indigenous Australians were both innovative and conservative in their approach to the work of politics, and in the multiple meanings of 'accountability'. Were these tensions endemic to 'self-determination' or were they 'contradictions' in the thinking of one intellectual? This issue has been raised by the debate on Indigenous policy that has flourished in Australia since 1999. In that debate, Coombs has become iconic, for some policy critics, of all that is flawed in 'self-determination' policy.

My two books on Coombs should cause readers to doubt such personifying accounts of policy eras, paradigms and traditions. For me, the study of Coombs' life has revealed much about problems that are intrinsic to twentieth-century liberal-democratic thought and practice. My intention in *Nugget* has been to continue to show that 'liberal governance' can be understood as an endless and unavoidable effort to deal with certain dilemmas of rule. In particular, I highlight two problems that were characteristic of Coombs' career as an economist with a deep interest in government – problems that give that career much of its energy and unity.

One problem was: how to secure within the political elite an economic rationality that was socially integrative and (later) ecologically responsible? I want to re-present Coombs as an 'economic rationalist'. This label will surprise those who equate 'economic rationalism' with the deregulation of markets for goods, services, labour and finance and with the promotion of market-based solutions to the allocation of hitherto collectively provided goods. Coombs enjoys iconic status among those opponents of 1980s and 1990s economic rationalism whom Paul Kelly has described as the 'sentimental traditionalists' of contemporary Australian politics. The 'sentimental traditionalists' included (in 1994):

> The academic Hugh Stretton, the commentator B. A. Santamaria, the *Age*'s economic editor, Ken Davidson, the Australian Democrats, the Kerry Packer-owned magazine *Australian Business*, virtually the entire ALP left and sections of the ALP right, most of the National Party's formal membership, sections of manufacturing industry, a number of powerful trade unions, the Melburnian conservative intellectuals based upon *Quadrant* magazine, the 'new class' teachers and public sector professionals, most of the literary establishment, the Fraser era Liberals, and the opponents of the 1980s dry revolution within the Liberal Party.[14]

Hugh Stretton dedicated his 1986 *Political Essays* to Nugget Coombs.

Although I share many of this constituency's deep reservations about the trends in Australian public policy since the 1980s, I have also had to distance myself from one feature of their political sensibility – their fondness for making Coombs an object of nostalgia, an emblem of imperilled or mourned political values. Jack Waterford, introducing what seems to have been Coombs' last published interview, described him as 'the last of a generation of public servants of enormous intellectual breadth'. He referred to Coombs' 'breadth of outlook, as opposed to the narrowness of the present day'. 'We need a few more public servants like him.'[15] Phillip Adams invited us 'to look again at the life of Nugget so we can see what values the neo-cons[ervatives] are so joyfully destroying, what skills they seem determined to lose'. Though at risk of being seen as 'an historic relic', Coombs' 'brand of political ethics remains indispensable to civilised life'. His writings were of 'increasingly urgent relevance to these mean-spirited times'.[16] I find these tributes ambivalent – ostensibly looking forward, but nostalgic and elegiac. To be hailed 'a national treasure' – as was Coombs – was a tribute tinged with bewildered regret.

In proposing that we see Coombs as an economic rationalist, we first have to detach that term from the right wing of the political spectrum and affix it instead to his professional identity. That is, I use the phrase 'economic rationalism' to refer to any way of thinking about public policy in which 'politics' is viewed from the standpoint of 'the economy'. 'The economy' is the object of knowledge that economists have produced since the eighteenth century; they claim to know its workings better than anyone else. Therefore 'economic rationalism' is the defining professional ideology of economics and of economists. This is as true of economists of the left, who promote public ownership and/or the mixed economy, as it is of economists of the right, who promote market-based allocations of goods. Left and right 'economic rationalists' differ in their accounts of what makes economies viable, but both evaluate public policy from the standpoint of the economy's ultimately undeniable demands.

In Part 2 of this biography, I show the steps by which Coombs became able to abstract 'the economy' from the rest of social life. In Part 3, I highlight, all too briefly, his peers' strongest claim to intellectual authority – their construction, between the world wars, of a statistics-based knowledge of 'the economy'. Entry into the profession of economists entailed Coombs' growing confidence in the political relevance of economists, that is, of a critical discourse about public policy based on knowledge of 'the economy'.

That there is nothing inherently right-wing about being an economic rationalist is clear from what followed as Coombs ascended, as an 'expert', into the political elite. Having to fight a war of survival from 1939 to 1945 made that Australian political elite needful of a model of the economy as a 'thing' that could be shaped, mobilised and governed, in order to avoid two problems of the previous world war: inflation and chaotic demobilisation. Coombs became a Keynesian – despite his theoretical reservations about Keynes' *General Theory* of 1936 – because Keynesian economics and the new categories of official statistics provided that model. It was good because it worked. His application of that model as Director-General of Post-war Reconstruction in the Curtin and Chifley Labor governments is my theme on pages 92–151.

The critical edge of Coombs' Keynesian economic rationalism emerged in the 1950s in his campaign, as Governor of the Commonwealth Bank, against the inflationary tendency that is built into any full employment economy. I have portrayed the political difficulties of Coombs' long (if intermittent) fight against inflation on pages 108–14, 200–27, 231–4, 243–8 and 302–7. That story starts with the policy failure of one Labor government – Curtin's unwillingness to entertain a new incomes policy mechanism in the 1945 White Paper *Full Employment in Australia* – and ends with the policy failure of another – Whitlam's approach to wage indexation and public finance, 1973–5. Between these two episodes are many moments when Coombs' quest to defeat inflation pitted him not against the trade unions (a political obstacle in 1945 and 1974–5) but against the various interests favoured by the Coalition government: the military, the States, the champions of immigration and of national development, the private banks and hire-purchase companies, and the pervasive culture of post-war consumer affluence. Coombs apprehended each of these interests as blithely risking Australia's hard-won social cohesion. As a Keynesian economic rationalist, his characteristic post-war anxiety, until the 1970s, was that Australians were unable and unwilling to structure their economy so that private activity was properly balanced by a strong public sector, so that industries were globally competitive and so that money kept its value.

He was therefore ambivalent about that great achievement of the post-war era, sustained economic growth. On the one hand, he was grateful for the social integration that it underpinned; he had witnessed the polarising miseries of the Great Depression not only in Perth but in London, and he was determined that they should not be repeated. On the other hand, he found in affluence an edge of wanton excess, of dispirited selfishness, of disregard for future generations; he saw a tendency towards 'private affluence and public squalor', to quote a kindred spirit J. K. Galbraith (to whom Coombs sent a copy of his 1970 Boyer Lectures). As it happened, the moment of Coombs' retirement as Governor of the Reserve Bank was also when scientists from the industrialised capitalist nations began to extrapolate from economic growth trends in order to warn of the ecological disaster that humanity was preparing for itself.

Coombs took this message to heart and found a new meaning for 'economise'. The mission of the economist was not to promote growth; that was a 'heresy' into which too many economists had fallen. To be an economist was to present conscientiously to the public answers to the question: how to revalue the resources we have so as to use them sustainably and equitably?

What then of 'economic man'? If economics were to rededicate itself to 'economising', in this sense, did it not require a new set of assumptions about human propensities? Not able to assure himself of an answer to that question in 1970–1, Coombs' recently awakened interest in Indigenous Australians developed a new intellectual relevance. Were not Indigenous Australians a living demonstration of the cultural limits of economists' usual assumptions about human nature? Indeed, were not Indigenous Australians an implicit reproach to the prosperity that economists' expertise had helped to bring about? As I show on pages 318–31, these were some of the questions that Coombs asked himself in the early 1970s. Readers will find in these chapters some of the philosophical context of the policy activism that I have narrated in *Obliged*.

This brings me to the other problem that bothered Coombs as an *economist* policy intellectual: how to sensitise the political elite to problems of governance that were at risk of inadequate representation in the terms of any economic rationality? I have already mentioned his wrestling with the relationship between ecology and economy. Before that question arose Coombs had been concerned with other issues of the 'quality of life'. Australia could improve the amenities of rural and remote regions (he was a child of both Perth and its hinterland, pages 12–34). Relations between men and women were not as they should be (women's stake in 'reconstruction', pages 99–105, and in full employment, pages 227–31). And would Australia not be enriched, in non-material and material senses, if it gave security and freedom to people who were scientifically and artistically creative (pages 166–72, 192–7, 254–85 and 296–300)?

If Coombs worked to ensure, intermittently throughout his career, that these 'non-economic' interests had a political voice, he was no less determined to see that they were well managed. For Coombs the tasks of representation and of management tended to be closely linked, in two senses. Not only would better governance flow from hearing from all interests, but marginal interests could help to secure their voice by showing how well they could manage themselves. Coombs' interest in neglected constituencies sometimes included his prodding 'prima donnas' (as he once affectionately called artists and academics) towards self-disciplines that were scarcely of their own imagining. This duality of management and representation is certainly characteristic of Coombs' approach to artists and academics, and his experience in those spheres informed his approach to Indigenous affairs.

It is more difficult, though not impossible, to formulate in these terms those episodes in which he showed sensitivity to the marginalisation of women. Certainly, Coombs conceded the rationality of admitting women as full members of the professional-managerial class (for that issue see pages 72–5, 99–104, 227–31 and 335–6). He also cherished what made women 'different' from men, and wished, during the war, to enable and enrich women's home-making in the new social order. The creativity and happiness of women in that sphere requires something of men that far exceeds what I could convey with the vocabulary of 'management', 'representation' and 'governance' that I have generally found illuminating of Coombs. Coombs as father and husband is this book's most elusive topic. I agreed, at his insistence, not to write in such a way as to invade the privacy of his family and of intimate friends. His papers, rich in so many ways, are a poor basis for a story of Coombs' emotions. I can only hope that a reader who looks at pages 140–4, 181–5 and 217–18 will find something in Coombs' metaphors and my silences.

In the last thirty years of Coombs' life – the post-retirement third of it – Coombs found ways to broaden the sensitivities of a political elite whose understanding of government had shrunk to the horizons of the major economic interests. In particular, in the years 1967–74, he consummated thirty years of arts advocacy and initiated thirty years of Indigenous advocacy. He witnessed sympathetically, and at times abetted, the assertiveness of youth and of women, and he found allies for the cause of conservation in a reformulated political economy and in the Aboriginal land rights movement. He became the self-conscious maverick of the Establishment. This was not merely an intellectual and political exercising of ageing muscles and brain cells. Coombs was energised – I suspect to an extent that surprised even him – by rediscovering the Australia he thought he knew, through repeated visits to Aboriginal communities in Arnhem Land, the western desert and the Kimberley, through friendship (and classificatory kinship) with Aboriginal people, and through a deepening understanding of what their art so beautifully expressed. His commitment to what he called their 'autonomy' was best expressed in his campaign, from 1979, for a 'treaty' to extinguish *validly* – with legislative and possibly constitutional guarantees of their rights – Indigenous Australians' sovereignty.

Coombs took the opportunity to theorise this work of mediation – that is, of making more diverse and complex the connections between the political elite and their subjects – when he became Chair of the Royal Commission on Australian Government Administration from 1974 to 1976. The Royal Commission's report postulated a new ideal of the public servant – the 'responsive public servant', and it called for the public service to have a more diverse recruitment base. The responsive public servant was the link between government and the interests and power centres that government needed to address. He or she was not simply an anonymous servant and adviser of the Minister, but an active agent, enabling and sustaining a channel of communication, and helping to adapt the interlocutors – government and social interest – to the demands of their dialogue.

It is possible to read this doctrine of the 'responsive public servant' as a resolution of one of the defining tensions of Coombs' career – that between the public servant and the public intellectual. Coombs held the following publicly mandated offices: bank economist (1935–9), Treasury official (1939–42), Director of Rationing (1942), Director-General of Post-war Reconstruction (1943–9), Governor of the Commonwealth and Reserve Banks (1949–68), Pro-Chancellor of the Australian National University (1959–68) and its Chancellor (1968–76), Chair of the Australian Council for the Arts (1967–73), Chair of the Australia Council (1973–4), Chair of the Council for Aboriginal Affairs (1967–76). Each one of them posed him the question: to what extent must I limit my campaign for better policy to the giving of confidential advice to the political authority under whom I work?

As the record of this book shows, there were periods in Coombs' life when he transgressed the public service rules of anonymity and confidentiality. In 1943 and 1944 he was outspoken in soliciting public support for increased powers for the national government. In contrast, he made no public addresses over five years,

1948–53, such was his cautious initial estimation of the conventions of Governorship. His campaign in the 1950s against inflation and for consensual bank regulation exhibited his tactical ambivalence about his office's public voice. As Chair of ACFTA and CAA, we see him finding different balances again between the need to rouse the public and the imperative to serve the Minister. From 1976, he occupied a new kind of public position, research academic at the university that he helped to found. Here the conventions of office leaned decisively in favour of being the outspoken 'public intellectual'. Perhaps *that* Coombs is now best remembered – the increasingly biting critic of governments who compromised Indigenous land rights. His fury at Liberals such as Fred Chaney, Ian Viner and Malcolm Fraser in the period 1978–81 was certainly no secret.

This story could be told as a 'progress' from constraint to freedom. To do so would be to miss the point that Coombs had good reasons to be an ambivalent mandarin. No matter how eager he might be to offer publicly his influential representations of the common good, he did not lose sight of the need for democratic legitimation of all his schemes. Without his own public mandate, he could not lightly dismiss the idea of the 'career service' – the duty of public servants to advise elected governments expertly and fearlessly, but anonymously. Careful calculation about when, where and how to speak was also vital to a program of elite education, such as his effort to woo the general managers of the private banks and hire-purchase companies to trust his policy of commercial self-restraint. His public chidings of the banks were almost pusillanimous in their decorum. There is no doubt that Coombs sometimes chafed against the contraints of this self-effacing model of public service. To retire from the Governorship in 1968, and to move from government to academia in 1977 were moments of personal release.

Coombs could find a mid-point between 'public servant' and 'public intellectual' by describing himself as an 'enabler'. Upon ceasing to chair the Australia Council in 1974, he responded to warm speeches of thanks by saying that he found it hard to recognise himself in the praise he had just heard. He denied that he was a connoisseur of the arts. 'I know they are important but they do not come easily to me.' (It had taken him years to find pleasure in Bach, he said.) Administrators, he pointed out, are 'enablers', and administrators of the arts, especially, must cultivate their humility. This was a well-developed theme in the Coombs persona, given special emphasis in 1973–4 because many in the arts constituency were questioning the pace, process and direction of Coombs' policy leadership. In 1971, Coombs had received the Arts Award of the Henry Lawson Festival at Grenfell, New South Wales. In his speech of thanks he admitted to feeling

> somewhat guilty about it. This is partly because when I look at the names of my predecessors I am conscious that in them the flame of creative energy burned in such a way which is not within the capacity of an administrator or the instrument of public patronage such as I am.[17]

He sometimes ironised his enabling centrality as 'conceit'. When Film Australia's Frank Heimans asked Coombs in 1991 to articulate the personal quality which attracted Prime Ministers to seek his advice and to entrust him with great tasks, Coombs answered: 'Well it's partly lucky, I know that I'm lucky ... and maybe my wife's comment is not without some relevance that I'm conceited enough to think that ... I can do these things.'[18] I have no idea how often, if at all, Mrs Coombs said such a thing, but there is no underestimating the power of spousal comment (whether gentle or caustic) to disarm those empowered by the world's praise. 'Distaff' can trump 'staff' every time, for every CEO with a family to go home to. Lallie Coombs told the ANU's *Convocation News* in 1976 that 'my part is that of Devil's Advocate – or a restraining influence'. She did not see herself as having succeeded entirely in keeping Coombs' 'feet on the ground'.[19]

Coombs worried about being part of the Establishment, rather than being among the critical resources ensuring society's constant renewal. Addressing the University of Sydney's graduation ceremony on 27 March 1969, when he was awarded an honorary Doctorate in Laws, he issued a warning.

> Boredom rather than exuberance is the danger of contemporary life, and pre-tentiousness and pomposity its besetting sins. From today you will be offered the safe way – the safe job, the accepted opinion, the conventional wisdom. The community will conspire to wrap you in a cocoon of conformity and the accumulating weight of responsibility may lead you to welcome its protection. You may even be given honorary degrees and invited to make pompous and sententious speeches at graduation ceremonies. However there is within you the qualities to resist this if you wish.[20]

There is more to this advice than 'don't be conformist'. Coombs offered himself as a possible instance of the Establishment's rhetorical flatulence. Was there within him 'the qualities to resist this'?

I can offer the reader little insight into that inward Coombs that lay beyond his self-effacing ways of writing and talking. Some biographies tell the reader what made the subject tick. This one does not. In this lack I am comforted by a man who knew him for about half a century, the academic John Passmore. When I asked him if he knew what made Coombs tick, he replied: 'No. I never knew. I just saw him as a series of admirable projects.' On pages 19–21 I offer a reading of two teenage essays by Coombs to suggest that he may have been ambivalent from adolescence about his own brilliant and effective agency. This is a rare and tentative moment of psychological portraiture, but I am encouraged by seeing the spirit of these essays in Coombs' remark, forty-eight years later, to a friend who had just commented on his draft Boyer Lectures. 'Microphones and captive audiences (even if imaginary) are corrupting things.'[21] 'Corrupting' is a power-fully censorious word typical of Coombs' puritanism. A series of admirable projects indeed.

Perhaps Coombs' persistent tactics of self-effacement are part of the truth of the inner man. Coombs was named a Companion of the Order of Australia in 1975. Being a good time-manager, he answered nearly all letters of congratulation with a thoughtfully composed form letter.

An old friend has reminded me that Alfred Deakin said that the only honours he would wish for would be those conferred upon him by the Australian people. This is a rather chauvinist view and I do not think I hold it, but the identification of the award with Australia certainly appealed to me. Despite the manifest deficiencies of us, its inhabitants, I am like James Macauley [*sic*], 'fitted to that land as the soul is to the body'. That sounds pretentious but I am afraid that awards often make men both pretentious and pompous. Ecclesiastes probably has the last word – see Chapter 1, Verse 2.[22]

Three quotations, his endorsement of two of them withheld in subsequent commentary ('rather chauvinist … sounds pretentious'). Here is a man evading the capture of his own rhetoric, extraordinarily sensitive to the possibility of hubris, whether national or personal. However, there is ('probably'), he says, a 'last word', though he playfully refuses to give those words. Depending on which English translation of Ecclesiastes they consulted, his correspondents would have read:

Futility of futilities, says the Preacher, futility of futilities, all is futile.

or

Completely meaningless, Qohelet said, completely meaningless. Everything is meaningless.

Either way, Coombs invoked the Bible's most heterodox voice in order to tilt his newly bestowed aura. Awarded a halo, Coombs turned it into a frisbee.

Part 1
Learning and teaching

Childhood and youth

THE CHILDHOOD AND adolescence of Herbert Cole Coombs were shaped by two modernising forces that transformed the landscape and social life of the south-west of Western Australia in the thirty years (1895–1925) after the Kalgoorlie and Coolgardie gold rushes: the spread of a railway system to open up land to intensive agriculture, and the systematic cultivation of children's minds, wherever their parents tilled the soil, in a comprehensive and newly profession-alised public education system. Coombs was the son of a railway employee, and by his eighteenth birthday, he had set his foot on the first rung of the teaching profession.

Coombs' father was Francis Robert Henry Coombs, known to all as Frank. Born around 1880 (he may have lied about his age to get a job) in England, Frank lost his father, a marine engineer, in an accident in a river in India. He grew up and was educated at an endowed school for the orphaned sons of members of the merchant navy. Having migrated to Western Australia, he joined the Western Australian Government Railways in January 1899 as a cleaner at Perth station.[1]

Frank Coombs joined a rapidly expanding concern. In the south-western corner of Western Australia the British Empire's migrants and investors, urged by enthusiastic governments, saw limitless promise. British investors who had missed the South African diamond and gold booms and who were wary of the slumps and industrial disputes of eastern Australia were turning in hope to the west of the continent. Encouraged first by gold discoveries at Kalgoorlie and Coolgardie, the investors' money

stayed in Western Australia to prime the growth of basic industries and public services, especially railways. By the time the goldfields passed their peak of pro-duction in 1903, the West was ready to benefit from William Farrer's experiments in New South Wales in breeding new varieties of wheat for areas of marginal rainfall. This gave credibility to what might otherwise have been the vain faith of Western Australians in their country's potential.[2]

Marketing the fruits of agriculture – not only wheat but other cereals, fruit and vegetables – required a railway system. To extend track was to access the earth's riches. In 1894 there were 324 miles of track, in 1931, 4181 (521 and 6731 kilometres respectively). This growth exceeded the rise in population (which was itself gaining quickly from immigration), so that in 1894 there were 209 persons for every mile of track and in 1931 only 100 persons per mile. The public debt from railway construction increased by a factor of twenty, again faster than the population: debt per head for the railways' proliferation tripled between 1894 and 1931. The pattern of railway intensification – a few main lines embellished with 'branch lines, loop lines and spur lines' – obeyed the social principle embodied in the *Homestead Act* of 1893: closer settlement, the conversion of large pastoral leases and mining regions to smaller agricultural holdings. For those plots to be viable, it was argued in the 1905 Royal Commission on Immigration and Land Settlement, they must be no more than fifteen miles from a rail service.[3]

The frequency of Frank Coombs' transfers is a cameo of the network's dynamism: the rapidly expanding railway system valued the unattached migrant. Eight months after starting as a cleaner at Perth Station, Frank became a porter (six shillings per day) at Chidlow, just across the Darling Ranges, about 50 kilometres east of Perth. Sixth months later he was 'night officer' at North Dandalup on £130 per year. Five months later, still a 'night officer', he found himself in Clackluie where he stayed for seven months, before being transferred to Spencer's Brook. In February 1902, after eleven months at Spencer's Brook, Frank was sent to York, one of the oldest towns in Western Australia, the heart of the agricultural and grazing lands of the Avon Valley.

It was was probably there that Frank met the young woman of eighteen whom he was to marry the following year, Rebecca Elliott.

Rebecca was the daughter of one of York's more distinguished figures, William Willoughby Lowry Cole Elliott. Born in Mullaghbane, Co. Fermanagh, Ireland, on 24 January 1856, Elliott had arrived in Western Australia in 1887. He lived first in the Canning district, where he lost his wife Annie Storey in March 1891. Moving to York, he was a Councillor and member of the York Local Board of Health from 1896 to 1910. In June 1910 the Board appointed him Health Inspector. Three years later he became Town Clerk, holding the job until he died in 1918, aged sixty-three. He 'commanded the highest esteem and respect of the community', and his 'unexpected' death 'cast a gloom over the town'.[4]

The town's sense of premature loss is echoed in Coombs' inaccurate recollection (seventy-seven years later) that Elliott had died relatively young, in his forties.[5] Coombs recalled Elliott's 'rather joking style towards children' with whom he was not 'enormously comfortable'. His mother's admiration for Elliott also impressed itself on him.[6] Rebecca Elliott had been only seven years old when her mother Annie had died. As Coombs once put it, 'she had the benefit of growing up in the company of her father who was a very well educated man, and a great reader'.[7] Though only twelve when W. Cole Elliott died, Coombs retained a definite impression of his Protestant grandfather's personality as 'intellectually innovative and emotionally conservative' and 'not a Home Ruler, but a rebel'.[8]

By the time Frank and Rebecca married in 1903, Frank was back in Perth, now on £150 per year. Their first child, Jimmy, was born in 1904. Some time in that year, Frank was made officer in charge of the station at Kalamunda, 300 metres above sea level in the Darling Ranges east of Perth. Private interests had built the trunk line to Kalamunda to facilitate timber-getting. By 1906 the town's guesthouses and hotel had become the haunt of 'visitors from the capital and from Fremantle who delude themselves in thinking that they go there for a change of air', in the words of Perth's Italian consul.[9] There Rebecca gave birth to a second child on 24 February 1906. He was christened Herbert Cole Coombs.

Other siblings followed at roughly two-year intervals: Annie Adelaide (Nancy) in 1908, Betty in 1910, then a five-year gap during which Rebecca miscarried at least once, before Jenny in 1915 and Phyllis in 1917.[10] In the year of Betty's birth, Jimmy died of diphtheria. Coombs could recall little of him in 1989 – a walk in the bush, when Jimmy let him get lost, and sitting in the sand together sketching a comet they had observed.[11] In 1974, Coombs recalled that Jimmy's death made him and his mother 'rather like companions' by the time young Phyllis was born. 'Effectively the oldest of the five children in our family ... I helped around the house.'[12] He recollected that in his childhood,

> I had fairly considerable domestic responsibilities, you know I looked after the girls and nursed the babies and ... I learnt to be a good cook. At the age of about 11 ... my mother had to go to hospital for an operation, ... and she was in hospital for some weeks, and I kept house, did all the cooking, cleaned the house and all that ... because my father ... was a kindly man, but he thought that a husband was performing properly if he stayed out of the kitchen, didn't interfere.[13]

It must have been difficult for Rebecca to find a social base for her mothering in a circle of other mothers, for the Railways kept Frank and his family on the move: to Bardoc, when Coombs was three months old, to Morgans when he was thirteen months and on to Kellerberrin shortly after he turned two. The loss of Jimmy and the frequent breaking of the family's outside attachments offered Coombs the chance to develop a sense of responsibility beyond his years, a quality that sister Phyllis warmly recalled to me in 1995.[14]

By the time young Bertie (as his family always called him) was eligible to go to school (six years of age), Frank Coombs was master of the station at Karrakatta, a non-residential area among the suburbs just to the west of the city of Perth. Instead of suburban cottages, this curious urban zone boasted a cemetery, a lunatic asylum and a military camp – but no local school. If little Bertie were to start his education, he would have to go to Claremont, a short train ride away. Coombs recalls being entrusted to an older child for this momentous journey. The boy told him that he would have to get out of the train quickly, once it stopped. Too eager, Coombs seized the handle of the 'dog box' in which they were seated before the train had come to a halt. The door swung open with his weight, and he found himself hanging onto the handle as the train dragged him along the platform. His arrival at the school with scraped and bleeding knees was a minor sensation. The teacher sent him home, with a note telling his parents that Bertie was too young for the journey to school. Although his parents were reluctant to accept this instruction, Bertie was kept home the next day. He went exploring, and was soon peering into an interesting-looking well, in which there was an inviting ladder. He climbed down, jumping from the bottom of the ladder into water which, fortunately, was not very deep. It was a few hours before he was found again. A distraught Rebecca put it to Bertie that if he were going to risk his life going down a well, he might as well risk it going to school.

Within a few months, the family moved once more, this time to Bridgetown. For the first time, the Railways Department let the Coombs family settle. Coombs was able to complete his primary schooling at the recently opened (1911) Bridgetown school, a five- to ten-minute dawdle from the station-master's wooden cottage.

Bridgetown, on the Blackwood River, prospered in the era of closer agricultural settlement that followed the 1890s gold boom. The rail line had quickened the conversion of land use from grazing to agriculture. Hilly and well-watered, the soils favoured orchards. When the first engine pulled into Bridgetown station in 1895, it passed under a 'specially built arch with the significant description "Our engine means development, advancement and prosperity to our town and country, Blackwood, the garden of Western Australia. God Save the Queen"'.[15] The railway had also encouraged the timber industry, a steam-driven mill commencing the same year as the rail service. Bridgetown had its first hospital by 1899, and in the decade before the war it began to be the administrative centre for a number of government services. In 1906 the Italian Royal Consul Zunini had come to the conclusion that this part of the State, particularly the adjoining district of Kojonup, was the prime destination for immigrant Italian farmers. Zunini pronounced Bridgetown to be 'probably the most picturesque town in Western Australia'.[16] There was soon a Mechanics Institute where a Mrs Ellis worked as librarian from 1906 to 1934. In 1911 the Associated Fruitgrowers constructed a packing shed near the railway station. The Bridgetown Cooperative Society formed in 1917, and a cider factory was built.

As the stationmaster of this bustling, pretty little town, Frank Coombs was assured a busy time. 'A very gentle sort of person', Frank was also 'a keen rifle man and collected several trophies', Coombs once recalled.[17] Whether Coombs joined Frank in target practice I do not know, but he shared his father's penchant for football and cricket.[18] Both parents left their mark on him. Coombs' love of sport was as inextinguishable as his love of reading.

Coombs' mother 'was interested in intellectual things and encouraged me to read widely'.[19] Dickens, Thackeray, Hardy and Trollope were her favourites.[20] If we can imagine young Coombs accepting many books over Mrs Ellis' counter, we know that he was also in contact with one of the town's most important figures, the Anglican Rector of St Paul's from 1911 to 1937, Fred Davis. A worldly parson, according to Bridgetown's historian, Davis was the first man to bring a car to the district 'and his service to the apple industry as a grower and fruit grower's representative was second only to his service as a spiritual leader and adviser'.[21] Frank Coombs had been raised a nonconformist Christian and made his way into Freemasonry, but Rebecca had brought him around to Anglican observance, and so the family worshipped together, with young Coombs in the choir and at Sunday school. When called upon to write a reference for Coombs in August 1921, Fred Davis could say that he had been 'in almost daily touch with [Coombs] for four or five years'. He praised the lad's 'integrity and steady application to his studies'.[22]

Rebecca's Christian faith gave pride of place to social justice – 'a kind of Christian Socialist'.[23] In 1974 Coombs described his mother (only recently deceased in 1971) as 'not a politically minded woman – few were in those days – she was disappointed that social institutions didn't reflect Christian values'.[24]

'She thought that Christ really meant it.'[25] Frank Coombs was also 'a good trade union man' with 'a general Labor Party type political philosophy'.[26] Coombs' pocket-money job of minding some cows also brought him into contact with a yardman who was a 'Wobbly' – a member of the Industrial Workers of the World. He recalled watching that man confront a visiting recruiting officer. 'I was astonished to find myself on the side of the yardman' as he denounced the imperialist war.[27] He heard the anti-conscriptionists vilified, but the first time he saw a photograph of Archbishop Mannix he found his face 'absolutely beautiful … the face of an aesthetic [ascetic?], the face of a saint'. Coombs' family were not 'actually against the war, but they certainly weren't enthusiastic about it'.[28] Coombs could recall ringing the Bridgetown school bell, in the final weeks of his primary schooling, on Armistice Day, 11 November 1918.[29]

Schooling

IN 1967 BRIDGETOWN'S *Civic Centre Bowling Club News* sourced the current Reserve Bank Governor's knowledge of book-keeping to the tuition of one Ted Swift.[1] A more substantial intellectual influence at primary school was the young head teacher who arrived when Coombs was 'about eleven I suppose' – W. N. Roberts, 'a very brilliant teacher' with 'the gift of making you feel that [your learning] was important to him'.[2] In 1954, Coombs recalled that 'it was his enthusiasm and confidence in my capacity which started me along the academic road.'[3] Roberts knew that the State's rapidly expanding school system held out the prospect of a career to bright boys and girls. In 1918, he set his sights on the fifty scholarships tenable at Perth Modern School, the only State secondary school in Perth at that time. As Coombs later recalled,

> because I'd been moved around …, I hadn't really reached the level of school which would have made me eligible even to sit for the examinations. But [Roberts] picked me out and he had a look at some of the things I'd done and he said 'you're going to sit for one of these scholarships' … I got the 49th out of 50.[4]

Roberts later commended Coombs as 'one of the most industrious lads I know, reliable, trustworthy and full of ambition. As a prospective Candidate for the teaching profession, there is no one I would more strongly recommend, but in any branch of work requiring brains and determination he should make good.'[5]

The Perth Modern School had opened its doors eight years before Coombs enrolled, in February 1911, in Subiaco, an inner western suburb of Perth, with Joseph Parsons as headmaster. Cecil Andrews, the State's founding Director of Education, thought 'Modern' was consistent with the teaching of science and modern languages.[6] It was modern in other respects also. After long service leave in the United Kingdom in 1914, Parsons concluded that our mode of discipline appears to be unique. In no boys' school did I find a system of discipline that was not based on a definite system of rewards and punishments, involving in most cases corporal chastisement, while the Modern School has been conducted for four years without any system of either reward or punishment, except in the inherent sense of … the feeling of work well or ill done.[7]

According to a fellow student of Coombs', Ralph Honner, Perth Modern School 'did not teach, it merely allowed you to learn'. Honner recalled a good library, which students were encouraged to explore. Knowledge was not drummed in, he said, there was no learning by rote. However, he also remembered few teachers with an aptitude for teaching. Charles Sharp, the English master (and Parsons' 'First Assistant'), was 'up in the clouds': he did not correct students' work, but rather asked them to read aloud their writing assignments in which they were meant to display a mastery of the style of the author whom the class had just been studying. According to Honner, homework was set, but it was not compulsory. Parsons did not allow prizes to be awarded in the school.[8] Parsons saw value in sport. As an inspector, he had written that 'a teacher who is willing to play with his children not only keeps his own youth but gains the confidence and affection of his pupils'.[9] In order to encourage a spirit of competition, he introduced factions into the school in 1915 – gold, blue, red and 'sphinx'. Coombs was in 'gold' (where else?).

Coombs entered the school on 7 February 1919, supported by the scholarship – £30 per year, with £5 a year book allowance. Coombs resided in one of Subiaco's approved boarding houses, first with a Mrs Shotter (a friend of the family at 164 Subiaco Road) and later with Mrs Brownless, at 142 Cambridge Street. For a thirteen-year-old affectionately bonded to his family, this time away from them must have tested his desire for an education. The fellowship of other students, many of them also in boarding houses, while reducing loneliness, also made demands. Phyllis Hatt tells that when Coombs said that he wished to continue to attend Sunday services, he was branded 'Holy Coley'.

What were his aspirations? Under 'Course Desired', a standard heading on the enrolment form, the school had noted 'Teacher or Journalist'. Teaching offered the opportunity of his quick return to his family, as a breadwinner. Shortly after he began to live in Subiaco, the Coombs family moved to Busselton. Coombs considered leaving Perth Modern as soon as he could to be a 'monitor' in Busselton, at the end of 1921. To return home, with only his Junior Certificate – the minimum requirement for becoming a monitor – was within reach of a lad with 'Junior' passes in English, French, mathematics, history, geography, drawing and physics. The bond between the young Coombs and his family was very strong. Coombs' sister, Phyllis, recalls that Coombs' holiday returns to the family home were celebrated occasions. Rebecca idolised him, and so did his sisters: 'It was impossible to love anyone more than we loved him.' 'He was the centre of everything.'[10] Coombs' wish to leave Perth Modern before matriculation – to work and be paid, and live with his family – must have been strong. His Education Department personnel file includes referees' reports written in September 1921.[11]

Coombs did go on to matriculate at the end of 1923, but his academic results were not so outstanding as to make him an automatic candidate for higher education. In Parsons' 'Loose Leaf Ledger' – 'a complete and detailed account of the student's progress'[12] – the Coombs record is unremarkable.

> April 1919: 'A good all round student but careless and dreamy.'
> July 1919: 'Possesses a good deal of ability but has not done well in exam.'
> December 1919: 'Passed.'
> April 1920: 'Is doing sound work.'
> August 1920: 'Is making sound progress in all subjects of study.'
> December 1920: 'Passed.'
> August 1921: 'Has done very good work except in French.'
> A 1922 entry: 'On last 1921 school day absent without permission. Dilatory and unsatisfactory attendance and punctuality. Spoken to on March 1 1922.'
> April 1922: 'Continues to do good average work except in English and History where he excels.'

Other 1922 and 1923 comments report his steady application to his work and predict his matriculation, but with some fears for his French.[13]

Sport was probably among the reasons for staying the extra two years at Perth Mod. In a 1995 interview with another 'old Modernian', Keith Kessel, Coombs illuminated Parsons' cryptic 'spoken to on March 1 1922'. The headmaster had wanted to know why Coombs had played cricket rather than take a maths exam. Coombs was then in the First Eleven, unusual for a lad in fourth year. To Parsons' accusation that he was 'impertinent and presumptuous', Coombs replied that he had not considered his behaviour in that way. 'Finally Parsons said to me: "Well Coombs, you're the only one of your kind – get out."' Parsons' leniency was consistent with his view of the importance of sport in generating a good school atmosphere and of self-motivation in scholarship. Coombs told Kessel in 1995 that 'I enjoyed my time at the School but not for the right reasons. Looking back, I found it intellectually very disappointing, the teachers not stimulating. The School was, I think, a bit obsessed by performance.'[14] But was not Coombs one of its star performers – in sport at least? According to Ralph Honner, Coombs became known throughout the school, from his second year, for athletic prowess.[15] Picked for the First Eleven in his fourth year, he was the only boy left from that Eleven at the start of 1923, and so became captain. 'Cricket Notes' in the December 1922 issue of *The Sphinx* mentions a fine partnership between Coombs and Calcutt, 'the two diminutive batsmen of the eleven', against Guildford Grammar School.[16]

Coombs was effective with both bat and ball. The traditional match against the masters, at the end of the 1922–3 season, saw his finest bowling performance; he took seven wickets for thirty runs, the last five batsmen falling to consecutive balls. (The students lost the match, nonetheless.) Coombs topped the bowling averages for that season – 21 wickets at 6.25 runs each. As captain, it was his duty to contribute a 'Criticism of the First Eleven' to *The Sphinx*. The team's 'main fault', he wrote, was 'over-eagerness to score. Players should play themselves in before becoming aggressive. Another section of the game which is open to criticism is the running between the wickets, which shows a complete lack of understanding between batsmen.' He then offered comments on each member of the team. It fell to the sportsmaster to sum up Coombs as captain: 'a fine success ... Coombs has quite a variety of successful shots all around the wicket. He is inclined to be impatient ... He is a fair change bowler and a good field.'[17]

Football was another Coombs enthusiasm. The sportsmaster wrote that Coombs 'has been handicaped by his lack of height, and has thus found difficulty in defeating taller opponents. He is, however, very fast, and plays a clever game on the wing.'[18] Coombs' responsibilities in the football season included being a member of the selection panel.

If secondary school offered challenges and recognition, it was more often on the playing field than in the classroom. The curriculum did not challenge him, he recalled in 1995.[19] Coombs' Leaving Certificate subjects were English, maths, history and physics. When Parsons was asked to write a reference for him, in 1924, he found it possible to praise Coombs' work in 1922 and 1923 as 'characterised by excellence on the English side. ... He is a particularly thoughtful and intelligent lad and as he also took a prominent part in sport he should make a good candidate for admission to Teachers College.'[20]

Self-possession

THE PERTH MODERN SCHOOL encouraged its students to write in *The Sphinx.* Two little essays signed 'H.C.' are of great interest if attributed to Coombs. The essays appeared in his fourth year at Perth Modern – 1922, when Coombs had decided to stay on to matriculate and when his zeal for sport was starting to be rewarded by precocious success with bat and ball. A May 1922 essay bore the title 'Expectation and Realisation'.

> *Expectation.* I was batting and enjoying myself immensely. The score board already displayed 50 opposite my name, and I quickly set to work to reduce the difference between that and the coveted three figures. Drives, cuts and hooks followed in such profusion that they became monotonous. I was batting brilliantly, scoring all around the wicket as if I was Hobbs, Macartney and Grace all rolled into one. To the accompaniment of a rousing ovation I reached the century, and continuing to treat the bowling with supreme contempt, I rapidly augmented our total until it was within a few runs of our opponents' score. With a magnificent 'agricultural' (à la Bill Smith [Coombs' team-mate]) followed by a square cut for six (my favourite stroke), I accomplished my object. The enthusiastic crowd of spectators now rushed on to the oval to bear me shoulder high from the ground as the saviour of the match and then – I woke up to find that the rousing cheers were only the combined frantic endeavours of Oscar, Poker and the Brat to rouse me from my pleasant dreams.

Realisation. It was the morning of the great match. My dream had placed me in a very optimistic frame of mind, and I eagerly awaited the opportunity to prove my worth. At last it was time for me to bat. I walked to the crease supremely confident in my own ability and the truth of my vision, and there prepared to face the bowling. The first ball I remembered I was to drive for four, and filled with a laudable determination to do so I awaited its delivery. It came – at least, I suppose it did – and the next things I noticed were that I was walking off without any enthusiastic reception, and that the scorer was placing a very large 0 against my name on the score board. 'I wish score-boards had never been invented,' I growled as I heard some new arrivals reading aloud what was there inscribed.[1]

The second essay by 'H.C.' was published a term later, 'Feelings on speaking at a debate'.

Having, by dint of much moral courage and determination, decided to appear at the debate, I hurried along to R [the room in which debates took place]. Naturally, as I expected to have a companion in misery, my partner failed to arrive, and I was seriously contemplating deserting at the eleventh hour while I still had the opportunity. These reflections were cut short by the entrance of the chairman. The die was cast, and vainly I endeavoured to compose my fears. I had in my hand, which I confess was rather shaky, a paper on which I had written notes concerning the things I wished to say. On hearing my name called by the chairman, I rose mechanically, and to my consternation I discovered that all the arguments and expressions, which I had so carefully prepared on the aforementioned piece of paper, had evaporated. Although I must have made some sort of speech, not only was it not what I intended, but also I am absolutely unable to recall a single word which I employed. My chief feeling was one of infinite longing to return to the seat which I had vacated, it seemed to me, hours ago. It is totally beyond my powers even to attempt to describe or analyse that feeling of overpowering relief which I conceived upon again finding myself seated. My next emotion was one of curiosity. I wondered how big a fool I had made of myself. In order to satiate this curiosity, I enquired of my neighbour, 'Did I make much of a goat of myself?' to which he replied, 'Not so much that you'd notice it.' This, of course, was a great relief, although I had my suspicions that there was just a little sarcasm underlying the reassuring tone which he adopted when answering.[2]

There is striking consistency between the two compositions. The narrator is in each case a public performer confiding some unease about the adequacy of his skills and, hence, about his standing with his public. He wishes to perform, but will he do so creditably? Perhaps the performance will amount to vainglorious nothing.

These two little essays in self-monitoring have in common a literary device which enacts their author's own quiet self-assurance: the first-person narrator is rendered as 'losing' himself: 'the next things I noticed were that I was walking off' and 'upon again finding myself seated'. This relaxation of narrative self-possession occurs at the emotionally critical moment, when the possibility of failure and public humiliation is highest. The narrator's 'public' then becomes the principal actor in each tale's conclusion – posting his duck on the scoreboard, casually adjudicating the cogency, or otherwise, of his speech. The 'I' of the story is thus put in its place by the narration's shift of agency.

Playfully confessional, both pieces present their question: does one dare to put oneself forward, before one's peers, as skilful? Anxiety about failure is here given something of the character of a moral dilemma. The essayist's sense that he might have what it takes is made to wrestle with the thought that confidence may be founded less in skill than in vanity. Acknowledging the perilous possibility of acquitting himself a fool, the two essays hold such a verdict at bay. Not only addressing the possibility of mates' teasing, the essays declare an ever ready *self-censure*. As contributions to the school magazine, they confidently position all peers as witnesses to an accomplished boy's capacity for self-knowledge.

Busselton

UPON GRADUATING FROM Perth Modern School, Coombs re-joined his family as a wage-earner. In 1924, the Education Department appointed him monitor at Busselton Primary School. A monitor (or pupil-teacher) was an apprentice who could study for formal qualification, via exams, as a 'C' level teacher; from there one might advance to Teachers College. Busselton School boasted 145 enrolments when Coombs took up his duties on 20 February 1924, four days before he turned eighteen. The head teacher, Mr H. Jeanes, rearranged classes in order 'to give Mr Coombs a small Class IV'.

Jeanes' record of the life of the school that year included the closing of the school on 7 November to celebrate the completion of the rail line from Busselton to Margaret River (surely a 'holy day' in that State), the decline of attendances to as low as 50–60 per cent when chickenpox, measles, flu and whooping cough made their usual appearances in the winter, the purchase of a gramophone in March, and the culling of old and dilapidated books from the library (and their replacement with new purchases). In a modest way, the school was a cultural centre for Busseltonians. Townsfolk were invited to fund-raising 'recitals' on the new gramophone in March and May; the proceeds were used to purchase records and to pay off the gramophone itself. School fund-raisings – a 'Bazaar' and a fancy-dress ball – helped pay for the piano and purchase books.

Founded in 1832, Busselton was one of the State's oldest ports, servicing the region's timber and dairy industries from the 1850s. From 1871, it was terminus of a private local railway (Western Australia Timber Company) and from 1894, there was a rail connection to Perth. In the 1920s, the region was undergoing one of the State's most ambitious and ill-fated experiments in social and economic transformation – Group Settlement. Commencing in September 1922, Group Settlement was the project of the British, Australian and Western Australian governments to transplant British migrants to the State's south-west. Selected migrants would be formed into groups and allocated portions of uncleared forest land. After getting rid of the trees, they would develop adjoining family-based farms. Sales of their produce – cow's milk and, later, pork – would be sufficient to enable them to repay the government's development costs. Before the scheme commenced, there were 'but a few hundred souls' sprinkled through the forests between Busselton and Augusta. Group Settlement gave impetus to the development of Busselton's hinterland, including the railway whose extension meant a day off for Coombs. The scheme was zealously advocated by the optimistic Sir James Mitchell (whose visit to the Busselton School on 23 May 1924 was no doubt the occasion for yet another speech promoting the land's promise).

There were insufficient grounds for optimism. 'A hundred years of [European] history bore testimony to the difficulties of settlement. The Western Australians who refused to pioneer that part of the country gave their tacit evidence; the thin sprinkling of inhabitants over the wide area was proof of it.' According to the author of these words, the scheme's 'eventual cost was extremely high in money and human suffering'. The signs of difficulty were not slow to appear: by April 1924, 31 per cent of the migrants and 42 per cent of the Australian participants had already left their holdings, defeated by the many unexpected technical challenges of converting the country to dairy farming. According to Jeanes, the school's client population was extraordinarily fluid in 1923–4.

> Since the present H[ead] T[eacher] commenced duties in February 1923, there have been 175 admissions. At that time the enrolment was 117, the present enrolment is 144 so that the school has retained only 27 out of 175 admissions or 15%. This means that a great deal of work has been expended by the staff on a drifting population which has remained from 1 day (in one instance) to varying longer periods.[1]

By 1926, coastal pastures south of Busselton had failed for the third season to supply fodder for dairy herds. Deluded by misleading advertising, ill-served by government administration, and thrown together from a diversity of backgrounds, the Group settlers became insecure and mistrustful.[2]

Coombs must have been aware of the human drama that was playing out around him. In one way, he and his family were among Group Settlement's beneficiaries: as Busselton's stationmaster, his father was a cog in the State's engine of development. However, trying to organise an education for the children of such a restless and disillusioned population might have stimulated Coombs' thoughts about the energies and excesses of this form of modernisation. 'Regional development' was to become one of his life-long interests.

All of Jeanes' quarterly reports about Coombs were favourable, though terse – 'a lad well worth training', as he put it at the end of Coombs' second quarter. According to Phyllis Hatt (who recalls being in a class monitored by her brother), the lad met Jeanes' challenge of 'taming' a few of the more intractable boys at Busselton.[3] Coombs was twice absent from the school during the year, taking examinations in Perth in August (five days missed) and November–December (two weeks absent), in order to get his 'C' levels as a teacher and to qualify for Teachers College. Of Coombs' work with class IV, Jeanes wrote:

> He has closely applied himself to master his profession, and he has achieved a very creditable result in his class work, exhibiting no little ability. Outside the classroom, also, his influence has been pleasing to note, he taking an active part in the organised pastimes of the boys.[4]

Claremont

THE WESTERN AUSTRALIAN government's commitment to the agricultural development of the south-west, from 1895 to 1930, was matched by a zeal to upgrade the education system. Gold rush migration increased enrolment almost sixfold, between 1890 and 1900, from 3352 to 18,557.[1] At the same time the government introduced compulsory education; the 1894 *Amendment Act* made the Education Department responsible for enforcing attendance, replacing 'amateur district boards' under which truancy had been high. A new Inspector-General of Education appointed in 1896, Cyril Jackson, argued the need for a regular census. Recorded attendance was 72 per cent when Jackson arrived; by 1902 it was 90 per cent.[2] No longer would the Department set a minimum number of days on which children should attend; the 1899 *Public Education Act* made education free and compulsory up to the age of fourteen years, and children had to turn up any day the school opened. Truancy persisted. The 1901 Census enumerated two thousand more children in the State than were on the roll.[3] Among struggling rural settlers, children were unpaid labour. To compete with parents' demands, the government had to place schools where families were farming. From 1893 to 1908 the number of schools in Western Australia increased from 100 to 400. Around 1905 there was rapid expansion in the agricultural districts; some schools were no more than tents holding up to twenty-five pupils.[4]

By the time Coombs enrolled at Bridgetown, schools had begun to become instruments of intensified social administration. Medical inspection of all schools commenced in 1911, and children's defective teeth were commonly noted. Schooling was also made longer. In 1912 the primary school curriculum was revised after a conference of inspectors and teachers. The new curriculum would take a child to the sixth standard and to the issue of a qualifying certificate, at age thirteen. The age of entrance was lowered from six to five years in 1916. The Perth Modern School opened its doors in February 1911, and the University of Western Australia commenced classes in makeshift premises in Perth's eastern end in 1913. East Goldfields High School took its first students in 1914. In 1917, a fifth year was added to the secondary curriculum of the State's two high schools.

Such developments necessitated a larger teacher force than could be imported from Britain and the eastern States. The process of making Western Australian teaching 'professional' dates from the early 1890s. In the struggle to end 'state aid' to the Catholic school system – an issue resolved in Western Australia later (1895) than in any other Australian colony – the Catholic Bishop, Matthew Gibbney, had been able to show that many Protestants preferred to send their children to the nuns and brothers, rather than have them languish at the hands of those employed by the Boards of Education.[5] The Department of Education, formed in order to succeed 'state aid', had to improve teacher quality – at first by paying them in a new way. From 1895, no longer would teachers collect fees from parents. Since its inception in 1871, 'payment by results' – attendance figures and examination results – had perpetuated bad teaching, argued teachers. Their short-lived Government Teachers Association had pressed for payment reform from 1892. Salaries were now to be determined by the teachers' levels of training, and school fees were phased out by 1899. These reforms launched teaching as a 'profession' – defined by its credentialled basis of expertise and recruitment – in Western Australia.

It would be many years, however, before all teachers in the Western Australian system were qualified. Cyril Jackson measured the heritage of neglect in 1897. Of 208 head and assistant teachers, only sixteen had been through 'a training college or a normal school'.[6] In 1893, as a form of in-service training, Jackson's predecessor, Chief Inspector James Walton, had begun to issue *Suggestions to Teachers*. As the population boomed in the 1890s, the colony was forced to recruit teachers from elsewhere in Australia, enjoying a good choice of credentialled men as the eastern colonies' economies slumped.

Jackson was critical of a teaching service which for so long had relied on learning on the job, the pupil-teacher system.[7] He initiated the *Education Circular* in 1898 for in-service education, and he imported experts from England to give instruction in teaching method. Jackson overcame a Minister who wished to stint teachers' salaries, and he encouraged the Public School Teachers Association (formed in 1896, and renamed the West Australian State School Teachers Union in 1899), believing such associations to be necessary forums of professional development.[8]

Professionalism in teaching required a local institute of training. In 1902, Claremont Teachers Training College opened, with residential accommodation for sixty students. In the same year, special classes for monitors commenced, quickly evolving into the Normal School which gave selected monitors two years of full-time secondary education. Graduates of the Normal School, after a short time in the classroom, were then admitted to the Teachers College. The Normal School was itself replaced, after four years, by Perth Modern School.

Initially, Claremont offered a form of secondary education, with special emphasis on teaching methods. The principal, William Rooney, formulated a curriculum in 1906 with three aims: liberal education (in English, languages, mathematics, sciences, history and geography); training in subjects taught in schools (music, drill, needlework, manual training and drawing); and 'to inculcate the attitudes and ideals of the teaching profession'.[9] With the formation of the Normal School and then Perth Modern School, this curriculum evolved further towards tertiary, professional training. Optional subjects were introduced, distinctions were made between training for infants and primary teaching, and practical classes – with criticism from observing lecturers – were included. By 1918, these initiatives had made teaching a locally based profession. For the first time, all new teachers required were supplied from within the State, and all future appointments could now be required to be formally trained and credentialled.[10] In 1921 a Royal Commission recommended that matriculation, followed by two years' training, be the minimum qualification for Western Australia's teachers. The Teachers Union agreed.[11]

Claremont's evolution gave it a unique and, in terms of its student culture, ambiguous position within the State's systems of professional training. The college was tertiary, like the new university, in that entry was open first to those who had matriculated through the Leaving Certificate (with monitors filling only such places as were left). Yet Claremont remained unlike the university in that 'even at the close of the Great War, in many respects such as range of subjects, content matter and text-books, the two year course did not far transcend the accepted boundaries of secondary education'.[12] The *Calendar* for 1926 stated that entrance could be gained with no more than Departmental 'C' levels and some probationary period as a teacher.[13] The ethos of Claremont was different from the university in another respect. The college was not only co-educational, but also, for many students, residential, making it necessary for the principal, vice-principal and the women's warden to maintain 'strict discipline and closely planned routine'.[14]

Enrolling at Claremont Teachers College in February 1925, Coombs, with his 'C' certificate earned at Busselton, joined the two-year course which would give him the 'B' certificate he needed to teach primary school children. The training that was not then open to him required either a university degree, or concurrent study full-time at Claremont and the university for three to four years (yielding both a degree and a teaching qualification). Both paths were barred by the relative poverty of his family. To get a degree from the university, he would first have to get a job – not to pay fees, for the university tuition was free, but to help his family. Training for that job would, in any case, deprive his family of his monitor's salary (£172 per year) for two years, but some sacrifice of his income was unavoidable. He would at least have his tuition, board and lodgings at the State's expense and £12 per year to spend on himself.

At Claremont Teachers College, as always for Coombs, sport was a must. In both 1925 and 1926, he played football and cricket (First Eleven) creditably. The football side was particularly successful, winning the Hugo Fischer Cup and the premiership of the Perth District Football Association in 1925; in 1926 the team was undefeated. Coombs was among six college men named as best player on the field in one of the ten matches played in 1925.[15] In 1926 he was awarded an 'honour pocket with badge' for cricket, tennis and football. When the football selection committee published notes on their victorious players they wrote that Coombs had played 'many brilliant games' on left wing. He 'displays fine judgment in leading [passing the ball] to his forwards and is rarely beaten; plays best in fast open game; this player is an accurate drop kick, kicking best when at top speed'. With Perth Modern School friends, Charlie Cook and Ralph Honner, he made up 'the best centre line in the Association'.[16] When the swimming events in the 1926 college carnival were organised by handicap, he also shone in the pool.[17] His dynamic physical presence provoked anonymous doggerel tribute:

> Though he's neither tall nor stout,
> He is exceeding roisterous,
> We wonder how it Coombs about
> That boys can be so boisterous.[18]

His athleticism in dancing was also memorable: 'he used to scoot across the floor', recalled Dorothea Heron (née Chandler.) (The efforts of one 'Pivoting Percy' had also stayed in her mind.) In 1995, Dorothea recalled Coombs and his friends Charlie Cook and Eric Underwood as 'sports fanatics'. As well as playing their own games, they were avid spectators of women's hockey. The anonymous reporter for the *WA Trainee* said of one women's final that 'the men students think they won the match' with their 'valuable assistance during the practices immediately before the final matches'. For every goal scored by Dorothea, Coombs and Charlie Cook shouted her a 'threepenny snowball'.[19] Ralph Honner recalled that sport was central to the social life of the college; few students had any money to spend, and sport was free entertainment.[20]

Sport was the domain of permitted high spirits. Honner remembered Claremont students being 'governed like children'. The college's daily routine, Monday to Saturday, was:

7.25 am	Prayers
7.30 am	Breakfast
8.50 am – 12.25 pm	Lectures
12.30 pm	Dinner
1.35 pm – 4 pm	Lectures (with Wednesday and Saturday afternoons devoted to sport)
4.00 pm	Afternoon tea
6.35 pm	Tea
7.30 – 10.00 pm	Private study
10.00 –10.15 pm	Dancing
10.15 pm	Prayers
10.45 pm	Lights out

The college claimed to keep 'a permanent register of punctuality and regularity in discharge of all duties'. Attendance at lectures was compulsory. Had Coombs wished to stay out of college on Saturday or Sunday nights, he would have needed a note from his 'father or guardian', and to post his name on the 'Exeat' list 'not later than Friday afternoon'. Sunday church was compulsory, and only illness reported to the Senior Student of his dormitory would have excused Coombs from attendance at prayers; another student wished to visit his sick bed, Matron's permission was required. According to recently issued notes on the history of the college,

Student life was characterised by financial hardship and lacked many of the freedoms now associated with student life. Relations between the sexes were governed by a strict, almost Victorian, moral code. Restrictions on social life were most keenly felt by resident students, whose activities were often supervised by tutors. During the 1920s, the practice of 'pairing off' with the opposite sex was discouraged. Male students were instructed to divide their attention 'equally among the women'. Furthermore, habits acquired at University in relation to such matters as retiring hours were not necessarily welcome at College.[21]

The layout of the college's residential first floor made it possible to maintain sexual propriety: the eastern wing was the 'boys' side', the western the 'girls' side'. Matron's sitting room and bedroom stood between them.

But young men and women mixed freely at other times – apart from minor differentiations of curriculum: women took kindergarten, needlework and domestic economy, while boys could get extra instruction in algebra, chemistry, physics and manual training. In the dining room, men and women sat together in groups of eight; it fell to men to carve the joint. Ralph Honner recalls being 'head' of his table. Such tables would be the basis of social outings. Also seated with Honner was Coombs' future spouse Mary ('Lallie') Ross. Lallie had grown up in Perth, converting to Catholicism in her teens. She had a well-developed interest in music and languages, and these passions remained throughout her life. (At Coombs' request I did not interview her. I have understated the part that she played in his life.)

There were only a few high schools from which the student population could be drawn. This added to the cohesion of the student body, to their sense of continuity with secondary school and thus to their *esprit de corps*. 'Editorial notes' in the May 1926 issue of the *WA Trainee* (edited by Coombs and Honner) record that 'the year began with the usual welcome-in social to the First Year and "C" Course. Immediately the feeling of unity between the courses began to display itself in a spirit of camaraderie which rendered the social a striking success. The newcomers settled down quickly into College ways.'[22]

The structure of the dormitories recognised individuality. Each person had a booth or cubicle, containing a bed, a chest of drawers and a folding stool. College rules expressly forbade using any light other than that supplied. This is mild regimentation, compared with that which Coombs would have experienced in the college's compulsory military training, which it pleased him to avoid. Upon entering college he had enrolled in training as a physical education instructor, 'attracted by the fact that satisfactory performance in the course gave exemption from military service'.[23]

Coombs relished academic work at Claremont more than at Perth Modern, especially in the new subjects: philosophy, psychology and economics. 'Suddenly I wanted to be a scholar.'[24] The lecture program was a full one: four per week (each lecture fifty minutes long) in Education (doubled in the second year); two hours of psychology; one lecture per week, for two out of six terms, in 'hygiene'; one per week of scripture (for four of the six terms); five lectures in language, literature and speech training; two each in history and in economics (first year only); some arithmetic, music, drawing and applied art, manual training, physical training, and practicals – with choices among Latin, French, geography, physiography, general science, and mathematics.

Coombs responded well to the 'small classes, close contact with staff and discussion in and out of class', for his mind worked best in a 'dialectic context'. He recalled hearing his economics lecturer (probably Gladys Wearne) give a mistaken exposition of some theory of price determination.

> 'That doesn't make sense,' I thought. 'She must have it wrong.' So I went to the library and read some textbooks. This confirmed my impression but also excited me as I realised that the economic system was 'a system' and that laws governing its operation were capable of being analysed and expressed. It was my first experience of the exhilaration which comes from the conviction that one holds the key to understanding what otherwise seems chaotic.[25]

His results were good, but not outstanding – a general percentage of 71.1 per cent.[26] He would be rated 'B2 provisional'. He had trouble with wood- and metalwork classes, not taking seriously the requirement that he attend them, until he was told that he was putting at risk his entire teaching qualification. 'I scraped through the practical test and did exceptionally well in the theory and mechanical drawing papers.'[27] Some time in 1925, the words 'an unfavourable impression created' appeared in his file. There is no clue there as to why or how. According to the concluding, unsigned assessment on his student file, Coombs had

> [a] forceful manner but lacks a striking appearance. Attainments very good indeed. Mr. Coombs exhibits much zeal both as student and teacher. He has much more insight than the average. He selects his matter well, presents it thoughtfully and is always sure of the aim he is making for. Gives good promise. Should make a capable assistant and would be useful as an organiser in the school. Upper school.[28]

Wheat Belt days

COOMBS' ADOLESCENT YEARS had given him many opportunities to reflect on the differences between city and country. He had grown up partly in the country, in Bridgetown, and partly in the city, Subiaco (with holidays in Busselton). His father's occupation was essential to the growth of rural enterprise, maintaining a link between city and country, but did this make the Coombs family 'country people'? His father would not have had many of the skills of rural living which fathers then passed on to sons – the skills which would have allowed Coombs to breeze through manual arts at Teachers College. Coombs' life had made him familiar with the country, able to mix it with the most ardent of its cricketers and footballers, but he was far from being a 'country boy'. His life spanned city and country, and he was creature of either.

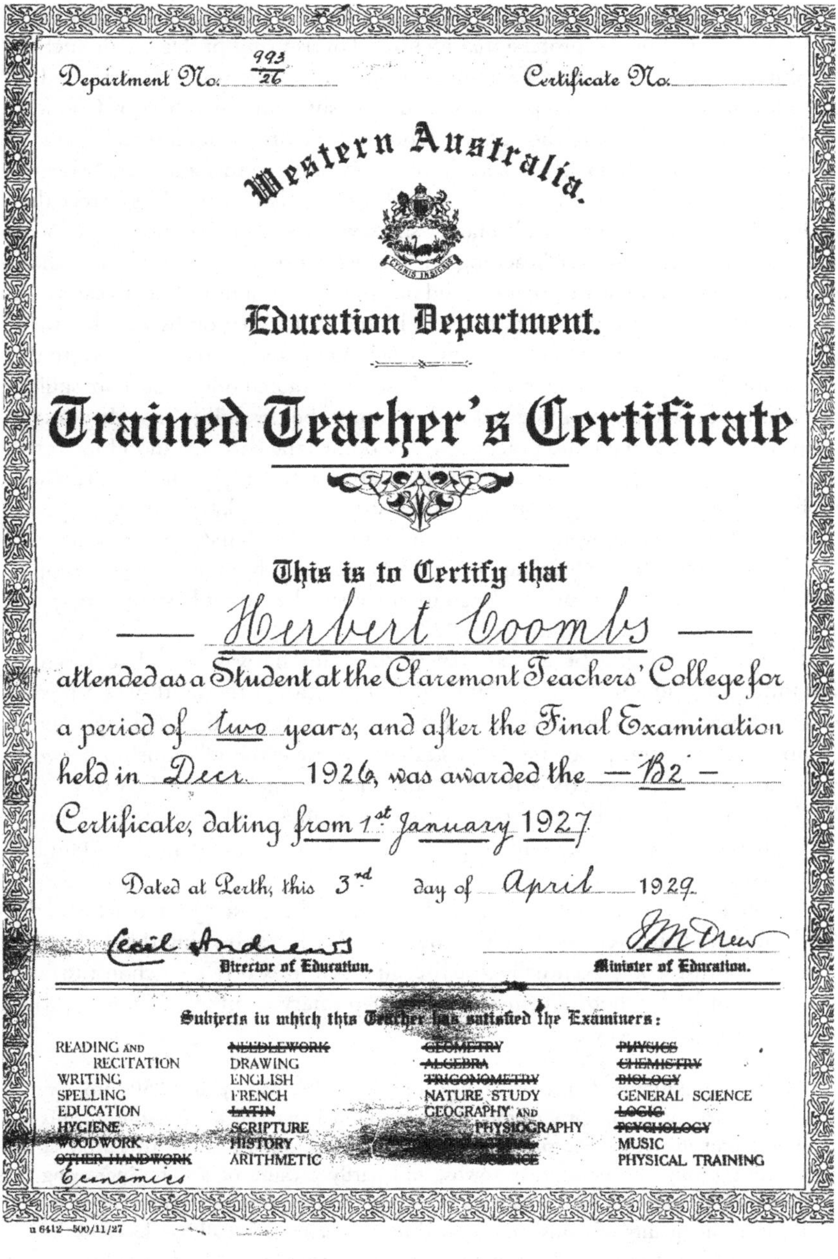

Department No. 993/26 Certificate No.

Western Australia.

Cygnis Insignis

Education Department.

Trained Teacher's Certificate

This is to Certify that

— Herbert Coombs —

attended as a Student at the Claremont Teachers' College for a period of two years, and after the Final Examination held in Decr 1926, was awarded the — B2 — Certificate, dating from 1st January 1927

Dated at Perth, this 3rd day of April 1929

Cecil Andrews
Director of Education.

J M Drew
Minister of Education.

Subjects in which this Teacher has satisfied the Examiners:

READING AND RECITATION	~~NEEDLEWORK~~	~~GEOMETRY~~	~~PHYSICS~~
WRITING	DRAWING	~~ALGEBRA~~	~~CHEMISTRY~~
SPELLING	ENGLISH	~~TRIGONOMETRY~~	~~BIOLOGY~~
EDUCATION	FRENCH	NATURE STUDY	GENERAL SCIENCE
HYGIENE	~~LATIN~~	GEOGRAPHY AND PHYSIOGRAPHY	~~LOGIC~~
~~WOODWORK~~	SCRIPTURE	[illegible]	~~PSYCHOLOGY~~
~~OTHER HANDWORK~~	HISTORY	[illegible]ENCE	MUSIC
Economics	ARITHMETIC		PHYSICAL TRAINING

u 6412—500/11/27

Coombs' first professional qualification.

Whether burdened or enriched by that complicated belonging, Coombs now faced a further choice – professional identity. For aspiring professionals such as Coombs and his class-mates, Claremont Teachers College was either the end of one's formal training or a step to more. Among surviving members of Coombs' milieu I found contrasting choices. For Dorothea Heron, 'B'-level teaching qualifications were enough. Her father, a schoolteacher, advised that a university degree would not equip her to teach any better. In 1995, after a rewarding career that included teaching music to Rolf Harris, she saw no reason to doubt his advice.[1] For Ralph Honner, however, 'teaching was the last resort of mediocrity'. A teacher's qualification merely ensured that one did not simply repeat one's father's career, he recalled in 1994; it was but the first step to higher callings. Coombs' decision to be a teacher 'was almost by default. ... Only teaching offered both easy access [to the professions] and professional training.'[2] He scarcely valued one of the core skills – the manual arts. He even discussed with Honner the possibility that they might both train in law and go into practice, with Coombs the barrister and Honner the solicitor. According to Honner, Coombs shared with many others at Teachers College a sense of being from an under-privileged background, nursing an ambition for self-improvement and for a better world.[3] That 'background' also entailed responsibility to help support his four siblings, through immediate application of his teacher's certificate. To go to university, he would have to enrol part-time. He did so at the beginning of 1927.

However, he would be an external student, for he was posted to teach at Katanning, a school with a large enrolment (420–430) at the south-western edge of the Wheat Belt. Coombs' time as a *rural* teacher nurtured a life-long interest in one of the central problems of Australian society – the relationship between city and country. As an arts student 'by distance' in small Wheat Belt towns, he held on to a thread of connection with metropolitan culture; yet his day-to-day concerns were with the children of farmers, and with the farming families themselves.

Through the extension of rail and through the posting of teachers, the landscape was being reworked as 'the country', that is, as the hinterland of a city. The city's thrust would eventually give rise, after World War II, to such institutions as the junior high school – primary and post-primary combined. One historian has sketched this process.

> The mechanisation of farms, which began in the 1920s, had by the 1950s brought about a decline in the proportion of the workforce engaged in agriculture. This was accompanied by a diversification of economic life in rural areas, partly a product of the growing size of country towns, and partly a cause of it. The increasing ownership of motor-cars in country districts, accompanied by a great improvement in the quality of roads, contributed to the decline of small hamlets and the growth of larger centres where shopping facilities were more varied and closer to city standards. In fact, what was taking place was an 'urbanisation of the countryside' that began in many areas to create a social structure not greatly different from that of the city.[4]

Coombs' brief career as a schoolteacher coincided with the beginnings of this change. A person in his position could feel in, but not of, the country. How the education system could best serve the rural population was a point for Coombs and his contemporaries to ponder. Intended to equip young men and women for life on the land, schooling was also to make them citizens of a wider world. His time in the Wheat Belt gave him food for thought for many years. In 1965, opening Wangaratta's thirteenth Arts Festival, he recalled his ambivalence towards the rural milieu of Katanning, Pingelly and Woodanilling.

I began my working life in Western Australia as a country school teacher and I became convinced then that in many respects the country town offered the best opportunity for a full life. In the immediacy of the contact with the people and resources of the country-side, in the accessibility of opportunities for physical exertion, in the sense of community, which a lively regional centre can develop, there are great opportunities for personal happiness. But in those days one was conscious that in the intellectual and cultural fields these centres, however vigorous, were cut off from the sources of experience and that civic consciousness was not sufficiently developed for the communities to organize for themselves an environment – physical and intellectual and cultural – in which their citizens could find the opportunities to fulfil and enrich their lives.[5]

His ready engagement, in the 1940s, with issues of regional development in the Department of Post-war Reconstruction can also be sourced to these dilemmas of city and country.

The first six months of Coombs' teaching at Katanning, from February to July 1927, went without remark in the journal of the head teacher, Edwin Stewart, apart from his occasional leaves of absence to take university exams in Perth.[6] Stewart was president and Coombs honorary secretary of the Katanning Branch Association of the State School Teachers Union of Western Australia (comprising 28 of the 1650 members of the union). The union's 1927 conference carried that branch's resolution 'that the Union establish a general (including fictional) library and endeavour to obtain privileges re distribution to country members similar to those enjoyed by the Railway Institute'.[7] Towards the end of 1927 Coombs was transferred to Pingelly (enrolment 180). There he was given duties in the fifth and sixth years, staying until the end of 1928. While at Pingelly, he resided at the Coffee Palace, spending many of his evenings poring over books sent by the University of Western Australia.

Coombs' few stories of his time in the Wheat Belt are about being slightly at odds with what was expected of him. To his dismay, he was asked to teach woodwork and metalwork. 'I spent a miserable year exposing my incompetence to a class of farmers' sons who were already adept bush carpenters and mechanics. They were on the whole remarkably tolerant.'[8] Opening an independent school in Birchgrove, NSW, Coombs recalled in 1973 that schools were about square pegs in round holes:

Educated people have usually become educated in spite of their schools rather than because of them ... there was little in my own brief but inglorious career as a pedagogue to convince me otherwise. In retrospect I seem to have spent my time champing at the snaffle of rigid curricula and inspectorial conservatism. I certainly quitted the profession with some relief and the hope that it might be easier to shape the future of the economic system than that of the rising generation.[9]

Such memories – perhaps inflected by the demands of the occasions – would have dismayed the parents of Woodanilling. In July 1927, Coombs was briefly moved from Katanning to Woodanilling, a one-teacher school, to replace a sick teacher. In his three months in that position he so impressed the locals that they petitioned the Department to keep him there.

During the short period in which he has been stationed here, the children have made wonderful progress with their work, and in their behaviour. Mr. Coombes [sic] is respected by both the Children and Residents of the District alike, and in view of the manner in which the effeciency [sic] of the children has improved since his stay here, we would humbly ask that your Department will retain Mr. Coombes for service at Woodanilling State School.[10]

Night student

THOUGH THE EDUCATION DEPARTMENT continued to transfer him often (just as the Railways had his father), it also recognised Coombs' need to be closer to the university, so that in 1929 and 1930 his postings usually kept him in Perth and its suburbs, within a bus ride of the buildings at the eastern end of Perth's city block that housed the university until the end of 1930. In March 1929 he was at James Street School, then, after a month, for two weeks at Thomas Street, then off to Midland Junction for two weeks. Stability in workplace came at last: in May 1929 he fetched up at Perth Boys School, where he remained for the rest of the year. In 1930, he was at only two schools – five months at Inglewood, the rest of the year at Leederville. In four years, after his initial placement at Katanning in February 1927, he had been transferred eleven times and served in ten schools. Nothing on his file suggests that his colleagues might have been keen to see the back of him. On the contrary, his adaptability and the fact that he was single made him useful to a Department which had to fill occasional gaps. The head teacher at Thomas Street School, where Coombs spent two weeks in April–May 1929, wrote to the Chief Inspector of his 'earnest spirit ... He not only worked thoroughly well with his class, but offered and gave, with training in sports, much valuable assistance out of school hours.'[1]

Offsetting these frequent moves were sources of stability. After his father was transferred from Busselton to suburban Maylands, he could live with his family. Coombs' sister Phyllis recalls that though Bertie had his own room in the Maylands house, he preferred to study in the family room where all gathered each evening.

And there was the continuing satisfaction of study itself.

The University of Western Australia had been established upon the recommendation of a Royal Commission of 1910. Arts, science and engineering classes commenced in March 1913 in temporary accommodation in Irwin Street, City. In a unique experiment in social liberalism, the bequest of Winthrop Hackett allowed tuition free of charge. However, physical conditions were at first deprived. Coombs' contemporary J. A. La Nauze has described the Irwin Street campus:

> A few one-storey weatherboard buildings had been hastily erected on a site within a few hundred yards of the elegant Town Hall. Others, weatherboard or galvanized iron, were to come in time, some transported from the once-busy scenes of decaying goldfields. It was a slum, a shanty-town set down in the midst of a small city, the more depressing because a stone's throw away, across St. George's Terrace, were the trees and lawns surrounding the pleasant Government House.

At the end of 1930, when the university moved to new buildings in Crawley, according to La Nauze, 'no tears were shed, no wakes were held in Tin Pot Alley [the space between the wooden buildings]. ... As the trees grew and the lawns spread around the buildings at Crawley it was difficult to suppose that anyone had ever thought of the University as being elsewhere.'[2] Coombs' four years as an undergraduate were the last four at Irwin Street, 1927–30. He was to enjoy only one year at Crawley, as he pursued his MA in 1931.

By the time it was possible for him to attend nightly classes at Irwin Street in 1929, Coombs had completed the first two years of English and the first two units in economics as an external student, filing assignments from the Wheat Belt and gaining distinctions in both subjects. As well, he had completed a course in 'Logic and Psychology'. In 1929, he pressed ahead with English and economics, supplemented by botany and French. In 1930 it was Economics Honours and Statistical Methods.

In this selection of courses, Coombs enjoyed the influence of two of the university's founding professors: Walter Murdoch (English) and Edward Shann (history and economics).

Shann's first year (Economics A) introduced political economy. Texts included Adam Smith's classic *Wealth of Nations*, Alfred Marshall's *Principles of Economics* and John Maynard Keynes' recent (1923) *Tract on Monetary Reform* – a critique of the international monetary policy known as the gold standard, 'perhaps the most respected and sacrosanct of all the mechanisms of nineteenth-century Capitalism'.[3] Economics C, which Coombs took in 1928, was about public finance; and Economics B, the third course in Coombs' sequence, was closer to economic history, demography and descriptive economics. Because English texts dominated the reading list, Britain's experience of capitalism furnished the most illustrations; however, Economics B included study of T. A. Coghlan's *Labour and Industry in Australia*.

Shann was 'a good man to argue with', and Coombs also recalled enjoying Merab Harris's teaching.[4] Shann's honours courses reflected his engagement with current issues of public policy. In 1927 and 1928, he got his best students to consider 'the tariff history of the United States, Germany, France and Australia'; in 1929 and 1930 (Coombs' honours year) the topic was 'industrial fluctuations and central banking'.

Edward Shann (1884–1935) was a Tasmanian, educated at the University of Melbourne and the London School of Economics. Upon his return to Australia in 1910 he was 'inspired by Fabian ideals and intense pariotism' and so was 'eager to participate in the building of a rational socialist society'.[5] Appointed as founding professor in history and economics at Perth in 1913, he was known in some circles as 'Bolshie Teddy'.[6] In the course of his research into Australian history, however, Shann began to reconsider his Fabian enthusiasm for state action to promote the collective good. *An Economic History of Australia* (1930), his most substantial book, depicts Australians as tempted to rely too much on state action, to the neglect of that essential ingredient of prosperity: individual and corporate enterprise.[7] His book of essays *Bond or Free?* (1930) challenged Australians to question that collectivist heritage.

It is likely that observation of Western Australia quickened Shann's scepticism about state action. In 1925 he reviewed the agricultural progress of the part of Western Australia in which Coombs had spent his boyhood. In particular he scrutinised the lending policy of the State's Agricultural Bank and other government financial incentives to agriculture after World War I – and Group Settlement. 'Group settlement', he complained, had lifted from the shoulders of individuals the burden of repaying the state's investment, making pioneers of 'gangs of men on Government wages'.[8] Shann praised the report of the 1924 Royal Commission into Group Settlement. He saw as Group Settlement's fundamental flaw, 'the attempt to do by mass action on the initiative of the State what has previously been done by individuals'.[9]

Coombs later questioned the profundity of his teacher's understanding of economics. In 1961 he recalled that Shann's 'equipment in this field was severely limited'; however, he praised Shann's 'capacity to stimulate one's excitement … and to discuss the issues involved helpfully, without any attempt to conceal his own incapacity to be of direct help.'[10] 'Not a great economist but … a very good teacher' was Coombs' verdict in 1991.

> He … liked argument, and we became very good friends, because he was, as an economist, very conservative whereas I was by that time very critical of the way the economic system was working … the classes were very small, the seminars were half a dozen people so that there was a great opportunity to discuss issues, and I … decided [what] I thought about things, by disagreeing with what he said. He had that gift of seeing debate as a pedagogic instrument.[11]

Coombs' contrast of Shann's conservatism with his own critical stance is exaggerated. Both were within the stream of Australia's social liberalism. Shann was neither dogmatic nor comprehensive in his scepticism towards government. He warned conservative critics of state action, in a 1933 lecture, that

> there is an … all-important contrast between an exchange-economy, however rich in public utilities, and a purely authoritarian one. The former leaves individuals free to judge what their fellows will pay for, and to set about providing these things. It leaves them free also to spend the reward as they will. A democracy may circumscribe these freedoms and canalize them along what it judges to be pro-social lines. In that it is correcting the errors and exaggerations to which its citizens are prone in rewarding debasing uses of freedom. But the net result of individual freedom so pruned by taxation and controlled by law is an enriched social service as well as the enjoyment of freedom.[12]

It is hard to imagine Coombs finding anything in that to quarrel with.

Finding the words

IN *TRIAL BALANCE* Coombs told a story about teaching poetry to Wheat Belt children who were soon to complete their compulsory schooling. Knowing their disdain for the poems in the set anthology, he tried them out on T. S. Eliot. 'The streak of toughness, phrases like "smells of steak in alley ways", "of faint stale smells of beer", rang bells with them. … The fact that I welcomed caustic and bluntly expressed criticism added zest to the occasions.' The children also enjoyed the licence to repeat words such as 'bloody' (used as a swear word in a poem by C. Day Lewis). A Departmental Inspector, pronouncing such poems 'decadent and corrupting', offered to show Coombs how to interest the children in the poetry from the set book. He chose 'a fatuous poem about hunting in England, pink jackets and all'. When he invited discussion, one boy mischievously commented that he and other lads sometimes hunted 'brush'. Because this school-yard word for girls was unknown to the Inspector, he briefly became the butt of a class joke, until 'I intervened to bring the puzzled Inspector up-to-date on Australian slang.'[1]

Literacy was essential to what was understood to be an educated person. When Leslie Melville and Edward Shann commented on Coombs' master's thesis, they attended not only to his economic analysis, but also to expression. Leslie Melville found it 'pleasing,…vigorous and clear, and at times he shows real penetration'. He applauded Coombs' 'happy and incisive' summaries; his work was 'accurate and concise'. Edward Shann, while praising 'a careful and valuable piece of work', lamented that 'it has few literary merits other than a rough vigour in marshalling the necessary facts and figures … If Mr. Coombs has any thought of publishing the thesis … he must be advised to submit it to a reader who is accustomed to editing youthful effusions.'[2]

Coombs enjoyed public verbal performance, in theatre and debating. Perth Modern School convened the Literary and Debating Society every second Tuesday afternoon. Paul Hasluck was library prefect and president of the society in Coombs' fourth year at Perth Modern, 1922. Under his leadership boys and girls joined issue over whether women should sit in Parliament, whether country life was preferable to town life, whether Western Australia should secede from the Federation, and whether ghosts were real or imaginary. At Claremont Teachers College, the Literary and Debating Club put on play readings. In third term, 1926, he took his part as John in J. M. Barrie's *What Every Woman Knows*: 'Self importance, sincerity and determination were the three characteristics which Mr. Coombs essayed to portray. And he did it well.'[3] The club's 'stump speech nights', made up of monologues both 'comic and serious',[4] also attracted him. Such training enabled him to put the case for 'the colonies to answer the call of the Mother Country' were she to participate in another European war. Coombs 'created a particularly fine impression' on that occasion with 'a really impassioned denunciation of all anti-Empire ideas'.[5] Later that year, he, Ralph Honner and a Mr. Horbury affirmed against a team from the university 'That democracy is a failure'.

> Mr. Coombs ... took up Lincoln's saying 'government of the people, by the people, and for the people' and, by discussing each section of the statement, he tried to show that Democracy in practice fell far short of its aims. Mr. Coombs' speech was, on the whole, a good one, tending a little towards ineffectiveness in the latter stages.

His 'reply' speech was better, stressing 'the results and not the aims of Democracy'. He also insisted that he was under no obligation to 'provide a constructive argument. All he had to do was to prove that Democracy had failed to do what it had set out to do.' Finally, 'on the vote of those present, the College gained the decision over the University, although it was generally agreed that Democracy is a success'.[6]

Debating is an insincere art, a persuasive performance of conviction. When *The Sphinx* (probably Paul Hasluck) urged Perth Modern School students' participation in debating 'in order to cultivate the power of being able to speak intelligently in public on the great questions of the day', it gave debating too solemn a rationale. Was 'Are Ghosts Real or Imaginary?' one of the 'great questions of the day'? It was as important to be playfully eloquent, irrespective of subject matter, as to be engaged with great questions. As a member of the community of debaters, one had to accept one's lot as the advocate, for one night only, of possibly obnoxious or ridiculous views. As well as training an elegant cogency of speech, then, debating developed a capacity for detachment from conviction, a facility for seeing the other side of a case. In this respect debating was and is a higher form of civic training.

In April 1931, the University Debating Society's topic was 'That the fiduciary note issue proposed by Mr. Theodore is sound finance.' T. Hartrey, P. Hasluck and Miss M. Battye spoke against, while Coombs, T. G. Wilsmore and D. Tangney spoke for Theodore. The Adjudicator, Dr Fowler, gave it to the No team by 311 to 279. 'An interesting general discussion followed.'[7] In August the Student Guild newspaper *The Pelican* announced a forthcoming feast of debating. In the last four days of that month a university team lead by Coombs would visit the Wheat Belt town of Merredin at the invitation of the local debating society. Two debates were to be held – 'That single men are happier than married men' (university to negate), and 'That the Lang policy is in the best interests of Australia' (university to affirm). Immediately upon their return, on 1 September, a debate was to be held between a university team and advocates of the Douglas Credit proposals. Coombs would be on the team denying 'That the Douglas Credit Plan is a Sound Monetary System'. They would be opposed by Messrs Butler and Bowe, with Walter Murdoch in the chair.[8]

The live pleasures of such displays of the spoken word were matched by *The Pelican*'s spirited reportage. In a debate 'That the accumulation of riches denotes success in life' a Labor member of the Legislative Assembly, A. G. Hawke, was the adjudicator, and Coombs 'gave a creditable impersonation of the Prime Minister, mouthing most convincingly an astonishing number of vague definitions, topped up with platitudes. Like that of Mr. Scullin, Mr. Coombs' voice has a distinct tendency to crackle when subjected to emotion.' Coombs' team-mate Paul Hasluck 'poured forth on the blessings of modern trade and commerce'. Summing up the affirmative case, Coombs, 'with a truculence which belied his inches, threw thunderbolts at his opponent, championing the popular cause of liberty'.[9]

Representing

COOMBS COMPLETED HIS Bachelor of Arts with first-class honours at the end of 1930. As well as his four years of economics, he had completed three years of English, one of 'Logic and Psychology', one of botany and one of French. From the commencement of the academic year 1931, once the University of Western Australia had moved from its old premises in Irwin Street to the new campus at Crawley, Coombs and other students had use of the most elegant and well-appointed student facilities in Australia. That year 1931 Coombs was to experience university life at several levels. He became a member of the academic staff. Shann's departure to advise the Bank of New South Wales in Sydney created the need for a tutor in economics – 'the only regular academic appointment I've ever had', Coombs assured me in 1995.[1] His salary, £200 per year, was one-fifth a professor's. 'Do not be afraid to apply the acid of criticism to the classes', urged Shann.[2] As President of the Guild of Undergraduates, as author of a master's thesis, and as a non-voting member of the University Senate, Coombs would be busy.

When the university was still at Irwin Street, Coombs had been President of the Sports Council, concerned with the sporting facilities at the new campus (tennis and hockey pavilions, and a cricket oval).

AT THE SHOP

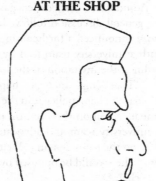

MR. H. COOMBS
President of the Sports Council

The Pelican*'s caricature of Coombs 5 September 1930.*

> As a critic Wee Nugget's ferocious,
> But in enterprise far from precocious;
>   Now building fund grants
> Have their teeth in his pants,
> We hope he'll do nothing atrocious.[3]

He had also proposed a new process for distributing Sports Council money. Any club seeking funds for 1931 would make an audited statement of claim including 'details of their past finance and estimates of coming need'. These would be circulated. The Council, made up of club representatives, would then be in a position to formulate a budget, to be ratified or rejected by the Guild. *The Pelican* reported ('The Coombs Rebuked') that the proposal 'was an active spark which caused explosions in the dark, and loud contention was soon rife, the Coombs invoking sharp retort for saying that the heads of sport (by this he really meant himself) unbiassed were in sharing pelf'.[4]

Sometimes Coombs' good sense outshone any attempt to make fun. In June 1931, *The Pelican* reported that when the library was losing books through theft, Coombs – 'full as ever … with bright suggestions' – had persuaded students to pay a yearly subscription to employ library attendants who would check books at the door, just as they did at Harvard.[5]

Under the editorship of Griff Richards (later to become editor-in-chief of the *West Australian*) and Jim Macartney, *The Pelican* was resolute in its good-natured mockery of Coombs and other student leaders. This atmosphere of determined irreverence did not always help Coombs' conduct of himself at a number of levels of university life. Richards and company's jocosity could easily turn to an abiding suspicion of any attempt to reconcile the staff (to be insubordinated) and the students (youth licensed to be naughty). Coombs, with emerging responsibilities up and down this hierarchy, might reconcile these established antinomies and spoil the fun.

Having impressed many students by his efforts to make Sports Council funding more transparent, on Monday, 30 March 1931, Coombs was elected President of the Guild of Undergraduates and member of the publications committee, nominally responsible for *The Pelican*. The Guild presidency was about to become a more important position. Responsible for the new facilities at Crawley, the undergraduate clubs and societies had to re-evaluate their resources and attitudes. At the first ever meeting of the Guild in its new premises, 13 March 1931, it was suggested that the University Senate be asked to nominate two of its members to the Union Council, the body responsible for the students' refectory. The suggestion had evidently emanated from the Vice-Chancellor, Professor Hubert Whitfield – classicist, engineer, metallurgist and sometime mine manager, a man accustomed to the persuasiveness of his authority. According to *The Pelican*, Coombs – who 'had abandoned thinking and was making use of his natural gift for talking' – supported the idea.

However, a subsequent Guild meeting found paternalistic implications in the proposal, and an amended version of the motion was carried. While welcoming more cooperation between the undergraduate body and the Senate, the students wanted a member of the Senate elected by undergraduates and a member of the Senate elected to the Union Council. As *The Pelican* commented,

> The Senate and the guild are separate entities. Neither owns the University; neither is the University. The aims of each differ widely, though their aims are coincident. The only spirit in which the affairs of one may become in the smallest part the province of the other is one of co-operation.[6]

The Guild wanted more autonomy. The Senators were wary. On 20 April, they discussed whether the Senate and the Guild should exchange representatives. To the Chancellor, Sir Walter James, it seemed that this would require an amendment to the *University Act*, and he invited a motion on the matter 'at a future meeting'.[7]

Among the bodies that made up university opinion was Convocation, an occasional assembly made up of graduates and current students. Coombs was among those who sought its reinvigoration. *The Pelican* reported on the first lively meeting of Convocation in living memory. On 15 May, in an atmosphere reflecting 'the youthful vigour of the standing committee' and the 'belated but welcome endeavours of graduate undergraduates', Coombs had accepted nomination for the Convocation standing committee.[8] While votes were being cast, he had moved a motion that the *University Act* be amended to create three new Senate positions, for the Warden of Convocation, the President of the Guild of Undergraduates (both *ex officio*), and an additional government appointee. After debate, Coombs withdrew the first and third of these new Senators, winning support for the Guild President's *ex officio* Senate membership.[9] *The Pelican* reported Coombs speaking 'comprehensively, convincingly, and deafeningly', with opposition only from a student who thought that the Guild was now the playground of 'red-raggers'. Out of the two members of Senate who were present (as graduates of the university and therefore members of Convocation), one (Miss Stevens) gave 'hearty support', while the other, Mr Gillett, though 'expressing sympathy with the motion, tended to evade the issues'.[10]

Some Senators were sceptical of the undergraduates' bid to manage their own affairs. In April, the Senate had received a letter from Coombs as Guild President asking for clarification 'as to the right of the Senate to amend or interpret the Guild constitution as approved by the Senate'. The Guild told the Senate that it had set up a sub-committee to revise the Guild constitution, 'and would like representatives of the Senate to meet the sub-committee regarding the matter'.[11] The Senate replied that it would be 'pleased to confer', but reminded the Guild that the Senate had power to alter unilaterally the Guild's constitution.[12] This testy atmosphere became more charged when the conventions of deference to Senate, notwithstanding the written rules of the university, appeared to have been set aside.

The 15 June Senate meeting heard a letter from Coombs setting out some recent changes in regulations governing student societies. One Senate member, Professor Ross, alleged that, from his knowledge of the Music Society, the Guild was already acting as if those regulations were accepted and in place. 'If they have passed these regulations and proceed to act upon them at once', grumbled the Chancellor, 'I think it is most discourteous to the Senate.'[13] This was not an auspicious climate in which to consider the Convocation motion about the Guild President being a member of Senate. In the *West Australian*'s report of this Senate meeting, it is clear that Coombs was himself beginning to be the issue – a graduate student and tutor as President of the Guild of Undergraduates?

As it happened, Ross's information about the Guild's new regulations was incorrect. The new regulations were administrative, not constitutional, and they were no more than the Guild's sympathetic response to a suggestion by the university's own auditor that university clubs show the Guild monthly financial statements. The real cause of Ross's disquiet was a dispute between the Guild and the Music Society. Nonetheless, there was now risk of ill-feeling between Senate and Guild.

Coombs thought it necessary to call a special meeting of the Guild Council on 16 June. He then wrote to suggest that 'the whole matter could be most easily cleared up if a representative of the Guild were invited to be present at the next meeting of the Senate'.[14] On 20 July, the Senate decided that the Guild President could attend the Senate, provided that he withdraw when requested by the Chair, and that the experiment would be reviewed at the end of the year.[15]

Recent public debate about the worth of the university may have prompted Senators' caution towards undergraduate initiatives. 'The doyen of colonial conservatism',[16] Sir Edward Wittenoom, had told his fellow Legislative Councillors in June 1931 that the State could balance the 1931/2 budget by abolishing the Arbitration Court and all industrial awards, by no longer providing post-primary education, and by ending its grant to the university.[17] Subsequent letters to the *West Australian* indicate that tertiary education was not, in all minds, a public good. Those who thought it was included the Secretary of the Western Australian Teachers Union, the State Executive of the Women's Service Guilds (and one of its members Bessie Rischbieth), an 'Old Modernian', a correspondent called '*Academicus*', the Secretary of the State Executive of the Australian Labor Party, a former Labor Minister for Education (now a member of the University Senate), the Australian Natives Association and Sir Walter Murdoch. Some asserted that Western Australia provided education comparatively cheaply, on a cost per head basis.[18] Others pointed out that Wittenoom's suggestion would discriminate against the poor, as only fee-charging schools would provide secondary education.[19] Free education equipped more people for citizenship, some argued, and for tackling the economic depression. The 'best brains of the people' were needed more than ever, and 'our failure is a failure of intelligence'. 'If he is serious', suggested one correspondent, Sir Edward 'should have suggested closing down all State schools, so that the future workers would not be intelligent enough to understand and appreciate the exploitation which takes place in the present state of society'.[20]

However, many found congenial Wittenoom's disregard for free mass education. 'Rusticus' of Bunbury thought it 'characteristic of human nature that privileges gained without effort and at little or no cost are very little appreciated'. Free university education had encouraged students to look on university 'as a right rather than a privilege, and to lower professional standards'. He quoted a recent report in the *West Australian* of the Senate's rebuke of Guild discourtesy and the alleged 'wave of discontent' among students, concluding that 'the University of Western Australia is becoming little more than a glorified high school at which students are equipped with sufficient knowledge to earn a living in the world'. He questioned the value of enrolling women.[21] To 'Hard Living High Thinking' of South Perth, free and compulsory education was responsible for 'governments ruled by Lang, Theodore, Scullin and Caucus' and for a lack of culture in Australia. He called for a more Spartan approach. There were 'far better educational harvests from oatcakes than from trifle'.[22] 'Rusticus' of Bunbury protested that 'A free University is a luxury which no other country provides.' Soviet and Italian education reform is aimed mainly at improving access to primary education, which was not in question in Western Australia. The benefits of education to our political life were not obvious: 'the attitude of Australian electors to national problems in recent years is not an inspiring one'.[23] '*Suum cuique opus*' of Perth protested that education was undermining both social hierarchy and the exploitation of the State's marginal lands. It was folly 'to educate every child away from the land'.[24] Several correspondents suggested that students pay for tuition.

On 28 September 1931, the Senate voted nine to five against a motion by one member (Justice Northmore) to introduce fees. Chancellor Sir Walter James – a New Liberal of Deakinite vintage – was among those opposed.[25] Six months earlier, in an address to a graduation ceremony, he had argued that students' hard work secured the bond between the university and its community.

> Every student should fully justify his or her privileges by hard work, and use every chance to its full measure in increasing personal efficiency … Generally speaking, the Western Australian student is a worker. To-day, every member of the University must be a worker, and the slacker must make room for the toiler. … Our training here is a free gift from the community, and for that reason, if for no other, the students and graduates should regard themselves as public servants in the broadest sense of the word. … In older countries the University and its graduates play a much greater part in forming the public mind than they do with us. Australia has not asked enough of her universities. Our political parties, for example, have rather preferred the wide waistcoat to the broad brow. (Laughter).[26]

It is not difficult to imagine young Coombs nodding assent. He had good reason to see himself as a 'worker' – in the sense of a 'toiler' – not a 'slacker', and he would readily have acknowledged the return that he owed society, his 'public service'. But did all his fellow undergraduates feel the obligation to serve the society that nurtured them? Students had to decide how they should conduct themselves before the divided public.

On the day James made these remarks the students performed *Trial by Jury*, followed by 'musical and humorous interludes by members of the Women's Club' with undergraduate songs (some with words by Walter Murdoch) 'interspersed throughout the proceedings'. The graduation ceremony followed these revels, and the evening was marked by a Graduation Ball at Government House, from 8.30 pm to 2 am.[27]

The *West Australian*'s correspondent appreciated this plan's compromise between decorum and hilarity. It had not been easy in recent years to combine within the one day the sobriety required for the conferring of degrees and the high-spirited celebration of student release. There had been a time when the graduation ceremony had been staged in the evening, but 'the undergraduates had been prone to be more disorderly than in the day, and it was even suggested that students be excluded from the proceedings altogether'. Then, from 1924 to 1929, the paper explained, Graduation Day had been marked by a procession through the city streets, followed by the formal ceremony. 'Intoxicated, as it were, by the excitement of the occasion, the Graduation ceremonies which followed later in the afternoon were very lively.' In 1930 (when Coombs' BA pass had been conferred) there had been no procession.[28]

Graduation Day 1931 having passed without reported incident, some students began to ask whether the Guild under Coombs was too tame? In May, *The Pelican* complained about the Guild's failure to plan student activities for

Commemoration Week, at the end of August. The Guild Councillors of 1931 were too cautious financially and were wary of 'incurring the public disfavour which might follow extensive 'Varsity celebrations'.[29] It is possible that Coombs judged that this was not the year to test the public's affection for youth's privileged playfulness. In any case, he had a full load, teaching courses he had not taught before, and he was trying to write a master's thesis, on a topic that required close study of primary sources, with his only a guide a supervisor living three thousand miles away. As President of the Guild he was responsible (with how much help it is not clear) for drafting a new constitution. As a member of the standing committee of Convocation, he was lobbying the university to introduce a course in political science. Coombs had also resumed debating on 22 April, and he is mentioned in *The Pelican*'s report of a play reading by the Dramatic Society on 23 June.[30] Finally, as we have seen, he aspired to sit on the Senate. So busy was Coombs, in fact, that he forgot to register his master's thesis topic. The urgency of planning a romping Commemoration Week may not have been obvious to him.[31]

Nonetheless, the Guild had a responsibility to increase the amenity of student life. In June 1931, a series of 'Guild Nights' commenced. Students would gather in the new refectory and, after 'a period of discussion on student matters at the University, a musical and dramatic programme is contributed by members of the undergraduate societies, followed by dancing and supper'.[32] In July, the Guild announced the program for Commemoration Week. Friday, 4 September, would see a procession in the morning and a cabaret at night, and the following day the students would stage a burlesque sports meeting, a mock court, and a Theatre Night. This final event – a gala 'musical and dramatic program' – would be open to the general public. Admission charges would raise money for the Lord Mayor's Unemployment Fund. To mark the occasion there would be a special issue of *The Pelican*.

According to *The Pelican*, these concessions to the student thirst for revelry had to be wrung from Coombs and his Treasurer T. G. Wilsmore. 'They fought every inch of the way, and they used every weapon at their command except the Council room ash-trays.' Their worry, according to *The Pelican*, was financial solvency. 'At first it appeared that these two financial cravens wished to confine the celebrations to a high tea for the women, and, maybe, a euchre party for the men.' But they had to yield to 'the Liberals, led by Mr. G. Richards', the editor of *The Pelican*.[33] The decision resulted in the biggest imbroglio of Coombs' crowded year.

Two things went wrong in Commemoration Week. At the fund-raising concert, some students in the audience engaged in 'buffoonery and offensive behaviour'.[34] And the 'Sruss Sruss', as the special issue of *The Pelican* was called, offended some in authority.

Coombs was directly involved in the concert: he played the part of the Chief Villain in A. A. Milne's one-act play *The Man in the Bowler Hat* which followed a violin solo and preceded interval. According to the *West Australian*, some students had hurled solid objects at the actors, 'mainly eggs, tomatoes, carrots and cauliflowers ... and a crayfish, long deceased'. It was reported that 'the thuds which accompanied their fall and the noisy comments and laughter of certain onlookers made it impossible to hear what the players said'. Stoically, the players continued.

> At the conclusion of the piece, one of the actors, Mr. H. C. Coombs ... addressed the rowdy element. He pointed out the filthy conditions of the stage which had to be cleaned before the program could be continued, said that it had been made so slippery as to be dangerous to those about to take part in a tumbling act, and appealed to all who had been 'enjoying themselves in their own way' to desist and give the other performers a chance to entertain those who had paid for admission. He was heard in a respectful silence and the general feeling was to be gauged from loud applause which followed his appeal. To the credit of the noisy faction be it said that thereafter their conduct was nearly perfect, only an occasional carrot finding its way on stage.[35]

However, the misdemeanours of the concert rowdies were overshadowed by the scandal of the 'Sruss Sruss'. The Guild had established *The Pelican* while the university was still at Irwin Street, in May 1930. A student, Griff Richards, thought that a student paper would oblige Vice-Chancellor Whitfield to listen more to students' views, in particular to their opposition to Whitfield's plan to move from Irwin Street to Crawley as soon as the building program allowed, that is, in the middle of the academic year, 1930. Richards had secured editorial liberty by declining the Guild Treasurer's offer to pay him ten shillings per week. Editing the paper for no payment, he had a free hand. The publications committee never met.

Richards set about establishing a readership through a style of reportage which was lively, teasing and bordering on the surreal in its whimsy. He then began a campaign to delay the date of the move to Crawley, from mid-1930 to the summer break of 1930–1. Anticipating that *The Pelican*'s arguments put his plans in jeopardy, the Vice-Chancellor called a meeting of students, where motions against the delay were carried. Richards persisted with *The Pelican*'s campaign, and soon the women rallied to his argument. In Richards' recollection, the Senate was therefore responding to student opinion when it overturned Whitfield's schedule and delayed the move to Crawley until the 1930–1 summer break. By the time the Guild announced plans for Commemoration Week of 1931, Richards had handed over the editorship to Jim Macartney. The Guild asked him to come back to edit the special issue. He agreed, but a football injury immobilised him for several weeks. Macartney stepped into his place, but he too fell ill with a poisoned thumb. Only a week before the paper was to appear, there was no copy other than a single poem, by Guild Treasurer T. G. Wilsmore. So Macartney and Richards wrote almost the entire issue in a week.[36]

The 'Sruss Sruss' featured boyish efforts to scandalise a moral climate which seems, now, rather prim. The issue was made up of items such as:

> She was only a sportsman's daughter,
> She lived beside the mill:
> There were otters in the water,
> But she was otter still.

Silly to the point of infantile though the 'Sruss Sruss' may have been, the Guild had to take responsibility for it when senior university figures decided to take offence.

Attempting conciliation, Coombs came to the Senate meeting on 21 September armed with a letter that, after an hour of discussion, the Senate decided to publish.

> The Guild of Undergraduates recognises fully its responsibility for the publication of the 'Sruss-Sruss'. We deeply regret the nature of some of its contents, and the offence it has given. We realise that at such a time it can have done the University's standing with the public nothing but harm.[37]

The 'Sruss Sruss' would be pulped, and the Guild would assert editorial control of *The Pelican*. The editors had resigned from the Guild.

Not satisfied with the Guild's measures, the Senate fined the Guild £10 and 'rusticated' (expelled) the editors for twelve months. (Their names were not published, and their punishment, in the event, was made less severe by the Vice-Chancellor.) The students who threw the missiles during the concert were fined £1 each. (Whitfield was quoted as saying that the four or five worst offenders 'had not been University students at all'.)[38] The Guild was asked to collect all fines and give them to the university for transmission to the Children's Hospital.

According to Griff Richards, there had at first been little reaction to 'Sruss Sruss'. However, the disruption of the concert had given the press a chance to report scandalous student behaviour, a story that could include the 'Sruss Sruss'. That paper's offensiveness, unlike the rowdy audience, could be studied and savoured at leisure as copies passed from hand to hand among respectable folk. When the size of the scandal became apparent to Richards and Macartney, they each wrote letters to the Guild President making it clear that they, not Coombs, were responsible for all that appeared in 'Sruss Sruss'. They were concerned, Richards recalled, that Coombs' Hackett studentship (awarded in April 1931, in recognition of the quality of his BA honours work) would now be in jeopardy. Coombs passed their letters on to Whitfield and to the Senate.

The students' honourable actions were not matched by procedural fairness on the part of the university. It was only via the newspapers that Richards learned that unnamed students responsible for 'Sruss Sruss' had been 'rusticated'. He went to Whitfield to complain that he and Macartney had been denied the opportunity to speak for themselves. Whitfield's reply, according to Richards, compared the pettiness of their concerns with the larger spirit in which politics had been conducted in Ancient Greece. In 1961, Coombs recalled that he had at first thought that he and Whitfield had agreed that

> the Guild Council should accept responsibility and should deal with its editors itself ... the Guild was to be fined 50 pounds and the fate of the editors was to be left to the [Guild] Council. This agreement was overruled by the Senate

Discipline Committee, under the influence of Professor Ross, and in addition to the Guild itself being fined, the editors ... were sent down from the University.

This left Coombs undermined and very angry with Ross.[39]

The Senate's sentence was eventually modified – not as a result of any advocacy by Coombs, according to Richards, but rather because the Guild's response gave Whitfield his objective – control of the undergraduate voice. In Richards' opinion, Whitfield behaved like a headmaster. And whereas Richards was trying to insist that undergraduates be treated as adults, Coombs was a little too quick, in Richards' recollection, to conciliate the headmaster's notions of good order. In the world as depicted in *The Pelican* Coombs could be lampooned as boringly sober and cravenly well-behaved. Coombs offered a decorous and deliberated version of student 'adulthood' for which some undergraduates had little sympathy.

In Richards' account to me in 1995, Coombs' attempted conciliation of Whitfield and the Senate, particularly his willingness to let Whitfield see *The Pelican*'s copy before publication, provoked a backlash from students who saw him as out of touch with undergraduate opinion. A special meeting of the Guild was convened. As President, Coombs was in the chair. In a written note, Richards foreshadowed to Coombs that he would be speaking for a motion censuring the Guild leadership for failing to insist on the independence of the undergraduate voice. Coombs, assisted by the long-winded oratory of student Tom Hartrey, made sure that the meeting was occupied with the proposed constitutional changes to the Guild. Students wearied of this, and the audience began to dwindle. The tram schedule imposed its own curfew. At last the meeting's main subject (in Richards' view) was brought up. Hartrey moved a motion of support for the Guild Council (a motion which Richards recalls was drafted by Coombs) and Coombs seconded it from the chair. A student named Barney Campbell moved a motion critical of the Guild. Richards did not speak. Another student, Jack Paul, moved an even more critical motion. Hartrey continued to speak at length. Richards gave up and went home. The Hartrey–Coombs motion was carried. A student loyal to the Guild leadership, Pierce ('Pike') Curtin, completed the Council's vindication by successfully moving that all remaining copies of the 'Sruss Sruss' be burned, and so they were.[40]

Richards and an unknown number of undergraduates were not the only ones who thought Coombs unrepresentative of student opinion; some members of Senate wondered whether a Guild of Undergraduates should have a graduate student as president. When the Guild and the Senate had their long-awaited conference about the proposed changes to the Guild constitution, on 30 October, Coombs' position was questioned by one of the university's founding Senators, the eminent public servant J.S.Battye, the Pro-Chancellor and State Librarian. Battye put the view of the Academic Board (which he chaired) that graduate students should be only associate members of the Guild. According to the *West Australian*, Coombs replied that 90 of the university's 700 students were graduates and that students had seen fit to elect some of them to Guild offices, to the benefit of the Guild's efficiency.

Confronted by this living example of the practical wisdom of older youth, the Senate–Guild conference rejected the Academic Board's scepticism about graduate leadership of the student body.[41] When the matter came to the Senate, Coombs continued to advocate the view agreed by this conference, arguing that 'older men' had the experience to perform executive work. It would be asking too much of the younger students to take on the responsibility of dealing with large sums of money; they could first acquire experience in running clubs and societies, and then move on to the Guild, he said. Coombs added that the Guild would suffer a significant fall in revenue were the graduate students to be denied membership. The Senate declined to ban graduate students from membership of the Guild and of its Council, ruling instead that no person could be elected as officers of the Guild more than seven years after first enrolling at the university.

These events were the first serious tests of Coombs' political skills, of his abilities to mediate forces that threatened to polarise.

Murdoch

COOMBS STUDIED ENGLISH literature under Walter Murdoch. In 1927, at Katanning, Woodanilling and Pingelly, he had to develop his responses to Chaucer (*The Clerk's Tale*), Shakespeare (*Coriolanus* and *Richard II*), Milton (*Samson Agonistes*), Macaulay (*Essay on Addison*), Wordsworth (a selection), Goldsmith (*Vicar of Wakefield*), Stevenson (*Virginibus Puerisque*). In 1928, he had on his desk in Pingelly's Coffee Palace such topics as 'the History of English Literature, 1780–1860', 'Shakespeare's Comedies', a book of Shakespearean criticism, some Romantic poets (Wordsworth, Keats and Byron), Hazlitt's *Table Talk* and Landor's *Imaginary Conversations*, and selections from Browning and Arnold. To get his distinction that year, he worked through English poetry of the eighteenth century.

Murdoch was a Scot whose family migrated to Australia in 1884, when he was ten. After taking a degree at the University of Melbourne, he taught in Victorian schools and then at the university. In 1913 he was among the University of Western Australia's founding professors. Throughout his academic career, he wrote essays for newspapers – first the *Argus* and later the *West Australian* and Melbourne *Herald*. A historian of literature studies in Australia judges that Murdoch's curriculum 'included more literature than was studied in other Australian universities at the time' but lacked the linguistic studies that were standard fare in other English Departments'.[1] Murdoch did not expose students to any author writing after the end of the nineteenth century. Only on the eve of his retirement, well after Coombs had graduated, did he include 'modern' poetry and the recently developed 'practical criticism' in his courses. Murdoch was neither a demanding teacher nor, in the usual sense of the word, an inspiring one. The consensus of university memoirs is that his lectures were dry and delivered in a monotone. His biographer, Coombs' fellow student John La Nauze, says that Murdoch never subordinated the enjoyment of literature to scholarship, that he was not interested in marking and that he became less and less interested in teaching. Yet Murdoch is well-remembered as one of the university's civilising influences, not only humane and humorous, but also committed to a vision of public life in which opinion and debate – clearly, forthrightly and elegantly expressed – were central.

As La Nauze points out, Murdoch's courses, like his writing for newspapers, extolled a great English tradition of non-fiction prose: Sidney, Dryden, Johnson, Coleridge, Lamb, Hazlitt and Arnold. An immersion in such work would encourage clarity and exactitude of expression – civic, as well as aesthetic, virtues. Perhaps Murdoch was attempting to capture this quality in his teaching – less a program of literary scholarship, and more an induction into forms of public discourse. In a 1963 converation with his daughter Catherine (King), he styled himself as 'Professor of Things in General'. 'It had long since dawned on me that English Literature meant books about things and that to interest students in literature you had to interest them in the things literature was about.' Murdoch recalled that his intellectual leadership was an attempt to address the hope of the university's founder, Winthrop Hackett, that the university might remain 'in touch with the community' and not become a white elephant.

> I had to show the public that a University Professor was not necessarily a person pedantic, detached, remote from the common interests of humanity. It seemed to me that by the nature of my subject I had a better opportunity of doing this than any of my colleagues and I took it and by taking it I lost all chance of becoming a recognised specialist in anything.[2]

This quest to improve the clarity and to moderate the temper of public speaking and writing grew out of Murdoch's considered liberalism, a political tradition on which he reflected explicitly in his 1937 John Murtagh Macrossan Lectures, *The Victorian Era: Its Strengths and Weaknesses.* Here Murdoch sifted what he thought was worth keeping of the Victorian intellectuals, whom he took to be at their best from 1850 to 1870. On the one hand, the Victorian era was unconscious of its limitations, smug and complacent; on the other hand, the best work of eminent Victorians was imbued with a spirit of criticism, of scientific rigour, exemplified by Charles Darwin. Murdoch tended to draw his examplars of Victorianism from non-fiction writing. John Stuart Mill provoked his most complex assessment. Though admiring of Mill, he castigated *On Liberty* for adopting

> an entirely inadequate view of the relations of the individual and society. He makes a sharp division between self-regarding acts and acts which affect others; we have come to see that there are no purely self-regarding acts, no acts which may not in the last resort affect others; purely self-regarding acts are only possible for Robinson Crusoe. ... He sees as the supreme end of life self-realization, the development of oneself to the fullest possible extent; he does not seem to see that the self can only be fully developed as a member of a society. ... Mill does not appear to see how often an interference with liberty may increase the sum of human liberty; as factory legislation did, and compulsory arbitration.[3]

Murdoch applauded Carlyle's and Arnold's critiques of this 'Victorian individualism'. After Shakespeare, Carlyle was the writer most frequently quoted in Murdoch's essays.[4]

Towards the end of his second Macrossan Lecture, Murdoch pronounced 'pathetic' the Victorian confidence in 'progress', especially their confidence that enlightened democracy would follow the spread of education.

> The idea that if people were taught to read they would read the right things, the idea that if all sorts of opinions were addressed to them they would choose the right opinions, the idea that they would adopt opinions at all, and the idea that a legislature elected by universal suffrage would give effect to the opinions so adopted – all these ideas have turned out to be fallacious.

But he closed on a note of admiration for the idealism he found among the Victorian liberals. The Spanish republicans, then pitted in bitter war with Franco, continued their quest for liberty, he suggested. 'When we are fighting for any real reform today we are fighting for an ideal which was first clarified and formulated and defined by the genius of the Victorian Era.'[5] Murdoch was active in the Perth division of the League of Nations Union, from the early 1920s to 1936 and President of the Kindergarten Union 1933–6.

In his essays, Murdoch was as much concerned to exemplify liberal virtues as to commend them. His light, economical manner in writing about his favourite themes – 'tolerance of views opposed to our own, social justice, the meaning of civilization and education, true patriotism, the aim of politics' – was 'free and friendly, neither extravagant nor sentimental', in the words of L. A. Triebel. The Professor of Everything's wide interests implied that one should, as Triebel put it, 'use leisure energetically and wisely, for the aim of true education should be to prepare us against, as well as for, our chosen calling, to make us less self-satisfied, to see life as a whole, to be less content to drift'.[6] Australia was lucky, in Arthur Phillips' opinion, to have a newspaper essayist who combined liberal humanist with Scots Presbyterian values. Addressing an Australian community 'which had achieved independence, vigour, and a shallow-rooted self-confidence, but which could not easily find its way forward to maturity', Murdoch did not 'chill them with an Anglican frostiness or rouse their debunking impulse with an Oxbridge air of superiority'.[7]

When Murdoch defended free university education from the attacks led by Wittenoom in 1931, he invoked the challenge of nation-building. Prussia's recovery from Napoleon's defeat showed the power of state investment in education, he argued, adding that educationists were watching with great interest the development of education in the Soviet Union, England and Italy (whose efforts even anti-Fascists could respect). 'Wherever you look … you see the great and civilised nations enduring hard times and resolutely refusing to allow the shortage of money to block the expansion of education.'[8] As a member of the University Senate, Murdoch also sympathised with Coombs' and others' bid for student representation at the June 1931 meeting.[9]

Murdoch took one stand on which he and Coombs could *not* agree: Douglas Social Credit. The English engineer Major C. H. Douglas had argued 'that the liabilities of a national economy could be offset by the value of its assets. It would thus be possible for a national credit agency to fund public services and to distribute a "national dividend" to all citizens.'[10] Professionals, farmers and small business owners found Social Credit an appealing alternative to communism. For many in the labour movement the theory, by pointing to the malign workings and inordinate political influence of financial institutions, reinforced hostility to 'the Money Power'.[11] Social Credit enjoyed a particularly strong following in the south-west of Western Australia. A leading exponent of Douglas Social Credit in Western Australia was a Congregational minister in Bunbury, the Reverend R. J. C. Butler, for whom Murdoch once expressed admiration.[12] A debate on Douglas Social Credit flourished in the *West Australian*, reaching its peak in the winter of 1934, when there were 200 branches of the Douglas Social Credit Movement across Australia. Murdoch pleaded the Douglas analysis of capitalism's ills in an essay for the *West Australian* – 'Fly Poker', published on 18 April 1931.[13] He 'wrote for the *New Era*, a Social Credit journal, and would speak in favour of that cause at meetings of its supporters. In the preface to *The Spur of the Moment* (1939) … he reiterated that he was "a believer in sane finance – which means, for me, some form of Social Credit."'[14]

While his two most important teachers – Murdoch and Shann – argued opposed responses to the Great Depression, the two professors shared in the same broad social liberal heritage. By exemplifying this heritage, in their different ways, they no doubt reinforced the Christian socialism and the unionism imparted by Coombs' mother and father.

Part 2
Liberalism's crisis

LSE student

COOMBS' HACKETT FELLOWSHIP survived the turmoil of 1931, so that, in December, he spent one momentous day marrying Mary (Lallie) Ross in the morning and embarking that evening for London. 'He only had cake and drinks that day, so he was sick as a dog on board', his sister recalled.[1] Coombs was off to write his PhD thesis at the London School of Economics (LSE). On board the *Moreton Bay* with Mr and Mrs Coombs was John La Nauze, Rhodes Scholar and Oxford-bound.

The three Aussies' introduction to the British class system began in Fremantle harbour. Their fellow passengers consisted of a 'party of English public-school boys on their way home from a world tour which had included a visit to Australia, no doubt permanently enlarging their conception of the British Empire' and 'disappointed immigrants, of the expansive 1920s, returning disillusioned with their families to an England as depressed as Australia'.[2] The lessons in social distinction would continue for as long as the Coombs stayed in London. As he recalled in 1951, 'The slums and the people in them were a shock to anybody from Western Australia. There was a depression at home, but it didn't go nearly as far in the direction of actually empty stomachs, cold and sordid misery and hopelessness for the future.'[3]

On a more personal level, these two years in London, though stimulating, turned out to be hard work. As he recalled sixty years later, 'I had the thesis to do, I had the work to do ... I had to ... be quite a lot in the household with my wife pregnant and the rest of it.' The Coombs' first child, Janet, was born in August 1933. There were 'a whole lot of things we wanted to do ... to go to theatre and to travel a bit here and there and to visit relatives of my wife and myself and so on, so that ... it was stimulating and I got great benefit from it'.

Coombs completed his thesis in two years, lightning pace by the standards of the research-based PhD. As well, to supplement his Hackett Fellowship, Coombs worked part-time as a casual teacher for the London County Council; he also attended seminars and lectures of his choosing and served as Vice-President of the LSE's Research Students Association. As usual, he was a busy man. Odd then, to see him writing to Shann a few months after settling in to the LSE that 'I feel very rested to have but one thing to devote my attention to seriously. It is a great help.'[4]

There were light moments. La Nauze stayed with the Coombs at least once, during breaks from Oxford. Both Alexandra Hasluck and Paul Hasluck – living in London at the same time as the Coombs – have recalled social occasions at the flat of yet another Old Modernian – Leslie and Coralie Rees. 'We were all in the forefront of young people going off to England on a shoe-string', Lady Hasluck recalled.[5] In their south London suburb, the Coombs were one node in this Old Modernian network, and so 'there were pleasant gatherings', Paul Hasluck remembered, '… at his home across the other side of London, and among other attractions, a baby to inspect. With "Nugget" and Mrs Coombs, my wife and I danced in the New Year's Eve, and later had a feed at a coffee stall somewhere in the vicinity.'[6] Lady Hasluck recalled a night at the Hammersmith Palais de Dance. 'Nugget wore tails, Paul a dinner suit, and Lallie and I, long evening dresses. … Although short, Nugget was a marvellous dancer and could steer one easily round the crowded dance floor'.[7] There was time for a modestly funded trip to Germany, via Belgium and France – 'travelling third class, sleeping on the slatted boards' – in the autumn of 1933.[8] Lallie, an accomplished musician and speaker of German, was able to take in a performance of the Ring Cycle – five days and nights of Wagner 'which I must say … I opted out of'.[9] Having 'parked' Janet at a well-to-do London nursery for about three weeks, they were disconcerted, upon their return, to find her wondering who they were. She inspected them, on the bus home from the nursery, 'with an undecided sort of air'.[10]

A few years after his return, Coombs drew on his London experience to advise Pike Curtin, his friend from the University of Western Australia, to live outside London and commute. In Bloomsbury students were charged high prices for small places. As for the LSE itself, he warned: 'you will probably be put in touch with the Dean of Postgraduate Studies, one, Robinson'. Lewis G. Robinson had not impressed Coombs. 'He is fat, pompous and lazy. He will try and push you off with a minimum effort to himself, but insist on getting a supervisor who satisfies you. If he is not the man you want keep complaining. They are used to it from Australians, and it pays.'[11]

Coombs' supervisor was John Coatman, Professor of Imperial Economic Relations. A graduate of Manchester University, Coatman had joined the Indian Police Service in 1910, served in the Frontier Constabulary, and then returned to study at Pembroke College Oxford. Back to India in 1926, he was Director of Public Information, charged with securing for the British authorities as sympathetic an indigenous press as he could cajole, and reporting annually from 1926–30 on Indians' 'moral and material progress'. Had Coombs been researching the politics of contemporary India, Coatman would have been a valuable resource, a voice of enlightened imperialism. In his chosen topic – a comparative study of Dominion banks' responses to the Depression – Coombs was on his own.

The LSE (and London in general) was well-equipped for readers of initiative. Coombs found the (non-borrowing) LSE library 'wonderfully efficient, and a pleasant place to work'. As well, a reader could get a ticket to the British Museum and join a local municipal free library.

> If the librarian is at all intelligent and helpful he can be very handy. For instance he got for me a number of official documents, including the evidence before the Macmillan Committee [on Finance and Industry, 1930–1, featuring an influential intervention by J.M.Keynes] which I was able to take home and read at my leisure.

Though Coombs found the school's lectures 'disappointing', 'The seminars … are quite different. Quite large numbers of staff attend them in their own and related subjects and the discussions are good', he later told Pike.[12]

Standing between undergraduates and staff, LSE research students such as Coombs were uncertain of their rights and status. Intellectually, the more capable of them were emerging as the peers of their teachers, but in the LSE's social order they remained supplicants of resources and dependent in their apprenticeship. Quite a few of them were from Asia, the white Dominions and the United States. Whether they got the best of the LSE's great minds depended partly on how particular staff took to them as individuals, and partly on how well each student negotiated opportunities and demanded attention. In 1932–3 Coombs was Vice-President of the Research Students Association, a body recognised by the school administration and including as members about one-third the school's 200 or so higher-degree students.[13] It was

> responsible for a Common Room (on the fourth floor of the main building), which is always open, and in which tea is served every Thursday. Meetings, at which outside speakers are present, are held from time to time, and 'week-ends' and walks arranged. … Adjoining the Common Room, there is also a Research Reading Room (with large desks) and a Locker Room. Research students may reserve lockers for their own books and papers.

Towards the end of 1932, the Research Students Association elected a delegation of six to meet with LSE senior staff to request better facilities and procedures for research students. Coombs was not recorded as taking part in that meeting of 9 February 1933. The students wanted better resources: more desks in the Reading Room and more tables and chairs in the Common Room; funds for a 'social push' during the first month of the session; 'a course of lectures … dealing with questions of research technique'. The social relationships of the school were also under question, and we can glimpse in the meeting's record some of the sources of Coombs' 1937 warnings to Pike Curtin. Under the heading 'supervisors, intercourse with staff' the following complaints were listed by a member of the administration:

(a) The system of allocation to Supervisors was stated to be not entirely satisfactory;
(b) Greater facility of intercourse with members of the staff was desired;
(c) It was asked that each Supervisor should set aside one hour a week exclusively for the use of Research Students;
(d) It was thought that Students who were not graduates of the School ought not to be allocated to a Supervisor during their first month at the School;
(e) In conjunction with (d) it was suggested that a number of Supervisors might be appointed to whom students might apply for general advice within their subject until such time as they should be allocated to a definite Supervisor.

Lionel Robbins, Professor of Economics, objected that 'postponement of allocation to supervisors would involve considerable administrative difficulties'. And Mrs Jessie Mair, the LSE's Secretary, recalled that 'a few years previously a request had been made in the opposite sense'. However, the Director, William Beveridge, saw the possibility of a concession, suggesting that 'allocation might be made provisional in the first place, in order to avoid any feeling of delicacy on the part of Research Students when applying for a change of Supervisor'.[14]

The LSE, whatever its reputation for producing 'socialist' intellectuals, was burdened with distinctions of power and status. One student complained in 1933, for example, that officers in the student union had been far too concerned with the issue of correct dress. Indeed, they had been

> notoriously, ... more snobbish than the academic staff. Presidents have made common cause with the administration in insisting on evening dress functions when Professors would have preferred a pipe and flannels. Even the year which saw the Labour Party sweep the poll – that year of enthusiasm which preceded the 1929 General Election – saw also the biggest evening dress debate in the history of the School.[15]

Beveridge, the Director, had become a rather 'forbidding' figure by the early 1930s, according to his biographer – 'at his best in policy-formation, as the architect of grand visions and designer of far-reaching schemes; ... at his worst in day-to-day administration, in accommodating the views of critics or opponents, and in his personal conduct of often trivial aspects of institutional affairs'. His assistant Jessie Mair strengthened rather than ameliorated this style of authority.[16]

Nonetheless, Coombs and other students found that the economic and political crisis of capitalism had stimulated at the LSE an unrivalled contention of histories, theories and prognoses of the capitalist system.

Politics versus Economics

COOMBS' BEST INTELLECTUAL experiences at the LSE included reading economic historian R. H. Tawney and attending the seminars of the Professor of Political Science, Harold J. Laski. However, in 1951, he parried the observation that he was a Laski socialist. 'My professors', he said, 'were those pillars of right-wing orthodoxy Lionel Robbins, John Coatman, and F. A. Hayek.'[1] This was neither playful evasion nor Cold War camouflage. The main product of Coombs' LSE years, his PhD thesis, demonstrated that he could adhere to one feature of 'orthodoxy'. In that work, as I will show, he restricted his consideration of 'politics' and 'society' in order to isolate technical questions of 'economy'. Coombs recalled in the early 1990s that during his time at the LSE, 'the economists and political scientists were really at daggers drawn'. Coombs chose to write in the tradition of economists, even though, as he recalled, at the LSE 'I was interested in politics, and well you can't be an economist if you're not. ...'[2]

We must be careful not to misconstrue Coombs' antithesis – economists versus political scientists – for Laski was not interested in engaging with economics. Born in 1893 in Manchester, Laski had been at the LSE since 1920, appointed after several years of teaching and studying in North American universities. Active in the Labour Party as an advocate of socialism, a chronicler and theorist of reform's vicissitudes, Laski was a prodigious writer and an inspiring talker. He had written frequently, on a great variety of issues, for the Labour-aligned *Daily Herald*, and in 1932 he became its regular columnist, thus connecting the seminar room with the public sphere. Laski 'was impossible to ignore. Students adored him; colleagues had strong feelings about him, not excluding envy and hatred; there were few subjects on which he did not express an opinion; his public views at least were often controversial and sometimes embarrassing to his friends, his Party, the School.'[3] His biographers, Kramnick and Sheerman, have written that Laski 'tempered the abstractions of continental Marxism with his own mixture of Anglo-American pragmatism and faith in democracy to become in the 1930s and 1940s the principal theorist of democratic socialism. ... He was also a legendary teacher, convinced that youth would break the age-old cycle of exploitation and suffering.'[4]

Coombs met Laski at a social function, and, after a chat, Laski invited Coombs to attend his seminars.[5] As he recalled, Laski 'used to lie back on a sofa, and just throw in a word when this argument seemed to be flagging'.[6] There was an element of 'holding court' in Laski's relationship with his students, which sometimes included inviting them to his home in Hammersmith. One student contemporary of Coombs, Ralph Araki, reported that

> the proceedings were not of a high intellectual order. Laski stands at the end of a small room, calling his wife 'dear' while she hands out cups of tea. There are little cakes and sandwiches. There must be 25 people there and everyone stands up. Then the company adjourns to a small long neighbouring room where Laski sits in a large chair and tells disconnected stories. Only one thing is really interesting and that is the library which is really very fine.[7]

One way or the other, Araki and many other students, including Coombs, found Laski's court stimulating. In 1937 Coombs suggested to Pike Curtin – hoping to research the topic 'Government and property in Locke and Tocqueville' – that he seek Laski out. 'He is a very approachable soul, and does a phenomenal amount of work as a supervisor.'[8]

If Laski defined political analysis at the LSE in those days, the ground of debate between economics and political science is difficult to see. Rather, the two disciplines were opposed in the sense of making rival and incompatible assumptions about the very terms in which to make sense of capitalism. The economists were more likely to conceive capitalism as a system of market forces, abstracted from 'society'. In that conception, labour was best conceived not as a social force but as just another commodity; and the state was peripheral, merely a given political and legal environment within which markets were the essential feature of interest. In a 1974 address to graduating commerce students at the University of New South Wales, Coombs recalled that his LSE teachers included some whose abstraction of 'the economy' from political and social realities was driven by their sense of the sheer beauty of their models.[9] He might have been thinking of F. C. Benham, Sir Ernest Cassel Lecturer in Commerce, who had remarked in a 1931 paper:

> As an economist, I have learned to love the way a flexible economic system, in which prices and wages are quite free to move and the quantity of money is fixed, automatically responds to changed conditions, to changes in consumers' wants, in methods of production and in factors external to man, such as good or bad seasons. I resent all attempts to hamper and distort the smooth working of this system by keeping particular prices and wages, or prices in general and wages in general, at a higher level than the free play of supply and demand would bring about; I resent opposition to more efficient methods or restriction of the free flow of migration and investment. I suppose I resent all this partly because I would like the real world to correspond more closely to the beautifully-working imaginary world.[10]

About this way of imagining the world we can make two different critical observations. On the one hand, it is not powerful in predicting and explaining behaviour. There are so many exceptions to the model (such as state-controlled or private monopolies, collective bargaining by trade unions to control the price of labour) that this kind of economic theory cannot tell us how the world actually works. On the other hand, Benham-style *laissez-faire* provokes critical reflection on the world's messiness. To model society as a market is to set up a norm of social rationality that politicians may be urged to realise through policies that outlaw monopolies, restrain state intervention and weaken the collective bargaining of labour. In short, economists, businesspeople and politicians trained to see the world as Benham evoked it would be critics of most if not all of the ways in which the modern state has come to answer the demands of voters and of organised labour for a fairer, less exploitative capitalism. On the one hand, an economics postulating free markets takes students of economics away from the messiness of politics and history, and so loses much realism. On the other hand, it leads its adherents right back into political engagement – as critics of those institutions of contemporary capitalism that 'interfere' with the orderly working of the market.

This way of thinking about economy, politics and society became very influential at the LSE in the 1930s. It was given intellectual depth by the newly recruited Friedrich von Hayek. Hayek belonged to an Austrian tradition of economic theory in which a number of English economists, including Lionel Robbins, had begun to be interested. Upon taking the chair of economics at the LSE in 1929, Robbins invited Hayek from Vienna to give a course of four lectures. The course was so well-received that Hayek was offered the Tooke Professorship of Economic Science and Statistics, and the lectures were quickly published as *Prices and Production*. In that book, Hayek endeavoured to show that the composition and level of economic activity was strongly influenced by decisions about the monetary forms in which people held their wealth. Such decisions were related by Hayek to the different times that it took to produce different commodities. For Robbins, the book's significance was that it explained trade depressions and, indeed, made them out to be necessary mechanisms by which the economic system adjusted itself. The book included no prescription for dealing with the

Depression, but it 'may make us more sceptical of the facile proposals for reform which are generally prevalent nowadays', to quote Robbins' preface.[11]

It is possible to present the rival political economies of the 1930s as a contest between the London economists Robbins and Hayek – worried about inflation and tolerant of unemployment – and the Cambridge economist John Maynard Keynes – worried about unemployment, and seeing no immediate risk of inflation flowing from state efforts to create jobs. Coombs' Hackett Fellowship from the University of Western Australia was too small to support himself and Lallie (and baby Janet). He needed to moonlight if he were to make ends meet. In London, not Cambridge, there was a market for his labour – casual teaching. Financial pressure trumped intellectual preference when Coombs made himself a student of Britain's more conservative political economists.

It is possible to exaggerate the fatefulness of this choice. It did not prevent Coombs from becoming Keynesian in his theoretical preferences. (The precise sense in which this was so will be explained in later chapters.) As well, Hayek and Keynes could sometimes agree on public policies. For example, they joined with a number of other academically prominent economists (including Robbins) in October 1932 in advocating increased public and private spending to create employment.[12]

Nonetheless, before, during and after Coombs' time at the LSE, he and other economists were witness to a contest between two schools of economic thought about how the underlying tendencies of capitalism should be conceived and managed. Keynes was keen to try measures which were 'unsound' from the point of view of orthodox opinion. For example, Robbins and Keynes were in clear and bitter disagreement in October 1930 about whether the British government should introduce a tariff. Keynes recommended one (10 per cent on all imports), while Robbins saw no good coming from such interference with the market. In the late 1920s and early 1930s – well before he published *The General Theory of Employment, Interest and Money* (1936) – Keynes had joined with Liberal Party politicians in advocating public works. The Robbins–Hayek seminar became a powerful and stimulating platform for a political economy of capitalism which stressed the difficulties and dangers of such government efforts to offset the cycles of the economy.

Coombs saw value in the Robbins–Hayek seminar. While finding Hayek 'very abstruse and confusing', he acknowledged in a letter to Shann that it was good to find a theorist 'emphasising the difficulty of monetary policy – in counteracting the tendency to believe that currency management can be achieved efficiently by rule of thumb. ... I am going to a class of his on monetary policy next term.' He was beginning to learn German. 'Whether I shall ever get to a sufficiently advanced stage to be able to read Hayek, Mises etc. in the original, is, I suppose, doubtful.'[13] Coombs later recalled Robbins as 'arrogant and dictatorial in style', but also as 'the clearest oral expositor of economic doctrine that I had encountered. His style of lecturing had a formal structure and a clarity which gave it great authority.'[14]

There were other voices among LSE's economists. Coombs recalled the young lecturer Nicholas Kaldor making Keynesian contributions.[15] For the LSE's Reader in Economics Hugh Dalton, who served as a Labour MP from 1924 to 1931, the intellectual trend of the Economics Department became steadily more alien to his political perspective. His biographer writes that 'there was little he could do to counter' what he called the 'Mises–Hayek anti-Socialist theme.' 'Not all the new staff members and research students shared Robbins' fiercely anti-interventionist sentiments. But in the intensely competitive atmosphere of the Robbins–Hayek weekly seminar, alternative views had little place.'[16]

As in Australia, the tragedy of Britain's Labour Party in the early 1930s was that it possessed no alternative political economy through which to actualise a socialist politics. One Labour MP, Oswald Mosley, developed an innovative political economy, to which Keynes was largely sympathetic, but Labour – with Dalton's hearty endorsement – rejected Mosley's unorthodoxies (and Keynes') and remained committed to deflationary policies that sacrificed working-class interests to the restoration of a 'sound' economy.[17] If Laski was the exemplar of the confluence of political science with socialist thought in Britain in the early 1930s, he also typified its unfortunate lack of any political economy suited to turning the capitalist crisis to the advantage of the working class.

If political science at the LSE offered an alternative perspective on capitalism, it was by bracketing off the economy and focusing on polity and history. Laski conceived capitalism as a historically developing contention of social forces. The state, not the market, was central to his analysis. The state's mediation of the social question determined the ways that capitalism was actualised as a system of pressures and possibilities. Coombs' memory of economics and political science as being at daggers drawn is thus best understood not as a depiction of two sides disputing a shared agenda, but as a remark about two disparate intellectual traditions. Students were challenged to choose.

The Money Power and its critics

IN 1930–1, IT BECAME the task of a small group of Australian economists to formulate a compromise between the demands of the labour movement and the wishes of the institutions controlling finance. The economists needed, on the one hand, to spread the hardships of deflationary policy (and thus comfort a Labor government horrified at having to reduce the basic wage), while, on the other hand, securing the cooperation of the banks. The banks thought that reductions in wages and public expenditure were the core of sound policy; they opposed government interference in their credit and currency policies. University of Melbourne economist D. B. Copland gave evidence before the Commonwealth Arbitration Commission in 1930, supporting the application made by Railway Commissioners of Victoria and New South Wales for a lower basic wage. In agreeing to a wage reduction, the Arbitration Commission 'endorsed the view – expressed by a number of economists – that all classes of income receivers should share in the burden of the loss of purchasing power'. According to Schedvin, the Commissioners were 'particularly impressed by the evidence of R. F. Irvine', one of the more unorthodox academic economists, that banks should be issuing credit more freely to both government and industry.[1] In 1931 the federal body that regulated all governments' borrowings, the Loan Council, asked Copland, Melville, Shann and Giblin to work with Treasury officials from each State except New South Wales to prepare a report on the financial situation of the Commonwealth and State governments. Their advice, offered in May 1931, was adopted as the Premiers' Plan. The banks would cut their interest rates on loans to the seven governments, as long as those governments cut spending on wages, salaries and pensions, and the Commonwealth increased taxes.

Were the economists extracting concessions from the harsh financial orthodoxy of the Commonwealth Bank and other banks or merely putting a popularly acceptable face on a hurtful deflation and income cut?[2] Suffering was not equally distributed among Australians: if you were unemployed or depended on a pension, wage or salary, you experienced hardship and insecurity to a degree that determined your view of life for ever more. There were other Australians who suffered inconvenience, perhaps, but not hardship.[3] Australia was polarised by class differences in the experience of economic depression. The poor had reason to envy, hate and blame the rich. Insofar as economists promoted themselves as saviours of this system and as authors of a recipe of all-round sacrifice, they damned themselves, in the eyes of the labour movement, as architects of oppression. The Depression nourished the popular story that 'the Money Power' was the nemesis of working men and women. Stretching from London to the board-rooms of the Australian banks, the Money Power now spoke through the economic experts. After the defeat of Labor in the 1932 federal election, the most common allegation within the ALP 'was that the Bank of England, the Commonwealth Bank, conservative politicians and economists had conspired to impose deflationary policies upon a Labor government as a means to enrich the Money Power at the expense of the people'.[4]

Coombs' perspective on the Money Power was that of an aspiring expert in monetary policy. The financial system was, to him, an intellectually feeble, rather than a socially ruthless, collective actor. Indeed, there is no doubt that the Depression challenged intellectually the leaders of Australian banking. The Australian banks' response to the Depression was at first based on convention, that is, the belief that the parity of the Australian pound with the British pound was fundamental to a sound economic system. 'Parity with sterling' meant that the British and the Australian pounds could buy the same quantity of goods; they had the same value. This sterling exchange standard (as it was known) rested on there being no marked long-term divergence between the demand for Australian pounds and the demand for sterling. Short-term changes in relative demand for the two currencies – caused, in particular, by fluctuations in the value and quantity of Australian exports – had been relatively easy for the banks to accommodate. Over time, they had developed the practice of maintaining a sterling currency buffer – holdings of foreign currency known as the 'London Funds' – and basing their readiness to lend to domestic customers partly on a consideration of the level of those funds. If the London Funds ran low (that is, if the demand for foreign currency was rising towards the point where it would be more valuable than Australian currency), the banks' valuation of their assets prompted them to reduce their domestic lending. This deflated the Australian economy, leading to a decline in the demand for imports and thus for foreign currency. The regulation of Australia's balance of payments thus rested on bankers' well-established accounting habits. Some called these habits 'principles', gilding them with a kind of moral grandeur. Others now suggest that it was more accurate to describe the banks' currency management practices as 'a mixture of prejudice, instinct, self-interest and common sense'.[5]

During the Depression, it became more difficult to practise 'parity with sterling' because, through a unique combination of adverse circumstances, the London Funds fell further and more sharply than banking officials had previously experienced. Were the banks to match this fall with a severe contraction in their lending to Australian customers, as customary notions of sound banking practice demanded? Or was it time to rethink their expectations about the normal relative values of the British and Australian pounds – that is, to devalue the Australian pound? Eventually, in January 1931, market forces combined with some intellectual leadership from the General Manager of the Bank of New South Wales, Alfred Davidson, to produce a devaluation of the Australian pound against sterling. Some economic historians have argued that this was the single most effective step taken towards Australian recovery from the Depression.[6]

The struggle over the 'sterling exchange principle', and over economic policies associated with it as 'sound finance', gave rise to a crisis in the Labor Party. In October 1929 the Australian voters had elected a Labor government, led by James Scullin. Scullin wished to honour Australian governments' debts to British investors, even if that caused hardship within Australia. He faced critics in his own party and in parties rivalling Labor for leadership of the working class. These critics wanted the financiers, not 'the people', to bear the burden of the Depression: could not loan repayments be suspended and rates of interest renegotiated? In 1930 and 1931 New South Wales' Labor Premier Jack Lang wanted to repudiate those debts which Australia had incurred through its participation in World War I and to suspend interest payments on other loans. The banks thought Lang's suggestions outrageous; they argued not only that all debts must be paid on schedule, but also that the Scullin government must cut government expenditure, if necessary, to cover the costs of such repayments. The contrary view was put by Labor MP E. G. Theodore in October 1930 – that the economy would recover more quickly if governments increased their expenditure, if the Commonwealth Bank helped them to do so by creating credit and if the private banks loaned money more freely to stimulate production. Scullin's Cabinet was divided over Theodore's proposal, and its electoral base was being seduced away from the Scullin–Theodore leadership by Lang's rival proposal of 'repudiation'.

The Commonwealth Bank Board, as scandalised as were the private banks by Lang, was no more friendly to Theodore's unorthodoxies. The Bank's intransigence was made all the more conspicuous to Labor's constituency by the fact that, though it was understood by many to be 'the People's Bank' and a publicly owned institution, its Board resisted Labor's policies of bank reform. Labor Party policy since before the Depression had included giving the Commonwealth Bank new responsibilities, such as holding the reserves of the private banks, competing with the private banks and being more subject to government policy. These changes would have given the Scullin government a powerful policy lever. But the Scullin government was thwarted in its two bills (1930 and 1931) to amend the Commonwealth Bank legislation because in October 1929 it had not won the majority in the Senate.

Beholden to Commonwealth Bank orthodoxy, Labor was less able to effect an anti-Depression policy that would put its own constituency first. The banks, including the Commonwealth Bank, thus appeared to politically conscious workers as defenders of rich people's privilege. By 1931 Labor MPs were divided between those who, with heavy hearts, accepted the banks' deflationary orthodoxies and those who attacked them; among the banks' critics there was an equally bitter split between the followers of Theodore and of Lang. Labor MPs sympathetic to Lang combined with the United Australia Party to defeat the Scullin government in November 1931. The Scullin government lost office at the election the next month. Labor had been weakened by internal disagreement about how to respond to the Depression, as much as by the conservative attack on its policies.

Observing Labor's political agony from Perth, Coombs had begun to wonder how government control over the banks could mediate between the demands of international finance capital and the needs of those whom Lang and Theodore had tried to defend. In 1989 he recalled that the Scullin government's difficulties in establishing a recovery policy had demonstrated to him 'that the Government lacked advisers who understood how the economic and financial systems worked'. His postgraduate studies would seek 'a way of being sure that the Government did have a source of advice which wasn't in fact more sympathetic to and more responsible to the Opposition'.[7] Examining developments in banking practices during the Depression in Australia, New Zealand, South Africa and Canada, Coombs proposed in 1932–3 a policy framework for Dominion central banking that took into account each economy's characteristic vulnerability – in its external accounts – to fluctuations in export incomes and in borrowings.

Coombs' PhD thesis was remarkable for its determinedly apolitical language, considering the political turmoil that inspired his inquiry. In a genuinely *political* economy of the external relationships of modern economies, one would describe the domestic social and political forces which any government would have to take into account when managing its loans from abroad and in setting the value of its currency. Indeed, such political sensitivity had been a feature of Keynes' many discussions of the significance, to Britain, of the gold standard. A practical economist such as Keynes could not help but consider such real-world factors as the difficulties of inducing British workers to accept cuts in the real value of their wages, or the competing claims of those industries advantaged and those disadvantaged by adherence to the gold standard. Not so Coombs in his thesis. His language was resolutely apolitical and sociologically blind. He thus projected the authorial persona of the apolitical expert that he aspired to be.

Rather than evoke Australia's policy dilemma as a contest of Lang against Scullin, arousing Theodore's contentious innovations, provoking the censorious voice of financial orthodoxy, leaving widespread hardship, a broken Labor Party and bitter disputes about 'equality of sacrifice', Coombs' language was almost comically bereft of historical and political vision. 'This forcible balancing of international payments was a severe task and entailed difficult internal adjust-ments.'[8] Elsewhere he acknowledged politics and the social question as 'difficulties of social adjustment of unpleasant magnitude'.[9] The social and political issues raised in the management of capitalism were thus displaced to the very margins, in order to highlight as technical the problems of getting 'the economy' right. To render the political and social as marginal, rather than integral, to 'the economic' is one of the defining intellectual achievements of a professionalising tradition among economists, a tendency exemplified in Lionel Robbins' *An Essay on the Nature and Significance of Economic Science* (1931).

The difficulty of sustaining this framing was evident when Coombs made explicit his criteria for policy 'success'.

> The primary task before the monetary authorities of the dominions is the main-tenance of external solvency. ... the second, no less important, task is to prevent the periodical fluctuations in the external position from exercising an unnecessarily great effect upon the level of internal prosperity.[10]

But if the 'second' task is 'no less important', then in what sense could Coombs assert the first task – external solvency – to be 'primary'? The latter word genuflects to one political orthodoxy, only to be, in effect, immediately withdrawn. The same uneasiness is evident in the question-begging phrase 'an unnecessarily great effect'. The language in this passage awkwardly evades the political issue – the social distribution of the costs of maintaining, in hard times, the collective obligation to sustain the flow of rewards to finance capital.

As if bothered by his own equivocation, Coombs conceded a few pages later that 'success in dealing with one of them implies to some extent the failure to deal with the other' – an oblique epitaph for British and Australian social democracy between the wars.[11]

In 1938, a Canadian student of Dominion central banking, A. F. W. Plumptre, distinguished three types of advocates of monetary reform in the same four Dominions as Coombs had studied.

> One class was of radical, perhaps socialistic, turn of mind; and regarded the operations of the private bankers as broadly anti-social and predatory. Another class was of small business men, farmers, and other clients of the banks who had reason, real or imagined, for dissatisfaction with the treatment which the banks had accorded them. The third class consisted of civil servants and members of governments who were similarly dissatisfied.[12]

The third group, which included academic economists, had proved the most 'immediately powerful' in the interwar struggles to reconstruct capitalist banking, Plumptre suggested. Coombs' PhD thesis can be understood as an artefact of this technocratic ascendancy. As Plumptre went on to say, the hopes of the first and second groups had been disappointed by the reforms drafted and implemented by the third group.

Among the first and second groups Major Douglas's Social Credit theory of financial reform would undoubtedly have been popular. Coombs came from one of Social Credit's Australian strongholds, the agricultural south-west of Western Australia, and so it had been an early and unavoidable step in his formation as an economist to work out what he thought of Douglas's theory of capitalist inequities. Douglas won many followers among those suffering economic hardship when he argued that financiers had a stranglehold on the capitalist system, that they siphoned income from the cycle of production and consumption and left the mass of people with too little income to buy the stock of goods produced. His model explained poverty and unemployment, and it proposed a solution: the public management of credit.

In his co-authored review of C. Marshall Hattersley's Social Credit tract *The Age of Plenty*, Coombs made two remarks that we should note.[13] Australians would find solutions to the Depression, he wrote, only if 'people are really thinking and not merely accepting the dicta either of the Douglas Plan or that of the so-called orthodox economists'. And 'any scheme which involves placing our monetary affairs more in the hands of vote-seeking politicians is, *from all experience of government finance*, damned at its inception'.[14] If not the Douglasites, not 'so-called orthodox economists', and not 'politicians' – who could Coombs deem to be rational and without self-interest? The implied position from which Coombs wrote was that of the class of experts into which he was moving as he commenced his graduate studies: the professional-managerial class, anchors of stability and reason in a politically volatile and irrational world.

Coombs observed in his thesis that in Canada (where Social Credit also enjoyed a popular following),

> It is curious that two movements for the creation of a Central Bank should be in existence at the same time: the popular movement being based on the belief in the inadequacy of existing credit and the faith in a Central Bank in extending it – and the academic based upon the apparently excessive use of existing facilities for credit creation. It indicates a nice problem as to whether the private banks, a Government department, or a Central bank, *is best able to ignore the discontent which the first of these movements expressed.*[15]

Coombs' thesis and his subsequent work in the 1930s affirmed the reform of central banking, by emergent experts such as himself, as the best response to popular discontent about the Money Power.

Poor Britain

COOMBS TRAINED HIMSELF to think and write as if social and political issues were peripheral to the 'economic', but he did not shut his mind to the turmoil of Britain's Depression. That was hardly possible. Not only could Coombs ponder a crisis of economy and polity from the comfort of the LSE seminar room, he was also confronted by a daily spectacle of poverty. Posted to London's schools as a casual teacher, Coombs was a minor manager of the social disorder of the working-class child. 'Getting around the schools for odd periods of a fortnight or ten days was an enlightening experience ... The whole atmosphere and way of life differed from anything I'd known ... They were horrifyingly gloomy times.'[1]

Forty years after he spoke those words, his memories were still vivid. The London County Council had sent him to teach in

> all sorts of places so that I saw a ... cross section of London life, kids, and it was not a very pleasant experience because the kids suffered very badly in the Depression. They were short of food ... rickets were common amongst the kids and you know they were pasty faced and skinny and miserable looking ... that was a distressing kind of experience ... it was enough [at] any rate ... to intensify my concern about the economic system and my ... conviction [that] it wasn't operating fairly ... but it was not even operating efficiently.

His time in London schools, Coombs recalled, 'intensified my anxiety to understand' the workings of the capitalist economy.[2]

East Enders' recollections substantiate Coombs' memories of the working-class school in Depression London. Ivy Alexander, born 1924, was a primary school pupil in the East End during the time when Coombs taught there.

> Classes were large and children were lethargic, no doubt through undernourishment and ill-health. Some were more deprived than others and were sent to the Fyfield Open Air School, in Essex. If they returned to Canning Town School they were quiet, well-mannered and subdued and spoke 'posh'. Homes were devoid of books, music, or even pencil and paper.[3]

Another East Londoner, who grew up in Bethnal Green in the 1920s and 1930s, recalls schools as regimes of health management as well as places of learning.

> In the mornings you had milk and biscuits, in the afternoons you had to go to sleep on rickety small beds while big green blinds were pulled down over the windows. At seven years old you graduated to the Juniors, you stayed there until eleven years old then you sat for exams to decide which pupils were average, above

average and brainy. ... The visit of 'Nitty Nora' was always a worrying time for
our mums. Would this huge woman in starched uniform with her steel comb in
a bowl of disinfectant have to start cutting your hair or have you sent to the
cleansing station?[4]

The duties of Ida Rex, who taught in Hackney from 1916 to 1923, included
social intervention. The picture is unlikely to have improved by the time Coombs
taught in Shoreditch.

We kept the hours of 9 to 12 in school. There were free dinners for those who
needed them in a special school nearby. It was not for those who could afford
dinners. The Head said who should go, in conjunction with the Social Care
Committee. Quite a lot of children went. They had to be deloused. There were some
very, very poor children. ... Teaching was looked upon as a type of social work in
the East end, far more so than it is now [mid-1970s].[5]

This was the system that Coombs experienced in 1932 and 1933. In 1934, he
described it to his colleagues back in Western Australia.

The first school in which I taught was the worst, but representative, I believe, of a
certain type. It was a Church school in the unsavoury district of Shoreditch. In such
schools, the staffs are chosen by the local church authorities, who determine the
nature of the education to be given, but salaries, materials, etc., are provided by the
Council. Each day here began with an hour devoted to prayers, hymns and scriptural
teaching. The children generally are ill-clothed, undernourished and exceedingly
dirty. As the head teacher swept into the assembly hall, the girls curtsied and the boys
touched their foreheads. (This was one of the few mixed schools I saw.) While the
school waited, time was beguiled by singing through the multiplication tables to a
peculiar tune which fitted satisfactorily until three figures appeared in the multiples,
and then the table was rushed to an end in an agonised, breathless gabble. Prayers
were long, but their burden was the same. Divine aid was invoked to make the
children 'respectful and obedient to their betters', and to make them live gratefully
in the state of life to which it had pleased God to call them. On the second day the
vicar called to assure himself that I was 'Church'. At the time I was so poor that had
he demanded my allegiance to Baal, I would gladly have forsworn myself. Reassured,
he dilated on the virtues of his school. 'This is a bad area,' he said, 'and though we
can teach but little, we do at least make the children respectful of their superiors.' At
this school, too, I assisted in a Cleanliness Week. On charts provided by the makers
of Lifebuoy soap, children recorded a cross each time they washed their *hands*, and
the child having the largest number of crosses at the end of the week was rewarded
with a badge. This ambitious project encouraged me to ask the class how many
cleaned their teeth that day. My question was met with a snigger of contemptuous
amusement. Speech was the purest cockney. No attempt was made to correct it.
Later I asked why, and I was told that it was useless. Correct speech to the Cockney
meant affectation and 'airs', and woe betide the child who tried it out at home. The
attitude of the teacher to the child was impregnated with what may be called the
'charity' point of view. Teacher and child were as foreign to one another as if of
different nationalities. Education here was little more than organised child minding

designed to keep him quiet and docile – at school and after. In this school I realised for the first time why the Russian Soviets have suppressed the churches.[6]

By the time he taught East Enders, it would have been clear to Coombs that the Labour Party had failed these people. The politics of unemployment between the wars was a struggle over the terms in which poor, working-class Britons maintained a dignified form of economic dependency and articulated politically their right to full social participation.

Under pressure to maintain the gold value of sterling, the McDonald Labour government (1929–31) had deployed notions of 'sound finance' that were no different from those of the men who controlled the world's capital markets. Financiers saw the budget as a test of the McDonald government's sense of responsibility. Needing financiers' support to borrow the foreign currency with which to keep buying sterling and so support the gold standard, Cabinet had cut expenditure. The unemployed were sacrificed. In 1931, the government introduced a household means test for unemployment relief. The welfare state's invigilation of the poor was intensified, as the completed household forms were checked for accuracy by visiting inspectors. From the point of view of the poor, this was an assault on their dignity and resilience. 'Where the maximisation of the earning potential of the subordinate members of the family had always been the most effective defence against hardship, now it was the major threat to the receipt of assistance.'[7] For the sake of sound finance, people were being asked to surrender their domestic privacy. 'The Means Test threw into reverse the momentum of change which had been set in motion before the First World War. Once more relief was made conditional on the exposure not just of the claimant's poverty, but on the whole structure of relationships and transactions which made up the family economy.'[8] The self-reliant poor were to be humiliated.

These perverse developments in social administration clarified the limits of popular sovereignty. Harold Laski of the LSE penned an anguished essay on 'the present position of representative democracy'. Over the last one hundred years, he observed, the unpropertied sections of society had been given the vote, free education and religious freedom. But could they now use these powers and liberties to transform society in their own interests? Could representative democracy challenge the selfish interests of property and bring about a peaceful transition to socialism? The problem, as Laski presented it, was not only that the propertied classes clung to their privileges. The institutions of modern capitalism were of such complexity and subject to such rapid dynamics as to expose the clumsiness of representative democracy's mechanics. The McDonald government's 1931 crisis had shown that 'the movements of finance had determined the course of events before ever [Parliament] could be summoned to grapple with its implications'.[9]

Yet, he continued, however clumsy an instrument of popular will a parliamentary government might be, the challenge to economic privilege could not indefinitely be deferred. Under pressure of nineteenth-century electoral reform, the propertied had made concessions which were not essentially threatening to their economic power, and they had been able to answer the democratic challenge with an improved standard of living. But no more. The capitalist system over which they presided was more and more trammelled by concessions to 'non-economic ends', such as social services and armaments. *Laissez-faire* was thus giving way to 'social control', and social control posed the question of equality: why, if the economy can be regulated, was it still regulated so as to maintain the comfort of the rich and the misery and insecurity of the poor? Laski concluded that the rich would soon face a forceful challenge from the poor.

But would representative democracy be their instrument? Under conditions of mass unemployment, 'the differences between men become final in character; the prospect of solving them in terms of reason instead of terms of power becomes a matter of extraordinary difficulty'.[10] British Labour's failure had made Laski's understanding of popular sovereignty more anxious and uncertain, his appeal to 'reason' less confident.

Among the British poor there grew well-based doubts about the adequacy of the trade unions and the Labour Party to advance their interests. As a large, growing and problematic constituency within the working class, the unemployed were isolated from both political and industrial wings of the labour movement. The National Unemployed Workers Movement (NUWM), founded in 1920 and led by communists, expressed working-class anger in a 12-point charter in 1929 and in a million-signature petition compiled for presentation to Parliament in 1932. The NUWM recruited many of its adherents at labour exchanges, where the needs of the unemployed were directly exposed to the strictures of social administration. In November 1931, the police began to discourage the NUWM's activities around the exchanges, and NUWM defiance occasioned violence, so confirming the Labour Party's anxiety about the politics of direct action. The organised unemployed struck fear in the hearts of the Labour leadership.[11]

Such was Labour's apprehension that in September 1932 the Trade Union Congress voted not to receive a NUWM deputation at its conference in Newcastle-on-Tyne. At the end of that month, a large march of the unemployed left Glasgow, headed for London to serve its petition on a Parliament that was now dominated by a cross-party coalition that included Labour defectors, such as Ramsay McDonald. The many skirmishes between marchers and mounted police culminated in a clash between police and 100,000 demonstrators at Hyde Park on 27 and 30 October 1932.[12] The mutual hostility of Labour Party and NUWM meant that the NUWM refused to allow any of Labour's few remaining MPs to present the petition to the House of Commons. Police action prevented the NUWM itself from presenting the petition.[13]

The Hyde Park clash was a contest between two modes of working-class mobilisation.

Whilst the NUWM and a number of local councils represented a more direct expression of the interests of the dispossessed than had been seen since Chartism and a more substantial threat to the authority of Parliament than was ever to be mounted again, they could not find a means of enforcing their demands on the national Labour Party or on the bulk of the trade union movement, and thus were unable to prevent a successful counter-attack by the state against such forms of participatory democracy. The central problem was not that the Depression demoralised the poor, but that their resentment demoralised those organisations capable of translating their grievances into a full-scale challenge to the assumptions upon which the inter-war economy was run.[14]

How were these dramas – seemingly definitive of the limits of popular sovereignty over capitalism – experienced at the LSE? For Laski, as I have shown, the politics of the Depression questioned the adequacy of liberal democratic institutions to compel concessions from the propertied classes. For the economists there were questions of a rather different kind: why should governments intervene, if trade cycles were an intrinsic part of the dynamics of capitalism? Was not ameliorative state action a danger to the integrity of a market-based social order? Writing in the LSE student publication *Clare Market Review* in 1933, 'Laodicean' feared that 'Marx and Robbins in alliance threaten to undermine the School's intellectual foundations.' That is, the school's intellectual inquiries depended on there being a political centre where reforms involving state intervention were imaginable. However, 'Laodicean' went on to doubt that Marxism had struck deep roots. 'Those slogans which we hear in the corridors are expressions of a hopeless indignation rather than an intellectual conviction.'[15]

One of the voices of (hopeful) indignation was the publication *Student Vanguard.* In the wake of the Hyde Park clashes over the NUWM petition, an anonymous correspondent reported a 'feeling of solidarity between students and workers'.

> One consequence has been the organization of a Students' Labour Defense Committee to organise further support from the students for the workers in their struggles, in the form of collections and protest meetings. The L.S.E. authorities have shown their alignment by refusing permission for a protest meeting in the Hunger March trials. All the Societies in the School are being approached to aid in securing the removal of this ban.[16]

A few months later, NUWM leader Wal Hannington was a guest speaker at the LSE, on 'Unemployment and organising the unemployed'. The *Morning Post* described the occasion: 'free fights occurred between the students and crockery was thrown about the hall ... A student told the *Morning Post* that the demonstration had been staged, not against Mr. Hannington, but against the Communistic tendencies of the Union, which were considered disproportionate to the opinions of its members.'[17]

I have seen no evidence that Coombs took part in any of these events, but they must have provoked his thoughts about the relationships of economics with politics, of reasoned analysis with demonstrative action. What did he make of it all?

In 1933, the *Old Modernian* published Coombs' reflections on 'The Decline of Liberalism'. These were some of his observations:

Wherein has Parliamentary government failed? It has failed to give security to the propertied classes. Does this not really mean that Democracy at last, from having been so long an empty mechanism, showed signs that it might become a reality? Why should communism be regarded as a menace? One explanation only can be satisfactory. The advocates of private property feared that they could not compete with those of Communism under the measure of equal opportunity which democratic governments afforded. And has all this passed England by? One is apt to take for granted England's reputation as the home of political freedom and tolerance. Certainly the outward display and symbolism of European fascism make little appeal to the English mind. Here also the menace to propertied classes is not as dangerous as it has been abroad. This is perhaps strange in view of the high development of parliamentary government in England. Paradoxically enough, I am convinced that despite this development the government of England is carried out practically by the same class of people as it was in the Eighteenth Century. The parliamentary system in England is remarkable for the way in which it admits – to the governing classes – the bricklayer without admitting the bricklayers. Further, by the time the bricklayer has reached responsible office, he has been so moulded, and influenced by the power of the traditions which surround him – that he is indistinguishable in any fundamental from the members of the class which he has joined. So it is then that the propertied class have had less need of complete Fascist organisation than they have had abroad. Nevertheless characteristic features of Fascism have appeared. In the Conservative press there is an agent of propaganda as ruthlessly and cunningly employed as any official organ in Germany or Italy. England is no longer free for political refugees. Trotsky was refused admittance. Justice has taken on a political bias. The imprisonment of Tom Mann and the leader of the Unemployed Marchers on trumpery charges are examples. Finally in the economic sphere – the present interference of the State in the interest of property owners in agriculture and industry is distinctly Fascist in character. … Even from Australia, far removed from the dogmatism and partisanship of European politics, we hear murmurs of similar intolerance and interference with freedom of opinion. Its methods are less brutal – less blatant. But subtlety and unobtrusiveness are no virtues here. It is necessary that those forces in Australia which stand for intellectual freedom should insist upon it for all types of opinion, and watch carefully that this intolerance does not become an accepted factor in our political life.[18]

The difference between the language and concepts of this essay and that of the PhD thesis shows the disciplinary gulf – economics versus political science – which Coombs had to negotiate. The 'social question' is as fully present in the two short articles he wrote for Western Australian readers (on London schools and on parliamentary democracy) as it was absent from the PhD he wrote for London examiners. Coombs never came any closer than in his *Old Modernian* article to expressing sympathy for the revolutionary overthrow of the capitalist. His quest, as for so many liberals of his times, was to find a way to bring social justice into a society which privileged the private ownership of the means of production, without sacrifice to liberty or reason.

Part 3
The experts we need

A vacancy?

WHEN HE RETURNED from London in the last days of January 1934, Coombs was in search of an academic job. Indeed he must have applied before leaving London for the position of Tutorial Class Lecturer at the University of Tasmania, for there is a February 1934 reference from Hubert Whitfield, Vice-Chancellor of the University of Western Australia, commending Coombs' 'exceedingly good work at the University, not only in the academic sphere'.[1] Meanwhile, for the sake of a salary, Coombs returned to teaching in the State school system. He found Perth Boys School interesting because his final-year pupils (7C) were socially aware and responsive to his experiments in teaching around issues of the day – 'my irregular or my unofficial agenda'.[2]

The university's attraction remained strong, however. Coombs lectured and supervised for the Economics Department on a voluntary basis in 1934 and 1935. Jock Hetherington, his maths teacher at Claremont Teachers College, coached him in calculus and in other aspects of mathematics that were becoming relevant to economics.[3] In March 1935, the *West Australian* (describing Coombs as a 'part-time lecturer in economics') reported his talk to the metropolitan branch of the National Party on the subject of his London thesis – the banking system's approach to fluctuations in the balance of payments.[4] As well, Coombs participated in the revival of the university's somnolent Convocation, which began to take an interest in curriculum reform.[5] In October 1934 he joined a committee formed by Con-vocation to investigate secondary schools' matriculation. The following month a second Convocation inquiry claimed his time. This one would look into the differentiation of Pass and Honours streams, the quality of lecturing, the useful-ness of examinations and the research opportunities of staff.[6]

In August 1934, his old teacher, Edward Shann, invited Coombs onto his Radio 6WF 'Economic commentary'. Prompted to 'say what impresses you most … about our situation?', Coombs replied:

> I'll tell you what *depresses* me most – and that is the fondness for palliatives here; the evasion of positive action towards recovery. By comparison with other countries Australia has done well so far but now when the situation cries aloud for constructive action there is a poverty of ideas and a dearth of enterprise that belies our traditional character. Are we, a young and vigorous people, going to continue to see the waste implied by the existence of 88,000 Australian workmen who are members of Unions but out of work, merely as a problem of giving relief? Of course relief is necessary but it does nothing – indeed less than nothing – to attack the real problem. We must see this question as one of *Employment*. These 88,000 unionists and each year's new recruits must be absorbed into industries which can cover their costs.[7]

He and Shann went on to agree that because Australia's London Funds had been rising at the same time as a growth in domestic deposits, the banks now had the opportunity (and – they implied – the duty) to stimulate the demand for jobs by reducing interest rates.

Meanwhile, Coombs was being observed by the Commonwealth Bank's economist, Leslie Melville. As examiner of Coombs' MA thesis in 1931, Melville's report had included words such as 'disappointing' and 'carelessness', not to mention the damning sentence: 'When Mr. Coombs makes use of economic analysis it is usually poor and often wrong.' Yet Melville had passed the thesis because of the author's 'happy and incisive' summaries and his ability to give 'an accurate though concise picture of the course of events'.[8] While in London, Coombs had met the author of this ambivalent evaluation, for Melville and Shann had attended the World Economic Conference in 1933. Coombs and Melville had discussed the possibility of his working at the Commonwealth Bank.[9] In August 1934 Coombs wrote to one of his PhD examiners, Cecil Kisch, seeking a reference because he was 'thinking of applying for an appointment in the Commonwealth Bank'.[10]

The Bank's intolerance of married women gave him his chance. Melville had employed an assistant, Wilmott Debenham, since January 1932. In December 1934 Debenham announced that she was soon to marry fellow economist John ('Jock') Phillips, research officer with the New South Wales Retail Traders Association. The Bank's rules required her to resign upon marriage in March 1935, so Melville began to search for an assistant. He took his time. In February 1935 he told Shann that he had still not made up his mind about Coombs: would he have the required 'flair for statistics and mathematics'?[11] There were other criteria to be satisfied. In June 1935, the Bank's Governor, Sir Claude Reading, asked the Commonwealth's Western Australian manager, R. A. Love, whether Coombs' 'instincts and general moral character are good and whether his repute amongst those people who know him is in every way satisfactory'. Sir Claude wanted someone 'trustworthy and discreet, quite apart from his academic qualifications'.[12] Whitfield assured Love of Coombs' 'integrity and good sense', and then revealed that the university too judged staff according to more than one standard. Coombs was unlikely to find a place at the University of Western Australia, Love believed, because of his 'lack of stature, plus a hard voice and the usual demeanour of a School Master'.[13] (These qualities had not prevented Whitfield from welcoming his voluntary teaching.) The federal Treasurer, R. G. Casey, took an interest in Melville's search, asking Fred Alexander about Coombs. Alexander later wondered 'whether I did Coombs as full justice as I might have'.[14] At least Alexander gave the Bank a copy of a reference from Coombs' supervisor, John Coatman: 'marked intellectual capacity, with a wide and accurate knowledge of economic theory, and with the power to think independently and fruitfully'.[15] Finding it necessary to visit Perth, Casey took the opportunity to interview Coombs himself in the Bank's Perth chambers, an appointment which Coombs later recalled as 'flattering'.[16]

Melville chose Coombs as his assistant. By August Dr and Mrs Coombs were on the *Karoola* bound for Sydney and the post of assistant economist, probationary for twelve months, at £500 per year. His first day in Martin Place was 16 August 1935.

Coombs had entered the middle class through that most meritocratic of portals, the teaching profession. He got his next big break – the Commonwealth Bank appointment – partly because the rule of merit was compromised by a rule of patriarchy. Since Coombs' relationship with feminism is one of the themes I wish to pursue in this biography, it is worth pausing here to reflect on this moment.

Why did Wilmott Debenham lose her job upon marriage?

In her book *Managing Gender*, Desley Deacon argues that public service employment has been one of the bases of the power of the Australian new middle class since the last quarter of the nineteenth century. She defines the middle class as

A third class standing rather uneasily between the bourgeoisie and the proletariat, the new middle class can be thought of in general terms as consisting of those workers who depend on the sale of educational, technical and social skills, or 'cultural capital'. It is 'new' because its members can be differentiated from the 'old' middle classes, the bourgeoisie and the petty bourgeoisie, by the fact that they do not own the means of production; and it is a 'middle' class because it is differentiated from the working class by the type of labour power it has to offer and by the culture and ideology which surround that work.[17]

Deacon shows that around the beginning of the twentieth century many influential public servants and professional members of the new middle class shared the view that governments should intervene into realms of social life where emerging professions were claiming technical competence: town-planning, public health, family welfare, education, and so on. The professional–bureaucratic alliance extended the administration of social life, from the 1890s to the 1930s, in two ways: public programs focused on the more efficient management of child-rearing; and sexually discriminatory labour markets were formalised. The combined impact of these developments was a new social ordering of gender, a reinforcement of certain notions of men's and women's complementary capacities and responsibilities.

Deacon argues that public sector employment has been most important in defining the professional-managerial class's social standing, political power and composition. The laws establishing the Australian public service boards and commissions (New South Wales in 1895, Tasmania in 1900, Victoria in 1902, Western Australia in 1904, South Australia in 1916 and Queensland in 1920) marked not only the dissolution of nineteenth-century habits of political patronage, but also the new middle class's capture of one of the political bases for its reproduction and self-definition. That is, the reformed traditions of public employment practice known as the 'career service' have made public service personnel management the foremost template of the new middle class.

Robert Parker lists four elements of public service personnel practices up to World War II: first, recruitment from below – so that most public servants began their public employment at a junior level; second, sex discrimination, so that married women were not employed and single women were generally confined to certain low-paid occupations; third, subject to this sex discrimination, recruitment was open to anyone who could pass an entrance exam; fourth, promotion through the ranks was every recruit's legitimate expectation, making 'classification' one of the defining activities of personnel practice and ensuring that 'seniority' was the main basis of an individual's upward movement. Although certain technical professions were exempt from the 'recruitment from below' rule, until the late 1930s there was little or no effort to recruit, as administrative generalists, people with advanced *non-technical* education (such as a Bachelor of Arts). The personnel practices of the 'career service' gave stable employment, a predictable career path and bureaucratic power to people who were men (with favouritism towards returned servicemen) including some professionals.[18]

However, two features of the 'career service' were vulnerable to new-middle-class critique. Recruitment from below and the rule of seniority starved the public service of talent, as they required graduates in most cases to start from the bottom and to expect no promotion advantages to flow from their advanced training. Why not give 'merit' a chance? However, if 'merit' were to be recognised, why stop at the merit of men? The argument of merit had a tendency to undermine traditions of male privilege. There was a slow build-up of pressure against sex discrimination in the public sector labour market. Here is an illustrative episode close to Coombs. The Western Australian Teachers Union, committed to impartially assessed merit, advocated equal pay for the sexes. In 1927, Coombs' first year as a qualified teacher, it brought this issue before the Public Service Appeal Board, which ruled that it was a matter for parliament. In the long term, sex inequality remained a difficult issue for the new middle class; its commitment to 'merit' and its opposition to any inherent privilege (including masculine privilege) are the defining features of its project as a class. Debenham's marriage created a vacancy for Coombs because in the 1930s the challenge of meritocracy against patriarchy was in its infancy. The issue would mature over the length of Coombs' career, as we shall see.

The economists

W̄HAT PROFESSIONAL COMMUNITY had Coombs joined?

'Until 1912, economics led a precarious existence between odd university courses mixed with philosophy and politics on the one hand and narrow commercial training in Bankers' Institutes on the other', writes Noel Butlin. 'The first formal Faculty [of Economics] was forced on a reluctant Sydney University by a combination of bankers, teacher training college and the State Government.' The University of Sydney appointed its first Professor of Economics, R. F. Irvine, in 1912 and created a Faculty of Economics in 1920. So did the University of Tasmania, the same year. Soon other universities followed: Melbourne (1923), Western Australia (1925), Queensland (1926) and Adelaide (1929). By 1930, these faculties and departments were graduating 75 students per year, and by 1940, 128 per year.[1] A relatively small number of city-based institutions – banks, State governments and industry lobby groups – employed them. The faculties' intellectual agenda derived from the tasks set by these bodies, but also from the wider work of the discipline. From 1925 the University of Melbourne published the *Economic Record*. 'Its audience was Australasian' and it included 'not only university academics but responsible men of political and commercial affairs. "Their" journal was intended to focus on what they thought they could do something about.'[2]

Between the two world wars, Australian governments began to see the usefulness of economists. The National Party government led by Stanley Melbourne Bruce in 1929 legislated for an economic research bureau, though that law was never implemented. However the Bruce government showed faith in economists in 1929 when it commissioned a team of them (J. B. Brigden, D. B. Copland, E. C. Dyason, L. F. Giblin and C. H. Wickens) to review the impact of the tariff on the pattern of Australian productive activity and to set out principles for a tariff policy. The resulting Brigden Report attracted favourable attention from the world's Anglophone economists. In 1930 the Queensland government set up a Bureau of Economics and Statistics, appointing Brigden as first director. Renamed the Bureau of Industry by the incoming Labor government, its job was to advise on loan expenditure and industry assistance. All States were stimulated to seek economists' research and advice by new efforts to bring order to federal financial relations. With the formation of the Loan Council in 1924 and the Commonwealth Grants Commission in 1933, officials of the Commonwealth and State governments were obliged to prepare reasoned statements about the recent past and near- to medium-term future of their industrial structures and public finances. In 1931 the Commonwealth commissioned L. F. Giblin to gather and analyse economic statistics and, the following year, created the position of 'economist' in the Bureau of Statistics.

Born in Hobart in 1872, Giblin was a graduate of University College London and King's College, in mathematics and science. His varied career included military service in France, instructing in jujitsu in London, prospecting in British Columbia, Labor member for the Tasmanian seat of Denison and Tasmanian government statistician. In 1929 he took up a new position at the University of Melbourne, the Ritchie Chair in Economic Research. There he straddled academia and government – as Acting Commonwealth Statistician, a foundation member of the Commonwealth Grants Commission, and member of the Board of the Commonwealth Bank. Giblin was a father figure for Australia's first generation of academic economists. His student, Richard Downing, recalled that he 'not only had academic excellence, but was also tolerant, cheerful, humane and equable. His simplicity and curiosity enabled him to get immediately on to terms with anyone. Critical and shrewd, there was yet no trace of the cynic in him.'[3] Giblin believed that economists had a duty to make the nature and limits of 'the economy' known to the ordinary waged worker. He was preoccupied with democracy, one acquaintance recalled. 'He thought about it continuously. It was the nodal point to which most of his interests led.'[4] A democracy needed experts who spoke plainly, he thought, though he feared that topics such as monetary policy were simply too technical for public discussion. He is said to have seldom referred to himself as an 'economist'; he preferred to define economics 'with reference to its impartiality and common sense'.[5]

When the Bureau of Statistics created the position 'economist' in 1932, Roland Wilson took the job. Another Tasmanian, his career began in 1925 when he assisted Giblin to advise the Tasmanian government on Commonwealth–State finances. In further training at Oxford and Chicago universities, he investigated the history of Australia's trade and investment relationships with the rest of the world. The basis of his earliest published work in 1930–2, this research, like Giblin's, involved the construction of 'new statistical series and discussion of conceptual matters relating to economic statistics'.[6] Upon his return he taught for a short time in Tasmania's Workers Educational Association, while looking for a university appointment. He preferred government to academia, however, and in 1932 he accepted Giblin's suggestion that he move to Canberra to be economist in the Statistician's Branch of Treasury – the Commonwealth's first senior appointment of an economist.

Banks also were beginning to recruit economists in the early 1930s, including Coombs' most important mentors – Shann and Melville. Melville was a middle-class Sydney boy who had studied economics at the University of Sydney in the early 1920s. Appointed South Australia's Public Actuary in 1924 (aged twenty-three) his early involvement in public policy, like Giblin's and Wilson's, was occasioned by a small State's efforts to justify access to Commonwealth grants. In 1929, he was the University of Adelaide's inaugural appointment as Professor of Economics. When the Commonwealth Bank decided to establish an economic research section, it recruited Melville in 1931. Melville had by then become part of the network of economists who met at conferences of the Australian and New Zealand Association for the Advancement of Science (ANZAAS) and warmed to the interest of the General Manager of the Bank of New South Wales, Alfred Davidson.

Davidson was foremost among Australian capitalists in seeking economic graduates and in cultivating the new professoriate. 'During the early 1930s Davidson regularly invited several leading economists to spend a week with him at Leura during the Christmas or Easter holidays to discuss economic topics of current interest.'[7] Among his guests were Copland, Giblin, Mills, Shann, Belshaw (Auckland) and Melville. Davidson set up an economic intelligence and statistical service within his bank, and he began publishing a circular in July 1930 in which his staff were encouraged to think independently. By the mid-1930s the economic department ('the first private sector economic research group in the country') had grown to as many as seventeen or eighteen economists and statisticians, and 'resembled a university', with freedom of expression for the senior economist.[8]

Even had there not been a Great Depression, the intricacies of Australia's federal financial relations would have demanded the recruitment of economists into government. However, the Depression promoted the new profession further by allowing economists to become the conspicuous authors of policies of wide and controversial relevance. Economists could celebrate the Premiers' Plan (June 1931) as the moment when the economics profession confirmed its political pertinence. D. B. Copland was particularly active in the 1930s promoting the story of economists' beneficial influence over public affairs. A New Zealander who had worked at the Universities of Tasmania and Melbourne, Copland had declared in 1923 that 'the economist is (or should be) king'.[9] Appointed Melbourne's Professor of Commerce (a position endowed by retailer Sidney Myer) in 1924, aged thirty, Copland opened his academic labours to worldly use, endeavouring to keep contact with both adult education (at which he had been assiduous in Tasmania) and Melbourne's financial and commercial interests. 'It did not mean that he became their mouthpiece', writes Marjorie Harper. 'He was above all an academic, and hoped always to achieve the objectivity which such an occupation would imply. He would stand above sectional interests as the informed and competent lofty leader. He would bare the basis of sectional conflict in an effort to confront it, minimise it, and promote consensus.'[10] To chair the committee that produced the Premiers' Plan was fully to vindicate an aspiration both personal and professional. In 1934, delivering Cambridge University's prestigious Marshall Lectures, he could proclaim to the world that economists' expertise had saved Australia. The world was impressed. One Indian economist, writing in the *Economic Record* in 1937, described Australia as 'the Utopia of practical economists'.[11]

Schedvin offers a corrective account. The economists' 1931 advice

> made compromise possible because it had the appearance of expertise and objectivity. In fact, however, the report [to the Premiers] was carefully framed so as to be acceptable to both parties: one side was offered wage cuts and the other a reduction in interest rates. The economists of their own volition had little influence on the broad principles of the plan; these were determined for them by political exigencies.

Schedvin argues that the economists worked within the Commonwealth Bank's orthodoxies, in particular the Bank's conviction that it was of supreme importance to maintain the value of the pound. If Australians hoped to pay overseas debts, they must cut their domestic expenditure, whatever the hardship among people living on wages, salaries and pensions. Against Schedvin's conclusion that the Premiers' Plan 'was in conception and design, if not in execution, the Bank's plan', we should place Copland's defence that he and his fellow economists had stood up to the banks by successfully proposing that those who lived by *lending* money should also suffer a fall in income.[12]

It is possible to see this public policy work by economists – the Premiers' Plan, the Brigden Report – as filling an ideological vacancy within Australia's utilitarian political culture. That was the view of a young professor of history, W. K. Hancock. In his book *Australia* (1930), the first generation of Australian academic economists emerges as a body of rational, tough-minded critics of the ruinous nostrums of a populist political ethos. Hancock lamented that there had never been in Australia a 'conservative' tradition to restrain populist public policies, such as public borrowing for infrastructure projects of dubious merit and wage-fixing that was answerable to union militancy rather than to employers' 'capacity to pay'. In passage after passage, Hancock contrasted the blind instinct of a people grown used to comfort with the cool inquiries of men trained to ask: where is the money to come from? *Australia* was hailed in the *Economic Record* as a book for 'every Australian adult' to ponder.[13]

Though the labour movement in the 1930s execrated economists as allies of the banks and authors of ruinous deflation, in their own eyes the economists' Depression interventions were politically judicious and technically sound. It was clear to them that they were not beholden to 'conservative' thought, as they conceived it. Had they not tried to overcome the Commonwealth Bank's intransigence on the exchange rate? Their collective technical self-confidence – based partly on the fact that they were the ones who were *constructing* a statistical artefact, 'the Australian economy' – included a strong sense of their political autonomy as worldly experts. Interviewed in 1992, Melville recalled the Premiers' Plan as a worthy compromise. Politically blocked from depreciating the Australian pound, 'we had to accept the alternative, which was cutting wages and cutting pensions, interest and everything else. But there was also, perhaps a case for it. We had to do some savage things and we had to get people to accept those savage things.'[14]

As authors of a deflation strategy shaped by such political pressures and convictions, the economists found their reputations were now as high in non-Labor circles as low among labour militants. The industrialist Sir Herbert Gepp celebrated them in a 1936 speech to the New South Wales regional group of the Institute of Public Administration. Economists were central figures, he argued, in the new 'administrative class' whose historic role was to reconcile the demands of democracy with those of a dynamic capitalism. Highly trained officials stood beside Cabinet and Parliament in order to inform them of the 'economic facts of their country before they make important economic decisions'.[15] To consolidate the preparation of such advice in Australia, Gepp proposed 'a bureau which includes experts in economics and statistical analysis combined with sound judgment and insight into the economic effects of policy decisions … an Economic Research and Advisory Council'.[16] He named Australian intellectuals suited to such a council: Roland Wilson, Douglas Copland, Leslie Melville and Arthur Smithies (soon to migrate to Harvard University). 'Government is a business', he continued, and its many 'shareholders' were sometimes 'swayed by psychological storms which result in the rejection of a whole board of directors'. Economists could stabilise governments, not only by reducing the frequency and magnitude of policy mistakes, but also by conveying to the community the reasons for policies, so that 'the psychological storms would become fewer and less destructive'.[17]

In a profession thus lauded, Coombs might well ask John La Nauze in 1937: 'Can I remain in a bank and retain my integrity?'

The question seems partly playful. Could Coombs have been deeply troubled by being part of the Commonwealth Bank? He found the Bank a stuffy and formal workplace, compared with a university, but in the ethos of the industry he had joined there were strengths as well. A certain restrained and conservative demeanour attested the Bank's staff as people of integrity. Thus the Bank's rules for staff disapproved of any employee residing at an hotel without the consent of the Governor or Chief Manager (no less). And 'officers who associate with questionable characters, or who are intemperate or improvident or of unsatisfactory habits will be considered guilty of misconduct and dealt with accordingly'. The desired soundness of character would be manifested in men's attire. Here the Bank struggled to reconcile English traditions of respectability with the realities of the Australian climate.

> Managers may approve of the removal of coats at any time hot weather conditions are experienced. Any decision to remove coats should extend to waistcoats and should apply to the whole of the staff in the public portions of the office ... The Bank expects all officers to co-operate in maintaining a reasonable uniformity of dress and the preservation of the businesslike tone of the office. Shirts of quiet tonings (preferably white) should be worn in such conditions, with suitable collars and ties. The Bank has no objection to the wearing of lightweight long trousers and soft shirts with collars attached (ties to be worn). If so desired, shirts may be worn with elbow-length sleeves. Belts must be worn instead of braces.[18]

Coombs, living in a Rose Bay flat with Lallie and Janet, had no pretensions to bohemianism, but after six months of the new job he confided to his old friend John La Nauze his fear of the effects of 'respectability'. Without regular news about new books, he might become 'an ossified banker'. He rejoiced in his budding friendship with Jock Phillips, with whom he visited art shows and with whom, over lunch, he liked to join 'in a chorus of abuse of Fascists and Conservatives'.[19] Differences of opinion enlivened his association with Melville. Just as he had learned economics partly by contesting the opinions of Shann, so he found in Melville's conversation occasions of further 'education by argument'.[20] When La Nauze was coming to work in Sydney in 1939, Coombs told him that Melville 'is much better than he sounds in print and correspondence and I think you'll find him very stimulating'.[21] Forty years later, Coombs publicly paid Melville ('my first boss') the following compliment.

> He was one of the few men that I have ever known who not merely liked to be disagreed with occasionally, but saw disagreement as a marvellous opportunity. When you were bold enough to disagree with him you could see him intellectually rubbing his hands while he waited for you to lay bare the basis of the disagreements so that he could take it to pieces. This was an eye-opener to me, not merely in the lessons I learnt in logic as well as in economics, but it was a lesson to me in personal relations.[22]

Phillips and Melville gave him much-needed conversational range, as 'I find it very hard to meet people with whom I can talk about things other than Banking' –

unlike in universities 'where one's contacts are so varied and made automatically'.[23] Coombs taught part-time in the University of Sydney's Economics Department in 1938 and 1939, his subjects including the history of political economy. He liked the academics he met there. Professor R. C. Mills – with whom he would work on education and cultural policy in the years 1946–9 – he described as 'a good Professor. Tolerant, loyal to his colleagues, willing to welcome new ideas even when he does not share them, and very honest'. He thought Sydney Butlin 'the best of them as a theorist – a good man altogether'.[24]

This university work helped to give him some emotional and intellectual distance from the Bank. Thus he could delight in the following story, shared with La Nauze.

> The Bank gave the Teachers Federation some money for their library but asked that the books when chosen be sent along to have the Bank's stamp and 'Presented By etc' engraved thereon. The teachers most unreasonably have bought a lot of subversive literature such as 'Marxism and modern thought'. Now the Bank is very worried. Can the B[an]k in view of its public responsibilities etc. present such books to the teachers? They have brought them to us for our opinion. I propose to read them at any rate – whether the teachers get them or not.[25]

Three months later, he remarked of *Australian Quarterly* that 'it might be good if wasn't so bloody respectable'.[26]

Defining himself as a little bit to the left of respectable, Coombs was none-theless aware of the Bank's status as a public institution with certain traditions of autonomy and liberality. Shann, who had come to know the world of commercial finance as adviser to Alfred Davidson, had advised Coombs in 1933 that he would do better to join the Commonwealth Bank: 'only there could a professional economist hope to maintain complete personal integrity'.[27] Possibly Shann had meant that within the Commonwealth Bank, one was more free to express one's opinions than under Davidson. In *Trial Balance* Coombs wrote that Common-wealth Bank Governor Sir Claude Reading had responded tolerantly to his unorthodox (for the Bank) sympathy for the report of the Royal Commission on Money and Banking in 1936. In 1992, he recalled that many people in the 1930s, without being Communists, looked hopefully on Russian social experiments. He had himself been described as a Communist by the New South Wales Agent-General in London, because he had dared to attack this man's views on British foreign policy at a Sydney meeting of the Economic Society. 'He went to the Chairman of the Bank Board', Coombs recalled, and the Chairman had dismissed the allegation as 'nonsense'.[28] The Bank's concern for 'respectability' underpinned a certain liberal strength. It might not be such a bad place to think.

From people's bank to central bank

BANKING WAS CENTRAL to the September 1934 federal election. Labor continued to highlight it, and the Country Party agreed that people on the land had grievances against the financiers. The United Australia Party, led by former Labor MP Joseph Lyons, had little choice but to promise an inquiry. The Royal Commission on Money and Banking began to take evidence in January 1936 and delivered its report in July 1937.[1] According to L. F. Giblin, 'it was the Commonwealth Bank itself which was most stimulated' by the Royal Commission's challenge to rethink Australian banking. It is hard not to have Coombs and Phillips in mind when we read that 'many of the Bank's younger staff were beginning to be interested in central banking matters which were outside their routine occupation. The Commission gave a great stimulus to this interest.'[2]

Melville, not Coombs, presented the views of the Bank's economists. However, Coombs' PhD thesis had argued in 1933 for an increase in the Bank's regulatory powers, and this view harmonised with the most far-reaching point, in practical terms, in the Bank's evidence to the Royal Commission: to enhance the Bank's powers over the management of the Australian banks' London Funds *and* over the credit policy of the banking system. Economists differed over the relative importance of these two regulatory faci. Some economists, made confident by Keynes' work, argued that the objective of a central bank should be full employment, through influence over the level of demand for goods and services.[3] That was not the view of Melville – the 'most vehement and articulate of the antagonists of fiscal and monetary action to eliminate unemployment'.[4] For Melville, the Commonwealth Bank should use credit controls to stabilise the exchange rate, and the Bank would urge on governments the complementary wages, fiscal and monetary policies required to maintain such stability. Whether such policies relieved unemployment was not, according to Melville, the primary issue. Giblin later described the Bank as 'reluctant to ask for really effective powers for fear of antagonizing the trading banks and perhaps frightening public opinion; it also was nervous lest strong powers should be too heavy a responsibility'.[5]

The Royal Commission was dissatisfied with the Bank's diffidence towards employment, making a sustained critique of the Bank's responses to the Depression. As S. J. Butlin read it, the report evoked an image of 'the [Commonwealth] bank digging in its toes, like a calf that won't be led, behaving as if it didn't want to be a central bank, and yielding only when it had to'.[6] The chief consideration of the bank, argued the Commissioners, should not be the traditional obsession with exchange rate stability but 'the reduction in fluctuations in general economic activity'. The Bank must expand credit in order to raise business activity and employment and contract it in order 'to prevent the development of boom conditions which are likely to end in a depression'. A stable exchange rate should be maintained only to the extent that it helped to smooth out the booms and slumps of economic activity in Australia.[7]

Both Bank and Royal Commission agreed that the Commonwealth Bank should have the power to hold deposits from the trading banks as a means to affect those banks' ability and willingness to lend. The Royal Commission wanted the Bank Board to set the level of those deposits within a limit decided by the Treasurer.[8] This would enable governments to control private banks' lending to a degree unprecedented in Australia, though not remarkable by comparison with other nations. The Royal Commission buttressed its 'reserve deposits' recommendation with others designed to give the Commonwealth Bank more information about each bank and to enhance its capacity for research and analysis of the banking system as a whole.

Economists generally welcomed these recommendations. The issue exciting most discussion was the relative responsibilities of 'experts' (such as might be appointed to the Bank Board) and the elected government. Reviewing the report for the *Economic Record*, Allan Fisher did not dissent from its statement of objectives for central bank regulation, but he worried that the Commissioners had understated the central bank's responsibility to *restrain* the booms which private trading banks were all too ready to feed. The report did not show a central bank when to apply the brakes, he complained, though he conceded that this was properly a decision for governments, not Bank boards.[9] Copland agreed that the Bank's experts were advisers to governments and that governments must have 'the last word', but he also urged that the Bank become a source of independent expertise with 'immediate' responsibility for policy. He thought the Commissioners wise to expect and to encourage a cooperative rather than coercive relationship between the Commonwealth Bank and the other trading banks. It was appropriate to a modern democracy, he wrote, that the state should have firm policies on private banks' lending. He likened the central bank to the Arbitration Court in its capacity for 'disinterested judgments' which 'will command public confidence in a policy that might be repudiated when proposed directly by governments'.[10] Sydney Butlin agreed that the government must ultimately be responsible for monetary policy, and he complained that the Royal Commission had passed too quickly over an issue raised by its critique of the banks' handling of the Depression: should the banks be nationalised? Generally, the economists warned against expecting too much of an enhanced central bank: economic fluctuations could be smoothed, but not eliminated.[11]

In the summer of 1937–8, Treasury, the Commonwealth Bank and the private trading banks conferred over the Royal Commission's recommendations. The government shouldered much of the trading banks' case against them. In the late 1930s, commented the Bank's historian, 'no effective control of monetary policy in Australia could be achieved by voluntary co-operation of the private banks, except perhaps in time of war'.[12] Indeed, it would be the outbreak of war in 1939 that made the Commonwealth Bank into an effective regulator of the banking system.

What did Coombs make of all this? His MA thesis was a progressive history of 'the development of the Commonwealth bank as a central bank'. The

Commonwealth Bank could, should and would become Australia's central bank because that was the only way to relieve Australia's sensitivity to externally induced economic shocks.[13] Coombs considered the Commonwealth Bank's responses to the two biggest challenges it had faced since it was established in 1911. During World War I, Australia suffered inflation. To what extent had the Bank been responsible? Coombs found this a 'difficult question'. 'In times of national emergency traditional finance goes by the board. No belligerent country escaped inflation; not even those with strong central banks with generations of experience and strong traditions of independence.'[14] The government's approach to war finance was not corrected by Commonwealth Bank advice because the Bank had then lacked the necessary power and prestige within government.

At least the pressure of the war had forced 'parliamentary theorists' to leave the bank alone to do its work.

> The war broke it free from the strings of parties and controversy and it emerged a national institution with a distinctive character and definite place in the Australian economy. It had been the government financial agent in its dealings with the trading banks, the Bank of England and with the Imperial government; it had raised, and administered the Government loans; it had acted as a representative of the trading banks and adjusted bank differences; it had controlled the export of gold in co-operation with the Bank of England. These were central bank functions. Even though the bank had not proved the restraining influence on Government finance that a fully developed Central bank might have been it nevertheless had done much to build up a reputation and a tradition of service which would enable it to wield a more active influence in the future. Long strides had been taken towards Mr. Denison Miller's ideal.[15]

The counterposing of 'strings of parties and controversy' on the one hand, with the closing image of purposeful officialdom (Miller was the Bank's founding Governor) on the other, is a cameo of Coombs' sympathy for the professional-isation of central banking, its liberation from politics through the assertion of disinterested expertise.

The questionable rationality of politicians was again his implication when he noted the incongruity, not apparent to Parliament, of two amendments to the bank's legislation separated by only a year (1924 and 1925): 'the one to convert the Commonwealth Bank into a Central Bank proper and another to extend the trading side of its activities [Rural Credits] into a sphere not only untouched by any such institution in the world but quite at variance with the general principles of central banking'.[16] He was soon to reverse this presumption that central bank-ing was, in principle, a stand-alone responsibility. In the 1950s he mounted a desperate defence of a composite central bank against the very 'principle' that he seemed to embrace in 1931.

When Coombs evaluated rival policies for recovery from the Depression, he expressed no sympathy for Theodore or Lang. He saw no good in Caucus's November 1930 'inflationary' resolution that the Commonwealth Bank give the government credit to meet its budgetary needs. He expressed no such disapproval of the Commonwealth Bank's refusing such credit, nor of the Bank's advice to Scullin to cut government expenditure. He inferred an unwonted policy of 'nationalisation of credit' in Treasurer E. G. Theodore's continuing quest for bank support for an expansionary budget.[17] He praised the Bank's leadership in persuading the trading banks in 1930 to mobilise their gold reserves and to ship them to London to fortify the ailing London Funds. However, he conceded, while this had served the needs of government to repay loans, it had done nothing to succour Australian producers nor to revive the domestic economy. Contrary to a labour movement story of the Depression as the triumph of banks over the people's government, Coombs in 1931 saw the banks as needing 'freedom from the incubus of Government deficits'. As well, he supported 'a vigorous attack on costs' and a 'free exchange' in order to 'give the export industries the opportunity to build up the required overseas surpluses'.[18]

Coombs' criticisms of the Commonwealth Bank in the Depression were not those voiced by the labour movement, but those of a historian who was partial to the Commonwealth Bank's perceived destiny. He criticised the Bank when it faltered in its assumption of 'the responsibilities of a national guardian of monetary sanity'.[19] From the Commonwealth Bank Board's point of view in 1929–31, Coombs was unorthodox. However, his was not the unorthodoxy of Theodore or Lang, but of Sir Alfred Davidson, the employer of his supervisor, Edward Shann.[20] Davidson and Shann emerged in 1930 as advocates of a fall in the value of the Australian pound, in order to boost exports. (The Bank of New South Wales had loaned heavily to export-oriented rural producers.) They were equally forceful, at that time, in their hostility to Theodore's 'inflationary' monetary and fiscal policy proposals. By opposing Theodore's 'inflationary proposals' and restricting further government borrowings, 'banking tradition had triumphed', wrote Coombs. 'In the victory the Commonwealth Bank itself had played no small part.'[21]

Coombs' scepticism towards Theodore was evident in his chapter on 'Nationalisation of banking'. Theodore's budget speech in November 1929 had 'forecast an attack on the very basis of the banking system'. Coombs thought that Labor's first bill to amend the Commonwealth Bank's legislation – 'appearing as it did before the whole scheme of which it was to form a unit had been announced' – had not disclosed the government's radical intentions.[22]

Coombs' conclusion argued that times of national crisis – World War I, the Depression – had been the making of the Commonwealth Bank as a central bank. In the second crisis it had had more stature and more influence than in the first. If it were to become an institution of relevance to normal times, he suggested, new policies would have to be developed: on short-term money, on the management of the overseas reserves, and on the coordination of government borrowings from abroad.

The central bank's management of Australia's external financial relations continued to be Coombs' theme in his PhD thesis, 'Dominions Exchanges and Central Bank Problems'. The Dominions' financial systems differed from Britain's in that the Dominions were heavily dependent on the world prices of a small number of exported commodities and on the capital of British and American investors. To manage that dependency, their banks had become tolerant of relatively wide fluctuations in the level of the London Funds. However, the Dominion banking systems had sometimes to consider how and when to make gross changes in policy. While short-term fluctuations in overseas funds could be dealt with by relatively minor changes in their supply of domestic credit, big rises or falls in the overseas funds required more careful consideration. Gross alterations in domestic credit policies would do great harm to each economy. Carefully considered, some changes in the levels of the Dominions' overseas funds were consistent with, indeed, were required by, long-term changes in the structures and prices of each Dominion's exports, imports and in access to overseas capital. Such structural shifts demanded of Dominion leaders a wider reconsideration of economic policies – including review of the exchange rate – than any single commercial bank had the capacity to offer. This was what made Dominion central banks necessary.

What responsibilities and instruments of control should they possess? While Coombs expressed some sympathy for a freely moving exchange rate, he was drawn to a more deliberative adjustment of domestic credit policies. Rates of exchange between currencies should be fixed, at least in the short term. When the causes of disequilibria between the values of currencies were discovered to be 'long term', bankers should, however, 'apply the mechanism of the automatic system – either through inflation or deflation, or through variations in the exchange rate'.[23] He favoured exchange devaluation or appreciation, but he recognised that governments and bankers could be slow to take such actions, and that their delay would make it likely that more severe correctives would be needed. How could the management of currency and credit be made more sensitive to long-term changes? A well-informed and analytically skilful 'monetary authority' was required, he suggested, to analyse 'continuously the relevant factors in the economic situation to detect possible causes of disequilibrium in the international position'.[24]

Was this 'monetary authority' necessarily a central bank? Coombs thought it should be, because any monetary authority holding all of a Dominion's overseas reserves in as liquid a form as possible would have to turn its eyes from the temptation to invest those funds at the most profitable rate. A central bank could give up the profit motive and be trusted by all the private banks to distribute fairly among them the burden of holding overseas funds in liquid form. A central bank would also be respected by the banks when it required access to their accounts and to other commercially sensitive information. A central bank could give disinterested advice about foreign borrowing, an important cause of disequilibrium in all the Dominions. It could also be the government's banker.

To maintain influence over the credit-creation and exchange-holding policies of the trading banks, a central bank should have the power to stipulate the minimum levels of trading banks' cash reserves. As well, Coombs wanted central banks to engage in 'open-market dealings in exchange within specified limits' and 'open market dealings in securities' and to wield 'a bank rediscount rate'.[25]

In 1936, the Royal Commission's recommendations coincided largely with Coombs' 1933 blueprint of an effective Dominion central bank. It recommended statutory minimum cash reserves (recommendations 9–11) and open-market dealings in securities and a bank rediscount rate (recommendation 15), but not an open market in currencies (exchange). However, Coombs' 1933 rationale for a strong central bank was closer to that of Leslie Melville than of the Royal Commissioners. That is, his thesis had focused less on the problem of maintaining employment than on the problem of managing each Dominion's external account. Nonetheless, the 'fit' between Coombs' and the Royal Commission's list of desired central bank controls is noteworthy. From his own historical studies he was converging with the most technically competent and politically respectable economists of his time.

Sweden and Australia

COOMBS CONCLUDED HIS pre-war writings in economics with two papers on Sweden's recovery from the Depression and one on Australia's.[1] Sweden, like Australia, was dependent to a high degree on its exports of primary products. As well, Sweden was of great interest in the Anglophone world in the late 1930s because of its inventive theoretical economists such as Gunnar Myrdal and for its policy history since 1929. Swedish policies had delivered recovery without inflation and from 1932 they had been the responsibility of a Socialist government.[2]

The most important feature of Swedish policy and practice, suggested Coombs, was the notion 'international margin' – 'that margin given to monetary authorities for expansive action because of the existence of a positive balance of payments'.[3] The margin is made up of the reserve of gold or foreign currencies, the expected income from exports, the flow of investment into the country, and the benefits of currency depreciation. Whereas banks, in the normal course of business, tended to concern themselves with only one of these constituents – the reserves of gold or foreign currency – a more sophisticated monetary authority, such as a central bank, could take them all into account in judging the risks of an expansionary policy.

Though the four entities making up the 'international margin' were variables familiar to economists, it was novel to lump them together as the 'international margin'. The very idea of the margin as an object for consideration and calculation presupposed a considering and calculating institution – a monetary authority or central bank – which had still to emerge in Australia. In drawing attention to the 'margin', therefore, Coombs was giving a name to the economic realities that the Commonwealth Bank, as a central bank, would be uniquely able to act upon.

So much for theory. But how much did actions taken by Sweden's Riksbank contribute to Swedish recovery? Coombs' answer is not entirely clear. On the one hand, he appeared to argue 'very little', and he seemed to come to the same conclusion about the significance of the Socialist government's deficit budgets after September 1932. The initial stimulus to Swedish recovery came from an improvement in export income – higher volume and better terms of trade. So 'Swedish experience … is inconclusive on the question of whether [monetary and fiscal] policy can itself be sufficient to bring about recovery. Too many extraneous factors enter into Swedish recovery.'[4] While drawing attention to these external factors, Coombs argued that it had nonetheless been important that Sweden had pursued a coherent and intelligent monetary policy. Swedish monetary policy was not based on any single objective, but its effects were to keep prices (cost of living index and wholesale price index) stable during 1929–37.

Was Coombs here equivocating about the significance of monetary policy, his interests as a central banker straining against the evidence of the relative un-importance of central bank policy in Swedish recovery? That is one possibility.

However there is another way to read his papers on Sweden, one which puts the emphasis on the word 'policy'. A policy is more than simply a set of govern-ment actions, it is also a reasoned discourse about intentions and means. And discourse is itself a form of political action. Coombs thought that 'monetary policy was useful because of the clear statements of the purposes for which that policy was designed'.[5] The important audience was the entrepreneurs deciding about investment. Stated monetary policy influenced entrepreneurs' expectations.

Coombs had a strong sense of the vulnerability and sensitivity of the entre-preneur. Contributing to a discussion of G. L. Woods' paper 'The American Experiment' in January 1939, he said that

> the entrepreneur in these days had become exceedingly sensitive. If there were any suggestion that the privileged position of the owners of property might be threatened, then the 'entrepreneur was likely to refuse to "entrepren".' Also, workers should not ask for higher wages, lest the entrepreneur's confidence be disturbed. Even 'pump-priming' to bolster entrepreneurial profits might prove unacceptable to those whom it was designed to aid. It was necessary to 'do your good by stealth'.[6]

It might be argued that 'doing good by stealth' implies *not* articulating the intentions of government policy. However, in the light of the following passage in his published paper on Sweden, I suggest that Coombs' remark applied only to state-phobic American entrepreneurs. One of the things he found most interesting about Sweden was the rapport between government, economists and entrepreneurs.

> One of the essential differences between modern Swedish theory and the 'general theory' now widely accepted in England is the different emphasis placed on 'expectations'. English general theory relates total income through the multiplier to investment. Investment is, of course, a composite factor, and Keynesian theory takes little account of the inter-relationship between various parts of investment, nor of variations in the multiplier, which can occur as during the period the trade cycle [*sic*].

Swedish theory, while coming substantially to the same conclusions, gives greater emphasis to *the importance of plans of entrepreneurs and influence of economic factors upon those plans.* If there is one factor characteristic of all phases of Swedish policy it is the attempt to provide a stable basis for entrepreneurs' expectations.[7]

Coombs thought it possible for entrepreneurs and economic policy-makers to build up a good mutual understanding of the purposes and directions of policy. Keynes' work in the 1930s is generally taken to have highlighted the theoretical significance of entrepreneurial expectations, but Coombs thought that the Swedes grasped this point better than the English. Coombs thus used the Swedish case to emphasise the importance of the *public exposition* of monetary policy. It was essential for governments, including central banks, to let entrepreneurs know what was going on.

Senior colleagues commented favourably on the first version of Coombs' discussion of Sweden. Brigden surmised that Coombs 'had local conditions and propaganda in mind'.[8] Copland, champion of the notion that articulate economists were central to good policy, sought to recruit Coombs to his cause of antipodean iconoclasm.

I have always maintained that, though Australian policy was much less deliberate and not as well planned, it contributed rather more to the problem of monetary policy in a depression than did the Swedish experiment. But Sweden gained caste in the eyes of the world. Swedes are respectable people. They have some highly respectable economists and they live in the Northern hemisphere. The uncouth and bad mannered Australians whose economists dare to question such renowned authorities as the Bank of England could not make any great contribution ... Now what you should do is write a preliminary account of the problem in Australia.[9]

In 1939 Coombs wrote but did not publish a paper on Australia's recovery. It emerges that 'the story of monetary policy in Australia during the depression is an illustration of the power of psychological factors in economic change'. The turning-point in investor confidence was in 1931–2, when

A number of changes took place which altered the background of the entrepreneurs' calculations. A balance was attained on international account and banking reserves abroad increased for the first time for some years. The fear of international insolvency was allayed. The Premiers' Plan in June, 1931, promised to make universal the reduction in wages and to reduce other costs and appeared to give greater stability to the future interest of property owners. Above all, it brought deficits 'under control'. The dispute between the Scullin government and the investing public over monetary and banking policy was finally resolved by the defeat of the Government in December, 1931. After a period of more intense uncertainty this was followed by the dismissal of the Lang Government in New South Wales in May, 1932. The way was now clear for business men to look optimistically upon the opportunities for investment.[10]

Coombs' ideas about central banking and monetary policy emerged from his close study of the political histories of five dependent economies – Australia, three other Dominions and Sweden – during the inter-war period. The lesson he drew was that monetary policy must be clearly *articulated* to be effective.

Part 4
New orders

Trusting the people

A NETWORK OF ECONOMISTS – some of them employed by universities, others senior officials of government – known as the Finance and Economic Advisory Committee (henceforth F&E Committee) deliberated on the war-time reshaping of Australia's economy. Set up in December 1938 within the Defence Department with Professor L. F. Giblin as Chair, the F&E Committee became the responsibility of Treasury in September 1939.

> The wisdom and experience of its chairman, Giblin, and his human qualities as well as his professional standing made the small room, at the sunny corner of the top of West Block, Canberra, where he crouched over his pipe among a litter of papers, not only a cell of economic thought but a place where many departmental and inter-departmental tangles were unwound by honest and straightforward common sense.[1]

Other members were Roland Wilson, Leslie Melville, D. B. Copland, J. B. Brigden, Sir Harry Brown, Daniel McVey, R. C. Mills and E. R. Walker.

In 1938 Coombs had been already at work on war economy problems as the Bank's representative on the Sea-Borne Trade Committee. When war was declared, the Bank seconded Coombs to Treasury. It was among his duties to be Treasury's link with the F&E Committee, whose deliberations had always been made known to him by Leslie Melville. Attending the expanded Committee's first meeting, Coombs contributed a paper on 'Import Control Plans'.

The F&E Committee met every few months in Canberra, and between meetings the members circulated papers and letters on a growing agenda of issues. Each member would be assigned to write a paper on a topic, perhaps concluding with some options for the government to consider. The others would contribute their opinions, and Giblin would try to formulate a consensus for advice to senior government officials. Hardly a meeting went by without the Committee discussing a concise paper by Coombs: higher taxation (including the possibility of a wealth tax), 'measures to check the tendency of prices to rise', the 'dislocation of trade with the UK', 'Should building be discouraged?', the sale of wool manufactures to the United States, the economic effects of the defence program.

No committee member doubted that government should now intervene, much further than in peace, into the workings of the economy. In his December 1940 paper on 'Banking system and war finance', Coombs considered how the banks might help the government raise loans from the public to finance the war. If they all raised these loans, then the government should set limits to their resulting profits; if the Commonwealth Bank alone bore the burden of raising the public loans, then the government would be entitled to regulate private banks' lending.

Either course of action would 'mean the conversion of the banking system into a public utility for the period of war'.[2]

It was up to each F&E economist to decide how much to consider the political meanings of technically sound policies. When they discussed how to curb private consumption, Coombs weighed alternative justifications. It would be 'more honest and more convincing to urge restrictions of imports and non-essential home production on the grounds that goods were needed for the expeditionary force', he advised, 'than on grounds that we should pay our overseas debt.'[3] Well might the economists ponder such issues, for the public was sceptical of their political masters. The October 1940 federal elections had left the governing coalition of the United Australia Party and the Country Party, under Menzies' leadership, dependent on the votes of two independent MPs. Menzies resigned on 29 August 1941, and his successor – the Country Party's Arthur Fadden – on 3 October.

By forsaking the Coalition, the two independents allowed John Curtin to form the first federal ALP government for ten years. Over the next year Curtin faced British Australia's worst military crisis, as the Japanese army swept through South-East Asia. By November 1941, the government had resolved to ration certain goods – clothes in particular – in order to release labour from the industries making, wholesaling and retailing those goods. Rationing had been considered too difficult politically by Curtin's predecessors. As Menzies told Curtin on 6 November 1941: 'I do not believe that any government will, in the present temper of public opinion in Australia, successfully attempt rationing.' How could Labor make rationing acceptable?[4] Coombs gave his answer in a February 1942 paper on 'Labour supply and rationing'. Only 'a relatively small proportion of the productive effort in the Australian economy is devoted to the actual production of goods', he argued. The government would divert more labour to war purposes were it to curtail effort in the 'distribution, financing, advertising' of consumer goods.[5] No trace survives of his brother economists' reception of this argument. Possibly Coombs' point was countered by the pragmatic argument that it was politically easier to intervene in consumer behaviour than to command firms engaged in 'distribution, financing, advertising' to cease their services. By limiting consumption of certain goods, the industries producing those goods could more amply service military needs and many retailing staff could be diverted to other occupations.

In the same month as this discussion took place, with the Japanese taking Singapore and bombing Darwin, Curtin announced a National Economic Plan with unprecedentedly comprehensive regulatory powers. In Hasluck's summary:

> No capital could be sold or invested without Government permission. Prices of all goods and services were pegged. Profits were pegged at a maximum of 4% on capital, and profits in excess of the prescribed maximum would either be passed on to the consumer in lower prices or taken in taxation. Interest rates were controlled, wages were pegged, although a 'margin of tolerance' was allowed to enable constituted industrial tribunals to complete current negotiations or to make adjustments to remove anomalies between industries, and the system of cost-of-

living adjustment of wages was continued. Control of manpower was tightened. Absenteeism in industry, for other than prescribed reasons, was made illegal for both employers and employees. Power was taken by the Government to proclaim any area under military control so that it could take effective action to meet an emergency. Speculation on commodities, such as forward dealings on foodstuffs, was prohibited.[6]

By 1 April 1942, with the Japanese poised to invade Australia, the Production Executive of Cabinet had decided to appoint a Director of Rationing. He would be advised by the Tariff Board. Coombs, Copland and others were critical of the plans outlined early in April by the Tariff Board's Chair, Hugh McConaghy. Curtin and Chifley found their comments persuasive, and 'to my surprise Curtin sent for me'.[7]

In accepting the offer to be Director of Rationing (his first day was 16 April 1942), Coombs made himself answerable to a Rationing Commission composed of three MPs – A. W. Coles (Independent), W. V. McCall (UAP) and J. I. Armstrong (ALP). Curtin announced on 8 May 1942 that rationing would be introduced, causing panic in the shops and raising doubts about the government's finesse in public relations. Coombs' hard work – he once spoke to me of working 16-hour days – ensured that coupon books were ready on 13 and 14 June to be issued – through post offices, commandeered churches and public halls – to every adult in Australia.[8] The rationing of clothing began on Monday, 16 June 1942.

Thus began Coombs' first taste of administrative responsibility (though he had had a small staff under him in Treasury). He later judged himself lucky to have been trained as a teacher.

> You know, you have a class of people to manage, and sometimes they're a hostile bunch of hooligans. But also, you have to design a discipline, or a way of controlling what they do, you have to be able to work out a program over a year, at least a year. … I think school teachers transfer to other jobs on the whole very readily.[9]

Not that his staff were 'hooligans' – merely 'an exceedingly radical group of people', he was fascinated to find. 'The very large proportion of them were people who were distressed by the war, were disinclined to be involved personally in it, and they saw this work as … an attempt to achieve a minimum of social justice, despite the war.'[10]

Coombs' ostensibly *administrative* mission – to install a rationing system – staged his emergence as a political figure. Rationing posed a political question – the popular acceptability of the new relationship between state and people. As Director of Rationing, Coombs became implicated in a discussion by politicians and intellectuals about the conditions of civilian morale.

In the early years of the war, the political elite found the public either lethargic or, when the press reported fresh danger, brimming with an excessive patriotism for which the government could find no outlet. The Menzies government, bruised by civil libertarian criticism of its early use of extraordinary war-time powers, had thought that 'the people were still mentally unprepared for war and that exceptional care would have to be taken to make certain that they would accept new burdens'.[11] Disaffection between government and people, Paul Hasluck has suggested, was a legacy of the bitter class divisions of the Depression and of World War I. If, for economists, that war had been a lesson in the dangers of inflation, for many working-class Australians, the Great War had demonstrated that all wars were tragedies visited on the people by profiteers and their political servants. Robin Gollan quotes a coal-mining labourer telling a war-time researcher that 'the war is a money-making show. There were more millionaires after the last war than before, and it will be the same this time.' Gollan comments that among miners (and the point holds more widely in the organised labour movement):

> the common view was a scepticism about the war, based on a long tradition of anti-war feeling and hostility to the bosses, coupled with a reluctant belief that the war must be won. For a considerable number the presence of Russia as one of the allies [after Russia entered the war against Hitler in June 1941] was in itself a reason for supporting the war and a guarantee that it would not result in a 'capitalists' peace'.[12]

The Menzies government – wishing to limit wage rises, to divert labour, to change working conditions and to discourage strikes – had failed in its efforts to forge a social contract with the trade union movement. It became Labor's responsibility to persuade the more militant sections of the trade union movement not to use the first favourable labour market in living memory to strike for better conditions and more pay. In 1941–2, Labor gathered strength. Since the Depression, the Labor Party in New South Wales had had to compete with Jack Lang for the working-class vote. In February 1941 Lang Labor voted to rejoin the ALP, and Curtin made sure there were Langites in his Cabinet. Russia's entry into the war brought the Communist Party – influential among workers on the wharves, in the coal mines and in the rapidly growing metals manufacturing industries – behind a determined prosecution of the war. Though the Curtin government never found a solution to the coalminers' restiveness – notwithstanding the help it received from the Australian Council of Trade Unions and the Miners Federation – as the war went on, strikes were, on average, settled more quickly.[13]

Curtin and his colleagues had rapidly to learn new rhetorics of command and appeal. Governments were intervening more and more restrictively in people's daily life; and the Curtin government's war finance policy included raising voluntary loans from the public, as a substitute for more onerous income and indirect tax schedules. How would the public respond? Percy Spender, former Treasurer in the Menzies UAP government, urged the government in April 1942

> not to display any semblance of *arrogance or tyranny*, either directly or through those to whom powers are delegated by it. It must avoid *class* discrimination in the implementation of war measures, and leave the citizen satisfied that cover is not being taken under them to introduce controversial measures not strictly necessary to the war.[14]

In his study *Our Opinions and the National Effort* (1941), Sydney University's Professor of Anthropology A. P. Elkin portrayed a cynical, disillusioned, apathetic citizenry. Writing to Curtin, Elkin cast about for a morale-boosting theme. Posters inspiring fear ('gorilla-like hands on faces') 'will terrify or worry people or cause them to act in some adverse emotional way. Fear stultifies real effort.'[15]

Early in 1942, a committee of concerned intellectuals, evidently led by medical practitioner Alf Conlon and including Elkin's fellow anthropologist Ian Hogbin, urged Curtin to arrest what they called the 'de-idealization of the war'. 'The citizen appealed to on the basis of saving his own skin is invited to regard talk about basic ideals as at least insincere.'[16] Curtin authorised Conlon to form a Prime Minister's Committee on National Morale on May 27 1942. Conlon's committee would formulate 'a far-reaching policy in matters of morale', coordinate the agencies for adult education and physical fitness, and 'mould those and other activities influencing public opinion into an essential weapon of national defence'.[17] In December 1942, Conlon proposed a Public Relations Authority to effect

> extensive and intimate relations between the Government and the people. Only the existence of an efficient public relations organization in *direct* contact with the people as organized in their various day to day activities can convert bewilderment into understanding and resentfulness into co-operation.[18]

In February 1943, Cabinet declined to set up Conlon's 'Authority', and Cabinet allowed Arthur Calwell, Minister for Information, to decide the extent to which the Conlon committee's ideas would be adopted.[19]

The Ministry of Information was not the only government agency to which Conlon's suggestions were relevant. Coombs' Rationing Commission, set up during the period of the Conlon committee's deliberations, had started to assume the qualities and functions of a 'Public Relations Authority'. By the winter of 1942 it had become the task of the new Director of Rationing to find the occasions and to fashion the voice in which a war-making government could address the people. Out of Coombs' nine months (April to December 1942) as Director, only eight or nine weeks were taken up in developing a coupon book and assigning every conceivable retail item its coupon 'worth'. The remaining seven months he spent justifying and adjusting the ration scale in the light of public comment. To ration was to enter into a dialogue with the people about duty and need.

In order to monitor public reactions, Coombs met deputations of retailers, manufacturers, unionists and housewives' associations in Melbourne, Sydney, Perth, Adelaide and Brisbane. The Rationing Commission's 'Investigation' staff examined in detail any reported anomalies in the ration scale, and proposed specific changes. Coombs told an assembly of Sydney 'housewives' that because he and his staff had worked 'in a very great hurry', there were 'defects' and 'anomalies' in the ration scales. 'We hope that they have not been very serious ones and we hope that when you see them you will tell us about them. ... [Rationing] is basically a democratic measure. It attempts to do justice to all classes of the community.'[20]

The Rationing Commission's market research revealed that rationing occasioned a ubiquitous, popular discussion of citizenship as equity in sacrifice. A Clothes Rationing Survey of five hundred people brought to light comments such as: 'A person who buys a luxury should not have the same advantage as one who buys a necessity.' 'A fur cape is 10 coupons and a pair of pyjamas is 13 coupons.' Factory hands were said to be advantaged because their clothes for work were counted separately from clothes for leisure, while this was not so for businessmen. On the other hand: 'A wealthy person can get the best because one has to give coupons to the same value for poorer material.' The Commission's survey report, written immediately after the scales became public, found that 'an undertone of frustration and resentment permeates the working-class homes, against their own "Labour Government" who, they say, have let the wealthy again score at the expense of the poor "wage slaves"'.[21]

Coombs found rationing to be a quotidian moral contract between government and people. As he told an audience of economists, 'Rationing must be acceptable. It must carry the conviction of equality as far as equality is possible. It must carry with it good-will, and there must be continuous interchange of thought, criticism, explanation and decision between the public being rationed and the rationing authority.'[22] He benefited from the retailing experience of one of the three Commissioners of Rationing under which he worked – Arthur (later Sir Arthur) Coles. Arthur and George Coles, who had founded G. J. Coles Pty Ltd in 1921, were leaders of the revolution in retailing which had begun in Australian cities between the wars. 'Nothing over 2s 6d' was the motto in their chain of stores – eighty-six in number by the outbreak of war. Arthur Coles counselled Coombs about policing of the black market. Should the Rationing Commission work with the police to hunt down every infraction and prosecute, as cheats of the war effort, those responsible? No, said Coles, for such breaches were analogous to shoplifting. Coombs later recalled Coles' point:

'It will always happen', he said, 'and mostly we treat it as part of the cost of selling and don't waste much effort on it. What you must watch for is when it rises above a normal percentage since that indicates an organised practice and professional involvement.' Indeed Coles thought the opportunity marginally to 'beat the system' introduced a kind of minor elasticity into rationing making it less absolute and therefore more acceptable.[23]

The modern arts of government were thus augmented by the nostrums of chain-store magnates.

When he did appeal to popular respect for authority, Coombs evoked not the relationship between 'government' and 'people' but the relations *among the people*. 'Every person who "tricks" the rationing scheme is not tricking the Government; they are tricking the poor and the needy … People who beat the rationing are … enemies of the people – not merely … of the Government.'[24]

Rationing exposed government to the most intimate test of its democratic character. The rationing government had little choice but to place its faith in the public. Coombs presented his authority as indeed a kind of vulnerability: the rationing imperium was beyond his enforcement. Questioned by the housewives about the likelihood of black markets, Coombs responded that 'the only adequate protection against the black market is a public which is determined not to buy from it'.[25]

The trade unions – the war-waging state's most challenging constituency – had reason to be sceptical of the Rationing Commission. Working in the hugely expanded munitions and metal fabrication industries took an especially heavy toll on work clothes. Unless the need for clothes was recognised by the Commission as, in this sense, class-specific, a simple notion of equity in entitlement to new clothes would discriminate against workers – and infuriate them. In dealing with the unions, Coombs benefited from Brian Fitzpatrick's help.

Born 1905, Fitzpatrick had emerged by the late 1930s as a champion both of civil liberties and of the left-nationalist strand of the Labor tradition. As a leading light of the Australian Council for Civil Liberties, he had protested the Menzies government's war-time regulations and its bans on political dissent. He joined the ALP in 1942. The Curtin government aroused his hope that something of permanent value could come from the way the country was being led in war. He 'saw in the state's extension a victory for reason over the irrationality of unmitigated capitalism, a victory for Australian nationalism over the parochialism of the states, and, perhaps, a victory for intellectuals over philistines'.[26] Coombs recruited Fitzpatrick to the Rationing Commission in September 1942 as its Industrial Liaison and Research Officer. 'I found Fitzpatrick likeable and interesting', Coombs later recalled.[27] The Commission made use of his union contacts and his journalistic experience. Even as a public servant Fitzpatrick remained a columnist in *Smith's Weekly*.

After a discussion between Coombs and the leaders of a number of unions in Melbourne on 1 October 1942, Fitzpatrick began to write radio scripts. In a series of ABC broadcasts, called 'Making the Best of It', selected unionists would read a Fitzpatrick text explaining why the clothing scale was necessary and how it was equitable. The series' signature tune was a jaunty rendering of the first few bars of 'The Internationale'. This was barely enough to satisfy the all-important munition workers, concentrated in Lithgow and Maribyrnong, whose oil-soaked and chemical-ridden work conditions severely shortened a fabric's life. There Fitzpatrick had to persuade management that they would not be bringing catastrophe upon their heads if they were to require workers to surrender precious ration coupons in exchange for the issued protective clothing. At Maribynong, in November 1942, he lost his voice addressing 'two somewhat turbulent meetings of women'. He came away optimistic that such encounters would soon bring compliance ('many workers unharangued so far').[28]

Reconstruction and feminism

WHEN PRIME MINISTER MENZIES returned from Britain in June 1941, he rallied Australians by foreshadowing 'the building of a new way of life in which men may live not only free from the fear of war but free from the fear of unemployment and injustice'.[1] In response, Curtin suggested that Parliament convene a Joint Committee on Social Security. This body began in July 1941 to discuss, with academic economists and others, policies for the future of a victorious Australia. Once in office, the Curtin Cabinet elevated the Division of Post-war Reconstruction (set up within the Department of Labour and National Service) to be a department in its own right. Curtin was prompted in part by Roland Wilson, that Department's Secretary, who found that his Minister, Eddie Ward, 'did not have a constructive bone in his body'. Wilson's suggestion was paralleled by the resolution of a special ALP Conference, in November 1942, that Post-war Reconstruction should be a department with its own Minister.[2]

Curtin chose J. B. Chifley as Minister for Post-war Reconstruction, and Coombs as his Director-General. Born in 1885, Chifley had been raised in Bathurst, where he began service with the New South Wales Railways. His application to self-improvement soon made him one of the youngest-ever first-class locomotive drivers. His reading also equipped him as a labour movement activist: an advocate and witness for his union in industrial tribunals, an office-bearer and State delegate for his union – the Australian Federated Union of Locomotive Enginemen (founded 1920). In 1928 he won the seat of Macquarie for the Labor Party. Minister for Defence in the Scullin government, Chifley had supported the Premiers' Plan rather than Theodore's alternative. Lang's popularity within the working class of New South Wales contributed to his loss of his seat in 1931. Out of Parliament for the next ten years, Chifley helped to rebuild the Labor Party in New South Wales, while continuing his reading of economics. His moderate views, labour movement contacts and articulate intelligence qualified him as one of the Royal Commissioners appointed by R. G. Casey to study Australia's banking system. Chifley went further than other Commissioners in recommending that the entire banking system be under public ownership and control. Early in the war, the Menzies government appointed him director of labour supply and regulation in the new Ministry of Munitions, from which position he resigned to contest the general election of September 1941. His return to Federal Parliament was part of the New South Wales resurgence of the ALP. Chifley brought to his new duties a familiarity with economics, and with economists, that had no parallel in the Commonwealth Parliament.

In anticipation of his new job, Coombs warned Chifley that a Ministry of Post-war Reconstruction would face three challenges: ensuring collaboration among its various commissions of inquiry; gaining bureaucratic credibility and winning the cooperation of other agencies of government; and developing a rapport with the public.[3] Broaching the third of these tasks, Coombs spoke to Radio 3AR listeners in December 1942. The war had set all Australians to work, Coombs pointed out; after the war there must be no idle hands. There would be more work 'to transform the setting in which our lives are lived – to change it from a setting adapted to the production, distribution, and exchange of an increasing flood of goods to one in which ... basic human activities can find full scope'. He foreshadowed 'the regional development of our national estate' as the resources of war were turned upon 'other enemies' – 'poverty, unemployment, and the degradation of the human spirit. Let us plan, too, for positive aims – to build in Australia a social environment in which the common life of our people will take on new colour, new intensity and new dramatic quality.'[4]

Officers of the Division of Reconstruction – in particular Gerald Firth, Arthur Tange and Finlay Crisp – briefed him on their contacts with other departments, with major interest groups and with the public at large. In December 1942, Firth suggested that the new Department might deploy 'special officers ... to collaborate with important groups in the community. Ideally, these officers should have ready-made contacts *with* the relevant groups, whilst not being too immediately *of* them. The first group to be tackled in this way might usefully be the trade unions with which at present we have hardly any contact.'[5] Eight weeks later, Firth told Coombs that the Division had received many letters from the public in response to ABC radio broadcast talks on reconstruction by H. V. Evatt, Professor Samuel Wadham and Kenneth Henderson. However, 'Ministerial indifference' (Eddie Ward's wet blanket) had thwarted their publications program, apart from Fin Crisp's articles in the armed services adult education publication *Salt*. Tange endorsed Firth's comments.[6]

From rationing's apologist to new order promoter was but a small step, Coombs told one of the last meetings of the Prime Minister's Committee on National Morale – convened by Conlon in December 1942. Coombs reflected on his recent soundings of public perceptions of the ration scale in Townsville. Of two committees set up there to deal with civilian morale, the Commonwealth government's had been much less effective than the local council's body for protecting 'the interests of civilians in things like food supplies, prices etc.'. The latter group had proved of 'much more use to [the Rationing Commission] ... because it had grown out of the situation where the people had felt the need for such a committee'. So 'community centres should be established from the bottom and not from the top'. Coombs also cited his liaison with the trade unions to make the point that 'indirect educational stuff is better than direct. If we can get a trade union leader to make a point that we want made in his paper, we regard that as ten times as good as us putting it over.'[7]

Coombs' experience at the Rationing Commission was not the only source of his thinking about the channels between government and people. He was also the beneficiary of feminism's enlivening impacts on Australian public life. Because of his interest in issues of population policy, Coombs was certainly aware of the (post-suffrage) agenda of Australian feminism. For example, during an economists' seminar discussing L. F. Giblin's May 1939 paper 'Trends in Population', Coombs is reported to have commented

> that the changed position of women was a fundamental cause of the declining birth rate, so that the attempts made in the totalitarian countries to increase the birth rate by methods which 'put back the clock' were doomed to failure. If it is desired to increase the birth rate, the changed position of women should be accepted as a postulate and it should be made possible for women to live fully and still have a family. This could be done by the provision of creches, nursery schools and other means.[8]

If 'the major achievement of post-suffragist feminism in Australia was the creation of a maternalist welfare state' – from the *Commonwealth Maternity Allowance Act 1912* to the national child endowment scheme introduced in 1941 – then Coombs' point made its own small contribution to that project.[9] Coombs' affinities with feminism went deeper than noting the nation-building pertinence of the feminist agenda, however. The political forms of feminism anticipated the political forms of Post-war Reconstruction.

Australian feminists between the wars were sceptical of the dominant forms of political mobilisation – parties standing candidates at elections and forming majorities in Parliament.[10] Rather, they favoured non-party associations in which women could be as active as their domestic responsibilities allowed. These associations held meetings and conferences, ran libraries and tea rooms, formed links with like-minded associations in other countries and other states. While the vote was important as *one* means to express the views developed through these clubs and associations, these bodies were *themselves* understood to be a form of political activity, enhancing the citizenship of all who participated. Associations of women enlivened civil society by developing political forms which presupposed a strong commitment to home life, rather than an aspiration to slough off domestic 'constraints' in order to enter public life as men conventionally conceived it. Historians Heather Radi and Marilyn Lake have judged World War II to be one of the high points of such feminist mobilisation in Australia.[11] Between the wars, women's 'citizens organisations' had thrived, for example: the Feminist Club, the National Council of Women, the Women's Service Guilds, the Australian Federation of Women Voters, the Council of Action for Equal Pay, the Victorian Women Citizens Movement, Housewives Associations, the League of Women Voters and the United Association of Women. Animators of civil society, these women prefigured and possibly helped to inspire the efforts of Coombs and his colleagues to constitute 'the people' as active formulators of a new social order.[12]

Jessie Street, born 1889 and married into a wealthy and powerful legal dynasty, had been one of the founders of the United Association of Women. In September 1941, she and seventeen men and women told Prime Minister Arthur Fadden that he should appoint 'an especially selected body of men and women … with the status and powers of Commissioners'. The 'indispensable' research already undertaken by the Division of Post-war Reconstruction should be expanded to include 'health, housing, employment, education, technical training, recreational facilities and social conditions generally'. Street and her colleagues were also seeking a more participatory research process, involving

> Trade Unions, housing societies, social work societies, kindergarten unions, hospital committees, societies dealing with the status and opportunity for women, girls' clubs, boys' clubs, etc., etc. The work of these organisations might profitably be included in planning for reconstruction.

A Reconstruction Commission would publish reports in order to garner 'criticism, suggestions and advice from expert and other members of the public. The fullest possible publicity will also tend to enlighten Parliament as well as the public.' Such a commission would have no administrative functions but would work through 'various committees consisting partly of Government personnel and partly of other qualified persons co-opted for special purposes from time to time'.[13]

When Fadden asked the Reconstruction Division to comment, one officer asked whether the Commission's suggested *modus operandi* was appropriate. A single body could not handle such a diverse array of policy issues. As well,

> It is impossible to disentangle from current policy the *basic* post-war issues in relation to economic development and international trade which are arising under the Lend-Lease agreements. These are matters of high Government policy which call for day to day decisions by Cabinet, and not by a public Commission.[14]

Such was the elitist temptation awaiting the economists recruited to the public service.

Coombs' contact with the rationed public in 1942 disposed him to respond more favourably to proposals, such as Street's, for new channels of influence between people and government. In 1943 and 1944, the Rural Reconstruction, Housing and Secondary Industry Commissions attempted to meld the perspectives of experts, bureaucrats and citizens, as foreshadowed in Street's letter to Fadden. The public relations section of the Department looked to discussion groups – some already lively, others requiring the Department's stimulus – to create a constituency for the new order.

Circulated pamphlets and published discussion pieces sustained this newly encouraged appetite for talking about the future. The armed services had the periodical *Salt*, and the Department also developed a working relationship with the ABC Radio producers of talks. When the United Association of Women endorsed Jessie Street's 1944 initiative to publish the *Australian Women's Digest*, Coombs told Street that the *Digest* would have 'a most important function in providing thoughtful articles and important information', some of it supplied by the Department.[15]

Not only were there affinities between second-wave feminist politics of animated civil society and the politics of reconstruction; their visions of social justice also resonated. Inter-war feminism had sought equality between the sexes via a more comprehensive welfare state (including financial support for women's work in the home), anti-discrimination legislation, sex education and improved sexual health services. Moral improvement was also a strong theme: the moralities of public and domestic life were crucial to sex equality, women reasoned, because the 'sexualisation' of women had long been an essential part of men's dominance and exploitation. The various demands on social policy made by feminists between the wars had been based on an implied concept of the mother as a rights-bearing political subject – a figure equivalent to the worker in labour movement discourse.[16] Of course, much of this agenda could be conceded by men without disturbing inequalities between men and women in their access to jobs and equal pay. Indeed, the agenda of a 'maternal welfare state' had the potential to confirm the family home as the primary site of women's mothering contribution to humanity.

In the 1930s and 1940s, however, feminists began to challenge any such complacency about the sexual division of labour. The emerging demand for equal pay was 'a major discursive shift' in Australian feminism, according to Lake. 'Men's lives became the standard against which feminists would measure women's progress, as their focus shifted from domestic relations to the conduct of public life.'[17] When the war-time shortage of labour made it essential to employ women in jobs previously reserved for men, the new threshold of sex equality came into view. However, women could not be assured of the Labor government's support. Within a few months of coming to power, Curtin and his Minister John Dedman were understood to say that women's war-time employment in men's jobs was only a temporary contingency. They were soon corrected by Jessie Street. She spoke for a whole generation of feminist critique of women's forced economic dependency on men when she urged the government to legislate against sex discrimination – in employment and in all areas of Australian life.[18] These ideas were expressed in the 28-point 'Australian Women's Charter' which issued from an unprecedented four-day conference in Sydney, 19–22 November 1943.

The notion that women had as much right to a job as men was an ingredient in Coombs' view that full employment was not only an economic but a social program. His vision of the post-war world honoured both sides of the feminist vision: full employment would make it possible for any *person* to get a job; and homes and communities, with good town and regional planning, would become enhanced sites for the nurturance of children and the enjoyment of family life, confirming the dignity and reducing the drudgery of motherhood.

In Coombs' war-time speeches, he asserted more vividly the theme of the enhancement of family life than the theme of every woman taking the job of her choice. In his June 1944 address to the Council for Women in War Work in Melbourne, Coombs began by endorsing the demand for an end to job discrimination. Society was obliged to provide women with jobs so that they could continue in 'very much the same sort of functions' as during the war, if they chose. There would be training for women and men, though the Department had received 'disappointingly few' applications for demobilisation training from women in the services. Coombs also addressed women's concerns about housing. The government was going to stimulate a rapid building program, but a shortage of houses, schools, kindergartens and hospitals would nonetheless blight the first five years of peace. The government was already facing 'a perennial house-wives' problem' – how to make a little go a long way and having to make hard choices.[19]

Coombs showed a thoughtful concern with the home as a workplace. Houses should be equipped to lighten the load of housework. The 'low engineering industry' – grown so much during the war – would supply labour-saving appliances. Coombs' recognition of housework as work led him to speculate on the future of domestic service. Acknowledging the war-time shortage of 'domestic help', he suggested that the era of 'the individual domestic servant is gone for ever and, I may say in my opinion, it is not very much to be regretted'. Perhaps the Country Women's Association was foreshadowing the future of domestic service by organising affordable domestic help on a collective basis – 'schemes in which women themselves will play a part in the organisation and in the planning'.[20] The social provision of relief in domestic work would be particularly useful to women 'at times of childbirth and to provide holidays for mothers of large families', he suggested in a 1944 pamphlet. 'It is probably true that nothing could contribute so much to the well-being of so large a number of people as provision which would make it possible for every mother to have four hours a day, one night a week, and three weeks a year free from her children.'[21] For homes to be good places to live and work, Coombs continued, there had to be community amenities. 'Once you add children [to a home] you multiply the link between the home and the outside facilities. It is not merely the baby clinic, there is the kindergarten and the nursery, the playground and the sporting field and, later on, the halls and the picture theatre.' The home was best conceived as a base from which to access such communal facilities. 'Mother has to shop; she has to attend baby health clinic; she needs a library; she needs a club, and other facilities for entertainment.' Better home life required better planning of urban land use. 'A town has generally speaking been regarded primarily as a place in which the economic processes of production and exchange have been carried on. It is necessary for us to see the town less as an economic unit and more as a human unit.'[22]

Coombs closed his 1944 talk to the Council for Women in War Work by urging women to be active in political life. 'I do not necessarily mean voting for members of Parliament, or becoming members of Parliament, I mean the whole of the activity associated with the common planning by people.'[23] He might well have referred to the composition of his own Department. Women officers under Coombs in September 1944 included: F. M. Grant (administrative assistant to Coombs), V. R. Wildie, G. Schneider, L. Byrne, M. J. Parris. G. F. Littleton, S. E. Swinney, F. Wilson, M. D. Riseley, D. Haslam, E. L. Higson, W. Phillips. E. C. Morgan and K. Best. Coombs put special effort into creating Best's job, which was to examine the particular problems of demobilising service *women*.[24]

Fighting for Yes

IN JUNE 1941, Chifley had argued publicly that to correct Australia's 'failed economic system' would require 'a wider national outlook'. In listing 'matters which affected the nation as a whole', he anticipated Labor Attorney-General H. V. Evatt's agenda of constitutional change.[1] The Powers Referendum of August 1944 would soon put Coombs' emergent, optimistic populism to a severe test.

In October 1942, Evatt introduced a bill for a referendum to vest in the Commonwealth many powers hitherto wielded by the States. His aim was better to effect 'the war aims and objects of Australia as one of the United Nations, including the attainment of economic security and social justice in the postwar world, and for the purpose of postwar reconstruction'.[2] However, the referendum was not the Curtin government's preferred option. In November 1942 Evatt convened a special Constitutional convention of Commonwealth and State parliamentary leaders of all parties. Would the States, acting under Section 51(37) of the Constitution, like to refer certain powers to Canberra – not just for the war, but for the peace? Had they all answered 'yes', a referendum would not have been necessary.

With a referendum to come, Coombs' ambition to dialogue with the public acquired new importance. Though the Curtin government did not commit itself to the Powers Referendum until the end of 1943 – encouraged, no doubt, by its crushing victory in the August 1943 general election – the Department's work in 1943 can be understood not just as research into new policies but also as canvassing public sympathy for Labor's vision of government. Coombs hoped that his Department was not only preparing policies for a new society but preparing a new society for those policies. In March 1943, Coombs told Chifley that both citizens and soldiers were eager to hear some 'Ministerial statement if not of policy [then] of broad objectives of reconstruction'. He wanted Chifley to tell them that 'reconstruction can't be got for nothing. It implies a continued willingness to sacrifice some private purposes to achieve social benefits and a willingness to accept the continuance of some at least of the war-time controls.' Citing a recent Gallup poll, Coombs suggested that the government should proclaim objectives in several areas: stability and security of employment, housing, large-scale development works, improved education, and improvements in rural life.[3]

The commissions of inquiry that Coombs initiated in 1943 – into housing, rural reconstruction and secondary industry – were not only conduits of popular advice to government; they also projected the government's intentions to the people. A 'Plan of Public Relations' prepared under his authority referred to 'using housing discussions and plans as a method of improving public relations with the Department, as well as educating the public on housing issues [including] ... to

build up public support for the government's proposal on reconstruction to prepare against the inevitable opposition that is developing towards the government's
proposals.'[4] Coombs believed that the popular hunger for housing, if handled
astutely, could be turned into a mandate for state intervention into the economy.

Coombs was convinced that Australians were undergoing an epochal shift in
political culture. 'They have during the war seen the whole of the economic system
directed towards deliberately planned social objectives.'[5] In a January 1944 speech
he predicted that 'in the post-war years there will be a strong element of instability
in the psychological make-up of the people'. Yet this would better dispose them
towards 'drastic action ... than they would be if their world were a more stable
one. They have become accustomed during the war-time years to accepting
changes which, when we look back upon them, are revolutionary in character.'
The people's readiness for change therefore should not be underestimated. 'The
most potent fear in the minds of most people, I believe, is that the war-time
willingness of governments to make radical changes will melt in the face of hostile
criticism from interests adversely affected.'[6]

An undated memo (probably written around October 1943) which may
have been issued by Coombs' office, argued that the public's interest could be
aroused if the proposed constitutional changes were linked to employment and
to memories of the Depression.[7] Advocates of change must pose the issue of
economic security. Labor's effective management of the crisis of 1942 – the
mobilisation of all Australians in the face of likely Japanese invasion – had been
endorsed by the electorate in August 1943. Unprecedented and centralised powers
had thus passed practical and political tests. Only if those powers were maintained
would Australia effectively prosecute the tasks of peace. The aims of reconstruction
should be detached from the aims of any political party: 'the public must be
encouraged ... to regard the issue as something above the partisan political
atmosphere'. The more controversial proposals issuing from the Department of
Post-war Reconstruction should be omitted from Labor's Yes campaign.

Yet Coombs' Department's neutrality was implied in other suggestions: that the
Department prepare material for short documentaries to be screened to the four
million people who weekly attended the cinema; and that a pamphlet sum-
marising 'all schools of thought' should be issued 'in the name of the Director [*sic*]
of Post-War Reconstruction, rather than in the name of the Government or any
individual Minister'. Coombs endorsed this strategy but added two cautionary
points. Anxieties about increasing Commonwealth powers could be assuaged by
envisaging a more decentralised post-war administration; and the campaign
should try to find a way to address women voters. A Gallup poll had found in
December 1943 that three times as many women (30 per cent) as men (11 per
cent) would not yet express an opinion on the national government's bid for
powers 'to make laws on both employment and unemployment'.[8]

The referendum campaign strategy envisaged a 'pre-referendum educational
campaign' using departmental material before the 'actual referendum campaign'
in which political leaders would be prominent. However, this neat separation
of 'education' from overt political advocacy proved difficult to sustain, and the

referendum campaign was conducted in a 'partisan political atmosphere'. The 'educational' discussion pamphlets from Post-war Reconstruction were long in production. They had still not been issued by the second week of April 1944, by which time the politicians were already loudly canvassing the rights and wrongs of Yes and No.[9] The Department's publications program was intended to feed a national movement of discussion groups made up of 'the type of person who is now joining conservation groups', recalled Wilmott Phillips in 1981.[10] By June 1944, Coombs' officers understood there to be 'several thousand' such groups. The Country Women's Association claimed to have spawned 800. In each capital city the Department established Advisory Councils to liaise between the Department and the local groups, to give them training, guest speakers, conferences and a steady supply of pamphlets. Coombs planned to avoid 'calling on the daily press, the radio, and the film interest upon whom the Government must otherwise largely depend for spreading information on Government plans'. Instead, group activity 'gives to large numbers of people a sense of participation in the work of reconstruction and consequently develops a tendency to identify themselves with the action subsequently taken by the Government'.[11]

When Coombs broadcast six two-minute scripts prepared by the Department of Information, he was introduced with a claim that repeated this rhetoric of popular involvement.

> The Director-General of the Ministry of Postwar Reconstruction (Dr. Coombs) has repeatedly stated that there must be a two-way flow of ideas between his Department and the public … so that each may assist the other in planning … so that each may contribute to Australia's happy future. Some weeks ago he invited the Australian people to assist in the work of planning for our common future. The response has been magnificent. From all corners of the nation have come letters to Canberra.

The scripts scrupulously avoided mention of the referendum, let alone the wisdom of voting Yes. They merely pointed to the necessity of the Commonwealth's taking a 'national' approach to such 'national' problems as housing and employment.[12]

Despite the early expressions of sympathy for a transfer of powers by many non-Labor politicians, and despite continuing disunity in the non-Labor ranks (with Percy Spender and William Morris Hughes continuing to advocate Yes), the conservatives' condemnation of Labor's constitutional reform appealed to a majority of voters (2,305,418 against 1,963,400) and a majority of States (only Western Australia and South Australia had Yes majorities). So was the Powers Referendum defeated on 19 August 1944.

And so the political post-mortems began. Had the Curtin government fed the fear mobilised by the No case by delegating so many of the new 'defence' powers to public servants? Cabinet Secretary Frederick Shedden told Curtin, ten weeks after the poll, that the vote expressed 'democratic jealousy' provoked 'by the manner in which officers of Departments have grown into the habit of making statements on Policy which are the province of Ministers'.[13] The wrong kind of person, argued Sydney University's Professor of Public Administration F. A. Bland, had been recruited to effect the new relationship between public service and people – 'officials recruited temporarily from newspaper officers, advertising agencies and political organisations' – to the detriment of the government's public standing.[14] Coombs had confided to an academic who supported his efforts to educate the public about the prospects for full employment that

> This is the reason both for our 'talking in public' and for our move on discussion groups. It is fairly clear from the re-action that we are getting at this stage that this departure from established Public Service practice is rousing considerable hostility. However, I believe that it is a risk which must be taken.[15]

If Shedden and Bland were correct, then Coombs' 'risk' had worked out badly.

It was not only sticklers for public service propriety who wondered at the Curtin government's public service populism. Lloyd Ross, Post-war Reconstruction's Director of Public Relations, told Coombs three months after the referendum that a recent factory visit had revealed that 'your booklets make little appeal'. Of the 150 workers in the factory Ross had visited, 60 subscribed to the Communist Party's *Tribune*. 'There is a feeling that this post-war literature is a trick – a "pie in the sky" stunt to divert attention from unpleasant restrictions.'[16]

In an address to staff, after the referendum, Coombs reflected on the pitfalls of being a visionary bureaucrat.

> There is a definite strain of the bureaucrat – using that word in its worst sense – in us all. It derives from the feeling that we alone can do the job – in a sort of intellectual contempt for other people; a feeling that if only we were allowed to do this thing, it would be better, more intelligently and more competently done. That may well be true in some cases; it is unlikely to be true in many, and even if it were true, it would not justify the result. People have a right to make their own mistakes, and that is a very important thing to a potential bureaucrat. If we are prepared to admit to people the right to make their own mistakes, it will be much easier for us to approach this problem of our relations with people in general in a more properly humble spirit. And I do not say that cynically, because I think that is the essential danger of the public servant, of the bureaucrat, a tendency to arrogance.[17]

Soldiers and workers

THE WHITE PAPER *Full Employment in Australia* (1945) has been celebrated as seminal – the blueprint of the post-war Long Boom (c. 1945–75). Yet the Chifley government was strangely diffident about circulating it. The New South Wales Department of Education set the White Paper for Leaving Certificate students in economics to read in 1946. When students wrote to the Department of Post-war Reconstruction for a copy, the small print run was exhausted and a roneoed precis was sent out instead.

Why did the Labor government want a White Paper? In an exchange of comments about an early draft in 1945, Coombs reminded his Director of Public Relations, Lloyd Ross, that the Minister was pushing for an early tabling of its commitment to full employment partly in order to answer the criticisms by the Australian Council of Trade Unions (ACTU) of the Curtin government's plans for demobilisation.[1] Through its forthcoming Re-establishment and Employment Bill, the Curtin government intended to give returned service personnel priority access to civilian job vacancies, *whether or not they were members of trade unions.* In refusing the ACTU's long-standing demand that trade union membership be compulsory for all workers, the Labor government wanted to assure the public that henceforth there would be jobs for *all* workers – unionised or not. The White Paper was intended partly to neutralise ACTU disquiet.

The Labor Party and the trade union movement were then in the final moments of a quarter-century struggle over the representation of working-class interests. During and immediately after World War I, Australian trade union leaders had debated the possibility of forming One Big Union. Labor politicians and some trade union leaders feared the One Big Union. When its advocates sought to replace small craft unions with large industry-wide unions, they threatened Labor figures who relied on a craft union power base. When pressure from militants in the Communist Party and in the Australian Industrial Workers Union in the early 1920s led to the formation of the Australian Council of Trade Unions in 1927, the Australian Workers Union disputed its ambition to be nationally representative. That union remained a significant force within the Labor Party, a bulwark against the perceived influence of communists within the ACTU.[2] It was ACTU policy to make union membership compulsory for all employees.

In short, the war, with its acute labour shortage and its Labor government (after October 1941), presented the ACTU with the best chance ever to advance three organisational strategies, each controversial within the labour movement: industry-based unions, a national body, and compulsory unionism. That is why 'throughout the whole of the War period the ACTU urged the government to use its powers to introduce absolute preference for unionists and to reject any preference for ex-service personnel'.[3]

However, the Curtin government resisted the ACTU's pressure; its *Soldiers Repatriation Act 1942* gave preference in Commonwealth employment to those who had served in combat zones. The government then incurred a further debt to servicemen and women when Curtin persuaded his party, in January 1943, that conscripts should be placed in overseas combat duty – overturning the deeply held anti-conscription convictions of a whole generation of the labour movement. In framing law and policy about mass demobilisation, the government was also motivated by memories of the homecomings of Australian servicemen and women after World War I, an occasion of significant social unrest. Determined not to repeat this debacle, the Curtin government formulated a demobilisation strategy that would give training and job priority to any who had served.

According to Coombs, his Department had generally been opposed to giv-ing employment preference to those who served because of its offence to trade unionists and because it implied doubts about the government's commitment to full employment.[4] Such objections did not prevail. Faced with two competing notions of the needs and rights of 'the people', the Curtin government chose to privilege war service to the nation at the expense of a fundamental mechanism of class solidarity. This was a most significant, but almost forgotten, moment in the history of Labor's representation of the working class. An employment policy that rewarded war service rather than union membership breached the traditions of the labour movement, as many trade unionists understood them, while no doubt addressing the popular patriotism of the times.

If one of the White Paper's immediate political purposes was to remove the issue of 'employment preference' from labour movement debate, then it would make no sense for the paper to include other proposals that might antagonise trade unions. The officials drafting the White Paper, including Coombs, were thus unable to confront straightforwardly one of the social democratic dilemmas of full employment: how to assure labour discipline – in matters of productivity and price – in the new conditions of full employment. Officials such as Coombs wanted the White Paper to consider how to reform the trade union movement's deep-seated understandings of wage-bargaining and social responsibility.

Coombs devoted most of his Joseph Fisher Lecture at the University of Adelaide on 29 June 1944, 'Problems of a High Employment Economy', to the problem of predicting and controlling the total level of investment. Towards the end of the lecture, however, he acknowledged the need to contain the cost and to encourage the productivity of a fully employed workforce. A wages policy, he suggested, should be based on frequent review of the basic wage, so that workers would be assured that their incomes were rising in step with increases in the productivity of their labour. Coombs did not envisage a redistribution of wealth through wages policy, but through progressive taxation. He hoped to limit workers' wage bargaining power by redistributing workers from places and industries where their bargaining power was relatively high to places and industries where it was low. A government employment service would see to that. Wage rises could be limited also if the prices of basic commodities could be subsidised.

Full employment might corrupt labour's efficiency, Coombs admitted. For 'a hundred and fifty years', labour discipline 'was based essentially on a threat'. High employment would remove that threat. Incentives to efficiency would thus have to be developed – partly through education. Workers should be brought to a better understanding of the relationship between efficiency and national income, and between efficiency and the survival of individual firms. They could be made more conscious of their 'participation in the total achievements of the economy' and of 'the principles on which [their] wages are based'. Welfare and safety on the job could be improved, and so could the quality of workers' housing and community facilities. Workers and management should be given 'common responsibility' for production and management.[5]

Coombs' remarks on labour's cost and efficiency under full employment drew on two internal papers from his staff – L. F. Crisp's 'Incentives and Full Employment' and Lloyd Ross's 'Trade Unions and Full Employment'.

Crisp had alerted Coombs to the propaganda tasks implied by a full employment policy. He argued that labour would be more disciplined if workers had general confidence that governments were advancing their interests across all policies. People should be 'instructed and interested' in how the national income was being spent on communal services. 'People want to feel satisfied with the directions of [government] spending – e.g. social services, houses ... etc.' As well, they must be 'constantly interested by the government in stories and figures of production, costs and efficiency – industry by industry and plant by plant (as in Russia)'. They should be persuaded of 'the need to boost national income as well as to distribute it more evenly'. People should be 'educated in the essential interrelationships of wages, productivity and inflation – this as much for the union leader's and the boss's sake as for the sake of the Government and of the community at large'. As for 'the man on the job', he 'must believe his work to be needed and significant'. He must also 'be convinced, not only that the boss is sincere in his attitude towards the full employment objective, but also that industry is subject to some degree of government planning and control which will ensure that it serves more than simply profit motives'. Crisp had mentioned the need for a policy on profits, to defend workers against exploitation, and some guarantees of the best possible working conditions. He had instanced housing, industrial welfare, safety, pay rising with productivity, reasonable hours and other matters of interest to employees. Finally, Crisp had argued, there might have to be incentives, in some situations, to keep the worker motivated. Managements must also be convinced of the soundness of full employment policy; they must be trained in consultative techniques and in the use of incentives.[6] Ross had captured the essence of Crisp's advice by telling Coombs that 'Public interest and the development of individual responsibility are in fact the motivating forces that must take the place of the old, harsh, purely economic incentives or of the present patriotic desire to win the war.'[7]

After Coombs' Fisher Lecture, this departmental conversation continued. In August, Firth argued that a new approach to wage-setting would be essential in the transition to peace.

> It will only be practicable (and in any case, only just) to maintain the 'wages stop' in transition provided that arrangements for the periodic review of wages generally are put in hand immediately. The 'politics' of this are obviously sticky, and we shall need to tackle the question in a big way if it is to be resolved.

As for the long term, the White Paper should discuss an issue that Coombs had neglected in the Fisher Lecture – 'periodic review of labour's "distributive share" of real income'. The Commonwealth Court of Conciliation and Arbitration could be instructed to review at least once in every twelve months the capacity of the economy to pay higher real wages and to adjust the basic wage in accordance with its findings.[8]

Further innovative thinking by Coombs' staff is evidenced by an unsigned note speculating that 'the problem of labour discipline is short-run; perhaps the sack was never the potent sanction some think it to be'. Rather, the note continued, might not 'reasonably good workmanship, attendance, etc. [be] largely a matter of custom, carrying its own social sanction'? If that were so, then perhaps the foreshadowed Commonwealth employment service could demand references from those for whom it was finding jobs. The writer suggested some 'short-term reinforcement' of labour discipline 'by more specific inducements such as piece-rates, bonuses and profit-sharing, fines (imposed preferably by shop committees)'. A full employment policy could not wait for 'a Change of Heart' to solve problems of labour indiscipline.⁹

From this May to November 1944 discussion, wholly within Coombs' Department, emerged a first draft of the White Paper (known as Draft 'A'), completed on December 14. Coombs' revisions of 'A' gave rise to Draft 'B'. On the issue of labour's cost and efficiency, Draft 'B' proposed to promote a new 'sense of responsibility' among trade unions by giving workers 'a fair share of the increased production which flows from the increasing productivity of labour'. This would require reform of the Conciliation and Arbitration Court in order to mandate five-yearly reviews of the basic wage. The reviews would take into account not only improved productivity but also changes in the terms 'on which Australia exchanged her exports for goods made abroad'. There was nothing to guarantee that the terms of trade would always improve for Australia. The authors were prepared to justify both rises and *reductions* (or at least slower rises) in the basic wage.¹⁰ The authors of Draft 'B' admitted to finding the long-term redistribution of wealth from capital to labour 'a complex and difficult question'. Wage increases in excess of productivity would probably be passed on to the consumer as higher prices, neutralising any rise in the real value of wages. The draft therefore argued that 'effective progress towards more equal distribution of goods and services is likely to come from the steady development of social services financed by progressive taxation'. Social services included 'education, free medical and health benefits, and the development of community facilities such as infant welfare centres, kindergartens, libraries, and the provision for leisure time activities'.¹¹

The authors of Draft 'B' consciously challenged labour movement thinking when they canvassed 'methods of payment based upon individual output':

> The Labour Movement in the past has generally been opposed to the development of such 'piece-work' systems of payment. The Government shares the fears of employees that such systems are capable of being used to undermine established standards and to develop an intensity of work which can impair the long-term health and efficiency of the individual. At the same time the Government is conscious that recent developments overseas suggest the possibility that where a strong trade union movement exists to protect the interests of the worker and modern methods of wage fixing are employed that it is possible to raise the general level of production and the wages and standards of living of the employees themselves. Before accepting such developments, however, the closest investigation is necessary to ensure that the long-term interests of the employed are not impaired.¹²

The authors were determined to include piecework in the government's full employment agenda.

The circulation of Draft 'B' within the Department in January 1945 stimulated criticism. B. W. Hartnell wanted the paper to make more explicit that social justice was subject to 'the limits set by productivity'. He suggested to Coombs that the Department consult the trade unions formally on some of the more contentious proposals on secondary industry, labour relations and the reform of arbitration. If the unions could agree to a delegation to study overseas experiments in labour discipline, issues such as piecework could be left open by the government, without political damage.[13] Notwithstanding Hartnell's advice, Chifley and Coombs decided against a 'formal' conference with unions.[14]

Crisp questioned the draft's approach to wage-setting. While payment by results was 'the ideal' regime, that ideal assumed a fundamental shift in the balance of power from capital to labour which was not in Australia's immediate prospect. On the contrary, a period of transition from war to peace, with its heightened economic insecurity, was 'second only to the depths of depression' as a circumstance giving advantage to capital. 'In those circumstances payment by results seems to me the entrepreneur's (indeed, more generally, the capitalist's) dream weapon for atomizing the trade union movement as a whole, and the trade unions individually (except for a fortunate few).' Crisp advised caution and respect for the Australian traditions of industrial relations, however much they 'pamper the "bludger"'. The present basis of wage fixation was simple and understood by both employers and employees, requiring neither side to 'build up large bureaucracies'. Moreover, it 'has the strength of longstanding custom and acceptance, and is grounded in the egalitarian social philosophy which for good or ill is extraordinarily deep-rooted in Australians generally and Australian workers in particular'.

In these words Crisp evoked one of the deep tensions within the Australian labour movement. The small unions that would be most threatened by a piecework system were among the ALP's staunchest supporters, and the larger unions (in the metal trades, mining and on the waterfront) who might cope with and accept piecework were Communist strongholds; they might welcome the chance to build up their bureaucracies with more Communist cadres in order better to implement a piecework regime.

> Whether or not it is in fact so, it seems to me it would be fatal for a Labour [*sic*] Government to come out for a principle which lends itself to slogans (in Lang's mouth, and in those of many solid Labour men, too) about smashing the Arbitration System and the gains of fifty years struggle.

The labour movement could be split by a debate on piece work, Crisp concluded, and so find itself in the political wilderness, 'with anti-Labour and the Communist Party as the gainers'.[15]

After four more drafts, under many hands, the White Paper *Full Employment in Australia* was tabled in the House of Representatives on 30 May. Crisp's estimate of Cabinet's sensitivities about labour discipline proved accurate. On the question of how to deal with labour discipline in full employment, Cabinet authorised an anodyne statement: 'The Government is considering the setting up of a special committee on which employers and employees will be represented to report on possible changes in the principles and machinery for making general adjustments in wages and industrial conditions.'[16] The surrounding paragraphs link rising wages to rising productivity; they also promote attention to social services as a supplement to wages.

In the brevity of this discussion we find the defeat of the officials' hope that a White Paper would explore the wider institutional implications of full employment and even question Australian traditions of wage-determination. The White Paper served its purpose if it ameliorated the hurt of an historic political defeat of the ACTU by the leaders of the Labor Party, in the long-term struggle over the instruments of working-class representation. The price of this political tactic was that Australian governments were left without an incomes policy with which to face inflation. Inflation, rather than full employment, was to loom large among Coombs' policy anxieties for the next thirty years.

Part 5
Internationalist

Labor's new internationalism

THE WAR THREATENED Australia not only with Japanese invasion but with US free trade policies. On 23 February 1942, Great Britain and the United States signed a pact of 'Mutual Aid in the Prosecution of the War against Aggression'. Its seventh article pledged signatories to

> the expansion, by appropriate international and domestic measures, of production, employment, and the exchange and consumption of goods, which are the material foundations of the liberty and welfare of all peoples;

and

> the elimination of all forms of discriminatory treatment in international commerce, and ... the reduction of tariffs and other trade barriers; ...[1]

In the words of Evatt and Chifley, if Australia were to receive US war aid, it would be obliged to 'work step by step with U.S.A. to expand international trade and to relax trade barriers'.

The world's largest economic power had been embarked, since the 1930s, on a 'free trade' crusade, particularly against Imperial Preference – the trade agreement among members of the British Empire. Hitler's aggression gave Roosevelt's trade policy the context it needed. The United States' 'lend-lease' loans to its allies were conditional. Roosevelt had assured Churchill that the United States was not asking Britain to sacrifice Imperial Preference in order to buy US economic war aid – 'the furthest thing from my mind' – but that is precisely what the United States expected in all subsequent diplomacy. Many US officials of liberal opinion saw themselves as breaking down one of the last bastions of 'imperialism'.[2] Like all nations in conflict with the Axis powers, Australia had no choice but to sign the 'Mutual Aid' commitment to free, or at least freer, trade. To fight the Axis powers, it had to yield to the United States' free trade imperium.

Whatever reservations the Australian government might feel about this assault on the trading preferences established among members of the British Empire, Evatt and Chifley judged it 'in our interests to show a sympathetic understanding of the American viewpoint'.[3]

Australia's Treasury officers welcomed the pressure for freer international trade. Increased efficiency of production, as each region specialised in what it was good at producing, would lead to a general increase in living standards. Some political interests within Australia would oppose free trade, Treasury anticipated, but the government should explain to the people that free trade's overall benefits would outweigh the damage to these sectional groups. Free trade would also promote world peace. Treasury was realistic in expecting opposition to free trade. Many economic interests, speaking through both sides of Australian politics, were dependent on some form of protection, including the preferential trading agreements within the British Empire that had been agreed in Ottawa in 1932. The Treasury paper conceded something to these interests when it argued that other countries would have to lower their trade barriers if Australia were to do so.[4]

Confidence in free trade stated one of the classical orthodoxies of economics: prosperity through regional specialisation. However, economists had begun to note problems in the theory. First, the pattern of international trade included a very large volume of buying and selling among industrialised nations, that is, between economies making the same kinds of goods.[5] The classical model of free trade as regional specialisation could not explain this pattern. Perhaps there were other determinants of international trade and of economic development than the natural and historical endowments of regions. Was it not within Australia's capacity to become a trader of manufactured goods through a policy of industrial development? Second, economists had begun to argue that it was not the presence or absence of trade restrictions which determined the volume of international trade, but the amount of money which people had to spend. Coombs was soon to make much of this point.

As Chair of the F&E Committee, Giblin solicited as many opinions as he could before settling down to draft a Committee consensus view of the approach Australia should take to Article VII. In particular, he drew attention to the possibility that Article VII would be interpreted as a mandate not only for free trade but also for 'expansion' – the stimulation of full employment. 'What dangers are there in suggesting "expansion" as a permanent post-war policy,' he asked, 'even if all countries keep step in expansion?'

Giblin's worries about expansion policies were in part technical. How could nations 'keep step', when conditions of post-war demobilisation and even weather patterns could vary so markedly between nations? The problem of international coordination could be tackled by a few similar countries grouping together, but Giblin feared a re-emergence of the 'Washington–London economic axis'. Another problem he foresaw would be that each country would be tempted to over-invest in capital goods – for defence reasons and as a measure to prolong employment. Australia would do better to disband or scale down, rather than perpetuate, some of its war-time manufactures. Full employment would unleash 'speculation and manufacturing enterprise', it would increase trade unions' powers, and it would encourage governments to try to control more things, to the detriment of efficiency. Nevertheless, Giblin concluded, a policy of expansion would be necessary 'for the reabsorption of the men now in the services, for the transfer of resources from war industries, for the maintenance of full employment and for the reduction of the real burden of the increasing public debt'.[6]

In the last week of June, Giblin distilled into a single argument the answers he had received from the other F&E Committee members. A meeting on 26 and 27 June 1942, which Coombs did not attend, discussed the issues. Giblin's 'draft report on Australia's position in relation to Article VII' followed shortly, dated 8 July. This paper was further revised and reissued on 29 July. Submitted to the

Inder-departmental Committee on External Relations, it had one more paragraph added to it before becoming the final briefing paper for Ministers on Article VII.[7]

Any response to Article VII must heed the recent emergence of a powerful political mandate to keep unemployment very low, the paper began. However, a responsive Australian government would then face the consequences of expansion: a high demand for imports and recurring difficulties in paying for them. To deal with recurring deficits in our external account, it would be necessary to vary the value of the Australian pound and to impose import restrictions. Recourse to import controls would be regrettable. Not only would it provoke other nations to raise trade barriers against Australian exports, it would also allow our inefficient industries to remain unchallenged by overseas competition. A high rate of employment – likely to lead to import controls – would probably cause resources to be wasted and average real income to fall.

Having argued the sad necessity to choose between full employment and higher living standards, the paper then suggested how such a choice might be avoided. If there were global increases in production and rates of employment, fortified (and not preceded) by the removal of trade barriers, Australian exports might increase. To make this possible, Australia should accept the risks of international collaboration. In the absence of 'definite proposals for international collaboration', the paper refrained from specifying these risks, though it alluded to the possibility that Australia would lose some protected secondary industries. It was up to the major international powers to make reassuring commitments, 'to make the whole plan worthwhile for Australia', and this would include their giving Australia and other middle-sized powers a say in the running of any machinery of economic collaboration.[8]

This paper did not outline the shape of any post-war international economic charter. Rather, it warned politicians whose instincts on economic matters were protectionist that they should now be prepared to risk some security for the gains that international collaboration could bring. Economists addressing politicians, at this early stage of post-war planning (July–August 1942), were trying to do no more than mount a qualified political defence of the very idea of deserting one kind of international collaboration – Imperial Preference, a system of mutual protections – for another, unknown system, promoted by US free-traders.

When Coombs attended the next F&E Committee meeting, on 4 and 5 September 1942, he told his colleagues that the briefing paper was too defensive and cautious. 'Coombs stressed the importance of "playing down" the implications for certain economic groups and "playing up" the general idea of full employment, rising living standards, security, etc. for everyone. Coombs undertook to draft a statement along these lines.'[9]

A few weeks later, in October 1942, Coombs circulated his view.[10] He did not take issue with the economic reasoning of the July–August briefing paper. Rather, he departed from its political defensiveness.

I feel … that it is essential to establish beyond all doubt that the Commonwealth

Government regards Article VII primarily as an undertaking to collaborate in the achievement of a clearly defined political objective, i.e. the raising of living standards.

Coombs was worried that 'Neither the implications nor the possibilities of Article VII are fully understood in Australia.' Discussions so far had put too much emphasis on the pros and cons of free trade, which he referred to as 'the negative aspects of Article VII'. Here he challenged the free-traders' assumptions about what was fundamentally at issue in trade policy. 'The level of income is a much more significant determinant of a country's demand for internationally traded goods than the level of the tariff or the existence of exchange control.' That being so, Australia could best rise to the challenge of Article VII if it were to persuade other nations to make full employment their objective. Australia should also urge 'government responsibility for providing food, clothing and housing at socially acceptable levels'. More state intervention into the organisation of production, distribution and exchange would be entailed by such commitments, Coombs conceded. He posed the political issue: was the degree of government intervention conceded by most people to be justified in the war against fascism also justified in the longer-term war against unemployment and poverty? For Coombs it was. 'The technique of production control for war supplies is capable of being applied directly [to the post-war provision of food, clothing and housing] without drastic social change.'

A commitment to global full employment would impose particular responsibilities on nations which exported more than they imported, he went on to point out. They would have to minimise their credit balances, that is, to spend their holdings of other nations' currencies much more freely on world markets than prudence had allowed them to do in the past. Coombs acknowledged that nations could not altogether do without credit balances. For example, it was legitimate for Australia to require that its credit balances (London Funds) remain high enough to accommodate sudden downturns in the prices of its exports. International monetary arrangements after the war would have to 'assist Australia and other countries similarly placed to meet adverse balances in bad years'. However, for the nations with long-term excesses on external account, the best policies would now be to make long-term investments overseas, to purchase abroad on a government-to-government basis, to continue and to extend the lend-lease principle, and simply to give money to poorer nations. This emphasis on full employment Coombs came to call 'the positive approach': *Australia must urge responsibility for world employment growth on the economic powers who were pushing a free trade interpretation of Article VII.*

Over the next six years, the relationship between the relaxation of trade barriers and the expansion of production and employment preoccupied Australian foreign policy makers and vaulted Coombs onto the international stage. His diplomacy, as we shall see, took up three issues on which he had formulated his underlying view by October 1942. One was control over exchange rates. The free trade doctrine, when zealously applied, demanded that each nation abandon exchange-rate controls. Coombs urged Australian resistance to that demand: nations wishing to regulate the movement of capital into and out of their country and to pay off loans from other countries would need to be able to set their currency's rates of exchange.

A second issue was industrial development policy. 'It would be necessary' Coombs insisted, 'for us ... to refuse to accept the judgment of established industrial countries as to the potentialities of our own resources.' To make this refusal politically possible, Coombs urged Australia to forge alliances with under-developed countries, particularly in the Asia-Pacific area.

Third, Coombs advocated a non-defensive stance toward the free trade threat to Imperial Preference. To accept the gradual dismantling of Imperial Preference would not affect Australia's major export industries (preeminently wool), he argued, only the smaller primary industries that were dependent on British consumers. Australia should be willing to abandon Imperial Preference, Coombs suggested, if that would achieve an international order shaped by a global commit-ment to full employment.

As Sean Turnell has argued, Coombs' 'positive approach' had roots in two earlier diplomatic campaigns by Australian economists. One had been the basis of Australia's approach to the Imperial Economic Conference in Ottawa in 1932 and the World Monetary and Economic Conference in London in 1933. There Australia failed to convince creditor nations that it was their global responsibility to beat the Depression with expansionary monetary policies. The other campaign had been led by Australia's League of Nations diplomats, S. M. Bruce and F. L. McDougall. In the five years leading up to the war, they had won wide support for 'the nutrition approach' – the dismantling of agricultural protection and the coordinated expansion of world agriculture.[11] Coombs' distinctive contribution to this tradition of advocacy was less in his economic than in his political analysis, that is, his seizing upon the new political fluidity – between nations and within them – occasioned by World War II.

Coombs questioned the assumption that Article VII was primarily a mandate for trade liberalisation. This assumption had either emboldened longstanding critics of protection or cowed those who shared with the labour movement a commitment to the welfare functions of protection. By imagining a world of sustained full employment, Coombs' paper presented the Labor government with a third, less defensive option. His emphasis on full employment as an international objective distinguished him from other F&E Committee authors, including Giblin, who had devoted only a few faintly hopeful paragraphs to the possibility of international expansion.

Labor needed to hear such an analysis. Coming out of the Depression, the most popular economic theory in the labour movement had been Social Credit, a political economy of fearful hostility to global Money Power and its experts. Several members of the F&E Committee had only confirmed such fears by authoring the 'savage' deflationary policies of the Depression – the Premiers' Plan. It would have offered Labor little, eleven years later, had the same men sketched Australia's post-war options as either free trade or a lower standard of living. Chifley's intellectual rapport with the government's economic 'experts' would count for nothing in the party if their advice could not be articulated in terms of Labor's aspirations. Fortunately for Chifley, for the ALP and for the economist advisers, Coombs saw reformist potential in Article VII. International full employment would enable painless trade liberalisation. The 'positive approach' might thus reconcile the Labor government to 'economics' and to the available cadre of economists. Coombs offered to Labor an internationalism of their aspiration, to substitute for the predatory internationalism that they feared.

The diplomacy of security

IN PURSUING 'the positive approach' and emphasising full employment, Australia would have to persuade the United States (and any other nation with a positive balance of payments) to spend, invest or give away their trading surplus. Roland Wilson was the first member of the F&E Committee to be sent abroad to discuss with other governments such schemes for the realisation of Article VII. In London in October–November 1942, he talked to officials of the British Dominion and Indian governments about Keynes' suggestion for an International Clearing Union and other possible post-war trade and currency agreements. However, under Chifley's instructions, Wilson was not to advocate the 'positive approach' at this meeting.[1]

When he returned, Wilson was sceptical of a diplomacy that sought commitments from great economic powers. 'It is just impossible for Governments to bind succeeding Governments on matters of this nature.' While Melville shared Wilson's scepticism, he saw tactical value in Australia's demanding that large economies take a 'full employment' approach, for it would make clear 'that the responsibility for any failure to implement the spirit of Article VII would be equally shared by the US'. That is, if Australia were to be criticised for opposing the push towards free trade, it could counter that the United States had proved unhelpful on the linked matter of global 'expansion'.

Faced with the not unreasonable *Realpolitik* of Wilson and Melville, Coombs conceded that 'the prospects of international collaboration after the war were extremely remote'. However, he advised his colleagues not to underestimate the dynamic potential of world opinion now that war had restored employment to a long depressed world economy. 'We should not just throw up our hands.' If Australians now agreed that 'the maintenance of employment and incomes is the primary social purpose', and that 'we could afford to have the less than perfect allocation of resources' that full employment policies might entail, then world opinion might be tending the same way. Wilson replied that it was not possible to turn widespread understandings into guarantees. Melville argued 'that unless we obtain the guarantees we ought to put ourselves in the position of leaving our hands entirely free to take any action regarding tariffs, exchange rates, exchange control, etc. which we may desire'.[2]

'The positive approach' was, if nothing else, tactically useful to a dependent nation fearful of losing its sovereign rights to economic self-protection. Events would show, however, that such tactical appeal was not sufficient to promote it abroad as an ethical and political cause for all nations to embrace. The challenge for Coombs was to advocate 'the positive approach' positively. He soon got his chance.

In the early months of 1943, Minister for External Affairs Evatt decided to visit Washington to persuade President Roosevelt to take seriously Australia's need for armaments and for influence in the Allied war effort in the South-West Pacific. If Evatt's trip were also to elicit US thoughts about Article VII, he would need intellectual support. Coombs was Chifley's choice, a decision he found 'rather upsetting at this stage'.[3] Chifley soon added to his instructions that Coombs attend the United Nations' first conference, on food and agriculture policy, at Hot Springs, Virginia, in May. Coombs admitted to being 'rather worried by the length of time which this will keep me away from Australia. The international aspects of post-war affairs are very interesting', but 'there is a very big job to be done in Australia and I think that that is where my heart belongs'.[4]

The origins of the Hot Springs Food Conference lay in pre-war arguments presented by Australia and other nations for a 'nutrition approach' to global economic recovery. Many years later Coombs learned that Keynes, having been shown Coombs' 'positive approach' paper by Australia's High Commissioner in London, Stanley Melbourne Bruce, had suggested Coombs to represent Australia at this conference.

Coombs was in Washington for several weeks before the Food Conference commenced on 15 May 1943. Meeting a range of US officials, including New Dealers whose sympathy for a 'positive approach' embattled them within the US Administration, his sense of the possible wider value of Hot Springs was confirmed. On 19 April, he told Chifley that some US officials hoped the conference would 'give [American opinion] the impression that the Administration is being pushed by international opinion' into something like 'the positive approach'. He cited US delegates' predictions that there would be a polarisation of perspectives between Roosevelt (who was thought likely to be re-elected in 1944) and protectionist Congressmen who were sceptical of Article VII. These officials' tactics 'appear to be to get established international machinery of the kind capable of giving effect to international collaboration when political conditions are appropriate'.[5]

While involved in these pre-conference discussions, Coombs met the authors of the United States' post-war currency alternative to Keynes' International Clearing Union, the Stabilisation Fund. From Australia's point of view, the Fund was a less attractive proposal because it neither obliged nor encouraged nations such as the United States to spend their enormous trade surpluses. The officials proposing the Fund also preferred to discuss a currency agreement separately from other international issues, such as employment.[6] Within a fortnight, Coombs was putting to US Treasury officials a detailed critique of the proposed Fund, dwelling on its failure to oblige creditor countries to pursue expansionary policies, and pointing out Australia's wish to preserve its freedom to vary its exchange rates.[7] When Coombs and Evatt urged that full employment be made an objective of the proposed currency body, the Americans thought this 'smacked of socialism' and of improper interference with US domestic policy.[8]

Coombs consulted Evatt on 14 May on what the Australian delegation should say at the Hot Springs Food Conference. If the conference agreed to international policies on the production and distribution of food, then it would be vital to agree also on a mechanism for enforcement – mandatory reporting by each nation to all other nations. And if nations would agree to report to each other on food policy, why not on 'other aspects of living standards, in particular to employment, public health, housing, and education?' Coombs asked.[9] Here Coombs drew on his discussions and correspondence with his co-delegate at Hot Springs, F. L. McDougall – 'a very interesting bloke, a bit of a charlatan, but a very appealing one and with an element of good sense in the line that he was taking'.[10] McDougall had observed the evolution of mandatory reporting mechanisms in the League of Nations.

The Hot Springs conference commenced on 18 May. Evatt – a notoriously unsparing taskmaster and 'a great late night talker' – had worked Coombs hard in Washington.[11] Hot Springs was a holiday resort, and comfortably distant from Evatt. Coombs could soon report to Chifley that he was in 'a lovely spot … I feel as if I am having a holiday', finding time to play golf and tennis.[12] According to John Burton, who accompanied Coombs, the Americans were keen to impress the Latin American delegations on whose voting strength they hoped to base their domination of this and future international bodies. Accordingly, the Hot Springs hosts made sure that few nights were without a well-lubricated party.[13]

Evatt, though distant, watched his officials. Coombs had to defend himself when Evatt queried references, in the Food Conference's draft resolutions, to the possible reduction of trade barriers.[14] He had also to respond to Evatt's 'doubts as to the wisdom of recommending that governments should seek to maintain an equilibrium in balances of payments and to achieve the orderly management of currencies and exchange'. This point had come up in the drafting of the Food Conference's Resolution XXIV, 'Achievement of an Economy of Abundance'. Coombs told Evatt that the words he queried were consistent with Australian economists' views that major economies would have to be obliged to spend on imports the money they derived from exports. He reassured Evatt that the resulting resolution was in any case 'empty of content since no indication is given of the objects to which that orderly management should be directed'. He concluded by saying:

> I feel quite confident that the [conference] report is likely to be of political advantage to the Government in Australia rather than an embarrassment since it amounts to recommendations to the governments of the world that they follow a policy which in general character is, as I understand it, the policy of the Australian government.[15]

Coombs' phrase 'as I understand it' suggests that he may have been advancing his own construction of Cabinet's views on Article VII. According to Butlin and

Schedvin, Evatt's ministerial statement to the Hot Springs Conference – a Coombs effort advocating 'international responsibility for maintaining a high level of employment' – went beyond Cabinet approval and so caused 'some discomfort in Canberra'.[16] Coombs made sure that both Evatt and Chifley (to whom Coombs wrote long letters weekly while abroad) knew what he was doing, and he believed that he had Chifley's full backing, if not Cabinet's.[17] Like his US counterparts, Coombs hoped that the resolutions of a global forum would reinforce the arguments he and others were making domestically.

According to McDougall, he and Coombs were responsible for 'the most significant of the recommendations made by the Conference' – the mechanism by which nations would report to one another, through the nascent Food and Agriculture Organisation (FAO), their progress in meeting the objectives set out in the other recommendations.[18] A contemporary historian noted of the Hot Springs gathering that 'it was the first time in history that a large group of nations [forty-four] had agreed to bring before the bar of international opinion their own records of achievement'.[19]

When Coombs returned to Australia, he told the F&E Committee on 11 September 1943 that at Hot Springs 'some delegations had mental reservations about the positive approach'. Some nations gave priority to industrial develop-ment, and the US delegates had been very sensitive about the words which could be employed to reconcile different readings of Article VII. A generally protectionist US Congress, he had found, was in the back of every American official's mind. As well, US officials had assured him that 'Congress would not accept any conditions written into [an international monetary agreement] because it would look too much like the New Deal by the back door and they would regard any sanctions on creditors as increasing United States obligations too far.' If the United States were to guard its sovereignty so closely, commented Coombs, Australia should also insist on retaining some discretions over its external economic relations before agreeing to a new currency arrangement. Hot Springs had assured Coombs that Australia, like other dependent economies, had some chips with which to bargain.[20]

Almost a year after his first brief statement of 'the positive approach' to his F&E colleagues, Coombs was able to reflect on his first diplomatic foray in a speech to the Economic Society of Australia and New Zealand on 'International Aspects of Reconstruction'. He questioned usual ways of distinguishing between domestic and international matters: 'the level of employment and incomes in the United States and in the United Kingdom is a matter of major concern to us, a far more important concern than other factors which are recognised as international in their character'. How, then, to subject these 'domestic' matters to international scrutiny? The Hot Springs conference – 'the first, as far as I know, international conference which was concerned primarily with domestic policy' – had made domestic action an international responsibility. By setting up an international body, the FAO, the conference had made sure that when reports of domestic action were tabled, the FAO could recommend improved courses of action. If nutrition policies could be so regulated, why not employment?

Aware that his 'positive approach' to trade liberalisation was vulnerable to the charge of being too idealistic, Coombs turned the tables, and dwelt on the naivety of the 'free trade' reading of Article VII. That is, Coombs presented free trade as a legitimate aspiration rendered vulnerable by its theoretical, political and psychological innocence. Advocates of free trade showed no understanding of the hunger for security. If people feel more secure, they will be more rational in their consideration of trade policy, he argued. People wanted security against military aggression and against economic threats. Coombs asserted that 'the most important factor affecting the level of international trade is the domestic level of employment and incomes in the major economic countries of the world'. Trade liberals must tackle the question of full employment, and not seek 'reduction of tariffs and other trade barriers with the same desperate earnestness as in the prewar period'. Coombs referred not only to the income and employment levels of Britain and the United States, but also to those of India and China. It was short-sighted for industrialised nations to fear the industrialisation of under-developed countries: the advance of weaker nations would add to the volume of world trade. Nations trading in primary products whose prices fluctuated a lot needed mechanisms for the stabilisation of prices, and they were entitled to a considerate treatment of their need for foreign currency reserves.[21]

Success in London

IN JANUARY 1944, Cabinet at last approved 'the positive approach' to full employment which Coombs and other Australian representatives had been pursuing, with the evident support of Curtin, Chifley and Evatt, in 1943. The time was ripe for Labor to risk such a constructive vision. The war gave Labor practical experience of effective government intervention that it had missed in World War I (because the party had split over conscription) and in the Depression (because of the intellectual and political hegemony of deflationary economic orthodoxies). The twentieth century's third great crisis found Labor again in power, prefiguring in the 'war economy' a form of government conducive to social justice. Measures justified in the war against fascism were no less justified in the longer-term war against unemployment and poverty, Coombs argued. Not all of his economist colleagues went along with this interpretation of the war's potential. Some of them doubted that war experiences would give rise to new senses of international and domestic responsibility among the world's governments. However, Coombs assembled around him men (and a few women) who agreed that war was precipitating a peaceful political revolution. The key to that change was the economic diplomacy of the United States of America.

In the last quarter of 1945, talks in Washington determined the size and the conditions of the US loan enabling Britain to reconstruct its war-ravaged economy. Aware of Britain's need, but wanting also to satisfy Congress that the

United States was not giving anything away for nothing, US officials such as the State Department's Will Clayton persuaded Britain to endorse a plan for a multi-lateral free trade agreement. As a partner of a major cotton-exporting firm based in Oklahoma, Clayton believed in free international trade. Like other US officials, he thought free trade would secure the post-war world for free enterprise; this would extinguish the vestiges of British imperialism and nip in the bud the creeping 'socialism' which he and his colleagues saw in British politics and in parts of the British Empire where Keynesian ideas of economic 'regimentation' had become influential.[1] The 'Clayton draft' of an International Trade Organisation (ITO) was an anti-Keynesian move in the diplomatic realisation of Article VII of the mutual aid pact.

The first phase of inter-Allied diplomacy, 1943–4, had ended in a triumph for US interests when the rules of the International Monetary Fund (IMF), agreed at Bretton Woods in July 1944, reflected the Stabilisation Fund proposal rather than Keynes' International Clearing Union scheme. Not only would the IMF *not* oblige creditor nations to spend their currency surpluses, but economically dependent nations, such as Australia, would have to justify to the IMF any effort to protect themselves, by alterations of their exchange rate, from adverse movements in global prices for the goods they imported and exported. Neither the United States nor Britain had paid much attention to Australia's 'positive approach' at Bretton Woods. They kept full employment off the agenda of world currency reform. Chifley (Prime Minister following Curtin's death in June 1945) thus found Cabinet hostile, in January 1946, to his first submission recommending that Australia join the IMF.

Would Australia's argument for the global economic responsibility of rich nations fare any better in the forthcoming international discussion of Clayton's draft ITO charter?

In calling for the formation of an International Trade Organisation, the Clayton draft gave some hope to Australian diplomacy. The ITO would

> promote national and international action for the expansion of the production, exchange and consumption of goods, for the reduction of tariffs and other trade barriers, and for the elimination of all forms of discriminatory treatment in international commerce; thus contributing to an expanding world economy, to the establishment and maintenance in all countries of high levels of employment and real income, and to the creation of economic conditions conducive to the maintenance of world peace.[2]

While the Cabinet sub-committee on trade and employment (consisting of Ministers Keane, Scully and Dedman) saw promise in these words, the govern-ment remained sensitive to protected interests; it bound Australian officials such as Coombs not to discuss publicly their hopeful approach to the Clayton draft, in case the negotiations turned out badly.[3] As Coombs recalled in 1980, 'the idea of scrapping the imperial preferences and the protective tariffs sent cold shivers at [*sic*] the spine of very many Australians. It was quite astonishing, the intensity, the reactions about it.'[4]

Meanwhile, Coombs' colleagues had been returning from conferences with a deepened appreciation of US hegemony. In Melville's account of the IMF's inaugural meeting, in Savannah, USA, on 8–18 March 1946, the United States had demonstrated its 'power and will to dominate the organisation'.[5] Would Australia join the IMF? Chifley's strategy was to delay further discussion of that decision, while seeking to insert full employment clauses into the ITO draft charter. Melville's co-delegate in Savannah, J. B. Brigden, rejoiced that Australia 'is now expected to be a kind of "enfant terrible"' in its pursuit of the full employment agenda.[6]

Coombs was soon to emerge as *chef des enfants*. He spent an extraordinary amount of his time, between February 1946 and March 1948, conferring with officials from other nations who believed that the ITO could be the framework of a new international economic order based on full employment. Other officials, particularly those from the United States, Canada and Great Britain, were primarily advocates of free trade and made concessions to the employment approach only because Australian delegates, Coombs in particular, were so tireless in expounding it as a necessary condition of freer trade. As well, there emerged in 1947 and 1948 a self-conscious bloc of underdeveloped nations, such as India, China and the Latin American states, whose leaders wished to develop a manufacturing base so that their economic fortunes would not be tied to the fluctuating prices of a few raw material exports. Australian officials were sometimes able to position themselves as leaders of their challenge to the free trade imperialism of the North Atlantic bloc.[7]

In 1946, Coombs chaired in Canberra an inter-departmental committee that would formulate Australia's amendments for the ITO draft charter. He got his staff to rewrite a draft international employment agreement that they had circulated within the Australian government in 1944. Coombs proposed to turn a brief version of that draft into a whole new chapter in the ITO charter.[8] Some senior Canberra officials, notably J. J. Fletcher from Trade and Customs, warned him of the risks. Pointing to the recent agreement between the United States and Mexico, Fletcher warned that Australia should not underestimate the US determination to pursue the free trade reading of Article VII.[9] Throughout 1946 and 1947, he and his Department expressed a continuing scepticism about the direction Coombs was taking.

Chifley called Coombs away from this work in late April and early May 1946 in order to accompany himself and Evatt to London and Washington to discuss Imperial defence cooperation. Coombs used the trip to find out how others were reacting to the Clayton draft of the ITO charter. He heard UK Treasury officials urge that Australia join the IMF, in order to add the Australian vote to those hoping to curb US dominance. The UK officials played down the IMF's threat to Australia's control over its exchange rates.[10] In Washington he discussed the US trade proposals at length with the State Department's Winthrop Brown. Upon returning to Australia, his accounts of such talks enhanced his standing within inter-departmental discussions of Australia's position. He told the Permanent Heads Committee (advising the Cabinet sub-committee on trade and employment) on 24 May that some issues of interest to Australia were still open to intervention. 'Neither [the] US nor [the] UK had any firm ideas on the machinery by which the employment and trade clauses could be effectively linked, or on how employment problems could be handled.' In this field of unsettled opinion Coombs saw Australia's diplomatic opportunity.[11]

As well as helping to draft Australian amendments to the ITO draft charter, Coombs chaired a Tariff Reviewing Committee which began on 26 June 1946 to review Australia's tariffs, item by item, in order to estimate the implications of tariff reduction for local industry – with and without the continuation of Imperial Preference. The Department of Trade and Customs had done preparatory work for this review in the second half of 1945. Coombs' task was to coordinate advice from Treasury (with involvement from the Commonwealth Bank), Post-war Reconstruction, Commerce and Agriculture, External Affairs, and Trade and Customs.

Coombs was now well-briefed to head the Australian delegation of twelve senior bureaucrats that arrived in London to confer with UK officials on 3–11 October 1946.[12] He and his team pressed the need to write into the ITO charter an international agreement on full employment. The full meeting of seventeen nations (known as the United Nations Preparatory Committee on Trade and Employment) commenced on 15 October. Coombs' address on 17 October began by enumerating five principles underlying the Australian approach: full employment as a condition of freer trade; a willingness by creditor countries to buy and invest abroad; a commitment to economic development; the stabilisation of commodity prices; and preventing international organisations from becoming the instrument of 'established interests'. Coombs pointed out that Australia had more to lose than the United States from the failure of such internationalism. 'We are too conscious of our exposure to the economic blizzards of the world.'[13]

Coombs chaired one of five specialist committees – on commercial policy – which worked closely with the committee revising the draft's passages on employment, economic activity and industrial development. The resulting changes in the ITO draft charter's Chapters Three, 'Employment', and Four, 'Economic Development', were regarded by the Australians as a breakthrough. Here at last they seemed to find international acceptance of 'the positive approach'. According to a contemporary American account, 'Australia took the lead in advocating the strongest possible employment undertakings and the inclusion in the Charter of provisions for affirmative action of an expansionist character for the maintenance of employment.'[14] The strength of the United Kingdom's support on the employment clauses surprised Coombs – 'a greater concession than I expected'.[15]

The London draft of the ITO charter challenged the underlying political logic of the IMF. Whereas the IMF empowered rich nations to prescribe deflationary policies for weaker economies, the ITO would oblige countries with favourable trade balances to spend their surpluses overseas and to allow weaker nations to protect themselves, under certain circumstances, from global competition. Australia went so far as to argue 'for penal action against countries failing to live up to their charter obligations on employment'.[16] Though US delegates opposed such enforcement, Coombs thought that international redress against an offending nation remained possible. As he told Minister for Post-war Reconstruction John Dedman,

> following a complaint by a country affected by the failure of another to maintain full employment, the nature and extent of the retaliatory action to be taken would be left to the ITO. I believe that if we can obtain the right for a review of obligations in these circumstances, we can accept the responsibility, at the time of the review, to convince the ITO of the extent to which we should be released from obligations under the Charter.[17]

As Coombs hoped, the ITO was emerging as a global advocate of the dependent economies, a Keynesian alternative to the IMF.[18]

Global temptations

URGED BY THE ECONOMIST Copland and by Armitage, the Governor of the Commonwealth Bank, Prime Minister Chifley had decided by the second half of 1946 to ask Cabinet again to sign Australia on to the IMF.[1] Eddie Ward evoked the IMF as the new vehicle of the Money Power. 'Whilst our men and women were making tremendous sacrifices to prevent the establishment of a world dictatorship,' Ward warned in March 1946, 'the International Financial Interests were working out the details of a plan – more insidious because they laboured unseen – whereby the whole world would come under their domination ...'.[2] Some Australian economists also nursed reservations about the IMF. Melville advised the government in April 1946 that Australia would benefit from joining the IMF only if the Anglo-American Loan Agreement and the proposed ITO had the effect of restoring world trade and economic stability.[3] By November 1946, the American loan to Britain was in place and, after Coombs' and other officials' work in London, a full employment mandate for the ITO seemed more likely. In a speech to London's Royal Institute for International Affairs before returning to Australia, Coombs argued that the IMF and the ITO were now 'two halves of a whole'.[4]

On 14 November 1946 Chifley drew Cabinet's attention to the international developments favouring Australia: the US Congress had ratified the loan to the United Kingdom, and the UK Chancellor of the Exchequer, Hugh Dalton, had given assurances to the Australian Ambassador in Washington that his government would withdraw from the IMF should it attempt to impose any policy inconsistent with full employment. The Bank of England was then coming under the control of the UK government, Dalton argued, and would follow policies consistent with full employment. Finally, the IMF had adopted the UK interpretation of a 'fundamental disequilibrium' – effectively licensing a member to change the rate at which its currency exchanged, in order to prevent unemployment.[5] Thus encouraged, Cabinet voted on 19 November to join the IMF as long as the government would review Australia's membership of the Fund when the *final* draft of the ITO charter was determined.[6]

Nine days after Cabinet's decision, Chifley urged the Federal Executive of his party to endorse Cabinet's decision. Of the trade and employment talks in London he said that 'we have got agreement on some things we regarded as vital, such as the pledge to maintain full employment and the right of undeveloped countries to protect new industries'. Not to join the Fund might exclude Australia from the benefits of trade liberalisation, under the ITO, he warned. To be in the ITO but not in the IMF would expose Australia to the charge that it wanted benefits without risks. Chifley urged the Executive to agree to Australia's joining the IMF now, with the proviso that it could quit, if further drafting of the ITO charter reversed the gains made by Coombs' delegation in London.[7]

Coombs continued to canvass overseas opinion on the IMF and ITO. As soon as the Preparatory Committee had wound up in London, he made a quick visit to Sweden. Over two days, 28–29 November, he talked with Gunnar Myrdal, the Swedish Minister for Trade, with Dag Hammerskjöld, economic adviser to the Swedish government, and the governor of the Riksbank, Mr Rooth. His long-standing interest in Swedish economic policy assured Coombs' rapport with Myrdal. Indeed he had recently asked Myrdal to find a Swedish economist for the nascent Australian National University.[8] Six weeks after returning from Sweden, Coombs told Chifley that the Swedes were still lukewarm about the IMF. As for the ITO, the Swedes liked its draft philosophy and rules but worried that becoming a member might 'interfere with harmonious relations with possible non-members'.[9] The most important likely non-member, from Sweden's point of view, was its neighbour and trading partner, the Soviet Union.[10]

In the first two months of 1947, Chifley was still debating the IMF within the ALP, for he wanted his party united. At last, he felt it safe to introduce a bill for Australia's ratification of the Bretton Woods (IMF) agreement on 20 March 1947. The Opposition taunted Chifley with the threat of a split party, and Jack Lang excoriated the Prime Minister's 'betrayal of Australia … [to] an international financial cartel'.[11] (Coombs later likened Lang, at this moment, to a 'jackal'.[12]) Chifley's reply promoted the Bretton Woods agreement as a measure for peace, part of the cure for 'one of the fundamental causes of war', economic instability: 'we must put our faith in these international organizations.'[13] As Crisp commented, Chifley implied 'the shoddy provincial meanness of Lang's attack'.[14] In Coombs' recollection, Chifley had been in favour of joining the Fund perhaps as early as 1943, when the two of them had first discussed the rival British and US currency proposals. Chifley had found, in 'the positive approach', 'a coherent and politically acceptable rationale' for his internationalism.[15]

Coombs' contribution to Labor's embrace of the IMF rested not only on his judgment of the trends in talks about the ITO charter, but also on his hopes about the United Nations. The Economic and Social Council (ECOSOC) of the United Nations had formed an Economic and Employment Commission in 1946 – Australia providing one of its Commissioners. Coombs' letters at this time, including at least one to Chifley, assessing this nascent UN agency, convey hope rather than confidence that it could be an effective advocate of international full employment. He was worried that all the new international agencies remained susceptible to a narrow 'free trade' interpretation of Article VII. Because the techniques of full employment policy were largely untried, it was possible that too little notice would be taken, in practice, of the chapters on full employment and economic development in the ITO charter.

Coombs travelled to New York late in February 1947 to gauge for himself the competence and commitment of the staff of the Economic and Employment Commission. External Affairs economist Arthur Tange was already there, helping ECOSOC to edit the London redraft of the ITO charter so that it could be submitted to further discussions in the forthcoming second (Geneva) round of the Preparatory Committee in April 1947. Tange had recently written Coombs a sobering analysis of Australia's success in London in revising the draft ITO charter. Perhaps Australian diplomacy was better in the writing of constitutions, he suggested, than in the effective exercise of the rights afforded by them.[16] The politics of translating fine words into national and international programs lay ahead of Australia. The fears of the Labor Party's IMF sceptics would have been confirmed had they seen Tange's words.

Coombs' time in New York – 'hurried but useful' – gave him a sense of ECOSOC's limitations. On 13 March 1947 he wrote to Chifley that the commitment of the Economic and Employment Commission to full employment was 'essential if the dependent economies, for instance, are to be able to obtain freedom to take protective action against outside deflationary influences with full international approval'. To his disappointment the Commission lacked the economic data essential to conducting reviews of global employment trends. He worried as well about the quality of the staff of the United Nations' economic division. He hoped that the arrival at the United Nations of (Poland-born but Britain-based) economist Michal Kalecki ('very capable on the theoretical side') would toughen the Economic and Employment Commission.

In correspondence and in person, Coombs had got to know David Owen, Assistant Secretary-General of the United Nations and responsible for the Economic and Employment Commission. Coombs thought Owen 'good, but he is not an economist and he is very heavily burdened with work of a non-economic character'.[17] Owen found Coombs so impressive that he wondered if Coombs would lead one of the nascent international economic agencies such as the ITO or the FAO.

Coombs took these speculations and offers seriously. His effective advocacy in London and later in Geneva and Havana must often have produced the fantasy that he could make effective the agencies that he was helping to design. 'If I am to do an international job', he told John Crawford in August 1947, 'then it would probably be best for me to save myself for the ITO. … From a personal point of view, I think I would just as soon stay in Australia.'[18] Coombs' considerations were no doubt partly personal, but one can speculate that he reserved his own doubts about international monitoring. What global body, if any, would preside over a new international economic order? Would it necessarily be the ITO? Would the ITO embrace the spirit, not just the letter, of full employment? By what mechanisms could it intervene to ensure domestic policies of full employment? In a letter to Owen at the end of May 1947 Coombs discussed his future. 'I think I can do my best work in economic administration of one sort or another.' He was prepared to lead the ITO if the position were offered, 'but ... I would very much wish that this should be regarded as strictly confidential'. As for working at the United Nations, as Owen's deputy, Coombs declined, alluding to 'aspects of [working in the United Nations] which make me hesitate even more than about the ITO job'.[19] He did not clarify 'aspects' in this letter, but he had shared with Chifley his worry that the United Nations was not yet intellectually equipped to be an effective actor on international economic issues.

The circularity of this objection – Owen's attempt to recruit Coombs presumably stemmed from his own sense of such a lack – recalls a perceptive remark made in 1944 by Wilmott Phillips, then a Post-war Reconstruction officer. Phillips had suggested that international reporting on each nation's employment conditions would have its best effect not as the basis for an international agency's sanctions, but as 'publicity' favouring those *domestic* interests that promoted full employment policies. Pursuing the implication of her point, she noted

> [the] minor problem ... that first class people will not be willing to take positions on the executive of the international organisation since they will realise the difficulties of achieving any satisfactory action and also since a position of this kind would cut them off from the administration of the employment policies of particular countries where it is possible that something may be achieved.[20]

This 'minor problem' was becoming a personal dilemma for Coombs. Could his internationalism sustain his move to an international agency, or would his public service as an economist remain more potent within Australia?

Geneva

IT WAS A MARK of Coombs' success in the London talks that his position, as he entered the next round of talks on tariffs and on the ITO draft charter in Geneva in April 1947, had become rather delicate. To Australian critics he seemed to risk the foundations of national economic security. To US and British free-traders his insistence on exceptions to the proposed commercial order seemed too ingenious, making him the special pleader *par excellence*. His was not, however, a strategy of duplicity. Coombs' internationalism was consistent. Since 1942–3, it had rested on two connected propositions: that if people felt secure they would be more open to discussing a deregulation of their dealings with other nations; and that full employment was a feasible domestic policy of economic security and a stimulus to greater volumes of international trade.

By 1947, diplomatic experience had added new dimensions to this internationalism. We can see it in the briefing that he offered Chifley in March.

Because the US economy now determined the fortunes of all nations, he argued, Australia's relationships with Britain and the Commonwealth must be rethought, outside the old Imperial framework. Australia would be affected less by what happened in Britain and more by the global demand, particularly US demand, for Australian goods. Britain's purchasing power was now so impaired by war that Australia, while supporting British reconstruction, should seek new markets for its exports. Coombs thought that Australia could not further its mutual interests with Britain by defending Imperial Preference. British experts, Coombs noted, agreed that Imperial Preference was no longer sacrosanct. (Indeed. 'Unless there is some contraction of the preference system', wrote UK Secretary of State for Dominion Affairs Addison eight days after Coombs' advice to Chifley, 'none of us will secure adequate concessions from the United States.'[1])

Coombs' London experiences as a spokesperson for a bloc of nations had taught him that Australia could be a broker between what we now call 'North' and 'South'. Australia was objectively aligned with underdeveloped countries. Asian nationalism, Coombs suggested, would set a political framework for economic development, to Australia's advantage. India would be particularly important. Coombs ended his letter to Chifley by considering the relations between the Soviet Union and the West. International arrangements should try to accommodate both capitalist and socialist economies and to ease trading relations between members and non-members of ITO. He gave the example of Sweden – likely to have close trading relations with the Soviet Union, and unwilling to comply with an international economic framework dominated by the interest of the United States.[2]

Coombs prepared himself emotionally as well as intellectually for another episode of diplomacy. He had learned in London how unwise it was to reside with co-delegates. Allowed a sitting room as well as a bedroom at the Hyde Park Hotel, he had found himself host not only to daily pre-session meetings but also to 'a drink and gossip at any hour of the day and night', and so the conference had become all-enveloping. Chifley, hearing of his resulting illness, permitted him to arrange things differently when he got to Geneva.

> I found ... a small flat – bedroom, kitchenette and bathroom – in one of the old houses, where I got my own breakfast and was able to establish a tolerable pattern of life with adequate sleep and freedom for a few hours on most days from the pressure and bustle of the Conference. As a result I became very fond of Geneva. I visited the market place in the early morning buying my rolls, milk, eggs and fruit ... I became a regular and rather pampered customer [at Le Plat d'Argent].[3]

In Coombs' opening speech at Geneva, on 10 April 1947, he summed up the three outstanding achievements of recent international economic diplomacy. First, it had been recognised that high levels of employment and effective demand would yield a high volume of world trade. Second, there was now a common understanding that the economies of the world were at different stages of development and were guided by different political philosophies. It was therefore necessary to formulate flexible international rules. Third, there was now a consensus that many trade barriers were based on legitimate considerations. Now was a good time to reduce protection, however, as world demand was surging. Advocates of full employment 'are in danger of being embarrassed by the fullness with which our prayers have been answered'. Delegates therefore need not assess concessions only in terms of the costs and benefits to their nation. Better to 'take into account the role which the tariff plays in the economy of the countries negotiating, to assess the purposes which it is designed to achieve and the fears which it is designed to quiet' and so 'to see in the achievement of those purposes and the quieting of those fears advantages from which they too can benefit'.[4]

Geneva's multilateral bargaining process might better be described as cumulative bilateralism. Country A would publish a list of exported items whose import Country B restricted or burdened with an import duty. B would do likewise to A. Countries A and B would then negotiate, matching each other's offers of lower levels of protection. The results were made known to Countries C, D, E and so on. If A lowered tariffs against B's exports of a product, then any other nation exporting that product had a right to the same terms from A. Article 24 in the ITO draft charter stipulated this 'automatic' extension. The difficulty in the early days of the Geneva talks was that no nation knew whether Article 24 would come into effect: the ITO charter was not to be discussed again until substantial progress had been made in reducing trade barriers.

Coombs, as leader of Australia's Geneva delegation, attempted to make light of this difficulty. However, more cautious members of the delegation, such as Trade and Customs officer Jacob Fletcher, demurred. Fletcher's notion of Australia's interests and position within the world economy had been moulded by the bilateral logic of the 1932 Ottawa Agreement. Under Ottawa's rules, Australia's concessions to Britain's manufacturing exports were clearly matched by Britain's discrimination in favour of Australian exports (notably agricultural produce). Although the Ottawa Agreement could be defined as a multilateral arrangement, in that it was a pact among a number of nations or dominions, it is more accurate to think of it as a series of bilateral arrangements – between Britain and Canada, Britain and Australia, Britain and South Africa, and so on. The full-blooded multilateralism implied by ITO draft Article 24 was something new. Although Coombs welcomed this novelty as part of the challenge and promise of a new international order, his delegation was accountable, through daily cables, to a committee in Canberra chaired watchfully by Roland Wilson. One of Coombs' first tasks was therefore to play down the significance of draft Article 24. He told Chifley and Dedman that US negotiators were privately admitting to being embarrassed about its threat to the free and adventurous spirit in which the talks on trade barriers were supposed to begin. Article 24, he advised, could be bracketed off, after diplomatic protest by Australia, for later argument over the ITO draft charter.[5] The United States had reason to be yielding on this and later sticking points, regarding Australia as one of eight key countries in the Imperial Preference system. 'Without a bilateral agreement with Australia, it would be politically impossible to convince Congress that there had been significant modifications of the preferential system.'[6]

Wilson then raised the problem of draft Article 14. That part of the ITO draft charter appeared to prohibit any increase in the height of preferences or tariffs that had not been subject of negotiation by the time the agreements then being negotiated in Geneva came into force. Such a rule, argued Wilson, was in 'direct conflict with the principle of reciprocal and mutually advantageous negotiations upon which we are taking our stand'.[7] Coombs did not say it in so many words, but his version of 'our stand' was rather different from Wilson's. The Geneva tariff negotiations had the potential to be 'mutually advantageous' in a way not acknowledged in Wilson's cable: if Geneva generated a momentum, among all delegations, towards less protected trade, then it would create a fruitful atmosphere in which to formulate a charter of international economic relations. More tariff reductions could well induce the United States to concede stronger commitments to full employment in the ITO charter. Wilson and the more cautious spirits of the sub-committee questioned these tactics. They were stuck in a tit-for-tat bilateralism that inhibited risk and rationed hope. They worried that Article 14 would constrain the British Commonwealth's future adjustment of preference margins among its members. In particular they feared that Australian primary producers would lose their price advantages in Empire markets, while Australian manufacturers faced keener competition from British exports.

Coombs was wary of letting loyalty to Imperial Preference hinder Australia's dealings with the United States. For Wilson's committee to make a fuss about it cramped him tactically. Facing the Americans, he wished to exercise his own judgment about which issues to fight and which to concede in Geneva's daily scramble for diplomatic advantage. He responded to Wilson by playing down the risk to Australian industry were British manufacturing imports to be made cheaper by lower tariffs and preferences. He speculated that Australian manufacturing was now more productive than before the war and thus more competitive. He had to concede, however, that Australia's future wage and price structure was 'obscure', and that the manufacturing productivity of many nations still recovering from the war had yet to be determined.[8] This was an uneasy reply to Wilson.

The force of Wilson's worries depended partly on the attitude of other Empire countries, especially Britain, to Imperial Preference. The British negotiators in Geneva were treating Australia in a rather hard-nosed fashion, seeking to go beyond the advantages their manufacturing exports had enjoyed under Ottawa.[9] Canberra eventually permitted Coombs to flag Australia's willingness to renegotiate the terms of the Ottawa Agreement while all Commonwealth nations were in Geneva.[10] He was not the only Australian official who thought it best to act on the assumption that Imperial Preference was in its demise. Arthur Tange concurred, telling John Burton on 17 May 1947 that there was no point making a fuss about Articles 14 and 24, other than as tactics: bargain tariff concessions as a reward for accepting them under protest.[11] Eventually, Coombs was able to point out that because Article 14 preserved preference margins not included in the Geneva negotiations (while capping them), it actually preserved the vestiges of arrangements made within the Empire. Britain and Canada were not perturbed by Article 14.

Coombs was not opposed to the principle that a nation should reserve some discretion to differentiate between its trading partners. Instead of defending 'Imperial' grounds for such discrimination, however, Coombs wanted Australia to promote economic criteria that US officials could not lightly dismiss, criteria essential to the 'positive approach'. When Nation A could trace its economic problems to the unfair practices of Nation B, then the ITO, he hoped, would give A permission to discriminate against B's exports. In the spirit of the emerging ITO, however, 'discrimination based on political or traditional associations would be debarred'.[12]

By the end of April 1947 it was apparent that the United States was not going to give commercial concessions easily, so powerful were the rural producers for whom the US Department of Agriculture spoke. Coombs reported several times his discussions with Clayton about the high US tariff on wool. His cables kept open the option of withdrawing altogether from the talks. If Australia could not get its most lucrative export more favourably placed in the world's biggest market, Geneva's promise was hollow. He returned to Canberra between 18 and 22 May for talks on brinkmanship.

According to Wheeler, Coombs' brief return to Canberra was 'fairly hectic. We were more or less continuously in committees of one sort or another.' Indeed, from the evening of 19 May to the afternoon of 21 May, Coombs gave a detailed account of his delegation's work to no less than four meetings of Wilson's committee and one meeting with the trade and employment sub-committee of Cabinet. Coombs' cool assessment of Imperial Preference made it all the more important that he win a concession from the Americans on wool. Australia would persist in bargaining hard on wool, and Minister for Post-war Reconstruction John Dedman would now lead Australia's Geneva delegation.[13]

Within a week of returning from Canberra with a renewed mandate for his strategy, Coombs wrote to Chifley on the political problem now facing his government: how to conclude the delegation's work in Geneva without implying to the Australian public that a whole new tariff structure, negotiated in secret, was being brought back as a *fait accompli*. It would be necessary to publish the proposed new tariff rates. Coombs made a number of astute suggestions about the arrangement of this information in order to maximise the public impression of other countries' concessions and to minimise Australia's.[14] As Chifley explained to Dedman, the emerging General Agreement on Tariffs and Trade (GATT) was 'still extremely vague so far as the public, the labour movement, Caucus and even the majority of Cabinet are concerned, not to mention opposition parties'. Chifley wished to avoid 'a full-dress tariff debate' in 1947. His ministry had to be prepared for one, however, and that would require an effort by his tired officials to put the results of Geneva into an intelligible and persuasive form. Timing was important: 'it would be bad tactics to have all the details announced and then left hanging in mid-air for everyone to shoot at through the Xmas recess'. Chifley's dilemma was partly a problem of multilateralism. If one government chose to announce what it had brought back from Geneva, it would be difficult for other governments, with some of its concessions thus revealed, to hold back publicising the concessions they had extracted from others. Multilateralism was a heady atmosphere for the officials thronging the Palais des Nations, but a political headache for individual governments. Chifley admitted to Dedman: 'like you I lean to bilateral agreements'.[15]

And still the US President delayed vetoing the legislation which upheld a high duty on wool. US officials assured Coombs and Dedman that the delay had to do with President Truman's re-election tactics, not with any lack of sympathy for the Australian case. When the decision came, however, at the end of the first week of August 1947, the United States conceded only a 25 per cent cut in the wool duty, not the 50 per cent for which the Australians had long asked. It took eight weeks for a solution to be found. On 5 October 1947, the Australian delegation reported that the US would cut the wool duty by 50 per cent if Australia would consent to a rise in the price (effectively) of its dried and canned fruit in Canada and Britain. Australia had probably paid too high a price for the wool breakthrough, the delegation admitted, but 'from a long-term point of view access to United States market for Australian major exports may be of critical importance'.[16]

Havana

THE CHIFLEY GOVERNMENT presented GATT to Parliament on 18 November 1947; the new tariff schedules came into effect the following day. The ITO draft charter, though amended further in Geneva, had now to be made final at a special conference in Havana, commencing 21 November 1947 and ending 24 March 1948, attended by fifty-seven nations. Coombs was second to John Dedman's leadership of a large delegation that included bureaucrats such as Arthur Tange, J. J. Fletcher and E. McCarthy, Lenox Hewitt and Alan Renouf. Coombs served as delegate or alternate on the committees dealing with Employment and Economic Activity, Economic Development, Commercial Policy, and Organisation. As well, he chaired a joint sub-committee of the committees on Economic Development and Organisation.[1]

The Australian delegation's task was to preserve the ITO draft charter as a carefully negotiated statement of rich nations' obligations. On 2 December 1947 Coombs told delegates: 'The United States' economy seems to us to be essentially unstable. That instability hangs over the rest of the world with the same threat as a thunder-cloud. We are all watching it.' He called the persisting balance of payments surpluses of the United States 'the outstanding problem of this era'. The Marshall Plan – a program of US aid to reconstruct Europe, initiated during the Havana conference – was one 'generous' effort to deal with this problem, he conceded, but it was a short-term measure. Through 'a higher level of purchases and a greater volume of long-term investment' by the United States, he sought 'a natural equilibrium' between the United States and those nations needing dollars for their trade.[2] The ITO draft charter seemed to the Australians to go as far as one could to bind the United States to that equilibrium.

Accordingly, notwithstanding Australia's alignment with other dependent nations, the Australians frequently joined US officials in explaining and justifying features of the ITO draft charter. Most of the fifty-seven nations attending Havana had not been at the London and Geneva sessions of the Preparatory Committee. While the Australians could sympathise with their fears of US hegemony, the one thousand amendments tabled in November 1947 risked unravelling the hard-won compromises of London and Geneva.[3] Against the hail-storm of amendments, Australia often backed Clayton in defending the draft as already meeting – to the limits of political possibility – the concerns of all dependent nations. For example, it was argued that the charter should include an Economic Development Committee to counter the disciplinary Tariff Committee. Australia joined the United States in opposing this suggestion, while sympathising with the impulses behind it, because a proliferation of such bodies within the ITO would detract from its ability, first, to adjudicate by reference both to commercial and to economic development principles and, second, to rule decisively on disputes among nations over the tensions between free trade and protection.

The powers of the ITO became one of the issues on which Australia found itself at odds with the United States. Geneva draft Article 24(2) dealt with the relationship between the IMF's and the ITO's deliberations over a nation's ways of dealing with a balance of payments problem. The United States wanted the IMF to be able to tell a nation when and how it could resort to exchange controls and import restrictions. Coombs and his colleagues, wary of US dominance within the IMF, thought that the ITO should rule. Coombs, Dedman, the Australian Ambassador to Washington Makin, and US State Department officials discussed ways to avoid forcing all nations to choose between the Australian and the US positions. By skilful drafting of this and related articles, a form of words was found which both governments could live with. Had the ITO come into existence, its relationship with the Fund would have been an immediate and difficult issue.

To the extent that such compromises left powers in the ITO's hands, the composition and voting procedures of the ITO Executive became issues of importance. Australia wanted the ITO to be elected by a franchise of one vote per nation. Other nations (including the United States) wanted either that votes be weighted by some criterion of economic eminence or that certain seats on the Executive be reserved for major economies. A version of 'reserved seats' triumphed when the United States did a deal with the nations of Latin America. In such passages of diplomacy, the Australians learned to be careful not to alienate the support of the Latin American nations who were frequently Australia's natural allies (as dependent nations) in the delicate task of wooing the United States to a sense of imperial responsibility.[4]

Australia's advocacy of US investment abroad is a cameo of its mediation between the richest and the most vulnerable of the world's economies. The Geneva draft, anticipating that rich nations' investments abroad could lead to exploitation of a host nation and loss of its economic sovereignty, had inscribed the rights of countries receiving investment. The US delegation sought revisions securing investors' rights, threatening that no investment would be forthcoming without such protections. Australia, at one point, scandalised US opinion by suggesting that US investors could purchase the currency, rather than the physical assets, of poorer nations. US delegate Clair Wilcox 'without prior notice' managed to isolate Australia and India on this question 'by his skilful reasoning'. Coombs 'fortunately had available a compromise text which still says nothing but presents a satisfactory optical illusion', as he later related to his departmental colleague Allen Brown.[5] That 'illusion' included foreshadowing ITO arbitration of any allegations that recipient countries had wrongfully appropriated foreign investments.

Coombs was five months in Havana, leaving in the last week of March 1948. He had Lallie with him, but the conference had been very hard work – six-day weeks, with conference hours from 10.30 am to 8.30 pm. The Australian delegation assembled for a daily meeting at 9 am, and Coombs found it necessary, somehow, to fit additional 'private discussions' into such a day. As well they had to get used to 'very humid and tropical weather'. 'We should be working under the normal conditions of a tropical climate', he complained, 'but we are trying to adhere to European customs and the result is not good.'[6]

The Havana final draft of the ITO charter was the zenith of the decade's liberal internationalism. Yet in May 1948, Coombs chose to emphasise its inconsequence.

(a) Tariff protection upon which Australia relies predominantly for industrial development is permitted substantially without limitation under the Charter;

(b) Measures in operation in Australia for the protection of primary production are permitted under the Charter;

(c) Our delegation by being able to present Australia's point of view in the first stages of the preparation of the Charter has been able to secure recognition for all Australian policies. As a consequence the Charter requires no change in our commercial policy and few minor changes in commercial legislation and practices.[7]

Was this the harvest of 'the positive approach'?

It was possible to present a more upbeat account of what Australia had achieved: commitments from the richest nations to full employment and to the development of the world's more dependent economies. On 30 September 1948, Dedman introduced the International Trade Organization Bill, conditionally ratifying the ITO charter. The wording of the ITO charter, he said, now met Australia's international objectives. That is, if the 'major marketing countries' failed to meet their charter obligations then Australia would be justified, in terms of the charter, in taking defensive actions and in urging the ITO 'to correct the decline in demand'. Article 4, he said, would require the United States 'to correct a disequilibrium between dollar and non-dollar currencies'. The failure of the United States to do so would be grounds for countries to take defensive action and to call upon the ITO to take (unspecified) actions. The United States, unlike nations damaged by the war, would be bound immediately by the charter. Australia was already on the Interim Commission preparing for the ITO's first conference, and it stood a good chance of being elected to the eighteen-member executive board.

Dedman's bill provided that Australia would not accept membership of the ITO unless the United Kingdom and the United States did so as well. The United States did not, and so the ITO lapsed. I know of no record of Coombs' feelings about this anti-climax.

Perhaps the Australians had succeeded too well. In 1952, trade policy analyst William Diebold suggested that the ITO charter never gained Congressional support and forfeited Presidential enthusiasm by December 1950, because it displeased not only protectionists (a powerful element of US politics) but also 'perfectionists' who thought too many concessions had been made to the enemies of 'free enterprise' and free trade. Defending as 'realism' the concessions made to dependent countries such as Australia, Diebold wrote that the Havana delegates 'produced a document that proved to be unacceptable to that reputed arch-realist, the American businessman'.[8] In Coombs' recollections thirty years later, he had begun to sense towards the end of the Havana conference that the United States was losing interest in the ITO, as the Cold War with the Soviet Union directed attention to Europe as the key region of contested hegemony. By 1948, 'the Marshall Plan for massive financial support for the rehabilitation of European industry and the pressure on European countries to move towards a Customs Union ... [were] commanding more political interest'.[9] It was through the Marshall Plan, not the ITO, that the United States' strategic interest produced an approximate version of Coombs' 'positive approach'.

An official community

BETWEEN 1942 AND 1948 Coombs became a central figure in an international community of government officials.

Consider the global context in which this official community emerged. British hegemony over the international system had been under challenge from the United States since early in the twentieth century. World War II brought the two nations into a curiously ambivalent relationship – on the one hand allies against the Axis, on the other hand, rivals in setting the rules of international commerce. A North Atlantic community of officials carried much of the responsibility for negotiating the tensions within this alliance/enmity. According to one account, they improved the chances of agreement over the new economic order, in the years 1942–8, by setting the agenda. That is, they ensured that the focus of discussions on Article VII of the mutual aid pact was initially on currency issues, over which there was more chance of consensus among British and US officials. The more contentious questions of free trade, Imperial Preference and full employment were not taken up until after Bretton Woods.[1]

To the extent that monetary issues were the ground of an emergent Allied consensus by 1944, Australian officials were marginal to this 'community'. Melville and Tange lamented the difficulty of pursuing Australia's full employment agenda at Bretton Woods. For them, and for Coombs, the monetary cart had been put before the employment horse, and the wisdom of Australia joining the IMF was contingent on how well the new rules of international commerce – the ITO charter – would bind rich nations to full employment and to economic development.

Between 1944 and 1948, Coombs and other Australian officials moved from the margins to the centre of this international official community. They formed an alliance with other dependent economies, and they benefited from the reasonable apprehensions of a British Labour government about the extent of the United States' hegemonic ambition. The diplomatic success of Coombs and his colleagues meant that they accrued power, as well, within the Commonwealth bureaucracy and so in Labor Party thinking. Their project was to modernise Labor's economic policy, according to the precepts and practices of contemporary economics. Coombs later recalled that

> [the] protectionist component in Labor Party policy was strengthened by the close association between Australian manufacturing interests and the Customs Department, which not merely administered the tariff on imports but had established itself as the major source of advice and the prime negotiator in matters affecting international trade – other than those concerned exclusively with major exports of primary products. One of the 'in-jokes' of the Canberra scene in those times was to refer to the Customs Department as the Australian manufacturer's lobby – a description which usually brought a somewhat self-satisfied smirk to the faces of Customs officials. Even in the rural field the Labor Party had its own internal 'Country Party' pressure group representing small-scale farmers engaged in dairying, horticultural, and similar activities, to whom the United Kingdom market and the preferential advantages it offered seemed vital.[2]

The Department of Post-war Reconstruction, with no administrative bonds to any industry sector, challenged these protectionists. By emphasising the ITO charter's challenge to the United States, Coombs and other officials wooed the Labor leadership to a Keynesian, full employment internationalism that entailed a challenge to protection.

Their rapport with Chifley rendered the Labor Party rather schizoid in the late 1940s. In a 1947 commentary, Bruce Miller emphasised Labor's heritage of isolationism and its fear of the power of international finance capital. According to him, Labor MPs and their supporters were uneasy at the evident contradiction between Labor's domestic approach to finance (exemplified in the greater government controls conferred by the 1945 *Banking Act* and the 1947 decision to nationalise the private trading banks) and the same government's readiness to accept the IMF's rules over Australian currency policy. 'There were no traditions of Labor thought to which the Government could appeal in asking for support for the agreement [to join the IMF].' Chifley drew heavily on official advice in persuading his party to a more optimistic and less Empire-centred international policy.[3]

Cables between Canberra and Geneva in 1947 included many references to the need for officials such as Coombs to return to Australia in time to help the politicians build a pro-GATT case in public. When R. F. Holder reviewed the public discussion of GATT, in January 1951, he noted that opinions among the primary industry lobbies had been divided and that manufacturers had lobbied against GATT. He found it curious that 'no general expression of opinion has come from the trade unions, which would most likely have been severely critical, in spite of loyalty to official Labor Government policy, if they felt that tariff reductions entailed a danger to employment and the standard of living'. Perhaps the trade unions' silence evidences the credibility, within the labour movement, of Chifley's assurances that Australia had done well in London, Geneva and Havana. Holder thought Jack Lang accurate in saying that the government had been led into GATT by departmental experts.[4] The official 'community' could stand apart from the traditional constituencies of the governments they advised.

One way to see Coombs, then, is as an exemplary participant of that community. Verbal skill is a defining quality among such officials. Over the five years from April 1943 to February 1948, Coombs spent many months at international conferences negotiating, with officials from other nations, the formulation of multilateral objectives. His 'positive approach', in its most concrete form, was a quest for mutuality among officials about the wording of multilateral principles and rules. Those officials had then to persuade their political masters and other officials back home that the compromise formulations of London, San Francisco, Geneva and Havana were politically defensible. The officials developed a culture of their own, a world defined by certain languages and ways of negotiating about language, a world of conferences, speeches, resolutions, amendments and the occasional frantic collaboration to find words which all present could take back to those to whom they were accountable. Their labour was at once combative and collaborative, their product an elusive mix of the factitious and the substantive.

For example, Coombs wrote to Chifley in June 1943 of the contention between the free trade and the full employment approaches at Hot Springs. After referring to Evatt's continuing sensitivity about Australian concessions to the free trade argument, Coombs told how he negotiated the wording of a particularly tricky conference resolution.

> The resolution dealing specifically with the reduction of trade barriers was introduced by the American delegation in terms almost identical with those used in the relevant section of Article VII. I suggested that in order to re-emphasize the prime importance of an expanding economy that the resolutions should be introduced by the phrase 'progressively with the achievement of full employment and the development of under-developed resources' and that no specific reference should be made to tariffs but to trade barriers generally, on the grounds that tariffs were a

legitimate means of maintaining employment when world economic conditions were unfavourable and a legitimate instrument of industrial development in less developed countries. The Americans at first were willing to accept these changes but subsequently withdrew their agreement on the grounds that this would have meant going back on an undertaking to which the majority of governments present were already committed in Article VII. I pointed out that Article VII quite clearly envisages that positive measures of increasing production and consumption would go with measures taken to reduce trade barriers and, accordingly, I suggested that the clause might be introduced with the phrase 'as part of this general programme'. The Americans accepted this and agreed to drop the specific mention of tariffs.[5]

Officials adroit in such semantic horse-trading did not kid themselves that the resulting deals confirmed unity of purpose and action among nations. Rather, such compromises were a step within a larger political process abounding in hazards. All the more reason for officials such as Coombs to welcome one another's verbal felicity and to nurture the hope that their combined rhetorical prowess would ease the passage, through contentious domestic forums, of the formulations concocted abroad.

The officials who sustained their global community were often pitted against those from their own countries who saw every concession to multilateral thinking as a weakening of the nation's defences against a threatening global environment. The most important gap between 'global' officials and fearful constituencies was to be found in the United States, where public servants imbued with Roosevelt's New Deal and Secretary of State Cordell Hull's free trade, had continually to look over their shoulders to a Congress that cherished protection and saw socialism in full employment policies. That most cosmopolitan of Australian economists, D. B. Copland, once penned a vignette of the gulf between such officials and many businessmen. Copland's contacts with like-minded officials and academics in the United States had not prepared him for the businessmen whom he met in New York in 1944.

> I tried in my most persuasive manner to introduce them to the idea of the soothing and stimulating effects of Governmental activity on certain well-defined lines. To my surprise it was received with very great resistance. We had a long and vigorous argument and for the first time, in spite of the party and an excellent dinner, I felt depressed about the state of opinion. They were certainly a lot of barbarians who look upon the Government of the United States with much more animosity than they would look upon the Government of Paraguay.[6]

The gap between such 'barbarians' and the academics and officials with whom Copland was more familiar helped to undermine such internationalist projects as the ITO. A growing sense of the fragility of the international official community – its lack of a politically firm and intellectually effective institutional base – helped to persuade Coombs not to take the leap into international public service in 1948.

Coombs the Keynesian

COOMBS HAS THE reputation of being a Keynesian economist. That is true, in the sense that he advised governments that they could and should *manage the total demand for goods and services* so as to assure paid employment to every willing worker, while avoiding inflation. Yet Coombs was not an uncritical follower of John Maynard Keynes' theories and prescriptions. Political engagement made him pragmatic in appraising economic theory. In *Trial Balance* he explained that

> The establishment of any conceptual framework as the basis for discussion about policy in the practical administration of public affairs cannot, as it might be in Academe circles, be a matter simply of rational debate. Discussion of theory as such does not occur – it emerges, disguised in layman's language, as the basis for choice between possible options. If a consensus develops about it, it does so because it helps resolve conflict and so provides a more widely acceptable basis for action.[1]

The transformative impact of Keynes' *General Theory of Employment, Interest and Money* (1936) on intellectuals such as Coombs has been much mythologised. His and others' memories of the 'Keynesian revolution' evince a yearning for an unproblematic alignment of economic and political reason. The phrase 'Keynesian revolution' evokes a golden moment in the twentieth century, in which liberalism seemed to have produced a practically workable model of capitalism, and in which economists owned that model and were being invited by governments to apply it. In 1967, the indexer of *The General Theory*, David Bensusan-Butt, recalled finding in *The General Theory* 'joyful revelation in dark times ... The mystery of contemporary iniquity had been unveiled by a masterpiece of sustained intellectual effort.' In Keynes' vision of a reformed capitalism, Bensusan-Butt had found 'everything and more the Fabian generation had looked for in socialism: it was morally speaking egalitarian, it was fully employed, it was generous and gay; it was a very new sort of capitalism controlled not by the greedy votaries of Mammon but by the intellect and *joie de vivre* of an intelligent and robust democracy'. *The General Theory* 'gave a rational basis and a moral appeal for a faith in the possible health and sanity of contemporary mankind such as the youths of my generation found nowhere else'.[2]

Three years later, Coombs spoke in similar terms to ABC listeners. For many of his generation, it had been hard to see 'in Stalin's Russia the model of a Utopia of which the young could dream and, as for revolution, its techniques had been taken over by the irrational right'. What Keynes offered

> was unexciting enough – only a new understanding of the workings of the economic system. But it gave us justification for and words to express our scorn for the

stupidity and ineptitude of our elders and the grounds to believe that we who shared this new enlightenment could end this miserable mean-spirited chaos of the great depression for ever. It made it possible for us to face the war without despair, believing that if we survived we could set mankind fair with following wind on the way to a new society.[3]

Ten years later Coombs remembered the publication of *The General Theory* as 'for me and many of my generation the most seminal intellectual event of our time'.[4]

In the memoirs of Bensusan-Butt and Coombs we find: (1) reasoned iconoclasm, taken up by (2) critical youth, and (3) applied to government in a far-reaching and ultimately effective reform of capitalism. That story simplifies Coombs' complex response to Keynes' work.

When he joined the Commonwealth Bank in Sydney, Coombs kept in touch with John La Nauze. In 1937 La Nauze sent Coombs a downcast paper titled 'Economic Theory and Economic Practice'. What could economics as a discipline do to win the respect of politicians and the public? La Nauze asked. After canvassing a number of explanations for economists' lack of authority, La Nauze was unable to point out any way forward. He led the reader towards the conclusion that economists' authority was ever fragile. Would the demands of the looming war lead to a better economics or to better standing for economists? La Nauze doubted it. Indeed, 'I do not think that there is likely to be any revolution by which the world will turn from its irrationality to the comparative rationality of economic theory.' It is most likely, he thought, that economists 'will be driven to escape into the worlds of elegant equilibria, or the history of doctrine, where we know we are safe'.

La Nauze was wrong in his prognosis: World War II was the making of economists, because it forced them into a relatively unified policy stance favouring a popular program – full employment – and because governments hired economists in order to run the war economy and to project a peace which might inspire hard-pressed citizens.

La Nauze's paper does not corroborate Coombs' and Bensusan-Butt's memory that at the end of the 1930s early career economists were seized with joyous optimism upon reading *The General Theory*. La Nauze's passing references to Keynes' book conveyed no such feeling.[5] Nor was Coombs immediately persuaded by Keynes' 'General Theory'. In June 1936 he told La Nauze that he was meeting weekly with Ronald Walker, Hermann Black, Sydney Butlin and Lesley Melville 'to chew this book over. … At the moment I am not impressed – but am trying to keep an open mind.'[6] Coombs evidently attached some notes to this letter, but they have not survived. Later, he wrote again on Keynes:

I hear from [Jock] Phillips that you have been wrestling with Keynes and find him a pain in the neck. I am struggling with him too … so far I am more irritated than anything. His habit of having half a chapter of close and difficult analyses and then slipping into general criticism of the system which does not follow from the analysis is damned annoying. Of course the crux of the business is the theory of interest and there I think he's about half wrong.

And later in this letter: 'By the way don't you think Keynes puts things into the mouths of Malthus and others when he seeks for his intellectual ancestors?'[7]

In two subsequent letters Coombs outlined his dissatisfactions with *The General Theory*. He doubted Keynes on the rate of interest.

> Keynes' work I found unsatisfying and yet it seemed to me to have one aspect of truth – that interest is predominantly a monetary phenomenon. He goes wrong in confining the influence of the quantity of money to the yield on fixed money claims. The idea that I have been trying to follow up is that money is one form of property – the others being fixed money claims, equities, durable consumption goods and goods for immediate consumption and that a person at any time distributes his available wealth between those different forms in the way which gives him the maximum net satisfaction from the point of view of liquidity, income, immediate satisfaction, etc. So that the rate of interest will not (as Keynes suggests) merely be the rate which will make it worth while for people to hold money balances equal in aggregate to the quantity of money but that rate which establishes a relationship of relative attractiveness of the various forms of property as a result of which people will hold money balances equal in aggregate to the quantity of money. What this means is
> 1. that the changes in the quantity of money affect the attractiveness of all forms of property
> 2. that equilibrium in money holdings is restored not by changes in the rate of interest only but by a reshuffling of all the forms of property
> 3. that the effects of any change in the quantity of money will be different according to where they come into the economy.[8]

Coombs was here pursuing a thought that would later be developed by Milton Friedman.[9] The theoretical background of his response to Keynes was certainly eclectic, 'the result as far as I can trace it of reading Cannan, von Mises and Melville'.[10]

Coombs' second substantive criticism of *The General Theory* concerned the problem of conceptualising and measuring the propensity to consume – a point on which he had published a short article in the *Economic Record*.[11] He thought it impossible

> to aggregate schedules of individuals whose actual incomes are widely different, since the range of income for which their respective schedules would be valid would not coincide. At best it may be possible to talk of the propensity to consume of a representative individual – a very doubtful concept.[12]

These were not minor points of disagreement. Keynes' thoughts on the determinants of the rate of interest and on the propensity to consume were central to his 1936 book and have been much debated.

Coombs also found Keynes, for all his critique of classical economics, limited by the framework of a discredited liberalism. Without mentioning Keynes, Coombs set out his thoughts on economics as a form of liberalism when commenting on La Nauze's paper 'Economic Theory and Economic Practice'. Coombs argued that history had eroded the critical authority of economics. Economists' credibility had been high when their *laissez-faire* assumptions and convictions had expressed the interests of 'the rising small capitalist class ... the most dynamic section of the community', Coombs suggested. Now that capitalists were bent on maintaining 'large-scale monopolistic units', they no longer welcomed liberal economists' strictures against interference with markets. And, if LSE political theorist Harold Laski were right in seeing the state as the instrument of 'predominant groups in the community', then economists could now expect no more sympathetic a hearing from governments. Because there could be no return to capitalism's earlier *laissez-faire* stage, Coombs concluded, it was futile for economists to 'cry for the moon of free competition'.

So to what critical relevance might economists aspire? he asked. Either economists could cease to make any critique of capitalism and simply describe, without judgment, its contemporary dynamics; or economists could develop a critical conception of 'welfare' and throw themselves into the political process.[13] The war enabled Coombs to do the latter.

A year later, Coombs suggested to La Nauze that if there were hope for economics it lay in:

1. the adoption of a theory of the state
2. the willingness to consider people making economic decisions in statistical groups about which it would be possible to make judgments as to behaviour which would have [hold?] true for the group but not necessarily for the individual
3. the willingness to abandon the search for certainty and to base economics consciously upon probabilities.
   Of course if Economists will do this – they will reject equally the fictions of liberal economics and the limited interventions of Keynes, Meade, Harrod and co.[14]

Although this is not as clear a comment as one might wish to read, it demonstrates that Coombs had not yet found what he sought in Keynes' liberalism.

We are entitled to doubt Coombs' recollections of his Keynesian hierophany in *Trial Balance*, and Melville's recollection that 'Coombs ... went the whole way with Keynes.'[15] Yet Coombs was Keynesian in another sense. The demands of war developed his understanding of economics from the point of view of the statesman. The war economy – full employment without inflation – required a social contract.

In his 1940 pamphlet *How to Pay for the War*, Keynes argued that the government needed to secure the British population's consent to the privations of war. 'In peace time ... the size of the cake depends on the amount of work done. But in war time the size of the cake is fixed. If we work harder, we can fight better. But we must not consume more.'[16] How to get the public to deny itself? Keynes admitted that in his first thoughts on the war economy – two articles in *The Times* in November 1939 titled 'Paying for the War' – he had ignored this issue, for he had been

mainly concerned with questions of financial technique and did not secure the full gain in social justice for which this technique opened the way. In [How to Pay for the War] I have endeavoured to snatch from the exigency of war positive social improvements. The complete scheme now proposed, including universal family allowances in cash, the accumulation of working-class wealth under working-class control, a cheap ration of necessaries, and a capital levy (or tax) after the war, embodies an advance towards economic equality greater than any which we have made in recent times.[17]

When four Australian economists – Butlin, Critchley, McMillan and Tange – reviewed the first twenty months of the war economy in 1941, they did not ask whether a program of social justice was essential to winning popular cooperation with the imposed privations of war. They set aside issues of the distributional effects of war-time taxes. They could not ignore completely the political challenges of the war economy, but where Keynes laid out a program which might woo the masses to its disciplines, Butlin and Co. evinced a fear and loathing of the public. Not for them Keynes' invocation of a public hunger for 'social justice'. Rather, these Australian economists were scornfully apprehensive of the public's tendency 'to be carried away by muddled catch-cries'.

> The economic superstition which passes for theory about the mysterious virtues of the Commonwealth Bank, the sedulously cultivated doctrine of 'maintain private spending', and the indestructible faith in unlimited idle resources, make it extremely difficult for any uncourageous government to avoid inflationary finance. Reinforcing the faith in witch words are the natural disinclination to face unpleasant readjustments of living habits, and the equally natural tendency to identify the interest of one's class with those of the community.[18]

Butlin and his colleagues favoured taxation as a way to raise war finance, but they did not declare support for any particular mix of taxes and so, unlike Keynes, they declined to let the problem of political consent to the war economy shape their consideration of that economy's fiscal techniques. When they turned, unavoidably, to the question of how to win popular consent to restrictions on consumption, the four Australian economists could appeal only to the necessity for government 'propaganda' – a term whose lame centrality to their discourse was not noticed by whoever compiled the book's index.[19]

Australia Foots the Bill differed from *How to Pay for the War* in the paucity of its political and social vision, and in its effective refusal to consider the psychological and ideological underpinning of a war economy. In their lack of political imagination, these economists were 'essentially unKeynesian'.

That is, until the last few pages of their book. There Butlin and his colleagues *did* express an opinion about the Menzies government's taxes: they were too regressive, and this was 'inefficient'. More money could be raised if the government would target the better-off. As well, the economists were critical of the Menzies government's decision to use loans from the Commonwealth Bank. To counter the inflationary effects of this increase in the money supply, Australians should be required to set aside some of their money until after the war. Less-well-off consumers could be invited to divert their expenditure into 'contributory unemployment and old-age insurance and similar social services'. Whatever was done to siphon off the public's money, its impact should be progressive: 'Any scheme of finance which does not conform to these principles is not a Keynes Plan.'[20]

In *Australia Foots the Bill* four Australian economists' stance towards the public was as defensive and contemptuous, until its final pages, as Keynes' was open and sympathetic. In Keynes' 1940 pamphlet the questions of fiscal technique and of popular acceptability are not separated. Rather, Keynes saw the policy's technical worth as inseparable from its political soundness. As Director of Rationing and as exponent of the 'positive approach', Coombs was rather more like Keynes in his willingness to consider popular political acceptability as integral to sound economic policy.

Does this mean that Coombs – whatever his doubts about Keynes the theorist – was Keynesian in his politics? Coombs' 'positive approach' to trade liberalisation is of Keynesian inspiration – but Coombs and Keynes were at odds in their full employment diplomacies.

Keynes was highly critical of nations that strove, above all, to maintain a large surplus of export earnings over import spending. There had long been an economic orthodoxy – associated with Britain's erstwhile dominance within the global economy – that, in order to keep the nation a net creditor in its financial dealings with the rest of the world, internal interest rates should be kept high (attracting other nation's currencies) and wages (a major cost of production) low. High domestic interest rates and low wages enabled a nation to attract more currency than it spent. Alternative ways to maintain a positive balance of payments, such as altering the value of the currency or restricting the flow of money in and out of the country, were regarded in British governing circles as not 'sound', because they compromised the sanctity of the pound sterling as a medium in which the value of other currencies was to be measured.

To Keynes the folly of such high interest/low wages policies had been demonstrated in the economic stagnation of the 1920s and 1930s. Recovery from the Depression would have been quicker had interest rates been kept low (to encourage investment), had governments spent freely, and had the value of wages been maintained (to encourage spending on the products from which investors hoped to profit). If such recovery policies caused a nation's balance of payments to fall into the negative, then either this was a short-term problem which should be tolerated, or, if the problem persisted, it was better to change the value of the currency or to intervene in the flow of money in and out of the nation.

Nations that refused to manipulate the value of their currency, while wishing nonetheless to avoid the social upheavals of a high interest/low wages strategy, were tempted to the only other apparent option. Keynes pointed this out in the penultimate chapter of *The General Theory* – aggressive trade policies. But that was a flawed option: aggressive trade policies required some nations to fail if others were to succeed, giving rise to 'increasingly internecine' international relations – war and/or increased protectionism.

Thus Keynes argued that governments should not be so obsessed with their balance of payments. The primary objective of economic policy should rather be to encourage investment, employment and consumer spending consistent with full employment. While the resulting prosperity of the domestic market would stimulate your imports, if other nations enjoyed full employment they would be prosperous enough to buy more of your exports. Keynes foreshadowed Coombs' 'positive approach', when he remarked that 'it is the *simultaneous pursuit* of these policies by all countries together which is capable of restoring economic health and strength internationally, whether we measure it by the level of domestic employment or by the volume of international trade'.[21]

However, during the war, Keynes enacted his internationalism by focusing not on the link between trade and employment but on the currency arrangements that enabled trade. Preoccupied with arguing for his International Clearing Union, Keynes neither declared nor even developed a view on the future rules of international trade until after the war, when he heard US government officials explain the trade policies they would expect Britain to endorse if the American public was to support lending Britain billions of dollars for reconstruction.[22]

Keynes' concern with currency was pertinent to the rivalry between Britain and the United States. Britain had damaged its own social fabric, he thought, by persisting in maintaining sterling as the currency in which much of the world's trading bills were paid. Keynes' proposed International Clearing Union would have created a genuinely international currency. No single country would have been able to hold so much of that unit of exchange that other nations had insufficient for their own buying and selling. In advocating the International Clearing Union Keynes attempted to make it unnecessary (and indeed impossible) for the US dollar to succeed the British pound as the world's financial centre.

In 1943, Keynes' pursuit of his reform determined his attitude to Coombs' first statements of full employment diplomacy. Coombs went to London after Hot Springs, in June 1943. He dined with Keynes in a restaurant off Piccadilly. Coombs recalled him as 'stimulating and charming' – 'making the colonial boy at home'.[23] In July 1943 Coombs wrote to Keynes asking if he agreed that there should soon be an international conference on 'international collaboration to maintain employment and incomes'.[24] On 3 September, having consulted his British colleagues, and sharing their uncertainty as to how to reply with tact, Keynes assured Coombs that although 'we do not differ about the importance of the subject [of employment]', the British preferred to tackle unemployment 'indirectly'. An international conference on global employment policy 'might find itself overmuch concerned with what were little better than pious resolutions'.[25] In 1943–4, Keynes' aim was to influence the US government. To advocate an international commitment to full employment to a New Deal administration that was already on the defensive domestically for its leanings towards socialism, would have placed an avoidable burden on British diplomacy. The Australian emphasis on full employment as a condition of free trade was seen by some North Atlantic officials as Australia's ingenious, but disingenuous, way to avoid the challenge of free trade. British officials such as Keynes could not afford to be seen to be proposing something as novel as 'the positive approach' while bargaining with the Americans on the design of post-war currency arrangements.

My final comparison of Coombs' and Keynes' approach to post-war policies concerns wages. In drafting the White Paper on full employment in 1944–5, Post-war Reconstruction officials, including Coombs, faced one of the puzzles of the Keynesian approach: in an economy in which the demand for labour slightly exceeds supply, how would governments limit trade unions' pursuit of higher money-wages? Stalking this issue through Keynes' published and unpublished writings, Richard Kahn concluded that Keynes' thoughts on the money-wage problem were 'unsystematic and unsatisfactory'. In a 1943 debate with Friedrich von Hayek, Keynes acknowledged that it 'remains to be seen' whether 'a capitalist country is doomed to failure because it will be found impossible in conditions of full employment to prevent a progressive increase in wages'. In correspondence in 1943 and 1944, Keynes suggested that the problem was not one for economic theory but for politicians to solve.[26] When the Australian White Paper on full employment appeared in 1945, Keynes remarked to McFarlane, Secretary of the Australian Treasury: 'One is also, simply because one knows no solution, inclined to turn a blind eye to the wages problem in a full employment economy.'[27]

As I have shown, Coombs and his colleagues did not turn a blind eye. Stimulated by another of Keynes' students, Joan Robinson, their early drafts of the White Paper explored the political economy of wage earnings in the new social order. However, the political sensitivities of the Labor Cabinet forbade all but cursory mention of wages policy, full employment capitalism's most important policy issue.

Part 6

From Labor to Liberal

Chifley's 'family'

COOMBS ONCE PAID sometime Treasury officer Frederick Wheeler a compliment: 'Fred was really good at drafting compromises.'[1] To be a high-level policy bureaucrat is to be a member of a rather fractious 'team'. The maintenance of such teams requires leavening the will to win with an underlying desire not to jeopardise the existence of the team itself.

Coombs' 'team' ethic is implicit in his assessment of Alf Conlon. Though he had Curtin's ear in 1942, Conlon's eccentricities of manner and his disposition towards the big picture rather than the administrative mechanism made him a legendary outrider of the political elite. Shortly after becoming Director-General of Post-war Reconstruction, Coombs confided to R. C. Mills that he was finding it difficult to decide how best to use Conlon because Chifley, 'while he regards him as a very pleasant fellow, is convinced he is quite mad'.[2] Six years later, Coombs told Chifley that Conlon had been

> badly spoilt by having too much influence and authority during the war and he acquired then an unfortunate habit of intrigue. Furthermore, he has a serious tendency to be extravagant in his approach to most questions. At the same time he is without doubt a man of very considerable ability. ... Despite his serious faults I feel that he is a vigorous and colourful personality with qualities which could prove of real value. I feel a little reluctant to see this colour and intelligence lost to the service of the government.[3]

In Coombs' phrase 'spoilt by having too much influence and authority' we find an ethic of collegial moderation. The advisers of government had not only to respect the ultimate authority of the elected politician, they had also to ensure each other's speaking rights. The culture of officialdom was a competitive collegiate. You 'intrigued' as little as possible, and you could be 'spoiled', over time, if your influence was inordinate, that is, unchecked by opposing arguments. The ideal product of intellectual combat within the competitive collegiate was consensus expressed in submissions to Cabinet. Consensus was more a victory for the collegiate itself than a triumph for any individual within it.

The culture of the senior Commonwealth public service changed in the 1940s. Up to 1939 the ethos of the public service had been determined by the policy of giving preference in recruitment to soldiers returned from World War I. 'Partly as a result of pressure upon the Government by returned soldiers' organisations and partly as a manifestation of Australia's rather tenacious pride in its ANZACs, veteran appointment [had] been a cardinal feature of Commonwealth recruitment policy.'[4] In 1933 the *Public Service Act* had been amended to authorise appointment of university graduates provided that they were from an Australian university and under twenty-five years of age, that they started on the base grade of Third Division and that such recruits did not exceed 10 per cent of the positions proposed to be filled in any year. The British Economic Mission in 1929 had reinforced the arguments in favour of graduate recruitment that the universities had been putting since 1925.[5] However, the Great Depression so restricted recruitment that by World War II the public service was still 'woefully ill prepared to confront the problems which lay immediately ahead ... the consequences of past recruitment policies had now become fully apparent'.[6]

Many of the more effective war-time officials were drawn from outside. There had been outside recruitment before, but until 1939 these 'lateral' recruits had tended to be doctors, engineers, lawyers, surveyors and architects – 'specialists', in the jargon of public administration. Among senior officers who had acquired expertise through part-time study, accountancy had been the common choice.[7] There were very few economists by 1939. Because of the war-time expansion of the public service, the composition of the higher officers was suddenly altered by an influx of graduate 'generalists', that is, those qualified for a range of policy areas by virtue of their general abilities in analysis and expression. This was particularly true of the Department of Post-war Reconstruction, which 'more than any other [department] epitomized the new administrative role of the federal government'.[8]

Though the distinction between 'generalist' and 'specialist' is fuzzy, the multiple tasks of mobilising and then demobilising a war economy made economics the basis for a general administrative competence. Crisp (with qualifications in both politics and economics) was typical of the new 'generalists' in having obtained his credentials by full-time study rather than at night while working in the public service. He later recalled this cohort's 'energy' and their 'wealth of diverse training and experience'. They felt no 'inferiority, uneasiness or defensiveness in the company of established Commonwealth Public Service professional specialists'. According to Crisp, their sudden influx transformed the atmosphere of the higher levels of the public service, giving 'the generalist side a morale "lift" and a sharper cutting edge'.[9] Coombs recalled the atmosphere of his own Department of Post-war Reconstruction – in 'staff conferences held over weekends' – as 'strangely pentecostal or revivalist ... I know that while I found the conferences physically and emotionally exhausting, they were at the same time, the occasion for a renewal of faith and a regeneration of energy.'[10]

These younger economists challenged the political culture of the Commonwealth public service, affronting both the free trade advocates in Treasury and the protectionists in such departments as Trade and Customs. According to Scarrow, the Department of Trade and Customs at first declined to 'follow the lead of other strategic departments in strengthening its central staff with new recruits'.[11] Treasury proved more responsive to the challenge. Comprehensively reorganised in 1943 – for the first time since 1901 – it now boasted a separate General Financial and Economic Policy Branch to rival the influence of Post-war Reconstruction.[12] As well, 'the positive approach' to employment implied a new federalism that allowed increased national coordination of State budgets.

The Department of Post-war Reconstruction could seem thrusting and theoretical with its novel conceptions of government and economic management. In 1980, Arthur Tange (who moved between External Affairs and Post-war Reconstruction) recalled that 'there was a lot of bitterness about the place and that is likely to happen I'd suggest, when a group of people arrive on the scene, detached from a specific ministerial responsibility ... and impose, or seek to impose, ideas on the rest of the community.'[13] Coombs at one stage 'pulled us all together and said we'd better do better in getting a better acceptance in the Canberra official communities'.[14] Indeed, at such a staff meeting in December 1944, Coombs warned that 'we [the Department of Post-war Reconstruction] are regarded as interlopers'. He urged his officers to persuade other departments 'that we are not out to grab – not out to build up our department at other people's expense'. Liaison with other departments was 'one of our most serious weaknesses'.[15]

In such adversity, Coombs appears to have been a source of strength to his junior officers. One of the binding forces of the competitive collegiate was men- torship – the deliberate cultivation of the talents and loyalties of younger men by older (or bureaucratically/politically senior) men. Some of these methods were informal. Crisp gratefully recalled in 1969 that

> In 1940–42 – the darkest and busiest years of the war – H. C. Coombs and L. F. Giblin made it their business in their own minimal spare time to bring together informally at night, once a fortnight, a group of recently recruited young social science graduates in Treasury, the Bureau of Statistics, and the Reconstruction Division of Labour and National Service to anatomize, write papers about and discuss recent books by J. M. Keynes, D. H. Robertson, and J. A. Schumpeter on theoretical or applied issues in political economy and public finance.

He recalled being persuaded 'that there was a value set by our Service seniors in intellectual exploration for its own sake as well as for the sake of our daily service tasks – that a career in the Service was intellectually satisfying and in that sense truly "professional"'.[16] In 1980 Coombs commented that J. L. S. (Luke) Heywood, a young officer in the Department of Labour and National Service and sometime secretary of the F&E Committee, had been this group's 'driving force'.[17] According to Trevor Swan, Coombs' fondness for such discussion and for 'intellectual exploration for its own sake' sometimes provoked the old hands' teasing. In 1948, Swan wrote to Coombs from London, reporting that the Secretary of the Treasury, McFarlane, seemed in a recent London conference on currency management to have become more sympathetic to economic planning. 'It was most refreshing to hear Mac plugging vigorously for the Sterling Area counterparts of the kind of approach which in Canberra he used to call "Coombs' Conferences" or "essay-writing".'[18]

Coombs encouraged promising officers to work in London and the United States when positions became available, and he helped to set up a system of exchange appointments for young economists between the Australian and British governments. When placing Noel Butlin in the care of F. L. McDougall, in

February 1944, Coombs wrote, 'I hope he turns out to be the best man for the job. He has a very good mind and a great capacity for work. He takes life a little bit seriously and is inclined to academic jargon, but to both these faults I am confident you will provide an invaluable corrective.'[19]

Coombs was impressed by Trevor Swan – 'one of the very best theoretical economists we have ever produced in Australia'.[20] Swan had graduated from the University of Sydney early in the war, taught there in 1940–1 and then moved on to the Department of War Organisation of Industry. Coombs saw some of him on the War Commitments Committee. 'His theoretical grasp of the structure of the economy, his mastery of statistical techniques, his gift of lucid exposition and his incredible capacity for work made him the effective mainspring of the War Commitments Committee', Coombs recalled.[21]

After the Department of War Organisation of Industry was absorbed into Post-war Reconstruction in 1945, Swan became Chief Economist in Post-war Reconstruction from 1946 to 1950. During Coombs' extended overseas trips 1946–8, Swan carried the Coombs perspective on the Investment and Employment Committee and on the committees overseeing the work of the Australian delegations in London, Geneva and Havana. His gossipy letters to Coombs included anguished accounts of other departments' obdurate protectionism and of Roland Wilson's iron chairmanship of the inter-departmental sub-committee on trade policy. Swan confided to Coombs that he thought he had let Coombs down during the GATT talks in Geneva because he had been so absorbed in combating Trade and Customs' protectionist approach that he had been unable to contribute effectively to the Investment and Employment Committee, a forum in which Post-war Reconstruction attempted to match Treasury in reading the movements of the Australian economy. The effect of these work pressures and feelings of failure, Swan wrote, 'has been a pretty sad state of depression, bad-temper, and near hysteria which has made life miserable for my family and myself and upset even in official matters both my capacity for work and my judgment'. Swan wondered whether he possessed the temperament to be a good public servant. His letter to Coombs in May 1947 was something of an act of self-therapy, in which he identified as self-destructive his 'myth of indispensability' and his associated feelings of guilt about wanting to get out of Canberra for a while.

Coombs had arranged with Sir Edward Bridges, the UK Secretary of the Treasury, for Swan to spend twelve months working in the Economic Division of the British Cabinet Office. Yet with Coombs taking longer in Geneva than anyone had anticipated, it was difficult to know when Swan should leave for London.[22] Coombs' concern for Swan's condition is shown in his request to the man who would be Swan's boss in London, R. L. Hall, that Swan enjoy 'a period of relative freedom from direct responsibility during which he can refresh himself physically and intellectually'.[23] After six months in London (he left Australia in August 1947), Swan reported to Coombs, then in the final stages of the Havana marathon: 'Knowing that you would not grudge me a little light relief, I have organised myself to Paris for a few days next week'.[24] Coombs, nominally the person to authorise Swan's travel, must have been delighted.

The senior officers who encouraged their juniors also cannibalised their best work. When Coombs received copies of Hartley Grattan's edited book *Australia*, in which he had a piece on 'reconstruction', he gave one to Gerald Firth, referring to that chapter 'which I contributed and you wrote'.[25] Writing speeches was a collective effort in which Coombs drew heavily on his officers' notes and verbal discussions. Named authorship was a perquisite of hierarchy. Looking after your best and brightest was therefore a matter of Coombs' self-interest, as well as expressing his affection and respect. In the jockeying for influence over Australia's post-war economy, Coombs' quest for good staff put him in competition with universities (he lost Firth to Tasmania in 1947) and with other Commonwealth departments.[26]

Chifley was the mentor of mentors. His 'very human characteristics together with an innate politeness … did more than anything else to build up such a firm line of respect and affection between Mr. Chifley and his chief official advisers', recalls William Dunk. 'One can say without detracting from rugged male relationship that we loved him'.[27] Crisp likened this network of officials orbiting Chifley to 'a sort of "official family"', that is,

> a group of ministers, senior, and even a few not so senior, officials who came in time, quite informally, to be marked out as part of the group one might expect to find meeting together at any of the Cabinet Sub-committees, Interdepartmental Committees or more or less unofficial *ad hoc quasi*-committee meetings where policy issues were analysed and thrashed out on their way to Chif or to Chif and his colleagues, for final determination.[28]

The family metaphor captures the element of mentorship (fathers and sons, older and younger brothers) as well as the network's blend of warmth and competition (for 'father' Chifley's ear). Crisp was not the only writer to be attracted to the family metaphor. D. B. Copland, in a letter to his protégé Dick Downing, referred to 'my family in Melbourne and my other family in Canberra'.[29]

If Chifley was the father of this family, who was mother? A diary entry by Mrs Giblin is piquant. On 19 July 1942, she and her husband were dinner guests at Copland's home. 'During the meal Mr. Chifley talked about electioneering experiences', she recorded. Chifley seemed to her 'a shrewd and honest man' but he was 'not used to talking to women. When he was sitting opposite me at table and telling these experiences he turned to DBC [Copland] and then to Dick [Downing], back and forth, back and forth.'[30] Indeed, the family seems to have been very much a man's world, its helpful informalities and solidarities under-written by the shared pleasure of masculine company – not only in committee rooms but in the Golf Club, the hotel bar and on the cricket field. Crisp's unpublished 1971 memoir of the war-time Canberra YMCA cricket team tells us that, by virtue of its composition, it became the *de facto* Post-war Reconstruction team in the local competition. It included, at times, Coombs, Allen Brown, Pike Curtin, Tange, Grenfell Rudduck, Colin Dean, R. Markham, Bill Palethorpe, Ron Mendelsohn, John Beaumont, Gerald Firth, Noel Butlin, Crisp, and sometimes Paul Hasluck.[31]

Officials such as Downing, Copland, Coombs and Crisp had to spend a lot of time away from their wives and children, in the service of the government, because the organs of state were spread over three cities – Canberra, Melbourne and Sydney. When Coombs was seconded to Treasury in 1939, he and Lallie moved to Canberra, in the suburb of Forrest. Coombs could walk to his office, threading his way through the grazing sheep, sometimes in the company of Gough Whitlam's father. For Lallie, Canberra was 'grim', a 'ghastly town'. Instead of attending composition classes at the Sydney conservatorium, she could now join a weekly sock-knitting group, or play bridge, with other stranded wives.[32] In 1942 the Coombs moved to Melbourne, Rationing's headquarters. At the end of that year, posted back to Canberra, Lallie said that since Coombs was so often away, she might as well live in the city of her choice. They bought a house in Cremorne, and Coombs continued to move between Sydney, Melbourne and Canberra – and occasionally overseas – knowing that his wife, at least, had what she regarded as a home. As Director-General, based in Canberra, he lived much of his life at an hotel, thus commencing an enduring pattern of domestic life that he described in 1989 as being his family's 'occasional visitor'.[33]

Senior Commonwealth officials, during the war, could not avoid this deracinated life. Melbourne had been the seat of Commonwealth government until 1927, when the Public Service Board began to transfer the central divisions of certain departments to Canberra. Most of the departments created after 1938, under pressure of impending war and then of war itself, were nonetheless based in Melbourne. There was simply no room for them in Canberra – neither office space nor staff housing. Thirteen new departments, including War Organisation of Industry, chose Melbourne, a centre of manufacturing, and only the new Prices Branch of Trade and Customs, External Affairs, Home Security and Post-war Reconstruction were set up with their head offices in Canberra. Coombs' desire that his department be in Canberra owes much to his anticipation of rivalry with Treasury and Trade and Customs, both of which had had their central staff in the bush capital since 1927.[34] Sydney was important not only as the other great manufacturing and trading city but also as the headquarters of the Division of Import Procurement and of the US Lend-Lease Mission. For Coombs and others, it was not unusual to have meetings in each of the three capitals in one week. Paul Hasluck, who was there, later wrote of senior public servants' 'eternal peregrination of 1,500 miles per week around the Melbourne, Sydney, Canberra triangle'.[35] Interstate train travel could give rise to valuable contacts among policy-minded intellectuals. When Coombs wrote to J. D. G. Medley in March 1944 to share his thoughts about policies to limit city sizes and to develop neglected regions, he was continuing a conversation which had commenced on a rail journey on the Spirit of Progress a fortnight earlier.[36] John Dedman 'was an enthusiastic train traveller because it was an opportunity to meet senior public servants like H. C. Coombs' (before Dedman became Coombs' Minister).[37] To be so much on the move, away from family and home, made convivial colleagues a family.

The binding of Chifley's family was the power of Cabinet itself. Coombs recalled with pleasure the inclusiveness of the Labor Cabinet's relationships with its senior officers.

I've known no other government which did it. They used Cabinet sub-Committees quite a lot as an instrument of Government during the war … the members of the Cabinet who are on it used to take at Chifley's request, their Senior Departmental officers. I always went to the meetings with this Cabinet sub-Committees on economic matters. So did several other permanent Heads, and the meetings were conducted in two phases. The first phase was a kind of discussion of the issues that they had before them in which the Public Servants participated almost as freely as the Ministers, but as you got towards the stage … approaching decision there was … almost unnoticed a … withdrawal, not physical withdrawal, where the officials sort of stepped back.[38]

Such authority was mediated by bonds between powerful individuals. The Chifley–Wheeler relationship was very important, Crisp recalled, though Wheeler could not necessarily count on Chifley's agreement. Sometimes Chifley preferred Coombs' advice, and sometimes he refused to choose. 'I remember on one occasion pressing Chifley to decide an issue about which Fred Wheeler and I had been battling for some time. He replied, "Doc, don't ask me to choose between you and Fred. Go away and fight it out." '[39] Paternal wisdom in handling filial rivalry.

Chifley sometimes called Coombs 'son'. When Coombs was in Geneva, in 1947, trying to persuade the United States to lower the tariff on Australian wool, he conveyed what he thought to be a good result to Canberra. Soon he was 'staggered' to learn from Chifley, over the phone, that Cabinet rejected his proposal.

After the months of work with their alternations of confidence and despair this decision was like a punch in the solar plexus at the end of a fifteen-round fight. I must have sounded defeated because Chifley said gently, 'You're pretty disappointed son?' 'Yes', I said, 'I thought we had got a pretty good deal.' 'So you have', he responded, 'but we think you can do better still.'[40]

Coombs did, and (for this and other services to the Curtin and Chifley governments) he was rewarded. On 23 November 1948, Chifley announced that he had appointed Coombs to be Governor of the Commonwealth Bank of Australia.

Coombs had now to consider the feelings of those who had mentored him. His senior by twenty-one years, 'Misery Mac' McFarlane – writing from his IMF directorship in Washington – seemed to congratulate not only Coombs but himself for Coombs' 'coveted honour and responsible post'.

I can derive some personal satisfaction out of the appointment when I remember how I discovered you in the Bank and after some persuasion induced the Chairman and Governor to let you come to me for twelve months. I also recollect them pressing strongly for your return, but I resisted, and continued to hand to you some of the cream of Treasury jobs which gave you your opportunity from which you never looked back. I was always sorry you left me and some day we might exchange impressions of why you did so.[41]

Coombs thanked him and added: 'Perhaps you can look on this as a return of the wanderer to the fold.'[42]

Douglas Copland, his senior by twelve years and by an academic generation, recalled his earliest conversation with Coombs – about the Bank, on a London bus in 1933 – and made the offer: 'You will need neither help nor guidance from people like me, but you will know that you will always have a word of friendly counsel on any matter on which it is possible to be of assistance.'[43]

By far the most difficult reckoning was with Melville – the mentor rivalled and surpassed. Melville had marked his MA thesis in 1931 and then become his 'boss' in 1935; he had been 'generous, friendly and stimulating in that role'.[44] In 1947, Coombs had suggested Melville to be the first Vice-Chancellor of the nascent Australian National University. He told R. C. Mills, chair of the university's Interim Council: 'I know you will recall him in more difficult days, and I know that he did have a gift for rubbing people up the wrong way in his more dogmatic youth, but he has mellowed a great deal and has learned in the Bank to deal in a friendly way with people who regard him with some suspicion.'[45] Now that Melville had been passed over for the Governorship, Coombs felt 'some anxiety' about his attitude.[46] No less an authority than Giblin said that the Governorship should have been Melville's, and that Coombs was the next best appointment.[47] Coombs agreed, assuring Giblin: 'I have given that advice in the appropriate quarter. Since, however, it was not taken, I am anxious that I should have the benefit of Melville's help.' He told Giblin that he would soon try to arrange a short-term academic appointment for Melville, to enable him 'to relax and refresh himself'.[48] The association with Melville was worth nurturing.

The commanding heights?

WITH THE ARRIVAL of peace, the Department of Post-war Reconstruction's days were numbered.

In 1944, the Curtin government had decided to absorb the Department of War Organisation for Industry into the Department of Post-war Reconstruction. Coombs had asked Chifley in September 1944 to consider the resulting agency (to be called Post-war Reconstruction) as 'a Cabinet staff for economic planning' responsible to the Prime Minister or to a senior Cabinet Minister who would chair a Cabinet sub-committee dealing with questions of economic and social policy. The plans issuing from this sub-committee would be for various departments to execute.

To deal with all such issues of the peace-time structure of government, Coombs suggested that Chifley form a special committee to report to the Prime Minister on the allocation of functions between departments, on ways to decentralise Commonwealth administration, on collaboration between Commonwealth, State, regional and local government, and on the recruitment, education, training and remuneration of public service officers.[1] In June 1945 the government set up a review under the Public Service Board's John Pinner to deal with the first of these topics.

As his Department's representative on the Pinner Committee, Coombs argued that Post-war Reconstruction should monitor the economic initiatives of all three levels of government and of all private firms. He named some of the staff required, including lawyer Allen Brown, who had been his 'investigations' officer in the Rationing Commission and whom Coombs praised as 'familiar with the wider social, institutional and legal background in which economic policy has to be carried out'. In addition, Coombs wanted Trevor Swan as his Director of Economic Research and Planning. He would draw other staff from the old Department of War Organisation of Industry. To direct the peace-time full employment economy he wanted staff who had controlled the war-time full employment economy.

Pinner recommended that Post-war Reconstruction be succeeded by the Department of the Prime Minister.[2] Until the change of government in December 1949, Coombs and Dedman continued to advocate Pinner's scenario. Their quest reflected both personal ambition and a critique of Treasury. According to Crisp, Dedman aspired to be Treasurer, and calculated that Chifley was more likely to relinquish that portfolio if he retained, in the Department of Prime Minister, a retinue of economists who could brief him as well as he had been briefed as Treasurer.[3] Dedman reiterated the point made by Coombs and repeated by Pinner: that in administering full employment 'many of the matters which arise are "economic"' and so were beyond the 'financial' responsibilities of Treasury.

> If Dr. Coombs had been during the last four or five years a senior Treasury official or the Head of an economic group with Treasury attachments his contribution to [full employment] policy would, I am sure, have been made more difficult. The Treasury is, by tradition, and rightly so, conservative. It is more concerned with the examination and criticism of policies and proposals formulated elsewhere than it is with the preparation of such policies itself.[4]

Treasury countered by suggesting that Brown and his economic policy staff come under their command, in association with their statistics officers. Treasury's advice would be contested, its job made more difficult, if the Prime Minister could rely on his own economists.

In his efforts to secure a commanding, non-Treasury, position within Commonwealth economic policy-making in the years 1944–9, Coombs had also to take into account that Australian federalism continued to allocate much of economic policy to the States. The failure of the Powers Referendum in August 1944 had set the Labor government the challenge of creating machinery for coordinating seven governments' expenditures on public works. In December 1944, Coombs had warned his staff: 'It is no good our resenting the fact that the referendum was defeated. It *was* defeated ... we do tend at times to forget that we did not win.'[5] After much internal discussion about how to phrase the Commonwealth's continuing ambition to coordinate economic policy, the White Paper on full employment had merely endorsed 'the existing machinery for consultation between the Commonwealth and State Governments ... for reviewing and co-ordinating public capital expenditure'.[6] Three weeks after the White Paper's tabling, Gerald Firth expressed dismay at Acting Prime Minister Chifley's evident reluctance to convene the Premiers to discuss its implementation. Chifley's 'statement, that he sees "little opportunity of having frequent conferences of Premiers", is hard to reconcile with government policy laid down in the White Paper,' lamented Firth.[7]

During the war, the seven Australian governments had cooperated through the National Works Council, whose administrative staff were drawn from the Department of Post-war Reconstruction. According to Butlin and Schedvin, the Council's national 'reservoir' of public works – a reservoir to be 'released' whenever and wherever regional unemployment threatened – was not what assured post-war full employment. In the late 1940s, the economy boomed for other reasons. For example, all governments agreed that the housing industry should be encouraged to meet extraordinary demands placed on it at war's end. The programs devised by the Department of Post-war Reconstruction – national works projects, regional planning, rural reconstruction (including soldier settlement), training and education, and housing – were not given the financial backing for which the Department had hoped (with the exception of the university-based Reconstruction Training Scheme). 'Chifley, who had done so much to encourage the flow of new ideas as Minister for Post-War Reconstruction, was primarily responsible, as Prime Minister and Treasurer … for cutting the cloth to fit the cost.'[8]

Whatever the limits of Chifley's vision, the 'official family' was at the height of its strength in the years 1946 to 1949, according to Crisp. The forums of economists' advice included: Full Cabinet, the Defence Council (replacing War Cabinet), and four Cabinet Economic Standing Committees – Trade and Employment, Investment and Employment, Secondary Industries, and Dollar Budget. Each Minister continued to be accompanied to these committees not only by his Permanent Head but also by a senior economist and his offsider. Because there was yet no Cabinet Secretariat, Treasury's Frederick Wheeler worked as a 'quasi-secretariat for the coordination of policy-making'.[9] The Commonwealth Bank was linked to the 'official family'; from 1945 to 1951 its Advisory Board included such officials as McFarlane, Coombs, Melville and (from 1948–9) Roland Wilson.

A central figure within the 'official family', Coombs' policy interests were too many for me to describe. However, one issue allowed him again to suggest to Chifley that Australia should plan its economic development.

As an effect of the war, Australia had accumulated considerable reserves of foreign currency, with the significant exception of US dollars. Through its loyalty to what was known as the 'sterling area' – an agreement between a number of nations, including Australia and Britain, which originated at the beginning of World War II – Australia would exchange its US dollars for British pounds. This maximised the British government's holdings of dollars and thus its ability to trade. A prospering Britain would import Australian produce. The immediate effect of these arrangements was that Australia's overseas funds were held mostly in sterling, facilitating trade within the Commonwealth, but restricting Australians' ability to import from the United States, Canada and Latin America.

Australia's loyalty to these arrangements was arguably contrary to its long-term interests. In 1946 and 1947, Coombs was telling Chifley that the recovery of the British economy was but one of many factors in Australia's long-term prosperity. Australia should be careful not to sacrifice its trading relationship with other countries – the United States now, Asia in the medium- to long-term future – in order to defend the pattern of British–Australian trade. However, Chifley saw reasons to help Britain. It was still Australia's largest customer, and Clement Attlee's Labour government was to be given a chance to carry out its reforms.[10]

Britain's problems were great. At the end of the war, Britain had needed to import from the United States goods of a far greater value than it could sell to the United States. The United States had helped Britain with a loan of $3.75 billion in 1946, as long as Britain promised to allow the free exchange of dollars and pounds. As soon as sterling became 'convertible' on 15 July 1947, the world's currency markets showed such a preference for dollars that Britain had to draw heavily on its US loan, in order to have sufficient dollars to continue to import from the United States. Britain's plunge into a crisis of dollar shortage and sterling weakness affected Australian interests. When Australia wished to convert some of its overseas funds (held in sterling) to dollars, to pay for imports from the United States, the British government appealed to Australia to borrow dollars from the IMF and to restrict imports from the United States. This request tested Chifley's sympathy: he did not want to persuade his party that loyalty to sterling had made Australia a mendicant of the IMF.[11] However nor was Chifley ready to prejudice Australian trade with Britain 'by too precipitately leaving the sterling area in search of an illusory relationship with the United States'.[12]

Coombs was sensitive to this dilemma. His economic diplomacy from 1946 to 1948 explored the potential for Australia to break free of its trade dependency on Britain, by persuading the United States to buy more wool and to maintain a high employment and high import economy. After returning from Havana in March 1948, Coombs accepted that it was not yet the time to leave the sterling area, so unpredictable was the conduct of US economic policy. He suggested that Australia plan economic development so as to minimise the need to import from North America. Some imports could be produced locally – tobacco, chemicals, motor chassis and tractors, tinplate, newsprint, paper and pulp, cloth and yarn – if the government would divert manpower, materials and equipment to them. Meanwhile, Australian exporters, including manufacturers, should be encouraged to target the US market. Thus Australia's post-war currency problems stimulated Coombs' thoughts as an economic development planner.

Coombs was well placed to push a national plan for economic development. Post-war Reconstruction provided the executive support for the Cabinet sub-committee on the dollar problem, and Coombs chaired the committee of departmental officials that serviced these Ministers. He suggested that Chifley convene a new Ministerial Committee made up of the Prime Minister (who was also then Treasurer) and the Ministers for Post-war Reconstruction, Commerce and

Customs, supported by a similarly composed inter-departmental committee. These officials would present economic development plans for Cabinet approval and then work with other agencies – the Bank, Immigration, Labour and National Service, Works and Housing – to implement them. As well, a 'full-time working party at a high level' would need to liaise with business. The government would finance the infrastructure of such a guided economy with borrowings from the International Bank of Reconstruction and Development (later called the World Bank).[13]

At the end of August 1948, Coombs learned that within the British government there was a parallel exploration of economic planning, raising the possibility that Australia and Britain could coordinate the strategic direction of their economies.[14] Coombs visited London in October 1948 for the Prime Ministers' Conference. His talks with British officials produced estimates of the likely shape of world trade in 1952–3, when the United States' economic reconstruction program for Great Britain and Europe (the Marshall Plan) was due to end. Because it was expected that there would still be a world shortage of dollars by then, Coombs and his colleagues began to envisage 'a multilateral trade and payments system for the world as a whole excluding the United States'.[15] Coombs' view of the United States in 1948 mingled hope with realism. In May 1948 he told an audience of Australian economists that he hoped still that the ITO would nudge the United States towards what he called 'more liberal trade policies.'[16] However, in his talks with British officials, six months later, he did not think that Australia should pin its hopes on the United States joining the ITO and honouring its charter.

These London talks marked the end of the trade-focused phase of Coombs' career as an economist. Coombs would be Governor of the Commonwealth Bank from 1 January 1949. In the event, the chief problem of global economic order which Coombs had faced from 1943 to 1948 – the willingness of the United States to spend its dollars on other nations' exports – was resolved by the United States' preparations for war with the Soviet Union. Needing an ally, the United States became less aggressive towards Britain, in 1949, in commercial and currency policies. Britain devalued the pound against the dollar in September 1949 by 30 per cent (with Australia following), making the sterling area's exports more attractive in the United States. Chifley borrowed dollars from the IMF as a substitute for cutting dollar imports.[17] These developments greatly enhanced the sterling area's ability to trade in dollars. With the opening of a military front against the Communist bloc in Korea in 1950, the alliance of capitalist nations, particularly the United States, became massive purchasers of Malayan rubber and tin and Australian wool.[18] In helping to relieve the world's dollar shortage, the Cold War eliminated one context in which Coombs had been developing policies for planned economic growth. From the beginning of 1950, the inflationary risks of re-arming for war became his main concern.

The Cold War and CSIRO

BETWEEN 1945 AND 1949, Coombs became an advocate of the interests of Australia's scientific community. The nascent National University and the Council for Scientific and Industrial Research (CSIR) fell within the portfolio responsibilities of the Minister for Post-war Reconstruction 1945–49, John Dedman. Coombs was involved in the formation of the university and in the reformation of the CSIR. He had to consider two questions facing post-war governments. What scientific research was in Australia's interest? And through what kinds of institutions might governments assure public benefits from science without stifling creative interactions among scientists?

From its founding in 1926 until World War II, the CSIR had contributed to technical advances in grazing and agriculture; in 1937 it began research relevant to manufacturing. The war added new tasks, and the CSIR's staff and budget multiplied by six between 1938 and 1948. In the 1940s, figures in the Chifley government began to ask whether this burgeoning body should remain a statutory corporation. In Britain the government's scientific work was done by a Department. This was not only an issue of administrative rationality. After Hiroshima and Nagasaki, science was more than ever subject to government security concerns.

In August 1943, Britain and the United States made the Quebec Agreement, limiting to themselves the results of research into nuclear weaponry. The United Nations tried to subject nuclear research to international control, but its Atomic Energy Commission lasted only from January 1946 to May 1948, in which month the British government announced that it would develop an 'independent nuclear deterrent'. The internationalist aspirations behind the Atomic Energy Commission were overwhelmed by the rapid polarisation between the Soviet bloc and the capitalist nations of Western Europe and the North Atlantic. In August 1946, by passing the (McMahon) *Atomic Energy Act*, the United States ceased to share classified atomic information with any other nation. In February 1948, a Communist regime was established in Czechoslovakia, and in June of that year the Soviet Union began to blockade Berlin.

It was no longer possible for scientists to present themselves, without scandal, as an international community unto themselves. Sir David Rivett, the CSIR's Chief Executive from 1927 to 1945 and Chair from 1946 to 1949, apprehended the demise of the ethos of science. This 'true son of the Enlightenment' in an address on 'Science and Responsiblity' on 25 March 1947, exhorted the students and staff of Canberra University College to maintain the tradition of pure and fundamental inquiry.[1] He distinguished between science pursuing knowledge for its own sake and science directed towards solving practical problems. 'Fundamental scientific work' was animated by 'a spark, and maybe in many cases a flame, of that divine curiosity that impels men to seek for knowledge, and ultimately for explanation, of all the puzzling circumstances by which he finds himself surrounded'. Science mobilised 'unrestricted, passionate, fearless and I would even venture to say, religious, enthusiasm'. Rivett thought that scientists doing fundamental research made up an ethical community. He lamented the war's attrition of 'feelings of international community (brotherhood if you prefer it)' whose highest expression had been gatherings of senior scientists. The application of science to war had seen scientists' 'enslavement ... accompanied by a rapid decline in the more or less chivalrous immunities recognised by both sides in earlier wars'.

The 'inevitable sequel' of the conscription of science, Rivett argued, was the imposition of secrecy. Nazi Germany had started it, and other countries had been forced to follow. Now science was locked in a struggle to restore the ethos of open exchange. For example, the Australian government was then pondering how to invest in nuclear physics. If it were to be a CSIR program, would the government impose secrecy? That would be both futile and dangerous. Rivett predicted that the technologies of nuclear energy would soon be grasped by scientists all over the world. The bomb was 'only a set of engineering procedures which other nations are certain to develop within a few years'. Humanity's hope lay not in confining nuclear capability to certain nations but in 'international control of nuclear energy ... and there can be no international control where there is national secrecy'. Rivett took heart from the UN Atomic Energy Commission, then fourteen months into its 27-month life. The ethos of fundamental science – the flame, the spark, the religion of humanity – would underpin the ethics of international relations – 'Science and Con-science'.[2]

Coombs saw the practical point of free exchange of information among researchers. In June 1946, he had advised Dedman that the CSIR should not be asked to research 'purely military problems'. Rather, the universities and the CSIR should be encouraged to undertake 'fundamental research', including nuclear research, and the CSIR 'must be free of restrictions on its scientific freedom of discussion and publication'. Military applications of science should be developed within 'specialised organisations closely linked with those to which research is directed'.[3] Coombs was not convinced that there was a 'security' problem that could not be fixed by setting up 'specialised organisations'.

The Australian nuclear physicist Mark Oliphant saw matters as Coombs did, suggesting to Rivett that 'all secret work and all contacts with secrecy' be transferred from the CSIR to the Supply Department, which could 'revel in red stamps and stultify work to their heart's content and CSIR would be free'.[4] Born 1901, Oliphant had been educated at Adelaide University before joining Lord Rutherford at Cambridge University's Cavendish Laboratory. During the war, he had been in the British group working on the Manhattan Project to develop the atomic bomb. Oliphant enjoyed intimate rapport with the Australian government. His advice during the war had prompted Curtin to develop a policy on the ownership and use of Australia's uranium deposits.[5] He and Coombs had been conferring since 1946 about the proposed Australian National University. Oliphant was then Coombs' most important contact with the world of science, and his advice was both forthright and brimming with the political confidence of a nuclear maestro.

Encouraged by Oliphant, Coombs made it his mission to talk Dedman out of making the CSIR into a department. He was not helped by Rivett's rather righteous approach, but nor was he expecting anything better. Coombs' scientist friends tempered their admiration for Rivett with exasperation at his style of leadership. University of Melbourne physiologist R. D. Wright, for example, referred to Rivett as 'little Davie' and described him as 'cranky as a wet hen and ... liable to shoot off his mouth publicly at any minute'.[6]

Dedman would not be an easy Minister for Coombs to turn, however. In the first week of June 1948, Dedman confronted Rivett with an allegation from within the CSIR – a memo written by the security-conscious British émigré scientist A. P. Rowe – that the CSIR's (in)security jeopardised Australia's access to US and British defence-related science. The CSIR Executive (Rivett, I. Clunies Ross, F. Mountjoy, F. White and E. V. Richardson) answered that only its aeronautics program currently had any bearing on defence. Apart from that,

> there is no need for CSIR to receive any secret information or classified material of military significance for carrying out its work, and it does not desire to have such secret information, the possession of which might well be merely an embarrassment. It goes without saying however, that any such material reaching us is meticulously guarded.[7]

Asked by Dedman to comment, Coombs warned against bringing all scientific work under the same 'secrecy' controls, as they would intimidate researchers and hinder their work. Any CSIR work which was currently of military significance should be hived off to the Department of Supply. However, Coombs conceded that there were administrative problems in the CSIR. Its recent rapid growth had rendered it unwieldy and over-centralised – dominated by 'Rivett's scientific stature and personality'.[8] It could be brought within the public service as a special division, structured so as to allow more delegation of research management to small units. He sketched a series of specialised units doing applied research rotating around a hub consisting of a central research institute doing pure research. Staff would move between them, and all would be served by a shared administration and financial staff.[9]

When Chifley talked to Rivett about the possibility of the CSIR becoming a department, he found Rivett fiercely resistant.[10] Coombs forecast 'very serious difficulties in the road' should Dedman persist. The government was beginning to panic, he thought, about 'criticism which to my mind appears substantially unfounded and hysterical'.[11] To Oliphant he wrote that 'these days when public attitudes on questions of security and political ideologies are somewhat hysterical, they [politicians] are continuously on the defensive'.[12] Coombs was worried that necessary administrative reforms would miscarry if security scandals licensed heavy-handed action.

'Hysterical' is an unusually critical word for Coombs to use of his political masters, but the advent of nuclear power generated an atmosphere of derangement. As Sheldon Ungar has reminded us, atomic power possessed a numinous quality in the 1940s: it exuded a sense of the holy in a world from which science had banished God, and it exemplified that powerful core of reality which was just beyond human reason. The numinous, Ungar argues, combines a sense of un-approachability with a sense of overpoweringness. For those who developed and first used it, the bomb was a sacred trust, and that entailed a duty to keep a secret – the 'atomic secret' which, if kept, guaranteed the United States an indefinite invincibility. Thus, in the years immediately after Hiroshima, 'Americans ... put their faith (and fate) in a numinous power and the secret of its creation. ... Loss of the secret was the most terrifying of all possibilities.'[13] Ungar emphasises the political potency of this belief in the existence of the 'atomic secret', until the Soviets exploded their first atomic device in August 1949. 'The idea of a secret was denied by scientists but believed by much of the public and the policy elite.' This perception gave rise to moral panics about the trustworthiness of scientists and about the susceptibility of science to espionage.[14]

The ripples of hysteria radiating from the North Atlantic bothered Coombs. Chifley should remember the CSIR's war service record before entertaining doubts about the loyalty of its personnel. Sure, the government had to address 'United Kingdom uncertainties however unwarranted', and it must also reply to domestic allegations of scientists' lax security. Coombs suggested that CSIR staff 'be required to make some form of affirmation that information coming to their knowledge as a result of their work should be regarded as confidential. This need not affect the full freedom of discussion in the conduct of research nor the right to publish.' The Minister could be empowered 'to ask that publication be *not* undertaken'.[15] In these words, Coombs looked for ways to please everyone.

Two weeks later, Chifley asked Coombs and William Dunk (Public Service Board) to write him a report on the CSIR's restructuring.[16] Rivett was uneasy about Coombs and Dunk, warning Dedman that 'unless they have had personal experience in the organisation and encouragement of scientific research work (and I mean original research work, not just technology) they may not prove to be sound advisers on the main issue'.[17] Rivett's parenthesis distinguished those who lived the ethic of knowledge from those of more instrumental disposition, those seized with the passion of free inquiry from those who had never heard the call of science, the highest of vocations. In ranking Coombs as an outsider to science, he played into Dedman's hands, for Rivett was unlikely to find a better ally against departmentalisation than Coombs.

Coombs sought the counsel of Mark Oliphant and of Henry Tizard, the scientific adviser to the British government.

Oliphant differed from Rivett in seeing no corruption of the ethos of science were scientists to work at times for the military, in secret, and at other times in the open community championed by Rivett. For example CSIR nutritionists could contribute 'secret work on chemical and bacteriological methods for destroying crops and animals, and on defence against such attacks'. Perhaps scientists should do 'a period of military service and then [go] back to a more open life'. Movement between secret and open research institutions would keep both places 'virile'. Scientists, 'like statesmen and civil servants, should be capable of living two lives, one the traditional open life of science, the other the way of military secrecy, if by so doing they can serve their country'. His own situation exemplified this principle: 'while I will have no secret work in the laboratory I consider it my duty and that of my colleagues to help with the problems of military science where our special knowledge is useful'. To Oliphant, Rivett seemed ill-suited, in habits and temperament, to lead a decentralised organisation.[18]

In the second week of September 1948, Coombs flew to London to discuss the future of economic cooperation within the British Commonwealth. Chifley refused his request that he talk with the United Kingdom's senior scientific officers. The Solicitor-General, Kenneth Bailey, was in London to review Australia's entire apparatus of internal security, and Chifley did not want Coombs to muddy the waters. Nevertheless, Coombs' membership of the Interim Council of the National University gave him reason to meet officials with an interest in the administration of research. Best of all, he was able to talk to Tizard, who, as it happened, was about to travel to Australia.[19]

While Coombs was in London, the 'hysteria' erupted again in Parliament. The Opposition (Fadden, Harrison, Cameron and Abbott) attacked Rivett and the CSIR in the House of Representatives on the last day of September. The CSIR's estimates included a paltry £31,000 for investigation of nuclear energy, but this was enough to trigger Archie Cameron's call for Rivett's head. The honourable members had discovered 'Science and Responsibility' and found it inflammatory. Rivett's defence of the free exchange of information seemed to Cameron to imply that he was not a servant of the Australian public but a law unto himself. Concerned at what the government might now do, Coombs cabled Dedman a preliminary report which essentially reiterated his previous written advice.

Dedman was not satisfied. He wanted Coombs to endorse the departmental concept and to sketch the practical steps to realising it. According to Dunk, who agreed with the line Coombs was taking, both Chifley and Dedman wanted the CSIR to 'come fully under the Public Service'. Dunk also told Coombs that Dedman was not passing Coombs' cable on to Rivett. We can infer that Dedman did not wish Rivett to know – if Rivett were capable of seeing it – the extent of Coombs' sympathies for CSIR and against departmentalisation.[20] Nor would Dedman give the permission Rivett needed to convene a meeting of the CSIR's Council to discuss the CSIR's future.

Meanwhile Coombs was gathering allies in the United Kingdom for his position. He showed Tizard what he was saying to Dedman, while writing to Dedman to urge him to await Tizard's assessment of the issue.[21] Coombs told Oliphant, whom he visited: 'I am doing my best to persuade the Ministers to go slowly.'[22] Acknowledging to Dedman that his advice had so far fallen short of his Minister's hopes, he continued:

> I am impressed with the cumulative evidence that scientific workers both governmental and non-governmental are against the departmental type of structure and Public Service employment for scientists. I think I understand more clearly than I did before the reasons for their objections. ... Whatever the government does should generally command the support of reasonable scientific people.

It would be worth sacrificing 'a little of logic' to preserve scientists' esteem for the Chifley government, he concluded.[23]

For the moment, Chifley and Dedman were content to amend the *Public Service Act* to allow portions of the CSIR to be removed to laboratories where security met military standards. Rivett worried that because the amendment did not specify that only defence-related programs were to be removed from CSIR control, it opened the way to the piecemeal departmentalisation of the CSIR, should the Coombs–Dunk report come down in favour of that option.[24] When pressed by Rivett to declare whether that was his strategy, Dedman made repeated reference to having to wait for Coombs and Dunk to finish their work. He did not, evidently, let Rivett know that Coombs had so far advised against departmentalisation.

An annotated record of a conversation between Dedman and Rivett, White, Clunies Ross and G. A. Cook (the CSIR Council's Secretary) on 11 October 1948 suggests that the linked issues of security and secrecy remained foremost. Coombs' invitation to focus on issues of structure and administration was taken up neither by Dedman (disappointed at Coombs' lack of interest in departmentalisation) nor by Rivett (not disposed to reflect critically on his own style of leadership). When the Minister expressed doubt about the 'expediency' of Rivett's address 'Science and Responsibility', Rivett countered by quoting from the third report of the recently defunct UN Atomic Energy Commission: 'Secrecy in the field of atomic energy is not compatible with lasting international security.' Dedman reported the view of the US Ambassador that the Australian government had insufficient control over its scientists. Dedman admitted that, personally, he did not like the segmentation of CSIR activities. But the Prime Minister had sought to reassure American opinion by putting the Division of Aeronautics under the Department of Supply and Development. Dedman remained worried about the security of knowledge on nuclear physics obtained by CSIR officers who were working at Harwell under Sir John Cockcroft. The CSIR men replied that their colleagues were bound by the British security measures at Harwell. When the CSIR men complained that Dedman had not yet authorised a Council meeting, the Minister replied that such a gathering would only give Council members 'information on a lot of the confidential matters under discussion'.[25] Here was no meeting of minds.

The CSIR Executive conferred with Coombs – now back in Australia – on 25 November 1948, and with Dunk on 2 December and 5 January 1949. Coombs and Dunk had produced a draft by 7 December 1948, listing the defects the CSIR would suffer if made a department. It would open the CSIR too much to political direction; it would inhibit a flow of staff between the CSIR and other institutions; and it would inhibit individual freedom and initiative. To deal with the problems of military research, Coombs and Dunk stuck to their earlier advice that the government should put work of a military character under the Department of Supply and Development, with provision for cooperation between that department and the CSIR on specific projects. Secrecy provisions should be used sparingly, and publication encouraged except where security considerations made it impossible. Coombs and Dunk suggested that the Minister be empowered to direct the CSIR to do work of military significance.

As well, Coombs and Dunk recommended that the CSIR and the universities share superannuation arrangements, and that more CSIR research work be allocated to universities. Postgraduate study should be accommodated within the CSIR. Finally, the CSIR should be administratively decentralised. Whereas Rivett had been Chair of both the Council and the Executive, these offices should henceforth be occupied by different individuals. The Public Service Board should take over from the Minister all decisions about salaries and conditions of service. CSIR employees as 'public servants' should 'subscribe to an Oath of Allegiance and be subject to the same security check as members of the Public Service proper'. According to Frederick White, discussions between Coombs, Dunk and the CSIR Executive in December and January centred on the proposed demotion of the Council and elevation of the Executive, and the authority of the Public Service Board over salary rates and conditions of service. Rivett, White recalled, 'found such changes impossible to accept'.[26]

Accepted by the Chifley government as the basis of its *CSIRO Act* of 1949, the Coombs–Dunk report saved the CSIR from Dedman's and Chifley's departmentalisation. Rivett, on the other hand, believed that the changes 'would destroy the organization's autonomy'.[27]

Coombs found late and qualified support for his liberal resistance in a long letter from Tizard that arrived while he and Dunk were trying to persuade Rivett to accept their report. Tizard was dismayed that Australian discussions of military secrecy in scientific work had become so fraught. He did not think it a problem that many scientists held left-wing political views. This was common in Britain, and 'it usually means very little'. In Tizard's view, Coombs and Dunk had conceded too much to the advocates of tighter security.[28]

Vice-Chancellor?

COOMBS WAS ONE OF the founders of the Australian National University. He could have been its first Vice-Chancellor.

In 1943 and 1944, the Department of Interior's C. S. Daley reminded an interdepartmental committee on Commonwealth education policies chaired by economist Ronald Walker that a university had long been intended for Canberra.[1] Daley proposed that it would teach arts, law and commerce, special courses for Commonwealth public servants and rehabilitation courses for ex-servicemen and women. There would be postgraduate research in international affairs (with emphasis on the Pacific), Oriental studies, public administration, economic aspects of Australian problems, and 'research in fields for which special facilities exist in Canberra namely nutrition, forestry, Australian history and literature'. Canberra's university would not include the large professional schools so prominent in the

State universities (such as medicine, law and engineering). It would be pre-dominantly a postgraduate and residential university, supplementary to the six in the State capitals.[2]

Coombs, a member of the Walker Committee, sympathised with Daley's emphasis on useful knowledge.[3] He asked Chifley to hear his officials explain how his Department's Building Research Station and Town Planning Bureau 'might ultimately form constituent parts of a post-graduate national university'.[4] Canberra's university would be one site for continuing research funded by the Department of Post-war Reconstruction. Further meetings of the Education Policy Committee, convened by Walker's successor R. C. Mills, confirmed this emphasis. The Mills Committee had added Institutes of Government and of Social Medicine by April 1945.[5]

Responding in December 1945, Cabinet found price tags on four postgraduate research schools (or 'Institutes'). The Institute of Pacific Affairs would have an annual budget of £50,000, the Institute of the Social Sciences £65,000, the Institute of Physical Science £50,000. They would be dwarfed by an Institute of Medical Research endowed with £250,000 each year. The Mills Committee's vision remained vocational, with emphasis on applied areas of teaching and research – 'schools of specialist training for the Public Service Board, Government Departments and other public authorities'. The university would 'provide under-graduate tuition primarily for students living in Canberra and the surround-ing regions'.[6] The modest commitment to physics – 'almost an afterthought', as Coombs recalled – was the suggestion of Dick Woolley (Commonwealth Astronomer) with whom he then shared a Canberra flat. The Mount Stromlo Observatory should be balanced, Woolley argued, by theoretical physicists who required 'little more than a room, pencils and paper'.[7]

Experimental physiologist Howard Florey, who had left Australia in 1921 and had since pursued a distinguished career at Oxford University (including sharing the Nobel Prize in 1945) was but one of the expatriate dons around whom Coombs and others hoped to build the four schools. Florey had discussed the future of Australian medical research with Melbourne University scientist R. D. Wright, an energetic and politically progressive visionary. The Institute of Medical Research would be the research base that university faculties of medicine, with their emphasis on graduating doctors, had been unable to provide. To lift research in the social sciences, the proponents of a national university looked to William Keith Hancock. Born in Melbourne in 1898 and educated at the Universities of Melbourne and Oxford, Hancock had been Professor of Modern History at the University of Adelaide from 1924 to 1933, then at Birmingham until 1944. He was now Professor of Economic History at Oxford. In physics, Mark Oliphant was their man.

When Coombs accompanied Chifley to London for the Imperial talks on defence and economic cooperation in April and May 1946, he visited Oliphant, Florey and Hancock, asking them to comment on the university draft bill. Oliphant's response caused Coombs to reconsider the Woolley vision for physics. Oliphant's interest in the university depended on it researching nuclear energy.

But what would it cost? The expatriate Australian physicist Harry Massie gave Coombs 'a real jolt' when answering that question.[8] What would Cabinet say? To find out, Coombs invited Oliphant to dine with Chifley, Evatt and himself at the Savoy Hotel. 'What they wanted to know, in particular, was the likely impact of the bomb on the balance of world power.' Coombs later recalled Oliphant as 'absolutely at his spell-binding best. ... We were all ga-ga!'[9] Chifley talked to Oliphant again, strolling in Hyde Park. Coombs recalled that 'the impact on Chifley was tremendous'. 'If you can persuade Oliphant to head the school', Chifley assured him, 'we will do whatever is necessary.'[10]

Coombs reported to the first meeting of the Mills Committee to be held after his return the interest expressed by Hancock, Oliphant and Florey.[11] He told Florey and Oliphant on 18 July 1946 that when the Committee defined the powers of the Directors of the Research Schools, they would certainly be consulted.[12] The budget for the Research School of Physics, he admitted to Oliphant, was less than Oliphant's current funds. Coombs reassured him that, nonetheless, the government was interested in nuclear research.

When the National University's Interim Council was formed in September 1946, it consisted of the former inter-departmental Education Policy Committee (Mills, Coombs, Kenneth Bailey, Treasury's H. J. Goodes, David Rivett), plus Sir Robert Garran and Daley, F. W. Eggleston, and three professors – J. D. G. Medley, Eric Ashby and R. D. Wright. Wright helped to keep a good connection with Florey. The Interim Council endorsed the strategy of getting the right 'men' and letting them build up the four research schools as they saw fit. They would invite Florey, Hancock and Oliphant to visit Australia. Oliphant was in any case expected in Australia in January 1947, to discuss atomic research with the Department of External Affairs. But would the provisional budget of the university entice him? 'It would be necessary to confer with CSIR and possibly with the Minister or Cabinet on the financial side', the Council recognised.[13]

Coombs attended further trade and employment talks in London in October and November 1946, returning to Canberra a week before Christmas. While in London he discussed the Research School of Pacific Studies with the fourth maestro, New Zealand-born anthropologist Raymond Firth, and with the Head of the Research Division of the Colonial Office. Firth was willing to visit Australia to advise.[14] Within a few days of this good news, Oliphant had arrived.

Oliphant asked a special Interim Council meeting for £500,000 for equipment over five years – £200,000–£300,000 of which was for 'special equipment for nuclear physics' – and £60,000–£65,000 for annual running expenses and salaries. The university faced a choice between four dynamic areas of physics research: nuclear, X-ray, low-temperature or high-pressure physics. Nuclear physics was the most important field for Australia, Oliphant told them. Coombs admitted to Chifley that the Interim Council had underestimated the cost of nuclear research. While it was difficult, he acknowledged, to estimate the financial benefits of Oliphant's work, 'it is clear ... that if Professor Oliphant's requirements could be met, we have an excellent chance of obtaining not only his services but those of Professor Florey ... and Professor Hancock ... and that this would establish a National University on a basis which would give it unprecedented standing in the international scientific world.' He sought an additional £400,000 in capital outlay for a Research School of Atomic Physics, if Oliphant were to accept the Interim Council's formal offer of appointment.[15] Cabinet soon agreed.

Coombs' vision of the new university, as he later recalled it, was utilitarian. If governments spent more money on the social sciences, they would govern better, as the war-time success of Keynesian economics demonstrated. And the medical and physical sciences, especially nuclear research, would enable science to 'serve humanitarian purposes as forcefully as it served those of mass destruction'.[16] However, Coombs was now resting his vision of the university on the recruitment of four distinguished expatriate antipodean intellectuals. Was their vision of the university the same as his?

Oliphant told the Interim Council, in a letter, his conception of intellectual leadership. Physics was the central discipline in humanity's knowledge corpus – 'the basic science, in terms of which all natural phenomena, inanimate or animate, must be explained'. Towards 'the problems of the less highly organized sciences', physics would be a mentor, helping 'to bring order and simplifying law into what are often purely descriptive disciplines'. Good work would be done in the new university only if that outpost remained organically connected to the current centres of knowledge-production. To import one distinguished individual per school would not suffice: each leader should be allowed to bring out a team of colleagues, that is, to import the communality of endeavour that a northern hemisphere network of men and institutions had made possible. The links among 'first-class men' sustained an '"atmosphere" which has grown in Europe over a very long period, and which is just approaching maturity in America'. Oliphant wrote that he, Hancock and Florey feared that the Interim Council failed still to appreciate the communal character of the pursuit of advanced learning. 'Council members should visit us in our laboratories and should endeavour to assess the reality of these more subtle factors.' As Director, he was to have discretion in spending the £500,000 on experimental equipment over the first five years. He hoped that the Physics School would be accepted by the physicists in the State universities. They would send their best students for postgraduate study in Canberra. No academic results were to be expected of his school until five or ten years had passed. Expensive equipment would have to be replaced as the frontiers of knowledge moved forward. The new university would flourish, Oliphant argued, to the extent that it would be insulated from the ethos of Australian universities. The Canberra University College was not to be incorporated into the ANU 'until such time, if ever, as the *academic* board of the National University shall determine'. Academic development in Australia had been constrained by the emphasis on undergraduate teaching, and by 'the necessity to cater for the expanding needs of the professions in a young country'. The ANU should not attach such importance to professional training. It was unfortunate that Australia lacked any equivalent to the Royal Society of London, 'which can establish and maintain standards of achievement by academic men and which give a reasonable measure of the success of any University'. Urging the Interim Councillors to relinquish their Australia-based conceptions of academic life, Oliphant challenged them to recognise 'how great a sacrifice is involved on the part of a senior academic man who moves from an established position in the United Kingdom to begin again in Canberra'.[17]

In March 1947 Coombs, back in England for more trade and employment talks, was able to assist R. D. Wright in further wooing the four maestros. In Oxford on 24–27 February, Wright reassured Oliphant, Hancock and Florey about the availability of men and materials, and about relief from administrative work. Wright and Coombs agreed that Wright should spend March in the United States examining the governing structures of certain US institutions. At the end of March 1947 Coombs and Wright proposed that the four maestros become an Academic Advisory Committee to work with the Interim Council.

Taking the word 'advisory' literally, Wright was keen to keep the founding decisions in the hands of the Interim Council. Pending the appointment of the Directors of the four schools, staff should be appointed by the Interim Council and dispersed to other institutions until the campus was ready.[18] This did not suit Oliphant and Hancock. Oliphant did not want his choices pre-empted, he told Coombs.[19] Hancock also began to set out his wishes to Coombs.

The possible links between the National University and the Canberra University College worried Hancock. He enjoyed undergraduate teaching, but 'what is alarming at Canberra is the juxtaposition of undergraduate work *at its very worst* (as you told us) and a research university which aims to achieve the best'. How would he select staff for such an odd combination of duties?[20] Three weeks later, he wrote again to Coombs that he still did not know whether his appointments (that he had not been empowered to make) would be expected to do undergraduate teaching.[21] Three months later, he set out further desiderata. The only undergraduate teaching he would countenance would be at an advanced level – something like Oxford's B.Phil. degree. The danger for the ANU was that 'it is cheek by jowl with a University College for pass men (mostly part-timers so I am told). … If I were to become the head of School, I should as a preliminary require an explicit guarantee that no pass work of any kind would be expected from any member of the School's staff, either at Canberra or anywhere else.' The National University should not include vocational training for the civil service. Nor should his social scientists be expected to do jobs for the government – except 'in time of great emergency or in exceptional cases'. Directors should only sparingly permit 'popularising' activity. 'Too frequent appearances by members of staff at the microphone or in the public press would do immense harm to the prestige of a Research University particularly in Australia.'

Hancock thought that to invite a colleague to join him in Canberra was like asking a musician 'to play the piano with one finger'. Library resources were poor in Australia, and the community of scholars was small. Australia was itself a limited object for study – 'a one-language, one-nation society with a local history occupying only a recent moment in time'. Canberra was a small, over-specialised community, with very limited facilities for cultured leisure. Sabbaticals would have to be generous. And what was the purchasing power of Australian salaries? Would his colleagues be able to buy the books, the housing and the domestic service which a don required? Canberra would need something like an Oxford college in which good work is possible because 'somebody else washes the dishes. I personally would not think of coming to Canberra unless I was assured that something equivalent was in working order there.' He proposed a mobile reserve of domestic labour that could be hired out to academic staff. Dons' wives (some of whom might be academics) would not go to Canberra to spend all their time in the kitchen.[22]

The Interim Council did not want to concede to Hancock, not yet a Director, the power to offer positions to his contacts in Britain and the United States. However, on 8 August 1947, it resolved to assure him that only in exceptional conditions would university staff perform commissions of the government. Nor would they be expected or encouraged to engage in press or radio debate. The Interim Council acknowledged a distinction between a graduate research school and a graduate vocational school. Evidently referring both to domestic service and to administration, the Council promised 'to secure to all research workers that measure of freedom from routine duties which is essential to success in original investigation'.[23] The Interim Council, eager for the maestros' pledge, was rewriting its vision of the university to match their 'advice'. Coombs' utilitarian conception of publicly endowed intellectual work was being qualified by a more patrician vision of what the Australian public owed Great Expatriate Minds. At least the State universities could not complain that the national university was duplicating their functions of professional and undergraduate training. However, there remained in Coombs a nagging ambivalence about the social purpose of academic privilege.

Perhaps this uncertainty about what the university was becoming helped him to make up his mind on one matter raised by the Academic Advisory Committee. The expatriate dons, doubting the Interim Council's executive capacity, wanted a 'first-class man' who could finalise the statutes and secure the building materials that were then so scarce. Wright shared their misgivings. 'When it comes to approaching anybody in Government circles,' he wrote to Coombs, Mills 'gives me the impression of a small schoolboy approaching the head master'.[24] Oliphant asked Coombs in April 1947 to 'father the University ... making much the same sort of break with your present work and career as the leaders of the Schools would be called upon to do'. By agreeing to be Vice-Chancellor, Coombs would help the maestros to commit themselves.[25] Wright became part of the 'Coombs for Vice-Chancellor' lobby.

Coombs was then in the thick of multilateral tariff negotiations in Geneva. 'I can conceive of nothing more satisfying than to become Vice-Chancellor', he assured Oliphant, but 'the Depression has been the most significant event in my life' and he was now engaged in preventing another. He did not believe in 'quitting before the real difficulties had appeared'. He hoped soon to discuss his options with Chifley and with the Interim Council.[26] Oliphant was glad to hear that Coombs remained open. To direct the new university was no less important than to advise governments on economic policy, he responded, 'if due account is taken of the long-term planning for Australia'. Perhaps Coombs could do both – 'after all your voice and counsel would always be available in Canberra' – or perhaps he could take up the Vice-Chancellorship in five years' time.[27] Medley, Mills and Wright wanted Coombs to be Vice-Chancellor, Wright told him.[28] Though Chifley had told Mills that 'it was for a man to choose what he wanted to do and no pressure should be put on him to do anything else', Mills insisted that Coombs was the Interim Council's 'unanimous choice'. In accepting the job Coombs would make a 'vital step' towards securing Oliphant and Hancock as Directors. 'Your appointment will make the University a success, and failing it, I think we shall be miles off our objective.'[29]

Crossing Mills' letter was Coombs' answer: 'I can make my most useful contribution in the governmental economic field,' Coombs wrote. '… I should stick to that type of work.'[30] He did not say whether he had any particular position in mind. Some months later, having reiterated his refusal,[31] and hearing that Samuel Wadham and Douglas Copland were being touted as possible Vice-Chancellors, Coombs told the disappointed Wright and Mills that Leslie Melville was the only Australian who, as Vice-Chancellor, would give 'me any feeling of confidence for the future'.[32]

D. B. Copland became the ANU's founding Vice-Chancellor in February 1948. By then, the interactions between the maestros and the Interim Council had written the charter for the ANU, an accord sealed at a face-to-face meeting between the Academic Advisory Committee and the Interim Council over Easter 1948. The university's biggest financial commitment was now the study of nuclear physics. The university was to confine its teaching to graduate supervision. By emphasising the formation of a small community of scholars with vital connections to similar communities in North America and Britain, the world of Australian universities would be held at a distance. So too, the world of public affairs: the academic virtue of advising governments and enlivening public debate was much contested in the ANU's first decade.

Coombs became Deputy Chairman of Council (succeeding Mills) in 1952. Since the first three Chancellors of the ANU lived in Britain, Coombs performed some of the functions of a Chancellor. He continued in that office (renamed Pro-Chancellor in 1959) until 1968, when he became, for eight years, the ANU's first Australia-residing Chancellor. We will follow some of his activities in these roles. His conception of the university continued to be unresolved – between a faith in the usefulness of knowledge to government and an aspiration to soar beyond the vision of political elites.

Reconstructing Papua New Guinea

IN OCTOBER 1944, Coombs became concerned that the Curtin government, in its first steps towards post-war reconstruction in Papua and New

Guinea, was drifting into a *de facto* restoration of a discredited colonial order. The Allied war effort had expelled the last Japanese troops from the Territory of Papua by January 1943. Over the next two and a half years, the Allies reclaimed more and more of the adjoining Territory of New Guinea. As the Japanese were driven back, the plantation owners, mostly expatriate Australians, began to return. By setting up a Production Control Board in May 1943 to help these returning investors restore supplies of rubber and copra, the Curtin government could not help but enact the interests of the plantation owners.

So the government received competing streams of advice – from the Board, and from the Australian New Guinea Administrative Unit (Angau). The Army was effectively in charge of New Guinea during World War II through Angau. In the eyes of many Angau officers Australia was now indebted to New Guineans for their assistance, as labourers, to the Australian military effort. On matters such as the diet scale for native labourers, for example, Angau and the Board clashed.

In February 1944 Cabinet spawned a sub-committee to formulate post-war policy for New Guinea. Coombs appealed to one of its members, Chifley, to clarify the government's priorities. The government had to decide either to renew and expand the old expatriate plantation economy – with its eyes on export and using indentured labour – or 'to develop to new standards, and on a new scale, native agriculture and industry', for home consumption. 'If the trend is to be away from White plantation development in favour of development of the native economy to more advanced levels with the aid of more advanced techniques', Coombs asked, 'what measures will be required to delimit white enterprise and how soon should and could such delimiting measures be taken?'[1]

Colonel Alf Conlon, Director of Research and Civil Affairs in the Australian Army, shared Coombs' concerns. Conlon's Directorate outlined how 'native welfare' could now be the goal of post-war policy. One Conlon associate, agronomist J. K. Murray, was appointed the Territories' Administrator in 1945. He recalled in the early 1960s that:

> It was a general impression prior to the war that the dark-skinned people of New Guinea were not only culturally deficient, but were lacking in capacity, lacking in IQ, in a way that was not characteristic of the white population. The work of the anthropologists on Colonel Conlon's staff, and of men with a wider view, definitely established that the native people should be regarded as having the same sort of endowment in intelligence as any other race, and secondly, that the government of the country should be in the interest of the roughly two million people who were indigenous to Papua and New Guinea.[2]

Under Chifley's External Territories Minister Eddie Ward, and consistent with Evatt's warm embrace of the principles of colonial trusteeship proclaimed by the United Nations from 1945, the Labor government disappointed the returning planters and others who wanted New Guinea to be a colony of settlement. Ward demonstrated the importance he attached to native welfare on 15 October 1945, when he cancelled all New Guineans' labour contracts, sparking a mass return to villages of origin. The people were to be encouraged to work for themselves, assisted by Australian funds for infrastructure, education and public health. The budgets of the 'provisional administration' of 1945–9 dwarfed Australia's pre-war expenditure.[3]

In his pursuit of 'pro-native' policies in these Australian territories, Conlon wanted Coombs to be Vice-Chancellor of the National University. In May 1947, while Coombs was in Washington talking to US officials about trade and employment issues, he heard from Conlon that Wright, Oliphant, Florey, Hancock and Firth wanted Coombs as Vice-Chancellor, for 'a stranger is out of the question. It must be one of ourselves.'[4] Even after Coombs rejected the Interim Council's informal offer of the Vice-Chancellorship at the end of May 1947, Conlon persisted.[5]

Conlon's 'ourselves' instanced the vocabulary of a consummate networker. As Brian Jinks has explained, by 1946, when he resigned his position in the Army, Conlon connected a circle – including Coombs – who shared a vision of post-war New Guinea. Coombs' place in the ANU's affairs now made him central to Conlon's strategy for revising Australia's colonial policy. Through academic research and training at the nascent Australian School of Pacific Administration (ASOPA), Conlon and his allies would inform the work of patrol officers and other officials who would govern the Melanesian territories after the war. Conlon had been influential in the formation of a Pacific Territories Research Council which, in turn, established the ASOPA. The Research Council first met in mid-1945, with Conlon as Chair. It included R. C. Mills, K. S. Isles, E. S. Hills, J. K. Murray, Camilla Wedgwood, Harvey Sutton, R. D. Wright, W. D. Forsyth, W. C. Thomas, H. C. Coombs and J. R. Halligan. Conlon's Council made bureaucratic enemies because it was perceived to cut across the responsibilities of the Department of External Territories. Conlon's direct access to the Minister, Eddie Ward, particularly vexed Halligan, the departmental Secretary. Conlon was demoted from Chair to Deputy Chair, and the Research Council's relationship to External Territories was firmly defined as 'advisory'. Mills succeeded Conlon in the Chair. In April 1947 the Research Council met for the last time, its functions transferred to the Council of ASOPA.[6] Conlon was not alone in aspiring to give ASOPA a research function. Without that, J. K. Murray told Ward in April 1947, Australia would have nothing more than 'a mid-Victorian colonial administration' in New Guinea.[7] Such hopes were consistent with the Mills Committee's earliest drafts of the National University as a facility for socially useful research, but in 1946–7, as we have seen, the four academic advisers were persuading the ANU Interim Council to distance the university from affairs of state. The Interim Council wrote warily to Ward in October 1946 pointing out that they had yet to discuss the National University's relationship with Conlon's school.[8]

I have seen no explicit comment by Coombs on ASOPA's purpose, but it is clear that Mills, Coombs and Wright were, on the one hand, wanting to woo the four academic advisers, while on the other hand, hoping to preserve some of their original vision of the university. The fifth meeting of the Interim Council reflected this unresolved issue. The Council declared its wish to be consulted about ASOPA's development; one day perhaps, the school's work could be taken over by the National University. By lobbying Coombs to be Vice-Chancellor, Conlon sought to keep this possibility alive.

It was a lost cause. In January 1947, the Interim Council 're-affirmed that the School of Pacific Administration should not be affiliated to the National University at least until the Research Schools were fully established'.[9] Mills' 'inferior advisers' were persuading him that ASOPA's aspirations were a threat to the National University, Conlon complained to Coombs. Conlon named Frederic Eggleston as one such 'uninformed opinion'.[10]

Would Coombs ever have been able to reconcile the wishes of the academic advisers with the vision of Conlon? With every letter Coombs received from Oliphant and Hancock in the winter of 1947, their disdain for any academic work other than pure research was becoming more plain.

Governor and father

UPON TAKING UP HIS appointment as Governor of the Commonwealth Bank on 1 January 1949, Coombs told John La Nauze: 'I have always felt that central banking was the work for which I was best trained, and in many ways the work I have done during and since the war has been an appropriate preparation.'[1] Coombs' other 158 replies to congratulators gave little insight into his emotions, other than a series of observations about his relationship with his family.

> I have not seen as much of them as I would have liked in recent years since my work has made it necessary for me to be away from home, and indeed, out of the country for long periods of time. One of the most pleasant things about my new position is that I will lead a more stable domestic life and this should enable me really to enjoy the pleasure of having a family.[2]

Economist Sydney Butlin congratulated both the Bank and Mrs Coombs on the good fortune of the appointment.[3] Giblin also noted 'the blessing to the family' if they could 'get you moored for a while'.[4] Coombs told his old friend from Claremont Teachers College, Ralph Honner, that more family time was a particularly pleasing part of the job.[5] In other letters, he was less solemn, perhaps even a little insecure about his and his family's adjustment to his return. 'The family think it's a good idea', Coombs joked to a Western Australian friend. 'I will be home more and we shall have our name on the pound notes. It's hard to say which is the more important to them.'[6] His family's pleasure, he conjectured to a colleague, 'might wear off after my presence around the place has lost its scarcity value. I understand that already my wife thinks that Saturday morning work will be an idea since it will keep me out of the house!'[7] To another he wrote that 'the kids think that [his presence at home is] nearly as good as having their name on the pound notes'.[8]

How did Coombs combine an active public life with being a husband and a father?

In 1991, Coombs recalled that in his life time the most significant division in Australian society had been the tension between Protestant and Catholic. This rift shaped Coombs' life because, although raised an Anglican, he had married a devout Catholic convert and remained married to her for sixty-six years, until his death. Lallie Ross observed her church's injunctions on worship and on sexual morality (no contraception, abortion or divorce) at some cost to marital harmony. Three of Mrs Coombs' four labours were fraught with medical complications. With contraception ruled out by her faith, sexual relations required of her a fortitude which, according to daughter Janet, astonished and impressed Coombs but did not always bind him to fidelity. Coombs obliged the Catholic Church's insistence that children of 'mixed marriages' be raised as Catholics, but he did not see himself as belonging to the confessional community that embraced other fathers and mothers of children at Loreto Convent and Saint Aloysius. Both Coombs' parents limited their involvement in the school community to attendances at prize-givings. On Sunday mornings, when the family went to Mass, Coombs played golf. Then they lunched together.

Like all Australians of his generation, Coombs had been exposed to intense sectarian polarisation, in both public and private life. In the early 1990s Coombs recalled that at Bridgetown – during the Great War's furious debates about conscription and Empire loyalty – the distinction between ('disloyal') Catholics and ('loyal') Protestants was strongly felt. Imperial loyalties were especially strong in Western Australia. While he was in primary school, the war demonstrated the civic and moral ideals that the Department of Education tried to propagate.

> The young could be got to understand the real meaning of the struggle, the high ideals of duty and the real self-sacrifice that actuated those who went to the front, the obligations of those at home to do their part and the honour that is due to those who fell. Before the War, teachers spoke of pariotism in connection with historical matters. The War with its concrete lessons vitalised the sentiment. Before the War the Empire was an abstraction – now it was a reality. There was never such an opportunity for training the young in ideals of good citizenship, social service and self-sacrifice.[9]

This climate of state-sponsored Imperial loyalty heightened Australia's sectarian divisions. Many Catholics opposed the most intrusive instance of Empire loyalty – conscription – because their Irish background had instilled a hatred of English imperialism. Coombs recalled that in his milieu it 'was proper to hate Catholics'.[10] 'I can remember being rebuked at the state school because I talked to the kids at the convent school.'[11]

Yet his (Irish Protestant) mother did not share these prejudices, and the 'atmosphere of the home and the sort of books that … were lying around for me to read … and conversations that took place [at] dinner … ran counter to prejudicial kind of attitudes'.[12] That Coombs' home life spared him an indoctrination

Coombs (far left of photo) looks to be about 14 years old. Possibly an excursion with Perth Modern School mates to a Perth beach? (Coombs family)

Coombs captained his School Eleven in 1923. (Coombs family)

Coombs with fellow trainees Kath Powell (left of photo) and Dorothea Chandler in the grounds of Claremont Teachers College in 1925 or 1926. (Dorothea Heron, née Chandler)

Coombs as university student, 1927–1931. (UWA Archives)

*Coombs and Mary
('Lallie') Ross married
in December 1931.*
(Coombs family)

*Janet Coombs was their first
child, born in London in 1933.*
(Coombs family)

Coombs concentrates on representing his country – probably London, October–November 1946. (Coombs family)

In 1953, Coombs, as Governor of the Commonwealth Bank, made his first of several visits to Papua New Guinea. (Coombs family)

The Governor receives a debutante in the mid-1950s. (Coombs family)

Frank and Rebecca Coombs in the early 1950s. (Coombs family)

in sectarian bigotry is borne out by his choice of Lallie Ross as his life-long partner. However, the incitement of sectarian loyalty did not fade from Australian life, and this affected Coombs' marital and family relations.

By the time Coombs became Governor, Australian Catholicism was climaxing one of its more militant phases. Patrick O'Farrell has described the Australian Catholic community as looking out with mounting alarm, in the first half of the twentieth century, at the moral ravages of secular liberalism and, in particular, at the trends in sexual morality. In 1930, the year before the Coombs wedding, his church's Lambeth Conference gave birth control qualified approval, while her Pope (Pius XI) condemned it in his *Encyclical on Christian Marriage*. 'By the 1940s Catholic spokesmen were frequently denouncing birth control and contraceptive practices', and in 1944 the *Catholic Worker* estimated that from 1922 to 1933 such practices accounted for the loss to Australia of 'nine whole Army divisions'.[13] Australian Catholics, from the 1880s to the 1950s, believed themselves to be 'the only great safeguard and the greatest moral force in the community'.[14] In 2000, Janet Coombs could recall the astonishing moment in her adolescence when her father patiently but firmly explained that on questions of morality there could be more than one reasonable point of view.

The Catholic Church entered a phase of worldly militancy in 1937 with clerical approval of the National Secretariat of Catholic Action, with two kinds of political effect.

First, when the Coombs children were growing up, in the 1940s and 1950s, the Catholics were in a particularly high state of mobilisation on questions of public and private morality – perhaps in reaction to what Marilyn Lake has described as World War II's effective incitements of female sexuality.[15] According to a civil libertarian with whom Coombs had worked happily during the war, Brian Fitzpatrick, 'Catholic action in 1947–55 was able to engineer changes in the obscenity/blasphemy laws of several states.' For example, in Victoria 'anti-Labor governments introduced, with support from Labor Parliamentarians who were Catholics, a Cinematograph Films Bill 1947 ... a Police Offences (Obscene Publications) Bill ... and a Public Entertainments Bill'. Each was withdrawn in the face of civil libertarian opposition to which Fitzpatrick contributed, but in 1954 a modified Police Offences Bill was passed in Victoria, following a similar law in South Australia in 1953. Further legislation against obscenity was passed in Queensland 1954 and New South Wales 1955.[16]

Second, Catholic Action began to mobilise within the Australian Labor Party, to save it from the perceived growing influence of the Communist Party of Australia. The resulting schism within the Labor Party culminated in the formation of the Democratic Labor Party in 1957 to unite those purged under Evatt's leadership between 1954 and 1957. The DLP vote helped deny office to the Labor Party until 1972. I have not seen a word by Coombs on the politics of the split, but it is unlikely that his relations with his wife, his children and their teachers were left untroubled by what O'Farrell calls 'sectarian and political explosions of a most damaging and destructive kind ... reviving the rancorous bitterness and fearsome phantoms that had characterised the sectarianism of the World War I period'.[17]

The two Coombs children with whom I have discussed this point differ in their memories of the ease or difficulty of discussing issues of religion and politics in the Coombs home. For Coombs the secular rationalist with Labor sympathies, these must have been difficult years. To deal with the potentially explosive differences – over public morality, the character of Labor politics and the civil obligations of Catholicism – between himself and his wife (and as they matured, his children), the Coombs family evolved a practical rule of toleration by which dinner table peace rested on a tacit embargo on certain topics. On other topics, it took some resolve to contest Father's views. Coombs was not a punishing father, but he could make his displeasure known.

For her part, Lallie Coombs evidently found ways to put Coombs' many public endeavours in a certain perspective. Both found occasions to be wry about this. When Film Australia's Frank Heimans asked Coombs to articulate the personal quality which attracted Prime Ministers to seek his advice and to entrust him with great tasks, Coombs drew on a lifetime of domestic commentary in order to deflect the question's flattery. 'Well it's partly lucky, I know that I'm lucky … and maybe my wife's comment is not without some relevance that I'm conceited enough to think that … I can do these things.'[18] Mrs Coombs told the ANU's *Convocation News* in 1976 that 'my part is that of Devil's Advocate – or a restraining influence'.[19]

Coombs' travels and his meetings – before, during and after his Governorship – required his frequent and prolonged absence from the family home. 'Oh Lord yes', answered Coombs when once asked whether 'your work ever took you too much away from your family?'[20] A family friend once observed that Coombs' family had made him 'a stranger in his own home'; but in the opinion of one of his children, it was rather that they had made him a 'welcome guest'. According to his daughter, Coombs was the only member of his household without a commonly agreed and regularly executed set of domestic chores. One son recalls, however, that his father 'regularly made breakfast' for the rest of the family. They loved and admired him, but they had no choice but to find ways to get along without him. In 1963 the *West Australian* quoted one of Coombs' sons: 'The war's well and truly over, Dad. When will the post-war be over so we can see you at weekends?'[21] Welcome in his family home, but emotionally and morally peripheral to it, Coombs required another domestic space that was neither 'public' nor 'private'. His Governorship gave him a flat in Canberra, for example (above the Commonwealth Bank branch in Northbourne Avenue). Eventually, he would set up homes within and near the ANU: a flat in University House, another in the adjoining suburb of Turner, and a winter domicile (for the northern dry season) in the grounds of the North Australian Research Unit, Darwin. The university and the Bank, between them, provided his second homes until 1995, when debility made that impossible and his family reclaimed him by admitting him to a North Sydney nursing home.

Chifley's man?

WHEN COOMBS ASSUMED the Governorship of the Commonwealth Bank on 1 January 1949, Australia was torn by controversy over who should control the banking system. In 1947, the Labor government had passed a law making private banking illegal, and in August 1948 the High Court had ruled that law constitutionally invalid. The government had appealed immediately to the Privy Council, commencing its plea 25 October 1948. The nation – few more attentively than Coombs – now awaited the Council's verdict.

Not many of Coombs' 158 well-wishers referred to the extraordinary uncertainties now shadowing the Governor's job. However, Leslie Bury – a future Liberal MP, and recently a public service colleague in trade and employment diplomacy – remarked that a nationalised bank system would be 'a wonderful machine at your disposal in a sphere where State powers could no longer frustrate'.[1] Another correspondent warned that the job 'may be something of a *damnosa hereditas*'.[2] Trevor Swan thought Coombs' appointment 'the best argument for nationalisation yet advanced'.[3] In the newspapers, some harsher notes sounded, reflecting anger at Chifley's essay in 'socialism'. One Victorian State Liberal MP complained that Coombs had served in neither of the two world wars. Whether he realised that Coombs had been twelve years old at the Armistice was not reported. A. R. Greene wrote to the *Sydney Morning Herald* to say that the appointment of a 'theorist' was 'indicative of the socialistic trend of our time'. Iris Hyde told the same paper that Coombs' appointment should worry 'the countless citizens who are bank depositors'.[4]

To be so identified as Chifley's socialist favourite bothered Coombs. 'I was conscious that my years in close association with Curtin, Chifley, and Dedman, had probably given me "an inside run". At the same time I believed that I had a contribution to make the job sufficiently distinctive for me to accept it without qualms.'[5] He needed to define a public persona appropriate to the office of Governor and consistent with his convictions.

> Not long after I became Governor of the Bank I went one Saturday afternoon to watch a cricket match at the Mosman Oval, and was embarrassed to find myself sitting behind a group of bank employees who were talking about me and the vicious purposes which I had been chosen to achieve. I listened for a few minutes wondering how I could have been 'translated' into this Machiavellian character on whom they were passing judgment. I toyed with the idea of tapping one of them on the shoulder and saying, 'Hey that's me you're talking about', but instead I just walked deliberately past them in line of vision to verify my belief that they would not even recognise me and turned my attention again to the cricket.[6]

A moment of relief from his problem, to be sure, but not a solution to it.

When John La Nauze congratulated Coombs on his appointment, he hoped that 'the enormous dignity of Governor does not mean that you will play no greater part in policy than other sorts of Governor'.[7] While Coombs was certainly not about to embrace vice-regal irrelevance, it must have struck him that his appointment converted him into a rather different piece on the political chessboard. The domestic political delicacy of his diplomatic work from 1946–8 had introduced him to a more discreet style of political action than in his conspicuous role in the campaign to pass the Powers Referendum in 1944. Now he had accepted another ostensibly 'apolitical' role. The Governorship was 'apolitical' only in the strict sense of being outside the party political contest; he would not be outside the spheres of effective political influence. But what were the rules of influence? The Governorship did not bar his speaking publicly, and he was allowed, in his *Annual Reports*, to say something about economic trends affecting the pursuit of the Bank's charter. His pre-war studies of Sweden had shown him how important it was that monetary policy be articulated, so that all significant actors understood the intentions of policy. He would have to make his own style of Governorship, in accordance with his view of the proper precepts of Australian central banking. But could he range beyond monetary policy to issues of economic structure and social policy?

However pertinent these questions were in developing and defining the style of his Governorship, they were overshadowed for a while by another issue. It was a peculiarity of the Chifley government's conduct of the Cold War that Coombs had not only to shake off the stigma of being a socialist pawn in Chifley's game against the private banks; he had also to distance himself – if only privately – from an illiberal feature of Chifley's attack on Australian communism: freezing the bank accounts of the colaminers' union in 1949.

In the 1949 coalminers' strike, the ALP's leadership of the organised working class was put to its toughest test since Lang's challenges in the early 1930s. The men wanted long-service leave, a 35-hour week, a wage increase of 30 shillings per week, and a reorganisation of their work amenities. The government insisted that this log – not radical by contemporary standards, according to Tom Sheridan – be submitted to arbitration (the Coal Industry Tribunal).[8] The employers' bargaining strategy featured their renewed demand that miners consent to the mechanical removal of pillars, an issue which set management's ideas about productivity against employees' concerns about safety. Disappointed by the employers' rejection of parts of the log and by their intransigence on the mechanisation issue, and concerned as well at an evident threat to their right to consult members in a stop work meeting, the Australian Coal and Shale Employees' Federation decided to strike in June 1949.

Chifley saw a dispute with the miners as a chance to crush Communist Party influence within the labour movement. The government and the mine owners were encouraged to resist ACSEF by many newspapers' allegation that the miners were acting under the traitorous influence of the Communist Party of Australia.[9] The strikers were handicapped politically by the ramifying public inconveniences of a shortage of electricity.

An old friend of Coombs', Neville Stuart, was then secretary of the Joint Coal Board, the regulator of the coal industry set up by the Chifley government in 1947. However, from this fact alone we cannot infer Coombs' sympathy for the tough line that the Joint Coal Board took against the union. Coombs later recalled his thinking that the New South Wales miners had previously abused their power and his feeling sympathy for a government whose 'patience had been tried to the point of exhaustion'.[10] However, as he relates in *Trial Balance*, Coombs had now to consider how his responsibilities as a banker were affected by the Chifley government's tactics under the *National Emergency (Coal Strike) Act*, passed on 29 June 1949. On 5 July union officials were ordered by the Arbitration Court – empowered by this law – to lodge with the Industrial Registrar union funds that they were suspected of using to support striking rank and file. Two days later, in an atmosphere fuelled by press stories and advertisements (paid by the Chifley government) depicting strikers as dastardly conspirators against the common good, the court began to jail non-complying officials.

Coombs was uneasy about the government's infringement of civil liberties. He was worried, in particular, about the government's expectation that the Bank would fall into line and freeze union accounts. Coombs' scruples about the sanctity of the relationship between depositor and banker prompted his close reading of the draft regulations under the *National Emergency Act*. He concluded that while they 'made it illegal for the unions concerned to draw cheques upon, or withdraw from, their accounts, they were silent about any obligations they imposed upon bankers with whom those accounts were held. ... My colleagues and our solicitor were inclined reluctantly to agree with my assessment.' The Solicitor-General, Kenneth Bailey, warned that any banker who honoured a miner's cheque would risk five years' imprisonment. Chifley dismissed Bailey's scenario – 'That will be the day – when we have the Governor of the Bank in gaol' – but got him to amend the regulations nonetheless, to ensure that they threatened any non-compliant banker. 'I remained unhappy at the bank being used in the dispute', Coombs recalled.[11]

Menzies' man?

COOMBS DID NOT WANT Chifley to nationalise the banking system. He had been happy with most aspects of the legal framework set out by the Labor government at the end of the war.

In August 1945, the *Commonwealth Bank Act* and the *Banking Act* retained many of the war-time controls: over the banks' liquidity and ability to lend (the Special Account); over the kinds of customers to whom they could lend (the Capital Issues controls); and over the price of credit (interest rate ceilings). As well, Labor continued the Commonwealth Bank's pre-war controls over foreign

Noel Counihan's vision of Coombs as the 'money jingler'.
(Courtesy Mick and Meredith Counihan)

exchange and gold. The Bank's Board welcomed the peace-time extension of firm monetary control through the Special Account requirement.[1]

Curtin had appointed Coombs to the Bank Board in 1942. Evidently, Coombs had found it a thoughtful forum, for during the preparation of the 1945 laws he had objected to Labor's replacing the Board with an Advisory Council of 'experts'. Writing to Chifley in October 1944, Coombs had passed quickly over their common ground – their mutual satisfaction with the 1936 Royal Commission's recommendations and with the war-time regulations – and asked Chifley to preserve the Board. He had conceded that the Bank should be under the government's authority, but he had explored more subtle means. He had suggested a preamble which would include stating that the Bank must help implement government financial policy; as well, Cabinet, through the Treasurer, should be empowered to issue written directives. The Bank should continue to be controlled by a Board, he had advised, because a well-chosen Board would take a wider point of view than would a panel of experts in banking. 'Bankers' were likely to be 'notoriously narrow in … outlook and inclined to rule-of-thumb methods'. Nor would an 'advisory' Board be sufficient. An intellectually diverse and powerful Board would occasion reviews and discussions, contributing to more thoughtful decisions. An effective Board would be one that could question the judgment of both the Governor and the Cabinet, since its members would not be under the immediate authority of either and would represent other points of view. Coombs had cited the example of trade unionists as Board members. It was a shame, he had told Chifley, that one such appointee, during the war, had been obliged to give up his trade union membership upon appointment.[2]

Coombs later reflected on the extent of his sympathy with Chifley's 1945 banking laws. He and Chifley were at one on the idea of setting up a 'mortgage bank' – recommended by the Royal Commission – to allow rural producers access to long-term capital. They had had discussions on this issue as long ago as the end of 1941, when Coombs was still a Treasury officer.[3] They had also agreed that the Bank be obliged to pursue full employment. They had agreed that formality and publicity should attend any Cabinet directive to the Bank, to afford the Bank a degree of autonomy. He had counted himself influential over Chifley's legislation of a division of industrial development within the Bank – executing a recom-mendation of Post-war Reconstruction's Secondary Industries Commission. He welcomed the legislation's endorsement of the 1936 Royal Commission's view that the Commonwealth Bank should compete with the trading banks in general banking business. The idea of 'greater Commonwealth Bank action in financing housing' carried the stamp of Post-war Reconstruction's plans for the housing industry.[4]

In so many ways, he had felt at one with Labor on banking policy. However, he had regretted the decision to extinguish the Bank Board – long loathed in the Labor Party as a capitalist incubus on the People's Bank. Chifley had heard him out 'patiently and impassively but decisions of Labor Party Conferences were not to be ignored without reasons of much greater weight'.[5] Most significantly, Coombs had shared the Bank's fears about that part of the 1945 legislation which compelled all government agencies to hold accounts only with the Common-wealth – Section 48 of the *Banking Act*. In this matter, he suspected, Chifley had been following the wishes of his party rather than his own judgment.[6] At first, the government had not proclaimed Section 48. However, it was soon Chifley's assessment that the trading banks were in only grudging compliance with his legislation and in August 1947, almost two years after the proclamation of the rest of the legislation, he brought the contentious Section 48 into force. Immediately, the Melbourne City Council, wishing to remain a client of the National Bank, successfully challenged this section in the High Court. The Chifley Cabinet responded by nationalising the banks, that is, by making all private banking unlawful.

Coombs regretted the resulting legal and political contest between the Com-monwealth government and the private banks. His discussions with French bank officials about their recent bank nationalisation had persuaded him that 'ownership of the banking system was largely irrelevant'.[7] Good monetary policy required not a certain form of bank ownership but a common approach to managing the business cycle. By making ownership the issue, the Chifley government was helping to delay the emergence of cooperative understanding among public and private bankers.

Upon becoming Governor in January 1949, with the constitutional validity of bank nationalisation not yet decided, Coombs had no choice but to prepare for the possibility that the Privy Council might uphold nationalisation. How would he implement a law which forbade private banking? In *Trial Balance* he said that he would have made such alterations to the senior levels of the private banks as would have enabled them 'to continue their operations with little change'.[8] He could have persuaded the general managers of the nationalised private banks to stay on, or found replacements for them from within each bank. Unpublished passages of *Trial Balance* reveal his thoughts about a deeper challenge in 1949 – the morale of rank and file bank staff. In 1948–9, the staffs of the private banks were being mobilised by their employers not merely against nationalisation but in opposition to the entire Labor government. Coombs wondered whether such staff could ever settle down to serve in banks controlled by appointees of the Commonwealth Bank, and he feared for the morale of Commonwealth Bank staff. He wrote to all branch managers about the need to maintain standards of service in such a polarised climate.[9] On the eve of the December 1949 general election that ended the Chifley government, he acknowledged in a letter to staff that:

> Some of you no doubt have uncomfortable times, but it is important that we don't allow our dignity or our good temper to be disturbed by things which unwise and foolish people may say. We are the staff of a national institution. The bank is owned by and exists to serve the people of Australia. I believe we can all be proud to be part of such an institution, and therefore when in the heat of controversy things may be said on this side or on that side which you find irritating, we need not let it get under our skin. The Bank is big enough, and we as its staff should be big enough, to let such things pass over, certainly without allowing them to affect our own equanimity or our own dignity.[10]

In reform, the first moves of the Menzies–Fadden government were modest – and welcomed by Coombs. Menzies introduced a bill in 1950 so that the Commonwealth Bank of Australia would again be governed by a Board consisting of the Governor (and Board Chair), the Deputy Governor, the Secretary to the Treasury, and seven government appointees (no more than two of whom could be Bank officers) serving for five years. Keeping continuity with the membership of Labor's Bank Advisory Council, Menzies and Fadden included former Councillors Melville and Wilson in the first Board. The government had power to direct the Board only in exceptional circumstances, after the Board had supplied the Treasurer with a statement describing the issue on which government and Board could not agree. The Treasurer would be obliged to lay before Parliament a copy of the government's overriding direction to the Board.

Deeply resenting the restoration of the Board, Labor used its Senate majority to fight it all the way to a double dissolution in April 1951. According to Chifley, Menzies and Fadden were showing that they hated the Bank because it was 'a purely socialist institution'.[11] The Board was a 'pay-off' to the private banks, he alleged, for letting their staff campaign against Labor in the 1949 election. Menzies' amendment did not disallow the five non-official Board members being shareholders in private banks, Chifley complained, and nor did it require the five appointees to have any knowledge of banking. They might merely be 'excellent polo players', he speculated.[12] Menzies and Fadden were assisting those wanting 'to cripple the Commonwealth Bank and impede its progress'.[13]

Such rhetoric obscured Menzies' moderation. It had been central to Menzies' anti-socialist rhetoric that he would overturn Chifley's bank legislation. Allan Martin estimates that Menzies 'clinched' his leadership of the Liberal Party in 1947 'when he dramatically portrayed resistance to Chifley's attempt to nationalise the private banks as the opening of a long fight against socialism'.[14] In 1949, the anti-Labor mood had comprised the private banks' campaign against bank nationalisation and the Opposition's campaign against the 'socialist' ambitions and achievements of the Chifley era. When they decried Menzies' Board as the restoration of the power of capital, Labor leaders were continuing the myth that their legislation had been socialist.

For Australian politicians schooled by Depression and war, the banks issue symbolised the clash of two rhetorics of freedom – the rightful liberties of free enterprise versus the emancipation of 'the people' from economic tyranny by the wealthy. Conservatives celebrated the December 1949 election as a mandate for the parties of free enterprise to vanquish Labor's socialism. For Menzies to throw out Chifley's banking policy would be their first step. However, in practice, Menzies was more responsive to his public service advisers than to his anti-socialist constituency. Coombs, with Treasury's assistance, proved adept in defending a policy orthodoxy – exemplified in the 1936 Royal Commission and in Chifley's 1945 legislation – from which Menzies proved loath to stray. Menzies' 1951 amendment gave Coombs what he had asked Chifley for in 1945 – a Board that included non-bankers.

Coombs believed that Chifley's attempted nationalisation had stigmatised him, in the eyes of many businesspersons, as a socialist bureaucrat to be whisked away by Menzies' new broom. Menzies' restoration of the Board allowed the Governor to start undermining that image. It was news to Melbourne industrialist and incoming Board-member Geoffrey Grimwade that Coombs had advised Chifley against abolishing the Bank Board in 1945. 'This was not in accord with gossip in Liberal Party quarters', recalled Coombs, 'where at that time it was normal for me to be seen as a power-hungry financial dictator whom the Board was being re-created to restrain. Geoff looked a little incredulous but was willing to accept the evidence of the documents.' Having to answer to a Board in the 1950s turned out to be 'not a difficult adjustment for me personally' because from 1949 to 1951, Coombs had 'tried to use the Advisory Council … as far as possible as if it had been a Board with executive responsibilities on policy issues'.[15]

From his experience of the new government in 1949–51, Coombs could be sure that his new Prime Minister was, on some matters of policy, listening to him. According to Coombs, Menzies' respect for him as Governor was based partly on the judgment of his brother Syd Menzies, a businessman whose dealings with Coombs during the war had left a good impression.[16] Such a personal explanation should not be allowed to obscure a weakness in Coombs' position. Coombs' survival as Governor demonstrated (and even embodied) something which was not conceivable within the available rhetorics of party politics: the continuities of Menzies with Chifley. In the polarised politics of 1951, neither side of politics could admit the extent of their pragmatic common ground, yet that is the ground on which Coombs stood. Thus his survival presented him with a problem. It would prove difficult to find parliamentary champions for his most cherished ideas about central banking.

Corporate Elizabethan

IN JUNE AND JULY 1954, Coombs told audiences of Rotarians in several Australian cities the following story about the inspiration of the Australian Elizabethan Theatre Trust – the performing arts patron and entrepreneur which he founded that year and chaired until 1967.

> About the time of the Queen's visit to Sydney, in a conversation among a number of businessmen, surprise was expressed that the Australian people had reacted so enthusiastically to the colour and pageantry of the Queen's visit. Not that there were doubts about the fundamental loyalty of the Australian people, but rather that Australians who had a reputation for being hard-boiled and unemotional had responded vigorously to the colour and pageantry. We said to one another: 'Surely there is something in this which should be kept alive. When the Queen leaves Australia we should not just drop back and forget the pleasure that her visit has given us.'[1]

Coombs did not mention his persuasion of the Chifley government in October 1949 to support a body very like the Trust. Rather, he postulated a new founding moment and new progenitors, people such as himself and his Rotarian audience.

Coombs had been among several economists advising the Curtin government to stimulate the arts. When Giblin and Copland had put their suggestions early in 1944, they attracted the support of the General Manager of the ABC, Charles Moses. He had embraced the idea of 'a national theatre of the sincere drama of the stage which has been almost entirely neglected by private enterprise'.[2] What the ABC had been able to do for live music, another government instrumentality might do for drama, ballet and opera. In July 1944, conductor Eugene Ormandy had asked for a Commonwealth plan for musical performance: the three levels of government, combined with public subscription, could build a hall in each capital.

In August, Curtin asked Copland, Giblin and New South Wales Supreme Court Judge Nicholas to comment on Ormandy's proposal. Their replies, received within days, had been buttressed by an admiring essay on the theatre in Russia by University of Melbourne historian R. M. Crawford.[3]

A lively constituency had continued during the war to demand a government arts initiative. Amateur repertory drama, requiring far less capital than ballet, opera and orchestras, had for many years been performing scripts inspired by plays of Ibsen and Shaw that addressed the great issues of the day. Professionally managed, but using amateur actors who lacked a school in which to train, the 'little theatre' or 'theatre of ideas' had become a vigorous expression of the desire for a more civil, thoughtful and just society. Some companies – such as the New Theatre in Adelaide, Brisbane, Melbourne, Newcastle, Perth and Sydney – were closely associated with the projects of the Communist Party and the Workers Educational Association for working-class emancipation.[4] Other drama groups expressed the commitment of Catholic clergy and laity to give wider and deeper expression to their faith. 'The 1920s and 1930s saw amateur theatre move from private enter-tainment to become a force in national consciousness', writes one historian, 'advancing questions of community and cultural improvement, social and moral justice, and the need for Australia's own playwrights and actors.'[5]

The word 'theatre' had then referred also to ballet and to opera, blossoming in Australia by World War II. From 1936 to 1940, the Ballet Russes de Monte Carlo – 'the best ballet to be seen in the world' – had visited Australia three times, with 'a lasting effect on the local public'.[6] The cause of opera had been championed by prominent citizens of Melbourne led by Gertrude Johnson, who in 1935 had established the National Theatre Movement, Victoria, renaming it the Aus-tralian National Theatre in 1940. Quickly attracting thousands of subscribers, the National Theatre had staged fifteen operas during the war.[7] Within this constituency there were differences of class, taste, religious affiliation, generic preference and political conviction. However, in its broad meaning 'theatre' had submerged such differences.

Leslie Haylen, the Labor MP representing Sydney's western suburbs, had denied that anyone advocating a subsidised National Theatre was peddling 'middle-class notions'. Rather, the journalist, novelist and playwright MP had insisted that Australians be enabled to be like the people of Britain, Russia and the United States who were strong because they 'know their own story'. Aligning 'theatre' with 'nation', Haylen's words had implied that if Australia's 'story' were to be told effectively theatre would be its best vehicle.[8] It was common, before television, for advocates of government support for 'Culture' to assume that live performance could enact, with heightened expression, the public life and shared character of the nation.

Building on Ormandy's concern for subsidised music, Coombs had suggested a 'Cultural Council' to coordinate existing Commonwealth efforts (such as the Art Advisory Board and the Commonwealth Literary Fund) and to develop new programs to deal with the demands of war and demobilisation.[9] A cultural policy would enhance country towns, he had argued, making them attractive for people whose migration to war-time work had awakened a taste for the cities' diversions. Coombs had seen 'cultural policy' as essential to cultivating the consituency of a 'New Social Order'. The Department of Post-war Reconstruction had shown films, fostered drama groups and exhibited new ideas about housing. If the Commonwealth were to continue in his Department's spirit, 'less emphasis should be placed on large-scale development than on assisting small groups of people who are doing a good deal, at the moment, to assist themselves and who will make possible a democratic development of culture by the masses of the Australian people'.[10]

Chifley had not assented to that committee's recommended Commonwealth Cultural Council. This had not discouraged the activists within Australia's many theatre groups, nor silenced advisers such as Giblin, Copland, Coombs and Ross. Writing to Coombs about Labor's long-term political strategy in 1945, Lloyd Ross had suggested that some appeal to the middle class through a cultural policy was precisely what Labor needed. The government, Ross suggested, was otherwise widening the division between Labor and non-Labor, making 'the middle-class voter (on whom the borderline seats depend) increasingly worried'.[11]

In April 1945, the enthusiasts for theatre had held a conference as the People's Council for Culture. Papers from its speakers were soon in Coombs' files. In January 1946 he had commended to Chifley the New Theatre League's draft national theatre policy. Chifley could ask the ABC's Frederick Clewlow to conduct an inquiry, he had suggested, and Clewlow should get help and advice from representatives of 'the Little Theatre and Amateur theatre Movement'; from adult education personnel (to help extend a National Theatre 'into trade unions, local governing areas' and to recognise 'the part that the theatre could play in community development and reconstruction'); and from 'a dramatist who has been concerned not merely with the grand idea of a National Theatre but with its application in a democratic way'.[12] Coombs' language thus aligned 'theatre' with 'nation' and 'democracy'.

Facing voters as ALP leader for the first time in September 1946, Chifley had promised a National Theatre. He had soon referred the issue to R. C. Mills' inter-departmental committee on education policy – the same group then developing a National University.[13] In October 1947, the Mills Committee had proposed to John Dedman (whose responsibilities included education) a National Theatre Board which would employ about sixteen actors, run a school of the theatre, and encourage ballet, opera, repertory companies and Australian dramatists. Costs of £70,000 per year would be offset by ticket sales. Commending theatre as moral and civic education, the Mills Committee had endorsed a claim 'that the best means of eradicating meanness and pettiness is by the representation of figures on a heroic scale, e.g. Lear and Macbeth'.[14]

Although the Prime Minister had told Dedman that he wished to avoid 'a sink for public money', he had not said this in public, so Coombs and Mills had continued to push the Committee's plan.[15] Coombs' persistence in arts advocacy had been encouraged by popular enthusiasm for the Old Vic company's 1948 tour of *School for Scandal*, *Richard III* and *The Skin of Our Teeth*. Public rapture over

Laurence Olivier and Vivien Leigh had made it 'an appropriate time for some action to be taken'.[16] Another of the Old Vic tour's benefits – money – had assisted the cause. The British Council was willing to donate the tour's surplus towards founding an Australian National Theatre. Would the initiative in establishing an Australian National Theatre have to come from Britain?

The Australian government had asked Old Vic Director Tyrone Guthrie to suggest how to develop a national theatre. His May 1949 report – after a return two-week visit – had argued that to raise the audience's standard of appreciation, nine to twelve distinguished productions should be imported from Britain and the continent over the next three years. Meanwhile Australian theatre workers would be trained in London and some would be formed into a London-based company, using Australian directors and retaining their Australian style of speech. Thus would an Australian national company gather the skill and authority for subsequent work in Australia.

Guthrie's 'import-export' plan would have Australians still in thrall to Britain, some critics had complained. Nonetheless, Coombs had begun to base recommendations on it. There were 'certain weaknesses in our present situation', he had written, 'which would militate against a high quality National Theatre being established at this stage'.[17] The ANU had just established a postgraduate training program in which promising young men and women were sent abroad. Were not the problems of theatrical and academic development similar? The government should set a date three years hence for a National Theatre, and it could meanwhile select and train personnel. Each State should have its own National Theatre Committee, and the Commonwealth should seek State contributions to a trust fund (matching Commonwealth money) to pay for imported productions and for scholarships. A business manager or theatrical organiser with commercial experience should be appointed, and a body of trustees selected.

Although Coombs had wanted public participation in the National Theatre, his conception of the public's role had by 1949 come to resemble Gertrude Johnson's National Theatre Movement more than the New Theatre's populism. The Trust would be financed by public *subscription* by 'many business enterprises and individuals and possibly trade unions and other organisations ... to a Guarantee Fund'. Were the National Theatre to be exempted from taxation 'as a non-profit-making body', it could sustain itself financially. However, if public subscription 'established claims to participation in the control of the scheme, ... this, we believe, could be overcome'.[18]

In this August 1949 vision of the National Theatre's popular base – tax-deductible subscription, with Trustees mandated to limit popular influence over management – Coombs had sketched what became, in 1954, the Australian Elizabethan Theatre Trust. The Chifley government had warmed to this mix of federal accord and private subscription, deciding on 25 October 1949 to invite the States to share the costs of a National Theatre Project. Coombs had been one of six Commonwealth nominees to a Board of Trustees made up of twelve (one nominee from each of the States). The other Commonwealth nominees had been Mills, Treasury's Bert Goodes, ABC Chair Richard Boyer, Leslie Haylen, and entrepreneur Hector Crawford. The Board would have brought 'high-class productions' to Australia and 'prepare[d] the ground for the establishment of an Australian National Theatre Company'. The Commonwealth would have provided £20,000 for scholarships for actors and technicians to train overseas, and the States and the public would have chipped in the rest.[19]

Within weeks of deciding on this model, the Chifley government had lost office. Menzies had not continued the initiative due to 'financial restraint, a narrow conception of Federalism and a scepticism about Australian cultural potential'.[20]

So it was that in 1953-4, Coombs seized upon the popular splendour of Queen Elizabeth II's Australian tour in order to reinvent the Trust to which Chifley had agreed. There was to be one significant difference: the initiatives of leading citizens, not the decisions of governments, would now determine the Trust Board's composition. In Coombs' 1954 rhetoric he adjusted to the succession of one public service culture – that of Post-war Reconstruction's melding of popular and government-sponsored 'new orders' – by another that emphasised non-government initiatives. Having ceased to be a populist promoter of new orders and having started to be a counsel to the private banking system and a chief executive in his own right, Coombs was developing a new rhetoric of reform and leadership. Mediating the relationship between government and people was less the job of public servants and more the task of the new corporate elite. His Rotarian *risorgimento* declared culture to be a cause and a duty for businesspersons and executives. As 'a project which sober-thinking people are convinced has a chance of standing on its own feet', the Trust would combine managerial with artistic expertise. Quality of cultural life would be assured 'by people with business and administrative experience interested in the theatre as onlookers, rather than as participants', and governments would not face an endless drain on public money.[21]

Coombs drew confidently on several months of networking among the leaders of Australian enterprise. In December 1953, five months before his first Rotary speech, Coombs hosted dinners, in Melbourne and Sydney, for owners and managers of large corporations. Their pledges of financial support made him confident in autumn 1954 to approach the Prime Minister, the Premiers and – with help from newspaper and radio proprietors and executives – the subscribing public. For the corporate elite to lead would appeal to the Coalition government. 'Those things which spring from and affect the mind and the spirit of man are the things which should be preserved most completely for private and individual effort. This should be the last aspect of human life to be subjected to any form of regimentation.' Thus Coombs made a virtue of lack of government initiative.[22]

The mission of the Trust, in Coombs' conception, was not only to channel public and private corporations' financial interest in the arts, but also to focus their executive competence. He assured one businessman in April 1954 that the Trust would back ventures in opera, ballet and drama only if 'satisfied about both (a) the professional quality of the performers; and (b) the adequacy of the management' because 'business organisations and individuals can only reasonably be asked to support the theatre through some instrumentality which is equipped … to judge both the artistic and management capacity of companies seeking support.'[23] To

Melbourne University's Keith Macartney he complained of 'the irresponsible attitude of some existing theatre organisations'. He continued: 'it is the hope of ensuring capable management of theatrical projects which gave birth to this particular project'.[24] The Trust would challenge the prevailing amateurism of the performing arts, channelling the executive competence of a new managerial elite into new fields of social service. Fred Alexander asked why the Trust should solicit small contributions from 'members' – £10 initially and £5 per year – as well as large donations from 'sponsors'. Among Coombs' reasons were that 'a number of people of the managerial class whom we approached said they would like to help but becoming a sponsor was beyond them'. As well 'many people in the professional occupations, while not prepared to be direct supporters of local theatre movements because they were not especially interested in the theatre as such, would like to have a hand in a national organisation of this sort'.[25] Coombs' 1954 Rotary speech owed something to Menzies' 1942 radio address, 'The Forgotten People'.

Yet he was adding something of his own. Coombs wanted the Trust to be a national body, building on capital-city-based cultural projects but going beyond them in scope and in excellence. Here we should take note of the personalities who worked with Coombs in first promoting the Trust. They were J. D. Pringle, editor of the *Sydney Morning Herald*, and Charles Moses, general manager of the ABC. As well, his former Post-war Reconstruction colleague, Allen Brown, now Secretary of the Prime Minister's Department, was an effective channel to Menzies. Accepting Pringle's account that he was a minor player, we can say that the Trust in 1953–4 was the initiative of the chief executives of two civil institutions of the Commonwealth – the ABC and the Commonwealth Bank – with assistance from a Commonwealth public servant schooled in the hopes of the Department of Post-war Reconstruction. Two national agencies, rallying business into a national trust, could lead the Commonwealth to national arts policies, transcending the (to Coombs) amateurish, coterie interests and intrigues of social elites in each capital city. The national government had recruited, in the forcing house of war, a retinue of skilled senior officials. In Coombs' vision they would contribute to the peace through their alliance with senior business executives with a national outlook.

Part 7
Other people's money

Inflation and war

SPEAKING TO THE Winter School of the Economic Society of Australia and New Zealand (New South Wales Branch) on 22 May 1948 on 'Australia's ability to avoid booms and depressions', Coombs lamented the political obstacles to Australia's control over inflation.[1] Budget surpluses, particularly by the States, were unpopular; farmers disliked stabilisation of the prices of their produce; and wages and prices were locked in mutual upward adjustment. Should prices start to rise rapidly, Australian politicians would either have to be brave enough to embrace measures against inflation, or learn to live with it. 'It is not always politically practicable', he regretted, 'to do things which economically appear necessary.'[2]

However, his was not an economic rationalist's counsel of despair about politics, for some of the stabilising instruments to which Coombs pointed hopefully in the second half of his talk were no less the creatures of politics. Should aggregate demand ever look like *falling*, its fall could be anticipated and/or offset. Social security payments would uphold consumer expenditure, and so would public expenditure on services such as education and law and order, and possibly health services. Government statisticians now had better data on private investment intentions. More enterprises were now in government hands (he instanced shipbuilding, coal mining and aircraft production) and large private corporations, like governments, were planning their investment over long terms.

We can read Coombs' speech as both a strong expression of confidence that Australia could solve the problem it turned out not to have (depression), and as a warning that Australia seemed unable to solve the problem that it was starting to have (boom). The Menzies government soon gave Coombs direct experience of governmental weakness in the face of inflation.

In July 1950, the Australian government committed ground troops to the UN force fighting Chinese and North Korean soldiers on the Korean Peninsula. Thus, in the first year of the Menzies government, the military potential of 'Cold War' was realised for Australia. While increasing the budget for defence, Menzies made a 'Defence Call to the Nation' in September 1950. Predicting a Soviet invasion of Western Europe, he began to prepare Australians for war. As well as introducing compulsory military training, Menzies assembled a National Security Resources Board (NSRB) in October 1950. Governor Coombs was among its founding members.[3]

Addressing the NSRB's inaugural meeting, Menzies said that the deteriorating international situation required Australia 'to superimpose an expansion of the immediate and prospective defence programmes on an economy already bearing the strain of ambitious programmes of development and immigration'. The economy, growing rapidly in the manufacture of consumer goods, would be restructured around the provision of capital and defence goods, 'to ensure that the national safety received the first priority'. Menzies did not think that war was inevitable. 'If war could be avoided in the short run, the soundest defence policy would therefore be to continue to build the economic and industrial foundations of the nation, while at the same time making all possible preparations for a future mobilization if this should be necessary.' There was something missing from the machinery of government, Menzies admitted – an 'organ to review the whole structure of the plans for economic mobilisation that would be necessary in the event of war'. He intended the NSRB to fill this gap. He recalled a parallel moment in Australian government – the years 1943–4, when 'the re-balancing of the war effort ... was only rendered practicable by the development of a man-power budget'.[4] Menzies chaired the NSRB and chose as his Vice-Chair Giles Chippindall, with Ronald Walker as Executive Member. Both men had been senior officers in the war-time Department of the War Organisation of Industry. So the Menzies era began in unexpected continuity with the Curtin government's priorities and personnel.

Geared up for World War III, from 1947 to 1953 public investment grew and private investment fell, as proportions of total investment. Agriculture was the greatest beneficiary of this accelerated development, for Australia's role in the anti-Soviet alliance included the production of food. Former Post-war Reconstruction officers John Crawford (now Secretary of the Department of Commerce and Agriculture) and Trevor Swan (Prime Minister's Department) were sent to the United States and Britain for detailed consultations about the demands that World War III would make on Australian farms. The NSRB also sought ways to ease Australia's post-war electricity shortage – at its worst in the years 1949–52.

It was Coombs' job to discuss the Bank's credit policy with the NSRB, to ensure that it was consistent with other actions advised by the Board. However, the NSRB was also a platform for his persistent concern that the government was not managing aggregate demand. In an early meeting, he suggested that to eliminate 'bottlenecks' in the supply of materials for building and manufacturing, Australia should simply reduce production.[5] Such advice displeased the military. Cabinet's Defence Committee criticised the NSRB for insisting that, in war preparations, the government's primary consideration was not how many Australian troops might be demanded by Australia's allies, but whether the economy provided a sound base for any increase in defence preparation. The NSRB also clashed with the Defence Committee on the possibility of Australian self-sufficiency, with the Board arguing for many goods to be imported, so as not to increase the inflationary strain on Australian production.

According to Ronald Mendelsohn, a public servant who replaced Walker as the Board's Executive Member just before its demise, the Board's failure to deal with inflation in 1951–2 was the greatest mark of its political weakness. Taking the years 1923–7 as the base years (100), one statistical series shows the size of the increase in retail prices in the six years 1948–53:

           1948   129.5
           1949   141.5
           1950   156.0
           1951   188.3
           1952   219.6
           1953   230.2.[6]

Average weekly earnings for men doubled in these years, and for women they more than doubled.[7] Among the reasons prices of labour and goods grew at these astonishing rates were a surge in the global wool price and the political difficulty of limiting aggregate demand.

Notwithstanding Menzies' apprehensions of war, the States would not let defence priorities limit their public works budgets, and the Commonwealth itself was not willing to curb the immigration program. Defence-related planning and spending were simply added to those commitments. The NSRB did not impose a new set of spending priorities; it never produced a full manpower and materials budget. One visitor to the Board's deliberations has told me that all those around its table gave the impression that they did not take its business seriously.

By the beginning of 1953, defence analysts concluded that the threat of World War III had receded. The increase in Australian armaments and military personnel between 1950 and 1953 was impressive. Had the Soviet Union made war, Australia could have sent almost three times as many personnel (to the Middle East, as requested by the Allies) in 1953 as it could have in 1950. But the demands made on production had been excessive. Inflation – at its most severe 1950 to 1952 – showed that Menzies' brief experiment in economic planning had been thwarted by all the economic interests that benefited from national development, immigration and defence spending.[8]

Wage-earners' democracy

WITH THE PROSPECT OF peace, and with full employment assured by the government, the organised working class had laid down its demands in June 1945. The ACTU Congress had sought a rise in the basic wage. At the same time the 1945 federal ALP Conference had resolved that workers' standard week should fall from 44 to 40 hours. Cabinet, while sympathising with workers' aspirations, had endorsed a strategy that Coombs put to Chifley, after much work by his departmental officers Gerald Firth and Allen Brown, in November 1945. The Arbitration Commission, when hearing the wages and hours demands, should be made aware of expert opinion about the economy's 'capacity to pay' and should review the principles for determining the basic wage. In particular, Cabinet had approved his suggestion that 'the Commmonwealth Arbitration Court should be authorised to employ trained staff to assist it to assess the evidence of an economic and statistical character'.[1]

The Chifley government's mandate to intervene directly in the markets for goods and for labour had then been waning. The trade unions had put up with wage-pegging in war-time, partly because it was matched by price controls. With the arrival of peace, employers had begun to concede wages above the wage peg, under pressure of unions and lured by buoyant consumer demand. The Chifley government had judged it no longer politically advisable for government to determine directly the cost of labour. In November 1946, Chifley had legislated to cease defence-related economic controls, including wage-pegging, by the end of 1947. His government had been told by the electorate, in a 1948 referendum, that it could not assume powers to determine the price of goods and of rent.

An inter-departmental committee that included Coombs had advised the government, early in the peace, to persuade the Arbitration Court to stagger the award of the gains sought by the labour movement, but not to resist them. A historian of industrial relations in this period, Tom Sheridan, argues that the Chifley government had found the cumbersome processes of the Arbitration Court useful in delaying the onset of the 40-hour week and the rise in the basic wage. Once hearings on these issues had commenced in May and November 1946 respectively, moderate trade union leaders counselled their members' patience.[2]

Although a political stabiliser, the Arbitration Court seemed to Coombs and other economists to be an inadequate instrument of economic policy. Thus, on Coombs' behalf (for he had then been in London), Allen Brown had complained to Dedman in October 1946 that even though the judges and their staff were not trained in economics they were effectively determining the government's incomes policy. To emphasise the absurdity of this delegation, Brown had made an analogy with monetary policy, appealing to a long-held Labor belief – expressed in Chifley's *Commonwealth Bank Act 1945* – that the Commonwealth Bank was better managed by experts in banking than by a board made up of business figures, graziers and private bankers. Should not incomes policy also be in expert hands? Brown and Coombs had suggested that the government should seek 'a periodical report from an expert Commission similar to the Tariff Board or the Grants Commission as to the desirable level of the basic wage or standard hours'.[3]

The trade union attitude to 'productivity' remained intractable to economists' reason. When the New South Wales Branch of the Economic Society devoted its 1949 Winter School to 'Incentive payments in Industry', the polarities of view were embodied in papers by Walter D. Scott (former member of the Secondary Industries Commission, an accountant and management consultant) and the President of the ACTU, P. J. Clarey.

Scott: 'A national duty devolves on all parties to overcome the disadvantages and objections to incentives so as to reap for Australia the undoubted advantages which incentive schemes can give.' Clarey: 'The development of the secondary industries of Australia ... has taken place with security for capital, to profits and to a lesser extent, to employees. It has in the main been done on the weekly wage system. The Trade Union Movement in view of its past experience is most unlikely to give its blessing to incentive payment systems.' Laffer (Sydney University economist): 'What chance is there of bridging the gap between Mr. Scott and Mr. Clarey? I have no doubt that this would be very difficult, but it is, I think, at least theoretically possible.'[4]

Coombs had considered 'productivity' when giving evidence on the effects of granting a 40-hour week. As a supporter of the unions' case, one of his tasks had been to comment on Giblin's prediction that output would fall by 5 per cent. On 2 September 1946 he had pointed to a number of factors – including the likelihood of industrial action were the 40-hour week not granted – which cast doubt on such a high figure. His argument had mingled economic description with observations about prevailing morale. He had told the court that he detected in Australians 'a "post-war" sense of unrest', a result, he thought, of 'war-time fatigue and a sense of frustration' that the material benefits of peace were yet impalpable. There was a feeling among workers that, while demand for labour was high, they were entitled to prosper. A reduced working week would so improve labour morale as to 'contribute positively to the re-establishment of efficient production'. The demobilisation of service personnel would not be hampered by a shorter week, he had argued. If anything, it would add to the demand for such people to enter the civilian workforce. If the buoyant demand for labour resulted in its higher price, employers would be encouraged to invest in labour-saving machines, to the benefit of productivity.

Coombs had been less apprehensive than Giblin about the effect of a shorter week on the balance of payments. Prices and costs were rising the world over, he had pointed out, so Australian exporters' competitiveness would not necessarily be lost if workers had shorter hours. Export prices (and rural incomes) were likely to benefit, he had forecast, from the post-war international economic agreements (on full employment, on development of Asia, on stabilisation of wheat and other commodities) that he had then been helping to formulate. Coombs had told the court in 1946 that the economy, in the last phases of demobilisation, was fluid and adaptable in structure – a good time to allow the rise in labour costs. He had concluded his advocacy with the pragmatic observation that 'standard hours will never be reduced if we insist upon waiting until every factor is favourable. When considering measures of this kind we are always faced with a balance of advantage and disadvantage.'[5]

These were the terms – pragmatic, shrewd, as well as informed by study of economic statistics – in which Coombs had played his public 'expert' role in incomes policy.

In the inflation that blighted the first year (1950) of the Menzies government, some economists found confirmation of their worst fears about a democracy of wage-earners. Controlling wage rises continued to be a topic of their wistful or despairing reflection. Such control was made more difficult by the Arbitration Commission's decision to index the basic wage to the consumer price index, guaranteeing wage rises to compensate for wage-earners' falling purchasing power. Indexation removed or severely blunted one anti-inflationary policy instrument: a reduction in consumers' power to purchase. Then, in October 1950, the

Arbitration Comission raised the basic wage itself by one pound per week for males; it had lifted the female basic wage from 54 per cent to 75 per cent of the male rate. Justice Foster defied economists' concerns when he declared that 'inflation and its control are matters for the Government'.[6]

Such disregard for economic reason appalled L. F. Giblin, confirming the fears that he had expressed in 1945.

> On the whole I do not see any class very likely to play the full employment game, except perhaps the managers and technicians, and, of course, the people that in Sydney you like to describe as bureaucrats. But their job is the planning; and the crux of the matter is the conduct of individuals. Most of us will need a new outlook. As of old, the Kingdom of God is within us.[7]

Five years of post-war boom had left Giblin no less lugubrious. In May 1950, while completing his commissioned history of the Commonwealth Bank, he circulated to Coombs and others a plan by which 'to halt, and then reverse, the continuing degradation of our economy'.[8]

The consciousness of the wage-earner – who 'in a democracy must be king' – was the fundamental problem, Giblin began.[9] Australian workers now contributed to 'the retarding of productivity (and therefore of material welfare generally)'.[10] Would their behaviour not improve if their thoughts were imbued with the wisdoms of economics, Giblin asked? 'A good many industrial disputes would not occur if the wage-earner had a better understanding of the economic effects of his action. This defect of understanding he shares with a majority of the community.' As remedy, Giblin suggested that 'a representative Committee of economists might be called to consider what they know with certainty – not merely as a deduction from the latest theory – about the facts of wages, profits, prices and income, so far as they are relevant to the subject-matter of industrial disputes'. The representative committee would then find a way to render this knowledge 'convincing to people unfamiliar with economics and suspicious of its conclusions.' The economists would 'confer privately with a few influential trade unionists, chosen, not for official position, but as likely to be sympathetic to the economic approach'. He looked forward to 'the machinery for friendly conference at intervals between the trade unions and economists'.[11] Reviving an idea that had circulated among the drafters of the White Paper on full employment, Giblin suggested a Royal Commission to discover and then address workers' objections to 'incentive' wage payment. He called for the installation of psychologists in the workplace; universities should study 'group tensions'. Perhaps there was some nostalgia for the moral disciplines of the war effort in Giblin's concluding declaration: 'Arbitration, like price control, can be reasonably effective only with the assent of the great majority of the people affected. That assent is not now forthcoming, and the main task is to encourage its growth.'[12]

In 1944 Coombs had voiced the same optimistic view of economics as popular pedagogy. In his Joseph Fisher Lecture, he had fantasised that workers would comply with an incomes policy if its factual basis were expounded by economists.

That presumption of popular awe of expertise had not survived such setbacks as the defeat of the Powers Referendum, a month after the Fisher Lecture. Coombs was now politely evasive in response to Giblin's paper. He saw 'a number of ideas … which it would be useful to urge on the government. … I think the main thing in these matters is to get some discussion going in the right places. Many of the conflicts can then be worked out and a commonly agreed course of action determined.'[13] He asked Melville to comment.

Melville was witheringly sceptical that economists had anything to offer trade unionists. He conceded the possibility that 'if the individual employee were able to appreciate fully what he would get from an increase in aggregate production he would choose the greater output rather than his present working conditions'. However,

> I am not clear just how this can best be brought home to the unions. I doubt whether a committee of economists would yield very much that would be helpful. I think that more research will be needed before the relevant facts can be assembled. There is so little on this subject that economists know with certainty … not until we have something more convincing than anything now available do I feel that it would be worth while conferring with trade unionists on the matter. Not much more than a general exhortation would now seem possible.[14]

Full employment had become not only an achievement for economists to be proud of, but a risky scenario for their impotent contemplation.

Horror budget

As AN OBSERVER and critic of economic policy in the 1950s, Coombs worried about 'balance' and about 'stability'. The main threat to balance was the excessive concentration of private sector development on the satisfaction of the desires of consumers, to the neglect of public and private investment in basic industries and infrastructure. The emerging enemy of stability was inflation – rapid rises in the costs of goods and labour, as demand exceeded supply.

In his last public speech before becoming Governor, in May 1948, Coombs had lamented the political obstacles to tackling inflation. In 1949, his first *Annual Report* as Governor (that for 1948/9) was pleased to note that 'inflationary pressure … appears to be slackening'.[1] The following year he noted how quickly Australian prices were rising. He attributed this partly to the September 1949 devaluation of the Australian and British pounds, which made dollar imports dearer, and partly to the effect of labour shortages in some industries whose markets were so strong that the employers were effectively bidding wages up. The Bank's 1949/50 *Annual Report* did not mention inflation.[2] That did not mean that it was not on Coombs' mind. In May 1950, he urged Treasurer Arthur Fadden to take five steps to curb inflation: limit public investment; budget for a surplus; tighten the money market through rises in interest rates; reduce barriers to imports; and appreciate the pound. Menzies and Fadden found all these suggestions politically unattractive.[3] 'Inflation' made an appearance in the 1950/1 *Annual Report*. However, only in one sentence was the problem acknowledged, as the Bank reassured the reader that the government was taking 'active measures' to solve the problem.[4]

This bland and uninformative sentence masked a vigorous campaign by Coombs and others. By the time the 1950/1 budget was brought down in October 1950, Coombs had been part of an unproductive policy debate behind closed doors. Menzies and Fadden did not want to raise interest rates, nor to curb immigration, nor to appreciate the value of the Australian pound.[5] The Korean war commitment in the second half of 1950 increased demand, however, making anti-inflationary action more urgent.

In keeping with his conception of a 'balanced' economy, Coombs' anti-inflation strategy rested on the government taking a firm hand against the private sector. A few days after Fadden's only 'marginally restrictive' 1950/1 budget, Coombs circulated a suggestion along these lines to Wheeler and Swan.[6] His covering note referred to it as 'my crack-pot idea'. He wanted to move back towards war-time direction of 'man-power'. The government should impose a penalty payroll tax on all wages paid to employees in excess of the number employed on a base date, exempting those industries Coombs thought crucial to the relief of energy and materials shortages: coal mining, electrical and other power production, iron and steel, building materials, transport, building. 'If effective, this measure might make a significant contribution to limiting the inflationary effects of our excessive developmental plans.' His objectives were: 'to concentrate as great a proportion as practicable of the increasing labour force in expanding production of basic requirements of industry and in breaking bottlenecks; to provide a rational basis for limiting public investment expenditure; and to reduce the excessive pressure of demand on labour supply'.[7] Though his proposal was not taken up, Coombs' advice on fighting inflation continued to imply a rebalancing of the economy, not just a restriction of aggregate demand.

From Melville came a more orthodox – but no less drastic – suggestion. Observing from Washington, where he was Australia's 'Director' of the International Monetary Fund, Melville reported to Fadden in December 1950 that 'the general view of the Fund and the bank technicians ... is that the Australian Government is likely to overcome inflation in Australia only by budgeting for a substantial surplus'.[8] Nine months later, this is exactly what the Menzies government did – with Coombs' support.

From the first weeks of 1951, the Menzies government knew that it had to deliver a heavy blow to the economy's excessive buoyancy. Wages and prices were now pursuing each other upwards at an alarming rate.[9] However, the double dissolution election of April 1951 (occasioned by Labor's Senate rejection of Menzies' bill to reinstate the Commonwealth Bank Board), further delayed government action. To reduce aggregate demand, by cutting expenditure and/or raising taxes, would have antagonised voters. The delay meant that the 1951/2 budget would now have to be, in Menzies' word, a 'horror'.

Coombs was becoming aware early in 1951 that were he to act against inflation within his own sphere of responsibility – by further tightening credit control – the private banks would complain that their business was suffering disproportionately because the government would not use the other obvious anti-inflationary weapons: raising taxes and/or reducing expenditure. For the sake of his long-term credibility as central banker Coombs could not ignore this point. He had to try to persuade the Treasurer to bring down a very restrictive budget in September 1951 and, possibly, to appreciate the Australian pound. Menzies continued to rule out the latter option. Within the Bank's Advisory Council (during its last months), Coombs advocated anti-inflationary action, including cuts in public works, increased sales taxes, a surcharge on income tax, and a national superannuation scheme (to increase saving). In the diversity of measures he canvassed, 'Coombs was encouraging the government to think more broadly and creatively.'[10]

Coombs was aware that many of the measures that he asked the government to consider 'go beyond the normal fields of responsibility of the Bank'. It would be no use budgeting a surplus, he argued, if restrictions on government expenditure freed the private sector to invest more on projects that were less essential to the nation than the works of government and semi-government authorities. He was pursuing a change in the structure of the Australian economy. 'I realise that these matters involve the Government's budgetary and economic policy, but ... we believe that drastic action is necessary on both lines if dangerous inflation is to be prevented.'[11]

Treasury's representative on the Commonwealth Bank Advisory Council, Roland Wilson, argued successfully that the Bank defer advising Fadden in such terms. 'No doubt Wilson's view was that the ideas trespassed too far into Treasury's territory', comments Schedvin.[12] Coombs' pursuit of a better 'balance' between private and public investment, between inessential and essential development, would have seemed to Treasury too much like socialist planning.

The compromise between Coombs and Wilson was that they both met with Fadden. At least Coombs had secured a seat at the table at which the 1951/2 budget would be outlined. Wilson, Coombs, Walker and Allen Brown prepared a paper framing an appropriately anti-inflationary budget. Though some of Coombs' proposals, such as a national superannuation fund, were casualties of this process, Schedvin has judged the 1951/2 'horror budget' a 'notable victory for Coombs'.[13] Yet, as we shall see, the budget surplus was not in itself sufficient to address Coombs' point that Australia's productive forces were growing in an 'unbalanced' way.

Coombs' was not given credit explicitly for the budget. Rather, D. B. Copland became the bad guy.[14] Copland had not been among those preparing the budget, but in an ABC broadcast he publicly congratulated Fadden for its deflationary bite. As well, Copland had given an address in Brisbane a few weeks earlier on 'Inflation and How to Curb It' in which he had anticipated some of the 'horrors'. The editorial of the *Sydney Morning Herald* called the budget 'the offspring of an unholy alliance between an improvident Government and a set of self-opinionated bureaucratic planners'. How sad, observed the editorial, that it was 'now becoming fashionable' to think that inflation could be restrained with a surplus budget.[15]

Yet that feature of the budget only exemplified Keynesian orthodoxy.

The Governor muted

FROM THE POINT of view of economists such as Coombs, inflation was a failure of government. As Governor of the Commonwealth Bank, could he say so? We have no record of Coombs giving public addresses between May 1948 and October 1953 – an astonishing period of silence for someone who, during the war, had so prolifically touted the possibilities of governmental action.

When Gerald Firth – the Post-war Reconstruction economist who had recently taken the chair of economics at the University of Tasmania – congratulated Coombs on becoming Governor, he confessed his fear that the Keynesian cause would now lose a champion. The immediate issue, for Firth at the end of 1948, was whether Coombs would still be among speakers at the Hobart ANZAAS meeting of January 1949. Firth hoped that Coombs would now 'find time to resume the "educational" programme at all levels – the job's barely started, and meantime we are all becoming a bit disillusioned. The Bank will give you a magnificent platform.'[1] To Firth's great disappointment, upon the announcement of his new job, Coombs cancelled his ANZAAS engagement. Firth, while conceding that 'the Governor of the Bank is surely in a position to decide … what he should do with his time', scolded him. 'I am convinced that you are quite wrong in deciding not to come … nor can I believe that you (of all people) hold the view that the Bank should remain aloof from controversy about economic policy. … I had hoped that this Bank job would leave you freer to stir people up as you undoubtedly did in 1943 and 1944.'[2]

In Firth's view, Australia's inflation showed that economists had yet to secure Keynesian principles within the thinking of governments. In a May 1951 paper he pointed out that inflation had come to Australia, during 1948–51, mainly from three sources: a build-up of unsatisfied consumer demand (and the means to pay) during the war; rising prices for exports; and the indirect consequences of migration (demand for housing, enhanced ability by public authorities to build large-scale infrastructure). In seeking to counter inflation, it was hardly possible, for a number of reasons, to expand the supply of goods to Australian governments, businesses and consumers, therefore it would be necessary to moderate their demand for goods. However all groups of spenders had been politically effective in blocking limitations on the growth of their powers to spend. Firth highlighted two causes of the political weakness of demand management.

First, economists had failed to educate the public about the full implications of Keynesian demand management. They had not tempered the propaganda of full employment with warnings that governments would sometimes do more good by spending less. Acknowledging that this implied self-criticism, he recalled in the period 1943–46 'an atmosphere in official circles more appropriate to an evangelical movement than to sober consideration of detailed plans for checking the development of excess demand'. Politicians' excessive promises had not been challenged by academic economists, and economists had not been willing to assign priority among the rival claims of investment, consumption and defence.

Second, Australian federalism unhelpfully allocated most power of taxation to the Commonwealth while leaving much of the power to spend to the States, among whose Ministers there seemed to be very little understanding of the problem of inflation. Rather, the States were yet another interest group clamorous for the opportunity to spend.

The underlying political problem, concluded Firth, was that 'no important interest group has shown any willingness to make concessions in the interests of stability'. Seeking to end on a positive note, Firth advanced two measures – one educational, the other institutional – for 'stiffening the morale of professional politicians without seriously damaging the effectiveness of democratic institutions in providing redress for genuine grievances'. Under the heading of 'educational', he hoped that interest groups would employ more economists and so become more amenable to the policy prescriptions that they were now reluctant to con-sider. As well, he hoped that publications able to carry economic discussion (he nursed little hopes of the press) might find the resources they needed to flourish. For 'institutional' solutions, he suggested that a 'semi-judicial' body, an Economic Policy Tribunal, should be set up in parallel with the public service economists, whose advice, Firth suggested, was far too attuned to the wishes of politicians. The Tribunal should be empowered to make whatever inquiries it judged necessary and to announce its findings if it wished. It should be small and be composed by fixed-term appointment (six years). Not all of its members should be economists. The Arbitration Court's settlement of major wage cases would be improved by the advice of the Tribunal, Firth suggested.[3]

Coombs approached cautiously the problem of reconciling his ambitions for policy relevance as an economist with the conventions and constraints of the office of Governor of the Commonwealth Bank. In the May 1950 Commonwealth Bank Advisory Council meeting, there had been 'full discussion on the responsibilities of the Governor in advising the Government and the form of advice appropriate to current and prospective economic conditions'.[4] Late in July 1950, staring at the inflationary effects of the Korean War commitment, Coombs wanted the Bank's *Annual Report* (to be released in September 1950) to canvass 'Problems of an Expanding Economy'. This section would have warned of the difficulties of sus-taining a large migration program when historic deficiencies in capital had still to be rectified. The government was in danger of losing control over prices, Coombs wanted to point out, and its population policy would only exacerbate excess demand. Saving levels were already high (20 per cent of national income) and unlikely to get higher. The London Funds were insufficient to increase imports. There were simply not enough resources for all that Menzies and Fadden were trying to do. Dollar borrowing could finance needed improvements to the nation's stock of capital, but this would carry the risk that stability would be dependent on a continuing flow of such borrowings, taking Australia back to its vulnerable condition of the late 1920s. Without constitutional powers to control investment directly, the government's options were: high taxes, restricted public investment programs and restriction on private investment, even on housing. 'The alternative is continuing inflationary pressure with consequent rising prices and deterioration in the real value of savings', Coombs wanted the Bank to say.

This warning was omitted from the *Annual Report* for 1949/50 lest it cause the government 'embarrassment'. According to Treasury's representatives on the Bank Advisory Council, Watt and Wilson, the draft would raise 'problems on which the Governnment was still in the process of formulating its policy'. They foreshadowed a government 'statement of general economic policy' (which Treasury would write). Coombs countered that a tough Bank *Annual Report*, coming out at the same time as that statement, would assist the government 'by bringing before the public the assessment by an independent but publicly responsible body of the difficulties facing the economy'.[5] He withdrew the contentious section of the draft, however, and the government deferred anti-inflationary action, as we have seen, until the following year, when it had to be much more severe.

This skirmish was repeated in 1951, when Coombs tried to get the Bank Board to endorse his favoured anti-inflationary options. The *Annual Report* published on the eve of that budget admitted that 'there are dangerous elements of instability growing within the economy', including public and private investment in excess of available savings. However, the government was now acting on inflation, said the *Report*. Omitted from this bland and brief assessment was the Governor's recommendation about how it should be acting. The burden of restraint should weigh more heavily on the private sector, he wanted his *Annual Report* to argue, not only because it was bigger, but also due to 'the greater degree of essentiality of many of the Government's plans, particularly for defence, development and migration'.[6] Again Coombs agreed to withdraw his contentious opinions. In these Council and Board debates, the Treasury (in particular, Roland Wilson) set limits to what Governor Coombs could say about government policy.

Coombs' earliest aspiration for the Bank's Advisory Council/Board resembled Firth's sketch of an Economic Policy Tribunal – an independent source of authoritative economic expertise, stiffening governments' Keynesian resolve in those moments when the Keynesian prescription was unpalatable to the country's powerful economic interests. Treasury countered this vision by offering Coombs a place in the formulation of at least one budget – and might there not be others? – provided that he fashioned his Governorship according to Treasury's notions of political discretion.

Hemmed in at the Bank by Wilson and other Treasury officers, Coombs sought to cultivate the Australian National University's capacity for independent economic commentary.

The university's founding chair of economics had been the notional responsibility of one of the reluctant maestros, the historian W. K. Hancock. In January 1949 Raymond Firth – with whom Hancock had had many discussions and with whom he shared many views as to academic development – had declined to become founding Director of the Research School of Pacific Studies. Hancock had asked the university to expand his brief to include appointing staff to that school as well as to Social Sciences. He wanted to be, for an indefinite interval, Director of the two schools, which would thus start as one. The Interim Council had refused, insisting that the two schools, though of obvious interest to one another, should be developed distinctly from the start, each with its own Director. When Copland had put this rejection to him in London, in April 1949, Hancock's interest in being Director of Social Sciences ended.[7]

Another of Hancock's disagreements with Copland was that he did not want Melville as professor of economics. Hancock had first met Melville as South Australia's Public Actuary in 1929 and had found him 'a man with an accurate grasp of facts and a capacity for clear thought' but lacking in 'adventurousness and originality of mind', he explained to Coombs in December 1948. Circumstances had not permitted Melville to publish much, but would he change if now appointed to a chair? wondered Hancock. 'Perhaps he is too old a dog to learn this new trick.' Would Melville be broad enough to work with others in the proposed school? How would Coombs rate Melville against Nicholas Kaldor (with whom Hancock was in touch)? What about Roland Wilson? Hancock had asked.[8] Before Coombs could reply, Trevor Swan (then working in London) had told him that he had recently spoken to some economists (including Nicholas Kaldor and Austin Robinson) whom Hancock had invited to consider the ANU appointment.[9]

Coombs had told Hancock that although he hoped Melville would stay with the Bank and although he would prefer to appoint Kaldor to the ANU, he thought Melville would make a good professor of economics. If Wilson were to join the ANU, it should be as a professor of statistics, for he was not 'in the same class as either Kaldor or Melville as an economist'.[10] In the event, the chair went to Trevor Swan, in 1950.

The leadership of economic research was undoubtedly a central issue for those intellectuals who founded the ANU. Coombs remained intensely interested in cultivating economic research outside the Commonwealth's two agencies of economic expertise, the Bank and the Treasury. In October 1952 he appealed to the private banks to combine with the Commonwealth in funding a different economist each year to visit the ANU.[11] In what seems to have been a related suggestion, Coombs approached Swan about an idea he had been discussing with a Swedish visitor to the Bank, the economist Erik Lindahl. Would the ANU like to publish a twice-yearly survey of the Australian economy, using money provided by the Commonwealth Bank? Coombs asked.

Swan agreed that a regular Australian economic survey was badly needed. The United States, the United Kingdom, Sweden, New Zealand, France and Canada benefited from such a publication, but in Australia 'the standard of public information and discussion is dangerously low'.[12] While welcoming the Bank's overtures, Swan was wary lest his Department's research program be overwhelmed by Coombs' suggested task. He sought to quarantine the resources for publishing the economic survey within a special unit to be attached to his Department. An Editorial Board drawn from 'three or four Universities' would supervise the work of a full-time editor (Swan thought a 'snake-charmer' would be necessary) working on manuscripts submitted from within and without the university. In

Swan's view, not only economists would have things to say in the quarterly publication he envisaged. It would be a mistake, he suggested, for the reports and studies to assume authority and formality. 'We cannot pretend to know all the answers. Without official inhibitions … a fresher and more selective kind of story-telling should be possible.' However, he did not lose sight of the kernel of Coombs' proposal: half-yearly reviews of the state of the Australian economy would appear in every second issue of *Australian Economic Reports*, signed by the editor. Swan anticipated 'friendly co-operation with the Bureau of Census and Statistics, the Treasury, the Commonwealth Bank and other Government institutions' in gathering data. He estimated that it would cost about £10,000 per year for *Australian Economic Reports*. Would the Bank like to commit itself to the first five years?[13]

Copland commended Swan's memo to the ANU Council, reassuring its members that the reports would not unbalance the Department of Economics' research program and would not imply that the university itself was adopting 'controversial views on current problems'. He rallied them: 'the prospect of controversy is one which must be faced boldly by any University worth its salt'.[14] Council soon authorised Copland to negotiate with Coombs the exact terms of the Commonwealth Bank's support.[15] Surprised by the size of Swan's budget, Coombs nonetheless assured his Board that the Bank would get its money's worth: informed independent analysis of the Australian economy.[16]

Although the ANU Council had been in unanimous support of the Coombs–Swan proposal, Councillor Roland Wilson soon had bad news from the government. As Coombs reported to Melville in June 1953, 'We are informed by Dr. Wilson that the Prime Minister and Treasurer both see political difficulties in the National University undertaking the publication of economic treatises which must, if they are to be of value, be prepared to be controversial.'[17] Years later, Coombs laid blame for the failure of the whole scheme at the feet of Treasury, whose officials had pooh-poohed the Reports as 'at best a kind of "fifth wheel" and at worst as a source of confusion'.[18] In an earlier, private retrospective he had also lamented not only 'quite bitter hostility in certain official quarters' but also a lack of enthusiasm among academic economists.[19] One observer has suggested to me that Swan was never really in favour of the idea.[20]

Coombs had to content himself with setting up a research fund within the Bank, from its profits, to disburse among applicant university economists. He valued as well the Bank's annual visitors from overseas (1953 Erik Lindahl, 1954 Thomas Balogh, 1955 Erik Lundberg, 1956 Raymond Goldsmith, 1957 B. H. Beckhardt, 1959 A. W. Phillips, 1960 R. F. Henderson and P. C. Mahalanobis, 1962 Arthur Smithies, 1963 N. Kaldor) and the occasional meetings of university economists, under the Bank's auspices, in the early 1950s. However, he never ceased to regret that, when Treasury and the Bank experienced their 'inevitable differences', there was no institutionalised academic 'third party' to help bring about consensus.[21] In January 1956, he asked Melville – who was then, as the ANU's Vice-Chancellor, visiting some northern hemisphere centres – to inquire whether Rockefeller or other foundation funds might be available to support an independent economic survey institute sponsored by the Social Science Research Council.[22] Coombs was pleased when, at last, the University of Melbourne supported an Institute of Applied Economic Research in December 1962.

Stern mentor?

WHEN COOMBS BECAME Governor of the Commonwealth Bank of Australia, it exercised five functions: Note Issue, General Banking, Rural Credits, the Mortgage Bank, and Industrial Finance. Alongside the Commonwealth Bank of Australia stood the Commonwealth Savings Bank, a separately incorporated entity. As a result of Menzies' hard-fought campaign through a double dissolution and an election, from September 1951 both banks were governed by the Commonwealth Bank Board, chaired by Coombs.[1] It was partly because this composite central bank structure seemed so wrong to the private banks that Coombs found the first ten years of his Governorship a struggle.

Replacing the Advisory Council with the Bank Board in 1951 hardly satisfied the thirst for reform of the private banks and many Liberal MPs. In a meeting with Menzies, Fadden and Roland Wilson on 9 August 1952, a delegation of general managers asked the government to repeal the *Banking Act* of 1945, and to replace it with an act to set up a central bank. A complementary act would set out the rules for all banks, including the Commonwealth Bank of Australia (stripped of central bank functions). Describing the 1945 bank laws as 'dangerous', their submission highlighted two issues.

First, the private banks thought that the General Banking Division competed unfairly with the trading banks. H. C. C. Marshall, General Manager of the Bank of New South Wales from July 1954, pointed out that since 1945 Commonwealth Bank advances had expanded over eight times, compared with the two and half times expansion of the private trading banks. The intimate association between the General Banking Division and the other parts of the Commonwealth Bank was an unfair advantage and must be terminated.[2] Second, the trading banks found the Commonwealth's regulative powers excessive. Under the 1945 act, the Bank could demand that the banks hand over, as a Special Account, as much as 100 per cent of the increase of their assets in each month since the commencement of the act. The Bank had not found it necessary to inhibit trading banks' lending to that extent, so that by December 1952 the banks' uncalled Special Account liability was almost as large as their total advances. Were the Commonwealth Bank to call that money in, any bank, or all banks, could be ruined. 'In effect, the power makes possible direct nationalization', the bankers protested. Though frequently canvassed by MPs and others who accused the Labor Party of harbouring socialist intentions towards the banks, this scenario had been made less plausible by Menzies' reinstatement of the Commonwealth Bank Board. To cripple a bank or all banks in this way, a nationalising Labor government would have to make the

Board – now including four appointed pillars of private enterprise – its instrument of destruction.[3]

Coombs took pride in what the private banks found offensive. The General Banking Division was expanding market share. Coombs never lost his conviction that this was not because the Commonwealth Bank combined the roles of referee (central bank) and player (trading bank) but because the Commonwealth was offering a better service. One of Coombs' aims in his autobiography *Trial Balance* was to vindicate the concept of the 'socialist competitor'. The Commonwealth Bank share of trading bank customers expanded, he argued, because the Commonwealth's savings and lending components (Mortgage Bank, Industrial Finance, General Banking, Rural Credits and Savings) combined to give customers a total service through a growing network of savings bank branches. As well, Coombs claimed to have inspired in his staff a more competitive attitude. He recalled counselling one young manager 'in a small but prosperous West Australian country town', who had queried: '"Do you really mean you want me to go out after business?" When I assured him that that was exactly what I hoped for his eyes lit up.'[4]

There is no doubt that the private trading banks' profits suffered under central bank regulation. 'The banks received a narrower margin between their lending and borrowing rates than they would have in an unregulated market, and ... they were required to deploy a higher proportion of their funds in low-yielding assets than they would have done if they were free to choose.' Competition from the Commonwealth Bank 'added insult to injury'.[5] But Coombs was not moved by such complaints. He had briefed Treasurer Fadden in 1950 on his notion of 'reasonable profits'.

> Generally, it has been the aim of the Bank to ensure that the effect of credit policy was not such as to deprive the banks of the possibility of earning reasonable profits. What level of profits would be 'reasonable' but not excessive is a matter for judgment and might differ according to the circumstances of the time ... Factors such as sharp changes in export income, import payments or the level of capital inflow, can affect profits substantially and to an unpredictable extent.[6]

Fadden reflected his rural constituency's resentment of the private banks' profitability. He told Coombs in 1956 that he had warned the private bank lobby 'that they were in an extremely vulnerable position in relation to profits and must expect severe criticism on that aspect of their operations if a banking bill came before Parliament'.[7]

In the 1950s debate about central bank regulation, the private banks found it easier to appeal to the public's sense of fair play than to try to cultivate public sympathy for their profits. They argued that it was not fair that the Commonwealth Bank was both regulator and competitor. The press generally supported their demand that central bank functions be separated. The scenario of nationalisation through a future government's abuse of the Special Accounts power was less prominent in the private banks' argument and in press comment. However, Labor

Party figures occasionally gave this line of attack a veneer of plausibility by ventilating a hatred of private banking. In November 1957, Arthur Calwell was quoted as saying that 'We [the ALP] dislike and distrust the private banking system as much as private bank directors have always disliked and distrusted the Commonwealth Bank.'[8]

For Coombs in 1952, the primary question was neither market share nor profits (and certainly not nationalisation) but: how to regulate? He wanted the trading banks to share responsibility for moderating the expansions and contractions of the economy. They would then earn the freedom to arrange their assets in the most profitable way.

When the trading banks outlined the amendments they wanted in August 1952, Coombs advised Menzies, Fadden and Wilson to retain the Special Account, but to reduce the banks' maximum liability; this would quash their fears of nationalisation, while keeping within the Commonwealth Bank's hands a potent weapon against inflation. Coombs was proud of the Special Account as a mechanism of credit regulation. 'I believe it is one of the major contributions to monetary management which Australia has ever made', he told economists in October 1953.[9] Coombs presented the Commonwealth Bank as a lenient regulator. He asked for the power, currently in the hands of the Treasurer, to give the banks 'reasonable' short-term rates of interest on their Special Accounts. Coombs also addressed the private banks' other charge – that the Commonwealth Bank's General Banking Division competed unfairly with private trading banks. The General Banking Division had been a comparatively liberal lender only to building societies and to individual home-builders, he argued, and that was in the national interest rather than in pursuit of profit. Such business was not highly prized by the private banks, he contended. As well, the General Banking Division was starting to behave, voluntarily, like a regulated trading bank, having opened up a 'Special Account' with the Central Bank. However, the government should not make this a legal obligation, he suggested, as the liquidity of the General Division could be useful in such emergencies as 'a threatened collapse of the building industry'.

Should the General Banking Division be made a separate entity like the Savings Bank? Coombs asked. Only if it assisted public *recognition* of the Division's effective autonomy from the rest of the Bank, he counselled. Should the Division be *completely* separated, with its own staff, Board and management? Coombs was opposed to this option, and his opposition throughout the 1950s became one of the defining struggles of his Governorship. He believed that by being a deposit accepter and a lender, through the General Banking Division, the central bank was directly effective in the finance market, not just indirectly effective through its regulation of the other banks. It was good, from the government's point of view, to have at least one lender whose aims were not to profit but to smooth out the booms and troughs of the economy. The Commonwealth Bank's market involvement also 'provides a salutary check on the practicability' of its central bank measures; it was thus helpful, rather than unfair, for trading, savings and central bank work to be performed by a single staff establishment under a single Commonwealth Bank Board. He cited the 1936–7 Royal Commission's praise for the composite structure of the Commonwealth Bank as 'essential to the efficient exercise of its functions as a central bank'.

Coombs warned Fadden that those lobbying against the 1945 and 1951 Bank laws, by politicising central banking, would hinder the public's gradual acceptance of it. If there were a 'period of freedom from political controversy and structural alteration', recently introduced practices and understandings would be 'confirmed into *traditions which are in the art of central banking more important than structural or legislative requirements*'. He hoped the government would avoid 'a new period of counteraction and reprisal' which might 'embitter the relationships within the banking system for another generation'.[10]

In October 1952, the Menzies government announced reforms that met some of the wishes of the private banks. The General Banking Division would be separately incorporated as the Commonwealth Trading Bank, with its own general manager and statutory functions. However, heeding Coombs, the government left the new Trading Bank under the Commonwealth Bank Board's authority and with a common pool of staff. The Commonwealth Trading Bank would submit to the same central bank controls as regulated the other trading banks. At the same time, those controls were to be modified. The government reduced the requirement that banks hold Special Accounts with the Commonwealth Bank. Menzies could present this as breaking the lance of would-be nationalisers.

Coombs saw no reason to be alarmed by Menzies' changes. It did not matter that the Bank would have less power to call increased trading bank assets into Special Accounts, he told senior staff in March 1953. Rather, this 'will oblige us to do what we have already been doing, that is, lean less heavily upon this instrument of control, and look to other means of getting the banks along the roads we want them to travel'. Nor did the separate incorporation of the Commonwealth Trading Bank compromise the Royal Commission model of a composite central bank. Here Coombs resorted to a homely metaphor. 'We, the officers of the Bank, remain one family with a single undivided loyalty – not the Commonwealth Bank as a central bank, not to the Commonwealth Trading Bank, not to the Commonwealth Savings Bank, but to the combined family of banks which constitutes the Commonwealth Bank as a whole.' And 'we remain one family, one family in the staff serving the family of Banks'. Efficiencies arose, he added, from the fact that 'we are a family'. Coombs worked hard at family relations. In unpublished passages of *Trial Balance*, he recalled that his first few years as Governor were devoted as much to establishing a clear division of labour among the Commonwealth Bank's various components as to any other issue.[11]

The family metaphor could be extended. In 1954 he defended 'the direct influence which the Commonwealth Bank exercises over the family of banks of which it is the head'.[12] He regretted that 'the relationships between the central bank and the Commonwealth Trading Bank are frequently misunderstood – putting it mildly'.[13]

Coombs' presentation of himself as the father of two families – the Commonwealth Bank and the banking system – expressed his ideal mode of authority: firm in his private discussions with the general managers, but moderate and tactful in his public statements. His purposes were educative, rather than combative, in the interest of establishing shared traditions. He later recalled his 1950s speeches and talks with the banks as 'a program which would enable those with whom we had to deal to participate in the processes by which judgments were made and policy formulated – reaching their own conclusions'.[14]

It was a mirror of Coombs' satisfaction with Menzies' limited 1953 amendments that the leaders of the private banks were disappointed by them. In November 1953, the President of the Bank of New South Wales, Sir Colin Sinclair, complained that there remained too much scope for 'governmentally-regimented banking ... the big disappointment over the legislation was the failure to create a central bank free from its own commercial or special bank responsibilities'.[15] The popularity of such sentiments among bankers prompted them to form the Australian Bankers Association in May 1954 (to replace the Associated Banks of Victoria).

Because the banks remained outspoken public critics of the Chifley–Menzies–Fadden legislation, Coombs faced a dilemma. On the one hand he wanted to assure the public, against private bank allegations to the contrary, that the Commonwealth Bank was a fair and able regulator and a good bank to do business with. On the other hand, he was worried that his explanations of monetary policy and his presentations of banks' social responsibilities would arouse controversy. He wanted above all to avoid his office being implicated in the rival philosophies and ambitions of the Coalition and the Labor Party. The Governor was supposed to be above and outside politics. Harold Levien, the editor of the monthly *Voice*, which Coombs admired and in which he held a small share, tried in July 1952 to get the Governor to write on 'The role of the Commonwealth Bank in the fight against inflation'. Declining, Coombs explained 'I have made it a practice since holding my present position to refrain from writing articles.'[16]

However, he began to make speeches. In October 1953 Coombs told economists that there had arisen two contrasting understandings of the purposes of the Special Account.

> It had been expected that if excess funds were taken from the private banks and immobilised in Special Accounts with the Commonwealth Bank, the private banks would base their policies on the funds left in their own hands. In practice the banks – *not unnaturally* – in considering their liquid position tended, *perhaps unconsciously*, to be influenced by the knowledge that they had large sums in Special Account. These funds, nominally immobilised, were in fact not regarded as frozen.[17]

The private banks could hear this as the mildest of scoldings.

Eleven months later, Coombs spoke again on this theme. On 15 September 1954, he delivered the inaugural English, Scottish and Australian Bank Research Lecture at the University of Queensland, 'The Development of Monetary Policy in Australia'; and on 29 November 1954 he spoke again, on 'The Role of the Central Bank in Australia', to the Bankers Institute of Australasia in Melbourne. Between these two occasions, he refused the *Sydney Morning Herald*'s invitation to write an article 'explaining the policy of the Commonwealth Bank and the need for a strong Central Bank policy'. Coombs justified his refusal as avoiding 'controversy of a political nature'.[18]

Yet both the public lectures of (September and November) 1954 could be read as responses to private banks' resistance to his regulation. Richard Downing, editor of the *Economic Record*, congratulated him on the ES&A Bank Lecture's 'clarity, simplicity and sanity'. It confirmed Downing's 'suspicions about the behaviour of the banks'. In Downing's opinion, if Coombs wanted to demonstrate to the banks the recklessness of their attitude to the Special Account, he 'ought to let just one bank go insolvent – preferably the National ... No doubt you in Sydney would prefer it to be the Wales'.[19] This was a pointed reading of Coombs' theme of private banks' resistance to credit control during the inflation of the early 1950s. 'Pointed' – because Coombs did not speak of 'resistance'. His diplomatic phrasing is exemplified in his naming, as an impediment to regulation, 'the absence of stable conventional standards generally accepted by banks as to their own asset structure'.[20] Downing was not the only economist urging Coombs to be tough with the banks. Melville had advised him from Washington to be 'a stern mentor and not a fairy godmother'.[21]

In considering the publication of his ES&A Bank Lecture we can see Coombs' continuing uncertainty about how forthright he should be. He wanted 250 copies of the lecture for the Bank. Though his staff talked him into taking 500 – as a long-term reserve – he opposed sending a copy to each Bank branch.

> The address bears very directly on a number of matters which have recently been the subject of public controversy. There is the real danger, therefore, that some managers after reading it will feel quite competent to enter the controversy, at least semi-publicly. This is likely to lead to further confusion in many cases and will certainly result in keeping the controversy alive.[22]

To keep controversy 'alive' would militate against the emergence of 'conventions'. Besides, Coombs saw more than one way to skin the cat: his Bank would exert influence by trading, not just by regulating.

The diplomacy of Coombs' Governorship was sorely tested by private bankers' continuing rancour against Menzies' 1953 preservation of the composite central bank. Sir Frank Packer's main writer on business, Roger Randerson, referred to 'the ill-gotten profits of the Central Bank' and to 'the morally indefensible expansion of the Commonwealth Bank group'.[23] In October 1955 a *Sydney Morning Herald* editorial referred to 'the essential dishonesty of the existing bank structure'. These were wounding words to use about the Bank and, implicitly, about its Governor.

Coombs lacked a parliamentary champion for the Royal Commission's notion of a composite central bank. Wishing to characterise Menzies as the people's bank's enemy, Labor did not concede how much Menzies had retained of Chifley's legislation. Coombs prompted Menzies to defend his own policy, in the *Sydney Morning Herald* or elsewhere.[24] However, it quickly became apparent that the Prime Minister 'probably would not wish to reply' to criticism of his 1953 amendments.[25] Diplomatically, Coombs endorsed Menzies' inaction, invoking the other horn of his political dilemma – that to reply to criticism would prolong acrimony and so delay the evolution of the conventions and common understandings on which regulation should rest.[26] When Bank staff examined the second-reading speeches on Menzies' 1953 amendments, they found that the government had placed much emphasis on the amending legislation's refashioning of the Commonwealth Trading Bank in the image of the private trading banks. However, Menzies had paid little attention to the point – more important to Coombs – that the Trading Bank and the other divisions within the Commonwealth Bank 'family' were all necessary instruments of central bank action.[27]

Menzies' unwillingness to defend the 1953 legislation in 1954 no doubt reflected the poor reputation of his banking policies within the Liberal Party itself. He could no longer ignore his party.[28] The Prime Minister informed Coombs in November 1954 that Cabinet would 'review the legislation and its workings' early in 1955. This hardly conceded the 1953 legislation the trial that Coombs thought necessary.[29] It is not surprising then that one of the most determined private bank lobbyists, the Wales' H. C. C. Marshall, found Coombs 'distinctly agitated' in a 14 February 1955 meeting with the banks. According to Marshall, Coombs showed 'signs of stress and emotion, as he poured out his grievances against the private banks' and against the successful lobbying of Menzies by the Australian Bankers Association.[30]

Coombs as boss

COOMBS FACED INFLATION not only as an economist/Governor, but also as an employer. By the early 1950s, the Commonwealth Bank's wage and salary structure had come to be regarded as the standard for the banking industry and for many insurance companies – with pay rates above the Arbitration Court's federal banking award. To play his part in defeating inflation, Coombs clashed publicly with his own staff.

In 1952, Bank officers sought pay increases – that is, increases in the margins, above the basic wage, to which their industry was entitled – in order to keep pace with the rising cost of living. The Bank's Classification Committee, after asking staff to document the impact of recent price rises on their household budgets, concluded that the case for a pay increase was very strong. However, that committee, on which the Commonwealth Bank Officers Association (CBOA) was represented, also felt a responsibility as the effective wage fixer for the industry. It therefore decided to defer any pay increase. In September 1952, at the CBOA's annual conference, Coombs 'met the delegates and explained the Bank's reluctance to lead the way in salary matters when it was known as a certainty that so many others would follow'.[1]

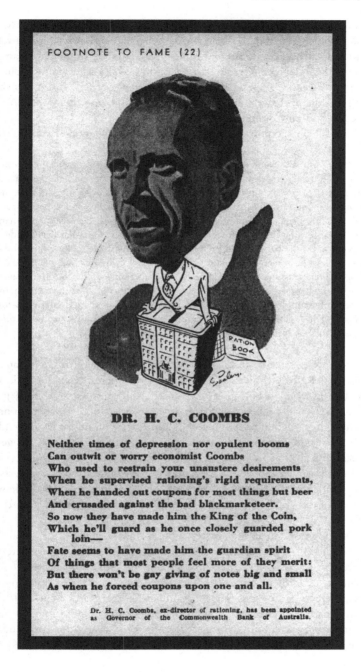

FOOTNOTE TO FAME (22)

DR. H. C. COOMBS

Neither times of depression nor opulent booms
Can outwit or worry economist Coombs
Who used to restrain your unaustere desirements
When he supervised rationing's rigid requirements,
When he handed out coupons for most things but beer
And crusaded against the bad blackmarketeer.
So now they have made him the King of the Coin,
Which he'll guard as he once closely guarded pork
    loin—
Fate seems to have made him the guardian spirit
Of things that most people feel more of they merit:
But there won't be gay giving of notes big and small
As when he forced coupons upon one and all.

Dr. H. C. Coombs, ex-director of rationing, has been appointed
as Governor of the Commonwealth Bank of Australia.

The austerity of Coombs' approach to boom times has been forgotten,
but it was predicted in this (best forgotten) doggerel of 1948–9.

Commonwealth Bank staff now looked to the Commonwealth Public Service Arbitrator, which referred the issue of marginal rates to the Commonwealth Arbitration Court. That avenue did not promise a quick response. Meanwhile public service employees covered by the New South Wales arbitration system were getting rises. By June 1953, when a special conference of the CBOA was called, many CBOA members were fed up with the Bank and with their representatives on the Classification Committee.

In August 1953, Coombs addressed this discontent in an open letter to staff.

The Commonwealth Bank above all must take into account the general economic and social circumstances in which it operates and cannot ignore the outside consequences of any actions it takes. The staff is aware that at the present time, the question of margins is a live issue over the widest possible range of occupations, and statutory authorities, Commonwealth and State, are, and have been for many months, concerning themselves with it. No significant decision has been made as yet. A move by the bank would be followed by many of the major 'white-collar' institutions who, in fact, now make a practice of following our salary scales. Such widespread repercussions would impinge on the functions of the Arbitration Court. There is a widespread concern at the relatively high level of costs in Australia and it is certainly true that a general upward adjustment of wages and salaries, before productivity has increased sufficiently, could start anew the upward spiral of price increases which is at present somewhat precariously halted.[2]

Coombs' letter must be read against the background of changes in the bases of wage-fixation. Following criticism of the 1950 increases in the basic wage and the female wage, in November 1951, the Arbitration Court's Chief Justice Raymond Kelly had convened a conference between employers and unions to discuss how they might attack inflation. Within a few months he had circulated his own conclusions from that discussion: a substantial cut in the basic wage over three years, and a parallel freezing of the 'margins for skill' – the payments which elevated many workers above the basic wage. So encouraged, the employers had formally applied to the Court, in June 1952, for a reduction in the basic wage, an increase in the hours of work and the abolition of the quarterly adjustments to wages.

The ensuing case, which took fifteen months to hear, persuaded the court that quarterly cost-of-living adjustments should cease and that future wage determinations were to be based on seven indicators of the soundness of the economy: employment, investment, production and productivity, overseas trade, overseas balances, the competitive position of secondary industry, and retail trade. 'The court's role had been changed ... from succouring the weak in industry to the enormous task of economic manager.'[3] Deferring a pay rise for bank industry employees, pending this reconsideration of the basic wage, Coombs angered many of his staff.

Because of his democratic style of Governorship, he was not shielded from this anger. The Bank's monthly staff journal *Currency* gave staff a voice. As Coombs stated in the first issue,

The interest and satisfaction which our job can give us are the greater if our understanding of the tasks and policies of the Bank is wide and thorough. Accordingly, to provide a stimulus and a channel for our officers' pride and satisfaction in their profession, the Bank has decided to issue this new Magazine. Its aim will be to keep you better informed on all aspects of the Bank's work and of life within the Bank. We hope it will help you to see how your particular job fits into the work of the rest and how the joint effort makes the Bank a vital unit in the national economy.[4]

So Coombs heard his staff debate the Bank's denial of a pay increase.

In September 1953 'Jape' listed staff perquisites available at other banks, arguing that the Commonwealth was not the source of all industry precedent, while 'One of Your Staff' detailed the indignities associated with a continuing low salary, concluding 'We are asking for a fair go.' In October 1953, A. G. C. Fraser portrayed Coombs as a *de facto* Conciliation Commissioner with a responsibility to seek wage justice rather than to apply what he imagined to be the government's anti-inflation incomes policy. L. T. Withers, in the same issue, accused Coombs of appealing to the 'bogy of inflation', commenting 'it is always the wage-earner who is the loser during a period of inflation, which might explain the present mood of the staff'. 'Suburban Manager' argued that the Bank's recent economies justified a pay increase. 'Mullum' asked the Bank to base its pay decision not on the 'economy' – a rationale implying that Bank staff were no more than 'clerks' – but on the Bank's interest in its officers' maintaining – in lifestyle and comportment – their image as 'leaders in the business or professional fields'. In the November *Currency* Lindsay E. Byrne disputed the Governor's implied view that inflation had come from higher wages, countering that higher wages would encourage productivity. In April 1954, 'Quo Vadis' asked: 'Does Dr. Coombs realise what a disgruntled staff he has?' This correspondent complained that 'the profit motive has become a fetish with our Bank'.

Most Australian economists were not CEOs and not *de facto* arbitrators of industry-wide pay scales. Governor Coombs was. More than most economists, he was exposed to the real impacts of Australia's essay in anti-inflationary incomes policy.

Carrots and sticks

IN COOMBS' PHILOSOPHY of regulation, the regulator should lead the regulated to relaxed acquiescence to a set of rules and conventions which the regulated would apply to themselves. As he made plain in his ES&A Lecture in September 1954, he was ready to discuss with the trading banks new, voluntary restraints on lending. They had taken a step in that direction in the first half of 1953, agreeing that in exchange for the government's moderation of the Special Account power, trading banks would hold one one-quarter of their deposits in the form of liquid assets or of government securities (LGS). Would this gentlemen's agreement develop the authority of a convention?

No. To violate the 25 per cent LGS ratio (as this agreement was known) proved too tempting for the banks. In 1954/5, the LGS ratio averaged only 18 per cent, as the banks competed for borrowers. Schedvin has pointed to a number of factors in extenuation of the banks' breach of the gentlemen's agreement.[1] However, we should not forget the political context. By November 1954, Menzies and Fadden had agreed, under pressure from the Australian Bankers Association, to review the banking legislation, so raising the possibility that the banks would soon be free of the hated Special Account. Might not the banks have judged that the entire Coombs' regulatory project was about to fail?

When Coombs realised that Menzies and Fadden were yielding to the call from the Australian Bankers Association for a review of legislation, he sought to delay the loss of the Special Account. In an internal paper of March 1955 the Bank considered the alternatives.

> If a move away from Special Accounts to a minimum reserve system is made, it may be possible to incorporate in the legislation a requirement for minimum holdings of cash, liquid assets or L.G.S. assets [that is, a ratio of liquid assets and government securities to deposits].

Alternatively,

> the banks might be prepared to accept long-term low-interest-bearing Government securities in exchange for part or all of their present Special Account balances. This would put a sharper edge to our reserve powers.[2]

Coombs further discussed alternatives to the Special Account with his Board in July 1955. He was authorised to keep talking to the banks on the basis

> a. that in the long run the banking system would be best served by a conventional standard of L.G.S. ratios, b. that this could not be effective without its acceptance by the trading banks, c. that, until the banks indicate their willingness and capacity to work to such a standard and while the need for restraint in lending continues, *Special Accounts be administered so as to keep pressure on the system generally* and, in particular, on the less liquid banks.[3]

In short, Coombs' credit policy in 1955/6 was aimed not only at curbing the inflation which once again threatened Australia, but also at persuading the banks to embrace an adequate substitute for the Special Account – an instrument of persuasion that might soon be taken from him.

For a while, during 1955/6, the Commonwealth Bank continued to use its Special Account powers leniently, as if the banks actually were observing the LGS ratio of 25 per cent. The danger of such diplomacy was that the trading banks would enjoy its liberality without adopting any of the self-restraint it was meant to encourage. The Bank soon found it necessary to be more demanding on Special Account. As Coombs later explained,

The Central Bank could not administer Special Account on the basis of a convention until there was firm evidence of the banks' willingness and capacity to observe it. In the absence of a convention, it could only revert to the practice of keeping the least liquid banks with little more than till money and thus continuously dependent on the Central bank for loans.[4]

The Commonwealth Bank now began to charge a punitive rate of interest whenever a bank found it necessary to borrow back some of its Special Account. Such a toughening stance on Special Account, he calculated, 'the banks could scarcely find palatable'.[5] Downing and Melville would have been pleased: no more fairy godmother. The banks' incentive to bind themselves to a high LGS convention was that the Commonwealth Bank paid them a very low rate of interest on their Special Account (and now charged them a relatively high rate when they had emergency recourse to that account). The higher the LGS ratio, the smaller the Special Account obligation could be, and the more income the banks could generate from the money they were not lending to customers. It cramped Coombs' tactics that he could not persuade Fadden to allow the interest on government securities to rise, to make credit self-discipline more financially rewarding for the banks.

The banks could respond to Coombs' combination of pressure and exhortation in two ways. One was to lobby the government to legislate to remove the big stick – Special Account – from Coombs' hand. The other was to take the LGS convention more seriously, hoping that this would so satisfy Coombs that he would not use his big stick.

In the short term, the banks preferred the former, more confrontational, course. In the ten years following Chifley's attempted nationalisation, with banks resenting every governmental encroachment on their business, cooperation and trust between government and banks was elusive. A generation of private bank leaders had been fired with suspicion in 1947–9. Worse, the Menzies government, although elected to restore free enterprise, had shown in 1953 how susceptible it was to the arguments of Chifley's men. Bad relations between the Commonwealth Bank and the private banks may also have been exacerbated by the Menzies and Fadden government requiring too much of monetary policy. According to Heinz Arndt,

> the ultimate responsibility for the renewal of inflation in 1954-5 lay neither with the central bank nor with the trading banks, but with the Government's failure to take any disinflationary action in its own sphere, whether through budget policy, direct controls, or an adjustment in the rate of immigration and development, thus throwing an impossible burden on monetary policy.[6]

In its most aggressive form, the banks' push against credit regulation became personal. In April 1955 a number of newspapers in Canberra, Melbourne, Brisbane and Newcastle reported an impending attack by Liberal MPs on the government's banking policy. The *Canberra Times* said that the backbenchers' demands included not only 'liberalisation of present credit restraint', separation of the central bank, and 'easing of Special Account', but also 'removal of present Governor' (whose seven-year term was to expire at the end of 1955). When the Bank tightened credit in September 1955, the *Daily Telegraph* headlined 'Dr. Coombs' plan is a gospel of mediocrity', and the *Daily Mirror* 'Public servant gives a policy of despair'. Randerson in the *Sunday Telegraph* profiled Coombs in critical terms.[7]

In 1955 and 1956, the banks reiterated the case the Australian Bankers Association had presented in December 1954 against Special Account. To replace it, they wanted a 'statutory reserve deposit', with a maximum of 15 per cent, allowing that the central bank could increase that ratio to 25 per cent, with three months written notice. Coombs told Fadden in April 1956 that this would be insufficient restraint. Reviewing the inflation of October 1953 – October 1955, he concluded that

> throughout the period the Central bank held in Special Account substantially more than the standard maximum and at times as much as the emergency maximum proposed by the Trading Banks. Despite this action, trading bank advances grew from 721m pounds to 936m pounds, a growth which was recognised here and abroad as a significant cause in the development of inflationary conditions in Australia.[8]

The Special Account powers were now 'barely adequate' and so should not be further cut.

It was difficult for Coombs to contrive just the right blend of carrot and stick. Fadden, a Country Party MP, felt the rural producer's distaste for and apprehension about the private banks. He was prepared to resist their calls for softer regulation. However, he was also unmoved by Coombs' plea, since 1953, to allow the banks to earn more interest from government securities. Coombs had good reason to declare his opposition to low interest rates. The direction of both monetary and fiscal policies sometimes required the Bank to soak up liquidity with attractively priced government bonds and to discourage the public's borrowing with tougher repayment schedules – both measures implying higher rates of interest. As we will see (pages 243–8), Coombs thought that hire-purchase firms, beyond his regulatory mandate, were advantaged in a low interest rate regime. The private banks favoured interest rate rises as a more profitable way to ration credit, when credit had to be tight. They expected Coombs to push their case, and Coombs welcomed any chance to ally himself with the banks when it suited his regulatory purposes.

Withstanding Coombs' assault on the low interest rate orthodoxy, Fadden and Menzies, backed by Roland Wilson, did not allow interest rates on government securities to rise until March 1956. Making that change, Menzies and Fadden showed their sensitivity to popular scepticism about banks' profits by decreeing a corresponding reduction in the rate of interest that the banks earned on the compulsory Special Accounts.[9] The Labor Party remained a steadfast supporter of 'cheap money', seeing the issue as 'the money-sellers' versus 'ordinary people'.[10]

It was the bane of Coombs' Governorship that he found it hard to secure a parliamentary champion for his blend of pressure and invitation.

The banks eventually embraced Coombs' alternative to abolishing the Special Account and adopted a mild form of the LGS convention. Coombs and the banks agreed to a ratio of 14 per cent (liquid and government securities to total deposits), to be operative by June 1956. Schedvin comments that although 14 per cent was lower than Coombs would have liked, it nonetheless secured the banks' support for a self-regulatory convention and so achieved his basic aim of elaborating a more cooperative credit policy.

Women at the Bank

IN 1958, COOMBS found a homely analogy for the central bank's relationship with the government. A central bank

> should go about her own housekeeping affairs independently, efficiently, expecting of her husband recognition of her sphere of responsibility but in matters where these touched upon those of the government she might like any wife cajole or wheedle – indeed even nag – but if such feminine devices failed she would wisely and gracefully bow to superior masculine wisdom and authority.[1]

Though casting himself in the wifely role, Coombs' implied norm of marital relations makes no concession to the ideals of sex equality espoused a century earlier by one of his intellectual heroes, John Stuart Mill (*The subjection of women*, 1869).

As Governor of the Commonwealth Bank of Australia (1949–59) and then of the Reserve Bank of Australia (1960–8), Coombs was an employer of thousands of men and women, most of them in white-collar jobs. The Bank recruited young men as clerks and tellers and young women as typistes. Most women married, so their time in the Bank was short, for Section 170(2) of the *Commonwealth Bank Act 1945* provided that except in 'special circumstances', 'every female officer shall cease to be an officer on her marriage'.

The Bank was thus part of the wider public service culture of male privilege. Women were typistes, stenographers and machinists who left work when they married; men were clerks and promotable throughout their 'career service' until retirement. Though World War II had forced governments to accept women doing 'men's jobs', the old practices of the 'career service' largely resumed at war's end. Three kinds of barrier to gender equity were central: women were expected or required to resign their jobs and leave the workforce upon marriage; certain jobs – characteristically poorly paid – were regarded as women's jobs, and others – better-paid – as men's jobs; and when men and women did the same job, men were paid more.

Each of these discriminations was contested during Coombs' time as an employer. For example, in New South Wales, equal pay was granted in principle in 1959 (and in practice, for teachers, in 1963); the bar against married women in the Commonwealth Public Service was removed in 1966; employees of the Commonwealth government were granted equal pay just after Coombs' retirement, in 1969. The Conciliation and Arbitration Commission granted restricted equal pay in 1969, extended it in the national wage case of 1972 and then, in 1974, extended the minimum wage to women. In 1973 the Commonwealth public service established maternity leave (twelve weeks on full pay). It proved harder to change established patterns of aspiration and workplace culture, which made certain occupations 'male' and others 'female', whatever the law said.

What was Coombs' contribution to these changes?

With a high turnover of women employees – partly a result of its own policy – the Commonwealth Bank had always been rather casual in selecting and training women. However, soon after Coombs became Governor, the Staff Department began to recognise problems of wasted potential and of supervision. In 1952, Coombs appointed a psychologist, Mrs Maxine Bucklow, to investigate whether 'the present employment conditions of women in the Bank constitute a career service'.[2] She would also counsel women staff about personal problems that lay beyond a male supervisor's competence. Bucklow escaped the ban on married women because her professional qualification and her expected role as an executive with empathy for typistes and stenographers made her a 'special case'. However, her employment status remained 'temporary', so that she was not entitled to superannuation and she remained outside the normal promotion stream.

Bucklow's survey of female Bank staff in New South Wales confirmed that all was not well with the Bank's women. In future selection of 'girls', she recommended, the Bank should recognise that many were now performing clerical and administrative duties, not simply typing or tending the new business machines. If more women could be streamed into clerical duties, men could be freed to work in classifications in which low turnover was desirable.[3] The distinguishing of clerical duties into those suited to high-turnover women (low skill, small investment in training) and those suited to low-turnover men (high skill, larger investment in training) scarcely contested established notions of gendered job entitlement.

In the pages of *Currency* the Bank showed off the few women holding jobs above the level of typist. In August 1953, Coombs' personal secretary since 1942, Mrs F. M. Grant, was featured, with a brief account of her distinguished career as a personal assistant to a series of powerful Canberra men. In December 1954, it was the turn of Mrs Bucklow's assistant, Miss Edna Hanscombe, the Bank's first female section officer. The first 'woman assistant staff officer' appointed in Victoria, Miss Muriel Yeates (previously head typist in the Accountants Department) was the subject of a warm profile in the February 1955 issue. These women were not mere tokens. As supervisors and counsellors of women staff, Bucklow, Hanscombe and Yeates were expected to help the Bank make better use of women employees, and that made them advocates of women's interests. Grant and Hanscombe reported to *Currency* readers the impressions they had gained, in recent overseas travels, of the employment of women. In Barclay's Bank, for example, women did not have to resign at marriage, and 'this is true of many of the banks I visited', Hanscombe reported. She made favourable mention of banks in Sweden, Norway and Finland, but found little to praise in France and Italy. In the United States, 10 per cent of the country's 105,000 executive bank staff were women.[4]

When the US economist and banking expert, B. H. Beckhart, visited the Bank in 1957, his wife, Margaret Myers Beckhart, who taught economics as Vassar, came too. At the end of their stay *Currency* published her account of Australia's gender relations. 'I've enjoyed some delicious afternoon teas in your homes, but do you know, there is so much satisfying work a woman could do in the time it takes to make seven kinds of cake.' She found Australian men 'insecure' and 'unsure of their virility' in their determination to keep women down; and in women she detected 'a strong undercurrent of bitterness', which she urged them to turn into political action. 'It is only a Nazi dictatorship or a caste system which forces individuals against their will into certain types of jobs, and excludes them from others.' She drew parallels between women's rights and Negro rights, and she held up Eleanor and Franklin Roosevelt as a couple who modelled respect for one another's intelligence.[5]

Currency's letter pages – more agitated by the tensions between graduate cadets and unqualified clerks, between the 'administration' and the 'branches', between those who liked contemporary bank advertising and those who found it un-dignified – printed a few responses to these overseas examples of fairer relations between the sexes. In an effort to rouse debate (or was it to quash it?) an anonymous contributor issued 'a challenge to women' in September 1958, inviting 'girls' to train in various fields, and aspire to go beyond the typing pool. The letter implied that their supine habits of mind retarded women – no mention of the Bank's power to end the career of any woman, no matter how well-trained, who made the mistake of marrying. In the same issue a correspondent, 'Only a woman officer', put it to the Bank that Hanscombe's articles on overseas practices had shamed the Bank. 'There can be no possible future for a woman here if present conditions continue', she asserted, describing as 'degrading' the rule against married women working. And why could women not be tellers?, she demanded to know.[6] The following issues contained no response to either piece. *Currency* continued to reflect in its cartoons a confidently male chauvinist office culture. In December 1960, a correspondent 'King Solomon' found many reasons, in responding to another piece by Margaret Myers Beckhart, to defend the male–female *status quo*. *Currency* offers stronger evidence of Bank staff's complacency about gender inequity than of discontent, but the discontent was there.

It was not until 'after separation' that either bank did anything about equal pay and associated issues. *The Commonwealth Bank Act 1959* restated the ban on married women (save in 'special' cases), but the *Reserve Bank Act 1959* omitted it. The issue for Coombs appears to have been whether inclusion or exclusion of such a clause gave management the more discretion. In July and August 1957, at the

same time as Beckhart was lambasting the Bank's sex discrimination, the Public
Service Board was warning Coombs to continue the bar against married women.
Otherwise the Bank might be obliged 'to employ all married women as fully
fledged members of the Bank's service' and to formulate 'special rules' on preg-
nancy leave and on 'leave to meet family crises, etc.'. The Bank's Staff Department
advised that 'it could prove embarrassing and not conducive to efficiency for the
Bank to be required to continue to employ female staff after marriage'. At first,
Coombs was 'strongly' in agreement. He asked for the Reserve Bank bill to make
marriage grounds for discharge of female staff 'unless the Bank considers it
desirable that she should continue'.[7]

Evidently, Coombs changed his mind. During the formulation of the bank
legislation, the Boyer inquiry into public service recruitment was hearing submissions from (among other women) Helen Crisp, spouse of Coombs' old
colleague Fin Crisp, arguing that the marriage bar was unfair to women in the
Third Division. The Boyer Committee recommended in 1959 that it was for
individuals, not the state, to decide whether or not a woman should be employed
after her marriage.[8] The winds of liberalism were blowing, and Coombs wished to
be free to respond to their redirection. Perhaps because it would no longer be his
concern, he agreed that the future Commonwealth Bank should continue to be
bound by a section allowing married women only in 'special cases', but the *Reserve
Bank Act* would say nothing about married women.[9]

No married woman had been appointed to the permanent staff of the Reserve
Bank by February 1962. Managerial discretion was secured and exercised con-
servatively in both the Reserve and the Commonwealth Bank. Section 67 of the
Reserve Bank Act allowed for some employees to be 'temporary' and 'casual'. In
practice, they were 'married women or people not eligible for permanent
appointment because of their nationality or on medical grounds'. They were thus
denied the pension benefits available to permanent employees and 'removed from
the normal promotional stream'. Mrs Bucklow, now with ten years' service,
continued to be employed as a Reserve Bank 'temporary'. The Bank began to
question this inequity in February 1962.[10]

The Commonwealth Bank Officers Association (which formed a Reserve Bank
Division upon separation) was not, in 1960, a champion of sex equality. Though
nominally in favour of equal pay, like the rest of the trade union movement at that
time, the CBOA devoted no resources to pursuing that goal. The CBOA was also
worried that it would harm the promotional prospects of single girls to lift restrictions on married women's employment. (That is, married women, being usually
older and more experienced, would win senior positions open to women.)

On 3 January 1964, in the interests of developing and using the talents of all of
its staff, the Bank set up a committee, with CBOA representation, to examine the
employment of women.[11] 'Second-class citizen' wrote to *Currency* in November
1964 querying this committee's failure to ask for submissions. However, the
CBOA solicited some submissions informally. The committee reported in January
1965 that there were indeed few women in clerical and administrative positions.
Women should be specially recruited for such work, it recommended, as well as

promoted from the ranks of typists and machinists, trained, and then paid the same as men. The pay for 'women's work' was not too low, opined the committee, but stenographers should be given more of a 'career', through the extension of the concept of the executive 'secretary' to more outstanding members of the typing pool, and through pay increments for length of service. The committee was notably cautious in advocating the interests of married women, falling short of stating that women had a right to continue in their jobs upon marriage. It counselled the Bank to continue its policy of discretion, but to become less arbitrary, by developing and stating criteria for retaining or discarding married women. Perhaps women above a certain salary level could be retained upon marriage, it suggested, with no loss of the entitlements of permanency. However, married women should be required to resign once they became pregnant, as maternity leave would be inequitable towards men.[12]

The Reserve Bank announced new policies on female employment within weeks, going further than the committee had dared. All women would now be allowed to stay in service after marriage. They could even be granted, upon application, one week's marriage leave and leave without pay before and after childbirth. However, the Bank, like the committee, remained cautious about the employment of married women after they had had a child. In October 1965, the Bank announced a trainee scheme to allow women in secretarial work to transfer to clerical and administrative duties.[13]

Coombs' time as Governor of the Reserve Bank was a period of intermittent discussion and cautious reform of the subjection of women. Under his leadership, the Bank was among the Commonwealth public service's *avant garde* in the matter of married women's right to a job, but only just. Cabinet decided 'in principle' to endorse the Boyer Committee's 1959 recommendation in November 1965 – under pressure of repeated questions in the House by Labor's Bill Hayden – and a bill to that effect was introduced to the Parliament in October 1966.[14]

A culture of inflation

WHEN GOVERNOR COOMBS broke his five-year silence on issues of economic policy – addressing Canberra economists on 26 October 1953 – he reformulated the aims of Australian economic policy as 'Full Employment without Inflation'.

> No one would wish to return to the wastes and injustices of unemployment of the kind experienced through the thirties. We have, however, seen that wastes and injustices – perhaps not as serious, but none the less devastating in their social and economic implications – flow from excess demand, from rapidly rising prices and all that goes with inflation.[1]

From the floor, Trevor Swan questioned Coombs' critical assessment of Australia's efforts, to date, to curb inflation. Given the huge export incomes earned during the Korean War's global raw materials boom, it would have been impossible for Australia to avoid price rises. Swan thought that government policies had done well to keep inflation as low as it had been in 1950–2. In reply, Coombs distinguished between two causes of Australia's inflation: the prices of its exported goods – which Australian governments could do little about – and the level of aggregate demand – the responsibility, undoubtedly, of governments. He did not want his fellow economists to let external factors obscure the failure of policy. Australia's inflation was no global accident, he insisted, but a result of internal political arrangements that Australians had to think about.[2]

The danger of inflation and the difficulty of curbing excess demand remained linked themes of Coombs' speeches throughout the 1950s. At the ANZAAS conference in August 1955 he set out some causes and consequences of inflation. When tracing consequences he argued that inflation contributed to a deterioration in Australia's balance of payments: that is, if Australian prices rose relative to world prices, its exports would be less competitive, export earnings would fall and Australians would lose some ability to import. His account of the causes of inflation highlighted excessive expenditure on development. Australia had to find more resources for development – by increasing productivity and/or savings and/or overseas borrowing and/or export production and/or import replacement. In each of these options he saw problems as well as opportunities, so that it was also necessary to ask the question he had been asking since 1950: how could development expenditure be restrained? He had little to offer by way of recommendations, seeing many weaknesses – 'partly constitutional, partly technical, but partly arising from our own attitudes' – in Australia's instruments of economic management. He was worried about Australia's 'healthy but exuberant tendency to want to do more than our resources will permit'.[3]

Three months later, his notes for an address on central banking referred to Australia's recent experience of 'severe inflation resulting in social injustices, distortions and inefficiencies in industry and a weakening of our competitive trading position'.[4] In July 1956 he again surveyed the recent tendency towards inflation, in an address to Newcastle accountants. Calling for reduced defence expenditure, he warned as well that Australia was becoming too reliant on overseas investment.[5] In his R. C. Mills Memorial Lecture of April 1958, he deplored the public reaction to tax increases in the 1955/6 budget. 'It is a sad commentary on the level of political and economic understanding that action which was no more than adequate to maintain the integrity of public finance and to avoid intensifying an already vigorous inflationary trend required political courage of such a high order.'[6]

Advocate of full employment in the 1940s, Coombs found it necessary to become Australia's anti-inflationary conscience in the 1950s.

Coombs' voiced understanding of Australia's inflation passed through three phases. At first, his emphasis was on structural factors. Unbalanced development of the economy combined with excessive demand to create shortages of labour and materials which helped raise their prices. In the early 1950s, his attention shifted more to the lack of political will to manage the level of aggregate demand. Towards the end of the 1950s and into the early 1960s Coombs shifted to a third per-spective, 'cost' inflation – a theory too often neglected by Australian economists, according to J. E. Isaac. 'Cost inflation' resulted from 'incompatible income claims between groups of wage earners and between wage earners and profit earners. ... Cost inflation can exist with or without excess demand.'[7]

Coombs reflected on inflation's challenge in his 1959 ANZAAS Presidential Address in Perth, 'A matter of prices', opening with the doleful question 'Must prices always rise?' Notwithstanding the conquest of hyper-inflation in 1952/3, Australian prices had continued to rise at about 3 per cent per year, he noted. If this slow deterioration in the value of money were now 'normal', then Australia faced 'a very serious economic problem'. As well as causing high internal costs that damaged Australian export performance, creeping inflation reduced the burden of investors' debt and thus boosted the profits of capitalists who borrowed their capital. This violated Coombs' principle that, while investors were to be rewarded for risk and entrepreneurship, it should be a transparent reward, with a clear assignment of the community's costs. Those profiting in this way were effectively diverting wealth from public investment into private consumption, he suggested.

Coombs worried that Australians had developed a tolerance for inflation. There was too little competitive pricing in Australia, because of monopolies, because consumers were insufficiently price-conscious, and because more was nowadays invested in packaging, advertising and retailing. Meanwhile, wage-earners were legitimately seeking to share in the rising productivity of their labour, with help from the Arbitration Commission. Taken together, the price-fixing practices of managers and the wage-seeking practices of unions promoted a wage-price spiral in which the real value of wages was persistently eroded. He urged wage-earners and managers to 'abstain from increasing one another's costs and ... as opportunity offers, reduce them, to their mutual advantage, by reducing their selling prices'.[8] Wage-earners' standards of living would be increased more effectively through better public services, he suggested.

Economists of the 1940s who absorbed Keynes' arguments about the im-portance of 'expectations' were necessarily cultural observers and social critics. In 'A Matter of Prices', Coombs' most developed essay in such social criticism, he directed listeners' critical attention away from politicians' fears (that to control aggregate demand would make too many political enemies) and towards the people's problematic hopes and expectations. Though he canvassed some policy changes – taxes to encourage savings, more public goods for wage and salary earners – the fundamental problems he identified in this address were attitudinal, rather than institutional. 'Fundamentally, prices rise because too many people wish them to rise and too few are anxious to resist.' The most important change required to beat inflation, then, was a 'change of heart'.[9] As Giblin had said in 1945, the Kingdom of Heaven is within us.

Portraying broad culpability for a culture of inflation, Coombs avoided blaming the trade union movement; nor did he condemn the Arbitration Com-mission as susceptible to union pressures. Yet F. L. Fitzpatrick, General Manager of Rocla Pipes, wrote to congratulate Coombs as if 'A Matter of Prices' had been a critical reflection on the economic irrationality of the Arbitration Commission. 'It seems truly deplorable that a court comprised of lawyers, and independent of the Country's financial controllers, can be allowed to produce a result so devastating to the best interests of the country and so unjust in its effects', wrote Fitzpatrick.[10] Another correspondent thought Coombs had underlined the danger that the Arbitration Court posed to the country.[11] These were self-interested and partial readings of Coombs' argument that the culture of inflation was sustained by the interlocking expectations and interests of unions, consumers and employers.

There remained the problem of Arbitration. Could it ever be the instrument of what economists regarded as a rational incomes policy? In January 1960, Liberal MP Leslie Bury declared that 'the decisions of the Arbitration Court in recent years have been one of the major contributory causes of price instability'.[12]

As always, Coombs pleaded for a softening of polarities. He told an Adelaide audience of businessmen in February 1960 that 'if we could review wage rates less frequently, there would be more time for industry to adjust its methods to counter increases in costs. ... The difficulty is to establish a sufficient trust on both sides of the labour market for this period to be allowed to elapse. I should not think this was impossible.'[13]

Separation

AFTER THE DECEMBER 1955 general election, agitation for the breaking up of the Commonwealth Bank revived within the Liberal Party and in the press.[1] Some newspapers continued to emphasise the lingering threat of nationalisation. Thus the *Hobart Mercury*: 'It would be quite possible for the bank by means of unfair competition to force the private banks out of business.'[2] However, this was a waning theme, and the *Age* explicitly rejected nationalisation as nothing more than a 'purely emotional undertone' to the otherwise laudable campaign for separation of central bank from other bank functions.[3] Public comment more commonly named 'trust' as the issue: if the Commonwealth Bank wanted to be both player (trading bank) and umpire (central bank), it could not expect the other players' full cooperation. Cautiously, Menzies acknowledged the persistence of this ferment throughout 1956 by announcing a series of conferences with the private banks, Treasury and the Commonwealth Bank in February 1957.

Coombs firmly rejected the argument that the Commonwealth Trading Bank was unfairly advantaged. The Bank's memorandum suggested that its success was 'due primarily to keen leadership of the present General Manager and enthusiasm on the part of a well-trained staff'.[4]

The private banks had told the government that they could not trust a central bank associated intimately with one of their competitors. The Bank replied:

Confidence can only be established between the Commonwealth Bank and the trading banks as a result of experience in facing the problems of the economic system together, and so long as it seems likely that banking legislation can be amended in ways favourable to the trading banks, it is unlikely that they will work whole-heartedly to make the present system fully effective.

The Bank appealed for 'an extended holiday from amendments to banking legislation'.

To the allegation that the Governor was distracted from his core central bank work, the Bank replied that the Governor delegated a great deal to the general managers of the Trading Bank and the Industrial Finance Department. Rebutting the charge that the central bank would gain in effectiveness if isolated from the activities of taking deposits and advancing credit, the Bank made four points. The central bank used Savings Bank funds to 'balance the needs of important sectors of the economy's investment programme: Government, semi-Government, local Government and housing'. Through the Savings Bank's purchase of securities, the central bank intervened in national liquidity. Lending by the Trading Bank could be a central bank weapon against depression. Central bank staff had a firmer grip on the realities of Australian finance by virtue of the central bank's composite structure.

However, the private banks were unremitting in their call for a stand-alone central bank in 1956 and 1957. The government was divided – the Liberal Party supporting the banks, the Country Party and the Treasury retaining some attachment to the 1936 Royal Commission's argument for a central bank with trading functions.[5] Complaining of Menzies' irresolution, financier Staniforth Ricketson wondered at 'the astonishing power and authority attained by certain bureaucrats in charge of Commonwealth departments and instrumentalities'.[6] It took until 10 April 1957 for Cabinet to agree that there had to be total separation of the Commonwealth Trading Bank from the central (Reserve) bank. The government had become convinced that if the Commonwealth Bank remained a composite of central and trading/savings functions, there would never be trust between private banks and their regulator.

With Coombs' Governorship renewed until the end of 1962, there was little political value in treating this decision as a rebuff to Coombs and a portent of his demise. The Financial Editor of the *Sydney Morning Herald*, Tom Fitzgerald, the Governor's not uncritical admirer, had written in February 1955 that the government's consideration of the separation issue did not imply 'dissatisfaction with the Central Bank Governor's personal administration of credit policy'. Rather, he suggested, history had handicapped the Governor's 'moral command'. 'We are still paying for the bank nationalisation episode, and we shall continue to suffer from its legacy of fear and suspicion until the remaining anomalies are cleared up.'[7] When the government announced separation, he looked forward to a 'Central Reserve bank purified as to its character and motives' which would 'participate in communal thinking and discussions much more than the Commonwealth Bank has done'.[8] The General Manager of the ANZ Bank, applauding Menzies' separation announcement, was careful to add that the banks' campaign had never been intended as any reflection on, or dissatisfaction with, the present administration of the central bank, or its present Governor.[9]

Coombs managed to save something of his vision. He argued that the Reserve Bank should retain a function that should not be entrusted, in the opinion of the Country Party, to the profit-oriented banks: a Rural Credits Department. Cabinet had also to decide the future of another Commonwealth Bank division valued by Country Party voters – the Mortgage Bank. Combined with the Industrial Finance Department, it would become the Commonwealth Development Bank in 1960 and join the Commonwealth Trading and Savings Banks as the subsidiaries of the new Commonwealth Banking Corporation. Though Coombs would rather have had the Development Bank in the Reserve Bank, under his authority, its very existence was a concession to his belief that national development required the dedicated stimulus of a public bank.

The four bills effecting the break-up of the Bank did not go smoothly through Parliament. In November 1957, they were rejected by a Senate in which Queensland Labor Party and Democratic Labor Party senators voted with the Labor Party. The same thing happened in May 1958. Labor's objections to the 1957 bank bills were three. First, in an associated amendment to the *Income Tax Assessment Act*, the government was making the Commonwealth Trading Bank liable for income tax, while retaining the older provision that half of its (after-tax) profits be paid to the Commonwealth Treasury. The Commonwealth Trading Bank was therefore to be more restricted than its competitors in its capacity to accumulate the capital needed to expand its operations.[10] Second, Labor objected that the revised credit controls were too weak. Evatt quoted from Coombs' ES&A Lecture of 1954, with its mild admonishment of private banks' credit policies, to cast doubt on the good faith of the private banks.[11] Third, a central bank was better at its regulatory functions if it had a trading arm. Some Labor speakers cited Coombs' observations on this point.[12] Coombs' quiet campaign of occasional addresses since 1953 had at last given the Labor Party a vision of bank regulation to articulate and to defend. Some Labor speakers asked why the public was not being told of the Governor's opinions of these changes.[13] Coombs remained scrupulously mute.

Not until the Coalition had won a majority of both houses, in December 1958, was it worth re-submitting the bills thus rejected. They were passed by April 1959, after parliamentary debate that ranged widely over the nature and purposes of the Australian financial system. The Reserve Bank commenced operations on 1 January 1960.

Bank historians Schedvin and Butlin have commented that the eclipse of Coombs' composite model of central banking was not a defeat for central banking itself. On the contrary, in the twenty-three years since the Royal Commission on Money and Banking, all sides of Australian politics and the private banks themselves had come gradually to accept the need for firm central bank regulation.[14] That is, it was not controversial, by the late 1950s, that the Reserve Bank should continue the Commonwealth Bank's power over credit, by means of statutory reserve deposits. Nor was it disputed that the Reserve Bank would continue controls over advances and enjoy authority over interest rates. 'Apart from separation', comments Schedvin, 'there is no hint in any of this of departure from Chifley's regulatory regime.'[15] In this assessment he concurred with Butlin, who also commented that the Commonwealth Trading Bank 'was to prove no less formidable a competitor' after separation.[16]

Butlin is far less plausible in finding 'little to justify the Labor complaint in Parliament that the government was obeying the behests of the private banks'.[17] That is precisely what the Menzies government did in 1957–9, because it judged that while the Commonwealth remained a composite Bank, the private banks would not provide (in Fadden's words) 'that close cooperation which ought to subsist between the central bank and the trading banks'.[18] In 1959, the *Sydney Morning Herald* described Fadden as having been 'a tenacious opponent of the whole concept of banking reform in the Cabinet and Government party discussions right to the end. He did not sympathise with the spirit of the reforms he undertook to draft.'[19] Evatt said of Fadden that he was unable to defend the bills of 1957–9 by referring to their real basis – the refusal of the private banks to cooperate until their regulator was reconstructed according to their demands.[20] Indeed, Coombs reflected in *Trial Balance* that the separation of the Reserve Bank from the Commonwealth Bank 'was followed by a significant improvement in our working relationships with the private banks'.[21] Nonetheless, the creation of the Reserve Bank was a defeat for his long-cherished model – a composite central bank – and it is interesting to speculate whether the private banks would have been quite so insistent in their demands had Chifley not antagonised them in 1947–9.

A Melanesian way?

IN 1965, CHARLES ROWLEY, Principal of the Australian School of Pacific Administration from November 1950 to March 1964, declared cash to be 'the Satanic power which breaches the limited cycle of desire and need in the village Eden'. The tree of knowledge was, in the New Guinea case, the 'trade store shelf laden with the dazzling array of industrially produced consumption goods'. In order to 'develop', the New Guinea villager 'has to forget his preoccupation with the great mystery of existence, and learn to add up his money and refuse it to his relatives and "one-talks". His reward is a place on the treadmill with the rest of us.'[1]

By the time Rowley penned this mordant prognosis for the people of New Guinea, Coombs had instigated, in the early 1960s, a mass education campaign to persuade New Guinea people that to save and to borrow money were necessary steps on their road to happiness. However, in a concession to Melanesian custom, Coombs and his Reserve Bank staff had encouraged people to save and borrow as members of a cooperative called a savings and loans society. Coombs' interest in Papua New Guinea engaged him in a post-war discussion about 'development'. Cooperatives were the hope of intellectuals who sought a Melanesian modernity.

Under the Native Economic Development Ordinance of 1951, the Australian administration encouraged cooperatives among the people of Papua New Guinea. A Registrar of Cooperative Societies encouraged producer cooperatives as a basis for the commercialisation of agriculture. Among the enthusiasts for cooperatives had been James McAuley, whose first visits to New Guinea had been as a soldier and then as a 'performing flea in A. A.Conlon's remarkable circus' in 1944. After the war, he became a lecturer in government at the Australian School of Pacific Administration, under Rowley.[2]

Cooperatives, McAuley hoped, would be an antidote to the characteristic faults of modernity.

> Co-operation ... contributes towards the deproletarianization of society by creating a widespread small ownership; and at the same time it creates centres of local autonomy which set limits to State encroachment ... What it is opposed to is easily stated: rank individualism; the pursuit of private gain without regard to the common good; the concentration of economic power into a few autocratic hands, and the consequent loss by the mass of people of economic property and self-determination.[3]

Cooperatives respected personhood, he further argued. In one kind of cooperative, credit societies, 'loans are made on the basis of personal character and not on the security of property'.[4]

However, by 1961, McAuley had lost confidence in any development program that Australia could offer. His own 'civilisation' was too 'shapeless', 'formless', 'unbelieving', 'disordered', 'meaningless' and 'irresolute' to guide New Guineans towards a better way to live.[5] While McAuley ascended into an abstract lyricism about 'tradition', Coombs continued to find a place for 'the cooperative' in his vision of a Melanesian monetary system.

Like McAuley in the early 1950s, Coombs had been worried by 'proletarianisation' of Papua New Guinea people. In 1953, accompanied by Mrs Coombs and several staff in the Bank's aircraft, he visited Port Moresby, Lae, Madang, Manus, Rabaul, Honiara, Espiritu Santo and Noumea, and travelled to the towns of Sogeri, Wau, Bulolo, Goroka, Nondugl, Keravat, Kokopo. Upon his return he wrote to the Administrator D. M. Cleland setting out his vision of New Guinea development. While there was little assistance the Bank could give white settlers, he told Cleland, it was keen to make loans to native councils and cooperatives. Acknowledging that none of these bodies had yet conceived projects that required finance, 'in the meantime I am anxious that the Bank should foster the development of native councils and co-operatives'. Could Cleland suggest how? Coombs raised the possibility of training their clerks, storekeepers and secretaries. Perhaps the Bank could institute 'an award of an honorific character to co-operatives or councils reaching certain stages in development'. He also offered to train natives in the work of the Bank itself. Finally, Coombs declared his faith in the social and economic importance of the village as 'a reasoned and conservative basis for realising the natives' own political and economic aspirations'.[6]

His sympathy for native 'conservatism' did not imply hostility to agricultural reform. On the contrary, he believed that if agriculture could be made more efficient, it would be good for the villagers themselves; and it would free labour for 'larger-scale white enterprises'. Believing that development should be village-based, he wondered what the government could do about a 'proletariat' that had begun to crowd major townships. On the one hand towns and their capitalist enterprises required a waged workforce. On the other hand, such people 'could be a danger and a source of deterioration in native standards as well as providing a medium in which difficult and anti-social influences could grow'. Perhaps the Administration could set up 'new native settlements on the fringes of major townships where the basic peasant agricultural pattern of native village life could be consciously re-built, thus avoiding the emergence of a proletariat completely dependent upon wages from casual employment'.[7] Coombs, like McAuley in the early 1950s, judged 'development' according to whether it conserved valued relationships among New Guinea people – sustaining 'the village', limiting the 'proletariat'.

In 1959 Coombs commissioned a Bank officer J. R. Thomas and a Sydney University anthropologist with New Guinea experience, Dawn Ryan, to survey the emerging indigenous uses of money and their need for credit. In Thomas' and Ryan's regional comparisons they described the desire to borrow for investment as 'sophistication' and as being 'advanced'. Two regions stood out: the Gazelle Peninsula and the town of Port Moresby. The Gazelle Peninsula Tolai seemed to be incipient capitalists. In a talk to the New Guinea Society in Canberra in October 1960, Coombs predicted that they could bring even more land under cultivation were they to borrow the capital from which to pay for labour. 'The Tolai people are efficient producers, shrewd bargainers and acquire an understanding of commercial and financial processes very quickly.'[8] In the other 'advanced' region – Port Moresby – Thomas and Ryan also found users of credit. However, they were not so much farmers as waged workers, fishermen, potters and consumers of the Western goods to whose attractions they had long been exposed.

What form could credit take? New Guineans interviewed by Thomas and Ryan cited Fiji's happy experience of credit unions. Thomas and Ryan suggested that credit unions 'function best where there is a common bond of association among the members'. In a society where land could not be collateral because it remained under customary and inalienable tenure, credit unions solved the problem of an absence of loan security. Decisions to lend could be based on 'the assessment, by the union's executive, of the credit worthiness of the member'.[9]

The Thomas–Ryan report made Coombs more confident that the banks could devise credit policies suited to 'speeding up the economic and financial development of the Territories'.[10] Why was 'speeding up' now presumed to be desirable?

As a trustee of New Guinea, Australia was answerable to a United Nations bent on decolonisation. In 1960 the UN General Assembly's 'Declaration on Colonialism' obliged colonial authorities to justify continuing tutelage. The Menzies government became sensitive to this pressure. Though he could point with pride to such developments as village councils, Menzies' Minister for External Territories, Paul Hasluck, had always avoided stating a blueprint and a time-table for New Guinea's national sovereignty. Now, to deal with the remaining pockets of European colonialism, the United Nations' Trusteeship Council began to ask

Australia for 'development target dates'.[11] Self-determination was understood to require an economic base. Hasluck told an audience of economists in October 1961 that 'if a nation is to have more than a mere pretence of independence, it has to reach a condition in which in matters of production and trade, in standards of living, and in matters of war and peace, its independent government can choose between alternative courses of action and give effect to its choice'.[12]

The formation of the Reserve Bank in 1960 coincided with this political impetus to economic development. Coombs saw an opportunity to give leadership to the private banks in a practical exercise of Australian responsibilities.

Before summoning the four banks working in New Guinea (the Bank of New South Wales, the National Bank of Australia, the Australian and New Zealand Banking Company and the Commonwealth) to a conference in September 1960, he visited New Guinea to gauge the Administration's preparedness to accept banks' help in accelerated development. On 29 August he answered written questions at a public forum convened by the Royal Institute of Public Administration in Port Moresby. Nearly all the questions came from senior officials of the Administration. In dwelling on the difficulties of mobilising indigenous investment, Coombs acknowledged that cooperatives – specifically, credit unions – might be very useful. They might help to mobilise small savings and thus stand as intermediary 'between the individual native and banks. ... Credit channelled through a credit union can give a better security than a loan made to an individual.' He added that credit unions would also be a 'stepping-stone to normal banking practices, so that as income and wealth grow people will come naturally to use normal financial institutions'.[13]

In these remarks, Coombs straddled two alternative perspectives on economic development. On the one hand, credit unions could be a transitional step towards familiarity with banks, on the other hand credit unions could be a *Melanesian alternative* to banks. To what extent was 'development' to be shaped by continuing respect for Melanesian custom? We have a clue to Coombs' thoughts on this issue in 1962. His old friend John Burton asked him to comment on a paper about the prospects of the world's 'non-aligned' nations. Coombs found particularly interesting Burton's discussion of a possible 'pattern of development in under-developed countries, based primarily on improvements in subsistence and village economies rather than by a switch to much more capitalistic forms of production'. That had long been his vision for New Guinea, he told Burton. However, there were two reasons to think that large-scale capitalist development should now be favoured by Australia's policy. Better nutrition and health policies were causing the New Guinea population to grow beyond 'reliance on subsistence and village economies ... without reducing already low standards'. And even 'limited develop-ment' required imported goods and services that must be paid for by exports. 'It is hard to see how an export sector can develop efficiently except on a completely modern technological and capitalistic basis.'[14]

Land tenure was understood by the Australian government to be the single most important impediment to development 'on a completely modern techno-logical and capitalistic basis'. In New Guinea in 1960, because the government had protected customary ownership, only 3 per cent of land was an asset that a group or an individual could alienate to another in sale or in default of a loan. Hasluck now aspired to increase that percentage. In April 1960, he announced a new land policy that would eventually replace customary with modern tenure. 'Native custom will not meet the needs of a society in which, to an increasing extent as the result of rapid economic progress, the native people are planting tree crops such as coffee, cocoa and copra, and engaging in cash farming.' Hasluck wanted to make land available to those of more entrepreneurial spirit – 'the people who need it and will use it'. The Administration, without forcing anyone to give up their customary ownership of land, would henceforth promote a single system of land-holding, 'providing for secure individual registered titles after the pattern of the Australian system'.[15]

This long-term plan to transform the customary bonds between people and land to a relation of alienable property is the background of the banks' monetary education campaigns, led by Coombs in the early 1960s. By promoting 'credit consciousness' they would sympathetically anticipate land tenure reform. Both developments would lead to New Guineans' unprecedented ability to amass capital for investment. This would not happen overnight. How would New Guineans secure loans in the meantime?

Returning from New Guinea at the end of August 1960, Coombs pointed out that land need not be the only collateral. Loans to councils could be secured against their (small but growing) ability to raise taxes. Loans to cooperatives (mostly trade stores and plantations) might require a guarantor – the Administration, the Reserve Bank or the 'association of cooperatives'. Perhaps the Reserve Bank could establish a 'common guarantee fund' for all the banks. There was some hope of securing loans to individuals, if the Administration succeeded in creating leasehold tenure for individual New Guineans of enterprise. However, the credit-worthiness of such individuals remained an unknown, he admitted. Individuals whose land tenure remained customary could be given credit, perhaps, in the form of hire purchase. Failing that, credit unions could lend to them. The banks could loan to credit unions, and they could loan, in turn, to individuals without assets. The credit unions could thus bear the responsibility for individuals' payments. 'This would provide for more effective examination of the credit-worthiness of individual borrowers and more effective discipline of possible defaulters', he suggested.[16] Coombs' senior administrative assistant, G. Lewis, said that many of New Guinea's 232 cooperatives had achieved 'credit consciousness' in that they had borrowed from banks and were meeting the repayment schedule. However, he continued, this did not instil 'credit consciousness' in the individual. That task remained.[17]

Coombs convened a meeting of senior managers of the National, ANZ, New South Wales and Commonwealth Banks on 15 September 1960. In his welcoming remarks he cited a recent conversation with the Prime Minister, in which Menzies urged New Guinea's 'progress to be expedited'. Thanking the banks in advance for being among the expeditors, Coombs invoked 'the winds of change' – British Prime Minister Macmillan's then famous metaphor for the rapid and inevitable passing of Empire as the colonised peoples seized liberty.

However, unlike Coombs, the banks were reluctant to concede the virtues of credit unions. They were unanimous 'that emphasis should be placed on the individual rather than the group in mobilising savings' and that it was necessary 'to break down the existing native collective ownership concept and to build up an individuality cult – asset-wise – in natives'. The people seemed to see no point in banks, they worried. Advertising and education were needed to persuade people to deposit their cash. In discussing prospects for lending, the banks looked with hope at the Gazelle Peninsula and Port Moresby, where people had 'advanced' to become money users, and to local government councils and cooperatives. Three of the four banks saw no sign that individuals were seeking loans. Though the banks conceded that Indigenous borrowing would remain a group matter for some time, they did not think that more credit unions should be encouraged, as the existing cooperatives were already sufficient 'at the present stage of native development'; 'the ultimate aim should be to encourage individual enterprise among the natives'.[18] The normal and desirable bank client, from these banks' point of view, was an individual or corporation with alienable property as security, and with prospects of income. Gradually, these clients would emerge in New Guinea society – no doubt stimulated by the Administration's effort to extinguish communal land tenure – and so the need for cooperatives would fade.

Unlike 'reformist' McAuley, who had seen cooperatives as the most desirable form of collective action for modern times, the banks saw 'cooperation' as at best a stage through which primitives might have to 'advance' in order to become 'normal'. This vocabulary made it difficult to conceive the savings and loan societies as an indigenous *alternative* to the services of the four Australian banks. There was only one modern approach to mobilising credit, in the long run, and the four banks were satisfied that their Australian practices exemplified it.

In the short run, however, cooperatives and credit unions could be part of Coombs' vision. He wanted the Bank 'to forge close links with the co-operative movement, the main indigenous economic institution and training ground in the Territory, which needs the stiffening which consultation on the spot with the Reserve Bank can provide'.[19] The Reserve Bank won Administration support. By June 1961, the Treasurer and Director of Finance was telling the Administrator that savings and loans societies would provide 'another weld in the community awareness of responsibility, self development and joint participation in the common weal'.[20] The Legislative Council of Papua and New Guinea passed the Savings and Loan Societies Ordinance on 28 September 1961, creating the position of Registrar. The Reserve Bank seconded a senior economist, M. J. Phillips, for that job. It had been feared that lack of competent staff would keep the savings and loans movement small. The four banks were persuaded to give staff. By January 1966, twenty-three Reserve Bank staff (excluding typists, and mostly indigenous New Guineans) were engaged full-time on the promotion and supervision of 319 savings clubs and 115 saving and loan societies.[21] However, the savings and loans societies mobilised only a tiny fraction of the credit that circulated in Papua New Guinea by the end of the 1960s.

Ultimately, and in contrast with gloomy McAuley, Coombs saw a happy convergence between (white) Australian and Melanesian ways. In an unpublished retrospective, Coombs recalled the New Guineans as 'natural small capitalists, with the peasants' desire to accumulate. Notions of borrowing and lending came to them more naturally than we expected.' He explained that 'Unlike the Aboriginal Australians, Papuans and New Guineans were not nomadic hunter-gatherers but gardeners and managers of livestock ... They had an understanding of property, and wealth was a source of status and power in their communities.'[22]

Poor man's overdraft

IN FULLY EMPLOYED, prosperous Australia, as Nick Brown has shown, the problems of inflation and wage discipline had another aspect – the undisciplined consumer.[1] Giblin had anticipated in June 1942 that consumers would have to be educated. Released from the privations of war, their pockets refilled weekly and fortnightly, people would have a tendency to spend unwisely, he feared. He hoped that 'some form of control or at least of consumers' education, above the level of commercial advertising' would accompany 'monetary expansion'.[2] Seventeen years later, Coombs' reflections on a decade of 'creeping inflation' echoed Giblin. Urging manufacturers to pass on some of their productivity gains as lower prices, Coombs called as well for 'revision of our attitudes as consumers'. He had long been 'puzzled at the passivity of the Australian public towards rising prices'. He hoped to see 'a more critical consumer's attitude towards prices and a greater scepticism to the incitements of the advertiser and the salesman'.[3]

Twice in the late 1950s, Coombs evoked this problematic consumer with the image of the ostentatious motor car.

> A gracious city – well equipped with well-planned roads and highways, with parks and playing fields, providing fine schools, universities, public buildings, theatres, and the like – may well give a better life for its citizens than one which lacks these amenities but sprouts television antennae from every roof top and whose streets are jammed with opulent chromium studded motor vehicles.[4]

In a speech to a conference on 'Design in Australian Industry' in 1958, Coombs offered, as an instance of poor design, the modern car:

> frequently over-elaborated, extravagant in relation to its purpose and a source of great discomfort and cost to contemporary society ... It has ... become a sort of symbol, something like a 41-inch bust, a symbol of gratification and prestige ... It is, I think, a pity to glorify mundane articles as symbols of status and gratification.[5]

Responsible for monetary policy, Coombs' practical encounter with the privatised, libidinous consumer took the form of a confrontation with hire purchase – high-priced loans for people to acquire such durable goods as family cars, refrigerators and television sets.

Hire-purchase companies grew rapidly in the 1950s. While advances by cheque-paying banks increased fivefold between June 1947 and December 1960, the outstanding balances of hire-purchase companies increased by a factor of 29.[6] Persistent full employment made people more confident that they could meet long debt repayment schedules. Desires grew commensurate with the capacity to requite them. The expansion of Australian manufacturing into the production of consumer durables had eased the transition from an economy of war to an economy of peace. Now such manufacturers were pleased to cooperate with any credit mechanism – and to help promote any change in popular expectations – that redefined refrigerators, radios, televisions and motor cars as necessities, not luxuries.

Hire-purchase charged high rates of interest, yet it was popular. In 1958, economist Richard Downing made sense of this paradox by suggesting that 'people find it so difficult to save voluntarily that it is not surprising they are willing to pay dearly for having someone force them to save'.[7] Through hire purchase, the less 'creditable' members of society had joined – expensively, but affordably – those better-off fellow-citizens who had long enjoyed the bank manager's confidence in their repayment ability. Hire purchase was sometimes described as 'the poor man's overdraft'. The child of full employment, hire purchase allowed the simultaneous democratisation of comfort and thrift.

Coombs' imagery about 'the consumer' sometimes hints at an innately puritanical disdain for some forms of consumer gratification. In 1964 Coombs recalled – evidently with a touch of self-irony – that hire purchase in the 1950s had presented 'problems we could not cope with. I thought it was wicked.'[8] However, whatever moral and psychological resonances unfettered consumption had for Coombs, the problem of hire purchase was practical and institutional. Hire-purchase firms did not fall within the law's definition of a bank. The expansion of 'non-bank finance' mocked his regulatory reach.

In 1949, the first year of his Governorship, Coombs had responded positively to an appeal from Ian Jacoby to allow the company of which he was general manager, Industrial Acceptance Corporation (IAC), to raise capital from the public. Jacoby and IAC were the Australian pioneers of hire purchase, associating themselves between the wars with the small market for luxury cars. Hire purchase was not unknown to Coombs. Indeed, the Bank was one of the IAC's keenest competitors in the late 1940s through its Industrial Finance Department. The latter helped small businesses and farmers to finance *capital* goods – such as a truck, van or tractor – by hire purchase. In March 1949, the IFD's I. A. McGregor summed up his prudential calculus as the 'commercial colloquial yardstick of the three C's':

> Character, Capacity and Capital. Character leading to the essence of the assessment
> and allied to the essential element of Capacity (to repay) with considerations of

Capital subordinated to the other factors which are the keystones, of which Character is the more important of the two.[9]

Jacoby and IAC were not content to confine their business to farmers and small traders. They had long serviced the market for family cars, a business growing in the late 1940s. How could the kind of assessment evoked by McGregor be applied to a customer whose hire purchase would pay not for a tractor but for a car to take the family on picnics, or for a fridge in which to chill beer? In 1950, the Bank ceased to see harm in expanding hire purchase to consumer goods. It erased the distinction previously made between 'industrial and farming machinery or equipment; motor buses and trucks; motor cars' and 'all other goods'.[10]

Jacoby's biographer, Tom Fitzgerald, suggests that the Governor and his staff could hardly have realised that in commending IAC to Treasury, in 1949, as a worthy borrower of capital from the wider public, they were letting a genie out of a bottle. Raising money with debentures in order to finance loans to consumers – both at relatively high rates of interest – IAC and similar firms flourished. To the extent that borrowing from the public freed them from having to borrow from the trading banks, companies such as IAC were moving outside the regulatory reach of the central bank. Had their business remained small, this would not have compromised the Australian system of financial regulation.[11] But they did not remain small.

It was argued in the mid-1950s (and later research confirmed) that hire purchase had a tendency to accentuate tendencies of both boom and contraction, contrary to Coombs' ambition to smooth the business cycle.[12] The private banks also were concerned – not only about the incursion of hire purchase into their own lending business but also about the extra regulatory pressure on the trading banks that was likely to follow indirectly from the dynamism of unregulated finance companies. In 1955, the *Sunday Telegraph*'s Roger Randerson, never slow to pick up a stick with which to beat the Commonwealth Bank, asked 'how the Central bank justifies its restrictions on bank deposit rates and the granting of bank overdrafts when this simply leads to other companies raising and supplying the finance?'[13]

One policy response, advocated by Coombs as we have seen, was to allow bank interest rates to rise. Low bank interest rates not only made it harder to curb the public's spending but also made it easy for hire-purchase companies to attract money that would otherwise have been deposited in a bank or used to purchase government securities.[14] The lower that interest rates were kept, the more Coombs had to rely on verbal persuasion. A conference with the 'responsible leaders in the hire-purchase field' might establish 'a sensible understanding, not of the intrinsic evils of hire purchase, but of the evils of an excessive use of it in an inflationary period', Menzies speculated to Cabinet in September 1955.[15] Some of the people Coombs had to persuade were his old antagonists, the trading bank senior executives, for the trading banks were beginning to respond to the challenge of non-bank financial services by buying equity in hire-purchase companies or by starting their own. 'Between 1953 and 1957, all the seven major private trading banks moved into the field of hire-purchase finance.' The banks envied the freedoms of this growing, unregulated sector of the finance market.[16]

And the new financiers were not deaf to talk of 'responsibility'. To be rich would be sweeter if respectability went with it. Finance company entrepreneurs had started to be regarded as more 'sound' by the established finance capitalists, according to Tom Fitzgerald in 1957. 'These finance companies seem to have gathered new lustre, a new investment regard, a sort of standing little below that of the banks ... The top-line financiers seem to be entering a new era of investment acceptance and some well-worn prejudices are being swept aside.'[17] Such convergence of old financiers with new offered Coombs little comfort. 'A practicable line of approach to solve the problems created by the growth of these institutions was not clearly apparent', his Board sadly concluded by September 1959. Not only did hire purchase make it harder to curb inflation, the Board continued, but 'the soundness and balanced development of the economy' were at stake.[18]

The latter complaint was a growing theme of discussion. The *Age* had complained in 1958 that, because of hire purchase, 'huge sums are being diverted from important areas of industrial and community development'.[19] The prolonged passage of Fadden's banking bills through Parliament made the House a forum for similar comments. Labor MPs, knowing that they no longer had the numbers in the Senate to block the bills for the break-up of the Commonwealth Bank, criticised the government for neglecting the most pressing new issue of monetary policy – hire purchase. 'How ridiculous it is that a man can get easy money – at a price, of course – for a car or a television set', Evatt observed, 'although he frequently cannot get the money for a home to put them in and although his children may have to take their school lessons under the trees or in cloakrooms.'[20] Whitlam, after pointing out that the trading banks had begun to invest in hire-purchase firms, drew the conclusion that because the central bank guaranteed the soundness of trading banks, it also, by extension, stood as guarantor of many hire-purchase firms. 'This Government is conniving at the by-passing of its powers of credit. It has created a completely parallel credit system.'[21] D. B. Copland suggested that the government might 'require all time-payment [hire-purchase] companies to devote a stated proportion of their assets to investment in public utilities which provided goods and services essential for the goods bought on hire purchase'.[22]

Coombs did not take up publicly the issue of the impact of hire purchase on the availability of capital for public purposes. Rather he pointed to problems in smoothing the business cycle, urging the general managers of the trading banks to be more prudent in their new non-bank ventures.[23] In October 1960, Coombs asked them to use whatever influence they had to persuade hire-purchase companies to lend more cautiously in the coming months. In June 1963, the Board authorised Coombs to put some principles of hire purchase lending before the general managers of the trading banks.[24] He invited the trading banks to talk to him about their diversification into non-bank finance. 'When a bank is contemplating some form of association with a non-bank concern, it should inform the Reserve Bank early enough for the Bank to comment.'[25]

Inviting such dialogue, Coombs' kept his public assessments of the hire purchase boom free of the censure heard from Labor MPs and from Copland in 1959. In 'A Matter of Prices', his 1959 critique of the attitudes engendering inflation, Coombs conspicuously omitted to mention (and thus to blame) hire purchase as an institutional prop to 'the passivity of the Australian public towards rising prices'.[26] In his 1964 address to the first National Instalment Credit Conference, he implied that the finance company managers had begun to satisfy his appeals to their 'social responsibility'. His expectations of them were modest. Noting that Australians were not well-provided with credit for two pursuits – industrial research and personal education and training – he doubted 'whether these are appropriate to your industry but the latter might be considered'. In commenting on the contribution of hire purchase to full employment and economic stability, he made a prudential appeal – to 'strengthen ... internal liquidity and capital structure and generally to refrain from emulating the reckless and the irresponsible'. Imprudent firms would eventually be punished by investors (refusing to subscribe capital) and by governments (unspecified 'punitive measures').[27]

In his retrospective essay on the post-war financial system – his 1969 Giblin Lecture – Coombs was at pains to see a logic and a benign order in the changes to financial institutions that mass consumption had stimulated. By then he could tell a story of an 'evolutionary process'.[28] At first, 'the authorities' (including himself) had fought inflation by restricting bank credit. However, this had opened the field of consumer finance to financiers that were not banks. It had been necessary for the central bank to engage with the short-term money market – a market immeasurably stimulated by Jacoby and others' eagerness to attract savings to consumer finance. This had made it prudent for the government to allow interest rates on government securities and bank deposits to rise in order to lure funds back from non-bank intermediaries. Once the trading banks and the central bank had ended their fifteen-year feud (1945–60), they had worked together to make the banks more competitive with non-bank finance, including allowing the banks to become more internally diverse in their ways of doing business – 'a conception of banks as functionally diverse intermediaries inter-penetrating the financial system in almost all classes of business'.[29] With such changes in practice, theory and legislation were also changing, though in what directions he did not care to speculate in 1969.

Coombs' 1969 Giblin lecture was his last public comment on Australian monetary policy. Tom Fitzgerald, after witnessing further financial deregulation in the early 1980s, has described Jacoby as 'an agent of change and eventual dissolution of the regulatory financial system'.[30] 'The inconsistencies Jacoby planted in the financial system contributed to its ultimate deregulation.'[31] Taking Coombs' and Fitzgerald's historical evaluations together, we can identify Coombs' Governorship as transitional between two regulatory philosophies, from Chifley's disbelief that the banks could ever assume public responsibilities to the Hawke and subsequent governments' scepticism about any central bank action that was not mediated by markets in finance and currency. Coombs' approach to banking from 1949 to 1968 assumed that the private banks' profitability and social responsibility could be reconciled in a regulatory regime resting on conventions backed by laws and entrenched by discussion.

In 1964, he saw no reason to apologise to the banks for his demands on them.

> You cannot lose if you put your money into an Australian Bank. It is as safe as the Reserve Bank. No other institution has such an absolute, certain market. Banks are exceedingly privileged people. They are – of all industries – the most privileged people. They are guaranteed against loss – and even guaranteed against competition.

But regulation must be established by persuasion, he insisted, not simply by legislation. 'The Americans call it the "Open Mouth Policy"', he joked. 'Understanding is the most important thing.'[32]

Frustrated internationalist

THROUGHOUT HIS Governorship Coombs remained interested in the problems of international trade and economic development that had kept him so busy during 1943–8. In 1959, his old friend Thomas Balogh, retained by the Bank as an occasional commentator on North Atlantic affairs, described the malaise of most international agencies – 'waste, frustrated labour, repetition of jobs and general demoralisation among experts who do not feel used to the full'. Western nations' influence over underdeveloped nations was likely to wane, in favour of the Soviets, Balogh predicted. 'It is not really that there is any ill will in the leading countries, but there is lack of imagination and a great deal of ideological resistance to anything which might smack of planning', he complained.[1]

Coombs continued to view Australian problems as those of a dependent, peripheral and 'developing' nation. Thus in a 1961 lecture at the Australian Administrative Staff College, he could phrase a generalisation: 'In most developing countries, such as Australia …'.[2] He introduced the theme of a March 1964 lecture to economic students in Karachi with the words 'In Australia, we tend to think of ourselves as an underdeveloped country – as indeed we are – but in ways quite different from the underdeveloped countries of Asia.' The differences, he went on to say, were that Australia's population was comparatively small and growing relatively slowly (apart from immigration), and that there was a comparative abundance of investment capital in Australia. Australia stood between the 'developed' nations of the North Atlantic and the 'genuinely underdeveloped' nations of Asia.[3] Coombs here reflected the Australian policy orthodoxy. As Capling points out, Australia's GATT diplomacy promoted 'better understanding of the particular trade and developmental problems of developing countries.' Australia chaired GATT's Committee III (1958–65) that sought solutions to such nations' deteriorating trade position.[4]

In the 1960s poorer countries used the United Nations, as well as GATT, as a forum for their economic interests. In December 1961 the United Nations declared 1960–70 the Decade of Development, and GATT adopted a resolution in the same month to promote, through trade agreements, the export capacity of developing countries. In Cairo in July 1962, a conference of thirty-one 'developing countries' of Africa, Asia and Latin America called for action to narrow the growing gap between the living standards of rich and poor nations. Western nations at first apprehensively saw in this sentiment the influence of the communist Soviet Union. However, gradually they yielded – the European nations were surprised by President Kennedy's sympathy for the Cairo Conference – thus allowing the UN General Assembly to convene a Conference on Trade and Development (UNCTAD) in 1964. Australia was a member of UNCTAD's 'Preparatory Committee', meeting three times in 1963 and 1964.

The precocious Argentinian economist Raul Prebisch (he held a chair in political economy in Buenos Aires by the age of twenty-four) set the agenda for the UNCTAD. Like Coombs in the 1940s, Prebisch had examined the global economic order from the point of view of the dependent or peripheral economies, seeking to counter the intellectual hegemony of North Atlantic economic theory and policy prescription. In contrast to Coombs, Prebisch was first a central banker (in Argentina, 1935–43) and then an internationalist, serving the United Nations from 1948 and working as Director-General of the Latin American Institute for Economic and Social Planning. Almost certainly, Balogh would have had such men as Prebisch in mind in 1959 when exempting certain Latin Americans from his critical remarks about international economists. In May 1963 Prebisch became Secretary-General of UNCTAD, and in September he visited Australia. He sought Coombs' views about UNCTAD's agenda.

Coombs had recently been discussing the problem of diminishing international liquidity with a visitor to the Reserve Bank, Nicholas Kaldor. 'Generally', he told Prebisch, 'I am attracted to Kaldor's idea of trying to get the wealthier countries to guarantee increasing availability of foreign exchange and to provide access to their markets for the manufactured goods of the newly emerging low-income manufacturing countries.' Prebisch's thesis was that the rich countries were then benefiting from a long-term trend for manufactured goods to trade at higher prices and greater volumes than the raw material exports of the less-developed nations. There was, he argued, a systematic and widening 'trade gap'. Coombs' sympathetic response to the Prebisch thesis was that the countries benefiting from this trade gap should resist the temptation to build up their reserves; rather they should make those reserves available to poor countries through aid, direct investment and low-interest loans.[5]

Prebisch and UNCTAD promoted reforms not only of trade but of currency policy. In February 1965, he invited Coombs to be a member of a group that he hoped would include several distinguished economists (R. F. Kahn, James Tobin, Mamoun Beheiry and I. G. Patel). They were to consider how the underdeveloped countries might be affected by proposed measures to relieve the emerging global shortage of liquidity. As well, they were to consider how these countries could benefit from more liberal trade arrangements.

The international currency arrangements of the post-war era were ripe for reconsideration. The US dollar had become, since the 1940s, the favoured unit of international exchange. The supply of dollars depended on the US government's continued willingness to owe its trading partners more than it earned by selling to them. But this deficit also risked undermining confidence in the dollar. Faced with this contradiction, Prebisch and others anticipated that international diplomacy would soon have to rewrite currency arrangements, as they had been rewritten during World War II. Would the developing countries be at the table, with a technically adequate proposal that favoured their interests?

Here was a chance for Coombs to return to his 1940s 'crusade'.[6] He replied that he was 'very interested' in Prebisch's idea. He would give a definite answer after exploring some 'problems'.[7]

Sydney Dell, UNCTAD's Director of Research, had spoken to the Australian UN Mission about Coombs' possible availability. When the Australian diplomats briefed Canberra, it became clear that Coombs had been right to anticipate problems. He soon received Roland Wilson's stiff teletype letting him know that the Australian government objected to Prebisch writing directly to Coombs. For Menzies, Coombs' proposed involvement in Prebisch's group was an issue of 'considerable importance from an international political point of view'. Wilson suggested that Coombs not write further to Prebisch 'until matters have been sorted out at the political level'.[8]

The Menzies government's restraint on Coombs' relationship with Prebisch illustrated something he had told trainee bankers in Karachi the year before. Central banks are a link in an 'international chain which spreads throughout the world and most central bankers feel that they belong to a family of central banks which accepts a moral tradition'. It is likely that in Coombs' eyes ex-central banker and tireless internationalist Raul Prebisch remained a member of that imagined fraternity. 'We should behave in conformity with the best features of that tradition', Coombs had continued, without saying what these best features were, 'and regard ourselves to some degree as accountable to our international colleagues for the quality of our work and our standards of integrity. However, our prime responsibility lies within the society in which we function.'[9] Would Australia now allow Coombs to join a project of that global fraternity?

Coombs tried to convince his masters of the importance of the issues they would be examining. World deflation was in prospect, Coombs warned Holt, because of the ways that the United States, the United Kingdom, some Western European countries and Japan were now restraining their economies and limiting their overseas expenditures. It would be in Australia's interest to urge Western European nations in particular to open their markets to the less-developed countries and to give and to loan more international capital. 'It is because of these anxieties … that I have been reluctant to refuse Dr. Prebisch's invitation.'[10] Holt was not moved: 'for various reasons the Government does not wish Australia to be associated with the work of this particular body'.[11]

Global vulnerability to the United States continued to trouble Coombs. He repeated his classic message of the 1940s: countries with persistent reserves had a duty to make them available, by one means or another, to countries with persistent deficits. The United States had recently become more reluctant to 'see its own reserves of gold fall heavily and to provide reserves for others by accepting dollar liabilities to them', he reminded a Bankers Forum at Georgetown University, Washington, in October 1965. 'If widespread and unbalanced by expansive action in the surplus countries, such restrictive action can create an unfavourable climate for world trade, with falling commodity prices and growing tendencies towards illiberal practices.' He applauded a recent suggestion that long-term credits be extended to countries 'in serious disequilibrium', in order that 'soberly and with humanity' they could 'reconstruct their economies', as the United States' Marshall Plan had allowed post-war Europe.[12]

Eleven months later, at a conference in Venezuela on international monetary reform, he was more openly critical of the way that the world's richest nations had been brushing aside the international liquidity problem. Again he noted that the role of the reserve currencies (US dollar and British pound) was declining and that some nations were seeking to build up their gold reserves. 'From this viewpoint – that the available supply of gold and gold substitutes is inadequate to meet the demands from those who wish to hold such assets – it does not seem possible to argue that there is no international liquidity problem.' He acknowledged that this unmet demand for gold was not yet having a depressing effect on international demand. However, he criticised the richer nations' pressing deflationary policies on countries with persistent deficits. It was equally incumbent on nations with surpluses to spend them: 'unless some of the responsibility for adjustment is shared by the surplus countries, the deficit countries may be forced to implement excessively restrictive policies to the disadvantage of the whole world'. An expansive climate could best be maintained by 'the continued flow of international capital to support development in the less developed countries'. International agreements should make more allowance for exchange rates to be reviewed and adjusted frequently.[13]

Without joining Prebisch's group, Coombs had found a way, in his October 1966 Venezuela speech, to take up UNCTAD's case against the wealthy nations. Yet, in the Reserve Bank's annual report on its 1966/7 activities, not a word was said of the Governor's visit or speech. Coombs' limited return to his 1940s internationalist themes lacked the blessing of his government.

Part 8

Managing creativity

Reasonable liberty

'EVEN BANKERS ARE HUMAN', Coombs remarked in 1959, but they needed to 'renew' their humanity 'by activity in other fields'.

> For my part I have turned to theatre and to universities – institutions abounding in 'prima donnas' and a passionate conviction of the value of their own work. This latter produces a fine contempt for financial limitations. I am amused from time to time at finding myself caught up in this enthusiasm and arguing to those who hold the purse-strings that whatever else goes short it clearly should not be theatre – or university, as the case may be.[1]

Coombs' playful presentation of the university as a theatrical space with its own prima donnas belied his serious concern for the institutional conditions of intellectual freedom.

By the time Copland's term as Vice-Chancellor ended in 1953, the ANU was still working through unfinished business with the four founding maestros. Of the four Academic Advisers to the nascent ANU, only Oliphant had committed himself to a Directorship, arriving in August 1950. Firth had resigned from the Academic Advisory Council (and declined to become Director of the School of Pacific Studies) early in 1949. Hancock had not been satisfied with Interim Council's response to his plans. On 1 April 1949, Copland had warned Coombs that Hancock had had 'assurances from people who are prepared to go out with him, but who will not go if he decides against it, and now both Oliphant and Florey are feeling uncomfortable, since if Hancock's defection is added to Firth's they would not be prepared to start on the scientific side'.[2] Then Hancock's talks with Copland had broken down, and he withdrew. For a while, Oliphant had wondered whether he had 'the patience to tackle the problems before us in the manner necessary to satisfy the political and Civil Service red tape of Canberra. ... I was hard hit by the withdrawal of Hancock.'[3] Although he soon committed himself, Oliphant's relationship with the university remained tinctured with a feeling that the University did not realise how much the UK-based maestros were giving up when they relocated to Canberra. Such men yearned for the university's unqualified sympathy for all their research ambitions.

Without definitely committing himself to the Directorship, Florey had advised the Interim Council about the building, equipping and staffing of the John Curtin School of Medical Research in 1947 and 1948. Copland had asked Florey in May 1948 to take the title Acting Director for the next five years, during which the school would be built. Florey had been happy to continue advising the ANU as a mere Academic Adviser, so that he did not have to give up his involvement in the Sir William Dunn School of Pathology at Oxford University. The ANU Interim

Council had allowed him to make appointments. In the absence of any building for such staff, Florey had used his connections to place these recruits in laboratories he thought suitable, such as the Commonwealth Serum Laboratories and the Walter and Eliza Hall Institute, both in Melbourne, and the Wellcome Institute in London. Florey had also pressed firmly and successfully his ideas about the design of the school building. He effected his influence through his Oxford colleague A. G. Sanders, who made three long visits to Canberra in the years 1950–3, and through helping to select the school's first Laboratory Manager A. F. Bunker. Florey's visits to Canberra in the winters of 1950 and spring of 1951 had reinforced his work at a distance. One of his early appointees, Frank Fenner, recalled that 'every time Florey came out the building would take a jump'.[4] Nonetheless, slow progress on the building – trouble with the architect, restrictions on funds – had wearied him of his advisory duties.

In October 1952, towards the end of his term as Vice-Chancellor, Copland asked Florey if he would like the position, temporarily, until Coombs could step into it. Florey was tempted; it would allow him to deal directly with the delays in the John Curtin School's development and to improve the ANU's overall administration. He was aware that, under Copland, some key figures in the university's service had found it difficult to work together. R. D. Wright feared that Florey would arrive to find them all 'still at the old muddling stage'.[5] Though Florey declined to be a temporary Vice-Chancellor, he visited Canberra in 1953, at the end of his five-year appointment as an Academic Adviser. By then, Melville was being considered as the next Vice-Chancellor. The choice of Leslie Melville to succeed Copland in 1953 split the Council between academic and 'official' members, with Coombs supporting Melville against Oliphant's man, Schonland.[6] Some academics feared Melville's financial discipline.

It is striking how prominent were economists in the early years of the ANU: Copland, Melville, Wilson, Coombs. More than other academics, they had enjoyed intimate experience of government at its highest level. That experience and their professional ease with financial planning gave them the confidence of government. Yet, they were not mere number-crunchers. They followed their exemplar Keynes in having a broad sense of the importance of intellectual creativity. Copland and Giblin, as I have shown, had been among the earliest advocates of a Commonwealth arts policy. The confidence of the economists could find brusque expression. In 1953, Florey's opinions on the appointment of the next Vice-Chancellor were spurned. On one occasion, Council member Roland Wilson pointed out that Florey had no right to attend a meeting of the Council to discuss that matter. Thus the econocrats challenged the maestros.

To the extent that men such as Melville, Coombs, Copland and Wilson were professionally sensitive to questions of cost, it was becoming a political virtue. The expenses of a university that had yet to produce one scholar had begun to attract unfavourable attention. The House of Representatives' debate on the estimates in September 1953 aroused some MPs to discuss whether the ANU 'indulge[s] in extravagant expenditure'.[7] Members had seen no justification of the proposed 1953–4 vote of £1.6 million. The university had not issued a statement of accounts for the last two years. Under the act, one MP pointed put, the ANU should get a mere £325,000 annually.[8] Menzies, supported by rookie MP Gough Whitlam, explained that the original estimates of the cost of the university had been too low.[9] The ANU's budget remained an easy target for backbench sniping. In November 1954, Mr Gullett protested that 'a ludicrously large amount of money has been very ill-spent'.[10] The university's administration and Council were beginning to be squeezed between professors wanting more, more quickly, and representatives of the taxpayer expressing dismay at the apparent extravagance to date.

When the building of the John Curtin School commenced in 1954, Florey refused still to accept or to decline the Directorship. He continued, however, to use his still considerable influence as an adviser. A talented Australian chemist, A. J. Birch, became available. Florey warned Melville that if Birch were snapped up by an overseas institution, 'you and Council will be subjected to very severe criticism'. Florey offered to have Birch in the John Curtin School until the ANU was ready to start a School of Chemistry. Melville thought the financial implications of such opportunistic recruitment had to be better worked out before he could put a proposal to Council. Florey and Oliphant (who was also in England at that time) were giving him different estimates of the initial scope of Birch's activities. For their part, Florey and Oliphant gained the impression that Melville was working to a budget ceiling so impenetrable as to hamstring their talent-spotting. Just the other day 'a very eminent pathologist' had stepped into Florey's Oxford office 'and was making serious enquiries about the possibility of working in Canberra'.

Oliphant soon added his own pressure, letting Melville know that if the university was going to match some of the figures he was hearing bandied about in the United Kingdom, it would have to forget about 'ceilings':

> I took part in a discussion at Harwell on the future accelerator policy for this country. A sum of 3m pounds is likely to be made available for such a program in Cambridge and I will be asked to lead it if arrangements are satisfactory. If I accept this would change the outlook in Canberra.

Oliphant cited Wright (then visiting Florey's laboratory) as supporting such a free-handed approach. 'After a few weeks here Wright admits that we lag sadly behind, dominated by Treasury and thinking always in such inadequate terms that we are overshadowed by CSIRO and by events abroad.' Oliphant reported happy British colleagues who 'could not spend more money if they had it!' Melville soon got another salvo from Oliphant, who'd been talking to the Chancellor, S. M. Bruce (resident of London) about the folly of Melville's 'ceiling'. Among the people with whom Oliphant was mixing, Australia was on the nose. 'News of our financial difficulties and of governmental interference is going the rounds and will undoubtedly harm recruitment.' One colleague had commented to Oliphant that Australians 'were more interested in a tidy balance sheet and good conservative politics than in the work going on in the University'.[11]

Melville was prepared to defend one form of 'government interference' – the budget ceiling – but felt ambivalent about another – limits on intellectual freedom. He had foreshadowed to Menzies the growth of the John Curtin School after it opened in 1957. 'This will, of course be dependent on the University maintaining good relations with the Government', he explained to Florey, adding 'I am not happy about the way in which we are going about this at the moment.'[12] The difficulty for Melville was that to some members of the Menzies government, ANU staff were not only spendthrifts but Communists. Melville was far less sure of his values when this was the accusation.

In those times, many thought it impossible to be both an academic and a Communist, and anyone on the left was under suspicion of being a Communist. Melville considered his duties as a liberal in his opening address to a summer school of the Australian Institute of Political Science on 29 January 1954. Liberalism included no principles for judging how 'in seeking to preserve our liberty we do not lose it' – to communists, he meant. Was it possible to safeguard liberty by denying it to communists?, he asked in genuine perplexity.[13] For him this was an unavoidably practical question. His staff were being scrutinised for their left-wing sympathies. In 1952, the ANU geographer Oscar Spate – a former Communist – had been denied appointment as First Commissioner of the South Pacific Commission. An anthropology student, Peter Worsley, was refused entry to New Guinea because of his 'political affiliations'. The University Council did not fight for Worsley. Rather it decided in June 1952 that it could not 'request special privileges for its members not available to other citizens' – a point reiterated in public by Copland.[14] Worsley was allowed to do his field work on Groote Eylandt. Left-leaning physicist Ken Inall was appointed on probation, provided that he would have nothing to do with politics. The university lost one promising research fellow (chemist Stephen Mason) while making up its mind about the significance of the man's Marxist sympathies.[15] In April 1954, when two ANU academics, Davidson and Fitzgerald, joined others in presenting in the *Canberra Times* an alternative to the official US and Australian understanding of Vietnamese politics, William Wentworth MP questioned their competence and their motives. Gullett MP (scourge of academic spendthrifts) found it 'intolerable that persons engaged in a *government instrumentality* should be able to contradict publicly leaders on both sides of the National Parliament'.[16]

The Menzies government was not necessarily hostage to such repressive voices. True, Hasluck followed his banning of Worsley from New Guinea in 1952 with a similar rejection of British anthropologist Max Gluckman in 1960 – to a volley of academic protest that Menzies ignored. Menzies (whose love of universities has been described as 'romantic' by Allan Martin) was difficult to pin down on the principles involved.[17] When Stan Keon MP described the ANU as a 'nest of communists' in August 1952, Menzies replied that his discussions with Copland had left him confident in a 'principle ... which will reconcile reasonable liberty with the general responsibility that devolves upon the Government'.[18] If this was not a ringing endorsement of academic freedom, nor did it hand university affairs over to the more censorious voices in the Parliament and wider community.

'Reasonable liberty' was broad enough in meaning to give both academics and their scrutineers hope. It named the ideological space within which Coombs manoeuvred. Coombs served on the Finance Committee of Council and was Deputy Chairman of Council from 1953 to 1959, when that office was renamed Pro-Chancellor. Coombs and Melville formed a robust political buffer between the academics and those in the Menzies government who remained unenchanted with academia.

Was there a trade-off between academic outspokenness and governmental largesse? To some, it seemed that if some academics were to be free to do their expensive research, then other academics might tactfully limit their freedom of speech. Among those ANU academics most critical of Fitzgerald and Davidson in 1954 were physicists whose work depended on the Menzies government paying for very costly equipment. The physicists basked in Cold War sunshine. Among MPs who thought the ANU a lavish playpen for politically dubious characters, there were those who could not praise Oliphant's program enough. In November 1954 W. C. Wentworth predicted that completion of Oliphant's Homopolar Generator would make Canberra, by 1960, 'the world centre of study of certain vital aspects of nuclear science'.[19] He pleaded that Oliphant be given more staff. Eleven months later, he made the same point, emphasising the machine's importance in the 'free world's race against Soviet nuclear science'.[20] His Liberal colleague and ANU Councillor Donald Cameron warned the House against 'imagining that we can set up a school of nuclear physics and not expect it to be extremely expensive'. The ANU's nuclear research would lay bare 'the ultimate secrets of science'.[21] Opposition leader Evatt hailed Oliphant as 'one of the great world figures' and complimented his 'genius' and 'patriotism'.[22]

Aware of the varied reputations his colleagues enjoyed in political circles, Melville sought to protect them all. According to Foster and Varghese, the Vice-Chancellor 'hinted [to a meeting of the Board of Graduate Studies considering Fitzgerald's and Davidson's article in 1954] that the government might withhold funds for salary increases'.[23] In representing the government to the ANU staff in such terms, Melville mediated external pressures as an invitation to self-censorship. The challenge Melville and Coombs faced was to assign weights to two different notions of academic responsibility: the financial and the ideological.

Coombs loathed McCarthyism. In June 1953, he told senior bank officers that the United States, from which he had just returned, was 'an exceedingly depressing place for an Australian to go to'.

> The general atmosphere is not in any sense, I feel, a healthy one. There seems to be a general state of suppressed panic about almost everything. … as far as I could see America was frightened of everything except war. … I have met Australians in America who … were strong advocates here a couple of years ago of the Anti-Communist Bill which the Government proposed here but, as a result of living in America over the last year or so, are horrified at the consequences if this sort of thing gets into bad hands and gets disproportionate.[24]

These are the words of a moderate anti-Communist, learning from US mistakes the institutional costs of intolerance. In a 1953 address, he lamented that

> Men and women throughout the world are being cajoled, threatened, and coerced by a range of instruments of persuasion. In some places one is exposed to propaganda and the powerful influence of social pressure; in others the threat of heresy-hunts and economic pressure and in others even force and concentration camps. And all this to persuade us to conform to the current orthodoxy. There is need to resist these pressures and to defend intellectual freedom not merely for ourselves but even more for those with whom we disagree.[25]

Thus he put the issue of intellectual freedom in the most general terms.

However, intellectual freedom is a problem of institutional design, as much as it is a matter of principle. Just as Coombs had tried to insulate the CSIR from the witch-hunting atmosphere of 1946–9 (and had succeeded, at least, in preventing its being made a government department), so would he resist the presumption of MPs such as Gullett that the ANU was a mere 'government instrumentality'. The ANU, like the Commonwealth Bank, was a statutory authority. Unlike the Commonwealth Bank, it generated no revenue and was financially dependent on Cabinet's vote. In the rhetoric of the university's parliamentary critics, there was an eager tendency to conflate intellectual with financial irresponsibility. If the ANU were to defend its autonomy as a community of scholars, its leaders would have to conduct with discretion their relationship with that ambivalent patron, the Menzies government.

When Coombs defended Melville and the financial ceiling against the continuing criticisms of Oliphant and Florey, he was seeking to secure their intellectual freedom.[26] In a 'very frank informal discussion' between himself, Menzies, Roland Wilson and Melville, the Prime Minister had suggested that the university 'concentrate on developing the four Schools to the scale of activity broadly contemplated in the original plans'. The ANU would then consolidate by filling vacancies in its establishment and by making other appointments needed for 'rounding out' the organisation. This was not a 'freeze', Coombs argued, but a reasonable plan for expansion within limits. Florey's suggested recruitment of Birch was currently beyond those limits. Coombs conceded that 'this may involve the loss of an outstanding man to Australia'. But it was more important to win government confidence 'not merely in our scientific and professional capacity, but also in the soberness of our administration'. He went on to express his high opinion of Melville – better than Copland, he assured Florey. His closing paragraph evoked a network of shared friendship. 'I have a letter or two from Pansy Wright who is getting a great kick out of his work with you. Both Melville and I miss him from the Council and its committees and will be glad when he is back. Mark has just returned and I am looking forward to a long yarn with him when next I am in Canberra.'[27]

Oliphant continued to be unhappy with the Coombs–Melville stance. His frequent visits to the United Kingdom stirred his ambivalence about the ANU.

'The Australian machine of government regards the ANU as just another minor department', he complained to Melville in August 1955.[28] He and Florey presumably encouraged one another's misgivings. Soon Florey made his decision: he would not take up the Directorship of the John Curtin Medical School.

The loss of Florey provoked his foremost Australian champion, Wright, to spell out the failure of Coombs' diplomacy. It was not only the ceiling that had bothered Florey, but the appointment of Melville and Melville's handling of the Fitzgerald–Davidson affair. Though Wright's letter was friendly in tone, it is clear that he thought Coombs was now aligned with the very people who made Florey apprehensive. Were Florey to come to the ANU – so Wright reported Florey's fears – 'there would be an endless fight, not pleasant especially in relationship to Sir Roland, to secure funds in an uncongenial atmosphere with Melville'. Melville might be a better administrator than Copland, Wright conceded, but he was not 'imbued with a burning desire to create a great research institution. I feel he would prefer tidy bookkeeping to great publications if they were alternative.'[29]

Coombs was awkwardly placed between Wright, Oliphant and Florey – on one side – and Melville, Wilson and Menzies – on the other. He liked and admired the first three, while respecting the way that Melville was handling the pressures exerted by Wilson and Menzies. Melville was, in his opinion, no mere book-keeper but an intellectual of substance buffeted by powerful, self-confident antagonists. Coombs was looking for common ground between political interests who were inclined to dismiss one another's concerns.

Visualising Australia

W HEN COOMBS BECAME Governor of the Commonwealth Bank, the corporate Christmas card struck him as 'rather pedestrian'. The paintings chosen for its cover 'conveyed little that was Australian to our international associates and … were surprisingly expensive'. He began to purchase original paintings, including their reproduction rights, 'to hang in offices which it was customary to adorn with reproductions chosen "as part of the furniture"'.[1] The Bank also offered a prize, for a painting with 'Australian content', to students of East Sydney Technical College. Bank records show that the Macquarie Gallery was the single most important source of Christmas card images: paintings by Kenneth McQueen (on the 1950/1 card), Margaret Preston (1952/3), Jean Bellette (1953/4), John D. Moore (1954/5), Donald Friend (1956/7). Works by Jeffrey Smart, Russell Drysdale and George Lawrence were also bought from Macquarie but not used on Christmas cards during Coombs' time as Governor. In the 1960s, Rudy Komon's and Barry Stern's galleries were also on the Bank's rounds, with Komon a particularly active lender of works he thought the Bank might buy. Many purchases were made from the artists themselves. Coombs counted among his friends and acquaintances: Margaret Preston (from whom he

When Coombs farewelled assistant Governor F. O. Walters in 1955 with a gift of a 'handsome radiogram', the editors of Currency *imagined that their 'modernist' Governor* might *have given a 'vivid Impressionist [sic] likeness ... worthy even to hang in the Board'.*

commissioned a work to hang in his own home, prompted by Mrs Coombs), Russell Drysdale (whose '"The Puckamanni", Melville Island' was purchased from the artist and used on the 1959 Christmas card), Sidney Nolan, Fred Williams, Clifton Pugh (for whom Coombs once secured the patronage of Mexico's central bank, and who was eventually to paint an intriguing portrait of Coombs), Sali Herman (whom Coombs assisted with a loan to buy a house), Gerald and Margo Lewers and Leonard French.[2]

Coombs helped Nolan on many occasions. When Nolan became fascinated by Mexican murals in 1957, he wrote a letter of introduction to the Director-General, Banco de Mexico.[3] The entrance to the Melbourne Reserve Bank office was adorned with a mural of the Eureka Stockade, rendered in enamelled copper. Coombs helped to arrange Nolan's Creative Arts Fellowship at the ANU in 1965. Sidney and Cynthia Nolan wished to use that fellowship to travel to the Australian interior. Though Coombs had hoped that Nolan would spend his fellowship working on campus, he helped arrange their trip.[4] In company with South Australia's Premier Thomas Playford and Delhi Australian Petroleum's Charles Easley, Coombs had recently visited the north-east corner of that State. He showed Nolan photos of the landscape and obtained the support of Easley's seismic testing team for the Nolans to go there – to look for a relic of the Burke and Wills expedition of a century before, the 'Dig' tree.[5] Soon after that, through Coombs' negotiations, the ANU acquired one of Nolan's greatest ever paintings – the 'River Bend' series. The ANU would pay him $4000 per year for nine years.[6] In much of his dealings with the Nolans, it was Cynthia who answered correspondence.

Another artist friend was Russel Drysdale. Not only did Coombs purchase personally at least one of his works, but when the bank loaned 'The Young Mourner' to a travelling exhibition in 1961–2, Drysdale loaned the Bank 'Mount White' to hang in its place. On a conservator's advice, the Bank declined to buy it.

Drysdale lost his son Tim in 1962 and then his wife Bonnie in 1963. Remarrying and recovering made him conscious of the support of friends, as he told Coombs in August 1965, after a 'hard year of work':

> For the first time for long years I feel happy and confident – I owe this to extremely staunch and loyal friends – not least yourself. I feel now I can thank you, and deeply for all the encouragement and interest you have given and showed to me during a period of life which seemed very dark and hopeless.[7]

Both Nolan and Drysdale were great travellers within Australia, journeying to their subjects in a way that prefigured Coombs' own rediscovery of Australia after his retirement. Of Nolan and Drysdale Coombs said in 1966 that their work reflected 'with sympathy and devotion, yet still with a healthy fear the force and magic of the landscape, the people who have become part of it and the myths with which they have sought to answer its silent questions'.[8]

As in so many other endeavours, Coombs' management style in art patronage tended towards the collegial. Recalling the early 1950s, he wrote: 'With the Deputy Governor, Leslie Melville the Bank's economist and adviser and others, I often visited a gallery during our "constitutional walk" after having lunch in the Bank's cafeteria debating the merits of the works we had seen.'[9] His keen interest in the Bank's growing art collection and his enjoyment of associations with artists and gallery owners did not stop him from delegating some of the work of acquisition and all of the work of collection management to the Secretary's Department, under hard-nosed lawyer Cliff McPherson. McPherson, in turn, delegated to Bill Judges, who became a kind of *de facto* arts officer for the Reserve Bank. Judges had joined the Bank in 1935. Having long been interested in theatre, he was able to help run concerts and 'recorded music recitals' during his war service in the Air Force. After demobilisation, he returned to the Bank and was an early executive cadet, working in the Staff Department. He was posted to Melbourne, then to London – to the benefit of his cultural interests – in the 1950s. Returning to Sydney in 1960, he was appointed assistant to the Secretary and 'keeper' of the Bank's collection of paintings and sculpture. He became Secretary of the Australian Ballet Foundation, and served on the NSW Advisory Committee on Cultural Grants. More than any other bank officer, his career reflects the Reserve Bank's activities in cultural patronage under Coombs.

The Reserve Bank's London officers became Coombs' go-betweens with Nolan when that artist worked abroad. Coombs also encouraged his capital city branch officials to take an interest in the art of their State, giving rise to acquisitions of Tasmanian paintings which hung in the new Commonwealth Bank building in Hobart in the 1950s and to G. R. Simpson's contact with Elizabeth Durack in Perth. Simpson, General Manager of the Reserve Bank in Western Australia, was a man of wide interests and sympathies. The cover image of Coombs' 1978 book of essays about Aboriginal affairs, *Kulinma*, is a photo by Simpson taken at Kalumburu in the late 1950s. When Simpson acquired the Durack painting

'Landscape at Evening' in 1960, he advised McPherson that this image would not be suitable for the Bank's Christmas card because it showed 'natives' in poor condition and 'it would not be a very good advertisement for Australia'.[10] Simpson also changed the painting's title to 'Evening', 'as the artist has portrayed the evening of a dying race with a background of sunset in a limitless land'.[11]

Coombs' own travels and contacts gave him opportunities to visit galleries outside Sydney. The Bank's purchase of work by James Gleeson resulted from Coombs' foray to the South Yarra Gallery in 1963. In August 1964, Baillieu Myer urged to him to have a look at what proved to be a very successful exhibition by Ray Crooke – paintings about Papua New Guinea – at the Brian Johnstone Gallery in Brisbane. When Coombs visited the exhibition, he declined to purchase, but declared himself interested in Crooke's future work.[12]

When someone offered the Bank a Conrad Martens in 1960, Coombs refused, explaining that 'on the whole, I think I would prefer to concentrate our purchases on building a representative collection of contemporary work'.[13] He leaned to the figurative; abstract modernism is not so well represented in that part of the collection purchased during his Governorhsip. There are exceptions – paintings by Leonard French, Margo Lewers, Carl Plate, sculpture by Lyndon Dadswell, Margel Hinder – but on the whole, the Governor and his staff would have sympathised with the 1959 'Antipodean Manifesto'.

> Art is, for the artist, his speech, his way of communication. And the image, the recognizable shape, the meaningful symbol, is the basic unit of this language … It is born of past experience and refers back to past experience – and it communicates. It communicates because it has the capacity to refer to experiences the artist shares with his audience.[14]

Indeed, only a few weeks before the Antipodeans' Melbourne exhibition (for which the manifesto was written), Coombs, in a humanist's salute to theatre, conveyed similar reservations about the abstract and anti-humanist tendencies within modernist painting.

> I like the theatre – it is a warm and living thing. In an age when the arts have become alienated from humanity – when our painters merely paint and our musicians compose organised noises – it is good that there is an art which is wholly and unashamedly devoted to mankind.[15]

Works by four of the manifesto's seven signatories appeared on Bank Christmas cards in Coombs' time: Arthur Boyd (1958–9), Clifton Pugh (1961), Charles Blackman (1965), and Robert Dickerson (1966).[16] The Christmas cards issued by Governor Coombs from 1949 to 1968 were his 'antipodean manifesto' – Australia finding humanity in modernity.

Nuclear matters

IN FEBRUARY 1947 Professor Mark Oliphant had presented physics as the central discipline in humanity's knowledge corpus:

> the basic science, in terms of which all natural phenomena, inanimate or animate, must be explained. ... While the prime purpose of an institute of research in physics must be to extend the frontiers of knowledge by investigation of the ultimate structure of matter, it must remain sympathetic towards the problems of the less highly organized sciences where it can help to bring order and simplifying law into what are often purely descriptive disciplines.[1]

Within ten years, one of those 'less highly organised sciences' and 'descriptive disciplines' – economics – was calling Oliphant's bluff.

Coombs had continued to be curious about the possibilities of nuclear energy since Oliphant's spell-binding lecture to himself, Chifley and Evatt over dinner at the Savoy in 1946. Howard Beale, Minister for Supply in the Menzies Government, invited Coombs to be one of the 'representative industrial leaders' available to the new Australian Atomic Energy Commission. Once or twice a year, the Commission 'would give an account of its activities and plans and would seek advice of the members of this group'.[2]

The Menzies government had set up the Australian Atomic Energy Commission in 1953 to succeed the Industrial Atomic Energy Policy Committee (1949–52), chaired by Oliphant, and an Atomic Energy Policy Committee, chaired by a senior officer in the Department of Supply, J. E. S. Stevens, in 1952. The Stevens Committee had established mining at Rum Jungle, south of Darwin, but Menzies judged that a statutory authority should be set up to manage Australia's further production of uranium. The Australian Atomic Energy Commission, legislated in April 1953, consisted of Stevens, Hugh Murray (General Manager of the Mt Lyell Mining and Railway Company) and the Vice-Chancellor of the New South Wales University of Technology, Professor J. P. Baxter, another veteran of the Manhattan Project. Its charter was not only to supervise exploration, mining and sales, but also to 'construct and operate plant for the liberation of atomic energy and its conversion into other forms of energy; to sell or otherwise dispose of materials or energy produced;' and to generate, with the universities and the CSIRO, a national program of training and research.

Australia's steps towards nuclear power required careful diplomacy with Britain. Keen to access Australian uranium deposits at Rum Jungle and Radium Hill in South Australia, the British government had agreed to share with the Australian Atomic Energy Commission research findings about the industrial application of atomic energy, so that Australia was by the beginning of 1955 'right up to date', in Stevens' words, 'saving Australia millions of pounds and many years of hard work'.[3] The Commission had begun to work cooperatively with the British Atomic Energy Research Establishment at Harwell, and the Menzies Cabinet had authorised the construction of a small nuclear reactor in Australia.

Stevens was cautious in his expression of the Commission's hopes. Any further steps towards peaceful atomic power in Australia, he told the first meeting of the Business Advisory Group, should be taken 'in the cold hard light of your business and professional experience'.[4] The principal issue to investigate, his Deputy Baxter told the assembly of business leaders, was whether it would be cheaper in Australia to produce electricity from nuclear reactors than from coal, oil or hydro-electric schemes. If there was one place in Australia where nuclear-fired electricity generation *might* be cost-effective, it was in South Australia, with meagre coal supplies, but enclosing a uranium deposit. Indeed, Baxter was confident that 'by 1960, South Australia will be able to look to atomic energy for all its new sources of power'.[5] Nuclear power stations would require 'subsidiary servicing industries' – chemical and metallurgical – to manufacture the uranium-based materials essential to the generation process, to fashion precision measuring instruments, and to fabricate the strong metal structures at the heart of every plant.

> How far it will be possible to develop these industries in Australia in the first two or three atomic decades it is difficult to say. At first, plant and services from overseas will, no doubt, have to be used, but ultimately the general industrial development arising from atomic energy should be considerable.[6]

Baxter was thus more expansive than Stevens, asking the Business Advisory Group not 'whether' but 'how'.

Baxter was not the only promoter of nuclear power. Harry Messel, Professor of Physics at the University of Sydney, urged Australians not merely to go for nuclear power generation but also, through 'our own basic native science', to develop their own technology for it. He armed colleagues against sceptics by an appeal to their sense of national destiny.

> 'Little tin men with little tin souls' may tell us that we cannot do it, that we are a small, backward, colonial nation which is incapable of doing its own thinking and standing on its own feet in science and technology. ... If we take their advice, we might as well clear out of Australia and hand the country back to the Aborigines, because we will be forced out before long at any rate. If we wish to hold this continent, we must develop it quickly and on a large scale.[7]

In 1955, the United Nations convened a conference in Geneva on the peaceful uses of atomic energy. Oliphant concluded from its discussions that Australia could instal nuclear power stations 'so soon as their practicability and economy have been demonstrated'.[8] The Commonwealth Bank's Don Parr, having obtained from External Affairs officials some reports of the conference, briefed Coombs on the issues highlighted there: the need to assure supplies of uranium (no problem for Australia), the huge initial capital costs (raising the question of long-term interest rates), the shortages of trained personnel, and the uncertainties about the appropriate depreciation period for nuclear plants.

When the Business Advisory Group next met, at the end of November 1955, Baxter's pre-circulated paper projecting costs of nuclear power generation drew Coombs' attention. A Bank accountant concluded from Baxter's figures that it was not yet possible to demonstrate that, in Australia, atomic generation would make electricity cheaper. 'It follows ... that if there was a decision to introduce atomic power at present, that decision must rest on other than commercial grounds.'[9]

Coombs' critical interest in nuclear energy prompted him to convene the Bank's Atomic Energy Committee, chaired by M. B. Moorfield, the Bank's Engineer Consultant, in January 1956. Moorfield's Committee began to gather data on the costs of generating electricity in Australia, comparing these figures with costs documented at the UK power station, Calder Hall, and publicised by British researchers through the International Bank of Reconstruction and Development. They concluded that the South Australian demand for electricity would have to grow much bigger before a nuclear plant there would be economical.[10] The Committee briefed Coombs before he attended the third meeting of the Business Advisory Group on 19 March 1957, where Baxter read a paper on 'The Development of an Australian Atomic Power Industry'.

Baxter's paper stated its assumptions:

(a) that Australia will commence to build its first atomic power stations within the next decade;

(b) that the rate of progress in this field is such that in from fifteen to twenty years the construction of atomic power stations in our main industrial areas will be normal practice, based on sound economic considerations.

(c) that the state of the world will continue to be such that Australia will be interested in the possibility of atomic defence.[11]

In briefing Coombs, the Bank's Atomic Energy Committee neither endorsed nor challenged these assumptions. Rather their analysis continued to focus on the possibility of measuring the economic benefits of nuclear technology – isotope production as well as power generation – without reference to the military benefits assumed by Baxter. The Committee told Coombs that if Australian reactors were to produce plutonium as a by-product of power generation, as Baxter envisaged, they would have to sacrifice some of the productivity of their fuel if they wanted to ensure that the plutonium by-product was of the high grade needed in weapons manufacture. The Committee also anticipated that to go nuclear for the sake of such a mixture of aims – electricity generation *and* defence capability – would 'further complicate Commonwealth–State relations'.[12]

The Bank was far from dismissing the ideas of the Australian Atomic Energy Commission, however. Early in April 1957, Coombs hosted a lunch at the Bank for its Chief Scientist, C. N. Watson-Munro, inviting him to explain how nuclear energy might be harnessed to derive fresh water from sea water.[13] When the Committee looked into it, they judged that Watson-Munro's cost estimates had been unduly pessimistic. Even so, and taking into account the value of the main by-products – salts and plutonium – it would cost Sydney 13 to 22 times as much to produce water by nuclear desalination as by pumping from Warragamba Dam (then under construction). Only cities in arid parts of Australia – Adelaide, Perth and some future city – could conceivably benefit from future refinements in nuclear evaporation technology, they concluded.

When Baxter decided to convene in Sydney an international symposium on peaceful uses of atomic energy, his agenda did not seem to the Bank's Committee to invite their contribution.[14] Coombs asked his staff to reconsider their inference that the economics of nuclear power was not on Baxter's agenda, and when the Committee, at the last minute, offered a paper on 'general economic and/or financial aspects of atomic power', it was accepted.[15] Coombs was unwilling to let slip the chance to publicise the analyses that his staff were producing. The Business Advisory Group was an infrequent forum – it did not meet between March 1957 and June 1958 – and Baxter, in his buoyant speculations and optimistic assumptions, had tended to avoid the kinds of hard-headed questions that the Bank officers thought he should face.

Don Parr, representing the Bank, told the Sydney symposium that 'on economic considerations alone, the present case for the early general adoption of nuclear power in Australia is not particularly strong'. Perhaps there were places – South Australia, north-west Queensland – where small reactors could be justified, but as a replacement for coal generally, uranium was costly. The capital costs of setting up an industry would be very high. There was no financial incentive to discontinue the energy source – coal – for which the capital already existed. Fuel processing in Australia would not be economic, given the size of the Australian demand for electricity, so Australia would have to rely on overseas fuel processing – a problem of security which Australia would not face were it to stick to coal-based technology. Parr conceded that his economic calculus did not settle every issue: 'scientific advancements may eventually override many of the current reservations and non-economic considerations arising from such aspects as national security, national pride and the practical limitations of international industrial specialisation could outweigh purely economic considerations'.[16]

After hearing the reactions of scientists and businessmen to the Bank's paper, Coombs congratulated his Committee: 'while I gather many disagreed with the general conclusion all were satisfied that the relevant considerations had been competently surveyed and that the analyses would prove of real value to those in the industry'.[17] If there is equivocation detectable in these words, it may have arisen from a general uncertainty, within the Bank, about the status of economic analysis and its relevance to the nuclear prospect. Were they the 'little tin men with little tin souls' against whom Messel had warned? Such uncertainty was evident not only in Parr's closing words, quoted above, but also in *Currency*'s report of Baxter's Sydney symposium. Of 108 papers, only three raised economic questions, or, as *Currency* put it, 'these three papers were the only ones of a non-scientific nature (is Economics a science?)'.[18] Disciplinary insecurity? or just a self-deprecatory joke for *Currency* readers? Perhaps it was both. In the 1950s, the hard and rigorous sciences of physics and engineering seemed the intellectual keys of the gates to the future. It was the dismal responsibility of economists to tax the visionaries with practical questions, rather than to follow their dreams.

Opera

WHEN THE Australian Elizabethan Theatre Trust formed in 1954, men of capital were champions of Australia's two main opera companies. The General Manager of the Rural Bank of New South Wales, C. R. McKerihan, had financed Sydney's opera company (calling itself the National Opera of Australia) 'to a much greater extent', he explained to Coombs, 'than would be regarded as coming within ordinary banking practice'. He hoped that, if the Trust allowed it to work, the National Opera could trade out of debt. 'The New South Wales body has suffered a good deal from lack of managerial control', he admitted, 'but it could be expected 'to function successfully'.[1] In Melbourne, Sir Robert Knox – company director (Dunlop, Commonwealth Steel, the Commercial Banking Company of Sydney, Noyes), office-holder within the Melbourne and National Chambers of Commerce, Melbourne Club member, confidant of Menzies, resident of Toorak – was President of the Australian National Theatre, Gertrude Johnson's opera company. In 1953, her company had offered seasons not only in Melbourne but in Sydney, Adelaide and Perth. Both the Victorian government and the ABC subsidised it, providing respectively cash and, for Melbourne performances only, orchestral services at a discount.

Perhaps Coombs' personal interest in opera was not strong. He once implied that he found it rather culturally derivative ('re-creation of works from abroad') and old-fashioned ('the idiom of and for audiences of earlier generations'). On that occasion he said he looked forward to more contemporary and more Australian work, with *West Side Story* as inspiration.[2] However, there is no doubt that in 1954 the condition of opera in Australia aroused his managerial interest. The Sydney and Melbourne companies were planning rival seasons again. Yet neither had covered its costs in 1953 and neither could afford to employ singers all year round. Their seasons coinciding, the companies divided the available pool of performers into two groups of intermittently employed talent. Having seen both the recent Sydney and Melbourne opera seasons, aficionado Anthony Gallagher found that his 'predominant feeling' was 'regret. No one would deny that there is fine talent in each of the two; but it has been just less than enough to raise standards from competency to inspiration. ... In combination, some really splendid work might have been done.'[3]

It was the very point of the Trust, as Coombs and Moses saw it, that State-based cultural loyalties would sometimes have to give way to a national vision. Coombs took on the difficult task of persuading both the Melbourne and the Sydney groups to sink their rivalries in a common venture. Each city's opera committee would be asked to attract subscribers, publicise performances and train singers. The State governments would redirect their support to subsidising the new national company's rail travel.[4] The Trust would not back either company, Coombs explained in a letter to the *Sydney Morning Herald* on 24 April 1954, but it would 'support projects for specific dramatic seasons jointly with such organisations if the required standards of performance and management are reasonably assured'.

Coombs had to consider the interests of such figures as Clarice Lorenz (National Opera of Australia) and Gertrude Johnson. Both accepted invitations to serve on the Trust's Opera Board, formed in 1954–5 and accountable to the Board of the Trust. Coombs was keen to persuade Johnson and her backer Knox that the Trust was a support, not a Sydney take-over of Melbourne's opera company. When the Trust's public subscription drive began in the winter of 1954, the Victorian results lagged far behind those of New South Wales. Coombs wrote to the editors or managing directors of three Melbourne dailies – the *Argus*, the *Age* and the *Herald* – to ask them to match the Sydney dailies' promotion of the Trust appeal. He assured them that the Trust 'offers the only effective hope for the continued existence of such organisations as the National Theatre Movement in Victoria'.[5]

By the first week of October 1954, the Trust was confident that 'agreement in principle' between the Sydney and Melbourne groups warranted a press announcement that an opera season, mounted by a company drawing on both cities, would commence in a year's time.[6] The Trust would guarantee an overdraft to finance the season, once it was satisfied about the season's timing, repertoire, budget, artists, management and State government support. Profits, if any, would go to the Trust. To theatrical entrepreneur Frank Tait Coombs acknowledged that losses from opera 'are very hard to avoid'.[7]

The Trust was still not assured of the support of some influential Victorians. Coombs had probably won the confidence of some notable Melburnians by asking Sir John Latham to be President of the Trust. Latham was near the end of a multifaceted career in public affairs, having been barrister, diplomat and National Party MP (fervently anti-Communist and anti-union). For a while seriously considered as leader of the conservative parties, he had been Joseph Lyons' Attorney-General from 1931. Appointed Chief Justice of the High Court in 1934, he had been in the minority when that Court declared Menzies' anti-Communist law unconstitutional in 1951. As well as chairing the Trust, Latham was foundation President of the Australian Congress of Cultural Freedom. While Latham was in one way an astute choice of Establishment patron, his cultural interests were constrained by his rationalist rectitude, as I will later illustrate. Coombs' strongest Victorian ally was retailer and fine art collector, Aubrey Gibson, from 1955 the Chair of the Trust Board's Victorian State committee. In February 1955 he urged Coombs to convene the Trust's second-ever Board meeting in Melbourne 'to demonstrate as soon as possible to the people of Melbourne that this is a truly national movement'. He urged that Hugh Hunt, who took up the Trust's Executive Directorship in January 1955, should also come as soon as possible to Melbourne, before he picked up the idea that Sydney, where the Trust's office happened to be, was the base of a national organisation.[8] The next full Board meeting was held in Melbourne.

These inter-capital difficulties were felt in the tensions between the Trust's Opera Board and the Trust Board itself. It was easy for Johnson, Knox and Lorenz to feel marginalised by the ways that the Trust was starting to make decisions about opera in 1955. Hunt told Coombs in November 1955 that though it was dependent financially on the Trust, the Opera Board was inclined to assert its autonomy from his and the Trust Board's judgment. He sought more powers, in particular Coombs' mandate that he use his own judgment in setting up the new company.[9] Knox soon saw Hunt as breaching the understandings under which the Trust had been founded – that it would support existing companies whose performance warranted it. There was no doubt in his mind that the National Theatre Movement was of such quality. Latham felt obliged to represent Knox's fears to Coombs. Hunt and Knox conferred in May 1955 about how to preserve the identity of the Movement in its cooperation with the Trust. Hunt was determined not to give up the Trust's ascendancy in artistic direction and in management.[10]

There was no shortage of issues on which some Victorians could take offence at the Trust. Was the Trust usurping the Movement's funding? By May 1955, Coombs had persuaded the Victorian (Cain) government to contribute £8000 per year over the next five years, if the Melbourne City Council gave £4000 per year.[11] When Hugh Hunt began to prepare a budget for the planned 1956 opera season, he consulted theatre owner J. C. Williamson's about aspects of the season's costs and so the traditional rivalry between Williamson's and the National Theatre Movement was inflamed. Why was Gertrude Johnson not being involved in the planning of the 1956 season, asked Victorian Trust Board member Myra Roper?[12] In August 1955, Coombs attempted to neutralise Melbourne's discontent. He wrote to Knox that he was 'personally disappointed that you were not among the Victorian members of the Board'. Coombs asked him to become a Vice-President of the Trust and thus an *ex officio* member of the Trust Board.[13] Knox accepted, but the position of the National Theatre Movement as an opera provider remained unclear. From Hunt and from the Trust's newly appointed opera manager Robert Quentin, Coombs heard that some in Melbourne were complaining that, by absorbing the Victorian government's grants and by winning access to Melbourne's ABC orchestra, the Trust was preventing the Movement from trading out of its financial trouble.[14]

Though it managed to stage a nationally touring opera season in 1956 – four Mozart operas, critically acclaimed – the Trust's relationship with the National Theatre Movement, and therefore with some leading members of the Melbourne performing arts community, continued to be delicate. Gibson persuaded Coombs and the Board that if the work of the Trust was to attract Melburnians, it was essential to open an office in that city. The 'Trust just cannot come into town like a visiting circus from time to time and expect the locals to crowd the tent!' The Trust's losses in Melbourne, he warned, might drag it into ruin.[15] Indeed, Melbourne audiences had attended the 1956 opera season at lower rates than the national average – a problem which Coombs presented to Menzies in February 1957.[16] The Trust had an office, staffed by the Director of Melbourne University's Union Theatre company, John Sumner, from May 1957.

When Gibson warned Coombs of Victorian sensitivities, Gertrude Johnson would certainly have been on his mind. No doubt heartened by the local resistance that worried Gibson, Johnson was not ready to give up the eminent position which the National Theatre Movement had attained. She lobbied the ABC for access to the Victorian Symphony Orchestra, and she made sure that Premier Bolte knew her grievance. Hunt saw a threat to the Trust's 1957 box office in Melbourne were the Movement to stage a season before the Trust's. The Trust's budget required a 96 per cent house to cover costs.[17]

Sir Robert Knox was the person most seriously embarrassed by this sharpening of rivalries between the Trust and the Movement, and on 2 April 1957 he resigned from the Trust Board. A meeting of the Trust Board discussed Knox's allegation, as presented to them by Latham and by the Victorian government's Director of Finance, A. Tennyson Smithers, that the Trust had been making an enemy of the National Theatre Movement. Coombs' difficulty was to give his staff – Hunt and Trust Opera Company Director Robert Quentin – room to do their job, while hoping to justify to the Victorians the two men's brusque indifference – as some Victorians saw it – to the Movement's claims.[18] Coombs urged Knox to remain on the Trust Board to resolve differences by discussion.[19] But Knox was not the only person he had to placate. The embarrassment of the Trust's Victorian State committee was prompting even Latham to consider resigning his Trust presidency.[20] And Hunt, after consulting each Victorian committee member, told Coombs that if Knox stayed, the Trust might lose Gibson. 'We can't buy Knox's cooperation except at a price which would be ludicrous', Gibson had told Hunt, '– namely Gertrude Johnson as Manager of Opera and Knox as Chairman of the Victorian Committee.'[21]

Coombs soon found out what a difficult opponent Knox could be. In June 1957, Knox and Johnson came to a Trust meeting in Sydney. 'I had a long talk with Knox first', Coombs later told Hunt,

and, frankly, found a good deal of difficulty in preserving my equanimity as he made criticisms and accusations which, in my opinion, are quite without substance. He repeated a good deal of this at the meeting with the other State representatives where, fortunately, it had the effect of antagonizing them against him rather than against the Trust.[22]

(Recall that private banker Knox and central banker Coombs would also have been clashing in another arena in the mid-1950s.)

The Trust's relationship with the ABC continued to upset the personnel of the National Theatre Movement. If the Movement were to retain an identity outside the Trust, it must mount its own productions; but if the Trust had first claim to the services of the Victorian Symphony Orchestra (VSO) then the Movement could not freely determine its season. ABC Managing Director Charles Moses backed the Trust, telling Victorian Premier Bolte in October 1959 that the Movement could use the VSO – but not at the time it had requested.[23] In May 1960, one of the Trust's Victorian Board members, the retailer and Coombs loyalist Eric Lampe, gave Coombs his account of a long talk he'd had with Gertrude Johnson. Johnson thought that, under Hugh Hunt's influence, the Trust had dishonoured Coombs' 1954 promise that it would 'supplement and not … replace the various State and national organizations for the development of the theatre, and will, wherever practicable, collaborate with them in the presentation of theatrical seasons and will hope to be the means of fostering and developing their activities'.[24] She regarded Melbourne as having established itself as the home of opera. She accused the Trust of manipulating the ABC and the Musicians Union in order to make the VSO unavailable to the Movement in February and March. Lampe, in reply, had stressed the Trust's national responsibilities and its successes in engaging and fostering talent and productions way beyond the capacity of a State-based organisation.[25]

Whether or not it was due to these Melbourne difficulties, the Trust found that it could not sustain a full-time professional, national opera company. From 1958 to 1960 the company worked under the musical directorship of Karl Rankl. Granting Rankl his wish for large and lavish productions, and honouring its commitment to tour, the Trust's losses were crippling. Consequently, 'during the four years 1959–62 the Trust Opera Company disbanded twice and was reassembled twice'.[26] Unable to offer a season in 1961, the Trust at least agreed to fund a Melbourne season by the National Theatre Movement. However, when Johnson, having agreed to present three operas, staged only one of them, *The Student Prince*, while still accepting the $10,000 subsidy, the Trust found its worst fears confirmed.

By the end of 1962, the Trust was in a similar position, financially, to that in which it had found the National Opera and National Theatre Movement in the early 1950s – broke. Maintaining its own Opera company nearly bled the Trust dry – an excess of expenses over receipts of $183,000, during the five years 1957 to 1961. It was not that the opera seasons had been badly managed by Trust staff. Coombs told Eric Lampe in February that over the three seasons 1959, 1960, 1962, 'our expenditure has proved to be within 1 per cent of estimated costs'.[27] Nonetheless, to mount a 1963 season, subsidy would be required. Encouraged by the corporate donations he had been able to solicit for the Australian Ballet in 1962, Coombs approached Australia's eight largest newspaper firms for £5000 each – 'prestige advertising combined with real public service', he called it.[28] The response was patchy, and with box office in 1963 at 'an all-time low', the future for a national opera company looked grim.[29]

So it is perhaps not surprising that Gertrude Johnson believed that she could do no worse than the Trust, and continued to fight. In April 1964, she again approached the ABC's Victorian manager asking for Movement access to the VSO's services in March 1965, by which time, she hoped, the Movement would have opened its own theatre.[30] Knowing that Coombs cultivated the support of her Premier, in order to get State contributions to the Trust, she told Bolte that the Trust had breached agreements with the Movement and the ABC.[31] But her lobbying could not break the Trust's crucial alliance with the ABC, and Coombs and Gibson were again adamant that their season should not be pre-empted by Movement productions. The Movement could participate in a production in the Trust's 1964 season, but the Trust must remain in artistic control, especially in light of the *Student Prince* episode.[32] Miss Johnson, Gibson reported to Coombs in 1964, 'seems to live in a kind of dream-world and cannot put out of mind past glories – and hoped for future ones. Yet, she was the focus of much loyalty, so that the Melbourne audience had learned to hate the Trust, whatever it did.'[33]

Though the Trust outlasted Gertrude Johnson's challenge, it did not find a way, until the very end of Coombs' period in the chair, to give financial security to a national opera company. In October 1964, Coombs told Menzies that the Trust could do no better in the short term than to see its singers employed by J. C. Williamson's in the 1965 season in which soprano Joan Sutherland would return in triumph to her homeland. 'It is however a holding operation only.'[34] At the end of 1965, the picture was still one of 'intermittent employment of artists, accepting the loss of standards and the wastage of artists overseas'.[35] In his last year in the chair, 1967, Coombs persuaded the Commonwealth to fund the Elizabethan Trust Orchestra, so breaking the Opera Company's dependence on the ABC. Also in that year, funds from the New South Wales government (looking forward to putting something on in its Opera House) and from the first ever subscription season made it possible, at last, for the Trust Opera to offer year-round work for its singers. In 1970, the Trust Opera Company was renamed the Australian Opera.

Although an unhappy saga from a managerial point of view, Coombs' efforts to found a national touring opera company were successful in raising audience expectations, according to John Cargher. The Trust gave access to opera to cities that a commercial entrepreneur would certainly have neglected. The Sydney–Melbourne rivalry was not usually a problem for Coombs. Though very much a Sydney man from the late 1930s, he had made good connections with Melbourne manufacturers during the war, and in the 1950s and 1960s he enjoyed rapport with Melbourne men of business, philanthropy and research such as Ian Potter, Ian McLennan, Kenneth Myer and R. D. Wright's Melbourne University colleague Derek Denton. Inter-city rivalry plagued his endeavours in opera because the Trust's national strategy expressed the power of two Sydney-based Commonwealth bureaucracies – the ABC and the Commonwealth Bank – and because Coombs had no choice but to delegate Trust work to others – Hugh Hunt and Robert Quentin, who saw no reason to defer to the strong personalities of the National Theatre Movement.

Ballet

COOMBS ONCE DESCRIBED ballet as 'an art which, more than any other, rejoices in its humanity, glorifies the human body, made resplendent by colour, light and music, inspired and enchanted by movement'.[1] 'When you're as ugly as I am you like to be surrounded by beauty', he remarked on another occasion.[2] However, supporting ballet was not the Australian Elizabethan Theatre Trust's priority in the 1950s because J. C. Williamson's company, the Borovansky Ballet, provided what the Trust thought to be an adequate service.

Some balletomanes were not happy with the standard of 'Boro', and saw hope in the Trust. Alan Brissenden, the *Sydney Morning Herald*'s ballet critic, complained that the Borovansky Ballet was neither trying out new material nor nurturing artists and musicians. He noted that nearly every capital city had a ballet group of some kind, usually based around a teacher. He thought that Melbourne's Ballet Guild, directed by former Borovansky principal Laurel Martyn, was particularly deserving of the Trust's support. Otherwise, the Trust would be 'failing in its avowed purpose'.[3]

In 1955 Melbourne scientist Derek Denton (known to Coombs through R. D. Wright) and his wife, the Ballet Rambert dancer Margaret Scott, contacted Coombs about the possibility of attracting English dancer Walter Gore, who had worked in Melbourne in the early 1950s, to stay in Australia.[4] Denton and Scott, with dancer Geoffrey Ingram, members of the Australian Ballet Theatre Group, soon began to formulate a submission outlining why the Trust should, and how it could, form an Australian ballet company. Hugh Hunt thought their ideas promising, and in December 1958 Coombs discussed with Ingram the prospects of an Australian company. In January 1959 Ingram stated to Coombs this Melbourne lobby's disquiet 'that no company exists which draws upon the full artistic resources of the community, or was subject to artistic direction which could, in time produce a first-class and representative Australian ballet'. To Ingram it seemed that Williamson's held the initiative, for now. If 'the Firm' continued to employ the Borovansky Ballet for 'at least another two or three years', then 'it would be unreal to attempt to create an alternative company'. It would be a good idea, he continued, to persuade Sir Frank Tait that a plan was needed for the supercession of Borovansky by a national company.[5]

When Coombs wrote to all the Premiers in November 1959, outlining the Trust's plans for the next five years, he mentioned ballet only to remark that, although it was popular (the Bolshoi tour of Melbourne, Sydney, Canberra and Brisbane in July and August that year had enjoyed good box office), it could not 'hope to be presented regularly on a profitable basis'. The Trust's 'basic activity', he told the Premiers, 'must be the sponsoring of quality touring companies in opera and drama'.[6] A few days later he conceded to Aubrey Gibson – evidently lobbied by the Melbourne ballet groups – that in Melbourne and Sydney 'there is a nucleus of sufficiently high quality to warrant support' by the Trust for ballet.[7]

The Trust had become aware of different priorities among the Melbourne advocates of ballet development. Gibson was hearing from the Ballet Guild's Laurel Martyn that the Trust's first step should be to help found a ballet school; others, such as Ingram, placed the emphasis on consolidating artistic vision and authority within the Borovansky Ballet, as the germ of a new national, Trust-supported company. Coombs, like Gibson, was at first inclined to favour Martyn's view.[8] Hunt's successor as Executive Director of the Trust, Neil Hutchison, urged Coombs to be cautious. By July 1960, it was clear that Borovansky's recent (December 1959) death was presenting an opportunity for institutional reform and innovation. Coombs hoped still that any Trust initiative would be in association with 'the Firm'.[9]

J. C. Williamson's imported Peggy van Praagh, a distinguished English performer and teacher of ballet with whom Margaret Scott had been in contact, to be the guest teacher of the Borovansky company. In September 1960, touring Perth with the Borovansky company, she persuaded Fred Alexander that the high-quality peformances, good houses and financial losses of that tour confirmed the need for the Trust to put some money into continuing the company.[10] Van Praagh did not confine her advocacy to such backstage conversations. In October 1960, sensing the end of the company and knowing her own contract soon to expire, she closed a Melbourne performance with an appeal from the stage for governments to subsidise ballet. Commonwealth Treasurer Harold Holt heard her plea from the front row of the circle. He was already well aware of the Australian Ballet Theatre Group's activism, as his wife Zara had collaborated with Margaret Scott in using Scott's ballet pupils to model clothes at her Toorak boutique.[11] Van Praagh's speech crowned years of south of the Yarra networking.

Hutchinson advised Coombs that he should talk to Tait before meeting with van Praagh.[12] In his annual letter to the Premiers, the following month, Coombs was still not foreshadowing the Trust's intervention into the field of ballet.[13] When Coombs finally conferred with James Tait in December 1960, the Borovansky balance sheet shocked him. Such grim figures warranted further study, he said; they prompted also his approach to Menzies, to discuss how to assure Australia a touring ballet company. Meanwhile, Coombs and Tait agreed that they should combine to ensure van Praagh was not lost to Australia after the Borovansky's last performance (*Coppelia*) on 18 February 1961. They would pay her a retainer, while she worked in Britain and France. By the time the retainer expired, Coombs suggested, the Trust should have made up its mind what to do, 'so that if the outlook is adverse we could stop at that point'.[14] Coombs warned van Praagh against assuming that ballet had a future in Australia.[15]

In London, van Praagh worked on that future, contacting Australian dancers and formulating, with Geoffrey Ingram, 'Preliminary suggestions for the operation of the proposed new company' – a document outlining the first twelve months of a three-year performance program. Melbourne and Sydney would get eight-week seasons, Brisbane, Adelaide and Perth four weeks. Dancers were to be on one-year contracts, with one-year options. There would be a summer school. Stars would be imported from overseas. Hutchison found this plan 'too ambitious', and he began to project how the work of a ballet company could be integrated with the Trust's opera and drama.[16] Within days of receiving Hutchison's advice, Coombs was writing formally to Menzies for financial support.

Coombs attempted to convince Menzies that the proposed ballet company was not a response to an emergency (which it was) but one element in a long-range Trust plan whose realisation had steadily been moving Australia to a new threshold in arts policy. The Trust's work now anticipated the construction of performing arts venues in several capital cities; and the Trust had recently got the State Education Departments to agree to a common Shakespeare curriculum. Now there could be annual seasons of opera, ballet and Shakespeare in all states – *if* the Commonwealth gave the Trust another £50,000 per year (matching a proposed extra £25,000 a year from the States).[17] At the same time, Coombs asked the Victorian government if Melbourne's forthcoming cultural centre could be made the home of the Australian Ballet Foundation 'at present in the process of formation'.[18]

Menzies was cool. His government had committed to the Trust £50,000 per year for five years, starting in 1959/60. Was Coombs prepared for the Trust to undergo a comprehensive review before any change to that arrangement were contemplated?[19] Of course, came Coombs' accommodating reply. And did not the Commonwealth's five-year commitment to £50,000 per year finish in June 1963? he queried. His earlier letter, he now explained, had been referring to the Trust's work beyond that date; he had not sought to break the five-year agreement – except, Coombs admitted, in his plea for ballet. Here *was* an emergency. Ballet could be lost to Australia if the money were not found to reconstitute a company and present a season in 1962. Coombs could see a way to finance that season without asking for money for that purpose. The Trust had arranged for the Leningrad Ballet to tour Australia, and Coombs hoped that takings would exceed costs (underwritten, as they were, by the socialist state). That anticipated surplus could be applied to the new Australian ballet's 1962 season, as long as the Trust could use its current reserves to pay the up-front costs of the Leningrad tour. The Trust would not mind using its reserves in this way, if it was confident that in 1962, when the government's review was over, 'governmental support would be available'. Coombs' letter was a masterly exercise in financial smoke and mirrors. He was effectively asking Menzies to prejudge the outcome of a review, in order to provide the money to save ballet for Australia.[20] He asked Holt to back him up.

By the middle of September, Coombs could tell van Praagh that he had won government support for a thirty-week season in the second half of 1962. He would be in London in a few weeks, with Hutchison, and they would discuss the program with her.[21] Evidently, those talks went well, for Coombs wrote to van Praagh upon his return to let her know she had his full confidence. She should not take too much notice of his suggestions, he warned. 'I am very conscious that these are matters for professionals and that it is important that the Chairman of the Board does not try to do the executives' job.'[22]

The Australian Ballet, an organisation jointly supervised by the Trust and J. C. Williamson's, offered its first season in 1962. High-quality ballet, like high-quality opera, was very expensive, so the Australian Ballet – however warmly welcomed – lost money in 1962 and 1963. By the end of 1963, the Trust was considering suspending its support. Van Praagh insisted on the continuous employment of the dancers. She found the Trust Board – with the exception of Coombs and two women – sexually prejudiced against her. Nonetheless the Trust did not want to lose van Praagh's services. At the end of 1963, it agreed to give the Australian Ballet a further twelve months, and foreshadowed a review.[23]

The enormous critical success, at the Adelaide Arts Festival in March 1964, of Robert Helpmann's *The Display* (with music by Malcolm Williamson and sets by Sidney Nolan) was a fillip in bleak times. Coombs and van Praagh had tried to persuade those handling the Queen Mother's tour of Australia to divide Her Majesty's time that evening between the Sydney Symphony Orchestra and *The Display*. Every bit of Royal patronage helped. But the Queen Mother could not be spread so thinly, her handlers decided, without 'embarrassment and chaos'. The premiere rested solely – and magnificently – on the quality of the staged work.[24] Eighteen months later Coombs boasted to an English audience that *The Display*

> draws upon elements indigenous to the land of Australia in a theme which our aboriginal forebears would have recognised; it links this emotionally with the Greek myths that are the heritage of all of western civilisation; it comments justly on aspects of Australian social life, throwing light on the universal theme of the place of the non-conformist outsider in a tightly knit society; all this in a work of art marked by grace, beauty and passion.[25]

Yet even such critical success could not assure the Trust's continuing financial support. The same financial crisis that jeopardised opera in the early 1960s prompted Stefan Haag to caution Helpmann in October 1964 that the Trust would not necessarily be able to 'guarantee the continued operation of the ballet company' as 'the existing contract, if it may be termed such, with the governments … does not allow us to assume beyond a year ahead'.[26] If anything saved the Australian Ballet, at this time, it was that Coombs and others persuaded the Menzies government that it was good for Australia's image abroad. When Australia was invited to participate in the 1965 Commonwealth Arts Festival, Coombs chaired a committee of 'artistic interests' which chose as Australia's representatives the Sydney Symphony Orchestra and the Australian Ballet.[27] Winning international critical acclaim on that tour (including the Grand Prix of the City of Paris for *Giselle*), the Australian Ballet became the first of the Australian 'flagship' companies, demonstrating (in the words of the Trust's Executive Director Stefan Haag) that 'Australian theatre has a valuable ambassadorial role to play in projecting this nation's image to the world.'[28]

In search of an audience

WHEN INTELLECTUALS URGED governments to support theatre, one of their most prominent arguments was that Australians lacked opportunities to understand themselves through the stage. In 1947 the University of Melbourne's Keith Macartney wished for theatre that 'gives utterance to the desires and preoccupations of its audience'. He complained that, unlike the Irish, 'we still lack a truly national voice in the theatre, the most social of the arts'.[1] On the eve of the Trust's formation Leslie Rees, the ABC's federal drama editor and Chair of the Playwrights' Advisory Board, had argued that 'the drama has a greater power than any other living art form to make direct contact with the minds and emotions of the people. Therefore, the drama's use in social criticism, its potential influence in reflecting and pointing community ideals and welding the people into a wholesome unity, cannot be overestimated.'[2] Playwright and poet Douglas Stewart thought that the playwright 'created' the nation. Shakespeare had created 'Elizabethan England – or rather, eternal England', and it was now up to Australian playwrights to form the minds and shape the lives of 'a new country such as Australia'.[3]

The Trust's commercial success in touring Ray Lawler's *Summer of the Seventeenth Doll* in 1956 seemed to fulfil these ideas. First performed by the Melbourne Union Theatre Repertory in November 1955, the play quickly became an emblem of an indigenous theatre. Critics celebrated *The Doll* as a moment of unprecedented empathy between playwright and audience. 'We are no longer faced with the problem of getting plays staged', wrote Wal Cherry. 'The playwright is no longer dissociated from the theatre. The Australian dramatist can now turn to the expression of a people in and through its own theatre.'[4] Alrene Sykes marvelled that 'Lawler's success has come out of the blue with a suddenness that is almost breathtaking, at a time when most people had become thoroughly accustomed to deploring the talents and the opportunities for Australian playwrights.'[5] For Harry Kippax the play's popularity demonstrated 'that Australian life could supply the themes and characters of authentic drama capable of interesting audiences, who, until then, had looked to importations for their drama'.[6]

In that moment of Australian theatre's evident coming of age, Hugh Hunt might have regretted the dismal prospectus for indigenous theatre which he had published only weeks before the curtain rose on *The Doll*. Hunt, after less than a year as the Trust's first Executive Director, declared that 'the mass of the public in the large cities, upon whom high-standard theatre must depend for its economic existence, has become so acclimatised to overseas star artists and to British and American plays, it will not readily accept the home-grown product'. An indigenous theatre is impossible, he wrote, if that means plays and operas written and performed only by Australians, about the Australian way of life.[7]

The Trust's losses from Australian plays, puppets and musicals amounted to £77,000 in the four and half years ending 30 December 1960; these were offset by profits of £65,000, most of it from one source – tours and film rights on *The Doll*.[8] *The Doll* was followed by another successful Australian play *The Shifting Heart*, a commercial and critical success when toured by the Trust in 1957. However, over the next four years, the Trust did not locate the pulse of the public with its subsequent ventures in indigenous drama. According to Leslie Rees, *Curly on the Rack, The Multi-coloured Umbrella, Lola Montez, Slaughter on St Teresa's Day, The Bastard Country, The Piccadilly Bushman* failed to make 'a really firm impression on the Australian public'.[9] Hunt's successor as Executive Director, Neil Hutchison, told Coombs in 1962 how demoralising it was to deal, on the one hand, with

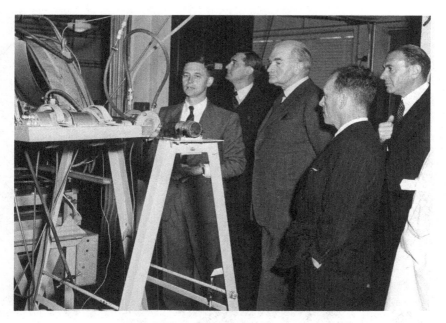

Machines that go PING!! Physicist Ernest Titterton (far left) shows Coombs and Vice-Chancellor Leslie Melville (far right) the work of the ANU's Research School of Physical Sciences in the late 1950s. (ANU Archives)

With Prime Minister Robert Menzies and a workman, laying the foundation stone of the Menzies Library, Australian National University, 11 May 1961. Two years later the new Coombs Building faced the Menzies Library. (ANU Archives)

An 'Elizabethan Night' at Sydney's 'Weinkeller' 20 April 1963. Lallie Coombs at left of picture. (Coombs family)

To keep fit, Coombs played squash and golf until his seventies, and for a time took up yoga. (Coombs family)

Making a decimal point. W. H. Wilcock of the Reserve Bank's Note Issue Department looks on, probably 1966. (National Library of Australia)

Soaring talents and their 'enabler'. With Gough Whitlam, the Sydney Opera House, and David Williamson in 1973. (Coombs family)

The enabler interrogates – as Chairman of the Royal Commission on Australian Government Administration, 1974 or 1975. (Coombs family)

On his eightieth birthday, the staff of the Centre for Resource and Environmental Studies (ANU) signed and presented Coombs a cricket bat. Coombs played one more staff social game after that.

With Lallie Coombs and May Grant, Coombs' personal assistant from 1942 to 1958, at a Reserve Bank Retired Officers evening November 1986. (Reserve Bank Archives)

*Delivering the Kenneth Myer Lecture 'Aborigines made visible: from humbug to politics',
National Library of Australia, 1991.* (National Library of Australia)

those who said the Trust had a duty to Australian playwrights ('I have already sponsored too many concessions to this point of view'), and on the other, with the 'conspicuous failure' of their plays.[10] So Hunt had been perceptive.

It is to Coombs' and the Board's credit that they took chances with indigenous drama. Offering guarantees against loss and paying the salaries of talented directors, the Trust encouraged repertory companies in the capital cities, many of them associated with universities. The 'little theatre' amateur tradition which had flourished between the wars was thus enhanced to the point of acquiring 'semi-professional' status. In its first ten years, the Trust assisted production of thirty-five Australian plays and produced twenty-five itself.[11]

Coombs' sense of what the Australian audience wanted in drama derived from two sources: his own experience of these plays, and his negotiations, sometimes difficult, with other leading Australians. In 1954, the Trust's President was Sir John Latham, recently retired as Chief Justice of the High Court and sometime conservative MP. The four Vice-Presidents were Dame Enid Lyons (first woman Minister in the Commonwealth Parliament on the conservative side, and now an ABC Commissioner), Sir Arthur Rymill (barrister and solicitor, President of South Australia's Liberal and Country League and Mayor of Adelaide), Sir Richard Boyer (grazier and Chair of the ABC) and Sir Robert Knox. The founding Board, chaired by Coombs, included three senior academics, three senior public servants, two trade unionists, and eleven company directors or general managers.

Drama, more explicitly than ballet and opera, is a form of political and moral discourse. One of the emerging features of the professional-managerial class which saw hope in subsidised drama was the readiness of some its members to see themselves as making cultural war on an artistically stuffy and morally censorious Establishment. Though the Trust was sometimes a vehicle for such challenges, the word 'Establishment' was less prominent in Coombs' vocabulary in these years than it was later to become. His rhetoric as Trust Chair was characteristically integrative rather than polarising. His chairmanship required him to bridge gaps that formed in the cultural leadership he had assembled in the Trust.

In 1956, someone proposed that Douglas Stewart's tragedy *Ned Kelly* be performed at the Comedy Theatre, with the Trust's help, to coincide with the Melbourne Olympic Games. However, in February 1956 several members of the Trust Board expressed doubts about the play's subject matter and the Board resolved to ask the opinion of the Olympic Festival Sub-Committee. The sub-committee's approval did not persuade all on the Trust Board, and there was further argument.[12] Latham could not reconcile himself to the play. Coombs urged him to consider how his stand might embarrass the Trust: 'For us to show reluctance in the face of clear and emphatic recommendations from our professional executive because some of us think the play may revive controversies best forgotten could, I feel, be gravely misunderstood and perhaps set a precedent for a sort of "political" censorship of the Trust's artistic policy.'[13] Latham reluctantly yielded, telling Coombs how much he regretted 'any support or countenance to the persistent attempt to represent Ned Kelly, thief, robber, and murderer, as a misunderstood, thoughtful, and really kindly man, worthy of respect and sympathy, and fitted to be regarded as a national hero'.[14] Coombs replied that 'there is less likelihood of the Kelly myth developing in a harmful way if it is brought out into the open and looked at frankly'.[15]

In Adelaide there were figures, some of them also eminent judges, who might have sympathised with Latham. A dissenting member of the Adelaide Establishment, Geoffrey Dutton, recalled it in its heyday as 'solidly monarchist and even more British than Menzies' and as 'narrow, inturned, smug and racist'.[16] In 1960 these men started their own Festival of the Arts and so became important if sometimes ambivalent partners of the Trust. The Governors refused to allow Alan Seymour's *One Day of the Year* to be performed in 1960, because its investigation of generational differences in the quality of the Anzac memory might offend the Returned Services League. The Adelaide Theatre Group, with help from the Trust, performed the play some months after the Festival. When preparing the next Festival in 1962, the Governors again defended their idea of taste and propriety by announcing that they could not accept Patrick White's *The Ham Funeral*. Again the Trust differed from the Governors. The Adelaide University Guild Theatre performed it in November 1961, with Trust support. This left some feathers ruffled, and Coombs had to smooth them. Sir Roland Jacobs, both a Festival Governor and a Trust Board member, was offended in 1963 when he thought that the Trust's Executive Director Stefan Haag was forming too cosy a relationship with the Adelaide University Guild Theatre 'behind our backs'. He was worried that the Trust would assist the Guild to produce Patrick White's *Night on Bald Mountain*, when the 'Festival people' had just rejected it for the 1964 Festival. White's plays, were, in his opinion 'not plays that one could be proud to produce'.[17] Coombs replied diplomatically.[18] The Guild performed the play in 1964 with Trust subsidy, after the Festival.

When the Queensland League for National Welfare and Decency found fault with the Old Tote Theatre's touring production of Edward Albee's *Who's Afraid of Virginia Woolf?* in 1964, Coombs told Premier Nicklin that it had been performed in other States, without provoking attending police officers to intervene. He referred to the police as 'the experienced investigators entrusted with official vigilance in these matters'. He then expounded the play's moral and psychological utility. *Virginia Woolf* was a moral play 'as it quite ruthlessly exposes issues which increasingly bedevil the institution of marriage in the modern world, it gives audiences clear recognition of these issues and, through this recognition, it may also help them personally deal with such difficulties in the real world'. It was likely that 'all drama – indeed, all art' would 'display matters which are ordinarily hidden' and so be 'therapeutic in its effects rather than damaging'.[19]

In his comments on the Stewart and the Albee plays (in 1956 and 1964), Coombs extolled theatre as the site of spiritually and morally empowering truth. Yet, his championing of Patrick White showed that this did not entail his exclusive allegiance to dramatic naturalism. White, having acquired Coombs as his Adelaide champion in 1962, was keen for him to attend the premiere of *A Cheery Soul* in Melbourne in November 1963. Coombs admired the performance of the play's star, Nita Pannell. He told her that he had found it 'the best Patrick White to date.

It is, I suppose, not surprising that from the audience responses I encountered after the show, it seems to have evoked the same violent differences of opinion as his previous efforts.'[20] Director John Sumner, to whom Coombs also wrote a congratulatory note, was depressed by the play's reception. The critics, he complained, were 'intolerant' of 'anything outside of the obvious general public comedy that goes down well at Russell Street ... any reception which requires deeper thought on the behalf of both critics and general public seems to meet with opposition in this city'.[21] He reported White to be in a similar mood of disenchantment with the public. Coombs implied in his note to White that the two of them could share the burden of public hostility.[22]

Re-designing Australia

IN DECEMBER 1958, opening a symposium on design in Australian industry at the University of New South Wales, Coombs declared that design 'is not a gimmick ... not something which is added irrelevantly'. Mass production was not inimical to good design, he added.

> The capacity of simple everyday objects to express in some way the character of the people whom they serve is something which adds greatly to the richness of everyday experience. ... When commodities produced here have something to say to the world, not merely about their own purpose but about the qualities of Australian people and Australian life, the world will want to buy them.[1]

By 1966, the words 'express the character of the people' had taken on a new and unexpected meaning, as the pursuit of the 'modern' took him to Darwin with a fishing basket.

During Coombs' Governorship, the Commonwealth and Reserve Banks commissioned several office buildings which became icons of post-war modernity. Speaking at the opening of the new Tasmanian head office of the Commonwealth Bank, 4 October 1954, he evoked the courage, persistence and vision of its architects (H. Riley and F. J. H. Crocker of the Commonwealth Department of Works), builders (Hansen and Yuncken) and workmen (he saluted the foreman-in-chief Dick Mason). He drew attention to the sculpture in the banking chamber, by Lyndon Dadswell, and a wooden panel carved by Hobart sculptor Stephen Walker. Proudly, he pointed out that the building was set back from its neighbours, endowing the city with a strip of land 15 feet wide. He asked the people of Tasmania to see the new premises as 'theirs to serve them and ... theirs to enjoy'.[2] An aerial photograph in *Currency* November 1954 shows the building dwarfing others.

The Bank's Hobart office attracted public attention of similar intensity to that devoted to the Sydney Opera House in 1971. The *Mercury* devoted sixteen pages to the building's splendour, reporting 'continuous streams of people walked through its corridors, opening doors and inspecting "their bank"'. One Saturday, during a ninety-minute inspection period, an estimated ten thousand Hobartians 'scrutinized every nook and cranny', even pausing to flush its toilets.[3]

The Bank was also proud of its next edifice, on a block bounded by York, George and Market Streets, Sydney – the subject of an eight-page supplement in the *Daily Mirror* on 18 April 1955. *Currency* celebrated its height ('a city landmark'), its innovative design features (such as an acoustic ceiling for the banking chamber, moveable light fittings and interior panels, stone, aluminium and glass facades). 'Each frontage will be adorned by sculptures in the modern manner' – by Lyndon Dadswell (in aluminium) and by Gerald Lewers (sandstone).[4] Coombs recalled in 1962 that the style of Dadswell's figures (symbolising trade) had occasioned criticism and satire. They were 'rather angular and with hollows where one might expect to see round protruberances. The cartoonists had a field day recording that this was what happened to those unfortunates who "got into the clutches of the banks".'[5]

In the early 1960s, the Reserve Bank built simultaneously its Melbourne, Adelaide, Canberra and Sydney office blocks – an orgy of design patronage. The January 1965 issue of *Currency* devoted twenty pages (and forty-two illustrations) to telling the story of the head office building, from the acquisition of the land bounded by Phillip Street, Martin Place and Macquarie Streets in 1958, to the building's completion in 1964. Sculptures by Bim Hilder and by Margel Hinder were chosen after a public competition judged in May 1962. Other buildings benefited from the Bank's interest in Australia's sculptors. The Canberra building got work from Gerald Lewers (completed by Margo Lewers), from Donald Brook (warmly recommended to Coombs by John Douglas Pringle) and by Milan Vojsk. Adelaide's and Brisbane's Reserve Bank branches were soon to be graced by Norma Redpath's works.

By the mid-1960s, the Governor and his Bank were exemplars of elegant, corporate modernism. In March 1966, the *Daily Telegraph*'s Ray Castle visited Coombs in his office and noted his taste. On the wall hung Leonard French's 'The Coming of the Turtle' and Dobell's 'Cockney Kid with Hoop' (the latter a personal loan from Russell Drysdale). There was also 'a tiny South Vietnamese screen – a thing of fragile beauty and painstaking lacquer', Milan Vojsk's 'Dreaming' sculpture and two glazed clay vases by Henri Le Grand, made from clay taken from the building's foundations. The furniture was made of Australian timbers.[6] In August 1968 *Vogue's Guide to Better Living* included the Governor's suite in a feature on the offices of senior executives.

Coombs' ideals of design – functional elegance, expressing national character – were most fully realised in his contribution to the appearance of Australia's new currency.

On 7 April 1963 the Treasurer, Harold Holt, announced that Australia would introduce decimal currency in February 1966. South Africa had begun a decimal system in February 1961, with banknotes only slightly redesigned. Would Australia also choose continuity? W. H. Wilcock, General Manager of the Reserve

Bank's Note Issue Department, told Coombs that it would be possible to produce notes of entirely new design, as long as his Department could buy the latest offset printing machinery and get plates made in Europe. Coombs immediately asked the Industrial Design Council of Australia for the names of possible designers of the new notes. He was told to see Alistair Morrison, Gordon Andrews, Richard Beck and Max Forbes.

Confident that he could assemble a design team, Coombs asked Treasurer Holt if Australia could be more adventurous than South Africa, whose design caution was probably influenced 'by the desire to make the change-over as simple as possible mainly because of the large native population'.[7] Coombs asked Russell Drysdale if he would represent the Bank on the design team that he was trying to assemble. Drysdale's work exemplified contemporary mainstream representation of Australia on canvas, and, as a member of the Commonwealth Art Advisory Council, he could personally reassure the Prime Minister and Treasurer of Coombs' design team's good taste. Coombs also got advice from Frederick Ward, design consultant to the ANU and to the Reserve Bank. Coombs' team came to consist of Gordon Andrews, Richard Beck, Max Forbes, George Hamori, with Douglas Annand and Hal Missingham as consultants to the four designers, and Alistair Morrison as the group's chair. Professor A. D. Trendall, a classicist and Master of University House, attended two meetings, at Coombs' invitation. Morrison had long been an important figure in Coombs' quest for the Bank to exemplify modernity. As the designer of the 1950 *Annual Report* of the Commonwealth Bank, of the first few years' Reserve Bank reports and (with Douglas Annand) of *Currency*, he was responsible, more than any other designer, for the Bank's visual 'house style'.[8]

Soon Morrison had his group poring over lists of names of Great Australians whose portraits (along with one of the Queen) should ornament the currency. There were five categories: Seafaring explorers (Tasman, Dampier, Cook, Flinders); Inland explorers (Sturt, Burke, Wills, Leichhardt); Governors (Macquarie, Phillip, King, Bourke, Mitchell, Hunter, Darling, Brisbane); 'National Identities' (Kingsford Smith, Charles Ulm, Edward Hargraves, Lawrence Hargrave, Douglas Mawson, Henry Kendall, Henry Lawson, Banjo Paterson, John Flynn, Hubert Murray, Nellie Melba, Peter Lalor, John Monash, Essington Lewis, and someone called Scott).[9] The final category had no names: 'Portraits of unidentified aborigines' – to be juxtaposed with specimens of their art.

Morrison devised a collaborative method for his team, balancing competition with cooperation. Each designer would sketch the front and reverse images of the four denominations and submit the eight designs to the rest of the committee for comment. The artist would then refine and revise his sketches in the light of comments. In order to achieve stylistic integration, the full suite of designs of only one artist would be chosen for recommendation to the Prime Minister and Treasurer. Coombs and some senior staff attended several of these meetings. He told the meeting on 8 November 1963 that there should be balance in the choice of themes, so that 'a range of life should be embraced'. He did not want, for example, too many explorers. Referring by way of illustration to the names

Kendall, Melba and Mawson, he hoped that the range of themes would reflect Australian 'folklore'.[10]

To get ideas about the Aboriginal theme, Morrison's group borrowed books and photographs from the library of the Australian Institute of Aboriginal Studies – a newly formed body which was about to receive its statutory charter in 1964. Karel Kupka's photographs of bark paintings impressed the committee members.

At that time, there was still little appreciation, beyond the circles of academic anthropologists, some missionaries and a handful of artists, of the Aboriginal artistic heritage. The Commonwealth Bank's Christmas card for 1951/2 had featured a watercolour landscape by Otto Pareroultja (though Bank records offer no clue as to how and when this work was acquired). In 1959 the corporate Yuletide greeting had sported Aboriginal motifs on its cover (with Drysdale's 'The Puckamanni' inside). But the Bank's collecting otherwise evidenced little interest in this visual tradition. The Reserve Bank did not publish an Aboriginal motif as a decorative device until the *Currency* cover of February 1968, and there is no record of the Bank purchasing the work of Aboriginal artists during Coombs' Governorship. In 1963–4, Aboriginal designs – apart from the ubiquitous boomerang – were largely untried by corporations, and by the nation itself. The inspiration offered by Kupka's photos was new.

In December 1963, the eventual 'winner' of Morrison's clever process, Gordon Andrews, had settled, in all but one particular, on the range of themes and personages. Andrews, at this stage, had considered Aboriginal motifs only as part of the background to the portrait of the Queen on the front of the one-dollar note. On the back of the dollar note he had placed a portrait of Nellie Melba surrounded by costumes from her career. Richard Beck had been more responsive to the Institute's stimulus; he had put an Aboriginal portrait and some bark paintings on the front of his two-dollar bill, and he had used Aboriginal art as background to portraits of Monash, Banks and Kingsford Smith. George Hamori had put Melba and 'Aboriginal bark painter' on either side of his fifty-dollar bill. Perhaps inspired by their example, by the end of January 1964 Andrews had dropped Melba, replacing her with 'an aboriginal scene with a reproduction of a bark painting of a number of fish'. After further discussion of that decision by the panel, Andrews again modified it to replace the fish with a kangaroo hunt.[11]

On 24 March 1964 the four sets of designs were approved by Menzies, Holt and Roland Wilson. Morrison then convened his advisers and all agreed that Andrews' work must be the nation's choice for going decimal in February 1966. Andrews further modified his one-dollar bill obverse, eventually contriving a faithful line interpretation of an Aboriginal bark painting as shown in a photograph printed from one of Kupka's loaned negatives, plus symbols and motifs garnered from Charles Mountford's book *Art, Myth and Symbolism*.

Morrison's currency designs triggered Coombs' recognition of Aboriginal art as a *living* tradition. On 11 February 1966, the *South Pacific Post* broke the story that Andrews' one-dollar bill obverse owed a great deal to a painting by Milingimbi artist, David Malangi. This work was now owned by the Paris Museum of Arts of Africa and Oceania, having been collected by Karel Kupka in

1963. The Bank, having just received this information from Kupka (who wanted payment for his photo), arranged for Malangi to be paid $1000 through the Department of Welfare in the Northern Territory. Coombs' letter to Director of Welfare Harry Giese required very careful wording, recalls Bill Judges. In August 1967, Coombs toured northern Australia to inspect the sites of mining, pastoral and agricultural investment. While in Darwin he was able to meet David Malangi and to present him with a medallion and 'a fully equipped fishing box' in recognition of his artistic contribution.[12] He came back wondering how Aboriginal people would survive the incipient 'boom in the North'.

Part 9
Labor's second chance

Retirement

BY 1966 COOMBS HAD exhausted the reformist possibilities of his Governorship. How might he have drawn up, in his sixtieth year, a ledger of achievement and frustration? He had lost the fight to keep the Commonwealth Bank composite, yet he had wooed the private banks to the semi-voluntary observance of what he regarded as their monetary responsibilities. By giving hire purchase its chance, he had presided over the start of the deregulation of the Australian financial system – an 'evolution' about which he was ambivalent. Though tempted by Raul Prebisch – surely a kindred, if distant spirit – to join the re-emergent forums that might consider again the North–South relationship, he had accepted his government's restraining hand. There was to be no late career replay of London–Geneva–Havana.

Coombs had become known for his amiable impenetrability. In 1961 Peter Hastings profiled him for the *Australian Financial Times*

> He is courteous to people and the sense of impending disapproval is merely illusion. He listens carefully to what people have to say and replies precisely and to the point in unmistakeably Australian accents. Sometimes he anticipates a question or the general drift of a conversation and breaks in quickly to make a point. But mostly he listens quietly and intently as he chain smokes or moves around in his chair. He smiles quite often, which robs his face of the severity it has in repose.

Hastings' strongest impression was of Coombs' 'unabashed Australianness'.[1] The *Age*'s John Hetherington judged that with 'inexhaustible reserves of cold detachment' Coombs would have been a good football umpire. 'His patience is said to be nearly inexhaustible. Few professional intimates have ever seen him show anger or any kind of displeasure stronger than momentary annoyance, expressed by a tightening of the mouth and a muttered "Hmph"!'[2] Laurie Oakes thought that 'nearly 20 years in the nation's top banking job has made him by nature tight-lipped'.[3]

The Reserve Bank's commemorative booklet on his retirement flavours Coombs' gubernatorial decorum with vignettes of fatherly modesty. Before an assembly of Bank staff D. A. Tate, Manager of the Establishment Department, presented a specially commissioned painting by Coombs' friend Leonard French. There was a 'buzz of disbelief' among assembled staff when Coombs declared that he did not deserve 'the generous things that you have said about me'.[4] Fondly, he evoked the milieu he had shared with staff.

> Here you live and work in an atmosphere which is pleasant, where things of beauty are a commonplace. ... You can hear laughter ringing in the halls and the rooms of this Bank, from the board room to the locker room. It is a simple human sort

of place. You can see in the entrance hall from time to time little mini-skirted girls holding hands with the boy friend and looking as if they thought that the miracle that was happening to them had never happened before.

A vignette of enlightened episcopacy: 'our staff does not suffer from the evils of pomposity'.[5]

The measured humanity of Coombs' persona as Governor did not satisfy those who wished that he had been more of an intellectual leader. 'The bank has sometimes maintained silence virtually for the full 12 months between annual reports which themselves have tended to be odd mixtures of platitudes, careful records of the economy's previous behaviour and occasional insights', wrote one journalist.[6] Nor would the financial editor of the *Sydney Morning Herald* forgive Coombs' self-control.

> Dr. Coombs' reluctance to say plainly what he had to say about policy has sometimes driven observers to distraction. There have been periods when the Reserve Bank had seemed a tower of mediocrity, an institution too much subordinated to the Governor's other interests. He has conspicuously failed to publish economic intelligence material anywhere comparable to that produced regularly by the British and U.S. central bank authorities. He has had to be pushed reluctantly into the development of some new functions in the money market.[7]

Coombs' circumspection made him vulnerable to ill-informed criticism. The financial editor noted as a low point of Coombs' Governorship his advocacy of cheap money. Records not available to that writer show Coombs to have been a tactful opponent of low interest rates from 1953. There was something personally stoic in that institutional 'mediocrity'.

It was a blessing to be free of the Bank. Trevor Swan congratulated Coombs in 1970 for becoming 'for public purposes yourself again, not the creature of cautious drafters or the victim of cautious blue pencils'.[8]

Coombs showed a critical awareness of what the Governorship had made of him when he told David Love of the *Australian Financial Review*:

> I don't think it makes good sense for a Central Bank to want to have both the role of a private confidential adviser to government and an outspoken public critic at the same time. These roles are incompatible. But, in qualification of this, let me say at once that I believe an informed public discussion or dialogue between government and other segments of the community on economic and financial policies is important. And I think the Reserve Bank should be freer – not to take direct public part in this – but to help facilitate it, to provide materials for informing it and within limits, privately to contribute to it.[9]

With characteristic sensitivity to the dilemmas of his position, Wilmott Phillips told him that 'only those who have been close to you can realise the value of what you have done in this field'.[10] Her husband, and Coombs' successor as Governor, Jock Phillips, listed for a colleague the Coombs virtues that only close workmates might see, the warm humanity of his approach to all problems, his ready sense of humour, his ability to see the central core of a problem through all the superficial complexities, and his energy and inventiveness. He always had on his desk – turned towards himself – a quotation from Cromwell saying 'I beseech you, in the bowels of Christ, to think it possible you may be mistaken'.[11]

There were strains of the puritan in Coombs' anticipation of retirement. To the Old People's Welfare Council of Victoria he had spoken in 1962 a manifesto for active, purposeful leisure shaped by thought of others' need. It was necessary to compensate for the inevitable loss of income, of status and – most dangerous – of purpose. He would begin to fortify his own self-respect by acknowledging that one's 'existence is justified by performance, at least to oneself. This is perhaps a puritanical thought.' Retirement activities were more likely to confer a sense of purpose 'when the focal point ... is beyond one's own immediate satisfaction'. Physical, mental and emotional exercise were essential, and 'there are many wrongs in the world to be righted; there are many weak and unhappy people to be pro-tected and comforted'.[12]

By the time his Bank colleagues were seeing him off, Coombs' plans fulfilled those words. Announcing in November 1967 that Coombs would retire the following July, Prime Minister Harold Holt welcomed Coombs as the founding chair of two new bodies, the Council for Aboriginal Affairs and the Australian Council for the Arts. Good works indeed. Coombs refused other offers. He declined to become, at $2000 per year, an investment adviser to the Prudential Assurance Company; and nor could he find time to work with economist Ronald Henderson to establish an Australian Innovation Corporation.[13] He hoped that his new responsibilities would 'stimulate my intelligence and give me the capacity for using any intelligence, character or enterprise which I may have'.[14] Russell Drysdale predicted of Coombs' 'retirement': 'God knows it will be a tough job.'[15]

Whitlam conscripts Coombs

As CHAIR OF TWO new Commonwealth policy advisory bodies since late 1967 – the Council for Aboriginal Affairs and the Australian Council for the Arts – Coombs experienced many disappointments.[1] Working under the unresponsive Peter Howson in 1971–2 required all his persistence. His personal prestige in the eyes of the public was a political asset. But any use of that asset put it at risk. Planning to visit Washington, New York and London, Prime Minister McMahon asked Coombs to accompany him. Coombs agreed to go as long as McMahon promised that the issue of Aboriginal title in Arnhem Land was not decided in his absence. McMahon agreed. Then, to Coombs' 'extreme irritation', McMahon referred publicly to him as 'a kind of guiding philosopher'.[2] Judith Wright offered her sympathy for what she described as Coombs 'being snatched to the upper atmosphere in a fiery propaganda machine'.[3]

The *Australian* soon restored him to a place 'above' politics by choosing him as Australian of the Year for 1971. Dominic Nagle profiled him as 'a kind of guru or house ideas man'. The editorial commended his work in 'Aboriginal advancement, development of the arts and better government in a rapidly changing society'. Coombs' disciplined vitality impressed Nagle.

> He behaves in such a confident way. When he moves, it's like a piston: well oiled, regular, got a job to do, no mucking about please, pow, pow … Even when he sits down, it's all go. He doesn't sit in a chair so much as bounce around just above it or on the edge of it. He is incisive and lucid; dates and figures pop out of him without his having to dredge around in his mind for them. He shoots his points out with short stabbing movements of his fingers or, like a teacher or general he ticks things off with the forefinger of one hand on the palm of the other.[4]

Among Coombs' many letters of congratulation, Russell Drysdale told Coombs that 'so many of your friends are tickled pink' about the newspaper's honour. The award restored Zelman Cowen's 'waning regard for that journal', while a Tom Bateman wondered why 'it has taken them so long' to find out that Coombs was a great man. Medical researcher M. R. Lemberg told Coombs that he would 'love and honour' him in spite of his having become Australian of the Year.[5] Harry M. Miller's letter opened with 'Dear National Hero!'[6]

Nagle found Coombs a rather circumspect guru, refusing to state personal views on issues. 'He slides away, his head down over his hands, his hands massaging each other in an "Aw shucks" way. It is really like watching steel shutters come down.'[7] Coombs was behaving as he had always thought a senior government adviser should, criticising the government from within, rather than in public. However, the McMahon government's intransigence on Aboriginal land rights tested his faith in that strategy. Coombs did *not* conceal his disappointment in McMahon's 26 January 1972 statement on Aboriginal Affairs policy. Nine months later, his well-reported lecture at the University of Sydney on 'The Future of the Australian Aboriginal' cast McMahon's Australia Day statement in a poor light.

Coombs and his fellow Councillors for Aboriginal Affairs – Barrie Dexter and William Stanner – had discussed since the winter of 1971 whether it was better to resign. Resignation might draw blood from a government they had learned to loathe. But Coombs had a better idea. He and Whitlam conferred in September 1972 about Coombs becoming Whitlam's adviser, should Whitlam win the forthcoming general election. With Coombs' consent, Whitlam publicised their agreement on 12 November, two days before Labor formally opened its election campaign. 'I shall personally be seeking the advice of Dr. Coombs on high economic matters', the PM-to-be was reported to have announced.[8] The press noted that only a year ago, Whitlam's 'Kissinger' had been McMahon's 'guiding philosopher'. Coombs' intention to serve Whitlam was seen as Labor's trumping of McMahon, not as evidence of Coombs' flightiness. Indeed, the *Australian Financial Review* demoted both politicians with the words 'Dr. Coombs, guru, finds new acolyte.'[9] Such a response to Whitlam's 'bombshell' (the word so often used) vindicated Stanner's advice: 'The PM [McMahon] may have dumped his quondam philosopher but the national media have not, and will not, do so.'[10]

In his press conference the day after Whitlam's announcement Coombs adopted a posture of public service propriety. He was still available to advise McMahon 'if he seeks my advice'. His agreement with Whitlam was only that he would seriously consider a request from Whitlam once he became Prime Minister, as long as Coombs saw in Labor 'a serious commitment to the improvement of the status and condition of Aboriginal Australians'. Coombs refused to comment evaluatively on either prime ministerial candidate; and he declined invitations to speculate on the election's outcome. 'I have always regarded myself as a Public Servant', he protested when asked if he would like personally to work with Whitlam. Nor would he comment on the McMahon government's Aboriginal affairs policies. Asked if he now *appeared* to be giving Labor his 'blessing', Coombs responded: 'I dare say that is possible but that is not my motive.' There was nothing improper about his announcing his conditional willingness to serve Whitlam, he argued. He was merely declaring his availability as an adviser to a Prime Minister other than the current Prime Minister. Coombs agreed that Whitlam's announcement 'could influence the outcome of the election', but he added that 'my refusing to act as an adviser could influence the election also'.[11]

As Alan Ramsey commented, 'in his present role as a public servant, Dr. Coombs clearly would become an automatic adviser to Mr. Whitlam if Labor were successful in the elections'. To the extent that Coombs was merely a public servant, in other words, Whitlam's announcement was entirely gratuitous. However, Coombs was not a public servant in any usual sense. He was paid from the public purse, but his powers and obligations as Chair of the Australian Council for the Arts and of the Council for Aboriginal Affairs had never been statutorily defined. To represent himself, in a press conference, as a 'public servant' – with all the refusals and silences that this permitted – was Coombs' way of effacing his own interest and highlighting the Aboriginal interest. It was a superb strategy, for all the work of promoting Coombs as personal 'philosopher', great Australian and personal 'adviser' extraordinaire was done by others – first McMahon, then the *Australian* and now Whitlam. The less Coombs said about his political role in that interview, the more his political virtue grew. His judgment on McMahon was widely inferred. The logic of the Channel Ten News was blunt: 'One of the country's most influential men, he's hardly the type to back a loser.'[12]

Whitlam's announcement struck some commentators as an attempt to assure the electorate that he could manage the Australian economy. Thus the *Sun-Herald*'s 'Onlooker': 'With that wise little man at his elbow, what incoming Prime Minister (so the inference ran) could go financially astray?'[13] The *Australian Financial Review* thought the announcement had lifted the mood of the stock market. 'Some serious reservations have been expressed in business and financial circles on the quality of the economic advice Mr. Whitlam can count on if he wins the next election. ... Dr. Coombs' influence would doubtless be seen by many such businessmen as a major gain to the ALP.'[14] Max Walsh, under the headline

'Whitlam Polishes Economic Image', more sceptically opined that Coombs' appointment 'underlines the ALP's lack of depth in the economic policy area'.[15] When Graham Perkin interviewed Whitlam for the *Age*, towards the end of the campaign, he asked if the announcement about Coombs was an attempt 'to persuade the electorate that you are respectable because you have one of the most significant public servants of the past 20 years beside you?' Whitlam's answer included the words: 'I've always respected Dr. Coombs. Everything I've read of his, everything I've noted he has done. I don't think there is an economist in the last quarter of a century who has been so impeccable or infallible. You can't recall an economic issue on which Coombs was wrong.' To Perkin's scepticism Whitlam responded that Sir Roland Wilson, not Coombs, had been to blame for a recession in 1962. And 'Coombs was not responsible for the '61 or the '56 or the '51 credit squeezes and the particular measures that were adopted then.' Whitlam summed Coombs up as 'a human, simple, unaffected person. No titles ...'. Coombs would also command the confidence 'of people in the investment and business fields where we will need cooperation'.[16] When the *Advertiser* published Helen Frizell's profile of Coombs, the same day Perkin spoke to Whitlam, the sub-editor dubbed Coombs 'the economist who cares about people'.[17] *Nation Review*'s Perth correspondent reported McMahon as telling a public meeting 'that Whitlam would make a hash of the economy'. An interjector shouted 'But he'll have Dr. Coombs behind him.' According to the reporter, 'others took up the cry of protest at the implied slur on Nugget's integrity'.[18] The intentions of the *Daily Telegraph*'s editorial triumphed over its inept wording: 'Dr. Coombs, as much as anyone else, has been the architect of Australia's economic growth over the past 25 years.'[19]

Trade reform

As WHITLAM'S ECONOMIC adviser, Coombs got a second chance at structural reform of the economy. In the 1940s, he had advocated trade liberalisation, provided that governments were allowed – compelled even – to pursue full employment. Though Australia had enjoyed full employment since then, Coombs told Whitlam in January 1973, Coalition governments had never developed a 'coherent and principled' international economic policy. Rather, governments had made 'ad hoc choices ... in a context of conflicting economic interests and ministerial and departmental rivalries. Australia's reputation as an enlightened member of the international community has suffered accordingly.'[1] The political alliance of primary producers, manufacturers and trade unions had continued to frustrate the generation of Keynesian economic rationalists that included Melville and Rattigan, successive Chairs of the Tariff Board.

In 1963, G. A. Rattigan, new in the Tariff Board's Chair, had begun to question the supposition laid down by successive governments that tariffs would 'diversify the Australian economy, employ a large number of migrants and protect the relatively high standard of living in the community.'[2] The Coalition government had spurned Rattigan's revisionism. Country Party leader John McEwen – whose Trade portfolio included the Tariff Board – had defended the protection of both primary and secondary industries as essential to all Australians' prosperity. The May 1965 report of the Vernon Committee had reiterated Rattigan's scepticism, recommending that tariffs above a 'benchmark' be justified and that their costs, as well as the benefits, be documented. Rattigan had gathered support not only from some Labor, Liberal and Country Party MPs but also from organisations representing wholesalers, retailers and farmers. The government had tried to silence Rattigan, but he had insisted in May 1967 that, as chair of a statutory authority, he enjoyed liberties not available to public servants. He continued to question tariff policy.

Labor's shadow Minister for Trade and Industry, Jim Cairns, accused Menzies and McEwen of being too close to manufacturing interests. McEwen countered that if Labor followed Cairns' support for Rattigan's critique, it would be forgetting the interests of workers. Cairns had changed his view by the end of 1968, deploring the possibility of the Tariff Board 'being allowed to run wild through Australian industry'.[3] However, his colleague Bill Hayden defended the Tariff Board in a November 1968 debate, and late in 1971, Whitlam and Rattigan began to converge in the view that a tariff review body such as the Tariff Board was essential to industry policy.

When Labor came to power in December 1972, it reflected these unresolved differences. On the one hand, Whitlam had announced in March 1972 that the Tariff Board – to be renamed the Protection Commission – would critically assess the protection of primary as well as secondary industries. On the other hand, he had announced during the election campaign that Cairns would be Minister for Overseas Trade and for Secondary Industry, a new portfolio set up at the suggestion of the protected manufacturers. Cairns wanted to treat the trade unions as partners in making industry policy; Whitlam was more sympathetic to letting market forces test the efficiency of Australian industries. On the first working day of the Whitlam government (4 December 1972), Rattigan urged Whitlam to place industry protection policy under the Department of the Prime Minister, not under Cairns.[4]

Coombs proposed that Cairns' new department be responsible for consumer affairs as well as for the Tariff Board. He cited the consumer advocacy of Ralph Nader and the planned Prices Justification Board as illustrations of ways to toughen the consumer lobby. With consumers to answer to, Cairns and his officials would be less likely to follow primary and secondary industry desires for protection through tariffs.[5] For several weeks Whitlam and Cairns struggled over which Department would write Cabinet submissions on Tariff Board recommendations.[6] Cairns offered to set up 'a series of industry panels' comprising 'not only … the industrial leaders and departmental representatives but also representatives of the trade unions and of consumers'.[7] Insisting that to consider and coordinate all interests was a prime ministerial duty, Whitlam sought Coombs' help.[8] Coombs consulted Rattigan when drafting Whitlam's conclusive rebuff of Cairns in April 1973.[9]

Coombs was then collaborating with Rattigan in another proposal that would soon result in the Tariff Board being reconstituted as an Industries Assistance Commission. In late February and early March they suggested to Whitlam that he ask Sir John Crawford, soon to retire as Vice-Chancellor of the ANU, to report on the future of protection policy in Australia. Coombs drafted the Prime Minister's letter of invitation to Crawford, with notes on how his inquiry might proceed and what it might set out to achieve.[10] Crawford's report, recommending the setting up of the Industries Assistance Commission, was ready by the middle of June, and Whitlam appointed Rattigan Chairman designate on 3 July 1973. Introducing a Bill for the Industries Assistance Commission on 27 September, Whitlam enlisted Coombs' help when a delegation of manufacturers presented their fears about its mission.[11] Disturbed by the ascendancy of the anti-protection forces within the Labor government, Cairns went on the attack publicly in July. Addressing the Australian Industries Development Association – a peak organisation of manu- facturers – he criticised the dominance of 'economists' in the making of industry policy. They were persuaded more by theories, he said, than by 'problems in human relations'. 'I think economists are too narrow in their view of life'.[12]

Inflation soon gave this debate a new context. In the summer of 1972–3, the economy was recovering from a minor recession – but how quickly? Coombs concurred with Treasury's advice that were the government to spend money now to soak up pockets of unemployment, aggregate demand would grow too quickly and the 1973/4 budget would have to be restrained. A moderate and slow recovery in employment, peaking in 1975, would leave room in Labor's first and second budgets for the many new programs promised during the 1972 election.[13] By June 1973 the economy was booming. In a six-page memorandum, 'The Budget and General Economic Strategy', Coombs pointed out the issue that Labor must now face: how to avert inflation, without abandoning promised expenditures on new programs? The government must find other ways to reduce excess demand. In Coombs' view, the best way would be to increase imports – by floating the exchange rate and/or by reducing tariffs. This would boost the supply of goods to Australia's consumers without requiring increased domestic production. Here he drew on a note to Whitlam from the ANU economist Fred Gruen.[14] Coombs' memo bridged two sectors of Labor opinion: those wanting to cut tariffs and those, such as Cairns, seeking to implement Labor's program without inflation. A cut in tariffs, Coombs suggested, would move Labor towards both goals.[15]

To win Cairns over, Coombs needed Whitlam to argue that a tariff cut was 'reasonable in the context of a wider strategy which included, for instance, significant cuts in defence expenditure and some increases in taxation.' The Prime Minister could also foreshadow restraints on private borrowing, imports from China, and 'a special tribunal to which firms whose total sales had been reduced by these tariff changes to levels which threatened total employment could apply for review'.[16]

Cabinet decided by a ratio of two to one to cut tariffs.[17] Whitlam and Cairns announced the 25 per cent across-the-board tariff cut – to take immediate effect – on the evening of 18 July 1973. Whitlam later deplored the 'knee-jerk hostility of sections of the trade union movement' to this announcement.[18] Bob Hawke, ACTU President and recently elected President of the Labor Party, began the day commanding his secretary 'Get me fucking Whitlam!', and finished it supporting the decision, with as much self-possession as 'somebody trying to sell an unroadworthy used car', according to the *Bulletin*.[19]

Two cultural constituencies

SINCE 1971, COOMBS had helped two constituencies – 'the Arts' and 'the Aborigines' – to become more articulate. When he became Whitlam's adviser in 1972, both challenged his concept of democratic participation in government.

The Australian Council for the Arts (ACFTA) was not quite what Coombs had asked for in 1967. He wished the government had conducted an inquiry into the arts, then formed a council with a statutory mandate to carry out its recommendations. Instead of a council specialising in the theatre arts, musical performance and 'the production of Australian television programs by live theatre and other companies engaged in the performing arts', he got the ACFTA, whose brief for the arts he found impossibly broad.[1] To an Adelaide forum in March 1968, Coombs complained that the ACFTA was the vehicle for the hopes of many artists and art forms. He admitted to being irritated when critics accused him – when he worked on his preferred narrow front – of merely perpetuating the Trust's pattern of subsidies. Yes – performing arts were the immediate beneficiaries of the ACFTA, but 'we cannot expect to move on the whole front at the same rate'.[2] Two years later he lamented that 'those concerned with the arts seem to have an infinite capacity for division'. He was responding to a speaker who had denigrated ballet. 'If there are some [arts] which give joy to others but leave us unmoved then let us, in decent humility, sorrow over our own inadequacy.'[3]

In its first distribution of grants in 1968, the ACFTA indeed favoured bodies that had flourished under the Australian Elizabethan Theatre Trust: the National Institute of Dramatic Art, the Australian Ballet School, the Australian Ballet, the National Opera Company, a permanent theatre orchestra and the Marionette Theatre of Australia, and the Trust itself. The performing arts companies who missed out – including some respected companies on Sydney's North Shore – became objects of sympathy in the newspapers of their city. In January 1969, Coombs defended the concentration of government subsidy on a few companies by arguing that it promoted 'excellence'. The ACFTA had received $3.5 million worth of requests and yet had only $1.5 million to do its work. Advised by experts to concentrate on a few areas of 'excellence', the ACFTA was nonetheless well aware of the danger of cultivating an Establishment – 'the beginning of atrophy', Coombs acknowledged. 'The pursuit of excellence therefore needs to be supported by the parallel pursuit of diversity.' Other sources of support for the arts – State

and local governments, universities and corporations – would increase the possibility of diversity, and the ACFTA was setting up a $160,000 Special Projects
Fund, for non-subsidised companies to dip into. 'Young Jimmy Sharman, the
liveliest and most adventurous of our young producers' was a fruit of 'diversity'.

> Sharman was with a group of youngsters responsible for *Terror Australis*, a theatrical
> event which Katherine Brisbane described as the bravest failure of 1968. It was a
> work which cast aside traditional forms of drama, borrowed freely from techniques
> of film, radio and the electronic arts generally and the outcome was technically and
> emotionally exciting. Its failure in the box office could easily reflect the uneasiness
> engendered in the consciences of those of us who watched it at the relentless
> exposure of aspects of our history and our contemporary life which instinctively we
> thrust below the surface of consciousness.[4]

Such gestures to 'diversity' were symbolically important – both warding off critics
of elitism and raising expectations that would be hard to meet. Under two successive Ministers, Prime Minister Gorton and then the Minister for the Environment, Aborigines and the Arts, Peter Howson, the ACFTA's budget grew to two
and half times its size from 1968/9 to 1971/2. However, there was no policy
framework, and Coombs' periodic defences and explanations in that period were
no substitute for one.

What were the proper sources of arts policy? Coombs rejected the suggestion
that arts practitioners should devise one. Instead, policy-makers should be people
with 'a wide and discriminating interest in the arts, … an understanding of the
problems associated with the support of the arts, and … a capacity to persuade
the Government'. Panels of practitioners, perhaps chosen by fellow artists, could
advise the Council, he conceded. However, he doubted that individual artists
would put up with the difficulties of playing such representative roles.[5] A persistent
advocate must 'accept cheerfully the decision of the moment and demonstrate a
capacity to live within it and to get value for money spent'.[6]

Sensitive to the sub-editors' label 'Arts Czar', Coombs pointed to the enabling,
not the determining, outcomes of his work. 'I don't regard myself in any sense as
a cultural leader,' he had declared in 1967 while still Chair of the Trust. But
in 1970 his old friend Dick Downing publicly applauded the ACFTA as a
'paternalistic bureaucracy'.[7] The ACFTA had chosen to support the 'excellent few',
and Coombs preferred to maintain the division of labour between manager/
advocates who knew the ways of government and 'practitioners' who focused, with
necessary selfishness, on their own artistic patch.

Under Labor these two issues became conflated. That is, many of those who
were missing out on government subsidy were inclined to think that better
distribution would come if policy was driven by forums of artists. Whitlam's 'It's
time' election campaign at the end of 1972 seemed to some to imply that
government would be run in such a new way.

Coombs had outlined his preferred Commonwealth arts policy in October
1972. It would bring together six Commonwealth 'cultural' bodies: the ACFTA,
the Commonwealth Art Advisory Board, the Commonwealth Literary Fund, the

Commonwealth Assistance to Australian Composers, the Interim Council for a National Film and Television Training School and the Interim Council for a National Gallery. He sought both to preserve each agency's freedom to act within its own field and to promote their collective consideration of issues which affected more than one field of the arts. The National Gallery and the Film School should be separately constituted, while the other agencies would be reconstituted as boards within a 'broad single Council'.[8] He named six Boards: Visual and Plastic Arts and Crafts, Film and Television, Theatre Arts, Music, Literary Arts, and 'Aboriginal or Ethnic Arts'. Membership of the Boards should overlap a little. Each Board would have its own delegated budget and enjoy the power to commission expert advice.

On Australia Day 1973 (26 January) Whitlam announced that he would legislate an independent Australian Council for the Arts. He would first appoint new members to the existing (ACFTA) Council, asking it to develop the detail of the proposed bill and to plan the staffing of the new body, to set out an initial budget and to suggest memberships for all Boards.[9] Coombs agreed to chair this interim body, with Jean Battersby continuing as his executive officer.[10] Whitlam and Coombs were immediately accused of pre-empting public consultation. There were too few artists on the Council, some complained. Clifton Pugh, Chair of the Victorian ALP Arts Policy Committee and a member of the new Council, described it as 'top-heavy with public servants and amateurs'.[11] The *Australian* headed Katherine Brisbane's article 'It's amateur hour in the arts world.'[12] The *Age* art critic, Patrick McCaughey, complained that Whitlam and Coombs had not consulted 'interested parties within the art world'.[13] Actors Equity was unhappy that it was not represented on the Council. 'Many of our members worked exceedingly hard to return a Labor government', the union's telegram explained, in the hope 'that they would have a voice in the structure and decisions of a reconstituted Council for the Arts.'[14] The President of the Artists' Guild of Australia, Paul Atroshenko, described Coombs as 'virtual dictator of culture'.[15] Publisher Andrew Fabinyi, in a more positive piece, labelled Coombs 'the Great Prompter' of arts policy.[16]

When the first meeting of the new 24-member Council (16 February 1973) announced the membership of six of the seven new Boards, Teresa Brennan wrote in *Nation Review* that 'the power of interested businessmen' had been 'reinforced'.[17] Joan Long of the Australian Writers Guild noted the absence of script-writers and playwrights.[18] A member of the Film and Television Board, Tom Jeffery, called for Board members to be elected.[19] George Whaley, Theatre Director at the University of Melbourne, saw the Council and its Boards as a poor substitute for 'a detailed investigation involving widespread consultation with professional artists and arts organisations'. He predicted that Coombs would 'steamroll the protesters'.[20] Dissent came from Colin Bennett who asked in the *Age* whether anyone could reasonably expect artists to be good at committee work and to be able to take a broad view of their Board's job?[21]

Before the Board members were announced, Pugh had visited Coombs and Whitlam in Canberra. The Prime Minister had then asked Coombs to fly to

Melbourne to talk to Pugh's ALP committee about the composition of the Boards. Pugh had also spoken his mind at the first meeting of the Council on 16 February. From the chair, Coombs had defended the inclusion of non-artists on the Boards. 'We are not here to create works of art. We are here to persuade and advise the Government on policies and when decisions have been made to give effect to them.'[22] Pugh publicised his disappointment. Rallying a number of artist co-signatories, he got a letter into the *Australian* ('only artists can understand their own ability to be and to give'). He supplied *Nation Review* with a caricature of ventriloquist Coombs operating dummy Whitlam. And he told *National Times* journalist Maureen Gilchrist that 'Nugget ... has a desire for power and an institutionalised idea of the arts, which is totally opposed to my idea of a new deal in the arts.'[23]

Coombs had once described himself as 'a friend and admirer of Pugh and his work'.[24] Pugh's slightly iconoclastic approach to portraiture appealed to him, and he had himself sat for Pugh in 1965 at Rudy Komon's gallery. When launching a book of Pugh's portraits (*Involvement* by Andrew Grimwade, Coombs' own portrait among those selected for publication), he had responded to an art critic's scepticism about whether portraits could really be works of art. 'I can recall long dreary lines of pompous and pretentious faces pompously and preten-tiously presented.'[25] Pugh was clearly exempt from that stricture, a kindred anti-Establishment spirit. In 1973 and 1974, however, Coombs became the object of Pugh's anti-Establishment scorn.[26]

In March 1973 Pugh helped to set up the Arts Action Committee. At its first public meeting in North Sydney's Independent Theatre on 8 April 1973, Coombs admitted that public consultation about Board membership had been 'incomplete and inadequate'. However, 'appointments to the Council and to the Boards did not exceed two years and almost half the nominees had terms limited to one year'. He was sceptical of the meeting's assumption that Board members were 'representatives'. It would be

> Dangerous ... to put a man in a position of giving advice to governments or making decisions on their behalf if he is to act as a representative. Not merely will this inhibit the integrity of his judgment but [it] can lead to the imposition of a particular philosophy or attitude towards art or society on the work of the Council.

In more pragmatic vein, he defended the rapid assembly of a Board and Council structure. By acting quickly, he argued, the ACFTA had been able to plan its 1973/4 budget. The Council would soon put forward proposals for legislation, in an interim report intended for public discussion.[27]

Coombs later gave Whitlam his impressions of the gathering. 'Although it is true that many of the people involved are not of great consequence in the field of the Arts, and some of them have views and motives which are clearly questionable, it is nonetheless clear that there is a body of opinion which still feels some anxiety about the Government's policies and the present situation.' The meeting's pro-posed 'national convention in Canberra to thrash out some of the issues at present causing concern' could 'give people a feeling of active personal participation'. However, to hand arts policy to elected bodies of arts practitioners would give 'insufficient weight to the general community and consumer interests in the Arts and to the value of drawing on the best traditions of quality and diversity in the Arts'.[28]

Pugh's clash with Coombs climaxed in his open letter to, and then resignation from, the Council at the end of January 1974. Accompanied by Battersby and the chairs of the seven Boards (the Aboriginal Arts Board having commenced work in May 1973), Coombs met Pugh's charges of 'elitism' and 'bureaucracy' at a press conference on 11 February 1974. Certainly, the arts were 'elitist'. 'At their best they are the work of the exceptionally talented and historically have been enjoyed relatively by the few.' However, the Council was seeking to widen access to the arts. As for 'bureaucracy' – the Council could hardly deny that the Council and its Boards were serviced by a bureaucracy whose costs absorbed a portion of the Council budget; but how else were grants to be administered?

In 1973, Coombs' policy initiatives suffered from the press appetite for scandal in the arts and from its sentimental regard for self-styled foes of the Establishment. As Denis O'Brien commented, after attending Coombs' press conference on 11 February 1974, few publications

> employ arts roundsmen in the way that they're strapped with police roundsmen, city-hall reporters, or racetrack touts. They provide no ready or substantial framework of reference about day-to-day developments in the arts. They dart in on such eruptions as the Clifton Pugh resignation, scatter the controversy randomly and then drop the subject, leaving no more than a pile of dandruff.[29]

The pugnacious populism of the arts consituency – at least, of those critical of Coombs – taught him a more conciliatory and consultative approach. When considering how Whitlam should go about formulating a statute for the National Gallery of Australia and choosing its Board, for example, Coombs drew on the bruising experience of early 1973 to warn of the need for consultations with artists and others.[30]

Shortly before Coombs was due to leave the Australia Council, he became concerned about the representation of another 'cultural' constituency – Aborigines. He had made sure, in his design of the Australia Council, that by May 1973 there was an Aboriginal Arts Board all of whose members were Aboriginal people. That breakthrough in 'Aboriginalisation' helped to put in question the politics of another Commonwealth cultural authority – the Australian Institute of Aboriginal Studies (AIAS).

The AIAS had been legislated by the Menzies government in 1964, with a charter to support the collection and analysis of information about what remained of traditional Aboriginal society. In the early 1970s, the AIAS began to assume greater importance both to Aboriginal people and to the Commonwealth. The registration of Aboriginal sacred sites became one of the AIAS's principal research programs, causing its funding from the Commonwealth to triple from 1972 to

1974. One founding member of the AIAS, anthropologist T. G. H. Strehlow, objected that, by gathering such knowledge, the AIAS would assist governments to usurp the proper Aboriginal custodianship of the registered places. Strehlow resigned from the AIAS in November 1973, blasting off publicly at individuals, including Coombs, whom he thought to be perversely influential in Commonwealth policy towards Aborigines.[31] He was the first to raise publicly the question: should not Aborigines be running the AIAS?

On 22 May 1974, Prime Minister Whitlam received an angry telegram from Charles Perkins condemning the AIAS as a 'racist, anti-Aboriginal exploitive organisation'. Perkins' specific complaints were two: there were no Aboriginal people participating in the 1974 AIAS conference, and the AIAS was considering shifting to quarters in Minerals House, with the Australian Mining Industry Council as its landlord.[32]

Coombs' Council for Aboriginal Affairs colleague Barrie Dexter thought the AMIC premises suitable in size and reasonable in rent. A closer physical association between the AMIC and the AIAS would be of mutual advantage. 'Over the past two years', he pointed out, the AIAS had 'developed close contact with the Mining Industry Council in relation to the Institute's task of identifying recording and protecting Aboriginal sacred sites throughout Australia, including on mining land'.[33] Dexter's advice exemplified the instrumental approach to the codification and 'protection' of Indigenous heritage against which Strehlow had warned.

Coombs was disturbed by Strehlow's and Perkins' charge that the AIAS was steered by academic and governmental rather than by Indigenous interests. He tried to persuade some of the AIAS's leading academic figures to place the AIAS under the control of a Society for Aboriginal Civilisation (SAC). The members of SAC should be 'nominees of Aboriginal communities chosen for their standing in ceremonial and related matters in their own communities. Academics also could be members of SAC. Initially 'the academic membership might be the existing members of the Institute', for the Institute was to be incorporated into SAC. The further admission of academic members would be subject to confirmation of the Council of SAC. SAC would also recommend the appointment of a majority of the members of the Aboriginal Arts Board and recommend the Aboriginal members of whatever Board or Council eventually governed the planned 'Gallery of Aboriginal Man'.[34]

ANU anthropologist W. E. H. Stanner, the third member of the Council for Aboriginal Affairs, told Coombs that he saw problems in SAC. Coombs' ideas about representation were flawed: in many regions Aborigines no longer assessed one another in terms of 'ceremonial' importance. Even in regions where there was an active ceremonial culture, men were unlikely to nominate others to 'represent their secret, jealously guarded, competitive and often materially valuable interests in ceremonies'. Thus 'the processes of choice might well produce some excellent members of SAC but I doubt if it would bring forward a majority of truly expert Aborigines, and I believe AIAS would suffer a blow from which it would be unlikely to recover'. Coombs' proposal would 'cause havoc in the research field ... not because it would Aboriginalize research but because it would politicize it'.

He added that because SAC would probably share members with the elected National Aboriginal Congress and possibly the Aboriginal Arts Board, it would add to the centralisation of Aborigines' political representation, to the detriment of 'local communities'.[35] Lacking support from Stanner (and others) for SAC, Coombs took the suggestion no further.

The Labor Party came to power in an atmosphere of world-wide debate about how political, economic and cultural elites could be made more accountable. The issues arose in most fields of Coombs' interest – higher education, conservation, the arts, and Aboriginal affairs – but we cannot find in these various engagements any formula by which he reconciled the tensions between producers and consumers, experts and 'the people'. Some of his peers thought him reckless in his radicalism or too susceptible to populist simplification. Others, such as Pugh, found him incorrigibly possessive of 'expert' prerogative. He could be impressive, however, in disarming critics (and charming friends) with a persona of candour and simplicity. 'I am an old man and my life in the administration of the arts, believe me, will be very short', he assured the audience assembled by the Arts Action Committee in April 1973. 'But I have had some experience and I believe I am a person who values the arts.'[36] When the Australia Council held a party to farewell him as Chair in June 1974, Coombs was gently teased by one speaker for having arrived carrying something in a plastic bag. It contained his weekend groceries, Coombs explained, adding: 'Even bankers have to have some real assets.'[37]

Wages and taxes

COOMBS' ECONOMIC ADVICE to Whitlam was not confined to one policy field, unlike when he had been central bank Governor under Menzies and Holt. Because inflation became the Whitlam government's greatest immediate problem, Coombs found himself fully extended, venturing even into incomes policy – the Keynesians' most intractable zone of statecraft – and into taxation policy – the social democrats' Achilles heel.

Coombs' respect for trade union power was well founded. Australian unions, like those in other advanced industrial countries, were at a peak in the late 1960s and early 1970s. Workers in manufacturing were well-organised, and their employers had been enabled by high tariffs to set prices which covered the cost of any wage rise. In 1967 a decision of the Conciliation and Arbitration Commission challenged the success of certain unions in winning levels of pay above the lawful award. Many union leaders were emboldened to pursue higher wages through militant action rather than through application to the Commission. The proportion of wage rises granted through general cases before the Commission began to fall, the number and duration of strikes began to rise, and direct action had become a norm of Australian industrial relations by the time Whitlam came to power. When unusual rises in food prices during 1973 helped general prices to rise by 13 per cent, trade unions' efforts to maintain the real value of wages, coupled with the liberty of employers to set prices, ensured that inflation persisted.

Initially, Coombs advised the government against imposing guidelines on the Arbitration Commission's granting of wage rises. 'The Commission's task is essentially to settle disputes', he reminded Whitlam, 'and it must seek a broadly acceptable resolution of the issues between the parties.'[1] Coombs recapitulated his cherished formula: persuade unionists that prices would not continue to rise at their recent rates and that their standard of living *was* rising due to more and better government services. The unions might then agree to restrict wage increases to productivity gains and 'to offset price increases which have already occurred'.[2]

In August and September 1973, Coombs and Gruen agreed that Whitlam would have to negotiate a wages indexation policy with the unions.[3] Whitlam, however, sought to enhance Commonwealth powers to regulate prices. When a Constitutional convention in September 1973 denied him the States' agreement, he announced a referendum. While helping to draft Whitlam's speech announcing the referendum, Coombs warned that a government with powers over prices would neglect other measures against inflation and would be blamed for all price rises. To the consternation of the unions, DLP Senators forced Whitlam to include incomes as well as prices in his bid for new powers. However, Coombs thought no more highly of government dictating to unions than he had government dictating to banks. To avoid the risks of pitting his government against the unions, Whitlam should *negotiate* wage indexation – and make the ACTU jointly responsible for wage restraint.[4]

Labor lost the referendum, antagonising the unions in the process. Returning to the alternative policy – negotiated wage indexation – Cabinet put forward a model under which any worker who was paid more than the minimum wage would suffer a gradual reduction in the real value of their wages. The Arbitration Commission was wary, sensitive to ACTU demands that no worker lose in the government's fight against inflation. Indicating his interest in some kind of wage indexation, however, Justice Moore on 2 May 1974 announced that on 7 and 8 August he would convene a conference to consider wage fixation. Treasury now warned the government against automatic indexation, *in any form* because it would add to inflationary pressures. Treasury wanted the National Wage Case to be the principal restraint: the rises determined in that case were to be discounted to the extent that any award had been increased since the last case, thus removing any incentive for unions to take action outside the one national hearing in which the government could argue the economy's (in)capacity to pay.[5]

Coombs searched for a wage indexation formula that might answer Treasury scepticism and yet appeal to the ACTU. On 22 July, he suggested to Whitlam that high wages could get a flat increase, and low wages a percentage increase, based on annual measurement of rises in the cost of living.[6] To his dismay, Cabinet continued to back Labour and Immigration Minister Clyde Cameron's flat version of indexation – effectively, a real wage cut for most workers. 'Frankly I do not believe that the Cameron proposal (or the modified alternative acceptable to

Cabinet) will command a consensus', Coombs told Whitlam. In anticipation of that failure, he wanted the government to circulate his proposal as a fall-back version of wage indexation, a gesture of leadership in a crisis: 'it might gather widespread support as the least of possible evils'.[7]

Coombs got a sense of the way things had moved in the Moore conference on 7 and 8 August by talking to Judge Moore himself. Neither employers nor unions had liked 'the Cameronian suggestion of flat money increases'. Employers and employees were now discussing full indexation, and Moore's mediation was taking incomes policy out of the government's control. Coombs had a suggestion. Would Whitlam ask Moore to table at the next discussions the Coombs version of indexation?[8] Unwilling to back a different wage indexation without Cabinet's approval, Whitlam nonetheless agreed to let Coombs and Gruen present their scheme to Moore on 19 August. They proposed that up to average weekly earnings wages be fully indexed; workers between the average wage and 2.5 times the average would get 50 per cent of the indexation rise, and incomes above that would get flat adjustments. Coombs and Gruen went further than Cameron and Cabinet in appeasing the unions; yet they also took something from Treasury's arguments. Their proposal allowed claims for wage rises on grounds other than cost of living, but National Wage Case increases would be discounted by taking into account such interim gains by any union or industry.[9] Cameron soon endorsed the Coombs–Gruen version of indexation.

The Moore conference was slow to resume, as both employers and unions wanted to see what was in the 1974/5 budget and then to confer with their constituencies.[10] Meanwhile, inflation continued to be high and to be matched by wage increases. Coombs' memos to Whitlam over the winter of 1974 implied that the Prime Minister was drifting, disabled by the novelties of inflation and by the diversity of proposed responses.

In particular, Coombs was worried that senior Ministers were now being panicked by the short-term forebodings of Treasury. On 15 July 1974, Treasury officer John Stone had given a chilling briefing to the Economic Committee of Cabinet. Now Whitlam had to address the nation on inflation, but in whose terms? Coombs found the flavour of Treasury's speech draft inadequate to Whitlam's political need. 'Treasury has suggested that I might draft some paragraphs for inclusion in the speech. I am reluctant to do this because I do not think the change in tone that I suggest can be achieved by minor surgery.' To suggest the spirit of an altogether different speech, Coombs reminded Whitlam of Cairns' recent point that (in Coombs' paraphrase) 'the deflationary elements in the action proposed must form part of a wider package or a wider programme which expresses in its aggregate the forward-looking philosophy of the Government'. Coombs urged Whitlam to rid the speech draft of Treasury's 'somewhat hysterical' tone. He should project the image of a Government blessed with many weapons against inflation and with undiminished confidence in its program.[11] Whitlam should distinguish between the short-term objectives of government – defeating inflation – and the long-term objectives of the Labor Party.

In his efforts to look further ahead than Treasury, Coombs returned again and again to the issue of taxation. The Whitlam government had come to power evading the question of assuring public revenue. In his memoirs, Whitlam recalled his 1972 campaign promise as 'not to increase taxes'. ACTU President Hawke had resisted such a commitment; he recalled that 'the campaign speeches were carefully written to avoid saying, We Will or We Won't. But the electorate got the message We Won't.' The Party's National Campaign Committee judged the electorate as needing such assurance, and income growth and the progressive incidence of income taxation seemed to guarantee the Commonwealth increasing revenue without changes in the income taxation scale.[12] This revenue strategy by default was not good enough for Coombs. He had been giving the problem of public revenue much thought.

Prime Minister McMahon had appointed Judge Asprey in 1972 to inquire into Australian taxation. Coombs' submission to Asprey argued that Australians did not save enough to finance immigration and national development. The deficiency was felt in poorly developed public services, increasing dependence on foreign investment, and a persistent tendency towards inflation. He wanted a tax policy that would persuade Australians to save. Taxpayers would be able to choose to increase their own assets rather than to pay a 'development tax' as long as those assets took the form of investment in development, such as government loans 'floated in competition with other claimants in the capital market'. There were other points in Coombs' Asprey submission. He proposed uniform rebates as a substitute for concessional deductions, in order to redistribute income. And he wanted all earnings of statutory authorities to be vested in a 'Commonwealth Estate' to be 'used for the uniform benefit of the community', either by a dividend to all or by financing socially beneficial works. If uniform rebates were combined with dividends from the 'Commonwealth Estate', they would amount to 'a greatly simplified system of social welfare payments. It would be possible to replace all such payments with a "minimum income after tax" which could prove more equitable and be administratively simpler and more economical.'[13]

Coombs' Asprey submission was his touchstone for reminding Whitlam of Labor's long-term vision of Australian society and economy. It was essential that Labor have a strategy to gather resources for socially beneficial investment. If the government were committed to a permanent lift in the proportion of gross national expenditure that flowed through the budget, it must reconsider the entire revenue base of government. Otherwise, it would always be making little improvements at the margins, and struggling with the inflationary effects of its budgets. He asked Whitlam to consider taxes on expenditure and on capital, and he wanted the definition of taxable income widened. Coombs looked forward to 'a tax system which would fall primarily on expenditure and encourage higher savings at all levels of income'. During the May 1974 election campaign, he urged Whitlam not to match the Opposition's 'dishonest' offer of tax cuts.[14]

In these memoranda to Whitlam, Coombs also began to question the goal of economic growth. Australian governments had tended to approve any investment as long as it created jobs. Yet 'unemployment has not at any time since 1945 been an important economic or social problem. Indeed only for a few months in years a decade apart has unemployment exceeded the stringent limit regarded as acceptable by contemporary Australian social attitudes.' Australians' fear of unemployment had been 'a significant source of the inflationary pressure ... the major problem of the past three decades'. It would be better to deal with unemployment through 'more generous unemployment benefits, to expand facilities for retraining and redeployment, and to establish more generously the means for local socially valuable work projects to deal with local and short-term unemployment'. A more discriminating economic development policy would, for example, be tougher on the resource-hungry car industry. With a more considered attitude to economic growth, immigration policy could be more discerning – a 'pursuit of special skills and social, intellectual and genetic diversity'.[15]

With the government in the final stages of preparing the 1974/5 budget, Coombs stated what he considered to be Labor's long-term aims. First, income redistribution – via social service payments, better public services, and changes in the tax system – and second, more public provision of goods not adequately provided by the market. Both goals implied a bigger public sector. Since there were no idle resources to be used by government and since the Australian propensity to save remained low, a bigger public sector must be based on increased taxation. If income were to be redistributed, then those extra taxes would have to come from middle and higher income earners. Such people must be made to feel that they had something material to gain from Labor's program.[16] We can understand Coombs' work as Chair of the Australia Council in part as his contribution to this strategy.

These winter 1974 memoranda were the high point of Coombs' strategic advice to Labor and the low point of his influence. From May 1974, his energies were increasingly diverted into chairing the Royal Commission on Australian Government Administration (RCAGA). He remained interested in the problem of incomes policy, however, with minutes to Whitlam on 20 September 1974 and on 20 and 29 January 1975. By January 1975 Coombs was satisfied that the government had generated a necessary degree of uncertainty about jobs. He urged Whitlam to defer negotiating an indexation deal and to rely on the fact that 'the bargaining power of Unions is weaker than for years'.[17] Wage rises could now be expected to be moderate, with or without an agreed incomes policy.

In May 1975, the ACTU Executive assented to a wage indexation agreement.[18] Coombs criticised its terms as too generous. Whitlam, he thought, had lost the battle for incomes policy. The persistence of mild unemployment remained Labor's best weapon against inflation. 'In crude electoral quantities, unemployment directly affects possibly four percent of the work force and their dependents. Inflation affects everybody except the powerful and the lucky who can perhaps manipulate it to their advantage.'[19] In December 1975, he told sociologists studying Australia's 'elite' that by 1978 Australia should have achieved a zero rate of inflation, with an unemployment rate of 3 per cent.[20] Coombs' opposition to 'inflation' was as militant under Whitlam as under Menzies, a quarter of a century before, but less effective.

The Whitlam government, Coombs concluded in 1975, had run up against weariness among Australian voters. 'The willingness of the community to adjust to and to accept social reform may well have already been overtaxed. There is, I believe, growing resistance even among those whom it is designed to benefit.' 'Overtaxed' was a significant pun, for Coombs' strategic thinking never lost sight of the central problem – Labor's approach to public revenue. 'In the longer term the expenditure of a larger proportion of Gross Domestic Expenditure through the Budget will require either a change in community attitudes towards tax levels or a change in the economic character of our society', he lamented. Such changes would be promoted by: slower rate of growth, less emphasis on attaining consumer goods as the means to 'the good life', and higher savings. The government should undertake studies of ways to promote these cultural changes.[21]

Labor, he was telling Whitlam, should confront the culture of the 'affluent society'.

Though Labor was closer to being Coombs' political 'home' than the Coalition, there are several pointers to Coombs' alienation from the culture of the labour movement. The wage indexation deal with the unions was one, and Labor's fudging of the problem of public revenue another. Worse was to come. Coombs must have been appalled at the noxious return of Labor's old hatred of the Money Power when Whitlam's fall in November and December 1975 was precipitated by a bizarre experiment in public finance. 'I never was happy,' Coombs reflected in 1989, 'because [Whitlam] didn't really understand ... financial matters at all ... and furthermore, he wasn't completely frank with me.' Whitlam did not ask Coombs to comment on his government's extraordinary decision in 1975 to raise loans, for huge infrastructure investment, from investors newly enriched by petro-dollars – the beginnings of the politically disastrous Khemlani affair.[22] 'Unfortunately the Labor Party had, very strongly at that time, and always has had I suppose, a suspicion of big financial institutions', Coombs later reflected.[23]

At the time, his disappointment in Labor was overshadowed by his horror at Labor's dismissal by the Governor-General.

> The breach ... of widely held expectations of political behaviour changed the Australian constitution from a symbol of national consensus to a weapon to be used by whatever interests possess the legalistic cunning, political opportunism, and/or access to power to do so. Until the constitution regains a form and status that is substantially neutral to political interests, and those interests can be relied upon to respect it, Australians will be divided by deep distrust ...[24]

The social fabric – not just 'social democracy' – was at stake in 1975.

Part 10

Rethink

The stuffed owl of Minerva

IN NOVEMBER 1966, Coombs apologised to ANU Registrar Ross Hohnen for not having been able to persuade Patrick White to accept an honorary doctorate. White had told Coombs that 'it is going to be difficult enough ... not to become "a stuffed owl"' without increasing that risk by accepting the ANU's honour.[1] Had White implied that Coombs now perched among the stuffed owls? In the years to come, years that included his retirement from the Bank and his appointment to the Australian Council for the Arts and the Council for Aboriginal Affairs, Coombs gave much thought to his relationship with the Establishment. He had reason to wonder whether Australia was being led wisely by the principal beneficiaries of the Long Boom. Coombs' rethinking of the tasks of leadership was reflected in public statements about new concerns – the environment, the place of Aboriginal people in Australian society – and in his renewed attention to older themes – the combining of elite and popular action in political reform, the possibility of an intellectual engagement with politics, the limits and possibilities of Economics.

In 1970, the ABC invited Coombs to deliver its annual radio lecture series – the Boyer Lectures. As Chair of the Council for Aboriginal Affairs, he would like to have used them to discuss the predicament of Indigenous Australians, but it was too soon after his colleague William Stanner had done so in his 1968 Boyer Lectures, *After the Dreaming*. Coombs decided to reflect on an issue at the centre of his life: the limits of enlightened leadership. They are my terms, not his. Coombs put it this way:

> Institutions ... provide the context within which the drama of our personal lives is played out. I want ... to consider their nature and the influence they have on human affairs; to look at the ways in which and the reasons why they can fail to serve man's purposes effectively; to consider various ways of responding to the challenges of these failures and finally to comment briefly on what appear to me to be the critical institutional problems of our age and the lines on which I believe their solutions should be sought.[2]

Institutions had a tendency to develop logics of their own, disappointing their founders and binding their leaders. He gave as example the ANU's straying from its original mission to be 'the power-house of social reconstruction'.[3] So complex were the workings of contemporary institutions that it was 'difficult, if not impossible, to find where the real power of decision lies'.[4] Nominally powerful people 'have only a limited range of choices open to them in the decisions they are called upon to make, and even when they are conscious of exercising power this consciousness may in part be an illusion'.[5] Coombs wondered whether he, and people like him, any longer commanded the institutions that empowered them.

Throughout the series his tone was impersonal. After reading his first draft, Stanner wished he would 'put more Ego into the talks'.[6] To question the possibility of intelligent social leadership was nonetheless a soul-searching.

As a war-time senior official, Coombs had exercised effective and enlightened power. He had set up a rationing system and found a voice in which to assure the people of its fairness. In the 'Keynesian Crusade' he had espoused popular desires for security and prosperity as the political basis of sound economic management. He had experienced a degree of alienation from the corridors of power in his struggle against inflation in the 1950s, but in the end Australia had prospered and he was given much credit. If the Liberal–Country Party Coalition, ruling from 1949 to 1972, had failed to defend his preferred model of a composite central bank, he had nonetheless found Menzies receptive to much that he had suggested about banking, the arts, research and higher education. In Coombs' view, leaders could emerge from either public or private institutions. As the would-be leader of monetary policy reform in the 1950s, he had continually to invest hopes in private corporate leaders' sense of social responsibility. As he had explained in 1956,

> Thirty years ago many people were concerned at the lack of responsibility associated with great economic power and thought that the answer was to transfer economic power to the agencies of governments so that by the processes of politics those to whom power was entrusted could be held responsible and accountable. More recent experience has led to some revulsion from this view as being likely to produce even more dangerous concentrations of power which the ordinary political processes are unlikely to be able to control adequately.[7]

Coombs welcomed the countervailing power of 'professional estates' such as the legal profession. He sought 'different ways of associating responsibility and accountability with power without leading to a situation in which all institutions become part of the State'.[8] From academia, from the public service, from corporations public and private there arose an institutionally diverse elite with whom he could work for a better society.

Coombs' speeches about leadership in the 1950s tell a story of meritocratic succession. In 1953, he had said:

> In past generations there was a privileged class in our society – a class chosen on the basis of birth – to whom were given amongst other things the privileges of access to learning and culture and the opportunity for leisure. That class had a motto 'Noblesse Oblige'. ... There is no doubt that the long list of scientists, writers, reformers, statesmen and administrators which this class has in the past produced, for example in England, is evidence of the vitality of a tradition that privileges should be balanced by an obligation to public service. The academic community of today, although differently selected, is in many ways the inheritor of many of the privileges of this class.[9]

It was not only among academics that he could discern the better qualities of this new meritocracy. When Harold Levien, editor of the monthly *Voice*, asked Coombs to help him raise funds, Coombs sent a list of 'broad-minded' corporate leaders: A. E. Symons (Waters Trading Co. Ltd), C. R. McKerihan (President, Rural Bank of New South Wales), R. J. Webster (Bradford Cotton Mills Ltd), D. McVey (Managing Director Metal Manufacturers), R. F. J. Boyer (Chair ABC), S. F. Cochran (Chair, Joint Coal Board), Sir Norman Mighell (Zinc Corporation), D. A. S. Campbell (W. & D. Hill, Australia), J. Malone (Chairman, Overseas Telecommunications), A. Thyne Reid (Chairman of Directors, Hardie Rubber Co.), and L. B. Robinson (Zinc Corporation). Soliciting a donation from BHP's Ian McLennan, Coombs described *Voice* as 'slightly Labour in tone, but aiming to provide serious and intelligent comment on economic, political and cultural affairs for persons of intellectual interests'.[10]

The hoped for patrons of *Voice* were the kind of men Coombs had tried to involve in arts patronage. In 1959, he explained to ABC television viewers the reasons for calling on the corporate elite to play such a prominent role in arts patronage.

> People in responsible positions and particularly people in industry and commerce and finance – indeed all those who are associated with enterprises which bring together great amounts of money and great incomes – have a responsibility to the community. ... Now ... the influence and control of wealth and income which used to be exercised by individuals has passed to the great corporations.[11]

In a 1966 speech on 'The Arts in Australia', he referred to institutional initiatives such as the ANU's recently established Creative Arts Fellowship, and to 'the growing acceptance by great corporations, public and private, that to them has been bequeathed the social obligation and privilege to act as patrons of the Arts'. He thought that that obligation 'could be honoured more widely.'

> These corporations are the inheritors of the nobility and the wealthy of the past – in that they alone to-day command great concentrations of wealth. It is inconsistent with the privileges which society confers upon them for the pursuit of their own ends that they should regard themselves as mere agents for the winning of dividends for their shareholders.[12]

As he reported with satisfaction in 1973, 'I have watched the attitude of company managers towards painting and sculpture change from one of contempt to one which suggests that no self-respecting company can be without its status-building collection or annual art prize.'[13]

Geoffrey Blainey remarked in 1976 that 'the increasing power of the professional manager – whether in big business, the civil service, the government corporation or trade unionism' – was 'one of the significant events in Australian history in the twentieth century'.[14] From the war until about 1970, Coombs saw his own ascendancy in hopeful terms. However, in the possibility that corporate leaders might be 'mere agents' we can see the germ of his Boyer Lecture question.

Had the corporate elite been too much moulded by their institutions? Rather than condemn fellow-members of the Australian elite as persons of little virtue and substance, Coombs' Boyer Lectures sketched a more fraternal sociology of the tendency of institutions to subvert the purposes of founders and to belittle the visions of leaders.

In tackling the themes of institutional inertia and atrophy of reflective purpose, he was voicing once more an old anxiety about 'the tendency towards concentration' in business and governmental organisation. Fourteen years earlier, at the Canberra University College's 1956 ceremony for conferring degrees, he had urged sociological studies of 'concentration and large-scale enterprises'. While 'inevitable or desirable from the point of view of efficiency', concentration posed the problem of how to combine 'responsibility with the power which goes with the control of the large unit'. Perhaps 'the public corporation offers a fruitful line of development', he had mused. It would be good to study 'the ways in which the charter of the corporation is established, the form of its accountability and the means by which it is exercised'.[15] He titled his second Boyer lecture 'Are Good Intentions Enough?'

> Every human institution is exposed to [the] risk of decay. Its social and moral purposes become blunted with use and familiarity; structures, methods and techniques once well adapted become rigid and obsolescent; a hierarchy of responsibility can become a mere Establishment of status and self-seeking power.[16]

Coombs made no reference to the Australian Elizabethan Theatre Trust, but he could have. By 1964, some observers of the Trust had been pointing out that its success in getting government grants raised the question of its public accountability. That issue had been posed in the *Bulletin* in April 1964 by Colin Badger, Director of Adult Education in Victoria. Badger had once presented himself unpersuasively to Coombs as a possible mediator between the Trust and the National Theatre Movement with which he was deeply associated.[17] While saluting Coombs' early leadership, Badger complained that in trying to sustain national companies, the Trust had effectively favoured Sydney and Melbourne. It exercised 'monopoly control, ... having plenty of money but no genuine public support', and it foisted 'official, government-sponsored art' on the public. The Trust, though receiving a lot of money from governments, was subject to no statutory accountability.[18] In August 1964, the *Sydney Morning Herald* had published Badger's letter and an unsigned feature article which compared the Trust unfavourably with the Canada Council, a statutory body formed in 1957.[19] The same month, Reid Douglas had devoted an issue of *Current Affairs Bulletin* to a critique of the Trust. As both a patron (receiving nearly all government performing arts money) and an entrepreneur, he argued, the Trust was blighted by a conflict of interests. Non-commercial theatre was at an impasse, as any new impulse was a threat to the Trust's share of the audience.[20] Labor MP Frank Crean, citing Douglas' critique, had asked the Government to explain 'how the money is spent'.[21] A politician for whom Coombs felt little empathy, Opposition Leader Arthur Calwell, had also asked him to comment on these complaints.[22]

Coombs had drafted a long reply and got comment from Aubrey Gibson, Lloyd Ross, Charles Moses, Fred Schonell, Fred Alexander, Judge Richard Eggleston, Neil Hutchison, G. F. Davies and Clyde Waterman and from the Trust's senior staff. He had pointed to the Trust's many grants to other organisations, and he had protested that the Trust exercised authority over its grantees only to ensure that they met the Trust's artistic objectives. Denying that the Trust 'encroached' on commercial theatre activity, he had insisted that it was sometimes in the Trust's interest to cooperate with commercial providers. The Trust was controlled by a Board of 'widely representative citizens', and its non-statutory status had allowed it to mobilise private donations from individuals and enterprises. Only one ballet and one opera company were sustainable, he had asserted. The Trust would like to devolve production responsibilities, he had declared, more than it had been able.[23]

If public accountability was one dimension of institutional vitality, size and complexity was another. In the late 1950s, ANU academics had discussed whether it was in the interests of the ANU to absorb the Canberra University College (CUC). Opinion had been divided. Coombs' initial view had been that the ANU should keep alive the incorporation option, but not rush into it. 'In the meantime we should do all we can to ensure that the two institutions work closely in harmony.'[24] Coombs and others had been urging Menzies for several years to develop a national policy for the funding of university teaching and research. At the end of 1956, Menzies had appointed a committee chaired by UK academic Sir Keith Murray to inquire and make recommendations. Warmly accepting Murray's September 1957 report, Menzies had put the ANU on notice that his government would soon make decisions about the relationship between the ANU and the CUC. Murray had doubted whether two universities were required in Canberra; he had urged the ANU and the CUC to devise a constitution which would allow pursuit of the fundamental purposes of each institution. In December 1957 and January 1958, Melville and CUC Principal Herbert Burton had met with Menzies to discuss Murray's recommendations, both arguing that the college be developed into a university in its own right.

At the time of Murray's 1957 inquiry Coombs had thought 'that some form of association between the two institutions would have been mutually beneficial and would have appeared more rational to outside observers'. He had since been impressed by the strength of the CUC staff aspiration to develop an independent institution. Coombs had become confident that the CUC would attract students from outside the ACT because, like the University of New England, its atmosphere would benefit from its small classes and from being 'genuinely residential'. As a regional university in Canberra, it would be especially attractive to students of government and public affairs. It could share with the ANU a site and many facilities, so delivering the efficiencies desired by the government. Without the threat of incorporation, there would be more cooperation between the two bodies of academics, with benefits, for example, in Oriental studies and in history. Coombs had hoped that the government would be satisfied with a form of association limited to the overlapping of the two institutions' governing bodies.[25]

Sensitive to criticism that his government was lavish on Canberrans, Menzies had insisted on amalgamation in 1960. Coombs had reflected on what had been at stake.

[A] big University is almost inevitably a poor University and a large University class means poverty in the quality of the teaching. Intellectual communication is a personal thing and it is in the study or round the laboratory bench rather than in the lecture hall, round the cafe table or in the small group on the grass by the pool rather than in the organised society meeting, that there suddenly passes from teacher to scholar or from scholar to scholar the intense excitement which comes from knowledge, from the pushing back of the darkness of ignorance or prejudice, both in one's own mind and in the collective mind of man. Let us keep our Universities small enough for the small group to be the characteristic pattern.[26]

Universities were not merely a case study in a sociology of institutions, as sites of intellectual training they were crucial to Coombs' conception of renewal and reflexivity. He devoted his fourth lecture, 'Shall We Join the Drop-outs?', to radical youths' challenge to established pedagogies and politics. Coombs had become Chancellor in August 1968. Only a few months before his formal installation, he had been moved, while on Reserve Bank business in Paris, by his direct exposure to students' political mobilisation. Citing the Nanterre campus graffiti 'They think, therefore I am', he aired his thoughts to Percy Partridge of the Research School of Social Sciences. Did not that slogan express 'dissatisfaction with a world which increasingly is completely outside their control or influence'? 'I am sure this sense of facing an impersonal and predetermined world is widely spread in the community running far beyond the students.' The university, at least, should try to ensure that its students and staff feel that 'there is a two-way relationship between the institution and its members', and it should also 'seek to understand and to devise ways of resisting the growth of this depersonalised quality in contemporary life'.[27]

In reply, Partridge doubted that students' unhappiness with universities reflected a widespread concern about a 'depersonalised' social order. Most people, he had observed, found in their affluence and freedom much compensation for modernity's ills. However, he agreed that students had a grievance. Their teachers were bored, and their courses failed to arouse curiosity and moral concern. Education had become democratised, banalised and oriented far too much to recruitment into the professions. The defect of this vocationalism and careerism 'is a moral point that some of the restless students are feeling in their bones and trying to articulate'. University education had become 'training, which can be quite incompatible with the freedom, leisure, intellectual play, *irresponsibility* in a certain sense, that ought to characterise the years a student spends in a university'.[28]

Coombs marked this passage and reproduced a version of it in his inaugural address as Chancellor. 'Do not let us grind our students into professionalism too soon.' Their learning should not present to students 'a packaged, predetermined destiny'. Coombs was not merely pleading for more stimulating courses. He was inviting his colleagues to see student activism as promoting their institution's salvation. He wondered if 'University leaders should not … invent "the moral equivalent" of student activism if it does not occur of itself.' He warned that

> a university must beware of being too completely identified with the society in which it exists … it is … a function of the university to observe our society critically – to question its unstated assumptions and its conventional wisdom. … A society, to remain vigorous requires inbuilt sources of regeneration – and the university is, by its traditions and the quality of its members, well equipped to provide one such source.[29]

This was a fine manifesto for a new Chancellor, free of the self-restraints of a Governorship not two months quitted.

Two years later, Coombs again consulted Partridge when writing his Boyer Lectures. He had been thinking about 'the difference between the emphasis of my generation on the establishment and modification of institutions as the technique of reform and that of the modern younger generation with its "whole or nothing" rejection of institutions'. He was ambivalent towards the political styles and rhetorics of the young. 'While I see no practical alternative to the "institutional" approach to reform I understand and sympathise with the more anarchistic approach and that it must have a place as a source of regeneration.'[30] It disturbed Coombs that somnolent universities could forfeit altogether the engagement of the young and thus extinguish one of society's main sources of political renewal – a critical intelligentsia prepared to work hopefully and confidently through available institutions. 'The Keynesian reform program', he remarked in his fourth Boyer Lecture, 'was the last hopefully inspired youthful revolt.'[31] He saw little in common between the 'optimistic – perhaps sentimental – imaginings of my own youth' and today's youth revolt. Among today's youth there was a variety of political orientations, from those who partook of the ANU's authorised 'student participation', to those 'who would wish to destroy or to reject much if not all of our society'. The latter were 'frequently the most articulate, the most persuasive, the most spectacular – the ones whose words, gestures, and actions are seized upon by the mass media. They are the ones who would wish to be and frequently are regarded as being representative.' However, he continued, their style and rhetoric disturbed those of Coombs' generation 'who learnt to distrust the emotional trappings of mass hysteria from their manipulation by Hitler and Mussolini'. Some charismatic youth 'use the same techniques and we find this distrust coming between us and them even when we would go along with the case they are pre-senting'.[32] Notwithstanding their 'irritating extravagance', it was best to listen 'quietly and rationally' to such young people. Their pessimism – notwithstanding their fondness for quoting those great optimists, the anarchists – and their 'lack of purpose' worried him.

As ANU Chancellor from 1968 to 1976, Coombs chaired a University Council composed of senior Australians with a more judgmental response to the young than this fine sifting of the sympathetic and the repugnant. ANU students occupied the Chancellory 18 April 1974 and made representations to Council the following day about staff-student control of course content, about student choice of means of assessment, about the need to repeat lectures, rather than limit enrolments, about the need for a women's studies course whose content would be decided 'by the women of the university'. On 8 August 1974, frustrated by the university's handling of these grievances, students occupied the university's telephone exchange. They did not damage it, but the university called police to remove them, and twenty-seven were arrested. The university laid no charges. The 138th meeting of Council 13 September 1974 considered these events. The minutes record Coombs as declaring 'that he wished that students would feel that better results could come from civilised methods but he preferred activism, even if impolite, to apathy. He believed the University had not been sufficiently active in seeking to resolve some of the complex issues raised by students.' Council then rejected Sir Norman Cowper's motion 'that a committee be established to consider whether the University should set out special "offences" relating to sit-ins; should consider the circumstances in which the police might be involved and to consider generally measures to protect University operations.' A motion that the Chancellor, Pro-Chancellor and Vice-Chancellor arrange a study of university decision-making was carried.[33]

From the point of view of at least one old friend of Coombs – Political Science Professor L. F. Crisp – the university had surrendered academic freedom in its response, during Coombs' Chancellorship, to student demands for participation in decision-making. Delivering the fifth John Curtin Memorial Lecture in the Coombs Lecture Theatre one month after this meeting of Council, Crisp distinguished between the 'social' and the 'academic' life of the ANU, insisting that students had rights to no more than 'consultation' in academic matters. He regretted that this view had been 'sharply rebuffed by some of the highest authorities in the University' as early as 1969. The ensuing 'landslide of progressive concessions' had now culminated disastrously in Chancellor Coombs not only giving 'a substantial blessing to student activism' but also reproaching the inactive ones for their apathy. Crisp felt 'humiliated' by what he saw as the surrender of proper academic authority.[34]

As Chancellor, Coombs was not only trying to give leadership in policy-making, he was also making an intellectual life for himself. To gather ideas for his Inaugural Address in 1968 and his Boyer Lectures in 1970, he held dinner parties in his University House flat (C.1) where colleagues – 'keepers of my conscience', he called them – had to 'sing for their supper'.[35] He urged his guests to follow up these conversations with letters. Picking brains was a well-tried technique of Coombs. He had begun it when writing speeches as Director-General of Post-war Reconstruction and continued it as Bank Governor. Now Coombs convivially combined the privileges of dinner host and Chancellor. Those who enjoyed such hospitality in 1968 and 1970 included William Stanner, Frank Fenner, Rutherford ('Bob') Robertson, Trevor Swan, and Percy Partridge – all at the ANU – and from out of town Derek Denton and Jean Battersby. Carillo Gantner's brief notes – for there were scribes as well as participants – on one of these occasions suggest that

Coombs played the role of provocateur. 'I have been in permanent rebellion', he is reported to have said, 'starting in Economics.' 'Society is obsessed with numbers, to the detriment of quality of life.' 'Anarchism is the only civilized form of government, in theory.' 'Personally I am an optimist. If there are things wrong there are things that can be done. I want to argue against numbers and for a diversity of values. There is excitement and joy in difference. I want, maybe irrationally, to preserve Aboriginal Institutions at Gove in the face of the profit motive.' 'The forms of stimulus we use in our society are not necessarily the only ones possible.' 'The one thing I distrust more than examinations is teachers.' (No place for Fin Crisp at that table!) 'Generally I think I approve of the current draft resistance.'[36]

Some letters from grateful guests were in frank disagreement. Trevor Swan doubted that Coombs was entitled to express disappointment that the ANU had not turned out to be 'the powerhouse of social reconstruction'.

> If the Interim Council had really wanted what you say would they have made the particular appointments which they did to the Advisory Committee in England? Would they have made most of the foundation appointments which occurred before there was an academic body to have a life of its own? Does your account square with the overwhelming importance in the early stages of the John Curtin School and the Physics School?[37]

Indeed, Swan could have gone a little further and reminded Coombs that he, as much as anybody, had been responsible for reconciling the Interim Council and the Chifley government, 1947–9, to the Advisory Committee's mandarin conceptions of how great minds, publicly endowed, would advance the public interest. Coombs' Boyer Lectures included moments of autobiographical reconstruction around the theme: how I avoided becoming a stuffed owl.

Nature and human nature

COOMBS TITLED HIS third Boyer Lecture 'Is Man a Crown of Thorns?' It had recently become widely known that the spread of the crown-of-thorns starfish was threatening the Great Barrier Reef. Coombs worried that 'the human species was like a cancerous growth reproducing itself beyond control and living parasitically on, rather than symbiotically with, the rest of creation and threatening to destroy not merely the environment but itself also'.[1] With these words Coombs publicly linked himself to the conservation movement for the first time. The Australian Conservation Foundation began to include excerpts from his lectures in its *Newsletter*.

The Australian Conservation Foundation (ACF) was an initiative of the Menzies government. In 1964, Prince Philip sought the Australian government's contribution to the World Wildlife Fund of which he was patron. Offering a small seeding grant, Menzies invited some scientists and businessmen to form an Australian chapter of the World Wildlife Fund. Francis Ratcliffe, founding head of the CSIRO's Wildlife Survey Section, combined with other Australian scientists to use the money to set up the Australian Conservation Foundation, and the ACF successfully sought membership of the World Wildlife Fund. Chief Justice of the High Court and former senior member of the Menzies Cabinet Sir Garfield Barwick was the first ACF President, and Ratcliffe was prominent in formulating and publicising its mission. Ratcliffe's 1947 book *Flying Fox and Drifting Sand* had included a 'sobering assessment of the limits of pastoralism in Australia'.[2] In his work for the ACF in 1965–70 Ratcliffe found a growing audience for his message that Australians must recognise the natural limits of their exploitation of the continent. With its combination of distinguished scientists, businessmen and professionals, the ACF was the elite expression of an Australian conservation movement that some historians have traced back to the late nineteenth century.[3]

The early concern of that movement had been to preserve selected areas of natural beauty. In August 1967, after returning from a tour of northern Australia's mining and agriculture boom sites, Coombs had urged Western Australian Premier David Brand to reserve many of his State's 'beauty spots' as parks 'before the localities were taken over by mining companies or other development schemes'.[4] However, conservationists had also begun to be influenced by the relatively new science of ecology. Ecological thought posed a deeper and more difficult question about the long-term viability of the human species.[5] Coombs became interested in this issue through the work of CSIRO and ANU scientists such as Ralph Slatyer, the ANU's Professor of Environmental and Population Biology.

Slatyer had recently come to the conclusion that 'man's future existence on earth is threatened by no species other than himself'.[6] Garett Hardin's influential article in a 1968 issue of *Science*, 'The Tragedy of the Commons', gave Slatyer a theory of human fecklessness: it was in no individual's economic interest to act so as to preserve the nature on which all humanity depended. 'Clearly the freedom of the individual in matters affecting other people cannot continue without restraint', Slatyer warned. 'The last great commons are the air and the sea, yet already changes are occurring to these.'[7] If 'man' were to survive,

> Firstly, he must regulate his numbers. Unless population stability is achieved, everything else must ultimately fail. Secondly, he must conserve and recycle the basic materials he uses to the greatest possible degree. Thirdly, he must ensure that his food supply is adequate for his regulated numbers, and that the means of its production are not in themselves leading to environmental deterioration.[8]

Coombs found immensely provocative Slatyer's question: 'where is the true economy of economics?'[9] In his 'Crown of Thorns' lecture Coombs pointed out why economists valued 'growth': 'a growing system most readily avoids the problems of depression and unemployment'. However, it was reasonable to value other goals as well. He ridiculed economist Fritz Machlup for criticising Australians' willingness to set such ephemeral things as the pleasures of the bushland, the beach, the theatre and the concert hall, the joy of solitude and of conversation, of the contemplation of the universe in all its splendour, above the urgent need to expand our industrial output. ... Thank goodness most Australians had the wit and understanding to laugh at this solemn pundit.[10]

Economists, he suggested, could envisage other values through the framework of their discipline.

Soon after the lecture went to air, Coombs was asked by Francis Ratcliffe to intervene in a public debate about whether the sands of Australia's eastern coast should be available for mining. The campaign against mining the Myall Lakes in New South Wales had begun to worry company executives and geologists, for whom mineral-rich sands were indisputably destined to be quarried. Two geologists from the Queensland Geological Survey published papers taking the conservation movement to task. Sir Maurice Mawby – Chair of Conzinc Riotinto Australia, member of the Australian Academy of Science and ACF Councillor – had commended these statements to Garfield Barwick, and Barwick had passed them on to Ratcliffe for comment. Ratcliffe and Melbourne University botanist John Turner thought it important that they refute the geologists, perhaps in ANZAAS's journal *Search*. Would Coombs help them? Ratcliffe reminded Coombs of their recent conversation in which 'you had views, which you might be prepared to commit to paper, on the lack of need to rush in and extract all our minerals as quickly as possible'. Coombs replied that he was unlikely to have the time to study the papers.[11]

His refusal was not through lack of interest. Though preoccupied with chairing the Australian Council for the Arts and the Council for Aboriginal Affairs, Coombs was still seeking to respond to Slatyer's challenge to find an 'economics' appopriate to ecological rationality. Plant scientist Sir Otto Frankel, Chair and General Secretary of the Pacific Science Association, may well have known this when he asked Coombs to address the Association's 12th Congress in August 1971. Doubting 'whether I have the range or depth of knowledge to add significantly to what has been said already', Coombs held one of his brainstorming dinner parties at University House and eventually spoke to the Congress – though 'weighed down with the whole exercise' – on 'Matching ecological and economic realities'.[12]

Citing Slatyer, Coombs argued that the ecological challenges revealed by science should now be met by raising the prices of non-replaceable resources. Not confident in the power of conservationists' exhortation, Coombs sought a valuation of 'the commons' that hard-headed accountancy would heed. He discussed the possibility of an *authoritative* revaluation of the natural estate. Perhaps a 'Scarce Resources Corporation' could be established to price such materials appropriately; or could taxes be imposed to discourage their use? Such actions would raise the cost of many finished goods, he admitted, and lower the general standard of living. People's values would have to change, if an ecologically rational structure of resource prices was to be secured by the popular valuation of natural heritage.

Was such value change within the possibilities of human nature? In posing this question, Coombs was testing the philosophical anthropology on which economics rested. On the one hand, Coombs made it clear that an ecologically sustainable economy did not have to renounce growth. It 'could still have (a) savings representing a significant proportion of total income; (b) a growing body of scientific knowledge and technological skills; and (c) a fund of organizational and entrepreneurial capacity.'[13] And 'man will continue to be, within his new ecological framework, still *homo economicus*, alert, diverting his libido into more ingenious combinations of known resources'.[14] On the other hand, towards the end of his talk Coombs envisaged that in surviving the ecological test 'man ... would become a radically different creature', valuing material welfare less. Not resolving this contradiction in his projections of human nature, Coombs' first essay in reconciling economics with ecology was an heroic failure.

Nonetheless, conservationists valued him as an eminent economist who had now joined their cause. Coombs was soon approached to say something about the future of the Great Barrier Reef.

In September 1967, the Queensland government had leased more than 20 million hectares of reef for oil exploration. A coalition of the Wildlife Preservation Society of Queensland, the Australian Littoral Society and the Save the Reef Committee opposed any such prospecting, and newsworthy oil spill catastrophes around the world had so boosted public support for their campaign in 1968 and 1969 that the Queensland government instituted a Royal Commission in 1970.

Coombs' October 1971 submission to the Royal Commission mingled principled and pragmatic reasoning. He praised two previous submissions by economists Stuart Cochrane and Alex Hunter, but found 'incomplete', in three respects, their framework for considering the contribution of reef oil drilling to the 'national product'. First 'the National Product ... does not incorporate some components of an income character which affect the quality of human life'; second, 'income alone cannot be regarded as the sole criterion of benefit', because 'wealth in the form of produced capital, discovered or imputed resources, and the nature of the physical and social environment' had also to be considered; third, the two economists' work did not discuss how to weight 'the needs of the community in the future against those of the present'. Developing each of these points, Coombs was trying to reform the calculus of cost and benefit with which Australians pondered the use of natural resources. They must measure more things, in calculating their fortunes, and they must consider nature as a form of 'wealth'. As well, Coombs challenged the Commissioners to redefine 'the community' to include 'representatives of the grandchildren of those at present involved and indeed the grandchildren of those grandchildren'.[15] Even if the Royal Commission were to conclude that oil below the reef was of such value as to be worth mining, Coombs pointed out, this did not compel immediate exploitation. Would it not be wise to keep Australian oil in reserve until global stocks had run out or become very expensive?[16]

Here and in 'Matching Ecological and Economic Realities', Coombs was trying out the thought that economists could and should be the conservation-minded conscience of capitalism. Economists who worshipped growth had 'been seduced into heresy'. Because 'the optimum use of scarce resources' had 'been the basic concern of his discipline',[17] economics could be purged of its growth fixation. The rational calculus of 'economy' could be reformulated to reflect the costs and benefits of using scarce resources. The price mechanism could be made to reflect the revised values of things. 'I see nothing intrinsically impracticable about a price policy designed to protect scarce resources', he declared in 1973, and in 1974 he offered a closely reasoned critique of the accounting convention known as 'discounted cash flow'.[18] Through such technical renovations, the markets for capital and for raw materials could be reconstructed to sustain Nature.

Coombs' links with the ACF had grown in the twelve months from October 1970 (when he delivered his Boyer Lectures) to October 1971 (when he stood before the Royal Commission). Now the ACF leadership gave him his first opportunity to bring conservation and Aboriginal policy within the one framework. The Council for Aboriginal Affairs (CAA) had become interested in the future of the western desert people living on the Petermann Reserve in the south-west corner of the Northern Territory. What industry might they adopt, in order to become economically self-sufficient? Through the work of Ratcliffe and of later rangeland ecologists, conservationists had learned to treasure those parts of arid Australia where bovine hoof had yet to tread. Would the Petermann Reserve now be invaded by cattle? Coombs and the CAA were looking for new options in the economic development of Northern Territory reserves – industries that would be both culturally and environmentally sympathetic. In December 1971, he pleased two emissaries of the ACF – Executive member W. D. L. Ride and Vice-President Frank Fenner – when he heard with sympathy their suggestions for avoiding ecological damage to the Petermann Range. He encouraged Barwick, President of the ACF, to write to his Minister, Peter Howson, about preserving the natural values of Aboriginal reserves in the Northern Territory, particularly the Petermann Reserve and the Arafura Swamp.

In the early 1970s, conservationists debated whether their political influence would necessarily take this form – interactions among members of Australia's governing elite. In a 1968 essay, 'Conservation and Australia', Ratcliffe had pleaded for mutual sympathy between 'nature conservation' and 'what might be termed economic or productive conservation'. That the Council of the ACF then included Sir Maurice Mawby must have encouraged him to believe that such reconciliation of priorities was possible. However, gentlemanly negotiations over the heads of the people were increasingly vulnerable to anti-elitist critique by the growing 'green' constituency.[19] Mawby left the ACF in 1974, on the grounds that it had become – at its 1973 annual general meeting – susceptible to 'hearsay, intolerance and sheer emotionalism, with little regard to facts and citizenship responsibilities'. Ratcliffe's project of elite integration around conservation goals was, for the moment, a failure.[20]

How were the ecologically enlightened to relate to a popular constituency?

It seemed to Judith Wright that Ratcliffe's enlightened minority needed the backing of an aroused public. A greatly respected writer of poetry and prose, Wright had been a founding member of the Queensland Wildlife Preservation

Society. The limitations of elite conservationism became a theme of her 1977 account of the saving of the Barrier Reef, *Coral Battleground*. The ACF and the Great Barrier Reef Committee had been far too susceptible to compromise with developers, especially when the political process shrank to a conversation between pro-drilling experts (who thought technology could minimise or eliminate risk of oil damage) and under-resourced scientists (who worried that they lacked sufficient information to assess environmental risk authoritatively). In an address published by the ACF in March 1970, Wright had framed the emerging issue for the conservation lobby – the accountability of elites – as a problem of combining reason with emotion.

> Scientists ... tend to retreat from the more 'unscientific' brand of conservationist, repudiate public campaigns, discredit lay efforts at conservation education, and look at conservation problems as matters of policy rather than publicity. They are right of course, but they are also wrong. ... once we know that real damage is being done and have the facts necessary to back up the claim, to refuse to enlist public feeling on our side is just as stupid as to try to enlist it on poor grounds.[21]

Coombs also wrestled with these problems – elites and masses, head and heart but with a characteristic misgiving about the possibility of his own elitism. 'Unregenerate economic man', he worried, was 'allergic' to moral exhortation from experts.[22] In 'Matching Ecological and Economic Realities', he declared that although the 'transformation of public attitudes on questions of conservation and pollution in the last few years' had exceeded 'the wildest hopes of the earnest few who pioneered these ideas', there was a long way to go in changing popular values.[23] Popular scepticism about the ecological critique had a point, he admitted. Many 'plain men' and economists were hearing the ecologists' arguments as 'a *cri de coeur* of a privileged class'.[24] Ecologists would therefore have to set an example through moderation in their own style of life.

Newspapers picked up on Coombs' suggestion ('a little flippantly') that the ecologically enlightened might consider doing without a motor car. In 1973, addressing the Wildlife Preservation Society of Queensland, he admitted to being 'astonished by the vehemence and hostility of the reaction the suggestion provoked'.[25] That year the ANU had tried to replace the Chancellor's Holden with an electric car, but had not found one.[26] In 1976, he returned to the issue of ecological elitism when launching a joint study by the three learned Academies (edited by Noel Butlin), *Sydney's Environmental Amenity*. 'There are many volunteer organisations concerned to protect the environment and valuable is the work they do. They are a continuous goad to governments and business enterprises.' However, 'sometimes I wonder whether the members of these organisations are not perhaps more concerned to tell others what to do than to do it themselves'.[27] In 1978 Coombs considered the alternatives to the 'exaggerated materialism of our life style'. Australians could 'live as abundantly but with less waste and extravagance, and therefore with less damage to the environment ... Perhaps to demonstrate that such a life style can be both rich and rewarding is the primary task conservationists should set themselves.'[28]

Coombs was not only warning ecologists not to be caught preaching to the public; he also urged people to make ecological politics a personal discipline. Although 'the major requirements of ecological behaviour probably lie largely outside the competence of individual decision',[29] it would be good if everyone started to live more simply. 'Perhaps there should be, parallel to the Club of Rome, a Club of Assisi composed of those who love the earth and its creatures, including man, and who are prepared, for the sake of its and their survival, to undertake to live simply, to abjure waste and to distrust the specious promises of technology.'[30] Here was emotionally familiar territory – the distaste for excess, pleasure thoughtfully taken.

When William Stanner read the first draft of Coombs' 'Matching Ecological and Economic Realities' he wondered what 'ecological man' might turn out to be like.

> The culture would have to be one which was very strong on taboos and blasphemies, commands and injunctions. ... It is all very well to conjure up an image of an alert, pushing, imaginative person diverting his libido into new methods of combining known resources by more imaginative methods into things, still profitable, but at lessening costs; all I can say is that, on all the models of man I have ever heard about, it seems improbable. ... He would have to be worshipful, fearful and self-limiting; imaginatively timid; an acceptor of authority; a searcher for safety in routine. The society would of course have to be severely hierarchical. The managing class would have a lot of fun deciding how to balance a thousand innovations on the head of a needle which would have been manufactured strictly in accord with the biologists' prescription.[31]

Utopia or Dystopia? that was Coombs' dilemma in evoking the cultural demands of ecological rationality. He incorporated Stanner's point into the conclusion of his published lecture.

> Man, who has genuinely 'internalized' the convictions and the disciplines necessary to live within a finite environment, might in fact prove to be a worshipful, fearful, self-limiting creature; imaginatively timid; an acceptor of authority; and a searcher after safety. I hope not, but I cannot be sure. Whether the things I have presumed are in fact compatible is a question to which the skills of the economist can give no answer. His view of man is too restricted.[32]

Economies and communities

WHEN COOMBS AGREED in 1967 to chair the Council for Aboriginal Affairs, he had few ideas about the economic future of Aboriginal people other than his conviction that, in some regions at least, they could and should be given choices about how they would fit in to the wider Australian economy. Making Indigenous choice central to better policy was not only ethically attractive but also scientifically necessary. Ethology – studies of animal and human behaviour, such as Konrad Lorenz's *On Aggression* – had convinced him that Aborigines had evolved over the millennia into a rather different kind of human being from the European colonists who now blithely expected them to turn into waged and salaried employees and small businessmen. Policy must respect such deep differences within human nature.

'Science and the Future of Man: The Role of the Social Scientist' – a paper he presented on 15 September 1969 at the Felton Bequest Symposium to honour Sir Macfarlane Burnet, 'Man and His Science' – is the most 'ethological' of his writings. Ethology promised to be 'an integrated chain of sciences of man – sciences which would study aspects of his existence from the bio-chemistry of sub-cellular units within his body, through to the developing cultures of multi-racial communities'.[1] Ethology told Coombs that human nature evolved and that 'the scope for learned behaviour is limited by the need to adhere to the basic inherited pattern'.[2] Therefore human behaviour could be poorly adapted to environments that had recently and rapidly changed. Australian Aborigines had evolved culturally and psychologically to fit certain environmental demands that had recently been radically altered. They were threatened by a 'disparity between the environment they must now live in and that for which their capacities have in the past been developed'. In particular,

(a) his mutual relationship with the land and the natural environment is destroyed;
(b) the 'cleverness' with which evolution endowed him ceases to have survival value, and 'industriousness', which in the past has been of neutral or negative significance, is regularly demanded of him;
(c) the natural and ritualistic outlets for his aggression are lost with his divorce from the land and the atrophy of his tribal and ceremonial life.[3]

Add the impact of diseases, European aggression and a sense of 'hopelessness and despair', it was no wonder that Aborigines had come close to extinction since the British had taken over their habitat.

Fortunately, their evolved capacity for 'wise passiveness' had proved adaptive 'in a situation where aggression had proved futile'. Policy-makers must learn 'enough of the inherited capacities and culturally modified behaviour of the Aboriginal people so as intelligently and humanely to make a place for them in our society'. Australians' new resolve to treat Aborigines with respect was thus a 'living test of the usefulness of ethology'.[4] When speaking to politicians, Coombs was more likely to put this argument in pragmatic terms. The 'full-blooded Aboriginal communities', he explained in September 1968, had a strong sense of belonging to their own distinct group 'and we must find acceptable economic prospects for them *within this context*'.[5]

The north and centre of the continent was the context he had in mind. In 1966, the Arbitration Court had ruled that Aboriginal stockworkers in the Northern Territory cattle industry be paid award wages by December 1968. This helped to reduce the cattle industry's demand for their labour. With improved access to cash welfare benefits, Aborigines were moving off the stations and into towns, settlements and missions. Was this their emancipation from pastoralists' peonage or the dissolution of the only community they knew? In August 1969 the CAA had debated whether Aboriginal people should remain on pastoral properties or be encouraged to live in townships and in 'villages' to be set up by governments. Two of the CAA's Aboriginal liaison officers, Reg Saunders and Philip Roberts, saw benefit in Aboriginal people moving to towns and villages where they would no longer be in thrall to pastoralist overlords.

Coombs was not convinced. Ethology postulated people's innate conservatism, contrasting with a liberal faith in the malleability of human behaviour no longer fettered by imposed rule. Coombs saw problems in developing new townships and he pointed to the 'attachment which many Aborigines had to particular areas now leased as pastoral properties'.[6] He visited some Central Australian cattle stations on 1–12 October 1969. His expectations were not high. Before leaving he had remarked to his daughter-in-law that Aboriginal people 'get less care and attention than the cattle'.[7] Nonetheless, the trip confirmed his cautious respect for the traditions of interdependence between pastoralists and station communities. Coombs concluded that 'the basic objective of policy ... should be to preserve the identification between the Aboriginal community and pastoral properties'.[8] That view applied also to Aborigines who, as citizens in training, lived at missions and settlements on the large reserves of northern and Central Australia. No economic development or policy should be allowed to extinguish the bonds among Aboriginal people living a neo-traditional life on land they regarded as their ancestral home. Coombs insisted in his Boyer Lectures that 'to impose on them the task of complete adaptation within a generation is, I fear, to invite their destruction'.[9]

Without being able to point to models of culturally appropriate Indigenous economic development at that time – other than the cattle stations, so low in liberal opinion – Coombs could be heard as a champion of Aborigines' stasis. The *Sydney Morning Herald* appreciated his Boyer Lecture remarks as a plea for 'conservation'. 'Dr. Coombs has aligned himself firmly with the conservationists. He wants us to conserve the unique treasures of the Barrier Reef and the unique culture of the Aborigines.'[10] Trevor Swan also found in drafts of the Boyer Lectures a plea for 'preservation':

> I simply cannot agree with your deeply held belief that the 'Way of the Aborigines' can be preserved, even if the developers are kept off their lands. To have any hope of preserving it you would have to build a new Wall of China and declare that beyond the wall there would be Australian citizens entirely deprived of education and social welfare, without which they have no means of knowing even what choices there are and can only be regarded as animals in a vast desert. I know I have no hope of convincing you of this.[11]

The CSIRO's Max Day asked Coombs to spell out the implications of his references to the Aboriginal way of life: 'what are you implying? Is it that we should tell them how lucky they are?'[12] Heinz Arndt found Coombs' draft Boyer Lecture remarks on Aborigines 'excessively romantic ... the overwhelming fact of life in most primitive societies is the oppressive and continuous fear of supernatural forces, ghosts, spirits, demons, in which the ordinary people live their lives'.[13]

Certainly, Coombs often evoked in positive terms the traditional Aboriginal way of life. However the charge 'romantic' does not engage the dual intellectual bases of his defence of 'tradition'. The first I have already described. Evolutionary theories of human nature are at odds with liberals' presumption of human malleability. As an admirer of ethology, Coombs' policy vision was often constrained by a sense of the pained slowness of behavioural change. Second, Indigenous Australians confirmed for Coombs the possibility of 'non-economic man' hypothesised in his 1971 paper 'Matching Economic and Ecological Realities'. What were the alternative possibilities of human nature? In 'The Quality of Life and its Assessment' (1977) and in 'Resource Management and Environmental Law' (1985), Coombs' passages about Aborigines instantiate humanity's variant potential.[14] 'It has been common to assume that [Aborigines'] way of life was poor and degraded – "nasty, brutish and short"', he told an audience of economists in 1977. But research had shown that 'this lifestyle was compatible with diverse physical and intellectual activity and a rich cultural experience'. The life of the hunter-gatherer was 'capable of satisfying the physical and psychic needs of those who lived it'. It was 'the simplest system which links human needs, the environment and human behaviour' and so 'provides a framework within which other lifestyles can be examined and assessed'.[15] It would be easy to misunderstand this last remark – as if Coombs was promoting traditional Aboriginal society as the ethical standard against which to evaluate the West. No – the 'framework' that the Aboriginal instance made possible was a 'philosophical anthropology', a revised set of assumptions about human nature. Aborigines in the north and centre demonstrated that the 'economic man' known to modern governments and assumed by economics to be universal was but one historically determined form of humanity. 'Economic man' did not exhaust the possible forms of human libido, values, and relationship with nature.

Coombs was cautious about claiming that he knew the potentials of Aboriginal humanity. To administrative trainees in October 1970 he explained that,

> Aborigines do not respond to the same persuasions as we do. Certainly not beyond a certain point. They work for a while until they have enough money for the immediate things they want; they tend at this point to stop. They do not see any virtue in an accumulation of property or of wealth. Tradition is that they don't own things except a few weapons and a few elementary tools. Sometimes it is said a man will not own anything that his wife cannot carry.

One trainee asked him if group involvement in work made Aboriginal people more motivated to stay in a job. 'We don't know', he admitted. 'This is one aspect of it we are very interested in. We think they will work for their own enterprises for things with which they are identified. We think this is something which is worth exploring.'[16] In the minutes of the CAA, from early 1970, we find the term 'sub-economic'. Though never defined, the word referred to Aboriginal community-based activities whose value lay not in their profits but in their creation of jobs and in their consolidation of Aboriginal communities *in situ*.[17] The awkward prefix 'sub' evokes Coombs' intelligent hesitancy about the political rationales and the social forms of Aborigines' economic development.

The CAA's approach to Aboriginal development tried to consider 'not only how Aborigines were housed etc. but the degree to which they were involved in the management of their community; their attitude toward traditional values; crime rates and criminality; their aspirations; and the stresses and anxieties most prevalent in their communities'.[18] Coombs was not opposed to Aborigines' economic development; he simply insisted that its foremost product must be 'community'. In the continuity of 'community' lay Aborigines' best hope for orderly adaptation to the novel challenges presented by Australians' new efforts to 'include' them.

This viewpoint underpinned Coombs' work on the Gibb Committee inquiry into the future of Aborigines on Northern Territory pastoral leases in 1970 and 1971.[19] Aboriginal people were increasingly superfluous to the pastoral industry, the report confirmed. To slow the attrition of their jobs, the Committee recommended more flexibility in employment and hiring policies, including more frequent payment of Aborigines as 'slow workers' – as allowed in the Cattle Industry Award. At the same time, the Committee recommended research into the potential demand for Aboriginal labour in other industries – tourism, urban development, public works, mining and fishing.

No Australian government found a way to avoid the rise of an economically redundant Aboriginal population in northern and central Australia. In the absence of a solution, the Whitlam and Fraser governments could only concede that Aboriginal adults were entitled to receive unemployment benefits.

Coombs wondered how unemployment benefit could be made to build, rather than to undermine, Indigenous community. There were two conflicting views of social security payments, he acknowledged in February 1974. On the one hand, Aborigines have an inalienable right to social service payments, wherever they meet the standard eligibility tests. On the other hand, 'where unemployment benefits are paid for long periods to Aborigines who are not really part of the workforce, it is damaging to their incentives and demoralizing'. Coombs sympathised with the latter view: 'the continued payment of unemployment benefits in circumstances where the people concerned are not (even if only temporarily) part of the workforce' was 'open to objection'. Perhaps the *Social Security Act* could be amended to empower the Minister to pay unemployment benefit in a different way in such circumstances. The Minister could make 'grants, like the grants for special work projects, to local employing authorities to meet the labour and related costs of works of special significance'. Such grants could be integrated with Department of Aboriginal Affairs' Special Work Projects, in Aboriginal communities, but they could also be available to non-Aboriginal communities who were experiencing prolonged, large-scale unemployment. 'This is no more than an idea and certainly bristles with problems.'[20]

Coombs' idea bore fruit as the Community Development Employment Projects (CDEP) scheme, introduced in some desert communities south-west of Alice Springs in 1977. Unemployment benefits would be pooled into a fund administered by the community. Coombs thought that the people of Warburton, Wingelina, Katta Ala, Blackstone, Giles and Jamieson whom he visited in the winter of 1977 would be enabled by CDEP 'to accept greater responsibility for their own affairs, to acquire the skills necessary to provide services for which they are at present wholly or largely dependent on resident or visiting white staff, and to develop greater economic independence'. To enable adaptation, economy must oblige community. Variant human lifestyles must not be made to bow to liberalism's blind propagation of 'economic man'.[21]

To postulate Aborigines as 'other' than 'economic man' did not bring Coombs to a confident empathy with their psychology and morality. After discussing the issues of unemployment benefit or CDEP with western desert people in 1977, Coombs admitted that his grasp of their views of welfare payments was, at best, tenuous.

> It would perhaps be pleasing to add that the Pitjantjatjara Aborigines were anxious to reduce their dependence on government subvention of one sort or another, but it is hard to do so. So long as that subvention appears impersonally, as do Pensions and Child Endowment, it tends to be accepted unemotionally. This may be evidence of the 'intelligent parasitism' of which Elkin wrote, but with few exceptions white citizens accept similar support without concern. The only suggestion of anxiety, expressed by Aborigines in my recent journey, related to Unemployment Benefit, and that could have originated in a desire to please the white visitor or simply from disappointment about the withdrawal of support for favoured projects. Thus there is little reason to believe that dependence on Unemployment Benefits is an important cause of concern to Aborigines or that where it exists it is likely to persist.[22]

An uneasy speculation, made no more comfortable by the connotations of 'parasitism'.

In later reflections on the Indigenous embrace of CDEP, Coombs rendered Aboriginal people as more knowable and morally familiar than this. In 1994 he wrote that CDEP 'helped Aborigines escape from the fear that the money they received was an unrequited gift carrying with it a potential obligation to repay, and to escape from the dependencies of welfare'.[23] In their use of CDEP they had shown 'intelligent opportunism'.[24]

Losing the master key

IN COOMBS' ACCOUNT of the 'Keynesian revolution', official statistics were fundamental. 'The application of theory is expedited', he told ABC listeners in 1970, 'when its concepts can be expressed quantitatively. ... Parallel with the emergence of Keynesian theory came the development of social accounts which brought together in financial terms the multitude of transactions which occur within the economic system.' Whatever their imperfections, they 'made possible the application to day to day policy of the basic principles of economic theory'.[1]

To lose confidence in these tools was to experience a loss of power. This is what happened to Coombs in the mid-1970s. In April 1974, Coombs told an assembly of Commerce graduates that now was 'not the easiest time to be entering upon the professional life of an economist' because the data that governments needed to manage the economy were not available.

> It is the statisticians rather than the theorists who have failed us. The Keynesian revolution in macro-economic theory became an effective instrument of policy because at the time it was being developed statisticians devised a system of social accounts which expressed quantitatively the concepts embodied in that theory and were able to develop principles upon which worthwhile judgments could be made about the way significant components of those accounts were likely to change in varying circumstances. No such fortunate coincidence has occurred in monetary theory.

Anti-inflationary theory and policy needed to start with flow of funds analysis, he continued. 'Statistics abound on the flow of funds in the past but no-one has evolved working principles upon which sensible anticipations can be made of the likely sources and channels of new purchasing power in different economic circumstances.'[2]

There was another, perhaps more profound theme in his disillusion with national accounts. From time to time in the 1970s – starting in his Boyer Lectures – he yearned for a 'human welfare index' to complement or even to replace the national accounts beloved of macro-economics.[3] He was hardly alone in questioning extant quantifications of well-being. In a March 1971 speech to engineers, Sir Garfield Barwick drew on conservative and romantic critiques of utilitarian thought to denounce the centrality of the gross national product in the imaginations of businessmen, politicians and economists. He even congratulated the younger generation for their 'realisation that the golden calf of growth is a false and unsatisfying god'.[4] When Coombs wondered whether an index of human welfare could be devised to enable governments to think in new terms about their policy goals, he caught the interest of Frank Horner, of the Bureau of Census and Statistics. Horner told him of recent efforts overseas to formulate such a measure. He doubted that people would ever agree on how to weight different measured factors that should comprise a 'welfare' index. We lacked 'precise community norms about social situations'.

> I have not thought about trying to include in an index some of the things you mentioned in your lecture – environmental pollution, civil liberties, intellectual opportunities, or artistic and cultural standards, for example. I think they would present greater problems of finding community norms than the elements I considered.[5]

Coombs had already received the same comment, more pungently worded, from Trevor Swan. 'No two people of any consequence are likely to agree' on weightings of different measures of well-being.[6]

However, others encouraged Coombs to work on ways to count the worth of 'goods' – such as environmental amenity – which had no market value. Whitlam's Minister for the Environment, Moss Cass, foreshadowed his Department's interest in the idea in 1973. Some of his officials were in touch with Coombs.[7] He never seemed to find the time to work on it. As he complained to Nancy Williams in March 1982, his new consultancy on the Central Land Council's corporate plan would delay yet again his commencement of such work. 'I was looking forward to some more leisurely and more "academic" activities in the economic – environmental – quality of life field for the balance of my [Centre for Resource and Environmental Studies] fellowship.'[8]

Coombs never did develop indices of human welfare nor of environmental amenity, but their in-principle possibility remained rhetorically important when he wanted to discuss the limits of economic reasoning. The absence of such indices raised the question of whether a truly enlightened governmental knowledge of the world – an alternative to an economics obsessed with expanding the output of priced goods – was now possible.

The responsive public servant

IN THE EIGHT YEARS following his retirement from the Bank, Coombs had several opportunities to engage practically with the problems of democratic participation, institutional atrophy, and the potential for critical renewal. These concerns came together when he chaired the Royal Commission on Australian Government Administration and formulated the notion of the 'responsive' public servant.

From the point of view of some in the Labor government, the Commonwealth bureaucracy, shaped by twenty-three years of conservative rule, was in need of overhaul. Mentioning in particular a recalcitrant Treasury, Paul Keating moved in Caucus in April 1973 that there be a Joint Parliamentary Committee of Inquiry into the Public Service. 'When our Ministers settled in, the Public Service Board gave them hell', he later explained. 'No one could get staff. But we are breaking through the old-boy network now.'[1]

The estrangement of reforming government from career public servants worried Coombs. In 1973, he had direct experience of it in Gordon Bryant's clash with the Permanent Head of the Department of Aboriginal Affairs, Barrie Dexter. In the last week of September 1973, just as the Bryant affair was climaxing in the Council of Aboriginal Affairs' trenchant and lethal critique of that Minister, Coombs had a chat with Bill Morrison, Minister for Science and External Territories, about the public service. Coombs told Morrison that Whitlam should consider setting up a Cabinet Office that would be not only a Cabinet secetariat but also a policy development unit and 'a channel through which new ideas and personalities could be introduced into the Public Service'.

> Possibly advisers provided for leading members of the Opposition could also formally be attached to it though working independently. They would move into the Office proper with a change of Government. The Office would then be composed for a particular government predominantly of persons sympathetic with their general political philosophy.[2]

He drew explicitly on what he recalled of the Department of Post-war Reconstruction – exemplary of rapport between Ministers and officials.

By December 1973, the Whitlam government was committed to a Royal Commission. Staff unions, the Public Service Board and the Priorities Review Staff offered their views on its terms of reference. Upon being re-elected in June 1974, the Labor government announced that Coombs would be the Chair, joined by four Commissioners: Peter Bailey of the Prime Minister's Department; Enid Campbell, a professor of law at Monash University; Joe Isaac, Deputy President of the Commonwealth Conciliation and Arbitration Commission; and Paul Munro, Secretary of the Council of Commonwealth Public Service Organisations.

It took Coombs, his fellow Commissioners, their ninety-three staff (not all concurrently employed), forty-eight consultants, five task forces, two advisory committees and one working group just over two years to produce a report. They read over 750 submissions, and heard 362 witnesses, mostly in public session, over fifty-four working days in Canberra, Melbourne, Sydney, Brisbane, Townsville, Albury–Wodonga, Hobart, Alice Springs, Darwin, Kununurra, Derby, Port Hedland, Perth, Adelaide and Salisbury (SA). Their 400-page report contained 337 recommendations, and it was accompanied by four substantial volumes of consultants' research reports. Halfway through the Royal Commission's life, when most written and all verbal submissions had been taken and the writing was about to begin, Coombs twice sketched his views of the condition of representative democracy in Australia.

On 13 May 1975, when opening the deliberations of the Task Force on a Regionally Based Australian Administration in Canberra, he argued that the cosy relationship between the bureaucracy and politicians was being disrupted by the entry of the public into government. As long as the general public had not been much interested in politics, the bureaucracy had held a 'substantial monopoly' over advice and information fed to the political elites chosen in elections. Now the public was more interested in 'the precise forms in which government policies are embodied', from the planning stage, through legislation or programming, to detailed administrative decision-making. Notions of participatory democracy were increasingly popular, especially among university students, and interests which had not previously lobbied politicians and bureaucrats were learning the value of doing so. As well, people were becoming concerned about the 'environmental' impact of government actions, that is, their impact on the whole pattern of life. Coombs concluded that 'if, despite the formal structure of representative and ministerial government, decision-making is to become the function of a wider range of groups, the exclusiveness of the relationship between bureaucracy and Ministers will be significantly eroded'.[3]

Nine days later, in an address to the Commonwealth Council of Public Service Organisations in Melbourne, Coombs spelled out changes that would follow if the relationship between government and bureaucracy ceased to be 'a kind of marriage'. As bureaucrats sought allies in a more complex advisory process they might lose their 'traditional anonymity and accountability'. Permanent Heads would need more autonomy from the Treasury and the Public Service Board. Departments would have to become more flexible internally; their hierarchical ethos had made them rigid and unresponsive to new tasks. Task forces could be set up, bringing together people from different positions in the hierarchy.

In the Royal Commission's report the summary term for a reformed democratic machinery of government was 'responsiveness' – a desirable quality not only of administrative machinery but also of the individuals within it. Asking 'Democracy – Can it be Participatory?', the Commissioners in the final report would not commit themselves to a definition of 'participation'. However, they implied a very broad notion of participation when they surveyed, in general terms, the proliferation of lobbying interests and the rise to lobbying effectiveness of such new interests as environmentalism, urban planning, women, migrants and youth – some of them using 'more violent and emotional demonstration techniques' than the longer-established interests such as the labour movement, the churches and industry groups.[4] If, in the interests of more responsive government, the new groups clamouring for attention were encouraged to be active, then public servants could say good-bye to their exclusive relationship with Ministers. Already governments were listening to a wider range of groups, the Royal Commission thought, groups expressing themselves in a more public manner than ever before. Officials wishing to maintain their influence in government had no choice but to become responsive to those groups with whom the bureaucracy competed for the ministers' ear. The new bureaucrat must learn 'to perform his tasks in a more open style, to be accessible, to be a good listener, and to act *as if he considered himself in part directly accountable to the community*'.[5]

The italicised words seem to me to fall short ('as if', 'in part') of endorsing 'participatory democracy' as a new doctrine of accountability. The Commissioners recommended a 'responsive' bureaucratic style, but they did not advocate new institutions of accountability to the public. Rather, they were urging a new ethic of public service, one that permitted and even encouraged the public servant to cultivate social awareness and breadth of sympathy. The term 'responsive' was sufficiently broad to apply not only to the way that public servants interacted with lobby groups, but also to the demeanour of officials who gave across-the-counter service to individual members of the public. That public was not merely seeking courtesy, it was increasingly assertive about 'the conditions of ... eligibility, priority and allocation' of public services.[6] To achieve 'responsiveness' it would be 'necessary to devolve responsibility and decentralise the focal points of decision'.[7]

In advocating 'responsiveness', the Commissioners made explicit their challenge to an older 'career service' ideal of the public servant – 'the simple image of the official as the instrument of ministerial authority, accountable to the minister alone, working unseen, unheard and anonymous'.[8] 'Career service' public servants were produced by a system of training made up of: 'entry governed by educational qualifications; promotion on the basis of assessed "merit"; security of tenure and the expectation that, with occasional exceptions, senior positions will be filled from those whose working life has been wholly or predominantly in the service of government'. Such personnel practices had cultivated a bureaucratic ethos in which senior public servants were a self-conscious 'professional class' – 'the guardians of the "public interest" and the central thread of political consensus around which political parties weave their colourful variations'.[9] New staffing policies were required in order to break that pattern of 'cultural and intellectual inbreeding' and to give rise to a new kind of public servant who was 'flexible and responsive as well as responsible'.[10]

Though the Commissioners' analysis of the defects of contemporary democracy flirted with notions of 'power elite' and 'ruling class', their recommendations focused on a narrower field of issues – the social composition, training and ethos of the public service. Research by the Royal Commission had revealed the under-representation, among the ranks of the service, of 'obviously disadvantaged groups such as aboriginals, migrants and women'; and at senior levels Catholics were under-represented, and 'persons educated at independent schools' over-represented.[11] Research had shown also that 'views expressed by senior officers on questions relating to the efficiency and fairness of practices in the Public Service and on "ethical" questions are markedly less critical of the *status quo* than those at lower levels; there is a similar division between older and younger officers'.[12]

The Commissioners also referred to the 'need to make the administration more responsive in its role as employer'.[13] They had found 'an increasing reluctance among employees to work within old-style strictly hierarchical organisations; ... a growing awareness of the need for ordinary people to find satisfaction and fulfilment in their jobs; ... the demands of individuals for more flexibility and variety throughout their working lives'.[14] There was good tactical sense in the Commissioners' attempt to extend the notion of responsiveness in this way. The notion 'responsive' was broad enough that the Commissioners could interpret employees' interests as consistent with the reforms they advocated, increasing the possibility that public service unions would endorse their recommendations.

Addressing the National Press Club on 11 August 1976, one week before the official presentation of the report, Coombs distinguished between the 'individual official' and 'the system' which 'so stultifies worthwhile human beings' because its centralisation of power 'is wasteful and destructive of much of the capacity and energy of the middle and lower levels of the bureaucracy'.[15] Coombs spoke as these public servants' champion; they were 'men and women of dedication and capacity struggling for a chance to serve governments and community more effectively. If our report frees them even in part for those tasks we will have been amply rewarded.'[16]

The Royal Commission's hearings gave these men and women a platform. Rosemary Walters closed her personal submission with troubled observations about the morale of the public service. Coombs asked her to elaborate at a public hearing in Canberra on 25 November 1974. She responded:

> I always feel when I say that I am a public servant that people will not think very much of that and will assume that I do not do very much, that I am a bludger on the taxpayers' money. I would like people perhaps to be more aware of what my department does and perhaps of the importance of some of the work I might be involved in. I think this would raise my morale.[17]

Months later, when the Commissioners sat in Darwin, they heard R. N. Wesley-Smith complain that public service discipline had constrained public debate about the effectiveness of government responses to the disruptions caused by Cyclone Tracy (24 December 1974). His superior officers had been able 'to lurk behind a wall of silence and secrecy'.[18] Unwilling to delegate to Branch heads, they had 'pursued reactionary courses of action against me for my free-thinking and actions'.[19] Coombs' reputation for openness and his Royal Commission's accessible methods of work had summoned Walters and Wesley-Smith to articulate discontent.

In promoting the idea of the responsive public servant, Coombs was drawing on his own experiences. As Director of Rationing and Director-General of Post-war Reconstruction he had seen himself as mediating a restive and volatile public to a receptively reformist government. More recently, since retiring from the Bank he had begun to rethink his relationship with the Establishment and to serve as a constructive interpreter of newly empowered constituencies: arts practitioners, Indigenous Australians and conservationists. I have mentioned his anxious thoughts about tensions between the elite and the mass in environmental advocacy; and I have outlined his difficulties with artists and with the Australian Institute of Aboriginal Studies. As Chancellor of the ANU and as Royal Commissioner, he had also taken up the cause of women.

Coombs is recalled by many as a man who liked and loved women in ways that they enjoy being liked and loved. He is credited with supporting their careers with good advice and commendations placed in the right ears. More than one female professional still active at the time of writing will use the word 'mentor' to describe the depth and helpfulness of his interest in their work. In Coombs' sensitivity to the impersonal tendencies of modern institutions we can see his affinity with feminism. Australian society was 'male-dominated' and

> 'male' values, in the form of power, status, force and greed, are most influential in our society. I believe that most men, and therefore their institutions, are more chauvinistic than they are aware of. I know I have to examine my own thoughts and actions to eliminate it in myself. I don't want to be a chauvinist.[20]

He described universities as 'quite conservative, often resistant to change and frequently dominated by male chauvinist views'. Sex discrimination had deprived the ANU of even one female professor. The stir that these remarks caused within the ANU's senior committees resulted in the university commissioning a study of the role of women in its affairs.[21]

While Chair of the Royal Commission on Australian Government Administration, he noted the sexism of the public service unions. Women made up the majority of the Fourth Division of the Commonwealth Public Service. The Commissioners challenged the Australian Public Service Association's male witnesses. Coombs asked had there 'ever been any discussion in your Association of the possibility or desirability of reserving a certain number of elected positions for women?'[22] And would the Association comment on 'the suggestion that has been put to the Commission that there is active and passive discrimination against women in the Public Service?'[23] Should not the Association call for female representation on departmental selection committees? he suggested. When the Association representatives responded that their federal executive had not heard of any complaints by women about sex discrimination, Coombs cited the Public Service Board's own figures to show male preponderance in selection for in-service training. He also asked if their women members had ever complained about being asked, when seeking promotion, about their plans for further children. He referred to submissions suggesting that the public service provide child care. He then asked 'Have you had proposals along these lines from your members?' Finding little or no response from the Association representatives, Coombs sent them away to consult their predominantly female members.[24]

Two days later (22 November 1974), hearing the male representatives of the Professional Officers Association, his fellow commissioner Peter Bailey took up Coombs' themes. 'We have been asking the associations … about their women members, whether they have them and whether they have certain views about what ought to be done, if anything, to promote their interests'.[25] Not hearing what he and the other Commissioners were seeking to hear, Coombs asked 'Have your women members been invited to consider whether they would want to put any issues before us as women members of the Professional Officers Association?' The men of the Professional Officers Association replied: 'If so, Sir, they have not informed us to that effect.'[26] Coombs had succeeded in unsettling them.

In these skirmishes with organisational sexism Coombs demonstrated something essential to his notion of 'responsive'. The work of representing interests was not passive but active. Settled understandings of this or that constituency and its concerns could and should be interrogated by a creative mediator in order to expose hitherto unrepresented features of that interest. Responsiveness involved interpretation, provocation, questioning – not just reflection of a given interest. In the case of the interest 'women', for example, he reserved his judgment about what the contribution of the feminine could be.

> Although I sympathise fully with the women's movement I don't like to see the extremist women's groups wanting power and to be like men. I realise that they, like other oppressed groups, may see the holding of power as the only way to bring about changes, but I hope it is only a transitional phase. I would rather see more

attention in our society paid to what might be called 'feminine' characteristics or values – tenderness, concern for others, kindness, sympathy – ideally found in both sexes.[27]

Coombs remembered these as the virtues of his own mother.

Active in linking new interests to the centres of power, the responsive public servant would help to shape the ways that interest was seen, and the way it understood itself. It is in these terms that we can understand some of Coombs' advocacy of Indigenous interests, as Part 11 shows. The stories to follow raise a doubt, however. It certainly helped Coombs' creative mediation of Indigenous interests that he was an 'elite outrider' of the public service – an adviser without statutory charter and a research academic. Was his work with remote Indigenous Australians a demonstration of the possibilities or the limits of the responsive public servant?

Part 11
Elite outrider

A Torres Strait agenda

WHEN FORMULATING HIS notion of 'responsiveness', Coombs was practising it as mediator of the wishes of the people of the Torres Strait.

Whitlam came to power in 1972 hoping to shift to the south a sea-border with Papua New Guinea that had hitherto included within Australia (and Queensland) all the inhabited islands of the strait. It would be fairer to the emergent nation of New Guinea, he thought, if the maritime boundary were to bisect the strait, ceding to New Guinea the islands of Boigu, Dauan and Saibai and much of the strait's fishery and seabed minerals. Coombs had an interest in the strait's economy. Since 1970, the Office of Aboriginal Affairs – the executive arm of the CAA – had been funding a zoologist from the Australian National University, Dr Robert Bustard, to experiment in the farming of turtles in the Strait. When Bustard left the ANU in 1971, the Office of Aboriginal Affairs recommended further funding for his project – now known as Applied Ecology. Bustard was necessarily in continuous dialogue with turtle-farming Islanders about how they saw their future.

The CAA considered the PNG–Australia border 'outside its responsibilities, but the principle it would recommend would be self-determination'.[1] The Premier of Queensland, Joh Bjelke-Petersen, informed by his officials that the Islanders would not like Whitlam's proposal, told the Prime Minister that he would not give a portion of his State to another country. No doubt he sensed the political benefit of championing the residents of Boigu, Dauan and Saibai against high-handed Canberra. Bjelke-Petersen proceeded on the assumption that in any discussion of a relocated border, the Torres Strait Islanders' self-determination would best be effected through the Queensland government.

Coombs told Whitlam how he might woo the Islanders' leaders – long beneficiaries of Queensland government patronage – to endorse Canberra's border change policy. The Islanders have 'genuine anxiety and concern' about the border change, he wrote, and they were evidently pleased to be spoken for by the Queensland government. The Commonwealth must find ways to sympathise with their interests.[2] Coombs recommended that Whitlam, while promoting the border change, also commit the Australian government to preserving the Islanders' existing 'privileges and benefits'. It would be to Australia's advantage if PNG leaders accepted some responsibility for persuading Islanders that the boundary should change. The best way for Whitlam to proceed, Coombs concluded, would be to set up a series of meetings: between the CAA and the Islanders, between the Islanders' representatives and members of Whitlam's cabinet (Whitlam; Bill Morrison, Foreign Minister; and Gordon Bryant, Minister for Aboriginal Affairs), and between PNG and Islander representatives. From such a sequence of meetings Coombs hoped that a settlement would emerge in which the Islanders would assent to the border change in exchange for security of land tenure, joint citizenship and the continuation of Australia's social service and other benefits. 'It would be important that Islanders' representatives see [the solutions resulting from these meetings] as successes won by their personal efforts. They would then be more likely to advocate them among their own people.'[3]

For the next nine months, Coombs tried to identify common ground between the Island Council Chairmen and Whitlam. He was handicapped by two difficulties. The Queensland government had every incentive to alienate these leaders from Whitlam and Coombs; and Whitlam's Minister for Aboriginal Affairs, Gordon Bryant, was trying to develop his own line of communication with an alternative set of Islander representatives that he judged less compliant with Queensland government wishes. Coombs saw no alternative to working with the Island Chairmen, even though he agreed with Bryant's assessment of them as susceptible to Brisbane's patronage. Whitlam could win their support for a border change, Coombs told Bryant, if the Commonwealth made more concessions to their desire for self-government than Queensland was prepared to make. The Commonwealth should legislate to acquire all Queensland reserves and to vest ownership in the traditional owners, he advised. This would clear the way for the Torres Strait to become a separate Commonwealth Territory, administered by a council made up of the thirteen Island Chairmen. The Islanders should also be assisted to set up their own inter-island transport cooperative. Their fishing rights in the strait should be ratified. All these moves would be subject to the Islanders' approval, in a referendum, after the Commonwealth had assumed control.[4]

Coombs got a grip on the Islanders' 'real' views through accounts supplied by Jeremy Beckett – an anthropologist who had visited the islands on several occasions since 1958, initially as a doctoral student under Stanner's supervision. In April, Coombs offered Bryant Beckett's distillation of Islander opinion: they wished their islands to remain within Australia, where they could continue to live and enjoy Australian citizenship entitlements; they were 'profoundly dissatisfied' with the Queensland government; they wished to hold title to the land which by custom belonged to them, and they were interested in 'the idea of an autonomous Torres Strait territory within the Commonwealth'.[5]

Coombs, Dexter and Stanner (as the Council for Aboriginal Affairs) met with the Island Chairmen in Canberra on 12 and 13 June 1973. Coombs' opening remarks reminded them that 'the Prime Minister had made it quite clear that he would not be a party to any settlement which the Islanders would not accept'. There is an element of Coombs' own wishes in these words. Whitlam's recent joint statement with PNG leader Michael Somare had said merely that the Australian government would be 'most reluctant'. The Islanders made it clear in this meeting that they were more than 'reluctant'. Rejecting any suggestion that, historically and culturally, they were linked with the Papuans, they said that they did not acknowledge Papuan fishing rights in the strait, though they admitted to tolerating Papuans fishing at Warrier Reef. They spoke proudly of establishing their supremacy over Papuans in nineteenth-century skirmishes. The strait's delegates were unanimous also in rejecting oil drilling in the strait as a threat to their maritime resources. When questioned on the possibility of petroleum royalties, they insisted that they were interested in survival, not in wealth. They wanted their Australian citizenship to continue, and they wished Australia to retain the uninhabited islands close to the Papuan coast, seeing them as belonging to residents of nearby islands.[6]

Coombs found something in this discussion that suggested a new approach. Perhaps there were changes even more frightening than a shift in the border to consider, Coombs pointed out to the Islanders, such as oil drilling. 'It may be possible', Coombs offered, 'that means other than retention of the present border might be found to provide the protection required.' He was hinting at something not yet disclosed – his proposal to Whitlam of a guarantee that the Islanders would keep their fisheries safe from any threat – whether environmental or political.

When Whitlam joined this Canberra gathering, he made clear that he was there to promote a border change. (We can see in his stance the same confident resolve that disposed of East Timorese independence in diplomacy with Indonesia two years later.) He cited UN interest in the border issue since 1971, and he foreshadowed that Papua New Guinea would get self-government on 1 December 1973 and full independence twelve or fifteen months after that. The Prime Minister also told the Islander representatives that Queensland, not the Commonwealth, had been promoting off-shore oil drilling in the Strait.[7]

Assessing these discussions for Whitlam, Coombs summarised the Islanders' position.

1. the land and sea is all one region owned by them;
2. they are ethnically distinct from Papuans;
3. they opposed any oil or mineral development of the seabed, at any price;
4. they feared PNG control over the seas, as Japanese interests would be given permission to fish;
5. they did not like the proposal to move the border, and nor did their Papuan friends see any point in the change.[8]

Coombs encouraged the Islander leaders to discuss their perspective with representatives of the communities on the Papuan coastline. A meeting was to take place on Yam Island in September 1973. Four weeks before then, Coombs suggested to Whitlam that he ask the Island Chairmen to make an in-principle agreement about environmental protection. Coombs wanted all three governments (Australia, Queensland and Papua New Guinea) to have to take into account a clearly expressed Islander wish for such a policy.[9] Coombs and two officials of the Queensland government were permitted to attend the Yam Island meeting. In his subsequent report to Bryant and Whitlam, Coombs attached a press release in which the Islanders and Papuans demanded environmental protection and announced their intention to continue sharing the strait. The statement further proposed that oil drilling and fishing by outsiders not be allowed in the Strait. According to Coombs, neither the Islanders nor the Papuans raised the issue of the border: their dominant concern had been to set up a 'kind of (marine) national park'. Coombs judged that both the PNG and the Australian governments could build an agreement around such a protective regime.[10]

It was time to put these promising developments into the form of a proposal. On 8 October 1973, Coombs circulated 'drafting notes' to the Secretaries of the Departments of Aboriginal Affairs, External Territories, Attorney-General, Foreign Affairs and Environment and Conservation. Referring to the 'unique and integrated environment on which the livelihood and the culture and traditions of the Islanders and the peoples of the South-western coast of Papua New Guinea depend', he outlined possible government guarantees of residents' free movement and fishing. He called for scientific scrutiny of 'economic projects', before any were submitted for approval by the Chairmen of the Councils of the Torres Strait Islands and of the coastal communities of south-western Papua New Guinea. Coombs proposed to restrict the licensing of marine harvesting to locals and to companies in which locals had at least 85 per cent equity. The Torres Strait would be administered 'as a National Park in accordance with internationally accepted practices for such Parks'.[11]

Three weeks later, these notes had been turned into the first draft of a formal 'Agreement between Australia and Papua New Guinea for the Preservation of the Environment in the Torres Strait Area and the settlement of other matters relating to the area'. The draft alluded to the wishes expressed at the Yam Island meeting 19 and 20 September 1973. In essence, Coombs was asking the governments of Australia and Papua New Guinea to forget about plotting a precise boundary and to declare the entire strait a shared environmentally protected zone that would include islands, sea, airspace, seabed and subsoil beneath the seabed. Those whose livelihoods were to be protected were referred to as permanent residents of the Torres Strait islands and the south-western coast of Papua New Guinea. The draft recognised 'traditional and customary practices of the local inhabitants with respect to the taking of fish and other living marine products' and the right of 'traditional and customary freedom of movement of local inhabitants' including navigation. 'New commercial projects' were to be vetted by a panel of three scientists (deciding by majority) advising a meeting of a Strait Consultative Council. To be approved, a commercial venture would have to be not less than 85 per cent owned by Papuan or Islander people. Disputes over custom (or any other matter) not resolved by this Council in three months would be referred to the two governments. The draft left open the composition and minimum meeting frequency of the Consultative Council.[12]

By tirelessly presenting this formulation of Torres Strait Islanders' economic and environmental interests (with details modified as the idea gained acceptance), Coombs laid the basis for Cabinet's decision, 26 February 1976, to endorse what became known as the Protected Zone. The strait was to have no sea-bed boundary through it, and there would be a moratorium on mining and prospecting. A treaty with Papua New Guinea followed in 1979. When all the relevant documents become available (in 2007), someone will trace Coombs' promotion through inter-departmental committees of this model of Torres Strait interests. His achievement was to persuade both the Islanders and the Commonwealth that the border was but a minor detail in a settlement that effected Islanders' economic and ecological sovereignty. Australia's maritime boundary with New Guinea is one of Coombs' greatest, but least-known, achievements.

Conservation and Aborigines

IN MAY 1970, COOMBS told readers of the *Australian* that 'When the Europeans first came to Australia they found a land where a balance existed between man and nature. ... The Aboriginal was conservative and a conservationist.' Did this mean that Aboriginal and conservation interests could be allied in contemporary Australian politics? The exhortation that 'Here, as indeed in other ways, we can learn from the first Australians' did not answer that political question.[1]

In 1977–8, an answer had to be found. When Kakadu National Park and Tanami Wildlife Sanctuary were claimed by Aboriginal traditional owners, the *Land Rights Act* permitted conservationists (and any other interest) to argue before the Aboriginal Land Commissioner that Aboriginal title would cause 'detriment'. Would the conservationists do so?

In October 1977, Coombs succeeded Sir Mark Oliphant as President of the ACF, after Oliphant had been President for only a year. One of Coombs' aims in accepting that office was to ensure that the ACF was not a hostile interest when the land claims were heard.[2] In November he wrote as ACF Chair to the Chair of the Northern Land Council asking for a meeting to discuss issues of common interest.[3] On 26 January 1978, at the ANU staff club, representatives of the Northern and Central Land Councils and the AIAS met with Coombs (representing the ACF) and a representative of the Friends of the Earth (FOE) to exchange views about how land under Aboriginal title could be managed to the satisfaction of both Aboriginal owners and conservationists. The talks went well, and Coombs soon sent to Galarrwuy Yunupingu (Northern Land Council) and Wenten Rubuntja (Central Land Council) a statement that he hoped conveyed points of agreement. 'It is intended to have this draft confirmed at a [ACF] Council meeting on 25th and 26th February', he explained. It would then be made available to the Judge hearing the Tanami and Kakadu claims.

> It would help the Foundation to ensure support for the statement if the two Land Councils would make a statement at the same time which expressed [the] Aboriginal intention to conserve the land and wild life as they have always done before. The two statements together would reassure some conservationists who have expressed anxiety and would have useful influence on the enquiries. Coming out together they should attract favourable press and media comment. Would you please ask your Council to consider this?

He attached a draft 'which your Council might find useful'.[4]

The two Land Councils soon made the following statement about their Kakadu and Tanami land claims.

We have lived on these lands for tens of thousands of years in harmony with it and its creatures. We have harvested its natural product for food and for other uses but do not take more than is strictly necessary. Aborigines do not kill or destroy for sport or for profit. Aborigines intend to maintain their ancient traditions in these matters and welcome the declaration of the areas as National Parks and Wildlife Sanctuaries. They will be especially concerned to help endangered species. Should problems arise Aboriginal owners are ready to seek expert advice and help. Discussions have already been held between representatives of the Northern and Central Land Councils and the ACF, and FOE about plans for continuing cooperation.[5]

When Coombs appeared before the Aboriginal Land Commissioner to state the ACF's support for the Warlpiri, he did not repeat his 1970 argument that Aboriginal people were, by virtue of their adaptation to the Australian environment, conservationists. That might have led to a debate about the character of Aboriginal civilisation. Instead, he evoked two political scenarios. 'To deny Aboriginal title because of lack of faith in Aboriginal integrity, understanding or capacity is to rely upon law and compulsion. To grant Aboriginal title and then to negotiate agreement is to rely upon consultation, mutual education and collaboration in agreed plans.'[6] Asked by counsel for his assessment of the management plan proposed for the sanctuary by the Territory Parks and Wildlife Service, Coombs insisted that it was important to elicit Aborigines' *unforced* agreement with any plan of management. They should enter negotiations with the Service after having gained strong title. Without their having 'final authority ... there will not be the necessary attempts to get them fully to understand what is involved in the issue'. We can hear echoes of Coombs the central banker in this: a regulatory practice had better obtain the cooperation of the regulated.

There were two risk scenarios for the Aboriginal Land Commissioner to assess, Coombs suggested. In one, the Aborigines would get title, but fail to cooperate with the service's conservation plan. In the other, their title would be denied or qualified, leading to 'an antagonistic and adversary relationship between the Aborigines and the wildlife authority'. He believed that the latter posed the greater danger to a sound land management plan.[7] Justice Toohey, granting the Warlpiri claim, explicitly agreed with this reasoning.

Although Coombs' 1970 article in the *Australian* could be read as depicting a spontaneous affinity between conservation and Aboriginal land use, that is not the position that Coombs adopted in 1978 – or subsequently. Rather, he thought that the relationship between traditional owners and the conservation interest had to be mediated – at two levels. It had to be mediated politically; that is why he had convened the Australia Day 1978 discussion and obtained both sides' consent to a joint statement. And it had to be mediated operationally. That is, government agencies charged with conservation had to form a working agreement with traditional owners. Such agreement was more likely to flow from discussions in which Aborigines participated as people with rights, rather than as people whose behaviour would henceforth be circumscribed by someone else's plans.

Bapa Dhumbul

IN 1978, THE COMMONWEALTH Office of Child Care funded the Aboriginal Family and Children's Heritage Project. Hosted by the ANU's Centre for Resource and Environmental Studies and supervised by Coombs, the project produced *A Certain Heritage* (1983), co-authored by Coombs, anthropologist Maria Brandl and teacher Warren Snowdon. Explicitly a manual in 'responsiveness' for public servants dealing with Aboriginal Australians, the book opened with a description of Aboriginal values and socialisation practices. Case studies of government service delivery followed – education, health care, economic and political development. The authors pointed out how the design of government programs could reinforce or undermine Aboriginal values.

Coombs' contributions included an essay on the development of new institutions of law and order among Yolngu at Yirrkala. His engagement with the Yolngu exemplifies 'responsive' mediation of a marginal social interest – the kind of activity that the report of the Royal Commission on Australian Government Administration enjoined on all public servants. His mediation was discriminatory. To be open to Yolngu values was not necessarily to be their captive.

Coombs had started to form a relationship with Yolngu at Yirrkala in 1968, and by 1971, he was leading the CAA's advocacy of their land rights.[1] Though Yolngu had secured their title by 1977, with the proclamation of the *Aboriginal Land Rights (NT) Act*, their domain remained compromised by the ineradicable bauxite mine, its dormitory town Nhulunbuy and that town's most destructive agency, the Walkabout Hotel. On 14 March 1975 a meeting of Yirrkala's Aboriginal Leadership Council had formulated a strategy to deal with Yolngu drinkers. Charles Rowley told the CAA that Yolngu authorities hoped 'to close the bottle shop for two years, to allow them to gear-up their cultural counter-attack. By then they hope to have their own written law, their own indigenous court, and their own "peace officers" … trained … for police work.'[2] Coombs and William Stanner visited Yirrkala in April and June 1975, seeking to write an informed case study of one Aboriginal community's steps towards self-determination. In their *Report on Arnhem Land* (September 1975), they reproduced Yolngu leader Roy Marika's account of 'the legal authority of the Council of Leadership and the orderlies' at Yirrkala.

Expounding this 'Yirrkala model', Coombs and Stanner had to decide whether to mention one troubling feature of Yolngu society – sorcery. Among Yolngu, the draft explained, untimely, unnatural and unexplained deaths provoke sorcery explanations and accusations. Coombs and Stanner recommended that the disorderly chain of death–accusation–sorcery–death could be broken by education – combatting magic with 'rational and comprehensible explanations of the deaths involved'. As well, 'magistrates in tradition-oriented parts of Aboriginal Australia [should be advised] of the need for post-mortems in cases of deaths likely to be puzzling or incomprehensible to Aborigines'. Such post-mortems would be conditional upon the family's consent.[3]

Ethnographers of the Yolngu have differed in the prominence they have given to sorcery. In 1975 Janice Reid was talking to Yolngu about their understandings of health and illness. She wanted to know how much their ideas had changed since the 1930s. Her conclusion – not available to Coombs and Stanner, but published in 1983 as *Sorcerers and Healing Spirits* – was that Yolngu belief in sorcery had persisted. The *marnggitj* or sorcerer remained a potent figure. Some deaths still occasioned Yolngu speculations that someone had ensorcelled the deceased. However, modern ways were having a complex effect on Yolngu thinking. On the one hand, untimely deaths associated with alcohol abuse provided new opportunities for people to attribute sorcery. On the other hand, Yolngu now had access to medical explanations. By 'naturalising' death and pre-empting sorcery accusations, the circulation of medical accounts could ameliorate social tensions. However, such modern explanations also had a tendency to undermine certain modes of Yolngu authority. 'The way the people of the community explain illness and death not only enables them to express their fears about the unsettling events which impinge on their lives', Reid pointed out, 'but to assert jurisdiction over their management.'[4] In Reid's account, sorcery beliefs and accusations were not only a source of division and dispute among the people of Arnhem Land, as the CAA *Report on Arnhem Land* presented them, they were also part of the idiom of a distinctly Yolngu jurisdiction.

Coombs and Stanner accepted the suggestion of anthropologist Nancy Williams, who had been making research visits to Yirrkala since 1969, that they delete references to sorcery. It was Coombs' intention to uphold and strengthen the practices of a Yolngu jurisdiction shorn of occult elements. In expounding the jural potential of Yolngu community the CAA chose not to address the politically more anarchic and cosmologically ambiguous, multipolar society that Janice Reid was trying to describe. The CAA presented a politically palatable and administratively calculable image of Yolngu sociality – the ideal subjects of the policy of 'self-determination'. The jural creativity of Aboriginal people impressed Coombs, and he wished to attest only to what he saw as its positive manifestations in Yolngu life.

In August 1974, addressing a seminar convened by the ANU's Law Faculty on 'Australian Lawyers and Social Change', Coombs had remarked on the ways that 'an Aboriginal Australian … lives under two law systems'. Was this remarkable situation not worthy of research, he asked?[5] Upon publication in 1976, Coombs' words grabbed the attention of the Law Reform Commission's Michael Kirby, who told Coombs that he was soon to talk with Minister for Aboriginal Affairs Ian Viner about the special problems of Aboriginal people in the Australian legal system. Coombs replied that, when his Royal Commission duties concluded, he 'hoped to maintain contact with some of the Aboriginal communities with whom I have been associated' and to 'co-operate in any way with your Commission towards "legal renewal" in this sphere'.[6]

Kirby discussed Coombs' paper with Gerald Brennan QC, who had written the Northern Land Council's submission to Justice Woodward's Royal Commission on land rights in 1974. Brennan was stimulated to circulate privately in May 1976 a proposal that the Law Reform Commission investigate 'The recognition of traditional Aboriginal law'. By the time the Commission began its inquiry (February 1977) Coombs had retired as Chancellor (in July 1976), and the CAA had been disbanded (in November 1976, at its own request). It was as a Fellow of the ANU's Centre for Resource and Environmental Studies that Coombs now started to document the ways that Aboriginal communities, on the periphery of Australian society, were living their life under two laws.

In April and May 1978, he visited a number of Aboriginal communities in Central Australia. Residents of the former Lutheran and government settlement Areyonga (established during World War II where western Arrernte and Luritja countries overlapped) told him of their fears and hopes about social control. Coombs suggested a local code of conduct to deal with 'tensions between drinkers and non-drinkers, between old and young, and between Aborigines and white residents'. Areyonga folk exhibited 'a strong tendency to seek greater Aboriginal authority and to fill with Aboriginal leaders positions previously held by whites'. This was 'the only significant existing aspiration capable of lending vitality to the community life at Areyonga'. People told Coombs that they wished 'to strengthen social disciplines'; and they seemed willing 'to accept responsibility for imposing them'.

Coombs' suggested code would bind all members of the community 'and other residents and visitors living in association with it'. The rules fell under three headings: protecting person, privacy and property; protecting peace and order; and protecting Aboriginal law or tradition. He suggested that wardens, appointed from each family group, would wield powers of preventive detention (until noon the following day) of persons judged likely to offend. The person to make that judgment was he or she 'who by Aboriginal law and tradition, has responsibility to guide and support the [likely offender]'. Coombs' notes also provided for a community meeting to hear grievances, which would then decide whether the grievance justified convening a community court. That court would comprise the community Chair (or his or her nominee), the family of the complainant (or their nominee), the family of the 'accused' (or their nominee), and senior men and women from other families. After hearing testimonies, they would impose compensation, a work order, a fine, or custody by senior member of the accused's family, or sequestration. Such punishment would have to be appellable to a magistrate, to ensure the accused's rights as an Australian citizen. To be binding, the community court's decision would have to be accepted by all its members and 'confirmed by the community'. Any convicted person not accepting punishment could be excluded from the community or handed over to police.[7]

Later in 1978 Coombs took these Areyonga notes to Yirrkala. Local linguist Joyce Ross told Coombs that she could find no equivalents for some of the Areyonga concepts, so he made a simpler version that emphasised 'the non-specific nature of the rules contemplated and the dependence of the procedures on traditional practices for the settlement of disputes'. A series of meetings between Coombs, Ross and 'a range of groups including both senior and more junior members of the various clans' further clarified Yolngu wishes. The result was Coombs' submission to the Australian Law Reform Commission on 2 January 1979.[8]

Coombs' submission gave examples of matters ('situations or offences') that Yolngu courts could deal with: violent behaviour while drunk; a young woman's refusal of her betrothed; sorcery accusations; petrol sniffing, and breaking and entering by children; 'misbehaviour away from community'; trouble occasioned by non-Aboriginal behaviour in Yirrkala. His submission contemplated the following corrective actions: rehabilitation and retraining on outstations; compensation; withdrawal of permits from offending visitors; 'strengthening the responsibility of families and clans for the behaviour of their members and for giving effect to decisions of the Court'.

The Yolngu rules were set out under a series of headings. The 'General rules about how to behave' were stated in terms of protecting persons, property, peace and order; they also included an injunction against 'anything forbidden by Aboriginal law and tradition or to do anything which will make the law weak'. There were also rules about 'Preventing wrong things', including conferring on 'the head of every clan or family' a 'duty to prevent wrong things being done by members of his clan or family. He shall name one of his clan or group to act as Warden to help him do this'. The Chair of the proposed local 'Law Council' would be given the responsibility to ask clan heads to take a likely offender 'into his care and control, until the next day, or until he thinks he will not do the wrong thing'. The community could hold a clan head responsible and punish him if he did not exercise authority in this way. The Yolngu rules also included the constitution of the court process ('When it is said that a wrong thing has been done') and set out the responsibilities of adults for misdemeanours by children ('When a wrong thing has been done by a child'). The submission also included the Yirrkala leaders' draft outline of the new authority that would deploy these proposed rules and procedures – 'a new Council which we would call the Garma Council', distinct from 'the Dhanbul Association which looks after our administration and business affairs'. The Garma Council would include two members from each clan but others could be present who could listen and speak.[9]

Over the next year, Coombs had to reconsider features of this model. He gave more attention to one potent threat to Yirrkala – children sniffing petrol. His accounts of Areyonga and Yirrkala had assumed the uniform integrity of each family. Families were assumed, in his model, to be sound units of authority that combined to form an aggregate authority called the 'community'. What if families varied in their capacity and willingness to supervise children? Mothering by young girls, he was beginning to find, was particularly problematic. Some men suggested that Yolngu be given authority to redirect child endowment payments from neglectful natural mothers to the actual carers over children. Considerations of the quality of mothering were, in Coombs' opinion, 'women's business'. Any authority over child endowment payments should therefore be composed of women – a 'court of Women' or a parallel 'Women's Council'.[10]

His realisation that men's and women's powers might have to be distinguished and that some families might require intervention led Coombs to reformulate the Yirrkala model. He submitted a new paper to the Law Reform Commission in May 1980, raising the possibility that the Garma Council could arrange for 'a Women's Council of older women from which it can obtain advice or to which it can refer matters' traditionally regarded as women's business. It is not clear whether Coombs' new model relayed the expressed ideas of Yirrkala's women. 'There are some sections of the community with which I am not fully familiar', he admitted, 'in particular women and to a lesser extent young men.'[11]

Petrol sniffing at Yirrkala illustrated the difficulty of making assumptions about Yolngu authority. For self-determination to work, it was not sufficient for white officials to withdraw; Yolngu and other Aboriginal people must also revitalise their influence over the young. Coombs was worried that, in this reassertion, Yolngu men might deal too punitively with petrol-sniffers. The Garma Council's authority should include non-judicial forms such as training children in traditional pursuits. Their authority must be nurturing.

The Council had experimented with a special school in which delinquent children were subject to round-the-clock surveillance. The money for that program having run out, the Council proposed to make a camp for sniffers on Bremer Island, removing them physically from petrol. Coombs told them that such a camp would isolate children from the beneficial influences of family. It could be a breeding ground for alienated and rebellious attitudes on the part of those confined. Coombs told Roy Marika that he could support only with reservations such a Yirrkala program against petrol-sniffing. He would talk to the Department of Aboriginal Affairs and to the Office of Child Care about Yirrkala's need, but he would suggest that Bremer Island be a last resort. Would it not be better, he asked Marika, to devise support for children within Yirrkala, perhaps with a Women's Council taking charge of craft and other recreation programs and organising sibling support for troubled children?[12]

When Coombs visited Yirrkala in September 1980, eighty to ninety children were reported to be sniffing petrol. Coombs suggested that their families be called before a community court appointed by the Garma Council. After discussion, the Council would recommend steps to strengthen the family's control over the child. Possibly a probation officer would be appointed to watch over and report on the family's treatment of the child, to assist the child to attend school. If that failed, then the child could be placed with another family or sent to the Bremer Island camp, and the Department of Social Security would be asked to redirect social security payments. Coombs recommended that the government pay for two probation officers and for some facilities to be erected on Bremer Island. The program should be funded for three years, then evaluated.

In Coombs' response to petrol-sniffing at Yirrkala we can see two features of his engagement with Yolngu.

First, Coombs was not content simply to relay to government agencies what Yolngu said to him; rather, he assessed what they proposed, asking what might or might not work and what would persuade government agencies. Although he affirmed that 'Aborigines backed by traditional authority are better placed than outsiders to implement plans and to assess its [*sic*] impact or failure', he sometimes offered Yolngu his critique.[13] Was Coombs then an 'insider'? Coombs and his most frequent correspondent, Roy Marika, used kin terms when writing to each other. Coombs addressed Marika as *gathu* (son) and signed himself *bapa* (father). These terms imply nurturing intimacy, closeness tempered by distance both generational and, in Coombs' case, cultural. It has been common to apply the term 'paternalism' to missionaries' and government officials' sustained assumption of tutelary authority. 'Self-determination' was supposed to end such paternalism. Yet Coombs' Yolngu kinship terms are so self-consciously 'paternal' as to suggest that 'paternalism' may be a relationship of many subtleties. I have seen nothing in Roy Marika's letters to Coombs (dictated to Nancy Williams) that suggest that Yolngu found him overbearing.

Second, petrol-sniffing seems to have challenged Coombs to develop a model of Yolngu authority as contestable and dispersed, rather than as a seamless web of customary law binding 'families' into a 'community' represented by a 'Law Council'. Coombs became unsure of the degree of 'community' homogeneity. Should a Women's Council have its own jurisdiction, with child endowment payments as women's business? Or was such a body's proper role to advise the Garma Council? Did his closeness to mature men, seniors of their clans, limit his empathy with other categories of Yolngu – the women, the young? Coombs was by then aware of Diane Bell's ethnography of the Warlpiri and Keytej of Central Australia, saying that women exercised powers and enjoyed a ritual life within their own domain. Prompted by sympathetic but probing questions from the Australian Law Reform Commission (to which Bell also was a consultant) Coombs, in March 1981, asked his Yolngu interlocutors how well senior men could represent all Yolngu opinion. Garma Council (comprising only men) responded, as he reported, that 'rules governing conduct in the community made by the Garma Council must be submitted to the community as a whole for confirmation' and 'that decisions of the Community courts will be reported to a community meeting and endorsed before being acted upon'. In other words, as a site of male authority Garma Council was a party, and no doubt a very influential one, within a wider political process of 'community' sovereignty. Its wishes were, in principle, contestable, its jurisdiction limited. If it were unable to command a community consensus, Garma Council would call upon the *balanda* authorities to resolve a dispute.[14] Dissenters thus had recourse to external authority, by virtue of their Australian citizenship. This was a more complex and open-ended model of Yolngu authority.

From 1974, when he and Stanner had examined the ways that Warlpiri and Arrernte people were taking up government invitations to 'self-determination', Coombs' work among Indigenous Australians taught him that 'self-determination' was not an easy project.[15] In one perspective the integrative norms of Aboriginal society were at risk of decay. Alternatively, they were robust, but ill-suited to the forms of self-determination that governments now made available. Coombs' engagement with the Yolngu shows him to have been discriminating in his appreciation of the policy significance of Yolngu words, practices and values. His was a fatherly responsiveness.

Conclusion

Histories nostalgic and hopeful

WHILE SPEAKING TO A Darwin conference on Indigenous health in September 1995, Coombs suffered a stroke from which he never fully recovered. He died twenty-five months later on 29 October 1997 in a Sydney nursing home at the age of ninety-one. For such an active man, the approach of infirmity and then loss of capacity seemed unmerciful. A few weeks before his stroke, he had remarked to me his frustration at having to cut back to an eight-hour working day. A few years before that, he had asked forgiveness for missing a publisher's deadline. 'You've got to remember I am now 84, and also I've got meetings in and around the Kimberleys next week and then I'm flying to the Northern Territory after that before I get back to Canberra.'[1]

In Coombs' last spoken intervention into Australian public life, he argued for the further empowerment of Aboriginal women. In Aboriginal communities with which he was familiar, women's concerns – in tradition and in their continuing practice – included the nurturance of children, the provision of most food, the curbing of alcohol consumption, and so on. It was not that individual men never shared such concerns; it was rather that these were the objects of Aboriginal women's collective practice. It followed that women should have certain community resources dedicated to their use. Why not reserve some of the CDEP budget for activities managed by the women?

If Coombs' public life ceased with the posing of that question or suggestion, it offers us a remarkable instance of continuity in the Australian tradition of liberalism. In February 1928, just as Coombs was receiving in a Wheat Belt town the first parcel of study materials of his second undergraduate year, his economics professor Edward Shann was making a similar point to the Royal Commission on Child Endowment. Shann supported child endowment as 'investment in the human capital of Australia'. He liked the idea of 'putting the maintenance fund of the community into the hands of the mothers'. His assumption was that women 'would spend it more definitely upon the upbringing of the youngsters than it is when distributed over the adult male workers of the community irrespective of whether they have families or not'.[2]

I offer this comparison as a corrective to overstating Coombs' singularity. He drew on and extended a shared intellectual inheritance.

Insofar as that tradition depended on intellectuals for its expression, Coombs worried about its survival. From his Boyer Lectures in December 1970 to his R. D. Wright Lecture of April 1993 – one of his last speeches – Coombs stated his revised evaluation of the corporate, academic and professional elites. Having promoted the promise of their meritocratic succession in the 1950s and 1960s, he began, in the 1970s, to dwell on the increasing risk that they would fail to lead and serve.

He had considered this theme – the subversion of social leadership – in his fifth Boyer Lecture, 'The Measure is Man'. If there were to be institutional reform, he insisted, not only moral vision but also intellectual discipline would be necessary. To renew society, one must study it, but how could society institutionalise such a regenerative intelligence? he asked. Our 'churches, political parties, universities, the press, radio and television and the spontaneous groupings of the young' were not, he lamented, effective. If they were not to become dependent on the gratuities and the income of the Establishment,

> They must be given, and trained to value and defend, an autonomy not merely of the government but also of the economic system and indeed of the whole corpus of the Establishment. This is possible only if:
> (a) their management is independent of government and of other sources of established authority;
> (b) their effectiveness does not depend on financial and economic subvention from government, industry or commerce;
> (c) their executives derive their authority from a community committed to professional standards of quality and integrity and are responsible to that community;
> (d) the members of the professional community are inspired by a faith in their long-term social purposes and therefrom derive the courage to resist the pressure of the Establishment to incorporate, intimidate and submerge them;
> (e) they keep open their doors, their ears and their hearts to those, particularly the young, who look with fresh and unprejudiced vision on the works of our hands.[3]

Coombs did not point to any professional estate that fulfilled these desiderata. (He could perhaps have mentioned his children's teachers, the Society of Jesus and the Loreto nuns.) We may take this as an aspirational statement – or as a prediction of the Establishment's inexorable subversion of 'regeneration'.

In Coombs' subsequent meditations on the fate of the intelligentsia, he was similarly caught between hope and despair. Speaking as President of the ACF in October 1978, for example, he characterised those with the knowledge to lead society as self-interested owners of a new kind of property. It was not only natural resources that made one wealthy in the last quarter of the twentieth century, he pointed out, but also 'the widely varying forms of assets – physical, intellectual, legal, political and conventional – which proliferate around the market-places of industrial and commercial society'. The elite that was now poised to gain most from technological progress was not 'a distinct and recognisable class of people' but 'the fortunate, talented, skilful or the powerful among all classes', including many white-collar workers.[4] Such men and women were beginning to estimate their social significance merely in terms of the material reward the market-place would now allow them, he warned.

In 'Science and Technology – For What Purpose?', an address to the Australian Academy of Science in April 1979, Coombs sketched modern life as the alienation of humanity from the machine-like structures of society. The corporation – typified by mining companies, he suggested – had subsumed the individual and suborned the mandated institutions of regulation. All institutions were tending to mimic the industrial corporation's division of labour, specialisation of function and hierarchical authority structures. 'Those who make decisions within it are constrained to serve its purposes – the primary one being the continuity and power of the institution itself.' In such an environment there was no place for 'the whole man or woman', only for those who had been moulded to be the specialised 'accessories' of corporate purpose.[5] The hope that Coombs held out was that 'growing numbers of people are seeking voluntarily to form groups small enough for those within them to care for and help each other; for self-reliance of individuals and of groups to be more significant; and for producer and consumer to be more often the same person'. Perhaps the revolution in information technology would enable such groups to proliferate, he speculated.[6]

In Coombs' R. D. Wright Lecture of 1993, this lament for a creative, selfless, intelligent leadership had become a series of nostalgic vignettes – for the University of Western Australia, when it was small, for the 'Research Department' of the Commonwealth Bank, when it was small, for the pre-industrial intelligentsia, when it consisted of small autonomous groups. He recalled the impact on his youthful mind of J. M. Keynes' *The Economic Consequences of the Peace* and Julien Benda's *The Betrayal of the Intellectuals*, and he urged, in the most general terms, a reappraisal of the social purposes of Australian economic policies. 'I've just about run out of steam', he acknowledged. 'I'm 87 and I'm getting old.'[7]

Imagine that in the 1980s Coombs had accepted a publisher's invitation to write a history of Australia's twentieth century. This theme – the meritocratic succession's rise and then ethical decline – would have been prominent. One could take Coombs as exemplary of that story: with his passing we lose touch with a humane and creative policy ethos. Hugh Stretton's retrospect on Coombs saw him as exemplary of a cohort of public service intellectuals. In his 1984 essay, 'Tasks for Social Democratic Intellectuals', Stretton wrote: 'Forty years ago, Labor governments recruited the likes of Coombs and Crawford and Crisp and Wheeler. They were broadly educated, Keynesian, and somewhat to the left of Menzies, who nevertheless trusted them.' However, these men were succeeded in the public service by persons more conservative than themselves. Why? Stretton asked. His answer drew attention to changes in the way intellectuals are educated.

> Coombs' generation, if they got to university at all, had to learn other things besides economics. … If they studied social sciences, those sciences were typically presented as means to improve the world. Improving the world required equal attention to ends and means, and the ends as well as the means of social reform got generous attention in the curriculum.

The economists they studied, including Keynes, 'presented economic theory as a reformist instrument … the best learners of that generation had a sensible understanding of the relation between their moral and social values and the other intellectual equipment which they brought to the study of government and social life'. Their successors have been educated more narrowly, Stretton lamented, and they have been invited to conceive their technical disciplines as best not encumbered by moral and political reflection. They have rarely been taught 'to understand the differences between the major schools of economic thought as intricate mixtures of technical and political disagreement'.[8]

As a historical explanation, this seems to me to pay too little attention to the context of Coombs' professional formation. The Depression and World War II provided Coombs' generation with the opportunity (the necessity, even) to experiment in unprecedented state interventions into the government of capitalism. Those years demanded, enabled and rewarded the application of the intellectual qualities evoked by Stretton.

Nostalgia for Coombs, as I pointed out in my introduction, is a theme in the historical consciousness of those disturbed by Australia's movement, since the 1970s, into a neo-liberal or free market approach to public policy. I prefer to loosen Stretton's link between the 'intelligentsia story' and the 'public policy story', or at least to show the link's contingencies. When Tom Fitzgerald spoke with Coombs in 1984 about the historical origins of a recent decline in the quality and morale of the Commonwealth public service, he asked if the 1940s had been an 'unrepeatable golden age' of government made by 'that wave of what were then called Laterals, chaps who moved in from outside the Commonwealth Public Service at a high level during the war and soon after the war. ... Is the fact that this cannot be repeated, part of the malaise?' Coombs: 'I certainly think so.'

Coombs went on to say that, having attained seniority while young, his cohort had been spared 'year after year of grind and disappointment and disillusionment. It was that, plus the post-war reconstruction atmosphere, the feeling that things could be different, partly because of things that were done during the war, unrepeatable for a great variety of reasons.'[9] Since the youth of Coombs there has been no equivalent professional socialising environment, within Australia, to the governmental challenges of 1930–45. Nor would one wish there to be, for they were desperate, bloody and wasteful years for so many. I see no way to make Fitzgerald's 'golden age' part of a hopeful historiography.

Is there another way of seeing Coombs' life as an illumination of twentieth-century trends? I think we can find one by critically considering Paul Kelly's influential, short account of Australian history in the twentieth century. The opening chapter of *The End of Certainty* (1992) argued that from 1901 to the 1980s, Australian political life was characterised by a 'settlement'. The Australian Settlement consisted of: White Australia, Industry Protection, Wage Arbitration, State Paternalism and Imperial Benevolence. Only by rejecting the institutions and policies of this Settlement in the 1980s, Kelly argued, could Australia 'stand on its own ability' and 'address the true definition of nationhood – the acceptance of responsibility for their own fate'.[10] In undermining the five terms of this Settlement governments were becoming 'smaller, less interventionist', enabling a more dynamic individual citizenry whose 'symptoms were a public sector surplus, an attack on government regulations, privatisation of public enterprise, needs-based welfare, deregulation of the labour market, and micro-economic reforms ... [in] energy, communications and transport'.[11]

This narrative of Australian history has critics. Has Kelly not dismissed the democratic benefits that the Australian Settlement institutionalised? Is the loss of these benefits adequately registered in Kelly's language when he writes that the Australian Settlement – 'introspective, defensive, dependent – is undergoing an irresistible demolition'?[12] One version of this critique of Kelly highlights the fact that the Settlement was 'Australian'; it accuses those who celebrate its demise as cultural cringers, caving in to an ethically shallow globalism. Another critique of Kelly's account argues that he has overstated the continuity of the Australian Settlement since Alfred Deakin. Kelly has ignored the way the Settlement was substantially renovated in the 1940s by Labor's changes in immigration policy, macro-economic policy, social security policy and foreign policy. In this view, the most obnoxious feature of dismantling the Australian Settlement is that we are being asked to abandon the goal of full employment without finding an alternative strategy for social cohesion.

What was Coombs' stance towards this Australian Settlement? To answer that question is to notice the ideological cunning of Kelly's narrative. He has ignored any alternatives to the Australian Settlement other than those now proposed by neo-liberal intellectuals in the 1980s. His story takes Australia from 'immaturity' to 'maturity', without raising the question of whether there could be alternatives to the market-oriented maturity to which we are being pulled – if only we were mature enough to acquiesce to its logic – by global forces. Coombs' career shows that the Settlement had been questioned long before the 1980s from points of view other than the neo-liberal economics that Kelly identifies with Australians becoming 'responsible'. In particular, Coombs' critique of at least two features of the Australian Settlement invoked a Keynesian political economy, not a neo-liberal one.

Let's go through the settlement point by point:

White Australia: Coombs did not, as far as I know, adopt any position on the issue of how immigration policy should determine Australia's cultural or racial composition. His main concern about immigration was that in the 1950s it contributed to inflation. However, in the 1960s, he did reflect critically on White Australia as a social policy ideal, first by drawing attention to the value of the Aboriginal artistic heritage and then by insisting that Aborigines be given choices about the economic and political terms of their adaptation to modern Australian society. He certainly eschewed the assumption that Indigenous autonomy should be sought through their joining the free market for goods and labour. His visions of Aboriginal and Torres Strait Islander autonomy put the emphasis on political settlements between peoples, not on the freedom of Indigenous corporations and individuals to join markets.

Industry Protection: Coombs became an economist at a time when Australian economists' studies of the costs and benefits of industry protection were winning international respect for their technical excellence. His critical attitude towards protection was not a naive free trade position, however.

Trade liberalisation was politically unsaleable, he argued, unless people were assured economic security. As Australia's most important trade policy official in the late 1940s, Coombs advocated international economic policies that would under-write Australians' economic security *while allowing a substantial reduction of tariffs.* Australia should not surrender its right to protect itself – by whatever means – unless it was sure that the world's great economic powers were committed to international full employment. In this diplomacy, Coombs sought the support of other 'developing' economies. In 1973, Coombs' (and other economists') con-tinuing scepticism about industry protection won the support of the Whitlam government. He was one of the architects of the July 1973 cut in tariffs of 25 per cent and of the Industries Assistance Commission. But such market discipline was, for him, only one ingredient of a good industry policy.

Arbitration: As one of the many authors of the 1945 White Paper *Full Employment in Australia,* Coombs considered carefully whether Australia's wage-setting system was suited to a full employment economy. He and his colleagues would like to have explored the alternative of setting wages according to economists' publicly accountable measurement of productivity and of the international terms of trade. They also wanted the labour movement to consider piece rates. When it became clear that the labour movement remained strongly committed to arbitration, Coombs accepted it as an inescapable feature of Australian economic management. He commended it for conciliating capital and labour and he pointed out that bringing wages down was not necessarily the best way to fight inflation. Nor was wage growth the best means to popular affluence. The tax system remained for him a pre-eminent instrument of both incomes and industry policy, as his neglected Asprey submission of 1974 showed. Like critics of the Australian Settlement, Coombs was disappointed by the culture of wage and price setting in Australia, as he made clear in his 1959 address 'A Matter of Prices'. He thought that Australians were rather fixated on their money wages and were not sufficiently interested in the social wage, the provision of public goods through the tax system. Good incomes policy would have to include a strong public sector assuring popular living standards through collective provision and thus obviating the fetish of the money wage.

State paternalism: Coombs believed in the mixed economy, with a strong public sector. Thus, one of the most important policy convictions of his career was that private banks should be regulated and that the central bank would be best able to regulate them if it were not only a rule-maker and enforcer but also a competitor of the banks it regulated. He fought those who wanted to separate the Commonwealth's regulatory and trading functions in the 1950s. However, Coombs did not think that it was important for the government to nationalise the banks. In fact, he found that the tensions of the nationalisation issue (1947–9) hindered his efforts at a cooperative style of regulation in the 1950s.

Coombs' approach to arts patronage exhibited a kind of state paternalism. That is, at his instigation, two great Commonwealth statutory corporations –

the Commonwealth Bank and the ABC – cooperated to create the Australian Elizabethan Theatre Trust. The Trust, founded in 1954, was difficult to classify as either 'public' or 'private', however. Its Board combined men and women from both public and private sectors, and its initial subscription combined public subsidy with private donations. It sought to cover its costs and to build up its reserves from profits, like a commercial entrepreneur, but it failed 'commercially' and sustained itself with larger and larger public subsidies. Despite becoming a 'public' body from the point of view of the sources of its funds, it remained 'private' in the sense of lacking any mechanism of public accountability – a point of criticism by 1964. Coombs finished his career in the arts by designing a public patronage body with much clearer procedures of accountability.

Kelly seems not to recognise the point that whether or not a state or private agency is 'paternalistic' depends largely on its accountability to the public that it is claiming to serve. So there can be (and there certainly is) such a thing as private corporate paternalism. A concern, often uneasy, about the accountability of public and private sector agencies is a thread running through Coombs' career. His work on the Royal Commission on Australian Government Administration (1974–6) was based on the conviction that the public had recently become much more interested in, outspoken about, and organised for, public affairs. In Kelly's narrative, Coombs could be counted as one of the great experimenters of paternalism, testing its benefits and limitations. Coombs' nuanced approach to paternalism is far more sophisticated than Kelly's glib identification of state initiative with 'paternalism' (and by implication, corporate initiative with 'freedom').

Imperial Benevolence: Coombs hated being called 'Bertie' (other than by his family of origin) because he found it a silly 'Pommie' name, and he refused Imperial honours. This modesty has its rewards. The Chair of Coombs' National Press Club session on 22 January 1969 said in his thanks: 'as you have refused the offer of a knighthood on several occasions, in the eyes of some this would probably make you even a greater Australian than some who have accepted it'.[13] Whitlam echoed this compliment in a 1972 interview.

More important (since I am discussing policy), Coombs' notion of Australia as a 'dependent' economy undermined any illusions of Imperial benevolence. For example, he concluded early in his career that Australia's economic institutions, in particular its central bank, should not be modelled on Britain's but designed according to the conditions typical of dependent economies such as Australia's. That conviction never left him. As a trade diplomat in the 1940s, his advice was based on the conviction that Imperial Preference was of rapidly decreasing worth to Australia. In a 1947 memorandum to Chifley, he projected Australia's economic future as dependent on trade with the United States and with the emergent nations of Asia. He attached particular significance to India's economic development. In the terms of Kelly's narrative, Coombs is an early and persistent sceptic of Imperial benevolence, a keen advocate of 'engagement' with Asia.

Kelly could have found in Coombs' career a critique of the Australian Settlement that owes nothing to neoliberalism. But what now is the political vehicle of such a critique? Neither Coombs nor Kelly is confident that the Labor Party can find a place in the Settlement's dissolution and replacement. But their reasons for that prognosis are different. In 1984 Coombs concluded his John Curtin Lecture by warning Labor about its recent efforts to 'pre-empt' the non-Labor parties. Particularly in its conservative approach to 'nuclear war, Aborigines and unemployment' the ALP was 'alienating not merely those in need and those whom society has injured but also the idealists, the intelligentsia and the radical reformers'. He predicted Labor's demise if it continued in this direction. 'The political vacuum on the left will be filled, per-haps for a while by a single-issue or splinter parties but before long by a more radical party outside the Labor Party.'[14] As Kelly saw it, by dismantling the Australian Settlement Labor was undermining its historic basis. If successful, policies embraced by Labor in the 1980s and 1990s 'would make the old Labor Party obsolete'.[15] Kelly cannot yet envisage a new agenda for social democracy. I'm not sure whether Coombs could either.

Kelly is rightly uncertain of the terms of a *new* Australian Settlement. One possibility, however, seems invisible to him because of the limited terms in which he has critically depicted the Australian Settlement. For all his rhetoric of innovation, Kelly remains captive to the ecological assumptions of the Australian Settlement. When Kelly declares his evidence against the Australian Settlement, his critique is strangely old-fashioned in its invocation of material living standards as *the* test of a sound economy. Has he not heard of another test – ecological sustainability? A most important strand of the Australian Settlement – all parties' and economic interests' ruinous assumptions about the bounty and malleability of nature – has gone unnoticed by Kelly. What we now know of the damage to the Murray–Darling Basin tells us that a new Australian Settlement will have to rethink that discredited relationship with nature, if it is to be viable. By exploring the distortions in markets for natural resources Coombs began to lay the intellectual basis for such a revision of the Australian Settlement in 1971. In that sense, he made it plain that it will require all of Australians' courage to become economically rational.

Notes

ABBREVIATIONS

AA ACT	Australian Archives, Canberra
BLPES	British Library of Political and Economic Science (Archives of LSE)
CPD-R	*Commonwealth Parliamentary Debates* (House of Representatives)
Collected Speeches	Three-volume set of many of Coombs' speeches while Governor of the Commonwealth and then Reserve Banks, held by RBA and in NLA Box 45
Coombs	Conversation with author, 2 September 1995
DAFP	*Documents in Australian Foreign Policy* (a series published by the Australian Government Publishing Service, by volume/document numbers)
Dexter	Barrie Dexter's papers, in the Menzies Library, ANU, by file number.
FAT	Film Australia Transcripts (on diskette, unpaginated, interviewers F. Heimans and R. Hughes)
GHC	Name of a series in RBA to do with Coombs' Governorship
Hatt	Phyllis Hatt (née Coombs) interviewed by author 23 September 1995
Heron	Dorothea Heron (née Chandler) interviewed by author 10 September 1995
Honner	Ralph Honner interviewed by author 22 January 1994
Minutes	A series of dated and numbered 'Minutes' from Coombs to Whitlam, 1972–75, held in NLA MS 802 Boxes 46 and 48, and in AA ACT M448/1 Box 18 (items 152, 153), box 19 (154–7) and box 20 (158–60).
NLA	National Library of Australia Coombs papers MS802, by box/folder numbers.
PWR	National Library of Australia Transcript of 1981 Post-war Reconstruction Seminar (TS 1096)
RBA	Reserve Bank of Australia Archives
RCAGA	Royal Commission on Australian Government Administration
RCAGA Transcript	Held in National Library of Australia
Richards	Griff Richards interviewed by author 23 September 1995

Rusden	National Library of Australia, Oral History TS 2392, Coombs interviewed by Heather Rusden
TB draft	Typescript of Coombs' uncut draft of *Trial Balance*
UWA	University of Western Australia Archives
WASA	Western Australian State Archives
Wilson	Coombs interviewed by Rosemary Mayne Wilson, *West Australian* 30 October 1974

AUREAM PARTICULAM

1 Hammond to Coombs 15 January 1972 NLA 16/118.

2 *The Sphinx* May 1922.

3 Renouf (1980, 37).

4 A. D. Hope 'The Prologue' in Trust's Tenth Anniversary Gala Concert Programme Elizabethan Theatre 29 September 1964.

5 Untitled verse 'drafted Heinz Arndt, polished by [A. D.] Trendall 1968', supplied by Professor Arndt.

6 Coombs to Sykes 16 November 1983 NLA 87/7.

7 FAT

8 Coombs to Herbert 21 January 1974 NLA 86/2.

9 Coombs to Murdoch 7 August 1964 RBA GHC-67-19.

10 Dated 1 May 1937, RBA P-C-1.

11 Rusden, 17.

12 H. C. Coombs 'The University in contemporary society' Address given at the graduation ceremony of the University of Western Australia, April 1960, Collected Speeches, vol. 2, p. 288.

13 Coombs to Toner 9 June 1992 NLA 87/7.

14 Kelly (1994, 661).

15 J. Waterford 'The man who signed the notes' *Eureka Street* 5(4) May 1995, pp. 26, 27, 30.

16 *The Australian* 14–15 September 1996.

17 'Speech by HCC in accepting the Arts Award of the Henry Lawson Festival at Grenfell 12 June 1971' NLA 23/184.

18 FAT.

19 *ANU Convocation News* 28 May 1976, p. 4A.

20 Speech to University of Sydney Conferring of Degrees ceremony 27 March 1969 NLA 44/372

21 Coombs to Partridge 16 November 1970 NLA 23/180.

22 The correspondence is to be found in NLA 3/26 and 3/27.

CHILDHOOD AND YOUTH

1 Autobiographical notes by H. C. Coombs (in author's possession, courtesy of Cecily Osborne).

2 Bolton (1972, 22).

3 Glynn (1975, 60–1, 69).

4 *Eastern Districts Chronicle* Friday 25 October 1918.

5 Most of the information in this paragraph comes from Coombs himself (conversation with author, 2 September 1995), but the dates are given in the Battye Library's biographical register.

6 Rusden, 5.

7 FAT.

8 Coombs.

9 Zunini (1997, 67).

10 Hatt.

11 Rusden, 6–7.

12 Wilson

13 FAT.

14 Hatt.

15 Gaines (nd, 14).

16 Zunini (1997, 171).

17 Rusden, 13; Coombs to Myers 12 December 1974 NLA 32/266.

18 Hatt.

19 Wilson.

20 Rusden, 15.

21 Gaines (nd, 18).

22 WASA Education Department file AN 45/5 2451/30.

23 FAT.

24 Wilson.
25 FAT.
26 FAT.
27 Rusden, 24.
28 Rusden, 25, 22.
29 Coombs.

SCHOOLING

1 Cutting in RBA GHC-67-8.
2 FAT.
3 Coombs to Dooling 6 May 1954 RBA GHC-67-23.
4 FAT.
5 W. N. Roberts' reference, 3 September 1921 WASA AN 45/5 2451/30.
6 Errington (1995, 6).
7 Watts (1982, 301).
8 Honner.
9 Watts (1979, 188).
10 Hatt.
11 WASA AN 45/5 2451/30.
12 Anon. (1921, 8).
13 From Coombs' student record, Perth Modern School. Thanks to Eric Alcock, Headmaster, and Elizabeth Green for helping me to consult these records in September 1995.
14 Kessel (1995, 12).
15 Honner.
16 *The Sphinx* December 1922.
17 *The Sphinx* May 1923.
18 *The Sphinx* August 1923.
19 Coombs.
20 Claremont Teachers College Student Register RS 00007/01/1, Edith Cowan University Archives.

SELF-POSSESSION

1 *The Sphinx* May 1922.
2 *The Sphinx* August 1922.

BUSSELTON

1 WASA AN 45/BUS (Busselton Head Teacher's Journal), 8 September 1924.
2 Hunt (1958).
3 Hatt.

4 WASA AN 45/5 Item 247–24, Jeanes' reference dated 10 September 1924.

CLAREMONT

1 Lake (1982, 204).
2 Lake (1982, 205).
3 Rankin (1926, 98).
4 Rankin (1926, 107).
5 Mossenson (1972, 75, 82).
6 Rankin (1926, 91).
7 Lake (1982, 197).
8 Mossenson (1972, 97–101).
9 Mossenson (1955, 21).
10 Mossenson (1955, 23).
11 Mossenson (1955, 30).
12 Mossenson (1955, 22).
13 Claremont Teachers College, *Calendar 1926* p. 109.
14 Mossenson (1955, 22).
15 *WA Trainee* vol. xvii, no. 3.
16 *WA Trainee* vol. xviii, no. 2.
17 *WA Trainee* vol. xviii, no. 1.
18 *WA Trainee* vol. xvii, no. 1.
19 *WA Trainee* vol. xviii, no. 3, and Heron.
20 Honner.
21 Edith Cowan University Archives, File 89/1473 part 1 folio 43.
22 *WA Trainee* vol. xviii, no. 1.
23 Coombs (1981, 16).
24 Coombs.
25 Coombs (1981, 187).
26 WASA AN 45/5 247/24, Director of Education to Coombs 7 April 1927.
27 Coombs (1981, 188).
28 Edith Cowan University Archives, Student file for H. C. Coombs RS 00007/01/1.

WHEAT BELT DAYS

1 Heron.
2 Coombs (1981, 185).
3 Honner.
4 McKenzie (1982, 332).
5 H. C. Coombs 'Opening Address' to 13th Annual Arts Festival, Wangaratta, 27 March 1965, author's files.

6 Information on Katanning School from WASA AN 45/KAT 1203/408 Head Teacher's Yearbook.

7 *WA Teachers' Journal* 12 September 1927.

8 Coombs (1981, 188).

9 'Remarks made by Dr. H. C. Coombs on the occasion of the official opening of Chiron College, Birchgrove – Saturday, 1 September 1973' NLA 25/201. (It is not clear whether Coombs' actual remarks conformed to this draft speech.)

10 WASA AN 45/5 247/24, J. G. Calhoun and 16 others to Director of Education.

NIGHT STUDENT

1 Orr to Chief Inspector of Schools WASA AN 45/5 247/24.

2 La Nauze (1977, 62–4).

3 Harrod (1972, 399–400).

4 Coombs.

5 Snooks (1988, 575).

6 Alexander (1968, 295).

7 See Schedvin and Carr (1995).

8 Shann (1925, 82).

9 Shann (1925, 90).

10 Coombs to Alexander 27 July 1961 RBA GHC-67-7.

11 FAT.

12 Shann (1933, 33–4).

FINDING THE WORDS

1 Coombs (1981, 189).

2 L. G. Melville (3 March 1932) and E. Shann (nd) examiners' reports, microfilm student file 2373, UWA.

3 *The WA Trainee* vol. xvii, no. 3, December 1926.

4 *The WA Trainee* vol. xvii, no. 2, August 1926.

5 *The WA Trainee* vol. xvii, no. 1, May 1926.

6 *The WA Trainee* vol. xviii, no. 2, August 1926.

7 *The Pelican* 22 April 1931.

8 *The Pelican* 13 August 1931.

9 *The Pelican* 13 August 1931.

REPRESENTING

1 Coombs.

2 Shann to Coombs 10 April 1931 Shann Papers Box 4.

3 *The Pelican* 5 September 1930.

4 *The Pelican* 5 September 1930.

5 *The Pelican* 26 June 1931.

6 *The Pelican* 27 March 1931.

7 University of Western Australia Senate Minutes, 13 March 1931, UWA.

8 *The Pelican* 22 May 1931.

9 Convocation Minute Book, UWA.

10 *The Pelican* 22 May 1931.

11 University of Western Australia Senate Minutes 20 April 1931, UWA.

12 University of Western Australia Senate Minutes 18 May 1931, UWA.

13 *West Australian* 16 June 1931.

14 *The Pelican* 26 June 1931.

15 *West Australian* 21 July 1931.

16 Bolton and Hirst (1990, 553).

17 *West Australian* 25 June 1931.

18 *West Australian* 26 June 1931.

19 In *West Australian* W. E. Thomas 26 June 1931; E. H. Barker 29 June 1931; W. Murdoch 4 July 1931.

20 In *West Australian* W. E. Thomas 26 June 1931, 'Old Modernian' 27 June 1931, E. H. Barker 29 June 1931.

21 *West Australian* 27 June 1931.

22 *West Australian* 7 July 1931.

23 *West Australian* 11 July 1931.

24 *West Australian* 17 July 1931.

25 *West Australian* 2 October 1931.

26 Sir Walter James' address reported verbatim *West Australian* 11 April 1931.

27 *West Australian* 10 April 1931.

28 *West Australian* 9 April 1931.

29 *The Pelican* 22 May 1931.

30 *The Pelican* 10 July 1931.

31 Shann to Clerk of records 22 October 1931, Coombs student file 2373, UWA Archives.

32 *West Australian* 16 July 1931.

33 *The Pelican* 10 July 1931.
34 *West Australian* 7 September 1931.
35 *West Australian* 7 September 1931.
36 Richards.
37 The text of the letter was reproduced in the *West Australian* 22 September 1931.
38 *Mirror* 26 and 27 September 1931.
39 Coombs to Alexander 27 July 1961 GHC-67-7.
40 This is Richards' version of the meeting. Guild records from the 1930s no longer exist.
41 *West Australian* 17 November 1931.

MURDOCH

1 Dale (1997, 58, 88).
2 The interview transcript is among the Oral History files, OH2, UWA.
3 Murdoch (1938, 32–3).
4 Triebel (1969).
5 Murdoch (1938, 64–6).
6 Triebel (1969, 211–12).
7 Phillips (1969, 222).
8 W. Murdoch *West Australian* 4 July 1931.
9 *West Australian* 16 June 1931.
10 Macintyre (1998, 194).
11 Love (1984,133–40).
12 Waterson (1979, 509).
13 La Nauze (1977, 116–19).
14 La Nauze (1977, 117).

LSE STUDENT

1 Hatt.
2 La Nauze Papers, folder 366.
3 *People* 28 March 1951.
4 Coombs to Shann (nd, but Shann's reply dated 10 May 1932) Shann Papers Box 4.
5 Hasluck (1981, 127).
6 Paul Hasluck 'Old Modernians Abroad', *Old Modernian* La Nauze Papers Folder 76, NLA.
7 Hasluck (1981, 127).
8 Rusden, 138.
9 Rusden, 141.
10 Rusden, 141.

11 Coombs to Curtin 17 July 1937 NLA 3/19.
12 Coombs to Curtin 17 July 1937 NLA 3/19.
13 File 67/8 A 'Research Students Association' 1924–37, BLPES.
14 File 67/8 A 'Research Students Association' 1924–37, BLPES
15 'Laodicean' (1933, 5).
16 Harris (1977, 263, 275, 281).

POLITICS VERSUS ECONOMICS

1 *People* 28 March 1951.
2 FAT.
3 Dahrendorf (1995, 224).
4 Kramnick and Sheerman (1993, 2).
5 Coombs.
6 FAT.
7 Ralph Araki letter 9/32, in file box labelled: 'LSE History 1930s: reminiscence, student life, occasions, etc General ethos' BLPES.
8 Coombs to Curtin 17 July 1937 NLA 3/19.
9 H. C. Coombs Speech at University of New South Wales Degree conferring ceremony 8 May 1974 AA M448/1 item 185.
10 Benham cited in Walker (1943, 59).
11 L. Robbins (1931, xi).
12 The signatories were J. M. Keynes, Alfred Pigou (Cambridge), Friedrich von Hayek, T. E. Gregory, Arnold Plant, and Lionel Robbins (LSE). Their subsequent letter furthered the argument by refuting their critics, Clarke (1988, 285).
13 Coombs to Shann nd, Shann Papers Box 4.
14 Coombs (1981, 43).
15 Rusden, 128–9.
16 Pimlott (1985, 161).
17 Pimlott (1985, 162–3), Skidelsky (1975, 151).

THE MONEY POWER AND ITS CRITICS

1 Schedvin (1970, 217).

2 See Cain (1983).
3 See for example Wheatley (1988).
4 Love (1984, 129).
5 Schedvin (1970, 79).
6 Schedvin (1970, 331, 346).
7 Rusden, 359.
8 Coombs (1933a, 116).
9 Coombs (1933a, 183).
10 Coombs (1933a, 181).
11 Coombs (1933a, 183).
12 Plumptre (1938, 193).
13 *West Australian* 12 June 1931. The co-author was 'T.W.', possibly Coombs' fellow economics student Wilsmore.
14 H. C. Coombs and T.W. 'Age of Plenty' *West Australian* 12 June 1931, my emphasis.
15 Coombs (1933a, 174 my emphasis).

POOR BRITAIN

1 *People* 28 March 1951.
2 FAT.
3 Alexander (1994–5, 7–8).
4 Greenhalgh (1984, 16).
5 Rex (1976, 24–5).
6 Coombs (1934, 255).
7 Vincent (1991, 77–8).
8 Vincent (1991, 78).
9 Laski (1933, 17).
10 Laski (1933, 25).
11 Vincent (1991, 68).
12 Kingsford (1982, 151–2).
13 Kingsford (1982, 165).
14 Vincent (1991, 101–2).
15 'Laodicean' (1933, 5–6).
16 *Student Vanguard* vol. 1, no. 2 December 1932, Box labelled 'LSE History: Incidents pre 1939', BLPES.
17 *Morning Post* 2 March 1933, Box labelled 'LSE History: Incidents pre 1939', BLPES.
18 Coombs (1933b).

A VACANCY?

1 Whitfield to Registrar University of Tasmania 5 February 1934, Coombs file 2373, UWA.

2 Rusden, 147.
3 Rusden, 145.
4 *West Australian* 29 March 1935.
5 FAT; Whitfield testimonial 28 March 1935 NLA3/19.
6 *Convocation Minute Book* 24 October 1934, 1 November 1934, 21 August 1935 UWA.
7 'A Discussion on Employment' broadcast from 6WF, 1 August 1934, Shann Papers Box 4.
8 Melville's report on Coombs' MA thesis, Coombs student file 2373 UWA.
9 FAT.
10 Kisch to Coombs 14 November 1934 NLA 3/19.
11 Melville to Shann 18 February 1935, RBA GGM-35-2.
12 Reading to Love 14 June 1935, RBA E-PR 68-33.
13 Love to Reading 28 June 1935 RBA E-PR 68-33.
14 Alexander to Casey 27 June 1935 RBA E-PR 68-33.
15 Coatman to Whitfield 27 December 1935, Coombs student file 2373 UWA.
16 FAT.
17 Deacon (1977, 4).
18 Parker (1990, 54–6).

THE ECONOMISTS

1 Butlin (1987, 1, 3).
2 Perlman (1977, 219).
3 Downing (1960, 47).
4 Garland (1960, 215).
5 Firth (1960, 211).
6 Cornish (2001).
7 Schedvin (1988, 338).
8 Schedvin (1988, 347).
9 Cited in Harper (1986, 41).
10 Harper (1986, 43).
11 Cited in Goodwin (1974, 236).
12 Schedvin (1970, 252). For Copland's evaluation of the plan, twenty years later, see Copland (1951, 20–2).
13 Portus (1931, 134).
14 Cornish (1993, 9).

15 Gepp (1939, 165).
16 Gepp (1939, 169).
17 Gepp (1939, 174).
18 Staff regulations (nd) RBA.
19 Coombs to La Nauze 12 February
   1936 La Nauze Papers folder 212.
20 FAT.
21 Coombs to La Nauze 27 October 1939
   La Nauze Papers (1996 acquisition)
   folder 79.
22 Unedited remarks by Coombs at ANU
   Council's farewell dinner for Dr and
   Mrs Coombs, 13 May 1976 NLA
   30/254.
23 Coombs to La Nauze 12 February
   1936, La Nauze Papers folder 212.
24 Coombs to La Nauze 27 October 1939
   La Nauze Papers (1996 acquisition)
   folder 79.
25 Coombs to La Nauze 18 March 1936
   La Nauze Papers folder 212.
26 Coombs to La Nauze 22 June 1936
   La Nauze Papers folder 212.
27 Coombs to Alexander 17 July 1961
   GHC-67-7 RBA.
28 FAT.

FROM PEOPLE'S BANK TO
CENTRAL BANK

1 The Commissioners were: Justice
  Napier (Supreme Court of SA);
  J. P. Abbott, NSW grazier and MHR;
  J. B. Chifley (former Labor MP
  in the Scullin government);
  R. C. Mills (Professor of Economics,
  University of Sydney); E. V. Nixon
  (Melbourne accountant) and
  H. A. Pitt (Victorian Treasury
  official).
2 Giblin (1951, 213–14).
3 Cain (1988, 6–8).
4 Cain (1988, 8–9).
5 Giblin (1951, 219).
6 Butlin (1937, 43).
7 Commonwealth of Australia (1937,
  204).
8 Commonwealth of Australia (1937,
  228–9).

9 Fisher (1937).
10 Copland (1939, 34).
11 Hytten (1939).
12 Giblin (1951, 228).
13 Coombs (1931, 20).
14 Coombs (1931, 58).
15 Coombs (1931, 67–8).
16 Coombs (1931, 89).
17 Coombs (1931, 116).
18 Coombs (1931, 111).
19 Coombs (1931, 116).
20 The affinities between Davidson and
   Shann are remarked by Schedvin
   (1988, 338).
21 Coombs (1931, 150).
22 Coombs (1931, 118–19).
23 Coombs (1933a, 214).
24 Coombs (1933a, 215–16).
25 Coombs (1933a, 284–5).

SWEDEN AND AUSTRALIA

1 H. C. Coombs 'Swedish Monetary
  Policy' paper presented to the
  Economic Society of Australia and
  New Zealand, 13 August 1937 (not
  published, RBA GHC-37-1); Coombs
  (1939); and H. C. Coombs 'Australia
  1928/1938' (not published, RBA
  GHC-39-1).
2 Coombs did not cite, but may have
  read, Thomas (1936) in which the
  notion of 'international margin' is
  prominent (see pp. 232–3).
3 'Swedish monetary policy'.
4 'Swedish monetary policy'.
5 'Swedish monetary policy'.
6 Coombs in discussion of G. L. Woods
  'The American Experiment' *Economic
  Record* (supplement) April 1939,
  p. 133.
7 Coombs (1939,148 my emphasis).
8 Brigden to Coombs 3 November 1937
  NLA 3/19.
9 Copland to Coombs 1 October 1937
  NLA 3/19.
10 H. C. Coombs 'Australia 1928/1938'
   (7 September 1939) RBA GHC-39-1,
   p. 10.

TRUSTING THE PEOPLE

1 Hasluck (1952, 452).
2 H. C. Coombs 'Banking System and War Finance' (December 1940) AA ACT CP184/5 Item 25/4.
3 Notes on F&E Committee meeting 25–26 April 1941 AA ACT CP 184/4/1 Bundle 1.
4 Menzies quoted in Butlin (1955, 473).
5 H. C. Coombs 'Labour Supply and Rationing' (February 1942) AA ACT M448/1 item 179.
6 Hasluck (1952, 115–16).
7 Coombs (1981, 15).
8 Coombs to G. A. Judkins 1 June 1942, Coombs to Archbishop of Melbourne 25 May 1942, and Coombs to Moderator Presbyterian Church 25 May 1942 AA ACT M448/1 item 175.
9 Rusden, 257.
10 Rusden, 179.
11 Hasluck (1952, 236, 237).
12 Gollan (1963, 222–3).
13 Hasluck (1952, appendix 6).
14 Spender (1942, 68).
15 Elkin to Curtin 17 December 1941, 14 January and 5 March 1942, AA ACT A1608/1 item AK29/1/2.
16 'Report of Committee on Civilian Morale made under direction of the Prime Minister' (presented 4 April 1942). The Committee was listed as consisting of K. Barry, C. E. W. Bean, I. Clunies Ross, S. Deamer, I. Hogbin, J. Stone and A. K. Stout, AA ACT 5954/1 item 328/21.
17 A. A. Conlon, Sydney Deamer (journalist), A. K. Stout, J. Stone, Ian Hogbin (academics), E. D. Roper (NSW SC judge), K. L. Barry (ABC), R. D. Wright, R. M. Crawford, W. E. H. Stanner (academics) made up this Committee's approved membership.
18 'Plan for a National Public Relations Service' (nd) AA ACT A 5954/1 item 328/21.
19 The fortunes of Conlon's proposal in Cabinet are reflected in correspondence in AA ACT A5954/1 item 328/21.
20 Transcript of address (19 June 1942) to Houswives Association of New South Wales, AA ACT M448/1 item 178.
21 'Clothes Rationing Survey' (nd) AA ACT M448/1 item 178.
22 H. C. Coombs 'The Economic Implications of Rationing' (nd) AA ACT M448/1 item 179.
23 TB draft, 56.
24 Transcript of address (19 June 1942) to the Housewives Association of New South Wales, AA ACT M448/1 item 178.
25 Transcript of address (19 June 1942) to the Housewives Association of NSW, AA ACT M448/1 item 178.
26 Watson (1979, 147).
27 Coombs (1981, 20).
28 Fitzpatrick to Coombs 21 November 1942, AA (Melbourne) MP5/42/0 T5/25.

RECONSTRUCTION AND FEMINISM

1 Hasluck (1952, 364).
2 PWR Reel 5, side 2, pp. 11–13.
3 Coombs to Chifley 22 October 1942 Crisp Papers Box V.
4 H. C. Coombs 'Seven million pairs of hands' 4 December 1942 AA ACT M448/1 item 101.
5 Firth to Coombs ('Notes on Coordination') 9 December 1942 Crisp Papers Box V.
6 Firth to Coombs 8 February 1943 and Tange to Coombs 10 February 1943 Crisp Papers, Box V.
7 Those attending the Hotel Canberra meeting on 19 December were: Major Conlon, Professors Julius Stone, A. K. Stout, R. D. Wright, Dr Keith Barry, Coombs, Lieutenant John Kerr, Sergeant Hook, Messrs J. V. Barry (KC), S. H. Deamer, Vance Palmer, Brian Fitzpatrick and someone named merely 'Dean'. See 'Notes of meeting held at Hotel Canberra, Canberra, on Saturday' in 'Anne Conlon folder 25' (unprocessed manuscript) National

Library of Australia. I am grateful to Michael Crozier for this reference.

8 Notes on speech by Giblin to NSW Branch of Economic Society of Australia and New Zealand 13 May 1939 on 'Trends in Population' RBA BM-43-1.

9 Lake (1999, 49).

10 Sekuless (1978, 117–19).

11 Radi (1990, 109), Lake (1995, 75).

12 See Lake (1996, 154–69).

13 Street to Fadden 12 September 1941 AA ACT CP43/1 item 43/170.

14 Anonymous file note AA ACT CP43/1 item 43/170.

15 Coombs to Street 11 November 1944, cited by Weatherburn (1990, 170).

16 Lake (1999, 71).

17 Lake (1999, 173).

18 Lake (1990, 22).

19 H. C. Coombs' 'Address to the Council for Women War Workers', Melbourne, 7 June 1944 AA ACT CP43/1/1/ item 43/1490.

20 'Address to the Council for Women War Workers', Melbourne, 7 June 1944 AA ACT CP43/1/1/ item 43/1490.

21 Coombs (1944b, 12–13).

22 Coombs (1944b, 14).

23 'Address to the Council for Women War Workers', Melbourne, 7 June 1944 AA ACT CP43/1/1/ item 43/1490.

24 Coombs to Parkes 17 November 1943, AA ACT M448/1 item 48.

FIGHTING FOR YES

1 Chifley (1941, 104).

2 Quoted in Bailey (1947, 102).

3 Coombs to Minister 30 March 1943 AA ACT M448/1 item 33.

4 'Plan of Public Relations' (nd) AA ACT M448/1 item 110.

5 'People and Planning' AA ACT CRS M448/1 item 237.

6 H. C. Coombs (1944, 77–8).

7 'Plan for Educational Campaign in relation to projected referendum appeal

for increased federal powers' AA ACT CP43/1/1 item 44/29.

8 'Report from Deputy Director – Melbourne' (nd) AA ACT M448/1 item 29.

9 Ross to Palethorpe 11 April 1944 AA ACT CP43/1 item 44/183.

10 PWR Reel 3, side 1, p. 32.

11 Coombs to Minister 23 May 1944 AA ACT CP43/1/1 item 44/29.

12 Radio script for broadcast 7 May 1944 AA ACT CP43/1 item 1944/434.

13 Shedden to Curtin 28 October 1944 ('The National War Effort and the Maintenance of Public Morale to Support It') AA ACT A5954/1 item 312/8.

14 Bland (1945, 53).

15 Coombs to Edwards 16 May 1944, AA ACT M448/1 item 40.

16 Ross to Coombs 14 November 1944, Lloyd Ross Papers Box 49, folder ii.

17 H. C. Coombs 'Opening address to Postwar Reconstruction Officers Conference' 15 December 1944 AA ACT CP73/3.

SOLDIERS AND WORKERS

1 Coombs to Ross 22 February 1945 AA ACT A9816/1 item 45/632.

2 Hagan (1981, 179).

3 Hagan (1981, 187).

4 TB draft, 98.

5 Coombs (1944c, 33–4).

6 L. F. Crisp 'Incentives and full employment' (7 June 1944) AA ACT CP43/1 item 1944/23.

7 L. Ross 'Trade unions and full employment' (nd) AA ACT CP43/1 item 1944/23.

8 G. G. Firth 'Price stability with high employment' 17 August 1944 AA ACT CP43/1 item 1943/23.

9 Anon. 'For the White Paper – Efficiency of Industry' 17 August 1944 AA ACT CP43/1 item 1944/23.

10 Department of Post-war Reconstruction White Paper Draft 'B'

(nd), AA ACT A9816/1 item 45/631, par. 178.

11 Department of Post-war Reconstruction White Paper Draft 'B' (nd), AA ACT A9816/1 item 45/631, par. 181.

12 Department of Post-war Reconstruction White Paper Draft 'B' (nd), AA ACT A9816/1 item 45/631, pars 198-9.

13 B. W. Hartnell to Coombs 19 January 1945, and to Coombs 9 February 1945, AA ACT A9816/1 item 45/632.

14 L. F. Crisp and others 'Policy Coordination – the case of the 1945 White paper' (nd) Crisp Papers Box V.

15 Crisp to Coombs 16 and 27 January 1945 AA ACT A9816/1 item 45/632.

16 Commonwealth of Australia *Full Employment in Australia* Parliamentary Paper no. 11, 1945, par. 178.

LABOR'S NEW INTERNATIONALISM

1 Crawford, Anderson and Morris (1968, 9–10).

2 Skidelsky (2000, 133).

3 'War Cabinet Submission by H. V. Evatt and J. B. Chifley, Agendum 88/1942, 10 February 1942' DAFP 5, 324.

4 Anon. 'The Future of International Trade: Dominion Office Circulars Nos 259 & 261' AA ACT CP 184/7 item B1/25.

5 Walker (1947, 172).

6 L. F. Giblin 'F&E 36k: Mutual Aid Article VII' AA ACT CP 184/7/1 item B1-25.

7 Report by the Interdepartmental Committee on External Relations 18 August 1942 DAFP 6/26.

8 L. F. Giblin 'Draft Report on Australia's position in relation to Article VII (revised 27.7.42)' AA ACT CP 184/7/1 B1–25.

9 Notes on F&E Committee meeting 5 September 1942 AA ACT CP 184/4/1 Bundle 1.

10 H. C. Coombs 'Notes on Article Seven' 5 October 1942 (F&E 36am) Crisp Papers Box V (file labelled 'San Francisco Conference').

11 These precedents are discussed by Turnell (1999). See Hudson (1980) for more on the 'nutrition approach'.

THE DIPLOMACY OF SECURITY

1 Smith (1982).

2 Notes on F&E Committee meeting 21 January 1943 AA ACT CP 184/4/1 Bundle 1.

3 Coombs to Mills 30 March 1943, AA ACT M448/1 item 122.

4 Coombs to Chifley 10 May 1943 AA ACT M448/1 item 122.

5 Coombs to Chifley 19 April 1943 AA ACT M448/1 item 122.

6 Coombs to Chifley 23 April 1943 AA ACT M448/1 item 122.

7 'Notes on conversation with Mr. White of Treasury Department (July 12, 1943)' Crawford Papers NLA Box 1.

8 Butlin and Schedvin (1977, 647).

9 Coombs to Evatt 14 May 1943 AA ACT M448/1 item 125.

10 Coombs interviewed by Sean Turnell 3 February 1993.

11 Coombs.

12 Coombs to Chifley 24 May 1943 AA ACT M448/1 item 122.

13 John Burton pers comm.

14 Coombs to Evatt 1 June 1943 AA ACT M448/1 item 125.

15 Coombs to Evatt 1 June 1943 AA ACT M448/1 item 125.

16 Butlin and Schedvin (1977, 649).

17 Coombs' interview with Sean Turnell 3 February 1992.

18 McDougall to Bruce 23 June 1943, DAFP 6/228.

19 Arne (1945, 21).

20 Notes on F&E Committee meeting 11 September 1943 AA ACT CP 184/4/1 Bundle 1.

21 'International aspects of reconstruction' (address by Dr H. C. Coombs to the

Economic Society of Australia and New Zealand, Sydney 15 October 1943) AA ACT M448/1 item 130.

SUCCESS IN LONDON

1 Gardner (1970, ch. 6).
2 'Proposals by the Department of State, U.S.A., developed by a technical staff within the Government of the United States in preparation of an International Conference on Trade and Employment and presented for consideration by the Peoples of the World', extract in Crawford, Anderson and Morris (1968, 51–2).
3 Cabinet submission by Keane, Scully and Dedman 11 January 1946 DAFP 9, 22.
4 PWR Reel 7, side 2, p. 13.
5 Report by Melville 26 April 1946 DAFP 9, 212.
6 Memorandum by J. B. Brigden 8 April 1946 DAFP 9, 176.
7 Capling (2001, 26).
8 The inter-departmental correspondence leading to the formation of this committee is to be found on AA ACT A9790/1 items 4112 and 4151.
9 Fletcher to Coombs 4 February 1946 AA ACT A9790/1 item 4151, part 1.
10 'Note by Coombs of Discussion with United Kingdom Treasury Officials' 1 May 1946 DAFP 9, 225.
11 Report on Permanent Heads Committee 24 May 1946 AA ACT M448/1 item 11.
12 The other eleven: E. W. McCarthy and G. W. Smith (Commerce and Agriculture), C. F. Morton, J. Fletcher and G. A. Rattigan (Trade and Customs), L. H. E. Bury (External Affairs), J. G. Phillips (Commonwealth Bank and Treasury), B. W. Hartnell and C. L. Hewitt (Post-war Reconstruction).
13 'Speech by Dr. Coombs on 17/10/46' AA ACT M448/1 item 306.
14 Brown (1950, 95).
15 Coombs to Dedman 26 October 1946 A9790/1 item 4151, part 3.
16 Brown (1950, 96).
17 Coombs to Dedman 26 October 1946, A9790/1 item 4151, part 3.
18 See Capling (2001, 22–7) for a more detailed account of the London talks.

GLOBAL TEMPTATIONS

1 Copland to Dunk, Chifley and Evatt 2 July 1946 DAFP 10/7; *Annual Report of the Commonwealth Bank*, released 30 June 1946.
2 Crisp (1961, 205).
3 Report by Melville 26 April 1946, DAFP 9/212.
4 H. C. Coombs 'The Work of the Preparatory Commission' Royal Institute of International Affairs, London 2 December 1946 AA ACT M448/1 item 306.
5 Cabinet Submission by Chifley (Agendum 669E) 14 November 1946 DAFP 10/215.
6 Strahan to Chifley 20 November 1946 DAFP 10/230.
7 J. B. Chifley Address to Federal Executive of ALP, Canberra, 26 November 1946 AA ACT M448/1 item 120.
8 Coombs to Myrdal 8 November 1946 AA ACT M448/1 item 304.
9 Coombs to Chifley 15 January 1947 AA ACT M448/1 item 304.
10 'Notes on discussion on 28th November, 1946, with Gunnar Myrdal, Swedish Minister for Trade' AA ACT M448/1 item 304.
11 Crisp (1961, 209–10).
12 TB draft, 210.
13 Chifley (1952, 146–7).
14 Crisp (1961, 211).
15 TB draft, 213.
16 Tange to Coombs 15 January 1947 DAFP 12/80.

17 Coombs to Chifley 13 March 1947 AA
ACT M448/1 item 14.

18 Coombs to Crawford 26 August 1947
AA ACT M448/1 item 14.

19 Coombs to Owen 29 May 1947 AA
ACT M448/1 item 14.

20 Phillips to Tange 13 November 1944
AA (ACT) CP 43/1/1 Bundle
51/1944/621.

GENEVA

1 Addison to Australian Government
19 February 1947 DAFP 12/85.

2 Coombs to Chifley 11 February 1947
DAFP 12/83.

3 TB draft, 267–8.

4 Coombs' speech 10 April 1947 AA
ACT M448/1 item 14.

5 Coombs to Chifley and Dedman 25
March 1947 DAFP 12/90.

6 Capling (2001, 29).

7 Wilson to Coombs 3 April 1947 DAFP
12/92.

8 Coombs to Cabinet Sub-
Committee on Trade and
Employment Conference 3 April 1947
DAFP 12/93.

9 See Addison to Australian Government
3 April 1947 DAFP 12/94.

10 Coombs to Cabinet Sub-Committee
21 April 1947 DAFP 12/97.

11 Tange to Burton 18 May 1947 DAFP
12/103.0

12 Australian delegation to Cabinet Sub-
Committee 14 May 1947 DAFP
12/102.

13 Wheeler to McFarlane 3 June 1947
DAFP 12/108.

14 Coombs to Chifley 29 May 1947
DAFP 12/106.

15 Chifley to Dedman 22 July 1947
DAFP 12/124; Australian Delegation
to Cabinet Sub-Committee 3 August
1947 DAFP 12/127.

16 Australian delegation to Cabinet Sub-
Committee 5 October 1947 DAFP
12/139. For Capling's assessment see
(2001, 30).

HAVANA

1 'Minute by J. J. Dedman 1/12/47' AA
ACT CP 855/2/1 Bundle 1.

2 'Speech by Dr. H. C. Coombs to
Committee II on 2/12/47' AA ACT
CP 855/2/1 Bundle 1.

3 Cable W4 from Havana 15 December
1947 AA ACT CRS A9790/1 item
4151, part 7.

4 Australian concerns over Article 24(2)
and about the composition of the ITO
Executive can be followed through the
inward and outward cables of the
Havana Delegation on AA ACT CRS
A1068/7 ER47/1/18a and ER47/1/33.

5 Coombs to Brown 16 January 1948 AA
ACT CRS A9790/1 item 4151 part 7;
see Brown (1950, 152–3).

6 Coombs to Brown 16 January 1948 AA
CRS A9790/1 item 4151 part 7.

7 Coombs to Dedman 4 May 1948
Dedman Papers Box 13.

8 Diebold (1952, 36).

9 TB draft, 295.

AN OFFICIAL COMMUNITY

1 Ikenberry (1989).

2 TB draft, 172.

3 Miller (1947, 39).

4 Lang: *Century*, 4 August 1950; Holder
(1951, 31–2).

5 Coombs to Chifley letter (extracts)
7 June 1943) DAFP 6/215.

6 Copland to Downing 26 October 1944
Downing Papers, University of
Melbourne Archives.

COOMBS THE KEYNESIAN

1 Coombs (1981, 148).

2 Bensusan-Butt (1980, 35).

3 Coombs (1970, 41–2).

4 Coombs (1981, 3).

5 J. La Nauze 'Economic theory and
economic practice' (1937) unpublished
typescript RBA GHC-50-1.

6 Coombs to La Nauze 22 June 1936
La Nauze Papers file 212.

7 Coombs to La Nauze (nd) La Nauze Papers file 212.

8 Coombs to La Nauze 9 September [1936?] La Nauze Papers file 212.

9 Friedman (1956). I would like to thank Sean Turnell, Michael White and Roy Weintraub for helping me to place this line of thought within the history of economic theory.

10 Coombs to La Nauze 9 September [1936?] La Nauze Papers folder 212.

11 Coombs (1937).

12 Coombs to La Nauze 20 September 1937 La Nauze Papers folder 212.

13 Coombs to La Nauze 9 June 1937 La Nauze Papers folder 212.

14 Coombs to La Nauze 4 June 1938 La Nauze Papers folder 212.

15 Cornish (1993, 19).

16 Keynes (1940, 4).

17 Keynes (1940, iii–iv).

18 Butlin, Critchley, McMillan and Tange (1941, 10).

19 Butlin, Critchley, McMillan and Tange (1941, 71).

20 Butlin, Critchley, McMillan and Tange (1941, 122).

21 Keynes [1936] (1974, 349).

22 Harrod (1972, 721–2).

23 Coombs, Rusden, 134.

24 Coombs to Keynes 17 July 1943, UK Public Record Office T247/84 15587. My thanks to Sean Turnell for a copy of this document.

25 Keynes to Coombs 3 September 1943 AA ACT CP 43/1 item 43/1324 part 1.

26 For references to Keynes see Kahn (1974, 379, 387–8).

27 Keynes to S. G. Macfarlane 5 June 1945, *Collected Papers of J. M. Keynes* vol. 27, p. 385.

CHIFLEY'S 'FAMILY'

1 Coombs.

2 Coombs to Mills 30 March 1943 AA ACT M448/1 item 46.

3 Coombs to Chifley 7/2/49 AA ACT M448/1 item 244.

4 Scarrow (1957, 37).

5 Scarrow (1957, 38–9).

6 Scarrow (1957, 108–9).

7 Scarrow (1957, 104).

8 Scarrow (1957, 111).

9 Crisp (1970, 207–8).

10 TB draft, 84.

11 Scarrow (1957, 116–17).

12 Crisp (1972, 302).

13 PWR Reel 10, side 1, p. 5.

14 PWR Reel 10, side 1, p. 6.

15 H. C. Coombs 'Opening address to Postwar Reconstruction Officers' conference Canberra, 15 December 1944' AA ACT CP73/3.

16 Crisp (1969, 138).

17 PWR Reel 3, side 2, p. 37.

18 Swan to Coombs 14 July 1948 AA ACT M448/1 item 50.

19 Coombs to McDougall 8 February 1944 AA ACT M448/1 item 46.

20 Coombs to Mighell 26 August 1947 AA ACT M448/1 item 50.

21 TB draft, 74.

22 Swan to Coombs 7 May 1947 AA ACT M448/1 item 50.

23 Coombs to Hall 27 August 1947 AA ACT M448/1 item 50.

24 Swan to Coombs 13 March 1948 AA ACT M448/1 item 50.

25 Coombs to Firth 28 April 1948 AA ACT M448/1 item 43.

26 Coombs to Swan 29 June 1948 AA ACT M448/1 item 50.

27 Dunk (1974, 118).

28 Unpublished paper 'Economic Policy Coordination 1946–49' Crisp Papers Box 105 (subsequently published as ACT Regional Group (1955).

29 Copland to Downing 19 November 1944, Downing Papers, University of Melbourne Archives, 'Letters from Douglas'.

30 Diary of Eilean Giblin vol. 2, 19 July 1942, NLA MS 366

31 'YMCA cricket team during 1939–45 war' unpublished typescript, 14 October 1971 Crisp Papers Box V.

32 Rusden, 267–8.

33 Rusden, 272–3.
34 Curtin (1954).
35 Hasluck (1952, 477).
36 Coombs to Medley 23 March 1944 AA ACT M448/1 item 46.
37 Spaull (1998, 55).
38 FAT.
39 TB draft, 176.
40 Coombs (1981, 99).
41 McFarlane to Coombs 30 November 1948 RBA GHC-48-2.
42 Coombs to McFarlane 29 December 1948 RBA GHC-48-2.
43 Copland to Coombs 23 November 1948 RBA GHC-48-2.
44 TB draft, 338.
45 Coombs to Mills 29 September 1947 AA ACT M448/1 item 248.
46 TB draft, 338.
47 Giblin to Coombs 23 November 1948 RBA GHC-48-2.
48 Coombs to Giblin 3 December 1948 RBA GHC-48-2.

THE COMMANDING HEIGHTS?

1 Coombs to Chifley 1 September 1944 AA ACT M448/1 item 109.
2 'Committee of review – civil staffing of war-time activities' (Pinner Committee Report, 9 January 1946) AA ACT M448/1 item 105.
3 Crisp (1967, 32).
4 Dedman to Chifley 30 March 1949 AA ACT M448/1 item 104.
5 H. C. Coombs 'Address by Dr. Coombs to Post-War Reconstruction Officers Conference' Canberra 15–17 December 1944 AA ACT CP73/3.
6 *Full Employment in Australia* Parliamentary Paper no. 11 (Group H) 1945, par 127.
7 Firth to Brown 20 June 1945 AA ACT CP43/1/1 item 45/275.
8 Butlin and Schedvin (1977, 711, 741).
9 ACT Regional Study Group (1955, 203).
10 Wheeler to Dedman 17 August 1949 DAFP 14/49 sets out how Australia has been better off as a member of the sterling area.
11 H. C. Coombs 'Notes on Prime Minister's visit to London as reported by Mr. Wheeler' 28 July 1948 AA ACT AA 9790 item 533/i.
12 Lee (1990, 184).
13 Coombs to Chifley 7 May 1948 DAFP 14/17.
14 Meeting of Interdepartmental Dollar Policy Committee 31 August 1948 DAFP 14/24.
15 Coombs 'Notes on first discussion of long-term programme' London 22 September 1948 DAFP 14/28.
16 Coombs (1948, 42).
17 Chifley to McFarlane 7 October 1949 DAFP 14/54.
18 Lee (1990, 192).

THE COLD WAR AND CSIRO

1 Schedvin (1982/3, 80).
2 Rivett (1947).
3 Coombs to Dedman 5 June 1946 AA ACT M448/1 item 263.
4 Rivett (1972, 2).
5 Cawte (1992, ch. 1).
6 Wright to Coombs 12 May 1947 AA ACT M448/1 item 257.
7 Rivett et al. to Dedman 'CSIR in relation to co-operation with defence service departments and with respect to classified information' 17 June 1948 Dedman Papers Series 6.
8 TB draft, 610.
9 Coombs to Dedman 29 July 1948 Dedman Papers Series 6.
10 Rivett (1972, 204).
11 Coombs to Breen 6 August 1948 AA ACT M448/1 item 241.
12 Coombs to Oliphant 10 August 1948 AA ACT M448/1 item 241.
13 Ungar (1992, 75).
14 Ungar (1992, 71).
15 Coombs to Chifley 11 August 1948 Dedman Papers Series 6.
16 Chifley to Coombs 25 August 1948 Dedman Papers Series 6.

17 Rivett to Dedman 17 August 1948 Dedman Papers Series 6.

18 Oliphant to Coombs 22 August 1948 AA ACT M448/1 item 241.

19 Correspondence between Coombs and Havelock, Landsborough-Thomson on AA ACT M448/1 item 137. See Dunk to Coombs 29 September 1948 AA ACT M448/1 item 241, for Chifley's response to Coombs' suggested meetings with scientists.

20 Dunk to Coombs 29 September 1948 AA ACT M448/1 item 241.

21 Coombs to Dedman 25 October 1948 AA ACT M448/1 item 241.

22 Coombs to Oliphant 27 September 1948 AA ACT M448/1 item 241.

23 Coombs to Dedman [nd] AA ACT M448/1 item 137.

24 Rivett to Chifley 1 September 1948, Rivett to Dedman 25 October 1948, Dedman Papers Series 6.

25 Notes by G. A. Cook on meeting held in Dedman's office 11 October 1948, Dedman Papers Series 6.

26 White (1975, 284).

27 Schedvin (1988, 400).

28 Tizard to Coombs 7 December 1948 RBA GHC-67-25.

VICE-CHANCELLOR?

1 The minutes and papers of this committee are in AA ACT A9816/3 item 43/1410 parts 1 and 2.

2 Memorandum by C. S. Daley 'Establishment of National University in Canberra' (nd, c. October 1944), AA ACT A9816/3 item 43/1410 part 1.

3 Coombs to Dedman 5 December 1944, AA ACT A9816/3 item 43/1410 part 2.

4 Coombs to Chifley 10 January 1945, AA ACT A9816/3 item 43/1410 part 2.

5 Minutes of inter-departmental committee 12 April 1945, AA ACT M448/1 item 248.

6 'Extract from the Report of the Interdepartmental committee on the University at Canberra' AA ACT A9816/3 item 46/139 (part 1).

7 Coombs (1981, 199).

8 Coombs (1981, 82).

9 Ellyard and Cockburn (1981, 145).

10 Coombs (1981, 83).

11 Minutes of 5 June 1946 meeting of Interdepartmental Committee on Education, AA ACT A9816/3 item 46/139 part 1.

12 Coombs to Florey 18 July 1946, AA ACT M448/1 item 257.

13 Minutes of the first meeting of the ANU Interim Council 13 September 1946 ANU Archives.

14 Minutes of the fifth meeting of the ANU Interim Council 10 January 1947 ANU Archives.

15 Coombs to Chifley 13 January 1947 AA ACT M448/1 item 248.

16 Coombs (1981, 199–200).

17 M. Oliphant 8 February 1947 'Comments on the foundation of a National University in Canberra, with particular reference to the proposed School of Physical Sciences' AA ACT M448/1 item 248.

18 R. D. Wright 'A sketch plan for the establishment of the Australian National University' AA ACT M448/1 item 257.

19 Oliphant to Coombs 16 April 1947 AA ACT M448/1 item 248.

20 Hancock to Coombs 31 March 1947 AA ACT M448/1 item 257.

21 Hancock to Coombs 21 April 1947, AA ACT M448/1 item 257.

22 Memorandum from W. K. Hancock to Interim Council 16 July 1947 AA ACT M448/1 item 260.

23 Minutes of twelfth meeting of ANU Interim Council 8 August 1947 ANU Archives.

24 Wright to Coombs 12 August 1947 AA ACT M448/1 item 248.

25 Oliphant to Coombs 16 April 1947 AA ACT M448/1 item 248.

26 Coombs to Oliphant 1 May 1947 AA ACT M448/1 item 248.

27 Oliphant to Coombs 6 May 1947 AA ACT M448/1 item 257.

28 Wright to Coombs 12 May 1947 AA ACT M448/1 item 248.

29 Mills to Coombs 30 May 1947 AA ACT M448/1 item 248.

30 Coombs to Mills 29 May 1947 AA ACT M448/1 item 248.

31 See Wright to Coombs 12 August 1947 AA ACT M448/1 item 248 for further entreaties to Coombs to become Vice-Chancellor; and Coombs' reply to Wright 26 August 1947 AA ACT M448/1 item 257.

32 Coombs to Wright 29 September 1947 AA ACT M448/1 item 257.

RECONSTRUCTING PAPUA NEW GUINEA

1 Coombs to Chifley 16 October 1944 AA ACT M448/1 item 40.

2 Cited by Thompson (1964, 108–9).

3 I draw here on Griffin, Nelson and Firth (1979, ch. 8).

4 Conlon to Coombs 6 May 1947 AA ACT M448/1 item 248.

5 Coombs to Mills 29 May 1947 AA ACT M448/1 item 248. Wright to Coombs 18 July 1947 AA ACT M448/1 item 257 refers to Conlon's continuing activism on this issue.

6 Jinks (1983).

7 Quoted in Wright (1999, 162).

8 Minutes of second meeting of Interim Council 18 October 1946 ANU Archives.

9 Minutes of the fifth (10 January 1947) and seventh (14 March 1947) meetings of the Interim Council ANU Archives.

10 Conlon to Coombs 6 May 1947 AA M448/1 item 248.

GOVERNOR AND FATHER

1 Coombs to La Nauze 15 December 1948 RBA GHC-48-2.

2 Coombs to Adams 29 December 1948 RBA GHC-48-2. See also Coombs to Armstrong 29 November 1948, same file.

3 Butlin to Coombs (nd) RBA GHC-48-2.

4 Giblin to Coombs 23 November 1948 RBA GHC-48-2.

5 Coombs to Honner 16 December 1948 RBA GHC-48-2.

6 Coombs to Dart 16 December 1948 RBA GHC-48-2.

7 Coombs to Lewis 29 December 1948 RBA GHC-48-4.

8 Coombs to Johnston 16 December 1948 RBA GHC-48-2.

9 Rankin (1926, 115).

10 FAT.

11 FAT.

12 FAT.

13 O'Farrell (1985, 377).

14 O'Farrell (1985, 378).

15 Lake (1995).

16 Fitzpatrick (1961, 108–10).

17 O'Farrell (1985, 394).

18 FAT.

19 *ANU Convocation News* 28 May 1976, p. 4A.

20 FAT.

21 *West Australian* 14 June 1963.

CHIFLEY'S MAN?

1 Bury to Coombs 24 November 1948 RBA GHC-48-2.

2 Crowther to Coombs 17 December 1948 RBA GHC-48-2.

3 Swan to Coombs 17 December 1948 RBA GHC-48-2.

4 *Herald* (Melbourne) 30 November 1948, *Sydney Morning Herald* 27 November 1948.

5 TB draft, 338.

6 TB draft, 340.

7 La Nauze to Coombs 22 November 1948 RBA GHC-48-2.

8 Sheridan (1989, 273).

9 Sheridan (1989, 291–2).

10 Coombs (1981, 130).

11 Coombs (1981, 130–1).

MENZIES' MAN?

1 Giblin (1951, 340–1).
2 Coombs to Chifley 6 October 1944 (file reference lost).
3 TB draft, 306.
4 TB draft, 345.
5 TB draft, 316.
6 TB draft, 321.
7 Coombs (1981, 117).
8 Coombs (1981, 119).
9 TB draft, 329–36.
10 'Address to a meeting of managers at Head Office, Sydney, 22/11/49' RBA GHC-49-2.
11 CPD-R 28 March 1950, p. 1239.
12 CPD-R 28 March 1950, p. 1236.
13 CPD-R 28 March 1950, p. 1245.
14 Martin (1995, 24).
15 TB draft, 316–17.
16 Rusden, 332.

CORPORATE ELIZABETHAN

1 H. C. Coombs Address to the Rotary Club Sydney Tuesday 27 April 1954 AA ACT M448/1 item 266.
2 AA ACT A571/130 item 44/1171 part 1, undated file note.
3 See AA ACT A460001/8 item AK344/1/12 part 1.
4 Herlinger (1988).
5 Brisbane (1988, 40).
6 Cargher (1977, 217).
7 Cargher (1977, 21–3).
8 CPD-R 22 September 1944, pp. 1324–5.
9 Coombs to Secretary Prime Minister's Dept 6 November 1944 AA ACT CRS A9790/1 item 8141 part 1.
10 Coombs to Chifley 23 November 1944 AA ACT A9790/1 item 8141 part 1.
11 Ross to Coombs 28 February 1945 Ross Papers Box 49 'Memos to Dr. Coombs and Cabinet submissions ii'.
12 Coombs to Chifley AA ACT A461/8 item AK344/1/12 part 1.

13 Shaw to Chifley 1 November 1946, Chifley to Shaw 19 December 1946, both in AA ACT A432/82 item 47/291.
14 AA ACT A432/82 item 47/291.
15 Chifley to Dedman 24 March 1948 AA ACT A432/82 item 47/291.
16 Coombs (cable) to Mills 30 June 1948 AA ACT A432/82 item 47/291.
17 Draft dated 8 August 1949 AA ACT A432/82 item 47/291.
18 Draft dated 8 August 1949 AA ACT A432/82 item 47/291.
19 Cabinet Agendum 1652 AA ACT A1361/1 item 5/20/1 part 2.
20 Coombs (1981, 222–3).
21 Address to the Rotary Club Sydney Tuesday 27 April 1954 AA ACT M448/1 item 266, and Coombs (1981, 237).
22 Coombs address to Rotary Club Sydney Tuesday 27 April 1954 AA ACT M448/1 item 266.
23 Coombs to Grimwade 15 April 1954 AA ACT M448/1 item 266.
24 Coombs to Macartney 10 April 1954 AA ACT M448/1 item 266.
25 Coombs to Alexander 15 April 1954 AA ACT M448/1 item 266.

INFLATION AND WAR

1 Coombs (1948, 42).
2 Coombs (1948, 48).
3 Full membership was: Menzies, chair; G. T. Chippindall (Director-General of Posts and Telegraphs) vice-chair; Coombs, Dunk (chairman of Public Service Board), Sir John Kemp (Coordinator of Public Works, Queensland), I. M. McLennan (General Manager, BHP), A. E. Monk (President of ACTU), Sir Frederick Shedden (Secretary, Department of Defence), A. S. V. Smith (Electricity Meter and Allied Industries Ltd), R. J. Vicars (Governing Director, John Vicars & Co. Ltd), R. C. Wilson (General Manager, Grazcos

Cooperative) and Roland Wilson
(Treasury).

4 Minutes of NSRB 18 December 1950
AA ACT A4940/1 C117.

5 Minutes of the first three meetings of
Board 18 December 1950, 8, 22
January 1951 on AA ACT A4940/1
C117.

6 Table PC 16-20, in Vamplew (1987,
213).

7 Table LAB 153–154, in Vamplew
(1987, 157).

8 As far as I know, Coombs never wrote
about the NSRB. His membership
obliged him to secrecy. I have relied
on Lee (1992), Lowe (1999, ch. 5),
and Mendelsohn (1958): 177–93.
Mendelsohn was also the author of
Defence and Development, 1950–1953
(nd, no place of publication).

WAGE-EARNERS' DEMOCRACY

1 Cabinet Agendum 992 (15/11/45)
AA ACT A9790/1 item 1434
part 1.

2 Sheridan (1989, 2, 44, 157–8).

3 Brown to Minister (Dedman) 22
October 1946 AA ACT A970/1 1434
part 3.

4 Scott (1950, 2), Clarey (1950, 29),
Laffer (1950, 44).

5 H. C. Coombs 'Forty hour week
evidence' AA ACT M448/1
item 9.

6 From an extract of his judgment
printed in Copland and Barback
(1957, 666).

7 Giblin (1945, 61).

8 Giblin to Coombs 10 May 1950 RBA
GHC-67-13. 'Crisis in Democracy'.
was published in Copland (1960,
94–8).

9 Copland (1960, 94).

10 Copland (1960, 95).

11 Copland (1960, 95–6).

12 Copland (1960, 98).

13 Coombs to Giblin 13 June 1950 RBA
GHC-17-13.

14 L. G. Melville 'Comment for Governor'
25 September 1950 RBA GHC-67-13.

HORROR BUDGET

1 Commonwealth Bank of Australia and
Commonwealth Savings Bank of
Australia *Report and Balance Sheets*
30 June 1949, p. 27.

2 Commonwealth Bank of Australia and
Commonwealth Savings Bank of
Australia *Report and Balance Sheets*
30 June 1950, pp. 20–2.

3 TB draft, 406–7.

4 Commonwealth Bank of Australia and
Commonwealth Savings Bank of
Australia *Report and Balance Sheets*
30 June 1951, p. 8.

5 Schedvin (1992, 169–71).

6 Schedvin (1992, 172). I have followed
Schedvin's account of the
Menzies–Fadden government's
response to inflation in the early 1950s
(1992, 167–202), and see Whitwell
(1986, 100–10).

7 Coombs to Wheeler and Swan
31/10/50 'A Direct Control – by
financial means' NLA 3/24.

8 Melville to Fadden 7 December 1950
(excerpt) in 'Memorandum for the
Advisory Council' Agenda and papers
of Advisory Council meeting
25 January 1951 AA ACT
AA1967/392 Box 5.

9 Wheeler to Secretary Treasury 26
February 1951 AA ACT A571 51/595.

10 Schedvin (1992, 186).

11 Coombs to Fadden 26 June 1951,
agenda papers for Commonwealth
Bank Advisory Board AA ACT
1967/392/1 Box 6.

12 Schedvin (1992, 187).

13 Schedvin (1992, 190).

14 Whitwell (1986, 106) says 'some
blamed Coombs', but I have not seen
evidence of that in Treasury's file of
newspaper cuttings.

15 *Sydney Morning Herald* 28 September
1951.

THE GOVERNOR MUTED

1 Firth to Coombs 25 November 1948 RBA GHC-48-2.
2 Firth to Coombs 26 November 1948 RBA GHC-48-2.
3 G. G. Firth 'Disinflation in Australia: a democratic dilemma' Section G of ANZAAS (Brisbane May 1951) Crisp Papers Box R.
4 Commonwealth Bank Advisory Council Minutes 29, 30 May 1950, RBA.
5 Commonwealth Bank Advisory Council Minutes 27, 28 July 1950, RBA. The draft *Report* was dated 25 July 1950.
6 Commonwealth Bank Advisory Council Minutes 24, 25 July 1951, RBA. The quotation is from p. 3 of the draft *Report*.
7 Anon. draft 'Note concerning the proposal that Sir Keith Hancock be invited to accept the Directorship of the Research School of Social Sciences' (nd) AA ACT M448/1 item 249. Other correspondence on this file establishes that this document came from Melville's office, if not from his own hand.
8 Hancock to Coombs 4 December 1948 RBA GHC-48-2.
9 Swan to Coombs 17 December 1948 RBA GHC-48-2.
10 Coombs to Hancock 31 December 1948 RBA GHC-48-2.
11 Coombs to Gandon (Bank of NSW, and other General Managers) 17 October 1952 AA ACT M448/1 item 258.
12 T. W. Swan 'The Australian National University "Australian Economic Reports": a proposal' papers for 16th meeting of Commonwealth Bank Board 15 December 1952 RBA BM-Pc.
13 T. W. Swan 'Australian Economic Reports: a proposal' 9 November 1952, paper for 16th meeting of Commonwealth Bank Board 15 December 1952 RBA BM-Pc.

14 D. B. Copland 'The Australian National University: review of business conditions in Australia' 27 November 1952, paper for 16th meeting of Commonwealth Bank Board 15 December 1952 RBA BM-Pc.
15 Hohnen to Coombs 12 December 1952, papers for 16th meeting of Commonwealth Bank Board 15 December 1952 RBA Bm-Pc.
16 'Memorandum for the Board: Economic Reports' 13 December 1952, papers for 16th meeting of Commonwealth Bank Board 15 December 1952 RBA BM-Pc.
17 Coombs to Melville 30 June 1953 RBA S-a-1916. Bank/ANU correspondence on this matter was included in the papers for 16th meeting of Commonwealth Bank Board 15 December 1952 RBA BM-Pc.
18 Coombs (1981, 178).
19 Coombs to Rowan 10 February 1961 RBA GHC-67-23.
20 By R. H. Scott, a research scholar in Swan's Department in the early 1950s, in conversation with author.
21 Coombs (1981, 178).
22 Coombs to Melville (telegram) 16 January 1956 AA ACT M448/1 item 259.

STERN MENTOR?

1 The first meeting of the newly legislated Board was on 20 and 21 September 1951.
2 Holder (1970, 891–2) and statement of the Bank's position 'Banking Legislation' (nd) RBA S-d-203.
3 The 'pillars' were then: J. W. Fletcher, Queensland grazier; G. H. Grimwade, Chair of Drug Houses of Australia; W. L. Sanderson, Managing Director of Elder Smith; and John Thomson, a prominent member of the Western Australian wheat industry.
4 TB draft, 364.
5 Merrett (1985, 131).

6 Coombs to Fadden 17 April 1950 RBA S-d-301.

7 'Discussion with the Treasurer', file note of 5 November 1956 RBA S-d-270.

8 *Age* 11 November 1957.

9 Transcript of discussion of 'Full employment in retrospect' 26 October 1953 RBA GHC-53-4.

10 Coombs to Fadden 27 August 1952, papers for 12th meeting of Commonwealth Bank Board 27 August 1952 RBA BM-Pc, my emphasis.

11 TB draft, 353–8, 362.

12 Coombs (1971, 24).

13 H. C. Coombs 'The role of the central bank in Australia' – Bankers' Institute of Australasia, Melbourne 29 November 1954 RBA GHC-54-7.

14 TB draft, 400.

15 Holder (1970, 891–2).

16 Levien to Coombs 16 July 1952, Coombs to Levien 29 July 1952, NLA 3/20.

17 H. C. Coombs 'Full employment in retrospect' address given to the Canberra Branch of the Economic Society 26 October 1953, RBA GHC-53-4, my emphasis.

18 Coombs' note on Pringle to Coombs 21 October 1954 RBA S-d-227.

19 Downing to Grant 5 September 1955 RBA GHC-54-5.

20 Coombs (1971, 22).

21 Melville to Coombs 27 March 1952 RBA S-a-1916.

22 Coombs file note 20 May 1955 RBA GHC-54-5.

23 *Sunday Telegraph* 19 September 1954 and 25 September 1955.

24 Coombs to Menzies 15 October, 4 November 1954 RBA S-d-227.

25 Coombs to Wilson 4 November 1954 RBA S-d-227.

26 Coombs to Menzies 4 November 1954 RBA S-d-227.

27 'Memorandum for the Governor: criticism of banking legislation' 27 October 1954 RBA S-d-227.

28 See Martin (1999, 302-5) for Menzies' difficult backbenchers in 1954 and 1955.

29 Menzies to Coombs 25 November 1954 RBA S-d-227.

30 Marshall cited by Davidson and Salsbury (nd) ch. 1.

COOMBS AS BOSS

1 Mobbs (1968, 254).

2 *Currency* August 1953.

3 D'Alpuget (1977, 136–7).

4 *Currency* vol. 1 no. 1, 1 June 1951. In fact the name *Currency* was first used in the third issue 1 August 1951.

CARROTS AND STICKS

1 Schedvin (1992, 215–17).

2 'Extract from memorandum headed "Banking legislation – special account provisions"' 8 March 1955 RBA S-d-269.

3 Board Minutes 27 and 28 July 1955 RBA Bm-Mb, my emphasis.

4 Coombs (1971, 37).

5 Coombs (1971, 37).

6 Arndt (1960, 201).

7 14 April 1955 file note RBA S-d-263.

8 Coombs to Fadden 28 April 1956 RBA S-d-270.

9 For the battle over interest rates, see Schedvin (1992, 230–9).

10 For example, Evatt CPD-R 7 November 1957, pp. 1989, 1994.

WOMEN AT THE BANK

1 H. C. Coombs 'Accountability, delegation and control in a statutory corporation – a survey of Commonwealth bank experience' address to Australian Administrative Staff College Mt Eliza 24 August 1958 RBA GHC-58-4. Coombs attributed this analogy to a former Governor of the Bank of England Montague Norman. He used it again in a March

1964 lecture in Karachi: Coombs (1971, 63).

2 *Currency* July 1952, article by W. H. Wilcock.

3 Wilcock in *Currency* June 1953.

4 E. Hanscombe 'Women's work in foreign banks' two-part article in *Currency* June and July 1958.

5 M. M. Beckhart 'Do women live too long?' *Currency* August 1957.

6 *Currency* September 1958.

7 See undated memoranda to J. G. Phillips re S. 71 RBA s-d-321.

8 Sawer (1996, 2–3).

9 File note on 'Employment of married women' (signature obscure) 8 August 1957 RBA S-d-341.

10 'Memorandum for Central Bank Advisory Committee: Staff – conditions of service' 1 February 1962 Attachments A and D, RBA S-d-321.

11 Chaired by L. T. Hinde with two representatives of the Bank (R. A. Knight and Miss Patricia Doughty) and two of the staff association (R. W. Davidson and Miss J. A. McCracken).

12 'Report of the committee on the basis of employment of women' RBA P-d-47.

13 I have drawn heavily on Mobbs (1968).

14 See Sawer (1996, documents 10–18).

A CULTURE OF INFLATION

1 H. C. Coombs 'Full employment in retrospect' address to Economic Society Canberra 26 October 1953 RBA GHC-53-4.

2 The Coombs–Swan exchange is recorded in a typed transcript of discussion on file RBA GHC-53-4.

3 H. C. Coombs 'Economic development and financial stability' ANZAAS address Melbourne August 1955 RBA GHC-55-2.

4 H. C. Coombs 'The role of the central bank in the economy' 8 November 1955 RBA GHC-55-3. The file contains notes towards a speech of that title, without information about where or whether it was delivered.

5 H. C. Coombs 'The present economic situation – a challenge to Australia' address to Australian Society of Accountants, Newcastle Branch 19 July 1956 RBA GHC-56-4.

6 Coombs (1971, 30).

7 Isaac (1977, 67).

8 Coombs (1971, 125).

9 Coombs (1971, 128).

10 Fitzpatrick to Coombs 22 January 1960 RBA GHC-59-7.

11 Geis (obscure) to Coombs 18 January 1960 RBA GHC-59-7.

12 L. H. E. Bury MP 'Discussion' in Australian Institute of Political Science *Australia, 1970 and beyond* Sydney: Angus and Robertson 1961, p. 23.

13 H. C. Coombs 'Monetary policy and the businessman' address to summer school of business administration University of Adelaide 17 February 1960, Collected Speeches, vol. 2.

SEPARATION

1 Schedvin (1992, 280–1).

2 *Hobart Mercury* 28 September 1956. See also *Bulletin* 20 February 1957, John Eddy in the Melbourne *Herald* 11 April 1957 and the *Mercury* again 11 April 1957 and 17 December 1958.

3 *Age* 6 September 1957.

4 Anon. 'The separation issue' 10 September 1956 RBA S-d-305.

5 On Treasury's view see Butlin (1983, 184).

6 Quoted in 'Press Reports: memorandum for the Board, December 1956 meeting' Commonwealth Bank Board Papers 1951–1959, 62nd meeting, 12 December 1956 RBA BM-Pc.

7 *Sydney Morning Herald* 6 February 1955.

8 *Sydney Morning Herald* 11 April 1957.

9 *Melbourne Sun News-Pictorial* 6 September 1957.

10 CPD-R 7 November 1957 pp. 1988–99.
11 CPD-R 10 March 1959 pp. 442–3.
12 By Bird CPD-R 14 November 1957, p. 2174; Bryant, same day p. 2189; Whitlam CPD-R 12 March 1959, p. 628; Cairns CPD-R 12 March 1959, p. 639.
13 Frank Crean asked for Coombs to be called before the House, CPD-R 12 November 1957, pp. 2065–6; Daly repeated this call, CPD-R 11 March 1959, pp. 517–18.
14 Schedvin (1992, 284).
15 Schedvin (1992, 290).
16 Butlin (1983, 190).
17 Butlin (1983, 189).
18 CPD-R 24 October 1957, p. 1766.
19 *Sydney Morning Herald* editorial 19 December 1958.
20 CPD-R 7 November 1957, p. 1988.
21 Coombs (1981, 140).

A MELANESIAN WAY?

1 Rowley (1965, 99, 188).
2 McAuley (1975, 163).
3 McAuley (1952, 501).
4 McAuley (1952, 502).
5 McAuley (1975, 172).
6 Coombs to Cleland 1 October 1953 RBA PNG-a-83.
7 Coombs to Hasluck 1 October 1953 RBA PNG-a-83.
8 Coombs (1971, 79).
9 J. R. Thomas and D. Ryan 'Report of a survey on the use of money and on the need for credit by the Indigenous people of Papua and New Guinea' RBA PNG-a-85 p. 88.
10 Coombs (1971, 79–80).
11 Hudson and Daven (1971, 159).
12 Hasluck (1962, 5).
13 'Address given by Dr. H. C. Coombs, Governor of the Reserve Bank of Australia, to the Royal Institute of Public Administration, Port Moresby on 29 August 1960' RBA PNG-a-91.
14 Coombs to Burton 12 September 1962 RBA GHC-67-8.

15 P. M. C. Hasluck, Ministerial statement on 'Land Tenure in Papua and New Guinea' CPD-R 7 April 1960, pp. 1019–1021.
16 H. C. Coombs 'Notes on New Guinea visit' 8 September 1960 RBA PNG-60-1.
17 G. Lewis 'Notes on visit to New Guinea'(nd) RBA PNG-60-1.
18 'Conference with banks represented in the Territories held at 2.30 pm on 15 September 1960' RBA PNG-a-39; Anon. 'Some impressions of the meeting with banks on Papua-New Guinea' 22 September 1960 RBA PNG-61-2.
19 'Report of the visit to Papua-New Guinea by Messrs Curtin, Phillips and Fleming from 21st November to 12th December, 1960', 16 January 1961 RBA PNG-a-84.
20 Reeve to Administrator 19 June 1961 RBA PNG-62-3.
21 Phillips and Ferguson (1969, 81).
22 TB draft, 468.

POOR MAN'S OVERDRAFT

1 Brown (1995, 101–11).
2 L. F. Giblin 'F&E 36k: Mutual Aid Article VII' (June 1942) AA ACT CP184/7/1 item B1-25.
3 Coombs (1971, 125).
4 Coombs (1971, 119).
5 H. C. Coombs 'Design in Australian Industry' opening address at the Symposium on Design in Australian Industry, University of New South Wales, December 1958, Collected Speeches, vol. 1 p. 180.
6 Runcie (1969, 20).
7 R. I. Downing 'Hire purchase in the Australian economy' (information paper for the Board, issued by Secretary's Dept 13 June 1958) RBA Bm-Pc.
8 H. C. Coombs 'Address to Council of Institute of Public Affairs 17 March 1964 at the Athenaeum Club' RBA GHC-64-3.

9 I. A. McGregor 'A few thoughts on hire purchase' *Banknotes* March 1949, pp. 35–7.

10 Commonwealth Bank Advisory Council Minutes of meeting on 30 and 31 March 1950 RBA Bm-Pc.

11 I draw in Fitzgerald (1988).

12 Memorandum for the Commonwealth Bank Board May 1955 meeting RBA BM-Pc. And see Runcie (1969, 14, 67–71, 122–5).

13 *Sunday Telegraph* 1 May 1955.

14 Commonwealth Bank Board Minutes 25, 26 October 1956 RBA Bm-Pc.

15 Menzies' Cabinet submission 'Economic Policy' 5 September 1955, RBA GHC-66-3.

16 Arndt and Harris (1965, 12–13).

17 *Sydney Morning Herald* 7 July 1957.

18 Commonwealth Bank Board Minutes 23, 24 September 1959 RBA BM-Pc.

19 *Age* 11 July 1958.

20 CPD-R 10 March 1959, p. 448.

21 CPD-R 12 March 1959, p. 631.

22 *Sun-Herald* 31 January 1960.

23 *Sydney Morning Herald* 14 January 1960.

24 Reserve Bank Board Minutes 26 October 1960 RBA BM-Pc.

25 Reserve Bank Board Minutes 19 June 1963 RBA BM-Pc.

26 Coombs (1971, 125).

27 H. C. Coombs 'Address to Council of Institute of Public Affairs 17 March 1964 at the Athenaeum Club' RBA GHC-64-3.

28 Coombs (1971, 64).

29 Coombs (1971, 73).

30 Fitzgerald (1988, 364).

31 'Address to Council of Institute of Public Affairs 17 March 1964 at the Athenaeum Club' RBA GHC-64-3.

FRUSTRATED INTERNATIONALIST

1 Balogh to Coombs 7 August 1959 RBA GHC-67-8.

2 H. C. Coombs 'The problems of external balance' address to Australian Administrative Staff College Mt Eliza 4 June 1961 RBA GHC-61-1.

3 H. C. Coombs 'Problems of monetary policy in underdeveloped countries' (1964) Collected Speeches, vol. 3, pp. 417–18.

4 Capling (2001, 85).

5 Coombs to Prebisch 23 December 1963 RBA GHC-67-22.

6 Prebisch to Coombs 11 February 1965 RBA GHC-67-22.

7 Coombs to Prebisch 1 March 1965 RBA GHC-67-22.

8 Wilson to Coombs 31 March 1965 RBA GHC-67-22.

9 H. C. Coombs 'Relationship of the Central Bank with the Government – Policy formulation and co-ordination of monetary and fiscal policies' Collected Speeches, vol. 3, p. 427.

10 Coombs to Holt 9 April 1965 RBA GHC-67-22.

11 Holt to Coombs 13 April 1965 GHC-67-22.

12 H. C. Coombs 'International Liquidity and its significance for world trade' Georgetown University, Washington, Bankers' Forum 2 October 1965 on 'Gold and the monetary unit' RBA GHC-65-8.

13 Coombs' speech in Venezuela ('Asamblea especial en el Banco Central de Venezuela el Viernes' 23 September 1966) is on NLA 7/39.

REASONABLE LIBERTY

1 Coombs (1971, 3).

2 Foster to Copland 1 April 1949 AA ACT M448/1 item 253.

3 Oliphant to Copland 19 December 1949 AA ACT M448/1 item 258.

4 Frank Fenner pers. comm.

5 Mackay to Coombs 12 May 1954 AA ACT M448/1 item 258, and Wright to Coombs 21 April 1954 AA ACT M48/1 item 258.

6 Foster and Varghese (1996, 117–18).

7 CPD-R 24 September 1953, p. 667.

8 CPD-R 24 September 1953, pp. 658–9.

9 CPD-R 1 October 1953 pp. 939–41.

10 CPD-R 3 November 1954 p. 2602.

11 The last few paragraphs are based on: Florey to Melville 19 May 1955, Oliphant to Melville 21 May 1955, Oliphant to Melville 23 May 1955, Melville to Florey 27 May 1955, AA ACT M448/1 item 249.

12 Melville to Florey 27 May 1955 AA ACT M448/1 item 249.

13 Melville (1955, x–xi).

14 Lewis (1969, 118–19).

15 Foster and Varghese (1996, 122–4).

16 Quoted in W. G. K. Duncan (1955, 10) my emphasis.

17 Martin (1985, 99–101).

18 CPD-R 28 August 1952, p. 725.

19 CPD-R 10 November 1954, p. 2847.

20 CPD-R 6 October 1955, p. 1393–4.

21 CPD-R 10 November 1954, p. 2849.

22 CPD-R 10 November 1954, pp. 2849–50.

23 Foster and Varghese (1996, 124–5).

24 H. C. Coombs 'Address – Visit Overseas – Senior Staff Commonwealth Bank – 18/6/53' RBA GHC-53-2.

25 H. C. Coombs 'Role of a regional university' Collected Speeches, vol. 1, pp. 13–14.

26 Florey to Melville 9 June 1955, Oliphant to Coombs 23 June 1955 AA ACT M448/1 item 259.

27 Coombs to Florey 23 June 1955 AA ACT M448/1 item 259.

28 Oliphant to Melville 17 August 1955 AA ACT M448/1 item 249.

29 Wright to Coombs 26 August 1955 AA ACT M448/1 item 249.

VISUALISING AUSTRALIA

1 Coombs (1992, 9–10).

2 Herman to Coombs 10 December 1960 RBA GHC-67-14.

3 Coombs to Gomez 21 January 1957 RBA GHC-67-20.

4 Adams (1987, 177–8).

5 Coombs to Easley 18 May 1965, Coombs to Nolan (telegram) 28 May 1965 RBA GHC-67-20.

6 Coombs to Nolan 17 May 1966 RBA GHC-67-20.

7 Drysdale to Coombs 14 August 1965 RBA GHC-67-10.

8 H. C. Coombs 'The Arts in Australia' (Address at Australian Citizenship Convention, 1966) Collected Speeches, vol. 3, p. 588.

9 Coombs (1992, 9–10).

10 Simpson to McPherson 29 July 1960 RBA S-a-2207.

11 Simpson to McPherson 15 August 1960 RBA S-a-2207.

12 Information from RBA S-a-2207.

13 A remark in an internal memo c. November 1960 RBA PF-P27.

14 Smith (1988, 195).

15 Coombs (1971, 3).

16 The other three signatories of the Manifesto were David Boyd, John Brack and Bernard Smith.

NUCLEAR MATTERS

1 M. Oliphant 'Comments on the foundation of a National University in Canberra, with particular reference to the proposed School of Physical Sciences' 8 February 1947 AA ACT M448/1 item 248.

2 Beale to Coombs 1 November 1954, Coombs to Beale 3 November 1954, RBA SAEC-a-9.

3 J. E. S. Stevens 'The functions, powers and charter of the Australian Atomic Energy Commission' address to first meeting of the Business Advisory Group Sydney 22 February 1955 RBA SAEC-a-2.

4 J. E. S. Stevens 'The functions …'.

5 J. P. Baxter 'The Research and Development Program' address to the first meeting of the Business Advisory Group 22 February 1955 Sydney, RBA SAEC-a-2.

6 J. P. Baxter 'The Research and …'.
7 Messel (1955, 13).
8 M. Oliphant 'Atomic energy for industry' *Voice* November 1955, p. 23.
9 Bank briefing papers, RBA SAEC-A-3.
10 'Large scale nuclear power' paper attached to Minutes of Commonwealth Bank Atomic Energy Committee 18 March 1957 RBA SAEC-A-12.
11 J. P. Baxter 'The development of an Australian atomic power industry' presented to Business Advisory Group in March 1957, RBA SAEC-a-4.
12 'The development of an Australian atomic power industry (comments on Professor Baxter's paper)' 16 March 1957, RBA SAEC-a-4.
13 C. N. Watson-Munro to Coombs 11 April 1957 RBA SAEC-a-4.
14 Minutes Commonwealth Bank Atomic Energy Committee 25 October 1957 RBA SAEC-A-12.
15 Minutes of Commonwealth Bank Atomic Energy Committee 23 January, 25 March 1958 RBA SAEC-a-12.
16 'Atomic power in Australia: some economic considerations' RBA SAEC-a-9.
17 Handwritten note on final page of 'Atomic power …' RBA SAEC-a-9.
18 *Currency* August 1958, p. 6.

OPERA

1 McKerihan to Coombs 9 February 1954 AA ACT A571/130 item 44/1171 part 2.
2 Coombs' statement to annual general meeting of Australian Elizabethan Theatre Trust in Sydney June 1964 AA ACT M448/1 item 282.
3 A. Gallagher 'Opera from Melbourne' *Voice* September 1953.
4 Proposed National Opera Project (evidently written by Moses, with amendments by Coombs, nd) AA ACT M448/1 item 266.
5 Coombs to Jones 5 August 1954, AA ACT M448/1 item 266. See also

Coombs to Horniblow 5 August 1954 and Coombs to Campbell 5 August 1954, on same file.
6 ABC news service item 5 October 1954 (copy) AA ACT M448/1 item 267.
7 Coombs to Tait 16 November 1954 AA ACT M448/1 item 267.
8 Gibson to Coombs 4 February 1955 Latham Papers series 72 folios 57–8.
9 Hunt to Coombs 22 November 1955 AA ACT M448/1 item 268.
10 Hunt to Knox 17 May 1955, Latham to Coombs 20 May, both on AA ACT M448/1 item 267; Knox to Latham 20 May 1955 (copy) Latham Papers series 72, folios 68–70.
11 Coombs to Bolte 17 June 1955 AA ACT M448/1 item 267.
12 Coombs to Roper 19 April 1955 AA ACT M448/1 item 267.
13 Coombs to Knox 5 August 1955 AA ACT M448/1 item 268.
14 Hunt to Coombs 13 September 1955 AA ACT M448/1 item 268.
15 Gibson to Coombs 6 March 1957 AA ACT M448/1 item 269.
16 Coombs to Menzies 11 February 1957 AA ACT M448/1 item 269.
17 Hunt to Gibson 28 March 1957 AA ACT M448/1 item 269.
18 Coombs to Gibson 6 October 1959 AA ACT M448/1 item 272.
19 Coombs to Knox 10 April 1957, Coombs to Knox 21 May 1957, AA ACT M448/1 item 269.
20 Alexander to Latham 15 July 1957 Latham Papers series 72 items 1234–6.
21 Hunt to Coombs 2 May 1957 AA ACT M448/1 item 269.
22 Coombs to Hunt 13 June 1957 AA ACT M448/1 item 269.
23 Moses to Bolte 19 October 1959 AA ACT M448/1 item 272.
24 Coombs (1954, 285).
25 Lampe's notes were dated 4 May 1960, AA ACT M448/1 item 273.
26 Cargher (1988, 70).
27 Coombs to Lampe 7 February 1963 AA ACT M448/1 item 276.

28 Coombs to Murdoch 1 February 1963 AA ACT M448/1 item 276.
29 Cargher (1988, 76).
30 Johnson to Whiteley 27 April 1964 AA ACT M448/1 item 278.
31 Johnson to Bolte 1 May 1964 AA ACT M448/1 item 278.
32 'Notes for chairman for discussion with Mr. Gibson' 10 April 1964 AA ACT M448/1 item 278.
33 Gibson to Coombs 4 May 1964 AA ACT M448/1 item 278.
34 Coombs to Menzies 21 October 1964 AA ACT M448/1 item 277.
35 Coombs to Menzies 18 November 1965 AA ACT M448/1 item 277.

BALLET

1 Coombs' speech when opening the Princess Theatre in Launceston 16 November 1970 NLA 28/232.
2 As relayed to me by Margaret Denton (née Scott) 16 November 2000.
3 Alan Brissenden 'Ballet in Australia needs vitality and assistance' *Voice* January 1956.
4 Coombs to Denton AA ACT M448/1 item 268.
5 Ingram to Coombs 12 January 1959 AA ACT M448/1 item 145, and Geoffrey Ingram (interviewed by Michelle Potter) NLA Oral TRC 2372, p. 53.
6 Coombs to Playford 6 November 1959 AA ACT M448/1 M448/1 item 272.
7 Coombs to Gibson 17 November 1959 AA ACT M448/1 item 272.
8 Gibson to Coombs 10 February 1960, Coombs to Gibson 16 February 1960, both in AA ACT M448/1 item 273.
9 Hutchison to (Margaret Scott) Denton 11 July 1960 AA ACT M448/1 item 145, and Hutchison to Coombs 7 April 1960 AA ACT M448/1 item 273.
10 Alexander to Hutchison 23 September 1960 AA ACT M448/1 item 273.
11 Information from Margaret Scott and Derek Denton 16 November 2000.
12 Hutchison to Coombs (enclosing Melbourne *Sun* cutting) 27 October 1960 AA ACT M448/1 item 273.
13 Coombs to Bolte 25 November 1960 AA ACT M448/1 item 273.
14 Coombs to Tait 5 January 1961 AA ACT M448/1 item 274.
15 Coombs to van Praagh (unsigned) 6 January 1961 AA ACT M448/1 item 145.
16 The van Praagh–Ingram paper is on AA ACT M448/1 items 145 and 274. Hutchison's costings dated 31 May 1961 are on AA ACT M448/1 item 274.
17 Coombs to Menzies 2 June 1961 AA ACT M448/1 item 274.
18 Coombs to Rogers 7 June 1961 AA ACT M448/1 item 274.
19 Menzies to Coombs 4 July 1961 AA ACT M448/1 item 274.
20 Coombs to Menzies 10 July 1961 AA ACT M448/1 item 274.
21 Coombs to van Praagh 15 September 1961 AA ACT M448/1 item 274.
22 Coombs to van Praagh 25 November 1961 AA ACT M448/1 item 274.
23 Sexton (1985, 136).
24 Van Praagh to Coombs 26 November 1963, Van Praagh to Coombs 13 December 1963, Coombs to King 8 January 1964, King to Coombs 10 January 1964, AA ACT M448/1 item 277.
25 H. C. Coombs 'The Arts in Australia' address to the Athenaeum Club Liverpool (UK) 22 September 1965 AA ACT M448/1 item 142.
26 Haag to Helpmann 30 October 1964 AA ACT M448/1 item 277.
27 Press Statement: Commonwealth Arts Festival in London – 1965 (date erased) AA ACT M448/1 item 277.
28 'Executive Director's report to members' Australian Elizabethan Theatre Trust *Annual Report and Financial Statements* December 1965.

IN SEARCH OF AN AUDIENCE

1 Macartney (1947, 93).
2 Rees (1953, 160–1).
3 Stewart (1956/1981, lv–lvii)
4 Cherry (1981, 111).
5 Alrene Sykes 'Lawler's Exciting Doll' *Voice* February 1956.
6 Kippax (1981, 137).
7 Hugh Hunt 'What is the future for Australian theatre? *Voice* September 1955.
8 Gibson to Coombs 18 July 1961 AA ACT M448/1 item 274.
9 Rees (1978, 298).
10 Hutchison to Coombs 24 May 1962 AA ACT M448/1 item 275.
11 Coombs to Calwell 31 December 1964 AA ACT M448/1 item 277.
12 Hugh Hunt's circular letter to Board 2 March 1956 Latham Papers Box 72/87-8.
13 Coombs to Latham 28 February 1956 AA ACT M448/1 file 269.
14 Latham to Coombs 6 March 1956 Latham Papers Box 72.
15 Coombs to Latham 15 March 1956 Latham Papers Box 72.
16 Dutton (1994, 225).
17 Jacobs to Coombs 5 August 1963 AA ACT M448/1 item 276.
18 Coombs to Jacobs 22 August 1963 AA ACT M448/1 item 276.
19 Coombs to Nicklin 24 November 1964 AA ACT M448/1 item 277.
20 Coombs to Pannell 20 November 1963 AA ACT M448/1 item 276.
21 Sumner to Coombs 25 November 1963 AA ACT M448/1 item 276.
22 Coombs to White 20 November 1963 AA ACT M448/1 item 276

RE-DESIGNING AUSTRALIA

1 H. C. Coombs 'Design in Australian industry' Collected Speeches, vol. 1, pp. 179, 181.
2 H. C. Coombs 'Official opening of Commonwealth Bank building'
Hobart 4 October 1954 Collected Speeches, vol. 1, p. 54.
3 *Currency* November 1954.
4 *Currency* August 1955.
5 Coombs (1992, 10).
6 *Daily Telegraph* 11 March 1966.
7 Coombs to Holt 20 June 1963 RBA S-a-766.
8 Other graphic designers should also be credited. Paul Beadle designed the annual reports for 1951–55, Gordon Andrews those for 1956–59, and John Saxton those for 1965–67. The covers of *Currency* displayed the works of artists in addition to those mentioned here.
9 According to the then current *Australian Encyclopaedia*, this could have been Alexander Scott, Ernest Scott, James Scott, Rose Scott, either of two Thomas Scotts, and either of two Walter Scotts. Scott of the Antarctic, much admired in Australia, was English.
10 Record of meeting on 'Decimal currency – new notes designs' 8 November 1963 RBA S-a-67.
11 'Decimal Currency – new notes designs' meeting 31 January 1964 RBA S-a-768.
12 *Currency* September 1967, p. 11.

RETIREMENT

1 *The Australian Financial Times* 15 May 1961.
2 *Age* 5 December 1964.
3 *Sun News-Pictorial* 2 July 1968.
4 Reserve Bank of Australia commemorative booklet *Dr H. C. Coombs, 1949–1968* RBA.
5 'Dr. Coombs' Farewell' in Reserve Bank of Australia commemorative booklet *Dr H. C. Coombs, 1949–1968*.
6 *Australian Financial Review* 3 November 1967.
7 *Sydney Morning Herald* 3 November 1967.
8 Swan to Coombs (nd) NLA 21/168.

9 *Australian Financial Review* 23 July 1968.
10 Phillips to Coombs 22 July 1968 AA ACT M448/1 item 56.
11 Phillips to Williams 19 March 1969 RBA S-70-1788.
12 Coombs (1971, 184, 186).
13 Coombs to Canfield 11 January 1968, Henderson to Coombs 13 June 1968, NLA Box 7/37.
14 'Dr. Coombs' Farewell' in Reserve Bank of Australia commemorative booklet *Dr H. C. Coombs, 1949–1968*.
15 Drysdale to Coombs 3 November 1967 RBA S-70-1787.

WHITLAM CONSCRIPTS COOMBS

1 See Rowse (2000) for an account of his engagement with Indigenous policy.
2 Coombs (1981, 285).
3 Wright to Coombs 10 November 1971 NLA 20/160.
4 *Australian* 1 January 1972.
5 Lemberg to Coombs 20 January 1972, Drysdale to Coombs 7 February 1972, Cowen to Coombs 4 January 1972, Bateman to Coombs 6 January 1972, NLA 16/118.
6 Miller to Coombs 18 January 1972 NLA 33/277.
7 Dominic Nagle, *The Australian* 1 January 1972.
8 *Advertiser* 13 November 1972.
9 *Australian Financial Review* 13 November 1972.
10 Stanner 'Mr Howson's note of 2 November' (nd) Dexter file 30, 4.
11 'Dr. Coombs' Press Conference at Kingsford Smith Airport Monday 13 November 1972' Dexter file 18, 1.
12 Records of press comment 13 November 1972, Dexter file 18, 1.
13 *Sun-Herald* 19 November 1972.
14 *Australian Financial Review* 14 November 1972.
15 *Australian Financial Review* 13 November 1972.
16 *Age* 28 November 1972.
17 *Advertiser* 27 November 1972.
18 *Nation Review* 25–30 November 1972.
19 *Daily Telegraph* 14 November 1972.

TRADE REFORM

1 Coombs to Whitlam 24 January 1973 Minute 32/73
2 Rattigan (1986, 16).
3 Rattigan (1986, 49, 51, 66).
4 Rattigan (1986, 148).
5 Coombs to Whitlam 6 December 1972, Coombs 'Machinery of government' 15 December 1972, NLA Box 46.
6 Whitlam to Cairns 16 February 1973 and Cairns to Whitlam 8 March 1973 AA ACT M448/1 item 62.
7 Cairns to Whitlam 6 April 1973 AA ACT M448/1 item 62.
8 Whitlam to Cairns 28 March 1973 AA ACT M448/1 item 62.
9 Coombs to Whitlam 11 April 1973 Minute 97/73.
10 Coombs to Whitlam 28 February 1973, Minute 59/73; Rattigan (1986, 153–4).
11 Coombs to Whitlam 22 November 1973 Minute 218/73.
12 *Australian Financial Review* 10 July 1973.
13 Coombs to Whitlam 23 January 1973, Minute 21/73; Coombs to Whitlam 2 March 1973, Minute 60/73; Coombs to Whitlam 8 March 1973, Minute 66/73.
14 'On the need to increase imports in 1973–4' (nd but response from Coombs dated June 1973) AA ACT M448/1 item 62.
15 Coombs to Taylor 20 June 1973 AA ACT M448/1 item 61.
16 Coombs to Whitlam 25 June 1973, Minute 145/73; Coombs to Whitlam 26 June 1973, Minute 126/73.
17 Whitlam (1985, 192).
18 Whitlam (1985, 193).
19 D'Alpuget (1982, 226).

TWO CULTURAL CONSTITUENCIES

1 'Council for the performing arts: Dr. Coombs' proposal' Appendix B of 'Proposal for establishment of an Australian Council for the Arts' NLA 7/46.

2 Comments by Dr Coombs at open forum 'Government aid for the arts in Australia' Adelaide 11 March 1968 NLA 43/372.

3 'Address given by Dr. H. C. Coombs on 11 April 1970 in Wellington New Zealand at the public session of "Arts Conference 70" arranged by the Queen Elizabeth II Arts Council of New Zealand' NLA 29/241.

4 Address to National Press Club Canberra 22 January 1969, NLA 43/372.

5 Comments by Dr Coombs at open forum 'Government aid for the arts in Australia' Adelaide 11 March 1968 NLA 43/372.

6 Address by Coombs to National Press Club Canberra 22 January 1969 NLA 43/372.

7 Brown (2001, 245).

8 'The Administration of the Arts in Australia – suggested pattern, draft' (nd) NLA 8/49.

9 Whitlam to Coombs 23 January 1973 NLA 8/50.

10 Coombs to Whitlam 9 February 1973 NLA 8/50.

11 Melbourne *Herald* 8 February 1973.

12 *Australian* 16 February 1973.

13 *Age* 3 February 1973.

14 V. Arnold letter to *Age* 4 February 1973.

15 *Sydney Morning Herald* 1 February 1973. He was praising an editorial (30 January 1973) 'Autocracy', which criticised Whitlam and Coombs for their lack of consultation with existing arts funding bodies.

16 Melbourne *Herald* 1 February 1973.

17 *Nation Review* 25 February 1973.

18 *Mirror* 20 February 1973.

19 *Mirror* 20 February 1973.

20 G. Whaley letter to *Age* 28 February 1973.

21 *Age* 24 February 1973.

22 'Opening remarks by Dr. H. C. Coombs at the first meeting of the newly-structured Australian Council for the Arts at the Commonwealth Centre in Sydney on Friday 16 February 1973' NLA 30/249.

23 *National Times* 26 February – 3 March 1973, *Age* 19 February 1973, *Nation Review* 26 February 1973.

24 Coombs to Browne 9 October 1970 NLA 7/40.

25 H. C. Coombs 'Remarks on the launching of "Involvement" Andrew Grimwade and Clifton Pugh' December 1968 NLA 43/372.

26 Allen (1981, 127–33).

27 'Remarks made by Dr. H. C. Coombs at a public meeting of the Arts Action Committee at the Independent Theatre, North Sydney, 8 April 1973' NLA 30/250.

28 Coombs to Whitlam 26 April 1973, Minute 103/73.

29 'Nugget polishes off the critics' *Bulletin* 23 February 1974.

30 Coombs to Whitlam 13 April 1973 Minute 100/73.

31 Rowse (1999, 101–2).

32 *Canberra Times* 22 May 1974. A copy of the telegram is on NLA 42/355.

33 Dexter to Minister's office (telex) 23 May 1974, NLA 42/355.

34 H. C. Coombs 'A Society for Aboriginal Civilization: notes for discussion' 15 July 1974 NLA 42/355.

35 W. E. H. Stanner 'A "Society for Aboriginal Civilisation": some points for discussion' NLA 42/355.

36 'Remarks made by Dr. H. C. Coombs at a public meeting of the Arts Action Committee at the Independent Theatre, North Sydney, 8 April 1973' NLA 30/250.

37 The speeches of Coombs, Whitlam, Menadue and Karmel are in NLA 27/216.

WAGES AND TAXES

1 H. C. Coombs 'Prices Policy' (nd, but likely 11 April 1973) Minute 96/73.
2 'Notes from Dr. Coombs' on Cabinet submission 285 nd AA ACT M448/1 item 161.
3 F. Gruen 'Inflation and prices and incomes policy in Australia' 29 August 1973 AA Act M448/1 item 161, and Coombs to Whitlam 11 September 1973 Minute 173/73.
4 Coombs to Whitlam 2 October 1973 Minute 183/73; Coombs to Whitlam 16 October 1973 Minute 196/73.
5 Treasury's views are reported in a paper written by an interdepartmental committee on wage indexation, in AA ACT M448/1 item 68.
6 Coombs to Whitlam 22 July 1974, Minute 119/74.
7 Coombs to Whitlam 7 August 1974, Minute 129/74.
8 Coombs to Whitlam 15 August 1974, Minute 132/74.
9 Coombs and Gruen to Moore 19 August 1974 AA ACT M448/1 item 63.
10 Coombs to Whitlam 17 September 1974, Minute 146/74.
11 Coombs to Whitlam 17 July 1974, Minute 117/74 AA ACT M448/1 item 157.
12 Whitlam (1985, 197–8), and D'Alpuget (1982, 211–12).
13 H. C. Coombs 'Notes for Committee on Taxation' (April 1973) AA ACT M448/1 item 193.
14 Coombs to Whitlam 26 April 1974, Minute 67/74.
15 Coombs to Whitlam (nd), Minute 47/74.
16 Coombs to Whitlam 15 August 1974, Minute 134/74.
17 Coombs to Whitlam 29 January 1975, Minute 3/75.
18 Hagan (1981, 404).
19 Coombs to Whitlam 18 April 1975, Minute 7/75.
20 Coombs' responses to the study by John Higley, Desley Deacon and Don Smart are on NLA 16/126.
21 Coombs to Whitlam 18 April 1975, Minute 7/75.
22 Rusden, 352.
23 Rusden, 355.
24 Coombs (1977d, v–vi).

THE STUFFED OWL OF MINERVA

1 Coombs to Hohnen 2 November 1966 AA ACT M448/1 item 250.
2 Coombs (1970, 10).
3 Coombs (1970, 11).
4 Coombs (1970, 13).
5 Coombs (1970, 14).
6 Stanner to Coombs (nd, c. October 1970) NLA 23/180.
7 H. C. Coombs 'The University in contemporary Australia' (speech to 27th annual conferring of degrees ceremony Canberra University College 27 March 1956), Collected Speeches, vol. 1, p. 94.
8 'The University in contemporary Australia', p. 94.
9 H. C. Coombs 'The role of a regional university' Fifth Albert Joseph Memorial Lecture, New England University College October 1953, Collected Speeches, vol. 1, p. 15.
10 Coombs to McLennan 31 March 1953 NLA 3/20.
11 *Currency* March 1959.
12 H. C. Coombs 'The arts in Australia' AA ACT M448/1 item 142.
13 H. C. Coombs 'Biological and Economic Man' (variant title 'Ecological and Economic Man') address to Wildlife Preservation Society of Queensland 29 March 1973 NLA 31/257.
14 Blainey (1976, 6).
15 'The University in contemporary Australia' pp. 94, 95.
16 Coombs (1970, 16).
17 Badger to Coombs 10 July 1962 AA ACT M448/1 item 275.

18 'You can trust the Trust – to make a complete hash of it' *Bulletin* 11 April 1964.

19 *Sydney Morning Herald* 14, 20 August.

20 Anon. (1964).

21 CPD-R 17 September 1964, pp. 1264–6.

22 Calwell to Coombs 1 September 1964 AA ACT M448/1 item 277.

23 Coombs to Calwell (roneoed draft) 29 September 1964 AA ACT M448/1 item 277.

24 Coombs to Wright 17 August 1955 AA ACT M448/1 item 263.

25 Coombs to Murray 5 May 1959 AA ACT M448/1 item 249.

26 'The University in contemporary society' address given at the graduation ceremony of the University of Western Australia April 1960, Collected Speeches, vol. 2, p. 287.

27 Coombs to Partridge 6 August 1968 AA ACT M448/1 item 250.

28 Partridge to Coombs 17 August 1968 AA ACT M448/1 item 250.

29 H. C. Coombs 'Speech upon installation as Chancellor of ANU', August 1968 AA ACT M448/1 item 250.

30 Coombs to Partridge 13 July 1970 NLA 23/180.

31 Coombs (1970, 38).

32 Coombs (1970, 40).

33 Excerpts from Minutes of 138th meeting of ANU Council 13 September 1974 AA ACT M448/1 item 251.

34 Crisp (1974).

35 Coombs to Swan 30 June 1970 NLA 23/180.

36 Material on this and other dinner parties can be found in Coombs NLA 23/180.

37 Swan to Coombs 13 October 1970 NLA 23/180.

NATURE AND HUMAN NATURE

1 Coombs (1970, 34).

2 Robin (1998, 66).

3 Hutton and Connors (1999, chs 1–3).

4 *West Australian* 16 August 1976

5 Dunlap (1999).

6 Slatyer (1970, 1).

7 Slatyer (1970, 17).

8 Slatyer (1970, 18).

9 Slatyer (1970, 20).

10 Coombs (1970, 33).

11 Ratcliffe to HCC 10 November 1970, Coombs to Ratcliffe 16 November 1970, NLA 7/40.

12 Coombs to Frankel 28 January 1971, Coombs to Arndt 27 August 1971, NLA 22/172.

13 Coombs (1990, 55).

14 Coombs (1990, 59).

15 Coombs' submission to the Royal Commission is in NLA 20/160.

16 Submission to Royal Commission.

17 Coombs (1990, 40).

18 H. C. Coombs (1974).

19 Hutton and Connors (1999, 106–8).

20 Strahan (2000, 335).

21 Wright (1970).

22 Coombs (1990, 49).

23 Coombs (1990, 51).

24 Coombs (1990, 52).

25 H. C. Coombs 'Biological and Economic Man' (variant title 'Ecological and Economic Man') address to Wildlife Preservation Society of Queensland 29 March 1973 NLA 31/257.

26 *Sydney Morning Herald* 7 January 1974.

27 'Remarks by H. C. Coombs at the launching of Sydney's Environmental Amenity' 9 October 1976, NLA 31/257.

28 *Australian Conservation Foundation Annual Report 1977–8* Melbourne: Australian Conservation Foundation.

29 'Biological and Economic Man'. NLA 31/257.

30 Untitled address to launch *Mankind at the Turning Point* (by Mihajlo Mesarovic and Eduard Pestel) (2nd report of the Club of Rome) Canberra 14 November 1975 NLA folder 44/368.

31 Stanner to Coombs (nd, c. June 1971) NLA 22/172.

32 Coombs (1990, 59–60).

ECONOMIES AND COMMUNITIES

1 H. C. Coombs 'Science and the future of man: the role of the social scientist'. Paper presented at the Felton Bequest symposium 'Man and his Science', in honour of the 70th birthday of Sir Macfarlane Burnet, Melbourne 1969 NLA 84/27.95.

2 'Science and the future of man'.

3 'Science and the future of man'.

4 'Science and the future of man'.

5 'Report of a discussion on 12 September [1968] between the government members Aboriginal Affairs Committee and Dr. H. C. Coombs and Mr. B. G. Dexter' Dexter file 27 (emphasis added).

6 CAA Minutes 5–8 August 1969 Dexter file 25, 1.

7 Coombs to (Margaret) Coombs 24 September 1969 NLA 7/38.

8 H. C. Coombs 'Aborigines on Cattle Stations in the Northern Territory' (October 1969) AA ACT CRS OAA 69/1(1).

9 Coombs (1970) 54.

10 *Sydney Morning Herald* editorial 14 November 1970.

11 Swan to Coombs 13 October 1970 23/180.

12 Day to Coombs 9 August 1971 NLA 22/172.

13 Arndt to Coombs 6 August 1971 NLA 22/172.

14 Coombs (1990, 59, 97–9, 103, 107–8, 112–17, 120).

15 Coombs (1990, 107–8, 113).

16 'Record of Dr. Coombs' discussion with the administrative trainees in Canberra on 8th October 1970' NLA 41/337.

17 CAA Minutes 20 February, 12 May, 2–3 July 1970 Dexter file 25, 1.

18 CAA Minutes 7–11, 17 December 1970, Dexter file 25, 1.

19 Commonwealth of Australia (1971). Chaired by Professor C. A. Gibb, the committee included W. de Vos, J. Taylor, C. Roberts, E. Milliken and Coombs.

20 Coombs to Sharp 20 February 1974 NLA 43/360 (crossed out so possibly not sent).

21 Coombs (1977a, 1).

22 Coombs (1977b, par. 5. 3).

23 Coombs (1994, 163).

24 Coombs (1994, 81, 165).

LOSING THE MASTER KEY

1 Coombs (1970, 46).

2 H. C. Coombs 'Speech at University NSW degree conferring ceremony for Faculty of Commerce' 8 May 1974, AA ACT M448/1 item 185.

3 Coombs (1970, 45–6).

4 G. Barwick 'Economic growth and the environment' ACF Occasional Paper 7 (an address to the 1971 Engineering Conference of the Institution of Engineers, Adelaide March 1971).

5 Horner to Coombs 10 December 1970 NLA 23/180.

6 Swan to Coombs 13 October 1970 NLA 23/180.

7 Correspondence on this project between Coombs, Cass and his officers can be found on AA ACT M448/1 item 60.

8 Coombs to Williams 5 March 1982 NLA 87/8.

THE RESPONSIVE PUBLIC SERVANT

1 Lloyd and Reid (1974, 244).

2 Coombs to Morrison 3 October 1973 AA ACT M448/1 item 188.

3 H. C. Coombs 'Address to opening session of the Task Force on a regionally based Australian government administration' NLA 44/368.

4 RCAGA (1976, 14).

5 RCAGA (1976, 15).

6 RCAGA (1976, 15).
7 RCAGA (1976, 26).
8 RCAGA (1976, 16).
9 RCAGA (1976, 16).
10 RCAGA (1976, 23, 17).
11 RCAGA (1976, 23).
12 RCAGA (1976, 23).
13 RCAGA (1976, 22).
14 RCAGA (1976, 17).
15 H. C. Coombs (1977c, 49).
16 H. C. Coombs (1977c, 52).
17 RCAGA Transcript, 336.
18 RCAGA Transcript, 2378.
19 RCAGA Transcript, 2379.
20 Wilson.
21 Sawer (1984, 24–5).
22 RCAGA Transcript, 136.
23 RCAGA Transcript, 136.
24 RCAGA Transcript, 139.
25 RCAGA Transcript, 270.
26 RCAGA Transcript, 271.
27 Wilson.

A TORRES STRAIT AGENDA

1 Minutes of CAA meeting 27–28 September 1972, Dexter file 26.
2 Coombs to Whitlam 10 January 1973, Minute 4/73.
3 Coombs to Whitlam 10 January 1973, Minute 4/73.
4 Coombs to Bryant 16 March 1973 Dexter file 9.
5 Coombs to Bryant 11 April 1973 Dexter file 9.
6 DAA notes on this meeting are included in Minutes to Whitlam NLA 46, between Minutes 135/73 and 136/73.
7 The 28-page transcript of the 12–14 June meeting of the Torres Strait Islander Council Chairmen in Canberra is in NLA 11/81.
8 Coombs to Whitlam 12 June 1973, Minute 127/73.
9 Coombs to Whitlam 22 August 1973, Minute 155/73.
10 Coombs to Whitlam 24/9/73 NLA 41/343.

11 H. C. Coombs 'Drafting notes on Torres Strait Border' 8 October 1973 NLA 11/81.
12 Coombs' Draft Agreement dated 29 October 1973 is on NLA 12/88.

CONSERVATION AND ABORIGINES

1 *Australian* 7 May 1970, reprinted in Coombs (1978a, 27–9).
2 As Coombs once told the author.
3 Coombs to Yunupingu 3 November 1977 NLA 77/22.8.
4 Coombs to Rubuntja and Yunupingu 16 February 1978 NLA 77/22.8.
5 ACF *Newsletter* vol. 10, no. 3, May 1978.
6 Coombs (1978b, 7).
7 Coombs (1978b) includes an excerpt of the transcript of the Warlpiri land claim hearing containing Coombs' evidence. See pp. 2123–4, 2125, 2134.

BAPA DHUMBUL

1 Rowse (2000, 46–8, 57–9).
2 C. D. Rowley 'Report on Yirrkala, 13–17 July 1975' NLA 42/350.
3 'Report on Arnhem Land' (unpublished draft 15 August 1975) NLA 18/146.
4 Reid (1983, 30).
5 Coombs (1976, 3).
6 Kirby to Coombs 13 April 1976, Coombs to Kirby 22 April 1976, NLA 43/362.
7 H. C. Coombs 'Notes for the rules and procedures of the Areyonga community incorporated' June 1978 NLA 75/21.1.
8 Coombs to Kirby 2 January 1978 (misdated) NLA 75/21.3.
9 Coombs to Kirby 2 January 1978 NLA 75/21.3.
10 H. C. Coombs 'Notes in Yirrkala visit – petrol sniffing' 1 May 1980 NLA 75/21.4.
11 H. C. Coombs 'Aboriginal control of law and order – Yirrkala' 28 May 1980 NLA 75/21.5.

12 Coombs to Marika 19 May 1980 NLA 75/21.4.

13 H. C. Coombs 'Notes on Yirrkala visit – petrol sniffing' 1 May 1980 NLA 75/21.4.

14 Attachments to Coombs to Debelle 29 April 1981 NLA 75/21.6.

15 Rowse (2000, 138–40).

CONCLUSION: HISTORIES NOSTALGIC AND HOPEFUL

1 Information from Robin Derricourt.

2 Royal Commission on Child Endowment. Minutes of Evidence, Perth, 3 February 1928 pp. 416–18.

3 Coombs (1970, 53).

4 Coombs (1990, 25).

5 Coombs (1990, 68–7.

6 Coombs (1990, 81).

7 Professor J. P. Coghlan of the Howard Florey Institute of Experimental Physiology and Medicine was kind enough to supply an unedited transcript of Coombs' R. D. Wright Lecture of April 1993.

8 Stretton (1987, 202–3).

9 *Sydney Morning Herald* 18 May 1984.

10 Kelly (1992, 13).

11 Kelly (1992, 11).

12 Kelly (1992, 2).

13 The Chairman's remarks are on the transcript of Coombs' speech to National Press Club, 22 January 1969 NLA 44/372

14 Coombs (1984, 58–9).

15 Kelly (1992, 15).

References

PERSONAL PAPERS

H. C. Coombs (NLA MS 802, AA ACT M448/1, RBA GHC series).
J. G. Crawford (NLA MS 4514).
L. F. Crisp (NLA MS 5243).
J. J. Dedman (NLA MS 987).
J. A. La Nauze (NLA MS 5248).
J. G. Latham (NLA MS 6409).
L. Ross (NLA MS 3939).
E. O. G. Shann (NLA MS 7347).

LOCATION OF RARE PERIODICALS

The Sphinx is in the Library of the Perth Modern School, Subiaco, WA.
The *WA Trainee* can be consulted at Edith Cowan University Archives.
The *WA Teachers' Journal* is held in the library of the State School Teachers Union of
    Western Australia, 150 Adelaide Terrace Perth.

OFFICIAL DOCUMENTS

Documents in Australian Foreign Policy (published by the Australian Government Publishing
    Service):
    Volume 5 *July 1941 to June 1942* (ed. W. J. Hudson and H. W. J. Stokes, 1982).
    Volume 6 *July 1942 to December 1943* (ed. W. J. Hudson and H. W. J. Stokes, 1983).
    Volume 9 *January 1946 to June 1946* (ed. W. J. Hudson and W. Way, 1991).
    Volume 10 *July 1946 to December 1946* (ed. W. J. Hudson and W. Way, 1991).
    Volume 12 *1947* (ed. W. J. Hudson and W. Way, 1995).
    Volume 14 *Australia and the postwar world, 1948–9* (ed. P. Andre and S. Langford).

BOOKS, THESES AND ARTICLES

ACT Regional Study Group (1955) 'Commonwealth policy coordination' *Australian Journal of Public Administration* 14, pp. 193–213.

Adams B. (1987) *Sidney Nolan: such is life* Hawthorn, Vic.: Hutchinson.

Alexander F. (1968) 'Hancock – some reminiscences' *Historical Studies* 13(51) October, pp. 291–9.

Alexander I. (1994–5) 'Old Canning Town' *East London Record* 17, pp. 2–10.

Allen T. (1981) *Clifton Pugh: patterns of a lifetime* West Melbourne: Nelson.

Anon. (1921) *Perth Modern School: course for study* Perth: Government Printer.

Anon. (1964) 'Culture in Australia: theatre and subsidies' *Current Affairs Bulletin* 34(8), 31 August.

Arndt H. W. (1960) *The Australian trading banks* (2nd edn) Melbourne: Cheshire.

Arndt H. W. and Harris C. P. (1965) *The Australian trading banks* (3rd edn) Melbourne: Cheshire.

Arne S. (1945) *United Nations Primer* New York: Farrar and Rinehart.

Bailey K. H. (1947) 'The Constitution and its problems' in C. H. Grattan (ed.) *Australia* Berkeley and Los Angeles: University of California Press, pp. 87–104.

Barwick G. (1971) *Economic growth and the environment* Parkville, Vic.: Australian Conservation Foundation.

Benham F. (1931) *Go back to gold* 'Criterion Miscellanies' no. 35, London.

Bensusan-Butt D. (1980) *On economic knowledge: a sceptical miscellany* Canberra: Research School of Pacific Studies, Department of Economics, Australian National University.

Bickel L. (1972) *Rise up to life: a biography of Howard Walter Florey who gave penicillin to the world* London: Angus and Robertson.

Blainey G. (1976) *The politics of big business* Academy of the Social Sciences Annual Lecture, Canberra: Koomarri Printers.

Bland F. A. (1945) *Planning the modern state* (2nd edn) Sydney: Angus and Robertson.

Blaxland J. F., Major G. and Phillips O. E. (1961) *Australia: 1970 and beyond* Sydney: Angus and Robertson.

Bolton G. C. (1972) *A fine country to starve in* Nedlands: University of Western Australia Press.

Bolton G. C. and Hirst W. (1990) 'Sir Edward Wittenoom' *Australian Dictionary of Biography* vol. 12 (ed. J. Ritchie), pp. 553–4.

Brisbane, K. (1988) 'Amateur theatre' in P. Parsons (ed.) *The companion to theatre in Australia* Sydney: Currency Press and Cambridge University Press, pp. 38–45.

Brissenden A. (1956) 'Ballet in Australia needs vitality and assistance' *Voice* January.

Brown N. (1995) *Governing Prosperity: social change and social analysis in Austalia in the 1950s* Melbourne: Cambridge University Press.

—— (2001) *Richard Downing: economics, advocacy and social reform in Australia* Carlton: Melbourne University Press.

Brown W. A. (1950) *The United States and the restoration of world trade* Washington, DC: Brookings Institution.

Butlin N. G. (1987) 'Human or inhuman capital? The Economics profession, 1916–87' *Working Papers in Economic History* no. 91, Australian National University.

Butlin S. (1937) 'The banking commission's report' *Australian Quarterly* 9(3), pp. 40–50.

—— (1955) *War economy, 1939–42* Canberra: Australian War Memorial.

—— (1983) 'Australian central banking 1945–59' *Australian Economic History Review* XXIII, pp. 95–192.

Butlin S., Critchley T., McMillan R. and Tange A. (1941) *Australia foots the bill* Sydney: Angus and Robertson.

Butlin S. and Schedvin C. B. (1977) *The war economy, 1942–45* Canberra: Australian War Memorial.

Cain N. (1983) 'Recovery policy in Australia: a certain native wisdom' *Australian Economic History Review* September, pp. 193–218.

—— (1988) 'Resistance to Keynesian initiatives: an episode in Australian policy advice, 1933–36' *Working Papers in Economic History* no. 115, September.

Capling A. (2001) *Australia and the global trade system: from Havana to Seattle* Melbourne: Cambridge University Press.

Cargher J. (1977) *Opera and ballet in Australia* Stanmore: Cassell.

—— (1988) *Bravo: two hundred years of opera in Australia* Melbourne: Macmillan.

Cawte A. (1992) *Atomic Australia* Kensington: University of New South Wales Press.

Chamber of Commerce of the United States (1948) *America and the International Trade Organisation* (Economic Institute) Washington, DC.

Cherry W. (1981) in P. Holloway (ed.) *Contemporary Australian drama: perspectives since 1955* Sydney: Currency Press, pp. 107–11.

Chifley J. B. (1941) 'Reconstruction after the war' *Public Administration* 3(3) September, pp. 103–8.

—— (1952) *Things worth fighting for* (ed. A. W. Stargardt) Carlton: Melbourne University Press.

Clarey P. J. (1950) 'The trade union attitude to incentive payment schemes' *Economic Papers* 9, pp. 22–9.

Clarke P. (1988) *The Keynesian revolution in the making, 1924–1936* Oxford: Clarendon Press.

Cockburn S. and Ellyard P. (1981) *Oliphant: the life and times of Mark Oliphant* Adelaide: Axiom Books.

Coombs H. C. (1931) 'The development of the Commonwealth Bank as a central bank' MA thesis, University of Westrern Australia (RBA).

—— (1933a) 'Dominions exchanges and central bank problems' PhD thesis, London School of Economics and Political Science.

—— (1933b) 'The decline of liberalism' *The Old Modernian* December.

—— (1934) 'Some impressions of London County Council schools' *The WA Teachers' Journal* 8 December, pp. 254–5.

—— (1937) 'A propensity to consume: a comment on the note by Dr. Smithies' *Economic Record* 13, June, pp. 250–5.

—— (1939) 'General theory and Swedish economic practice' *Economic Record* 15, April, pp. 135–51.

—— (1944a) 'The economic aftermath of war' in D. A. S. Campbell (ed.) *Post-war Reconstruction in Australia* Sydney: Australasian Publishing Company Pty Ltd, pp. 67–99.

—— (1944b) 'The special problems of planning' Pamphlet no. 2 in the series *The realities of reconstruction*, Melbourne University Press.

—— (1944c) *Problems of a high employment economy* Joseph Fisher Memorial Lecture, Adelaide: Hassell Press.

—— (1948) 'Australia's ability to avoid booms and depressions' *Economic Papers* 8, pp. 36–55.

—— (1954) 'The Australian Elizabethan Theatre Trust' *Meanjin* XIII(2), pp. 283–5.

—— (1964) 'Instalment credit growth in Australia: a central banker's view' in N. Runcie (ed.) *The Management of Instalment Credit: the Australian experience* London: University of London Press, pp. 199–203.

—— (1970) *The fragile pattern: institutions and man* Sydney: ABC.

—— (1971) *Other people's money* Canberra: Australian National University Press.

—— (1976) 'Opening remarks' in D. Hambly and J. Goldring (eds) *Australian Lawyers and Social Change*, Sydney: Law Book Company, pp. 1–4.

—— (1977a) 'The Pitjantjatjara Aborigines: a strategy for survival' CRES Working Paper no. 1, Canberra: CRES and Australian National University.

—— (1977b) 'The application of CDEP in Aboriginal communities in the eastern zone of Western Australia' CRES Working Paper no. 3, Canberra: CRES and Australian National University.

—— (1977c) 'The Commission Report' in C. Hazlehurst and J. R. Nethercote (eds) *Reforming Australian Government: the Coombs report and beyond* Canberra: Royal Australian Institute of Public Administration, pp. 49–52.

—— (1977d) 'Foreword' in S. Encel, D. Horne and E. Thompson (eds) *Change the rules: towards a democratic constitution* Penguin Books, pp. v–vi.

—— (1978a) *Kulinma: listening to Aboriginal Australians* Canberra: Australian National University Press.

—— (1978b) 'Submission to the Commission on the Warlpiri Land Claim' CRES Working Paper no. 8, Canberra: CRES and Canberra: CRES and Australian National University.

—— (1981) *Trial Balance* South Melbourne: Macmillan.

—— (1990) *The return of scarcity: strategies for an economic future* Melbourne: Cambridge University Press.

—— (1992) 'Foreword' *The Reserve Bank of Australia Collection* Sydney: Reserve Bank of Australia, pp. 9–10.

Coombs H. C., Brandl M. M. and Snowdon W. E. (1983) *A certain heritage* CRES Monograph 9, Canberra: Australian National University.

Coombs H. C. and Stanner W. E. H. (1975) *Report on Arnhem Land* Council for Aboriginal Affairs.

Coombs H. C. and 'T. W.' (1931) 'Age of plenty' *West Australian* 12 June.

Commonwealth of Australia (1945) *Full Employment in Australia* Parliamentary Paper no. 11.

Copland D. B. (1939) 'The Commonwealth Bank – cooperation or compulsion' *Economic Record* (special supplement) April, pp. 21–39.

—— (1951) *Inflation and expansion* Melbourne: Cheshire.

—— (ed.) (1960) *Giblin: the scholar and the man* Melbourne: Cheshire.

Copland D. B. and Barback R. H. (eds) (1957) *The conflict of expansion and stability* Melbourne: Cheshire.

Cornish S. (1993) 'Sir Leslie Melville: an interview' *ANU Working Papers in Economic History*, no. 173.

—— (2001) 'Sir Roland Wilson: a biographical essay', not published.

Crawford J. G., Anderson N. and Morris M. G. N. (eds) (1968) *Australian trade policy, 1942–1966* Canberra: Australian National University Press.

Crisp L. F. (1961) *Ben Chifley* Croydon: Longmans, Green and Co.

—— (1967) 'Central co-ordination of Commonwealth policy-making: roles and dilemmas of the Prime Minister's Department' *Australian Journal of Public Administration* 26, pp. 28–57.

—— (1969) 'Public service as a profession' *Australian Journal of Public Administration* 28, pp. 122–40.

—— (1970) 'Specialists and generalists: further Australian reflections on Fulton' *Australian Journal of Public Administration* 29, pp. 197–217.

—— (1972) 'Politics and the Commonwealth Public Service' *Australian Journal of Public Administration* 31, pp. 287–309.

—— (1974) 'Gravediggers and undertakers – then and now' Fifth Annual John Curtin Memorial Lecture, 14 October, roneo typescript, Chifley Library, Australian National University.

Curtin P. W. E. (1954) 'The seat of government' in H. L. White (ed.) *Canberra: the nation's capital* Sydney: Angus and Robertson.

Dahrendorf R. (1995) *A history of the London School of Economics and Political Science, 1895–1995* Oxford: Oxford University Press.

Dale L. (1997) *The English men: professing literature in Australian universities* Toowoomba: Association for the Study of Australian Literature.

D'Alpuget B. (1977) *Mediator: a biography of Sir Richard Kirby* Carlton: Melbourne University Press.

—— (1982) *Robert J. Hawke: a biography* Melbourne: Schwartz.

Davidson L. S. and Salisbury S. (n.d.) Unpublished MS on history of Westpac.

Deacon D. (1977) *Managing gender: the state, the new middle class and women workers, 1830–1930* Melbourne: Oxford University Press.

Diebold W. (1952) *The end of the ITO* Essays in International Finance no. 16, October, Department of Economics and Financial Institutions, Princeton University.

Downing R. I. (1960) 'Giblin as Ritchie Professor' in D. B. Copland (ed.) *Giblin: the scholar and the man* Melbourne: F. W. Cheshire, pp. 39–48.

Duncan W. G. K. (1955) 'Freedom of the mind' in J. Wilkes (ed.) *Liberty in Australia* Sydney: Angus and Robertson, pp. 1–42.

Dunk W. E. (1974) *They also serve* Canberra: privately published.

Dunlap T. R. (1999) *Nature and the English diaspora* Cambridge: Cambridge University Press.

Dutton G. (1994) *Out in the open* St Lucia: University of Queensland Press.

Ellyard P. and Cockburn S. (1981) *Oliphant: the life and times of Sir Mark Oliphant* Adelaide: Axiom Books.

Errington S. (1995) 'School grew from inspector's vision' *The Perth Modernian* 1, August.

Firth G. G. (1960) 'Giblin and the post-war problem' in D. B. Copland (ed.) *Giblin: the scholar and the man* Melbourne: F. W. Cheshire, pp. 204–12.

Fisher A. G. B. (1937) 'Twentieth century banking in Australia' *Economic Record* (13)25, pp. 159–67.

Fitzgerald T. M. (1988) 'Ian Mathieson Jacoby' in R. T. Appleyard and C. B. Schedvin (eds) *Australian financiers: biographical essays* Melbourne: Macmillan, pp. 364–87.

Fitzpatrick B. (1961) 'Catholics in political controversy' in H. Mayer (ed.) *Catholics and the free society* Melbourne: Cheshire, pp. 104–14.

Foster S. and Varghese M. (1996) *The making of the Australian National University, 1946–1996* St Leonards, NSW: Allen and Unwin.

Friedman M. (1956) *Studies in the quantity theory of money* Chicago: Chicago University Press.

Gaines C. (n.d.) 'Bridgetown: one hundred years of history', typescript, Battye Library, Perth.

Gardner L. C. (1970) *Architects of illusion* Chicago: Quadrangle Books.

Garland J. M. (1960) 'Giblin and John Smith' in D. B. Copland (ed.) *Giblin: the scholar and the man* Melbourne: F. W. Cheshire, pp. 213–22.

Garratt E. (1982) 'Cecil Rollo Patton Andrews: the first Director of Education' in L. Fletcher (ed.) *Pioneers of education in Western Australia* University of Western Australia Press, pp. 221–54.

Gepp H. (1939) *Democracy's danger* Sydney and London: Angus and Robertson.

Giblin L. F. (1945) 'Financing full employment' *Economic Papers* 5, pp. 59–67.

—— (1951) *The growth of a central bank: the development of the Commonwealth Bank of Australia, 1924–45* Carlton: Melbourne University Press.

—— (1960) 'Crisis in democracy' in D. B. Copland (ed.) *Giblin: the scholar and the man* Melbourne: Cheshire, pp. 94–8.

Glynn S. (1975) *Government policy and agricultural development* Nedlands: University of Western Australia Press.

Gollan R. (1963) *The coalminers of New South Wales* Carlton: Melbourne University Press.

Goodwin C. (1974) *The image of Australia* Durham: Duke University Press.

Greenhalgh D. (1984) 'Around the bandstand' *East London Record* no. 7, pp. 14–20.

Griffin J., Nelson H. and Firth S. (1979) *Papua New Guinea: a political history* Melbourne: Heinemann.

Hagan J. (1981) *The history of the ACTU* Melbourne: Cheshire.

Harper M. (1986) 'Melbourne economist in the public arena' in A. G. L. Shaw (ed.) *Victoria's Heritage* Sydney: Allen and Unwin, pp. 37–55.

Harris J. (1977) *William Beveridge: a biography* Oxford: Clarendon Press.

Harrod R. (1972) *The life of John Maynard Keynes* Harmondsworth: Penguin.

Hasluck A. (1981) *Portrait in a mirror* Melbourne: Oxford University Press.

Hasluck P. (1952) *The government and the people* vol. 1: 1939–1941 Canberra: Australian War Memorial.

—— (1970) *The government and the people* vol. 2: 1942–1945 Canberra: Australian War Memorial.

—— (1962) 'The economic development of Papua and New Guinea' *Australian Outlook* 16, pp. 5–15.

Hawker G., Smith R. F. I. and Weller P. (1979) *Politics and policy in Australia* St Lucia: University of Queensland Press.

Herlinger P. (1988) 'The New Theatre' in P. Parsons (ed.) *Companion to theatre in Australia* Sydney: Currency Press and Cambridge University Press, pp. 400–4.

Holder R. F. (1951) 'Australian opinion and the G.A.T.T.' *Australian Outlook* 5(1), pp. 22–36.

—— (1970) *Bank of New South Wales: a history* Sydney: Angus and Robertson (2 vols).

Holloway P. (ed.) (1981) *Contemporary Australian drama: perspectives since 1955* Sydney: Currency Press.

Hudson W. J. and Daven J. (1971) 'Papua and New Guinea since 1945' in W. J. Hudson (ed.) *Australia and Papua New Guinea* Sydney: Sydney University Press, pp. 151–77.

Hudson W. J. (1980) *Australia and the League of Nations* Sydney: Sydney University Press.

Hunt H. (1955) 'What is the future for Australian theatre?' *Voice* September.

Hunt I. L. (1958) 'Group settlement in Western Australia' *University Studies in Western Australian History* III(2) October, pp. 5–42.

Hutton D. and Connors L. (1999) *A history of the Australian environmental movement* Melbourne: Cambridge University Press.

Hytten T. (1939) 'The limits of monetary policy' *Economic Record* (special supplement) April, pp. 76–93.

Ikenberry G. J. (1989) 'Rethinking the origins of American hegemony' *Political science quarterly* 104 (Fall), pp. 375–400.

Isaac J. E. (1977) 'On the neglect of social forces in wage determination' in J. P. Nieuwenhuysen and P. J. Drake (eds) *Australian economic policy* Carlton: Melbourne University Press, pp. 66–82.

Jinks B. (1983) 'Alfred Conlon, the Directorate of Research and New Guinea' *Journal of Australian Studies* 12, June, pp. 21–33.

Kahn R. (1974) 'On re-reading Keynes' *Proceedings of the British Academy* LX, pp. 361–91.

Kelly P. (1992) *The end of certainty: the story of the 1980s* St Leonards, NSW: Allen and Unwin.

—— (1994) *The end of certainty: power, politics and business in Australia* St Leonards, NSW: Allen and Unwin.

Kessel K. (1995) 'Nugget "mad keen" on sport' *The Perth Modernian* 1, August.

Keynes J. M. (1940) *How to pay for the war* Macmillan: London.

Kingsford P. (1982) *The Hunger Marchers in Britain, 1920–39* London: Lawrence and Wishart.

Kippax H. (1981) 'Australian drama since "Summer of the Seventeenth Doll"' in P. Holloway (ed.) *Contemporary Australian drama: perspectives since 1955* Sydney: Currency Press, pp. 137–52.

Kramnick I. and Sheerman B. (1993) *Harold Laski: a life on the left* London: Hamish Hamilton.

La Nauze J. (1977) *Walter Murdoch: a biographical memoir* Carlton: Melbourne University Press.

Laffer K. (1950) 'The economic aspects of incentive payment schemes' *Economic Papers* 9, pp. 30–44.

Lake M. (1982) 'Cyril Jackson: professional administrator' in L. Fletcher (ed.) *Pioneers in education in Western Australia* Nedlands: University of Western Australia Press, pp. 187–220.

Lake Marilyn (1990) 'Jessie Street and "feminist chauvinism"' in H. Radi (ed.) *Jessie Street: documents and essays* Sydney: Women's Redress Press, pp. 20–5.

—— (1995) 'Female desires: the meaning of World War Two' in J. Damousi and M. Lake (eds) *Gender and war* Melbourne: Cambridge University Press, pp. 60–80.

—— (1996) 'Feminist history as national history: writing the political history of women' *Australian Historical Studies* 106, April, pp. 154–69.

—— (1999) *Getting equal: a history of Australian feminism* St Leonards: Allen and Unwin.

'Laodicean' (1933) 'LSE and politics – a five years retrospective' *Clare Market Review* 14(1), Michaelmas, pp. 5–6.

Laski H. J. (1933) 'The present position of representative democracy' *Where stands socialism today?* London: Rich and Cowan Ltd.

Lee D. (1990) 'Protecting the sterling area: the Chifley government's response to multilateralism, 1945–9' *Australian Journal of Political Science* 25, pp. 178–95.

—— (1992) 'The national security planning and defence preparations of the Menzies government, 1950–53' *War and Society* 10(2), October, pp. 119–38.

Lewis M. J. (1969) 'The Australian National University, 1946–60, including an account of the development of Canberra University College and the University Movement in Canberra', unpublished typescript, Crisp papers, NLA MS 5243 Box 106.

Lloyd C. J. and Reid G. S. (1974) *Out of the wilderness: the return of Labor* North Melbourne: Cassell Australia.

Love P. (1984) *Labour and the money power: Australian labour populism, 1890–1950* Carlton: Melbourne University Press.

Lowe D. (1999) *Menzies and the 'great world struggle'* Kensington: University of New South Wales Press.

Macartney K. (1947) 'Louis Esson and Australian drama' *Meanjin* 6, pp. 93–6.

McAuley J. (1952) 'What are cooperatives?' *South Pacific* December, pp. 499–503.

—— (1975) *The grammar of the real* Melbourne: Oxford University Press.

Macintyre S. (1998) 'Douglas Credit' in G. Davison, J. Hirst and S. Macintyre (eds) *Oxford Companion to Australian History* Melbourne: Oxford University Press, p. 194.

McKenzie J. A. (1982) 'James Albert Miles: pioneer of rural education' in L. Fletcher (ed.) *Pioneers of education in Western Australia* Nedlands: University of Western Australia Press, pp. 313–39.

Martin A. W. (1990) 'R. G. Menzies and the Murray committee' in F. B. Smith and P. Crichton (eds) *Ideas for histories of universities in Australia* Division of Historical Studies, Research School of Social Sciences, Australian National University, pp. 94–115.

—— (1995) 'Menzies the man' in S. Prasser, J. Nethercote and J. Warhurst (eds) *The Menzies era* Sydney: Hale and Iremonger, pp. 17–32.

—— (1999) *Robert Menzies: a life*, vol. 2, Carlton: Melbourne University Press.

Martin, B. (1986) *Intellectual suppression: Australian case histories, analysis and responses* North Ryde, NSW: Angus and Robertson.

Melville L. (1955) 'Preface' in J. Wilkes (ed.) *Liberty in Australia* Sydney: Angus and Robertson, pp. ix–xi.

Mendelsohn R. (1958) 'The allocation of resources as an administrative problem' *Australian Journal of Public Administration* 17, pp. 177–93.

—— (1954) *Defence and development, 1950–53* (no publication details).

Merrett D. (1985) *ANZ Bank: an official history* St Leonards, NSW: Allen and Unwin.

Messel H. (1955) 'The place of nuclear power in Australia's future' in N. R. Wills (ed.) *Australia's power resources* Melbourne: F. W. Cheshire, pp. 1–14.

Mobbs C. L. (1968) 'Conciliation can work: a history of the Commonwealth Bank Officers' Association', unpublished manuscript, Reserve Bank Archives.

Miller J. D. B. (1947) 'Australian public opinion – the Bretton Woods controversy' *Australian Outlook* 1(3) September, pp. 31–41.

Mossenson D. (1955) *A history of teacher training in Western Australia* Melbourne: Australian Council for Educational Research (research series 68).

—— (1972) *State education in Western Australia, 1829–1960* Nedlands: University of Western Australia Press.

Murdoch W. (1938) *The Victorian era: its strengths and weaknesses* Sydney: Angus and Robertson.

O'Farrell P. (1985) *The Catholic Church and community: an Australian history* (2nd edn) Kensington: University of New South Wales Press.

Oliphant M. (1956) 'Foreword' in E. W. Titterton *Facing the atomic future* London: Macmillan, pp. ix–x.

Parker R. S. (1990) 'Recruitment, training and staff development in the Australian Public Service before Coombs' in A. Kouzmin and S. Prasser (eds) *Dynamics in Australian public management: selected essays* South Melbourne: Macmillan, pp. 50–62.

Perlman M. (1977) 'The editing of the *Economic Record*, 1925–1975' in J. P. Nieuwenhuysen and P. J. Drake (eds) *Australian Economic Policy* Carlton: Melbourne University Press, pp. 218–30.

Phillips A. A. (1969) 'Walter Murdoch: the art of good-humoured devastation' *Meanjin Quarterly* 28, pp. 221–3.

Phillips M. J. and Ferguson P. S. (1969) 'Savings clubs and savings and loan socieities in Papua and New Guinea' in N. Runcie (ed.) *Credit unions in the South Pacific* London: University of London Press, pp. 75–89.

Pimlott B. (1985) *Hugh Dalton* London: Macmillan.

Plumptre A. F. W. (1938) 'The arguments for central banking in the British dominions' in H. A. Innes (ed.) *Essays in political economy in honour of E. J. Urwick* Toronto: University of Toronto Press, pp. 191–204.

Portus G. V. (1931) Review of W. K. Hancock *Australia, Economic Record* 7, May, pp. 131–4.

Radi H. (1990) 'Organising for reform' in H. Radi (ed.) *Jessie Street: documents and essays* Sydney: Women's Redress Press, pp. 107–17.

Rankin D. H. (1926) *The history of the development of education in Western Australia* Perth: Carrolls Ltd.

Ratcliffe F. N. (1968) 'Conservation and Australia' *Australian Quarterly* March, pp. 58–64.

Rattigan G. A. (1986) *Industry assistance: the inside story* Carlton: Melbourne University Press.

RCAGA. (1976) *Report of the Royal Commission on Australian Government Administration* Parliamentary Paper 185.

Rees L. (1953) *Towards an Australian drama* Sydney: Angus and Robertson.

—— (1978) *A history of Australian drama* vol. 1, Sydney: Angus and Robertson.

Reid J. C. (1983) *Sorcerers and healing spirits* Canberra: Australian National University Press.

Renouf A. (1980) *The champagne trail: experiences of a diplomat* Melbourne: Sun Books.

Reserve Bank of Australia (1968) *Dr H. C. Coombs, 1949–1968* (commemorative booklet, RBA).

Rex I. (1976) 'Ida Rex: school teacher' in *Working Lives Volume One: 1905–45* Hackney WEA, pp. 23–30.

Rivett D. (1947) *Science and responsibility* (address to 18th annual Commencement ceremony, Canberra University College, 25 March) Canberra.

Rivett R. (1972) *David Rivett: fighter for Australian science* North Blackburn, Vic.

Robbins L. (1931) 'Foreword' to F. A. Hayek *Prices and Production* London: George Routledge and Sons.

Robin L. (1998) *Defending the Little Desert* Carlton: Melbourne University Press.

Rowley C. D. (1965) *The New Guinea villager* Melbourne: Cheshire.

Rowse T. (1999) 'The collector as outsider: T. G. H. Strehlow as "public intellectual"' *SRC Occasional Paper* 2, pp. 61–120.

—— (2000) *'Obliged to be difficult': Nugget Coombs' legacy in Indigenous affairs* Melbourne: Cambridge University Press.

Runcie N. (1969) *Economics of instalment credit* London: University of London Press.

Sawer M. (1984) *Towards equal opportunity: women and employment at the Australian National University* Canberra.

—— (1996) *Removal of the Commonwealth marriage bar: a documentary history* Canberra: Centre for Research in Public Centre Management.

Scarrow H. A. (1957) *The higher public service of the Commonwealth of Australia* Durham: Duke University Press.

Schedvin C. B. (1970) *Australia and the Great Depression* South Melbourne: Sydney University Press and Oxford University Press.

—— (1982/3) 'The culture of CSIRO' *Australian Cultural History* 2, pp. 76–89.

—— (1988) 'Rivett, Albert (1855–1934) and Rivett, Sir Albert Cherbury David (1885–1961)' *Australian Dictionary of Biography* vol. 11, pp. 398–401.

—— (1992) *In reserve: central banking in Australia, 1945–75* St Leonards, NSW: Allen and Unwin.

Schedvin C. B. and Carr J. E. (1995) 'Edward Shann: a radical liberal before his time' in S. Macintyre and J. Thomas (eds) *The discovery of Australian history* South Carlton: Melbourne University Press, pp. 49–70.

Scott W. D. (1950) 'Incentive payments operating in Australia' *Economic Papers* 9, pp. 6–22.

Sekuless P. (1978) *Jessie Street: a rewarding but unrewarded life* St Lucia: University of Queensland Press.

Sexton C. (1985) *Peggy van Praagh: a life of dance* South Melbourne: Macmillan.

Shann E. O. G. (1925) 'Group settlement of migrants in Western Australia' *Economic Record* 1, November, pp. 73–93.

—— (1933) *Quotas or stable money?* Sydney: Angus and Robertson.

Sheridan T. (1989) *Division of labour: industrial relations in the Chifley years, 1945–49* Melbourne: Oxford University Press.

Skidelsky R. (1975) *Oswald Mosley* London: Macmillan.

—— (2000) *John Maynard Keynes: fighting for Britain* London: Macmillan.

Slatyer R. (1970) 'Man's place in nature' in *Man and the new biology: university lectures, 1969* Canberra: Australian National University Press, pp. 1–21.

Smith B. (1988) 'The antipodean manifesto' (1959) in B. Smith *The death of the artist as hero: essays in history and culture* Melbourne: Oxford University Press, pp. 194–7.

Smith J. P. (1982) 'Australia and the war-time planning for a new international economic system', thesis, Australian National University.

Snooks G. D. (1988) 'Shann, Edwin Owen Giblin, 1884–1935' in *Australian Dictionary of Biography* vol. 11 (ed. G. Serle), pp. 574–6.

Spaull A. (1998) *John Dedman: a most unexpected Labor man* Melbourne: Hyland House.

Spender P. (1942) 'Is there anything wrong with Australia?' *Public Administration* 4(2), June, pp. 63–70.

Stewart D. (1981) 'Prologue: the playwright in Australia' in P. Holloway (ed.) *Contemporary Australian drama: perspectives since 1955* Sydney: Currency Press, pp. lv–lvii.

Strahan F. (2000) 'Mawby, Sir Maurice Alan Edgar (1904–1977)' *Australian Dictionary of Biography* vol. 15 (ed. J. Ritchie), pp. 333–5.

Stretton H. (1987) *Political essays* Melbourne: Georgian House.

Sykes A. (1956) 'Lawler's exciting doll' *Voice* February.

Thomas B. (1936) *Monetary policy and crises: a study of Swedish experience* London: Routledge.

Thompson J. (1964) *Five to remember* Melbourne: Lansdowne.

Triebel L. A. (1969) 'Walter Murdoch: essayist' *Meanjin Quarterly* 28, pp. 209–20.

Turnell S. (1999) 'Monetary reformers, amateur idealists and Keynesian crusaders: Australian economists' international advocacy' PhD thesis, Macquarie University.

Ungar S. (1992) *The rise and fall of nuclearism* Pennsylvania: Pennsylvania State University Press.

Vamplew R. (ed.) (1987) *Australia: historical statistics* Sydney: Fairfax, Syme and Weldon.

Vincent D. (1991) *Poor citizens: the state and the poor in the twentieth century* London and New York: Longman.

Walker E. R. (1943) *From economic theory to policy* Chicago: University of Chicago Press.

—— (1947) 'Australia and the world economy' in C. H. Grattan (ed.) *Australia* Berkeley and Los Angeles: University of California Press, pp. 171–83.

Waterson D. B. (1979) 'Butler, Robert John Cuthbert, 1889–1950' *Australian Dictionary of Biography* vol. 7 (ed. B. Nairn and G. Serle), pp. 508–9.

Watson D. (1979) *Brian Fitzpatrick: a radical life* Sydney: Hale and Iremonger.

Watts O. F. (1982) 'Joseph Parsons: pioneer headmaster of government secondary education' in L. Fletcher (ed.) *Pioneers of education in Western Australia* University of Western Australia Press, pp. 285–311.

—— (1979) 'J. Parsons – the teacher' in L. Hunt (ed.) *Westralian portraits* University of Western Australia Press, pp. 186–90.

Weatherburn H. (1990) '*Australian Women's Digest'* in H. Radi (ed.) *Jessie Street: documents and essays* Sydney: Women's Redress Press, pp. 166–71.

Wheatley N. (1988) 'All in the same boat? Sydney's rich and poor in the Great Depression' in V. Burgmann and J. Lee (eds) *Making a life* Melbourne: McPhee Gribble/Penguin, pp. 205–25.

White F. W. G. (1975) 'CSIR to CSIRO – the events of 1948–1949' *Australian Journal of Public Administration* 34(4), pp. 281–93.

Whitlam E. G. (1985) *The Whitlam government, 1972–1975* Ringwood, Vic.: Penguin.

Whitwell G. (1986) *The Treasury line* St Leonards, NSW: Allen and Unwin.

Wright J. (1970) *Conservation as an emerging concept* Parkville, Vic.: Australian Conservation Foundation.

Zunini L. (1997) *Western Australia as it is today, 1906* (trans. Melia and Bosworth) Nedlands: University of Western Australia Press.

Index

Printed in the United States
By Bookmasters